RACISM IN COLLEGE ATHLETICS

THE AFRICAN AMERICAN ATHLETE'S EXPERIENCE

2nd Edition, 2000

Dana Brooks, Ed.D.
WEST VIRGINIA UNIVERSITY

AND

Ronald Althouse, Ph.D.
WEST VIRGINIA UNIVERSITY

Editors

Fitness Information Technology, Inc. • P.O. Box 4425 •
Morgantown, WV 26504-4425 • USA

Library of Congress Card Catalog Number: 99-71259

ISBN: 1-885693-19-2

Copy Editor: Sandra R. Woods
Cover Design: Bellerophon Productions
Developmental Editor: Geoffrey C. Fuller
Production Editor: Craig Hines
Proofreader/Indexer: Candace Jordan
Printed by: Sheridan Press
Printed in the United States of America
10 9 8 7 6 5 4 3 2 1

Fitness Information Technology, Inc.
P.O. Box 4425, University Avenue
Morgantown, WV 26504 USA
(800) 477-4348
(304) 599-3482 (phone/fax)
Email: fit@fitinfotech.com
Website: www.fitinfotech.com

About the Editors

Ronald Althouse is a professor of sociology, chairperson of the Department of Sociology and Anthropology, and director of the Survey Research Center at West Virginia University. He received his M.A. and Ph.D. in sociology from the University of Minnesota. Dr. Althouse's research interests and publications have focused on workers' risk and workers' health, health care delivery, and health systems. He has contributed to the literature on athletic participation and is committed to efforts focused on social justice in sports. In his leisure time, he enjoys bicycling and jazz, and is an avid science fiction reader.

Dana Brooks is a professor and dean of Physical Education at West Virginia University. He received his B.S. from Towson State University (1973), and M.S. (1976) and Ed.D. (1979) from West Virginia University. He has published and presented nationally and internationally in sport sociology and sport social psychology. Dr. Brooks served as chairperson of West Virginia University's Athletic Council, and was a member of a special task force to review the feasibility of a student-athlete academic learning center, the Black Community Concerns Committee, and Affirmative Action Committee. In addition, he served as Minority Recruitment Coordinator in the Office of the Provost. He is project administrator for the National Youth Sport Program at West Virginia University. Dr. Brooks is a member of the North American Society for Sport Sociology; ICHPER-SD; and the American Alliance for Health, Physical Education, Recreation and Dance. He enjoys tennis, basketball, tole painting, fencing, and photography.

Contributing Authors

Robertha Abney is the associate athletic director and assistant professor at Slippery Rock University. She has distinguished herself as a leading writer, presenter, and authority on women and minorities in leadership roles in sport. She has served in many capacities in the area of athletics and girls and women in sport. Dr. Abney has served as president of the National Association for Girls and Women in Sport (NAGWS). She has international experience, having been selected to represent the International Council of Health, Physical Education and Recreation in Beijing, China. She continues to publish and be very active professionally and to hold numerous professional memberships. Dr. Abney has received many awards in her profession, a tribute to her commitment, involvement, and expertise.

Audwin Anderson is an associate professor in the Department of Sociology, Southwest Texas State University. He received his Ph.D. from Texas A & M University in 1990. Dr. Anderson's research, publications, and professional presentations include issues dealing with the African American student-athlete, medical sociology, and racism in law. His most recent publication, a coauthored piece titled "The Swain Case as a Model of Institutional Racism," was nominated for the *Sociological Spectrum* paper award for 1996. From 1986 to 1990, he was a member of the editorial board of the *Journal of Applied Research in Coaching and Athletics*. He is past president of the Psych-social Committee of the National Sickle Cell Disease Centers. Currently he serves as chair on the Committee on Minorities for the Mid-South Sociological Association. For hobbies, he enjoys all sports, reading, and jazz.

Doris R. Corbett is currently a professor of sport sociology at Howard University. She received a Ph.D. in sociology of sport from the University of Maryland. Dr. Corbett served as a congressional research fellow at the United States Capitol Historical Society, Washington, DC; a distinguished visiting professor at West Point, New York; and visiting professor at Nanyang Technological University, School of Physical Education, Republic of Singapore. Her many professional associations include serving as president of DC-AHPERD, NAGWS, EDA-AHPERD, AAHPERD, and international president of ICHPER.SD. Dr. Corbett has delivered more than 150 invited keynote addresses throughout the continental United States and abroad and has been the recipient of numerous honors and awards including the AAHPERD Luther Halsey Gulick Medal in 1997. Her publications include one book, *Outstanding Athletes of Congress;* several textbook chapters; and numerous articles that focus on ethics and moral issues in sport, as well as gender, race, and sport. For leisure and relaxation, she enjoys tennis, reading, and international travel.

Timothy Davis is currently a professor of law at Wake Forest University School of Law. He received his B.A. from Stanford University and his J.D. from the University of California at Berkeley School of Law. He began his teaching career at Southern Methodist University School of Law, where he served on the university's athletics council for 8 years. The recipient of two teaching awards at SMU, Professor Davis has also published numerous law review articles that apply legal principles to intercollegiate athletics. His recreational interests include exercise and travel.

D. Stanley Eitzen is professor emeritus of sociology at Colorado State University. He received a B.A. in history from Bethel College in 1956, an M.S. in social science from Emporia State University in 1962, and an M.A. (1966) and Ph.D. (1968) in sociology from the University of Kansas. While an undergraduate, he lettered in three varsity sports: football, basketball, and track. Dr. Eitzen's scholarly interests include the sociology of sport and social problems, especially social inequality, elite deviance, and political sociology. He has authored or coauthored 15 books, including 2 in sport: *Sociology of North American Sport*, sixth edition in 1997 (with George H. Sage); and *Sport in Contemporary America*, fifth edition in 1996. He is currently working on a new book, tentatively titled *Paradoxes of Sport*. For recreation, he enjoys golfing, watching sports, painting with watercolors, and creating contemporary sculptures from wood.

Tina Sloan Green is currently a professor of physical education at Temple University and former director of the National Youth Sport Program. In addition, she is cofounder and president of the Black Women in Sport Foundation. She received a B.S. degree in physical education from West Chester University and an M.Ed. in physical education at Temple University. As head coach of Temple's women's lacrosse team (1973–1992), she led her team to three National Championships and 11 consecutive NCAA Final Four appearances. Professor Green has coauthored two books, *Black Women in Sport* and *Modern Women's Lacrosse*. She was inducted into the Halls of Fame at both Temple and West Chester Universities as well as the Lacrosse Hall of Fame. Professor Green competed on the U.S. Women's Lacrosse Team (1969–1973) and the U.S. Women's Field Hockey Squad (1966). For recreation, she enjoys travel, tennis, and walking.

Othello Harris, Ph.D., is associate professor and chair of the Department of Physical Education, Health, and Sport Studies at Miami University. His research interests include race and sport involvement, especially the extent to which sport enhances or impedes opportunities for social mobility for African Americans. His work has been published in *The Black Scholar, Sociology of Sport Journal, The Journal of Social and Behavioral Sciences, Journal of African American Males, Masculinities,* and *Sociological Focus.* In addition, he has authored chapters in numerous books.

Debra A. Henderson, Ph.D., is an assistant professor of sociology at Ohio University. Her Ph.D. is from the Department of Sociology, Washington State University, Pullman, Washington. Dr. Henderson is currently working on a paper addressing the issue of "stacking" in Major League Baseball and revising her doctoral dissertation on interracial marriages. She is an avid reader and spends her leisure time listening to jazz.

William Johnson is an assistant professor of physical education at Howard University. He received his M.S. and Directorate of Physical Education degrees from Indiana University and has completed further graduate study at George Washington University. As an undergraduate, he lettered in football, track, and gymnastics. He was head track and field coach, head gymnastics coach, and head defensive football coach at Howard University. His academic work is anatomy, kinesiology, and curriculum development in higher education. He is a member of numerous professional organizations, including a life membership in AAHPERD. Professor Johnson's leisure activities include golf, tennis, bowling, and gardening.

Carole Oglesby is professor and former chairperson of the Physical Education Department at Temple University. In physical education, she completed a B.S. and an M.S. from the University of California, Los Angeles, in 1961 and 1964, and a Ph.D. from Purdue University in 1969. In counseling psychology, she is near completion of a Ph.D. from Temple University. She is a certified consultant to the Association for the Advancement of Applied Sport Psychology, and is on the Sport Psychology Registry of the United States Olympic Committee. Dr. Oglesby has been president of the National Association of Girls' and Women's Sport and the Association of Intercollegiate Athletics for Women, and has served terms on the Board of Trustees of the Women's Sport Foundation and the Board of Directors of the United States Olympic Committee. She has edited, published, and presented widely in gender, racial, and sexual identity as well as participated in political advocacy concerning human rights in the realm of sports and development. She is an avid jogger, tennis player, and in-line skater.

George Sage is a professor emeritus of kinesiology and sociology at the University of Northern Colorado. He received his Ed.D. from the University of California, Los Angeles, in 1962. From 1958 to 1969 he held head basketball coaching positions at Pomona College (1958–62) and the University of Northern Colorado (1963–1968). He left coaching in 1969 to pursue his academic interests in sociology of sport. He has presented over 50 invited speeches and has been the recipient of numerous honors and awards. His publications include numerous articles and 14 edited, authored, or coauthored books, including revisions; and he has contributed chapters to 12 edited volumes. His books include *Sport and American Society*, *Power and Ideology in American Sport: A Critical Perspective*, and *Sociology of North American Sport* (coauthored with D. Stanley Eitzen). In addition to memberships in many professional organizations, Dr. Sage relaxes with travel, reading, and golf.

Gary Sailes, Ph.D., is a sport sociologist in the Department of Kinesiology at Indiana University. He is director of the Center for the Study of the African American Athlete and editor of *The Journal of African American Men*. Dr. Sailes has lectured extensively across the country, published in several scholarly journals and books, appeared on national and international television and radio, and is frequently quoted in the press. Dr. Sailes presided over a congressional hearing on the African American athlete during the Black Congressional Caucus in Washington, D.C. Dr. Sailes sits on the Board of Directors of the National Council of African American Men. He is currently writing his fourth book, entitled *Betting Against the Odds: The African American Sports Experience*.

Diana Schrader is currently studying for a Ph.D. in sport psychology at Temple University. She received the master of creative arts in therapy degree from Hahneman University, Philadelphia, Pennsylvania, specializing in dance/movement therapy. She has worked for the past 13 years as a psychotherapist and activity therapist with severely mentally ill patients in both partial hospital and inpatient psychiatry programs. She spent a year living in Tanzania, where she enjoyed studying Kishwahili and getting to know people of another culture. She has long been concerned with issues of racism, social justice, and intercultural cooperation. In her leisure time, she enjoys modern dance, aerobics, hiking, travel, and British murder mysteries.

Robert Sellers is currently an associate professor of psychology at the University of Michigan. He graduated with a B.S. degree in psychology from Howard University in 1985. While at Howard University, Dr. Sellers was an All-American football player. After graduating from Howard, he went on to earn a Ph.D. in personality psychology from the University of Michigan in 1990. Dr. Sellers has published several research articles on life experiences of student-athletes, stress and coping, and racial identity; and he has served as consultant to the National Collegiate Athletic Association (NCAA) Presidents' Commission's Study of the Life Experiences of Student-Athletes, NCAA Research Committee. Dr. Sellers serves as the principal investigator for two projects: (a) Student-Athlete Life Stress Project and (b) a national study evaluating academic support programs for student-athletes at NCAA Division I institutions. In addition to his research on student-athletes, Dr. Sellers has published research articles on such topics as stress and coping, and African American racial identity.

Kenneth Shropshire is an associate professor of legal studies at the Wharton School at the University of Pennsylvania and acting director of the Afro-American Studies Program at the University of Pennsylvania for 1997–98. He joined the faculty in 1986. Professor Shropshire received his undergraduate degree in economics from Stanford University in 1977 and his law degree from Columbia University in 1989. He holds an honorary master of arts degree from the University of Pennsylvania. He was formerly in private practice in Los Angeles and prior to that was an assistant vice president with the Los Angeles Olympic Organizing Committee. Professor Shropshire has written several articles on sports, entertainment, and business issues. The articles have focused on topics such as sports franchise relocations, international sports leagues, and problems within the NCAA. His award-winning book, *Agents of Opportunity: Sports Agents and Corruption in Collegiate Sports*, was published by the University of Pennsylvania Press in 1990 and won the *Choice* magazine outstanding academic book award.

Earl Smith, Ph.D., is the Debbie and Mike Rubin Professor of American Ethnic Studies; Director of the American Ethnic Studies Program; and professor and chair of the Department of Sociology at Wake Forest University, Winston-Salem, North Carolina. Dr. Smith is a former dean, Division of Social Sciences at Pacific Lutheran University in Tacoma, Washington. He also chaired the Department of Sociology. The first part of Dr. Smith's career was spent at Washington State University in Pullman, Washington. He was professor of sociology and chaired the Department of Comparative American Cultures during the 14 years he spent at WSU. Dr. Smith is the secretary of the North American Society for the Sociology of Sport (NASSS) and serves on the Editorial Board of *The Journal of Sport and Social Issues*. Dr. Smith is a morning walker, and on the walks he listens to fiction and nonfiction books on tape.

Yevonne R. Smith, Ph.D., is an associate professor in the Department of Kinesiology at Michigan State University, East Lansing, Michigan, where she has taught since 1990. Dr. Smith earned her Ph.D. from the University of Michigan, Ann Arbor, and has presented many scholarly/research presentations at the North American Society for the Sociology of Sport (NASSS) and at the American Alliance for Health, Physical Education, Recreation and Dance (AAHPERD) conventions. She has also been a National Association for Sport and Physical Education (NASPE) Sport Sociology Academy chairperson. Dr. Smith has published articles in *Quest*, the *Journal of Physical Education, Recreation and Dance, NASPE News,* and the *NAGWS National Coaching Institute Applied Research Papers*. In addition, she has served on the *NASSS Journal of Sport Sociology, QUEST,* and *JOPERD* editorial boards.

Donald South is a professor of sociology at the University of South Alabama. He received his M.A. and Ph.D. from Louisiana State University. He has served on the university athletic-academic committee for 15 years. Dr. South has participated in baseball, basketball, and boxing. He has published extensively, contributing to books and authored monographs. In addition, Dr. South has been active on editorial boards of sociological journals and has served as editor of *Sociological Spectrum*. He has held offices in regional professional organizations. For relaxation, he enjoys gardening and watching sports on TV.

David K. Wiggins is a professor in the Department of Health, Fitness, and Recreation Resources at George Mason University. He received B.A. and M.A. degrees in physical education from San Diego State University and a Ph.D. in sport history from the University of Maryland. Dr. Wiggins' research has focused primarily on the history of African Americans in sport and physical activity. He is History and Philosophy Section editor for the *Research Quarterly for Exercise and Sport* and is the editor of the *Journal of Sport History*. Dr. Wiggins has authored *Glory Bound: Black Athletes in a White America* (Syracuse, NY: Syracuse University Press, 1997); edited *Sport in America: From Wicked Amusement to National Obsession* (Champaign, IL: Human Kinetics Publishers, 1994); and coedited, with George Eisen, *Ethnicity and Sport in North American History and Culture* (Westport, CT: Greenwood Press, 1995). For recreation, he enjoys tennis, running, and attending movies with his family.

Table of Contents

SECTION 1: HISTORICAL ANALYSIS OF RACISM AND CRITICAL EVENTS

SECTION 2: RECRUITMENT, RETENTION, AND LIFE AFTER PARTICIPATION

SECTION 3: GENDER AND RACE INTERSECTIONS IN COLLEGE ATHLETICS

SECTION 4: ANALYSIS OF RACISM AND PROSPECTS FOR CHANGE

**To the legacy of Jackie Robinson and all of the African American
male and female athletes, coaches, administrators, and parents
who struggle for equal opportunity. Keep the faith!**

Preface

The first edition of *Racism in College Athletics: The African American Athlete's Experience,* published in 1993, became the first textbook to break new ground in race relations applied to college athlete participation. It was significant because it not only identified social injustice in college athletics, but also offered practical and constructive courses of action for change. The new edition of *Racism in College Athletics* is an extension of the original project; essays are updated and the contributions from new authors strengthen the text.

The text is arranged into four themes that systematically organize the literature dealing with problem areas facing the African American college athlete: (a) Historical Analysis of Racism and Critical Events; (b) Recruitment, Retention, and Social Mobility in Collegiate Sport; (c) Gender and Race Intersections in College Athletics; and (d) Analysis of Racism and Prospects for Change. Essays found under each of the four sections identify plans or strategies and various courses of action that are proposed to ameliorate or even eradicate conditions contributing to racism, sexism, and other forms of oppression directed toward the African American college athlete. Each essay provides the reader with a distinctive perspective on racism, sexism, and classism.

Historical Analysis of Racism and Critical Events

Essay 1 identifies critical and historical events (e.g., signing of Jackie Robinson by the Brooklyn Dodgers in 1945; *Brown v. Topeka Board of Education* in 1954; Civil Rights Movement of the 1960s) affecting racism in college athletics.

Essay 2 provides a social and historical overview of factors leading to African American predominance in college athletics. The consequences of stereotyping and "stacking," as well as academic concerns (low graduation rates for African American student-athletes), are discussed in detail. The essay concludes by offering the reader suggestions to address academic problems faced by African American student-athletes.

Essay 3 discusses the role of the media in perpetuating racial stereotypes in college sport. The author offers an excellent conceptual and theoretical analysis of racial differences related to athletic participation.

Essay 4 looks at the persistence of stacking in college athletics. A critique of previous stacking literature is viewed in the context of marginalization and discrimination against African American athletes.

Essay 5 presents an in-depth look at the hiring practices and policies currently utilized by NCAA member institutions. It becomes very apparent that African American men and women are underutilized in the coaching and administrative positions at the collegiate and professional level.

Essay 6 explores the upward mobility patterns of African American female coaches and administrators. Clearly, barriers (i.e., inadequate salary, sexism) have been constructed, forming a "glass ceiling" for African American females wishing to enter the coaching profession.

Recruitment, Retention, and Life After Participation

Essay 7 studies the psychological and sociological problems African American athletes face when they retire from college athletics. The author offers the argument that athletic experience will have a positive effect on the quality of postathletic life.

Essay 8 provides an outstanding discussion on the social meaning of African American maleness and the sport experience. The essay challenges NCAA member institutions to eliminate all forms of oppression and exploitation in college athletics.

Gender and Race Intersection in College Athletics

Essay 9 is a groundbreaking piece of work and provides an excellent sociohistorical analysis of the African American elite female athlete. Biographies of notable African American female athletes such as Althea Gibson, Wilma Rudolph, and Lucinda Adams add to the significance of this essay.

Essay 10 explores the interaction of sexism and racism in college athletics. This essay is an extension of Essay 9 and reminds the reader that structural barriers such as lack of role models, lack of access to facilities, and poor media images must be overcome if the African American female is going to achieve parity in college sport.

Essay 11 provides an excellent analysis of the African American female sport experience. The author, a nationally recognized athlete, coach, and administrator, demands that current leaders fight against all forms of social injustice and support programs encouraging African American female opportunity.

Analysis of Racism and Prospects for Change

Essay 12 is written by an attorney and invites the reader to explore the legal and racial consequences of compensating student-athletes for services rendered to the athletic program. The essay is extremely well-written and challenges the entire amateur concept serving as the foundation for NCAA participation.

Essay 13, similarly, is written by an attorney, without all of the legal jargon. The author takes the position that traditional civil rights laws are largely ineffective for protecting the interest of African Americans. The essay makes a significant contribution to the literature by challenging leaders to turn to nonlegal alternatives to eliminate all forms of oppression in college sport.

Essay 14 is a very powerful and thought-provoking manuscript. Not only do the authors provide an excellent summary of the current status of race relations literature, they also confront power and privilege vested in the dominant culture. The essay provides a refreshing spiritual journey.

Essay 15 is written by a world-recognized scholar and provides an excellent summary of the status of race relations in American sport. Just as important, the author provides some outstanding strategies to bring about position change ultimately enhancing the African American sport experience as we move to the next millennium.

The epilogue provides a brief survey of all fifteen essays presented in this text. In addition, the authors were interested in determining how much progress was made by African Americans in college and professional sports since Jackie's signing with the Dodgers in 1947.

Target Audience

The target audience for this text is college, high school, and community sport coaches. Students enrolled in African American sport courses and upper division undergraduate courses in sport sociology will find this textbook an important supplement to their course of study.

The co-editors express appreciation to Dr. Andrew Ostrow, President, Fitness Information Technology, Inc. for his encouragement and support. We would like to thank Ms. Linda Hetrick for her secretarial and managerial contributions to this textbook.

The quality of this text resides primarily with the contributing authors: Dr. George Sage, Dr. David K.Wiggins, Dr. Othello Harris, Dr. Gary Sailes, Dr. Earl Smith, Dr. Debra Henderson, Dr. Robertha Abney, Dr. Robert Sellers, Dr. Audwin Anderson, Dr. Donald South, Dr. Doris Corbett, Mr. William Johnson, Dr. Yevonne Smith, Ms. Tina Sloan Green, Mr. Timothy Davis, Mr. Kenneth L. Shropshire, Dr. Carole Oglesby, Ms. Diana Schrader, and Dr. D. Stanley Eitzen.

Dana D. Brooks

Ronald C. Althouse

Coeditors

A Personal Statement

John B. McLendon
Cleveland State University
Basketball Hall of Fame Inductee

When reading *Racism in College Athletics* I am at once struck by the collection of writers whom the authors have solicited for comment and the range of their coverage of an American phenomenon, namely, collegiate sports. Each chapter represents some area of social conflict to which their own experiences bear witness and addresses how issues of discrimination and equal opportunity, at least to some extent, affect the lives of all citizens. The fact gives added credibility to their comments.

The word *racism* requires review because it is an idea often rather loosely applied, or at times, misapplied in its usage. Racism refers to "any discordant racial action of prejudice, bigotry and ignorance directed by any one or more persons toward any one representative of a group or the group itself because of ethnic origin, custom beliefs, religion, politics, nationality, skin color, etc."

With regard to American or USA sports, each of the essays supplies examples of what racism has been and is. It seems to be more prevalent in sports than in many other life pursuits, probably because of its visibility. Often the noise and brashness of negative advocates are matched by noisier, attention-getting special interest. The public reflects or deflects both negative and positive aspects of the news media situation, strengthening or weakening the position of an individual or an organization, and even the nation (see the Jasper, Texas tragedy). In part, the public is more often aware of the fortunes and misfortunes of sports figures, but even when discriminatory practices are less discernible—and may be more difficult to deal with—by those "outside the system," the revelation of actual as well as perceived racial practices that are dealt with in this collection of essays can rivet awareness on how widespread racism in sports, even college sports, continues to be at the end of the century. It requires daily attention in our education, thus allowing a chance for problem solving.

In *Racism in College Athletics* there are various factual depictions of "wrong versus right" allied with "White versus Black," although its explicit concern is college sports and the Black athlete. A number of essays that reflect on gender also make it clear that racism is not bound by color lines. On one level, these essays remind us that racist practices (prejudice, bigotry, and ignorance) may be on the rise (e.g., Catholics v. Protestants, Hutus v. Tutsis, atheists v. believers, Jews v. Palestinians, Hindus v. Christians), but the majority of contributions are most concerned with "USA sports" and racial barriers that have been created as a matter of traditional practice or policy in colleges, universities, and the professional arenas.

You need to use *Racism in College Athletics* to recognize and understand prejudice and racial barriers. Read and reflect on the Jackie Robinson, the Hank Aaron, the John McLendon, or the Charles Sifford stories in baseball, basketball, or golf respectively and follow each of them or other sports heroes and legends through the following steps of their experiences.

- Consideration of the possible entrant. Someone must propose the entry of the individual into the structured programs (e.g., Branch Rickey's influence on Jackie Robinson's career).

- Consideration of the actual entry. Managing the entrant into the operation. Example—approval or disapproval by governing body (e.g., NCAA rules).

- Consideration of the positioning of the entrant. Where to involve, merge, or play the entrant into the operation. Where in the competition for placement does an entrant best serve success and her/his group's advantage?

- Consideration of administrative/managerial post-action careers. Presentation of qualifications of experience and expertise without bias.

These *four aspects of consideration* are discussed and represented over and again in this volume of essays. If you think about the prejudice African American athletes have dealt with and the range of discrimination they have encountered, you then can consider what was, and what is to shape what is to be. If you find that some analyses of problems in the past seem unlikely or even fictional, count that observation as progress. Those who lament our present place in the world of equality by saying, "We are still in the pre-King world of inequalities and injustices," or that our progress has been inconsequential will confront a challenging account of experiences among African American collegiate athletes. People need to read this collection of essays because once done, readers will be likely to conclude that what may seem "a long way to go" has been shortened to "It is not as far as it has been."

Introduction

George H. Sage

Intercollegiate athletics has been a source of frustration, disappointment, and despair for African Americans as they have struggled against the discrimination that has historically been a part of intercollegiate sport. It has also been a place of courage and achievement for African American athletes, coaches, and athletic administrators who have been given the chance to play, coach, and administer college sports. Finally, it has been a place of opportunity and hope; opportunities continue to open up, creating hope that the injustices of the past will disappear in the future. Deeds of the past need not be visited upon African Americans in the future; but for full equality and opportunity to be achieved for African American college athletes, coaches, and administrators, a number of still unresolved problems must be resolved.

The widespread interest in the study of racism in college athletics generated by the first edition of this volume created a need for the second edition. The growing literature on this topic and recent social changes also needed reporting. The editors, Dana Brooks and Ronald Althouse, have been able to secure updated essays from nine of the original authors, which they have supplemented with six new essays for this edition.

Contemporary Sport in the United States

The subject of intercollegiate sports requires that we begin by framing the discussion at a level much broader than college athletics. Intercollegiate athletics must be situated within the context of contemporary American society, including the pervasive racism that has been systemic in American culture for the past 375 years.

Among the various popular cultural practices in American society, sport is undoubtedly the most ubiquitous. Over 25 million young boys and girls participate in youth sports programs each year; another 5.5 million high school athletes compete in over 25 different sports; and more than 300,000 college athletes toil for their institutions. Add to those participants the elite-level athletes who represent the United States in international competition, as well as professional athletes, and you have an enormous number of athletes engaged in organized sports. The major form of involvement with sports is not as participants. It is as spectators—the millions who watch sporting events, either by actually attending contests or by viewing them on television.

Beyond participating in sports in various ways, Americans invest a great deal of their time and emotions in understanding the intricacies of sports while following their favorite teams and athletes. They are knowledgeable about rules (or at least think they are); they are able to recite "their" teams' strengths and weaknesses and chances for winning the championship of their league; and they are enthusiastic admirers of certain athletes. Much of this knowledge and enthusiasm is fueled and sustained by the mass media, which cover several thousand hours of sporting events each year.

Understanding Sport as a Cultural Practice

In spite of the various ways in which Americans know and follow sports, they are not encouraged to critically examine the prevalent attitudes, values, myths, and folklore about this cultural practice.[1] Throughout American society, people tend to be unaware of the social relations of control in sport. To a frightening degree, there is a naïveté to the social context and material conditions underlying sporting practices. Although sports embody specific and identifiable purposes, values, and meanings, they are typically viewed by both participants and fans as ahistorical and apolitical in nature. This is largely the case because most of the written and broadcast information about sports in American society does not confront us with questions about the larger social issues and political and economic consequences of modern sports. Instead, we are fed a diet of traditional slogans, clichés, and ritualized trivia about sports. Although these can be comforting to the devoted fan, they do not come to grips with the social reality of contemporary sport.

Another obstacle to understanding American sports is that sport and society have traditionally been seen as discrete social phenomena, with sports often thought of as a pristine and isolated activity that is (or should be) uncontaminated by problems and issues of the wider society. Americans have tended to cherish the illusion that sports are just "fun and games," and those who have held the power and influence in sports have vigorously fought any attempt to change this image.

Attempting to understand sport as a cultural practice must begin with an assumption that it cannot be examined as a practice isolated from the social, economic, political, and cultural context in which is situated. As a set of social practices and relations that is structured by the culture in which it exists, any adequate account of sport must be grounded in a knowledge about its location within society. Thus, understanding sport as a cultural practice necessitates studying it as part of a larger political, economic, social, and ideological configuration. The essence of sport is to be found within the nature of its relationship to those broader societal forces of which it is a part. Relevant issues involve how sport is related to social class, race, and gender, as well as the control, production, and distribution of political, economic, and cultural power. Professors Gorn and Oriard (1995) argue that "the study of sport can take us to the very heart of critical issues in the study of culture and society" (p. A52). The critical issue that is the central focus of this volume is the persistence of racism in American intercollegiate athletics.

Racism in American Society

The racism that has been a salient part of college athletics throughout its history is only one dimension of an institutional racism that has been a pervasive part of the American experience since its beginnings. To really understand the role of racism in college athletics, it must be seen from the larger cultural context in which it is situated. Thus, it is important to historically situate and culturally locate racism in American society.

There are many racial and ethnic minorities in the United States, but African Americans are the largest minority population. Currently, there are approximately 34 million African Americans, who make up about 12% of the total U.S. population. A persisting thread running through the garment of the American experience is discrimination against African Americans; racism is rooted deeply in America's history. African Americans are the only racial group that has been subjected to an extended period of slavery; they are the only racial group to have segregation laws passed against them that were supported and fully sanctioned by the Supreme Court (Bell, 1992; Wilson, 1996). Of course, African Americans are not the only minority group in America that has had to struggle for basic civil rights (e.g., Native Americans), but theirs has been a unique and insidious heritage of injustice.

Black Africans were first brought to colo-

---

1. Parts of this section are drawn from my *Power and Ideology in American Sport: A Critical Perspective* (2nd ed.), Champaign, IL: Human Kinetics Publishers, 1998.

nial America in 1619, only 12 years after the establishment of the first English settlement at Jamestown. By the middle of the 17th century, a slave system among colonial plantation owners had begun, and by the end of that century enslaved Black Africans had become a major source of labor and a fundamental component of colonial agricultural and commercial interests. A racist social structure, with Blacks at the bottom, was thus created by slave owners of the agricultural South, together with Northern trading and shipping firms.

When the colonists challenged British rule in the latter part of the 18th century and finally established independence, a system of racism was incorporated into the basic documents of the newly formed United States. The Declaration of Independence and the U.S. Constitution condoned racial subordination and discrimination against African Americans. So, in spite of what was considered an enlightened stance toward human rights at that time, the framers of these documents saw no contradiction in espousing a liberal view of liberty for Whites while denying it to African Americans, who totaled 20% of the population when the United States became an nation. Slavery was sanctioned, and African Americans were denied all of the rights of citizenship.

It took a civil war and the passage of the 13th Amendment to the U.S. Constitution in 1865 to officially end the slavery system. Although slavery was abolished by the 13th Amendment, in the latter decades of the 19th century, many states passed Jim Crow laws mandating racial segregation in almost all areas of public life. In effect, then, Jim Crow laws legalized White domination and thus left racism essentially intact. A "separate but equal" system replaced slavery and became an even more efficient instrument of domination and subordination than slavery had been.

It was not until 1954 that the "separate but equal" doctrine was successfully challenged. In that year, the U.S. Supreme Court in the *Brown v. Board of Education* decision ruled that separate schools are inherently unequal, thus setting the stage for desegregation of American schools. This decision set in motion a series of challenges to discrimination against African Americans that culminated in sweeping civil rights legislation in the mid-1960s. So it has only been in the past 25 years that the civil rights of Black citizens have been protected by law (Berry, 1994; Wilson, 1996).

Even though laws protecting the civil rights of African Americans now exist, and provide improved conditions in some private and public sectors, domination and subordination of African Americans are still institutionally systemic in American society. Race is still a fundamental determinant of people's position in the social structure. African Americans are still defined as racially different by the White majority and singled out for a broad range of individual and institutionalized discrimination (Rowan, 1996; Rowe & Jeffries, 1996; Steinberg, 1995).

Although that last statement may seem to overstate current conditions, it actually does not. A poll by opinion analyst Louis Harris found that 75% of high school students indicated that they had seen or heard about a racial act with violent overtones, either very often or somewhat often, in the previous 12 months. Fifty-four percent of African American high school students reported that they had been a victim of a racial incident. The National Institute Against Prejudice and Violence, a group that monitors racist acts, reported that there are typically racial incidents on over 50 college campuses each year (and college students are supposed to be the most enlightened sector of the population!) (Donaldson, 1996; Harris, 1993).

There are widespread perceptions that things are getting better for African Americans, but in fact the economic gap between Whites and Blacks has actually been widening in recent years. African American families have actually lost ground economically to Whites over the past 20 years. The poverty rate among the nation's African Americans in 1996 was 33.1% compared with 12.2% for Whites.

African American household income was only 62% that of Whites, and it has changed very little during the 1990s. The jobless rate for African Americans has consistently been over twice that of Whites. Not only are African American twice as likely to be unemployed, but those who are employed are overrepresented in jobs whose pay, power, and prestige are low.

Although less common today than in the past, token integration in workplaces is more prevalent than demographic balance, even among occupations that are integrated. One noted researcher has argued that "although there has been some erosion of white . . . advantages in the workplace over the last two decades, they remain substantial" (Tomaskovic-Davey, 1993, p. 3). Only a smattering of African American managers have moved beyond middle levels of authority and control in the private sector of American business. Less than 3% of company senior-management positions (vice president and above) are African Americans. Out of 17 million U. S. business firms, only 2% are owned by African Americans. One social scientist recently noted,

> All of the evidence points to the fact that the [economic] winners are predominantly White and the biggest losers are Black. A wealth of recent material demonstrates that Black American [sic] have lost out to such an extent as to make a mockery of free enterprise, and the gap between Black and White incomes, if anything, has widened. (Hadjor, 1995, p. 13)

So, although some African Americans have made gains economically, politically, and in educational achievements, many barriers remain to social equality, and these barriers are rooted in institutional patterns and practices of racial discrimination that are deeply ingrained in the structure of American society. (Rowe & Jeffries, 1996). This was vividly illustrated in 1996 and 1997 with revelations of a racist corporate culture at the highest levels at Texaco, Avis, Denny's, and several other corporations. These incidents demonstrate that America has not yet conquered its heritage of racial inequality.

Where racism coexists with class stratification, as it does in the United States, the evidence is convincing that it is more basic to social structure and, therefore, the ultimate determinant of inequality between racial minorities and the dominant class. The basic fact is that much inequality and discrimination against African Americans continue, regardless of whether one uses income, employment rates, educational attainment, or political office-holding as measures. African Americans remain among the most disadvantaged groups in American society, and it is *racial barriers* that block Black achievement, not merely economic or class barriers. Martin Luther King Jr.'s dream that "one day racism would end in America" has not been fulfilled.

Racism, then, is a salient aspect of the structure of American society. The most important aspect of this form of stratification is that it excludes people of color from equal access to socially valued rewards and resources. They tend to have less wealth, power, and social prestige than do other Americans. Moreover, racism has built-in policies and practices that systematically discriminate against people in employment, housing, politics, education, health care, and many other areas. These conditions result in fewer human resources and diminished life chances for African Americans.

Racism in American Sport

Despite pervasive and systematic discrimination against African Americans throughout their history in North America, they have played a continuing and significant role in every era of American sport history, as David Wiggins (Essay 1) and Othello Harris (Essay 2) eloquently document in their essays. Their analyses suggest that this involvement can be divided roughly into four stages: (a) largely exclusion before the Civil War, (b) breakthroughs immediately following the Civil War, (c) segregation from the last two decades of the 19th century until after World War II, and (d) integration after World War II.

Sports relations between Whites and African Americans during the slavery era (1619 to 1865) centered on two sports: boxing and horse racing.[2] Plantation owners frequently selected and sometimes even trained one or more of their male slaves and entered them in boxing matches held in conjunction with festive occasions. The Black boxers, under such conditions, were merely used to entertain their White "masters" and their friends. Horse racing was also a popular colonial sporting event. Horses were, of course, owned by Whites, and when training occurred, much of it was done by Whites, but African Americans were used as jockeys. There was little status and there were no significant material rewards for jockeying, because slave labor of any kind was free and unpaid; it was viewed as basically a mechanical task, so Blacks could be trusted with a task that Whites did not care to do anyway. Social relations, then, can be seen as distant, with Whites in control and African Americans in subordinate roles, pleasing the dominant White groups (Wiggins, 1997).

As both Wiggins (Essay 1) and Harris (Essay 2) note, after the Civil War, African Americans made contributions to the rise of spectator sport as boxers, jockeys, and team players, but they were clearly exceptions. Society and sport remained racially segregated by custom and in some places by law (e.g., Jim Crow laws). Freedom had little effect on the social relations between Blacks and Whites in sports in the late 19th and early 20th centuries. Although a number of African Americans played on professional baseball teams in the early years of the National League, Jim Crowism gradually raised its ugly head. White players threatened to quit rather than share the diamond with Black men. Finally, by 1888, major league club owners made a gentleman's agreement not to sign anymore African American players. This unwritten law against hiring Black players was not violated until 1945

when Branch Rickey, general manager of the Brooklyn Dodgers, signed Jackie Robinson to a contract (Peterson, 1992). As other professional sports emerged, they too barred African Americans from participation. Among a number of consequences of excluding African Americans from professional sports, one was that it perpetuated privileges for Whites, because White athletes did not have to compete with an entire segment of the population for sports jobs.

When African Americans were barred from professional baseball, football, and basketball in the late 19th and early 20th centuries, they formed all-Black teams and leagues (Gardner & Shortelle, 1993; Peterson, 1992; Rust, 1992). The Harlem Globetrotters and the famous players of the Black baseball leagues, such as Satchel Paige and Josh Gibson, emerged from this segregated situation. When Jackie Robinson broke the color barrier, first in 1946 in the minor leagues and then in 1947 in the majors, he received much verbal and physical abuse from players and fans who resented Blacks playing on an equal level with Whites. The great major league player Rogers Hornsby uttered a common White attitude at the time:

"They've been getting along all right playing together and should stay where they belong in their league" (quoted in Chalk, 1975, p. 78).

Obstacles to African American participation in sport have fallen in almost every sport and in most sport organizations over the past 50 years. African Americans' presence in sport far exceeds what anyone would have predicted in the early decades of the 20th century. Indeed, African American athletes now dominate several sports at the high school, intercollegiate, and professional levels. Some of the most renowned current athletes are African American; they are heroes to millions of Americans—Black, White, Hispanic, and all other minorities.

Sporting opportunities have improved for African Americans in the past few decades, but

2. Parts of this section are drawn from my (coauthored with D. Stanley Eitzen) *Sociology of North American Sport* (6th ed.), Madison, WI: Brown & Benchmark, 1997.

racist attitudes appear to persist, albeit in more subtle forms. African Americans' success in sport has led many to seek an explanation for this phenomenon, and one section of Harris's essay traces the twists and turns of this controversy. He indicates that although some scientists have claimed that the African Americans possess physical characteristics that are advantageous for athletic performance, most social scientists are of the opinion that sociological and psychological factors are the primary reason for African American athletes' rise to eminence. Fundamental to this view is a recognition that most African American athletes come from the low socioeconomic classes; here, recreational outlets for the young are mainly sports, so many hours are spent playing in the streets, recreation centers, and playgrounds. Furthermore, excellence in sports provides one of the few opportunities for African Americans to escape from the slums and ghettos in which many of them live. Thus, hours devoted to honing sports skills, combined with the desire to escape from their childhood environment, seem to cause many African American youths to approach sport with greater motivation to excel than is found with middle-class Whites.

The essay by Gary Sailes (Essay 3) takes up this theme of racial myths and stereotypes about African American athletes. He argues that social myths and stereotypes are common ideological mechanisms that tend to support dominant interests. African Americans have been subject to various myths and stereotypes whose purpose was to intimidate and subordinate them while providing justifications for racial attitudes and discrimination.

Throughout American sport history, African American athletes have been subjected to various myths, at first to explain why they "couldn't" play with White athletes and, more recently, to explain why they are such a dominating presence in the most popular American sports. Sailes discusses the sociocultural conditions involved in the African American athlete's rise to prominence in American sport.

Intercollegiate Sport: The Beginnings

The elaborate system of intercollegiate sports popular in the United States is a unique phenomenon. In most countries of the world, sport plays a minor role in institutions of higher education. In the United States, games and sports became a diversion from the boredom of classroom work and limited social outlets during the first half of the 19th century. Students played a variety of sports, first as unorganized and impromptu games and later as organized intramural and interclass activities. As the number of colleges and their geographic proximity to each other increased, the next logical step was for the students at one college to challenge the students of a nearby school to a sports contest.

The first officially recorded intercollegiate sports event was a rowing race between Harvard and Yale in 1852. At the beginning, intercollegiate sports were organized by the students, usually over faculty objection. In time, with increased organization and the proliferation of sports teams, faculties assumed administrative control over sports.

African American athletes were largely absent from intercollegiate sports for most of the 19th century. During the late 19th and early 20th centuries, college sports were dominated by White, upper-class, Protestant males. A few Ivy League and other Eastern schools had African American athletes at an early time, but they were exceptions. This was an era of Jim Crowism and segregation, and collegiate sports remained segregated, except for isolated instances, until after World War II. At the University of Michigan, for example, from 1882 to 1945, there were only four African American lettermen in football and none in basketball. In 1948, only 10% of college basketball teams had one or more African Americans on their rosters. This proportion increased to 45% of the teams in 1962 and 92% by 1975. The transition from a segregated program to an integrated one is perhaps best illustrated by the

University of Alabama: In 1968, there were no African Americans on any of its teams, but its 1975 basketball team had an all-African American starting lineup (Eitzen & Sage, 1997).

For the most part, though, over the past 100 years, most African American college athletes have played at historically Black colleges in Black leagues (they were known as Negro colleges and Negro leagues). Of course, the only reason that all-Black colleges existed at all was racial prejudice and discrimination. Nevertheless, the Black colleges fielded teams in all of the popular sports, and they played a leading role in women's sports, especially in track and field. Tuskegee, with Wilma Rudolph, and the Tigerbelles of Tennessee State are prominent examples.

Although the system was segregated, Black colleges provided an avenue to athletic prominence for many African American athletes, male and female, and they have developed more outstanding African American athletes than any other agency of higher education, though many of the athletes were never known outside the African American press and African American community.

Expanding Opportunities

The impact of World War II, the 1954 Supreme Court decision forbidding separate educational facilities, the massive commercialization of collegiate sports, and the desire by White colleges and universities to benefit from talented African American athletes in building commercialized athletic programs resulted in more and more schools searching for talented Blacks to bolster their teams; consequently, Black colleges lost their monopoly on African American athletic talent. The best found it advantageous to play at predominantly White schools because of their greater visibility, especially on television. This visibility meant a better chance to sign a professional contract at the conclusion of their eligibility. The result was depleted athletic programs at Black colleges, forcing several of them to drastically modify their athletic programs and some Black leagues to disband.

The growing number of African Americans receiving college athletic scholarships in the past two decades at predominantly White schools has been a mixed blessing. On the one hand, a few athletically talented African Americans have been given the opportunity to attend and graduate from colleges that would otherwise have been inaccessible to them. This has allowed some to achieve social mobility and monetary success. On the other hand, the evidence is clear and abundant that many African American college athletes have been exploited in various ways by their institutions. As the essays by Robert Sellers (Essay 7) and Kenneth Shropshire (Essay 13) clearly document, African American athletes have been recruited lacking the academic background to succeed in higher education, and they have been advised into courses that will keep them eligible but that are dead-end courses for acquiring a college degree. African American athletes have been "stacked" into specific positions in the sport they played, limiting the number who were on the starting team. The essay by Earl Smith and Debra Henderson (Essay 4) provides an example of stacking in intercollegiate baseball. When athletes' eligibility has been used up, or they have become academically ineligible to compete for the team, they have been discarded and ignored by the coaches who recruited them.

There is little doubt that many opportunities are available in college sport for African American athletes that were not available a generation ago, but racism in college sport has not been eliminated, as the essays in this volume clearly document. Many college sports teams still have very few African American participants and coaches, and even fewer in administrative positions. The college sports with few participants and coaches tend to be linked to upper class patronage, but class linkage is not the entire explanation for African American underrepresentation in these sports. Powerful political and economic interests have the wherewithal to insulate themselves against those with whom they do not wish to associate.

Laws that prevent African Americans from being kept out do not assure that they will get in. There is compelling evidence demonstrating that those who control intercollegiate athletic programs have created barriers to African American participation and administrative positions in a number of sports and universities, thus reproducing some of the more odious features of racism.

Although racial discrimination has always been incompatible with the ideals of American sports, widespread intercollegiate sports opportunities for African Americans emerged only when discrimination became incompatible with good financial policy. In those team sports in which "revenue producing" has come to dominate, the contribution of outstanding African American athletes to winning championships and holding public interest has opened up opportunities to African Americans in college sports. Sports more closely linked to upper-class patronage and with less spectator interest have been slow to attract and integrate Blacks.

Academic-Athletic Conflicts

In the evolution of college sports, increasing commercialization and the demands for winning teams to generate more and more revenue have produced what is called big-time college athletics. Accompanying this trend toward a form of commercial entertainment sponsored by colleges and universities has been a tension between the goals and integrity of higher education and the economic interests and values of big-time sports. For many who view the mission of higher education as the promotion of scholarship and academic training for careers, there is more than just a tension; there is an inherent incompatibility between an economically driven activity that uses college students as a labor force, which big-time college sport does, and the mission of higher education in promoting scholarship and academic achievement. Audwin Anderson and Donald South (Essay 8) locate their essay within this academic-athletic conflict, with a specific focus on re-

cruitment, retention, and graduation rates of African American male athletes. They cast their analysis of the issues and problems within a current situation in which nearly twice the percentage of White athletes graduate compared to African American athletes. In an attempt to bring some meaning to the statistical data on graduation rates, Anderson and South focus on forces such as the social meaning of African American maleness, recruitment practices, Propositions 48 and 16, and the economic and academic exploitative nature of big-time college sport to questions having to do with graduate rates. Finally, they problematize the meaning of graduate rates.

Limited Opportunities in Leadership

Access to intercollegiate sport for African American athletes has expanded greatly in the past quarter century, but very few opportunities have been made available in positions in the upper levels of the sport hierarchy. Efforts to eliminate discrimination through the legislative and judicial systems tend to produce immediate results, but the results are most noticeable at the lower levels of the social formation. The higher levels, where the greatest power, prestige, and material rewards reside, are more insulated from direct scrutiny, so those who control access to the higher levels tend to employ subtle ways of maintaining discriminatory practices. Thus, the oppressed group typically has a difficult time penetrating the higher paying and prestigious positions. As the essays by Dana Brooks and Ronald Althouse (Essay 5) and Robertha Abney (Essay 6) clearly demonstrate, in the case of intercollegiate athletics, coaching and management jobs are under the control of those who presently have the power for determining who gets selected to these upper-level positions. African Americans in coaching positions are scarce in intercollegiate athletics, and of those who are college coaches, they are overwhelmingly stacked as assistant coaches, and many coaching staffs have only one African American, a small nod to affirmative action.

Managerial positions in intercollegiate sports continue to elude African Americans as well. Again, Brooks and Althouse and Abney document the scandalously low percentage of African American athletic directors in collegiate sports. Most executive vacancies continue to go to Whites, sometimes by thinly disguised ploys that eliminate African Americans from serious consideration for the positions. These authors describe how several factors appear to have affected the career mobility patterns of African American head and assistant college coaches. Although they are unable to identify any models that clearly explain why intercollegiate sports has been so slow in incorporating Black coaches and athletic administrators into its system, they emphatically affirm that African American men and women have been underutilized and underrepresented in college athletic leadership positions.

The Legal System and African American College Athletes

Social theorist Antonio Gramsci (1971) argued that the state "tends to create and maintain a certain type of civilization and citizen . . . and to eliminate certain customs and attitudes and to disseminate others," and the law is "its instrument for this purpose" (p. 246). Certainly, the law has been an instrument of the intercollegiate athletic establishment throughout its history. In the process, African American college athletes have been the victims. The essay by Timothy Davis (Essay 12) explains that despite the persistence of racism in intercollegiate athletics, traditional civil rights laws have been largely ineffective for protecting the interests of African American college athletes. Davis also examines the implications of the constraints of traditional civil rights laws and an increasing judicial hostility to affirmative action for African American college athletes. In closing, Davis proposes legal and nonlegal approaches for remedying racism in college sport.

Shropshire's essay (13) also deals with legal questions. His specific focus is on the issue of compensation for African American college athletes at major universities, especially in football and basketball. He discusses the various legal issues behind the claim of the National Collegiate Athletic Association (NCAA) that payment to college athletes is unnecessary, and the contention of athletes and their supporters who believe athletes should receive monetary compensation rather than merely an "athletic scholarship."

Women in Intercollegiate Sport

The essays by Yevonne Smith (Essay 9), Doris R. Corbett and William Johnson (Essay 10), and by Tina Sloan Green (Essay 11) all center attention on the historical and cultural conditions for female African American athletes. The intersections of race, gender, and class in the socialization and achievement experiences of African American elite sportswomen are explored in Smith's essay. The sociohistorical timeline Smith has developed summarizing African American women's sporting achievements is a unique and useful feature of the essay.

An observation that is frequently made about African American women is that they suffer "double jeopardy," meaning that they are subject to both sexism *and* racism. All three of these essays amply confirm this observation. As Corbett and Johnson demonstrate, there is a further twist in the cultural milieu of African American females: They are viewed and treated differently from White females, and this has had consequences with respect to expectations and treatment of them as athletes. A main theme of Corbett and Johnson is the inadequacy of the literature about female African American athletes, and, they argue, what little exists largely fails to contextualize and give meaning to African American women's experiences in sports. Instead, the focus is primarily on describing the achievements of an elite group of African American women athletes who have achieved international status in their sport. The media have been instrumental in making celebrities of a few female African American athletes, while reinforcing traditional stereotypes of both female and Black athletes.

A useful list of 12 racial and sexual barriers surrounding the involvement of African American female athletes is enumerated by Corbett and Johnson. The list is useful because the items could be used by various groups in formulating new policies and procedures for redressing the inequalities that now exist for African American female athletes.

Tina Sloan Green's speculations about the future of African American women in sport offer a hopeful, largely optimistic portrayal, but she does emphasize that increased opportunities are largely contingent on economic conditions, not only economic prosperity in the societal marketplace but also improved economic status for African Americans. Even where low-income conditions continue to exist, Green foresees improved access to sports through community-based organizations.

High school and college sports have broadened and expanded over the past 20 years to give greater access to female athletes, but African American female athletes have benefitted only marginally at this point, mainly due to social- and gender-related barriers. Green expects many of these barriers to be overcome in the future. Still, careers in sports for African American women, as athletes, coaches, administrators, sportscasters, etc., will be extremely limited and difficult to attain, according to Green.

College Athletics and Life After College

Participation in college athletics has long been touted as good preparation for life after college, but this notion has been based mostly on faith and public relations. As Sellers (Essay 7) notes, there has been little empirical study of college athletes after they leave the campus, and what little exists does not confirm the popular portrayal that college athletes, because of their collegiate sporting experiences, lead happy and contented lives and become successful in their chosen careers. Moreover, there is the possibility that African American and White student-athletes have quite different postcollege lives and careers.

After describing the unique characteristics of the African American student-athlete, Sellers reviews the relevant research about athletic retirement. He then develops a framework for evaluating whether college student-athletes are provided reasonable compensation for their participation. In Sellers's view, African American student-athletes' postcollege lives are influenced by whether they were provided sound educational opportunities or whether they were merely exploited by the institution. The key to providing educational opportunity, according to Sellers's criteria, is whether the opportunity for a college education is present. Three elements compose the opportunity for a college education: opportunities for developing personal competence, opportunities for upward mobility, and opportunity to earn a college degree. Sellers's assumption is that to the extent to which these educational opportunities exist, the athletic experience will have a positive effect on the quality of postathletic life. To the extent that they are absent, athletes are being exploited, and personal and economic problems will plague the athletes in their postathletic life.

Sellers devotes the final pages of his essay to recommending interventions that he believes can enhance the quality of life after student-athletes leave the campus. Recommendations are directed to sport sociologists and psychologists, the NCAA, colleges and universities, and the families of athletes.

What About the Future?

The essay by Carole Oglesby and Diana Schrader (Essay 14) calls on White Americans to end the denial, disregard, and resistance they have historically used, and still use, to maintain and sustain racism in our society at large and in sports particularly. They insist Whites have the power to make a difference in racial matters, and they must begin with acknowledging and accepting responsibility for White domination. For sports, it must begin, according to Oglesby and Schrader, by confronting the reluctance of the White sports establishment to acknowledge and confront racism. For too long, this has been the tactic for refusing to seriously address the widespread racism in sports.

They argue that in order to enhance a multiracial future, we all need to commit some of our professional work to antiracist activity. They propose three types of steps: personal, research-oriented, and programmatic. An example of the first would be pursuing historical and cultural understanding through courses in African American studies. Excerpts from a class journal one of the authors wrote for a course she took devoted to expanding awareness of and commitment to improved race relations in sport provide a case study of the values of education. Examples of the research-oriented step would include engaging in research, employing various methodologies, about African Americans. Examples of the third step include antiracist action programs designed to counteract and even eliminate institutionalized, cultural, and individual racism. Programs of this kind already exist, and the authors identify and describe a couple of very successful ones. These steps can make a difference and can be first steps on the path to personal empowerment for Whites as well as African Americans.

The final essay, written by D. Stanley Eitzen (Essay 15), is a thoughtful, broad-ranging essay examining race relations in American society and big-time intercollegiate athletics. In the first section, Eitzen discusses the interracial contexts of American society and big-time college sport, the two contests in which African American athletes participate. He clearly shows how African Americans are disadvantaged in both settings. Next, Eitzen describes the trends in American society, the universities, and intercollegiate athletics that will affect future race relations. Five major societal trends that will shape race relations in the future are identified and discussed by Eitzen. In the last section of his essay, Eitzen lists 22 recommendations for reforming intercollegiate sports that, if adopted, would help eliminate racism and the exploitation of African American student-athletes in big-time college sports programs.

The Unique Contributions of This Book

This volume makes a valuable contribution to the literature on American sports, primarily because there is no other single book that focuses on the African American athlete in college athletics. Furthermore, each of the essays makes a specific contribution to understanding the structure of intercollegiate athletics and the complex role of African American student-athletes in that enterprise. Of course, college athletics is only one form of sports in which African American athletes participate; millions participate in youth and high school athletics, and a few thousand are professional athletes at any one time. Some of the same issues and problems that African American athletes encounter in college athletics are also encountered at the other levels of organized sports, but those stories deserve separate treatments.

Study Questions

1. Understanding the role of racism in college athletics requires an understanding of racism in the larger American cultural context in which it is situated. Drawing on the description of racism in American society in this chapter and the knowledge you have acquired about this topic from other sources, historically situate and culturally locate racism in American society.

2. Throughout their history in North America, African Americans have played a continuing and significant role in every era of American sport history. Describe and discuss African American involvement in American sport: (a) before the Civil War, (b) immediately following the Civil War, (c) the last two decades of the 19th century until after World War II, and (d) after World War II.

3. Focusing specifically on African American involvement in intercollegiate sports, describe and discuss the involvement of African Americans in intercollegiate sport from the late 19th century to the present.

References

Bell, D. (1992). *Faces at the bottom of the well: The permanence of racism.* New York: Basic Books.

Berry, M. F. (1994). *Black resistance, white law* (Rev. ed.). New York: Penguin.

Chalk, O. (1975). *Pioneers of black sport.* New York: Dodd, Mead.

Donaldson, K. B. (1996). *Through students' eyes: Combating racism in United States schools.* New York: Praeger.

Eitzen, D. S., & Sage, G. H. (1997). *Sociology of North American sport* (6th ed.). Madison, WI: Brown & Benchmark.

Gardner, R., & Shortelle, D. (1993). *The forgotten players: The story of black baseball in America.* New York: Walker & Co.

Gorn, E. J., & Oriard, M. (1995, March 24). Taking sports seriously. *The Chronicle of Higher Education,* p. A52.

Gramsci, A. (1971). *Selections from the prison notebooks* (Q. Hoare & G. N. Smith, Eds.). New York: International Publishers.

Hadjor, K. B. (1995). *Another America: The politics of race and blame.* Boston: South End Press.

Harris, L. (1993). *Racism and violence in American high schools.* Baltimore: Project TEAMWORK Responds.

Peterson, R. (1992). *Only the ball was white: History of legendary black players and all black professional teams.* New York: Oxford University Press.

Rowan, C. T. (1996). *The coming race war.* Boston: Little Brown.

Rowe, A., & Jeffries, J. M. (Eds.). (1996). *The state of black America 1996.* New York: National Urban League.

Rust, A., Jr. (1992). *Get that nigger off the field: The oral history of the Negro leagues.* Brooklyn: Book Mail Services.

Steinberg, S. (1995). *Turning back: The retreat from racial justice in American thought and policy.* Boston: Beacon.

Tomaskovic-Davey, D. (1993). *Gender and racial inequality at work.* Ithaca, NY: ILR Press.

Wiggins, D. K. (1997). *Glory bound: Black athletes in a white America.* Syracuse, NY: Syracuse University Press.

Wilson, C. A. (1996). *Racism: From slavery to advanced capitalism.* Thousand Oaks, CA: Sage.

SECTION 1

HISTORICAL
ANALYSIS
OF
RACISM
AND
CRITICAL
EVENTS

Critical Events Affecting Racism in Athletics

David K. Wiggins

Abstract

This essay examines the involvement of African Americans in sport from the latter half of the 19th century to the present. Particular attention is paid to the critical events that have influenced the status of African American athletes at both the amateur and professional levels of sport. A number of outstanding African American athletes distinguished themselves in a variety of different sports during the latter half of the 19th century. Hardening racial policies, combined with a number of other societal factors in the late 19th century, forced African Americans to form their own teams and leagues in a number of different sports. Although a few African American athletes were able to overcome racial barriers and compete in predominantly White organized sport, the large majority participated in sport behind segregated walls throughout the first half of the 20th century. The signing of Jackie Robinson by the Brooklyn Dodgers paved the way for African American athletes to reenter predominantly White organized sport in increasing numbers. African American athletes shed their traditional conservative approach to racial matters and became involved in the Civil Rights movement during the latter part of the 1960s and the early 1970s. African American athletes eventually received a great deal of attention from academicians and became the source of much debate as they realized increasing success as participants, yet continued to endure frustrations wrought by racial discrimination.

Key Terms

- Social Darwinism -
- Historically Black colleges -
- Civil Rights movement -
- Black athletic revolts -
- African American athletic superiority -
- Academic performance and graduation rates -
- African American sports agents -

Figure 1

Carl Lewis, shown here at the 1984 Olympic Games in Los Angeles, is one of America's most decorated track and field performers. He garnered worldwide acclaim at the Los Angeles Games when he duplicated Jesse Owens's great performances by capturing gold medals in the 100 meters, 200 meters, long jump, and 4 x 100 meter relay. Photo courtesy of Amateur Athletic Foundation, Los Angeles, CA and Robert Long AAF/LPI 1984.

Introduction

The history of the African American athletes' involvement in sport has been marked by a number of major successes interspersed with bitter disappointments. Initially exposed to different sports on southern plantations or in larger cities in the eastern half of the United States, a number of outstanding African American athletes distinguished themselves in highly organized sport at both the amateur and professional levels of competition in the years immediately following the Civil War (Ashe,

1988; Betts, 1974; Henderson, 1939, 1972; Lucas & Smith, 1978; Malloy, 1995; Rader, 1983; Somers, 1972; D.K. Wiggins, 1979, 1985; Zang, 1995). By the latter years of the 19th century, the large majority of African American athletes were, for various reasons and under different circumstances, excluded from participating in most highly organized sport and forced to establish their own teams and leagues operated without White interference. With the notable exceptions of boxing and international athletic contests, African Americans established their own organizations behind segregated walls in such sports as football, basketball, and baseball. These separate institutions were a source of great pride to the African American community and served as visible examples of Black organizational skill and entrepreneurship during the oppressive years of the first half of the 20th century (Ashe, 1988; Betts, 1974; Henderson, 1939, 1972; Lomax, 1998; Lucas & Smith, 1978; Malloy, 1995; P.B. Miller, 1995; Rader, 1983; Rayl, 1996; Ruck, 1986; Somers, 1972). The historic signing of Jackie Robinson by the Brooklyn Dodgers in 1945 was the beginning of the end for the separate sporting organizations, but it also helped usher in the reintegration of sport in this country. Robinson's signing with the Dodgers, combined with the integrationist policies in the post-World War II era, triggered the reentry and gradual acceptance of African American athletes into various sports. The following two decades witnessed unprecedented growth in the number of African American athletes participating in sport, a growth that proceeded at an uneven rate depending on the particular sport and location (Grundman, 1979; Lowenfish, 1978; Spivey, 1983; Tygiel, 1983; D.K. Wiggins, 1983, 1989).

Toward the latter part of the 1960s, African American athletes became involved in the Civil Rights movement by actively protesting racial discrimination in sport and the larger society. The two major forums for protest were the Olympic Games and predominantly White university campuses, where African American athletes staged boycotts and spoke out against the racial discrimination experienced by them and other members of the African American community. Although their personal involvement in civil rights issues slowly abated under the weight of the women's rights movement and issues associated with inflation and unemployment, the role of African American athletes in organized sport continued to be of great interest to both academicians and laypeople alike. In recent years, African American athletes have garnered front-page headlines, particularly in regard to their exploitation by educational institutions, inability to assume managerial and upper-level administrative positions in sport, and restriction to particular playing positions as well as sports (Coakley, 1990; Edwards, 1973 a, b; Leonard, 1993; Spivey, 1985; D.K. Wiggins, 1988).

A Taste of Success in Late-19th-Century Sport

The African American athlete's first real taste of highly competitive sport took place in the

Figure 2

"The Knockout," Jack Johnson vs. Jim Jeffries (Fight of the Century), Reno, NV, July 4, 1910. Photo courtesy of Nevada Historical Society.

years immediately following the Civil War. Although some African American athletes had achieved fame prior to the great war between the states, it was not until the bloody conflict ended that large numbers of them would realize national and even international acclaim in a wide range of sports. The newly found freedom following the war and the lasting sporting traditions established during slavery created an atmosphere in which African Americans were more readily accepted into horse racing, baseball, and other sports popular during the period. For example, Peter Jackson, the great boxer from the Virgin Islands by way of Australia, continued the tradition of outstanding Black fighters and became a household name among pugilistic fans through his well-known ring battles with such men as James J. Corbett, George Godfrey, and Frank Slavin (Ashe, 1988; Betts, 1974; D.K. Wiggins, 1985). Isaac Murphy and a number of other diminutive African Americans dominated the jockey profession, capturing the Kentucky Derby and many of horse racing's other prestigious events (Ashe, 1988; Betts, 1974; Hotaling, 1995; Somers 1972; D.K. Wiggins, 1979). Marshall "Major" Taylor, the great bicyclist from Indianapolis, seized the imagination of racing fans on both sides of the Atlantic with his amazing feats of speed on the oval track (Ashe, 1988; Betts, 1974; Ritchie, 1988; Taylor, 1928). Moses "Fleetwood" Walker and his brother Weldy became Major League Baseball's first African American players when they signed contracts with the Toledo Mudhens of the American Association in the mid-1880s (Malloy, 1995; McKinney, 1976; Peterson, 1970; Zang, 1995).

By the latter years of the 19th century African American athletes were being excluded from highly organized sport. Even those African American athletes who had achieved great success were either eliminated or pressured to drop out of their respective sports. The reasons for their elimination from highly organized sport were many and varied, including the dominant culture's belief in Black inferiority, general deterioration of Black rights, and eventual separation of the races in late-19th-century America (Davis, 1966; Lucas & Smith, 1978; Rader, 1983; Somers, 1972). The southern Black codes, established shortly after the Civil War to insure legal restrictions against the newly freed slaves, became easier to implement towards the end of the century as northern Republicans abandoned their previous commitment to Black rights. Further deterioration of Black rights resulted from decommitment by the United States Supreme Court toward the latter part of the 19th century. In 1883, the Supreme Court affirmed legislation overturning the 14th Amendment, citing that prevention of discrimination against individuals by states did not prohibit discrimination by individual citizens. In 1896, the famous *Plessy v. Ferguson* case legally sanctioned separation of schools by race and upheld "separate-but-equal" accommodations on railroads. In 1898, the Supreme Court kept many African Americans out of politics by upholding poll-tax qualifications and literary tests for voting (Logan, 1965; Meier & Rudwick, 1963; Woodward, 1966).

The Supreme Court decisions took place in an increasingly more hostile environment where African Americans were being "proven" inferior to Whites. The exclusion of African Americans from sport, like the exclusion of African Americans from all walks of life, was given a philosophical rationale based on a combination of social Darwinism, the rise of imperialism around the world, and the spread of pseudoscientific writings by academicians and others. Such well-known thinkers as Herbert Spencer and William Graham Sumner gave support to the belief that African Americans were on the lowest rung of the evolutionary ladder, incapable of surviving in a competitive society due to their intellectual and emotional inferiority (Cochran & Miller, 1961; Logan, 1957; Meier & Rudwick, 1963; Woodward, 1966). Social Darwinism was supported in principle by various members of the dominant culture who believed "nonwhite" people of the new territories annexed during imperialist expansion were merely savages in

need of education and cultural enlightenment. The belief in African American inferiority was further "substantiated" by a number of racist treatises and academic studies completed during the period. Prejudiced Whites received all the support they needed from academicians in such divergent fields as history, psychology, sociology, biology, and anthropology, who were busily trying to prove African American inferiority through their various writings (Cochran & Miller, 1961; Logan, 1957; Meier & Rudwick, 1963; Woodward, 1966).

Striving for an Equal Share in the American Dream

The segregation of highly organized sport did not stop a select number of African American athletes from continuing to achieve success in certain sports at different levels of competition. Throughout the first half of the 20th century, a number of outstanding African American athletes gained prominence in professional boxing, in college sport on predominantly White university campuses, and in Olympic competition (Ashe, 1988; Betts, 1974; Chalk, 1976; Davis, 1966; Fleischer, 1938; Young, 1963).

Involvement of African Americans in boxing had a long tradition, extending back to the early years of the 19th century when Tom Molineaux, with assistance from Bill Richmond, another famous African American pugilist and trainer of boxers, fought for the heavyweight championship against the Englishman, Tom Crib (Brailsford, 1988; Cone, 1982; Goodman, 1980; Gorn, 1994; J.W. Rudolph, 1979). A sport that fit nicely into the dominant culture's stereotypical notions of African Americans and legendary traditions of gladiatorial combat, boxing provided a better life for some African Americans while at once helping delimit the conditions of African American identity within American culture and reflecting the racial realities of society in general. African Americans withstood the segregationist policies of the late 19th century and continued to engage in matches, drawing worldwide attention from audiences especially interested in bouts where at least one of the fighters was Black (Early, 1989; Sammons, 1988).

The two most prominent African American fighters of the first half of the 20th century were the similarly legendary, yet decidedly different, Jack Johnson and Joe Louis. Johnson, the powerfully built boxer from Galveston, Texas, became the first African American to capture the world's heavyweight championship, holding on to the title for some 7 years before losing to the Pottawatomie giant, Jess Willard, in 1915. As great as Johnson's exploits were in boxing, it was outside the squared circle that Johnson gained the most attention and caused the greatest controversy. He has often been referred to as a "Bad Nigger," a man who played on the worst fears of the dominant culture by marrying three White women and having illicit affairs with a number of others, often prostitutes whom he treated with an odd mixture of affection and disdain. He was absolutely fearless and attracted to dangerous escapades that challenged White conventions and mores. Although a hero to many members of his race, Johnson drew the wrath of segments of both the African American and White communities because of his unwillingness to assume a subservient position and play the role of the grateful Black. He was eventually convicted of violating the Mann Act for transporting a White woman across state lines for illicit purposes and was forced to leave the country for a short time before returning home to serve a jail sentence at the federal prison in Leavenworth, Kansas (Farr, 1964; Gilmore, 1975; Roberts, 1983; W.H. Wiggins, 1971).

The bitter aftertaste from Johnson's career, combined with continuing racial discrimination in American society, made it virtually impossible for African American boxers to secure championship fights over the next two decades. That all changed in 1937, however, when Joe Louis, the superbly talented boxer from Detroit, became the second African American heavyweight champion by defeating James Braddock. Louis was a decidedly different champion than Johnson. Possessing enormous strength and boxing skills, Louis was a quiet, dignified man

who assumed the more subservient role Whites expected from members of his race, but he became a hero of almost mythical proportions in this country's African American community by demolishing White fighters with remarkable regularity and serving as a symbol of possibility for those subjugated by continuing racial discrimination (Capeci & Wilkerson, 1983; Edmonds, 1973; Mead, 1985).

Whereas Louis and Johnson gained fame as possibly America's finest pugilists, a number of outstanding African American athletes were competing in intercollegiate sport on predominantly White university campuses across the country. Following in the tradition of William Henry Lewis, William Tecumseh Sherman Jackson, and other great college performers of the late 19th century, such African American athletes as Fritz Pollard of Brown University; Paul Robeson of Rutgers; Jerome "Brud" Holland of Cornell; Eddie Tolan and Willis Ward of Michigan; William Bell, David Albritton, and Jesse Owens of Ohio State; Ralph Metcalfe of Marquette University; and Kenny Washington, Woody Strode, Jackie Robinson, and Ralph Bunche of UCLA established lasting reputations for their exploits in intercollegiate sport and, in some cases, Olympic competition. Owens's victories, for example, in the 1936 Olympic Games are legendary, ranking among the most significant individual performances in sport history (Baker, 1986; Behee, 1974; Carroll, 1992; Chalk, 1976; T.G. Smith, 1988; Spivey, 1983; Strode & Young, 1990; D.K. Wiggins, 1991).

The great success of African American athletes was sometimes overshadowed by the insensitivity and various forms of discrimination they experienced on their individual college campuses and outside the halls of academe. African American athletes at predominantly White universities invariably experienced the loneliness and sense of isolation that come with being members of a small minority in a largely White setting. A large number of African American athletes found White campuses and their environs insensitive to their needs, not always providing the suitable living arrangements, satisfying social and cultural activities, and educational support services necessary for academic success (T. Davis, 1995; L. Miller, 1927; Spivey & Jones, 1975; D.K. Wiggins, 1991; Wolters, 1975).

Perhaps even more traumatic for African American athletes than on-campus injustices were the racially discriminatory acts committed against them by White opponents from other institutions. The most noteworthy of these involved the refusal of southern White institutions to compete against northern institutions that had African American players on their teams. In 1916, for example, Washington and Lee College of Virginia threatened to withdraw from a football game against Rutgers because Paul Robeson was on the Rutgers team. Rutgers coach George Sanford eventually acceded to Washington and Lee's request, and Robeson was forced to sit out the game, apparently without any protest from the Rutgers community (Fishman, 1969; Gilliam, 1976; D.K. Wiggins, 1991). Approximately 13 years after the Robeson incident, coach Chuck Meehan of New York University acceded to the demands of the University of Georgia by withholding his star halfback, Dave Myers, from a football game between the two institutions. This incident resulted in much debate and protest, including protracted negotiations between the National Association for the Advancement of Colored People (NAACP) and university officials (Spivey, 1988; D.K. Wiggins, 1991; Wolters, 1975). In 1941, New York University complied with the wishes of Catholic University of America by withholding its three African American athletes from a track meet in Washington, DC. In the same year, Harvard University's outstanding African American lacrosse player, Lucian Alexis, Jr., was withheld from a match against the Naval Academy because of that institution's refusal to compete against African American players (P.B. Miller, 1991). The Alexis decision caused a great deal of protest on Harvard's campus and ultimately resulted in the university's announc-

ing that it would never again "countenance racial discrimination" (Brower, 1941, p. 261).

Sport Behind Segregated Walls

As a select group of African American athletes struggled to realize a measure of success in predominantly White organized sport, the African American community established its own separate sporting organizations behind segregated walls and out of view of most members of the dominant culture. Although remarkably similar to White-controlled institutions, these sporting organizations reflected special African American cultural patterns, attesting to the strength and vibrancy of the African American community during the oppressive years of the early 20th century (Ashe, 1988; Gems, 1995; George, 1992; Henderson, 1939; Lanctot, 1994; Lomax, 1998; P.B. Miller, 1995; Peterson, 1970, 1990; Rayl, 1996; Rogosin, 1983; Ruck, 1987).

Prime examples of African American sporting organizations were the athletic programs established at historically Black colleges. Originally organized during the late 19th century, athletic programs at historically Black colleges were similar to those at predominantly White institutions in that they began as informal, student-run activities and evolved into highly structured and institutionally controlled phenomena. They were also much like intercollegiate athletic programs on White campuses in that they included a wide variety of sports, were eventually controlled by elaborate bureaucratic organizations, and were rationalized along both educational and social lines. Most historically Black colleges competed in all the major team sports, including football, which was one of the most popular sports in the African American community. The annual Thanksgiving Day football games between various schools, including the classic match between Howard and Lincoln (PA), drew thousands of spectators from around the country, contributed to a sense of institutional pride and national reputation, and stimulated school spirit by bringing students, faculty, and alumni together to share in the excitement of common pursuits. Organizational structure was first brought to Black college sport in 1912, when the Colored (later Central) Intercollegiate Athletic Association (CIAA) was formed among such well-known institutions as Howard, Lincoln (PA), and Hampton Institute. Shortly after the creation of the CIAA, similar athletic associations were organized, which led to the further legitimacy of Black college sport (Ashe, 1988; Captain, 1991; Chalk, 1976; George, 1992; Henderson, 1939; P.B. Miller, 1995).

Differences between athletic programs at historically Black colleges and predominantly White institutions were almost as great as their similarities. In contrast to their White counterparts, Black colleges lacked the funds necessary to hire large coaching staffs, purchase the latest equipment, and build elaborate athletic facilities. The financial circumstances of most Black colleges made it impossible for them to outfit well-equipped teams like those at predominantly White institutions. Sport at historically Black schools was also different from athletic programs at predominantly White institutions in that the exploits of many outstanding Black college athletes never became known to a larger American audience. Although many of them became household names in the African American community, Black college athletes were forced to perform behind segregated walls, which obscured their many exploits from public view and usually minimized the attention they received from the powerful White press (Ashe, 1988; Captain, 1991; Chalk, 1976; George, 1992; Henderson, 1939; P.B. Miller, 1995).

The last major difference between the two forms of intercollegiate sport had to do with gender and participation in the Olympic Games. Few, if any, male athletes from Black colleges participated in the Olympics. Male athletes from Black colleges were left at home whereas John Taylor, John Woodruff, and other great performers from predominantly White universities traveled the world competing in the most famous of all athletic festivals. Why

there were no male Olympians from Black colleges is open to speculation, but it partly stemmed from the fact that predominantly White institutions recruited the best of the elite African American athletes (Ashe, 1988; Chalk, 1976; Henderson, 1939).

Ironically, African American female athletes who participated in the Olympic Games often came from Black colleges rather than predominantly White universities. The first wave of African American women Olympians, including high jumper Alice Coachman, the first African American woman to capture an Olympic gold medal, had been members at various times of Cleveland Abbott's great track teams at Tuskegee Institute. The next outstanding group of African American women Olympians, including such great athletes as Wilma Rudolph, Barbara Jones, Martha Hudson, and Lucinda Williams, were products of Ed Temple's famous Tigerbelles track teams from Tennessee State University (Cahn, 1994; Gissendanner, 1994, 1996; W. Rudolph, 1977; Thaxton, 1970). The large number of women Olympians from historically Black colleges perhaps resulted, as Cahn has suggested, from the fact that African American women athletes were seemingly more accepted in their community than White women athletes were in their own. Although "middle-class White women" avoided track and field because of its reputation as a "masculine endeavor," African American women athletes were training and honing their talents under the watchful eyes of African American male coaches like Cleveland Abbott and Ed Temple (Cahn, 1994, p. 112). Unfortunately, the acceptance of African American women in a sport such as track and field "also reinforced disparaging stereotypes of Black women as less womanly or feminine than White women" (Cahn, 1994, p. 112).

Holding out as much interest to the African American community as college sports were the all-Black professional teams and leagues that were organized in early-20th-century America. A legacy from the late 19th century, a number of all-Black teams and leagues were established in the three major sports of football, basketball, and baseball. Of these three, baseball was the most highly organized and popular among members of the African American community; the sport enthralled thousands of fans, who found the game a meaningful experience and pleasurable counterpoint to the drudgery of everyday life (Bruce, 1985; George, 1992; Holway, 1988; Lanctot, 1994; Lomax, 1998; Peterson, 1970, 1990; Rogosin, 1983; Ruck, 1987; White, 1996).

Black baseball's first successful league was formed in 1920 by Rube Foster, the once-great pitcher and manager of the Chicago American Giants. Foster organized that year the National Negro Baseball League (NNL), an organization patterned along the lines of Major League Baseball and composed of teams from Chicago, Detroit, St. Louis, Kansas City, and Indianapolis. The NNL collapsed under the weight of financial instability and a host of other problems in 1931, just 3 years after the rival Eastern Negro League (ENL) ceased operation. In 1933, a second NNL was organized and 4 years later was in competition with the newly created Negro American League (NAL) (Bruce, 1985; Holway, 1988; Lanctot, 1994; Lomax, 1998; Peterson, 1970; Rogosin, 1983; White, 1996).

These two leagues were the cornerstone of Black baseball over the next two decades, representing at once some of the worst features of American racism and the best creative energy of the African American community. The NNL and NAL, although quite stable through much of the 1930s and 1940s, were never able to realize their financial potential, because clubs lacked ownership of baseball parks and were forced to engage in bidding wars for the services of outstanding players. Clark Griffith and other moguls in Major League Baseball never allowed Black teams to establish significant profit margins because of the high rent they charged for the use of their ballparks. This situation caused a myriad of other problems, including inadequate working and living conditions for the league's African American players, who already suffered the indignities associated with being members of one of this country's least esteemed minority groups. The players were forced to make long, confined road trips in buses and beat-up old cars, stay in segregated and sometimes dilapidated hotels, and survive on limited meal money. They also had to cope with the frustrations that resulted from being denied service at restaurants, hotels, and other public accommodations (Bruce, 1985; Holway, 1988; Lanctot, 1994; Peterson, 1970; Rogosin, 1983; White, 1996).

African American baseball players, however, overcame the numerous limitations of their separate leagues to carve out meaningful professional careers and more rewarding ways of life. Relative to many other members of the African American community, players in Black baseball often enjoyed satisfying lives characterized by adulation and pleasurable experiences. The players who participated in Black baseball were like most athletes in that they enjoyed the camaraderie of their teammates, the competition against other talented

Figure 3

African American women have contributed significantly to the growth of women's professional basketball in this country. Lisa Leslie, shown here with a large smile and conversing with teammates on the bench, is one of the most famous of the African American women professional basketball players.
Photo courtesy of Amateur Athletic Foundation, Los Angeles, CA.

performers, and the travel to different parts of the country. The more talented African American players participated in the greatest spectacle in Black baseball, the annual East-West All-Star Game. First played in 1933, the All-Star Game pitted the finest players in Black baseball against each other, allowing Josh Gibson, Cool Papa Bell, Judy Johnson, Buck Leonard, Satchel Paige, and other legendary performers to showcase their talents to thousands of fans (Brashler, 1978; Bruce, 1985; Holway, 1975, 1988; Peterson, 1970; Rogosin, 1983; White, 1996).

Campaigns to Reintegrate Lily-White Sport

Coinciding with the creation of all-Black sporting organizations were bitter campaigns waged by various individuals and groups against the color line in White organized sport. Of all the groups that hammered away at organized sport for its exclusionary policies, perhaps none were more significant than sportswriters from such well-known African American weeklies as the *Baltimore Afro-American*, *Chicago Defender*, *New York Amsterdam News*, and *Pittsburgh Courier Journal*. Clamoring loudly for an end to discrimination in baseball that symbolically, and in actual practice, was most important to the African American community, they led the battle against racism in White organized sport (Brower, 1940; Reisler, 1994; Simons, 1985; Tygiel, 1983; D.K. Wiggins, 1983).

In the late 1930s, for example, the *Pittsburgh Courier Journal*'s Wendell Smith began a fervent campaign to eliminate the color barrier in Major League Baseball. From the moment he wrote his first article on baseball's color ban in 1938, to the ultimate integration of the sport some 9 years later, Smith waged a fierce battle against the bureaucrats in the national game for their exclusion of African American players. Like other members of his race, Smith abhorred the discrimination in Major League Baseball, believing it symbolized the degraded status of African Americans in this country. He pointed out, through various

means, that African Americans could not be considered true American citizens until they gained entry into organized baseball. Although realizing that participation in the national game would not necessarily eradicate political and economic inequality, Smith believed that the desegregation of baseball would help give African Americans the sense of dignity and self-esteem essential for the ultimate elimination of racial discrimination in this country (D.K. Wiggins, 1983).

Smith's campaign to desegregate organized baseball was remarkably aggressive and took many forms. He was suggesting by the beginning of 1939 that African Americans form a National Association for the Advancement of Colored People (NAACP) on behalf of African American players and attack the color line as vigorously as possible. Shortly after announcing his plans to organize an NAACP on behalf of African American players, Smith conducted an exclusive interview with the president of the National League, Ford Frick. The interview with Frick, which was characterized by the typical rhetoric voiced for years by leaders in Major League Baseball, provoked Smith into conducting a series of interviews with eight managers and 40 players in the National League to determine their views on African American players. Culminating in a series of articles in the *Courier Journal* entitled "What Big Leaguers Think of Negro Baseball Players," the interviews were illuminating in that the only person who believed African Americans should be barred from organized baseball was Bill Terry, manager of the New York Giants (D.K. Wiggins, 1983).

In the years immediately following the interviews with National League managers and players, Smith became even bolder in his campaign efforts. He admonished Clark Griffith, owner of the Washington Senators, for his blatantly racist view of African American ballplayers; called upon President Roosevelt to adopt a "fair employment policy" in baseball just as he had done in war industries and governmental agencies; helped arrange a meeting between the baseball commissioner, Judge Kenesaw Mountain Landis, and the Black Newspaper Publishers' Association; assisted in arranging a tryout for three African American players with the Boston Red Sox; and suggested to Branch Rickey that Jackie Robinson would be the ideal player to integrate the national game (D.K. Wiggins, 1983).

The Walls Come Tumbling Down

The efforts of Smith, as well as those of others involved in their own campaigns to integrate organized baseball, finally paid off in 1945 when Rickey signed Robinson to a contract with the Brooklyn Dodgers. The signing of Robinson was received with unabated enthusiasm by the African American community and immediately catapulted the former UCLA and Kansas City Monarch baseball star into the national limelight. Like Jesse Owens and Joe Louis before him, Robinson became a much needed example of achievement and symbol of possibility for African Americans. He had an uplifting effect on other members of his race by becoming a participant in the sport considered the great leveler in society and America's national pastime (Falkner, 1995; Frommer, 1982; Polner, 1982; Rampersad, 1997; Robinson, 1972; Tygiel, 1983).

The most important outcome of Robinson's signing was that it paved the way for further desegregation of White organized sport at various levels of competition, a process that would not be completed until the latter half of the 1970s. Five months after obtaining the rights to Robinson, Rickey signed two more African American players, Roy Campanella and Don Newcombe, to contracts with the Dodgers, and about a year later, Bill Veeck began integration of his Cleveland Indians organization by signing Larry Doby. Other major league teams were slow to follow the examples set by Rickey and Veeck, and integration in organized baseball proceeded very deliberately and at an uneven pace. During the latter part of the 1940s, absence of financial incentives coupled with the racism and conservatism of base-

ball executives limited the number of teams that were willing to take chances on African American players. By 1951, however, the pace of integration quickened as more teams were stimulated to seek African American talent on account of the impressive performances of Robinson, Campanella, and others. Three years later, 12 of the 16 teams in Major League Baseball had African American players on their rosters. In 1959, the curtain finally dropped on baseball's color line for good when the Boston Red Sox promoted the talented African American infielder, Pumpsie Green, from their minor league affiliate in Minneapolis (Moore, 1988; Tygiel, 1983).

The desegregation of Major League Baseball would be duplicated in other professional and amateur sports over the next two decades. For example, the year after the signing of Robinson by the Brooklyn Dodgers, the color line was broken in professional football. The Los Angeles Rams of the National Football League, under pressure to field African American players and fearful of losing its lease of the Los Angeles Coliseum, signed Kenny Washington and Woody Strode to contracts. The two African American stars were, ironically enough, former teammates of Robinson's at the University of California at Los Angeles. In the same year the NFL was integrated, the Cleveland Browns of the newly organized All-American Football Conference signed two African American stars, fullback Marion Motley of the University of Nevada at Reno and lineman Bill Willis of Ohio State University (Gems, 1988; T.G. Smith, 1988; Strode & Young, 1990). The American Bowling Congress allowed African Americans to use its lanes for the first time in 1949 (Lucas & Smith, 1978). A year later, Althea Gibson became the first African American to participate at Forest Hills in the United States Tennis Championships, and the color line was broken in the National Basketball Association when the Harlem Globetrotters' Nat "Sweetwater" Clifton signed with the New York Knicks and Chuck Cooper of Duquesne University inked a contract with the Boston

Celtics (George, 1992; Gibson, 1958; Lucas & Smith, 1978; Salzberg, 1987). Art Dorrington became organized hockey's first Black player in America when he signed with the Pennsylvania Johnstown Jets in 1952. Some 22 years after Dorrington took to the ice with the Johnstown Jets, Lee Elder became the first African American golfer to participate in the prestigious Masters Tournament in Augusta, Georgia (Lucas & Smith, 1978).

Perhaps the most significant battles against White organized sport took place in intercollegiate athletics in the southern part of the United States. For years, African Americans who participated in intercollegiate sport competed for either historically Black colleges in the South or predominantly White universities in the North. The chance to compete in intercollegiate athletics for one of the schools in the prestigious Atlantic Coast (ACC), Southwestern (SWC), and Southeastern (SEC) conferences was out of the question for African Americans, who found themselves thwarted by southern racial policies and segregation (Ashe, 1988; Chalk, 1976; Henderson, 1939; Martin, 1993, 1996; D.K. Wiggins, 1991).

By the early 1960s, however, integration slowly began to take place in southern athletic conferences (Martin, 1993, 1996; Paul, McGhee, & Fant, 1984; Spivey, 1983; D.K. Wiggins, 1991). The *Brown v. Board of Education* school desegregation decision in 1954, combined with the fledgling Civil Rights movement and the desire of educational institutions to achieve prominence in sport, resulted in the gradual integration of athletic programs at schools that had historically refused even to compete against African American athletes. In 1963, the color line was broken in the ACC by football player Darryl Hill of the University of Maryland (Spivey, 1983; D.K. Wiggins, 1991). Two years later, Texas Christian basketball player James Cash became the first African American athlete in the SWC (Martin, 1993; Pennington, 1987; Spivey, 1983; D.K. Wiggins, 1991).

The last major conference to integrate its sports programs was the SEC, a traditional stronghold of both athletic excellence and racial prejudice. Conference schools had received much notoriety for their athletic achievements through the years, but were equally famous for racial intolerance and acts of discrimination committed against African American athletes from northern institutions. Perhaps nowhere was the color line drawn tighter than in athletic programs of SEC schools, which operated against a backdrop of burning crosses and robed Klansmen as well as large stadiums intended for White players only. In spite of these circumstances, segregation in the SEC slowly toppled under the weight of the Civil Rights struggle just as it had in the ACC and SWC. The University of Kentucky, the northernmost school in the conference, led the charge against segregation when football coach Charlie Bradshaw signed African American high school stars Nat Northington and Greg Page in 1966. Over the next few years, African American athletes began to appear in different sports at other SEC schools, with Vanderbilt basketball coach C.M. Newton being the first person to recruit African Americans in significant numbers and the University of Mississippi being the last member of the conference to integrate, in 1971 (Martin, 1993, 1996; Paul et al., 1984).

African American Athletes and the Civil Rights Movement

Integration of southern athletic conferences shared the spotlight with Black athletic disturbances that took place on predominantly White university campuses across the country. By the latter part of the 1960s, African American athletes were creating chaos on college campuses by becoming active participants in the Civil Rights movement and protesting racial discrimination in sport and society at large. Inspired by the examples set by such outspoken individuals as Jim Brown, Bill Russell, and Muhammad Ali, African American college athletes shed their traditional conservative approach to racial matters and vehemently protested everything from the lack of African American studies in the curriculum to the dearth of African American coaches and athletic administrators (Brown, 1964; Gorn, 1995; Russell, 1966). This path was sometimes paved with dire consequences, many African American athletes enduring the wrath of university administrations and jeopardizing their careers for speaking out on behalf of themselves and other members of their race. The protests also defied easy classification, as they took place on different-sized campuses, in both urban and rural settings, and from one end of the country to the other. Black athletic rebellions occurred, for example, on the campuses of Syracuse University; Oregon State University; Michigan State University; San Francisco State University; University of Washington; University of California, Berkeley; University of Kansas; University of Wyoming; University of Texas at El Paso; University of Arizona; and Oklahoma City University (Edwards, 1969, 1970; Scott, 1971; D.K. Wiggins, 1988, 1991, 1992).

Rebellious African American athletes sometimes took their protests off campus and into larger settings where they could better publicize their fight for racial equality. Certainly the most celebrated protest of this type was the proposed boycott of the 1968 Olympic Games in Mexico City. In the fall of 1967, Harry Edwards, then an instructor at San Jose State College and now a well-known professor of sociology at the University of California, Berkeley, assembled a group of outstanding African American athletes who threatened to withdraw from the Games in Mexico City unless certain demands were met. The demands included the removal of Avery Brundage as president of the International Olympic Committee, restoration of Muhammad Ali's heavyweight boxing title, exclusion of Rhodesia and South Africa from Olympic competition, appointment of at least two African Americans to the United States Olympic Committee, complete desegregation of the New York Athletic Club (NYAC), and addition of at least two African American coaches to the men's Olympic track and field team (Edwards, 1969, 1980; Sendler, 1969; Spivey, 1985; D.K. Wiggins, 1992).

Edwards and his band of African American athletes, who termed their movement the Olympic Project for Human Rights (OPHR), got their protest off to a fast start by successfully organizing a boycott of the NYAC's 100th Anniversary Track Meet in February, 1968. It became increasingly apparent following the NYAC boycott, however, that there would be no agreement among the disgruntled African American athletes as to whether to boycott the Mexico City games. As serious as they were about making a contribution to the Civil Rights movement and protesting racial discrimination, African American athletes found it impossible to forgo Olympic competition and not represent themselves and their country against the best athletes in the world. For most of the African American athletes, the Olympic games were the ultimate in athletic competition, representing years of preparation and bringing them potential glory and unmatched worldwide acclaim. To sacrifice the potential acclaim was extremely difficult, even for the most racially conscious African American athletes (Edwards, 1969, 1980; Johnson, 1972; Spivey, 1985; D.K. Wiggins, 1992).

Academicians and African American Athletic Performances

The protests of African American athletes declined in number by the early 1970s. Desegregation resulting from civil rights legislation of the 1960s, coupled with the fledgling women's rights movement and problems associated with inflation and unemployment, took some steam out of the Black athletic revolt just as it had the larger Black Power movement (Rader, 1983; Roberts & Olson, 1989). African American athletes continued to fight racial discrimination, but they increasingly became the topic of discussion among people of both races who had become sensitized to racial issues emanating from the athletic protests of the previous decade. One of the legacies of the athletic protest movement of the 1960s was that the problems of African American athletes were made more visible to the American public. The result was an outpouring of research studies and more popular essays dealing with the various forms of discrimination committed against African American athletes, rather than any substantive changes made in sport itself (Johnson & Marple, 1973; Loy & McElvogue, 1970; Pascal & Rapping, 1970; Skully, 1974; Yetman & Eitzen, 1972).

Topics receiving a great deal of attention from academicians and others interested in African American athletes were the phenomenon known as stacking, unequal opportunities and inadequate reward structures in sport, and differences in sport performances between African American and White athletes (Coakley, 1990; L.P. Davis, 1990; Leonard, 1993; Sailes, 1991; D.K. Wiggins, 1989). In 1971, Martin Kane, a senior editor for *Sports Illustrated*, ignited the age-old debate over alleged African American athletic superiority by claiming in an article titled "An Assessment of Black Is Best" that "there is an increasing body of scientific opinion which suggests that physical differences in the races might well have enhanced the athletic potential of the negro in certain sports" (p. 72). Drawing on the expertise of sport scientists, coaches, medical doctors, and African American athletes themselves, Kane argued that the dominance of African American athletes in sport was the result of racially linked psychological, historical, and physiological factors. The outstanding performances of African American athletes, in other words, were based on racial characteristics indigenous to the African American population (Cashmore, 1982; Hoberman, 1997; Kane, 1971; P.B. Miller, 1998; Sailes, 1991; Smith, 1995; D.K. Wiggins, 1989).

Kane's essay resulted in an angry response from Harry Edwards. In a series of articles, Edwards (1972, 1973a,b) claimed that Kane's theories suffered from serious methodological problems and were based on questionable assumptions about racial differences. He refuted Kane's argument that African American athletes possessed innate psychological and physiological skills that predisposed them to certain

physical activities and accounted for their outstanding performances in sport. Kane's assertions were ludicrous and implied that African Americans, while physiologically talented, were intellectually inferior to their White counterparts (Cashmore, 1982; Edwards, 1972, 1973a,b; Hoberman, 1997; P.B. Miller, 1998; E. Smith, 1995; D.K. Wiggins, 1989).

To Edwards, the outstanding performances of African American athletes stemmed from a variety of societal conditions rather than innate physiological or psychological characteristics. Edwards claimed, among other things, that African American youth placed a high value on sport, and the result was a channeling of a disproportionate number of skilled African Americans into athletics at both the amateur and professional levels. In contrast to their White counterparts, African Americans had less visible prestige role models, fewer job opportunities, and a more limited range of occupational choices. The upshot of these conditions was that African Americans viewed sport, and, to a lesser degree. entertainment, as their most achievable goals and the quickest path to stardom and wealth. This career path, unfortunately, has often been paved with bitter disappointments for aspiring African American athletes, the vast majority either ending up back in the ghetto because they lacked the talent to become superstars or dropping out of sport altogether because they refused to comply with the racist American sport establishment (Edwards, 1972, 1973a,b; Hoberman, 1997; D.K. Wiggins, 1989).

The exchange between Kane and Edwards did not put an end to the debate over African American athletic superiority. The increasing number of African Americans participating in sport throughout the last two decades has continued to spark much controversy among academicians and lay public alike (Cashmore, 1982; L.P. Davis, 1990; Hoberman, 1997; MacDonald, 1981; P.B. Miller, 1998; Price, 1997; Sailes, 1991; Shropshire & Smith, 1998; E. Smith, 1995; D.K. Wiggins, 1989). In 1972, for instance, Harvard psychiatrist Alvin F. Poussaint argued in an essay titled "Sex and the Black Male" that the need of African American males to display physical power has accounted for their outstanding performances in sport. Stripped of any social power, African American males have focused their attention on other symbols of masculinity, particularly on America's playing fields (pp. 115–116). Two years after Poussaint's article appeared, Jesse Owens, the man whose great performances on the cinder track in the 1930s contributed to initial discussions about African American athletic superiority, told members of the American Medical Association that desire rather than innate physiological differences accounted for the disproportionate number of African Americans in sport ("Byline," 1974).

In 1977, *Time* magazine published an article titled "Black Dominance" in which the opinions of various people, including famous African American athletes, were gathered concerning the issue of African American athletic superiority. A majority of the African American athletes interviewed argued that physical differences accounted for the outstanding performances of African American athletes ("Black Dominance," 1977). Academician Legrand Clegg suggested in a 1980 essay in *Sepia* magazine that the superior accomplishments of African American athletes resulted from large amounts of melanin in their systems. Citing the work of several African American scholars in the School of Ethnic Studies at San Francisco State University, Clegg believed melanin, rather than simply serving to protect skin from the harmful effects of the sun, was capable of absorbing a great deal of energy that African Americans used to achieve great speeds in track. In 1982, sociologist James LeFlore argued in an essay titled "Athleticism Among American Blacks" that the disproportionate number of African American athletes in certain sports, although obviously influenced to some degree by genetic, environmental, and economic factors, was determined primarily by the cultural setting in which African Americans found themselves and the type of information available to them and their particular

subculture. Some 6 years after the publication of LeFlore's article, Jimmy "The Greek" Snyder, at that time sports prognosticator and announcer on CBS's *The NFL Today* show, caused an uproar when he told an interviewer at a restaurant in Washington, DC, that African American athletes were superior to their White counterparts because of the way they were bred during slavery (L.P. Davis, 1990; Hoberman, 1997; P.B. Miller, 1998; "Of Fingerprints," 1988; Rowe, 1988; Sailes, 1991; E. Smith, 1995; "What We Say," 1988; D.K. Wiggins, 1989). In 1989, Tom Brokaw, partly in response to Snyder's controversial interview, hosted an NBC special devoted to the issue of African American athletic superiority. The special, which included such guests as Harry Edwards, Arthur Ashe, anthropologist Robert Malina, and sports activist Richard Lapchick, received widespread coverage in the popular press and resulted in mixed reactions from both the African American and White communities (Brokaw & Entine, 1989; L.P. Davis, 1990; P.B. Miller, 1998; Sailes, 1991; E. Smith, 1995; D.K. Wiggins, 1989). In 1995, Roger Bannister, the first person to break the four-minute mile, and later a well-known neurologist, noted at the conference for the British Association for the Advancement of Science that

> As a scientist rather than a sociologist, I am prepared to risk political incorrections by drawing attention to the seemingly obvious but under-stressed fact that Black sprinters and Black athletes in general all seem to have certain natural anatomical advantages. (quoted in "Bannister," 1995, p. D5)

Finally, in 1997, *Sports Illustrated*, in two essays, "What Ever Happened to the White Athlete" and "Is It in the Genes?," raised once again the question of innate physiological gifts and African American athletic performance (Price, 1997a,b).

Continued Forms of Discrimination

Just as controversial as the debate over African

American athletic superiority has been the recent flurry of interest concerning the academic preparation of African American college athletes and dearth of African Americans in coaching and high-level administrative positions within sport. In 1983, the National Collegiate Athletic Association (NCAA) attempted to remedy the poor academic performance and low graduation rates of college athletes by passing a rule known as Proposition 48 (Coakley, 1990; Figler & Whitaker, 1991; Leonard, 1993). Implemented for the first time in 1986, Proposition 48 declared that all freshman athletes would be ineligible to participate on varsity sports teams if they had not achieved a score of 15 on the American College Test (ACT) or 700 on the Scholastic Aptitude Test (SAT). This rule allowed athletes who satisfied just one of these requirements to be accepted into college and be given athletic aid, but they were not allowed to practice with their team as freshmen and forfeited a year of athletic eligibility. In 1989, the NCAA toughened its standards even more by passing Proposition 42, which prohibited universities from providing athletic aid to athletes who did not meet both the GPA and test-score requirements (Coakley, 1990; Figler &Whitaker, 1991; Leonard, 1993).

Propositions 48 and 42 were ultimately designed to encourage high school athletes to commit themselves to academics as well as sports and to insure that universities recruited athletes who were prepared to do the work expected of all students in institutions of higher learning. The two propositions have seemingly had a positive effect at the high school level, where they have encouraged young athletes to take academics more seriously and fostered the development of academic support programs by coaches and sports administrators. Both propositions have been heavily criticized, however, for being unfair to African American athletes (Coakley, 1990; Figler & Whitaker, 1991; Leonard, 1993). The passing of Proposition 48 had no sooner taken place than many African American educators and civil rights activists began lashing out at the rule for its discrimina-

tory nature. The National Alliance of Black School Educators, the National Association for Equality of Opportunity in Higher Education, and such well-known African American leaders as Jesse Jackson, Benjamin Hooks, and Joseph Lowery were critical of the rule because they believed it was formulated without African American input. They also claimed that the ACT and SAT tests were culturally biased in favor of Whites. It was their belief that the scores required for both tests were unfair to African American athletes because nearly 75% of African American students score below 15 on the ACT and more than 50% score below 700 on the SAT (Coakley, 1990; Figler & Whitaker, 1991; Leonard, 1993).

These charges, however, were countered by an equally sincere cadre of African Americans who argued that the propositions were not racially discriminatory and were a step in the right direction (Edwards, 1985; Hackley, 1983). Edwards was a very outspoken advocate of the rule changes and there were a substantial number of other African American academicians who also supported the tougher academic requirements for student-athletes. For instance, Lloyd V. Hackley (1983), chancellor of the University of Arkansas at Pine Bluff, had difficulty understanding how people could link Proposition 48 to racism. He implied that critics of the new rule were unintentionally "retarding the progress of deprived peoples" by claiming racism and arguing against higher academic standards (Hackley, 1983, p. 37). He believed that the only way to improve the academic performance of African American athletes was to support the tougher eligibility requirements included in Proposition 48 rather than decry the unfairness of testing procedures. Anything else was exploitation and nothing less (Hackley, 1983).

The African American community's concern about the academic preparation of African American athletes has been matched by its continuing frustration over the lack of African Americans in coaching and administrative positions within sport. Serious concern over the limited number of African Americans in coaching and administrative positions has been regularly expressed by African Americans since at least the latter half of the 1960s, but has become a cause celebre the last few years. In 1987, Al Campanis, a top executive with the Los Angeles Dodgers, brought national attention to the topic when he suggested to Ted Koppel on the *Nightline* television program that the scarcity of African Americans in baseball management positions resulted from their lack of abilities: "I truly believe they may not have the necessities to be, let's say, a field manager or perhaps a general manager" (quoted in Chass, 1987, p. B14). The public outcry following the interview was so great that Campanis was fired by the Dodgers, and Baseball Commissioner Peter Ueberoth hired Harry Edwards to study the problem of racism in Major League Baseball and increase the number of African Americans in management positions (Figler & Whitaker, 1991; Hoose, 1989).

The Campanis interview also helped spark formation of the now well-known Black Coaches Association (BCA). In 1988, two separate groups of socially conscious African American football and basketball coaches merged to form the BCA (Lederman, 1988). Since its inception, the BCA, under the leadership of Executive Director Rudy Washington, has addressed racial inequities in sport and fought to secure coaching and administrative positions for minorities at the high school, college, and professional levels of participation. The BCA has focused much of its attention on the NCAA and mounted an aggressive campaign against the organization in 1993 by boycotting a meeting of the National Association of Basketball Coaches and voicing its concerns about racial inequities in sport with the congressional Black Caucus. More recently, the BCA has charged that researchers hired by the NCAA are racially biased, called for a reexamination of the previously mentioned academic standards established by the NCAA, and threatened another boycott in protest of the NCAA's refusal to restore to 14 the number of scholarships for teams in Division I basketball (Blum, 1993, 1994a,b; T. Davis, 1995).

One of the most intriguing concerns emanating from some African Americans, in addition to the questions about the dearth of African Americans in coaching and managerial positions, involves the negative portrayal of African American sports agents and their relationship to African American athletes. Kenneth L. Shropshire, in his *In Black and White: Race and Sports in America* (1996), argues persuasively that African American sports agents have suffered from criticism leveled against them by White sports agents and refusal of African American athletes to utilize their services. Although they have started to recruit more clients, African American sports agents have been slow to realize success because of what Shropshire terms the "negative race consciousness" historically prevalent in the African American community and the socialization process of African American athletes (p. 130). Like other African American businessmen of the past, says Shropshire, African American sports agents have lost African American clients because of the African American community's belief that members of their own race are less competent than Whites "in positions requiring good faith and expertise" (p. 129). In addition, African American athletes have likely not sought the services of African American sports agents because of the controlling nature of their mostly White coaches and the "typical media portrayal" of sports agents as competent White males (p. 135).

Shropshire's analysis, which he provides in a wonderfully titled chapter, "The White Man's Ice Is Colder, His Sugar Sweeter, His Water Wetter, His Medicine Better: Sports Agents," seems correct from a historical standpoint. Examples from the past would confirm the African American community's apparent lack of trust in their own professionals, both within and outside the world of sport. For instance, Edwin Bancroft Henderson, the distinguished physical educator who wrote the first books on the history of African Americans in sport, constantly lamented the fact that members of his own race preferred White officials in athletic contests between Black schools (D.K. Wiggins, 1997). Henderson argued that the preference for White officials resulted from the African American community's belief that African American officials lacked the competence, trustworthiness, and ability to cope with the intense confrontations that invariably occurred in athletic contests.

> How it happens that our pigmy-minded, victory-at-any cost, blinded race people imagine the work of White officials superior to that done by Savoy, Gibson, Westmoreland, Washington, Abbott, Robinson, Pinderhughes, Wright, Morrison, Trigg, Coppage, and Douglas, and many others is a puzzle to me.
>
> The only advantage arriving from the use of White officials is from the fact of the peculiar psychology that presents itself when White officials work which causes the poor driven cattle to become blinded to the same errors of commission and omission that would not have escaped had the officials been of the colored race. (Henderson, 1927, p. 20)

The link between Henderson and Shropshire is important because it makes clear that in regards to race, the more things change, the more they stay the same. Although more overt forms of discrimination against African American athletes have decreased over the last few decades, it is apparent that many people still hold to their racist beliefs and deep-seated stereotypical notions about African Americans in both sport and the larger society. More African Americans have assumed coaching positions and even find themselves in some upper-level management positions, but the same racist beliefs that resulted in years of segregation in sport are still evident today. The belief that the success of African American athletes results from innate physical skills rather than dedication and hard work has been slow to die out in this country (Chass, 1987; L.P. Davis, 1990; Hoberman, 1997; P.B. Miller,

1998; Sailes, 1991; Shropshire & Smith, 1998; E. Smith, 1995; D.K. Wiggins, 1989). So has the notion that African American athletes, like other members of the African American community, are docile, savage, deceptive, child-like, or oversexed, or a combination of all the above. The simple truth is that people, both African American and White, continue to insist on differentiating between human beings based on race (L.P. Davis, 1990; Early, 1980; Herrnstein & Murray, 1994; P.B. Miller, 1998; Sailes, 1991; Shropshire and Smith, 1998; E. Smith, 1995; D.K. Wiggins, 1989). Although the scientific literature does not support such claims, people are still convinced that a person's color defines his or her very being and separates the person from others both emotionally and physically. This is what accounts for the attraction of interracial athletic contests, but also explains the racially insensitive remarks uttered by well-known sports prognosticators and top-level baseball executives (Early, 1989).

Based on the historical experiences of African American athletes, only time will tell when the insensitive remarks will finally cease and the last vestiges of racism will be eliminated from sport in this country. The involvement of African Americans in sport has been a turbulent one at best, characterized by major successes as well as a host of problems stemming from continual prejudices and unfounded beliefs in the inequality of the races. As has been shown, African American athletes during the second half of the 19th century realized many triumphs on the athletic field only to have the door of opportunity closed on them by believers in Jim Crow and White supremacy. This process was repeated in one form or another throughout much of the first half of this century and beyond. Although great sums of money and adulation were realized by a select number of African American athletes, the large majority of them were either forced to endure the racial discrimination evident in White-controlled sport or retreat into all-Black sporting organizations where they could realize success among their own group. This was unfortunate because African American athletes, like their White counterparts, merely wanted the opportunity to compete against the best athletes regardless of color and realize the numerous benefits resulting from successful participation in sport. In many regards, the critical events for African American athletes often took place off the field, where their physical abilities were unable to shield them from the racial discrimination in American society. Perhaps the best that can be hoped for at this point in time is that African Americans and Whites come together to have a serious dialogue about racial discrimination so that it can finally be purged completely from sport and all other areas of American life (Hoberman, 1997).

Suggested Readings

Baker, W. J. (1986). *Jesse Owens: An American life*. NY: The Free Press.

George, N. (1992). *Elevating the game: The history & aesthetics of Black men in basketball*. NY: Simon & Schuster.

Gorn, E. J. (1995). *Muhammad Ali: The people's champ*. IL: University of Illinois Press.

Hoberman, J. (1997). *Darwin's athletes: How sport has damaged Black America and preserved the myth of race*. MA: Houghton Mifflin.

Roberts, R. (1983). *Papa Jack: Jack Johnson and the era of white hopes*. NY: The Free Press.

Sammons, J. T. (1994). Race and sport: A critical, historical examination. *Journal of Sport History, 21*, 203–278.

Shropshire, K. L. (1996). *In black and white: Race and sports in America*. NY: New York University Press.

Tygiel, J. (1983). *Baseball's great experiment: Jackie Robinson and his legacy*. NY: Oxford University Press.

Wiggins, D. K. (1997). *Glory bound: Black athletes in a White America*. NY: Syracuse University Press.

Study Questions

1. What societal factors contributed to the elimination of African Americans from sport during the latter stages of the 19th century?

2. Why were a select number of African American athletes allowed to continue participating in professional boxing, predominantly White intercollegiate sport, and the Olympic Games during the first half of the 20th century?

3. Why did the first African American female Olympians come from historically Black colleges? Why did the first African American male Olympians come from predominantly White universities?

4. What were the differences and similarities between sport in historically Black colleges and sport in predominantly White universities during the first half of the 20th century?

5. Why was the integration of organized baseball so important to the African American community and society at large?

6. Why did Harry Edwards and African American athletes propose a boycott of the 1968 Olympic Games in Mexico City?

7. Why do people continue to insist that the outstanding performances of African American athletes are the result of innate physiological gifts?

8. Why, according to some scholars, have African American athletes been reluctant to employ African American sports agents?

References

Ashe, A. (1988). *A hard road to glory: A history of the African American athlete, 1619 to present* (3 Vols.). NY: Warner Books.

Baker, W. J. (1986). *Jesse Owens: An American life*. NY: The Free Press.

Bannister, R. (1995, September 14). Race may play role. *The Washington Post*, p. D5.

Behee, J. (1974). *Hail to the victors!: Black athletes at the University of Michigan*. MI: Swink Tuttle Press.

Betts, J. R. (1974). *America's sporting heritage, 1850–1950*. MA: Addison Wesley.

Black dominance. (1977, May 9). *Time*, 57–60.

Blum, D. E. (1993, October 27). Black coaches head to congress to press charge of bias in college sport. *The Chronicle of Higher Education*, p. A36.

Blum, D. E. (1994a, January 26). Battle over an additional scholarship symbolizes a much larger struggle. *The Chronicle of Higher Education*, pp. A39–A40.

Blum, D. E. (1994b, March 30). Black coaches and NCAA agree to discuss disputed rules. *The Chronicle of Higher Education*, p. A38.

Brailsford, D. (1988). *Bareknucles: A social history of prize fighting*. Cambridge: Lutterworth Press.

Brashler, W. (1978). *Josh Gibson: A life in the Negro leagues*. NY: Harper & Row.

Brokaw, T., & Entine, J. (1989, April). *Black athletes: Fact and fiction*. NY: National Broadcasting Company.

Brower, W. A. (1940). Has professional football closed the door? *Opportunity, 18*, 375–377.

Brower, W. A. (1941). Prejudice in sports. *Opportunity, 19*, 260–263.

Brown, J. (1964). *Off my chest*. NY: Doubleday and Company.

Bruce, J. (1985). *The Kansas City Monarchs: Champions of Black baseball*. KS: University Press of Kansas.

Byline. (1974, December 2). *New York Times*, pp. B13–B14.

Cahn, S. K. (1994). *Coming on strong: Gender and sexuality in twentieth-century women's sport*. MA: Harvard University Press.

Capeci, D. J., & Wilkerson, M. (1983). Multifarious hero: Joe Louis, American society and race relations during world crisis, 1935–45. *Journal of Sport History, 10*, 525.

Captain, G. (1991). Enter ladies and gentlemen of color: Gender, sport and the ideal of African American manhood and womanhood during the late nineteenth and early twentieth centuries. *Journal of Sport History, 18*, 81–102.

Carroll, J. M. (1992). *Fritz Pollard: Pioneer in racial advancement*. Urbana: University of Illinois Press.

Cashmore, E. (1982). *Black sportsmen*. London: Routledge & Kegan Paul.

Chalk, O. (1976). *Black college sport*. NY: Dodd & Mead.

Chass, M. (1987, April 9). Campanis is out: Racial remarks cited by Dodgers. *New York Times*, pp. B13–B14.

Clegg, L. H. II. (1980, July). Why Black athletes run faster. *Sepia, 29*, 18–22.

Coakley, J. (1990). *Sport in society: Issues and controversies* (4th ed.). MO: Times Mirror/Mosby.

Cochran, T. C., & Miller, W. (1961). *The age of enterprise*. NY: Harper & Row.

Cone, C. B. (1982). The Molineaux Cribb fight, 1918: "Wuz Tom Molineaux robbed?" *Journal of Sport History, 9*, 83–91.

Davis, J. P. (1966). The negro in American sports. In J. P. Davis (Ed.), *The American Negro reference book* (pp. 775–825). NJ: Prentice Hall.

Davis, L. P. (1990). The articulation of difference: White preoccupation with the question of racially linked genetic differences among athletes. *Sociology of Sport Journal, 7*, 179–187.

Davis, T. (1995). The myth of the superspade: The persistence of racism in college athletics. *Fordham Urban Law Journal, 22*, 615–698.

Early, G. (1989). *Tuxedo junction: Essays on American culture*. NY: The Ecco Press.

Edmonds, A. O. (1973). The second Louis Schmeling fight: Sport, symbol and culture. *Journal of Popular Culture, 7*, 42–50.

Edwards, H. (1969). *The revolt of the Black athlete*. NY: The Free Press.

Edwards, H. (1970). *Black students*. NY: The Free Press.

Edwards, H. (1972). The myth of the racially superior athlete. *Intellectual Digest, 2*, 58–60.

Edwards, H. (1973a). The sources of the Black athlete's superiority. *The Black Scholar, 3*, 32–41.

Edwards, H. (1973b, November). 20th century gladiators for white America. *Psychology Today, 7*, 43–52.

Edwards, H. (1980). *The struggle that must be: An autobiography*. NY: MacMillan.

Edwards, H. (1985). Educating Black athletes. In D. Chu, J. O. Segrave, & B. J. Becker (Eds.), *Sport and Higher Education* (pp. 373–384). IL: Human Kinetics Publishers. (Reprinted from *The Atlantic Monthly, 252*, 31–38.)

Falkner, D. (1995). *Great time coming: The life of Jackie Robinson from baseball to Birmingham*. NY: Simon & Schuster.

Farr, F. (1964). *Black champion: The life and times of Jack Johnson*. NY: Charles Scribner's Sons.

Figler, S. K., & Whitaker, G. (1991). *Sport & play in American life: A textbook in the sociology of sport* (2nd ed.). IA: Wm. C. Brown.

Fishman, G. (1969). Paul Robeson's student days and the fight against racism at Rutgers. *Freedomways, 9*, 211–229.

Fleischer, N. S. (1938). *The story of the Negro in the prize ring from 1782 to 1938* (3 Vols.). NY: The Ring Book Shop.

Frommer, H. (1982). *Rickey and Robinson: The men who broke baseball's color barrier*. NY: MacMillan.

Gems, G. R. (1988). Shooting stars: The rise and fall of Blacks in professional football. *Professional Football Research Association Annual Bulletin*, 1–18.

Gems, G. R. (1995). Blocked shot: The development of basketball in the African American community of Chicago. *Journal of Sport History, 22*, 135–148.

George, N. (1992). *Elevating the game: The history & aesthetics of Black men in basketball*. NY: Simon & Schuster.

Gibson, A. (1958). *I always wanted to be somebody*. NY: Harper and Brothers.

Gilliam, D. B. (1976). *Paul Robeson: All-American*. Washington, DC: New Republic Book Company.

Gilmore, A. T. (1975). *Bad nigger! The national impact of Jack Johnson*. NY: Kennikat.

Gissendanner, C. H. (1994). African American women and competitive sport, 1920–1960. In S. Birrell & C. Cole (Eds.), *Women, Sport, and Culture* (pp. 81–92). IL: Human Kinetics Publishers.

Gissendanner, C. H. (1996). African American women Olympians: The impact of race, gender, and class ideologies, 1932–1968. *Research Quarterly for Exercise and Sport, 67*, 172–182.

Goodman, M. H. (1980). The Moor vs. Black Diamond. *Virginia Cavalcade, 29*, 164–173.

Gorn, E. J. (1994). *The manly art: Bareknuckle prizefighting in America*. NY: Cornell University Press.

Gorn, E. J. (Ed.). (1995). *Muhammad Ali: The people's champ*. Urbana: University of Illinois Press.

Grundman, A. H. (1979). Image of intercollegiate sports and the Civil Rights movement: A historian's view. *Arena Review, 3*, 17–24.

Hackley, L. V. (1983). We need to educate our athletes! *The Black Collegian, 13*, 35–37.

Henderson, E. B. (1927, January). Sports. *The Messenger, 9*, 20.

Henderson, E. B. (1939). *The Negro in sports*. Washington, DC: The Associated Publishers.

Henderson, E. B. (1972). Physical education and athletics among Negroes. In B. L. Bennett (Ed.), *The History of Physical Education and Sport* (pp. 67–83). IL: The Athletic Institute.

Herrnstein, R., & Murray, C. (1994). *The bell curve: Intelligence and class structure in American life*. NY: Basic Books.

Hoberman, J. (1997). *Darwin's athletes: How sport has damaged Black America and preserved the myth of race*. Boston: Houghton Mifflin.

Holway, J. B. (1975). *Voices from the great Black baseball leagues*. NY: Harper and Row.

Holway, J. B. (1988). *Blackball stars: Negro league pioneers*. CT: Meckler Books.

Hoose, P. (1989). *Necessities: Racial barriers in American sports*. NY: Random House.

Hotaling, E. (1995). *They're off: Horse racing at Saratoga*. NY: Syracuse University Press.

Johnson, N. R., & Marple, D. P. (1973). Racial discrimination in professional basketball. *Sociological Focus, 6*, 6–18.

Johnson, W. O. (1972). *All that glitters is not gold: The Olympic Game*. NY: Putnam.

Kane, M. (1971, January 18). An assessment of Black is best. *Sports Illustrated, 34*, 783.

Lanctot, N. (1994). *Fair dealing and clean playing: The Hilldale Club and the development of Black professional baseball, 1910–1932*. NC: McFarland.

Lederman, D. (1988, April 13). Black coaches' movement gains momentum: First annual meeting attracts 300. *The Chronicle of Higher Education*, pp. 43–44.

LeFlore, J. (1982). Athleticism among American Blacks. In R. M. Pankin (Ed.), *Social approaches to sport* (pp. 104–121). Toronto: Associated University Press.

Leonard, W. (1993). *A sociological perspective of sport*. NY: Macmillan Publishing Company.

Logan, R. W. (1957). *The Negro in the United States*. Princeton: D. Van Nostrand.

Logan, R. W. (1965). *The betrayal of the Negro from Rutherford B. Hayes to Woodrow Wilson*. NY: Collier Books.

Lomax, M. (1998). Black entrepreneurship in the national pastime: The rise of semiprofessional baseball in Black Chicago, 1890–1915. *Journal of Sport History, 25*, 43–64.

Lowenfish, L. (1978). Sport, race, and the baseball business: The Jackie Robinson story revisited. *Arena Review, 2*, 216.

Loy, J. W., & McElvogue, J. F. (1970). Racial segregation in American sport. *International Review of Sport Sociology, 5*, 523.

Lucas, J. A., & Smith, R. A. (1978). *Saga of American sport*. Philadelphia: Lea & Febiger.

MacDonald, W. W. (1981). The Black athlete in American sports. In W. J. Baker & J. Carroll (Eds.), *Sports in modern America* (pp. 88–98). MO: River City Publishers.

Malloy, J. (1995). *Sol White's history of colored baseball with other documents on the early Black game, 1886–1936*. Lincoln: University of Nebraska Press.

Martin, C. H. (1993). Jim Crow in the gymnasium: The integration of college basketball in the American south. *The International Journal of the History of Sport, 10*, 68–86.

Martin, C. H. (1996). Racial change and bigtime college football in Georgia: The age of segregation, 1892–1957. *The Georgia Historical Quarterly, 80*, 532–562.

McKinney, G. B. (1976). Negro professional baseball players in the upper south in the gilded age. *Journal of Sport History, 3*, 273–280.

Mead, C. (1985). *Champion Joe Louis: Black hero in white America*. NY: Charles Scribner's Sons.

Meier, A., & Rudwick, E. M. (1963). *From plantation to ghetto*. NY: Hill and Wang.

Miller, L. (1927). The unrest among college students: Kansas University. *Crisis, 34*, 187–188.

Miller, P. B. (1991). Harvard and the color line: The case of Lucien Alexis. In Ronald Story (Ed.), *Sports in Massachusetts: Historical essays* (pp. 137–158). Westfield, MA.

Miller P. B. (1995). To bring the race along rapidly: Sport, student culture, and educational mission at historically Black colleges during the interwar years. *History of Education Quarterly, 35*, 111–133.

Miller, P. B. (1998). The anatomy of scientific racism: Racialist responses to Black athletic achievement. *Journal of Sport History, 15*, 119–151.

Moore, J. T. (1988). *Pride against prejudice: The biography of Larry Doby*. NY: Praeger.

Of fingerprints and other clues. (1988, February 15). *Fortune, 117*, 123–124.

Pascal, A. H., & Rapping, L. A. (1972). *Racial discrimination in organized baseball*. CA: Rand Corporation.

Paul, J., McGhee, R. V., & Fant, H. (1984). The arrival and ascendence of Black athletes in the Southeastern Conference, 1966–1980. *Phylon, 45*, 284–297.

Pennington, R. (1987). *Breaking the ice: The racial integration of Southwest Conference football*. NC: McFarland.

Peterson, R. W. (1970). *Only the ball was white*. NJ: Prentice Hall.

Peterson, R. W. (1990). *Cages to jumpshots: Pro basketball's early years*. NY: Oxford University Press.

Polner, M. (1982). *Branch Rickey: A biography*. NY: Atheneum Publishing Company.

Poussaint, A. F. (1972, August). Sex and the Black male. *Ebony*, 114–120.

Price, S. L. (1997a, December 8). Is it in the genes? *Sports Illustrated, 87*, 53–55.

Price, S. L. (1997). Whatever happened to the white athlete? *Sports Illustrated*, 31–52.

Rader, B. (1983). *American sports: From the age of folk games to the age of spectators*. NJ: Prentice Hall.

Rampersad, A. (1997). *Jackie Robinson: A biography*. NY: Alfred A. Knopf.

Rayl, S. (1996). *The New York renaissance professional Black basketball team, 1923–1950*. Unpublished doctoral dissertation, Pennsylvania State University, State College.

Reisler, J. (1994). *Black writers/Black baseball:An anthology of articles from Black sportswriters who covered the Negro leagues*. NC: McFarland.

Ritchie, A. (1988). *Major Taylor: The extraordinary career of a champion bicycle racer*. CA: Bicycle Books.

Roberts, R. (1983). *Papa Jack: Jack Johnson and the era of white hopes*. NY: The Free Press.

Roberts, R., & Olson, J. (1989). *Winning is the only thing: Sports in America since 1945*. Baltimore: The Johns Hopkins University Press.

Robinson, J. (1972). *I never had it made*. NY: G. P. Putnam.

Rogosin, D. (1983). *Invisible men: Life in baseball's Negro leagues*. NY: Atheneum Publishers.

Rowe, J. (1988, April). The Greek chorus: Jimmy the Greek got it wrong but so did his critics. *The Washington Monthly, 20*, 31–34.

Ruck, R. (1987) *Sandlot seasons: Sport in Black Pittsburgh*. Urbana: University of Illinois Press.

Rudolph, J. W. (1979). Tom Molyneaux: America's "almost" champion. *American History Illustrated, 14*, 8–14.

Rudolph, W. (1977). *Wilma*. NY: New American Library.

Russell, B. (1966). *Go up for glory*. NY: Coward-McCann.

Sailes, G. (1991). The myth of Black sports supremacy. *Journal of Black Studies, 21*, 480–487.

Salzberg, C. (1987). *From set shot to slam dunk*. NY: E. P. Dutton.

Sammons, J. T. (1988). *Beyond the ring: The role of boxing in American society*. IL: University of Illinois Press.

Scott, J. (1971). *The athletic revolution*. NY: The Free Press.

Sendler, D. (1969). The Black athlete—1968. In P. W. Romero (Ed.), *In Black America, 1968, The year of awakening* (pp. 325–338). NY: Publishers Company.

Shropshire, K. L. (1996). *In Black and white: Race and sports in America.* NY: New York University Press.

Shropshire, K. L., & Smith, E. (1998). The Tarzan syndrome: John Hoberman and his quarrels with African American athletes and intellectuals. *Journal of Sport & Social Issues, 22*, 103–112.

Simons, W. (1985). Jackie Robinson and the American mind: Journalistic perceptions of the reintegration of baseball. *Journal of Sport History, 12*, 39–64.

Skully, G. W. (1974). Discrimination: The case of baseball. In R. G. Noll (Ed.), *Government and the sport business* (pp. 221–247). Washington, DC: The Brookings Institute.

Smith, E. (1995). The self-fulfilling prophecy: Genetically superior African American athletes. *Humboldt Journal of Social Relations, 21*, 139–163.

Smith, T. G. (1988). Outside the pale: The exclusion of Blacks from the National Football League. *Journal of Sport History, 15*, 255–281.

Somers, D. A. (1972). *The rise of sport in New Orleans, 1850–1900.* LA: Louisiana State University Press.

Spivey, D. (1983). The Black athlete in bigtime intercollegiate sports, 1941–1968. *Phylon, 44*, 116–125.

Spivey, D. (1985). *Black consciousness and Olympic protest movement, 1964–1980.* In D. Spivey (Ed.), *Sport in America: New historical perspectives* (pp. 239–262). CT: Greenwood Press.

Spivey, D. (1988). End Jim Crow in sports: The protest at New York University, 1940–1941. *Journal of Sport History, 15*, 282–303.

Spivey, D., & Jones, T. (1975). Intercollegiate athletic servitude: A case study of the Black Illinois student-athletes, 1931–1967. *Social Science Quarterly, 55*, 939–947.

Strode, W., & Young, S. (1990). *Goal dust.* MD: Madison Books.

Taylor, M. M. (1928). *The fastest bicycle rider in the world.* MA: Wormley Publishing Company.

Thaxton, N. (1970). *A documentary analysis of competitive track and field for women at Tuskegee Institute and Tennessee State University.* Unpublished doctoral dissertation, Springfield College, Springfield, MO.

Tygiel, J. (1983). *Baseball's great experiment: Jackie Robinson and his legacy.* NY: Oxford University Press.

What we say, what we think. (1988, February 1). *U.S. News & World Report*, 27–28.

White, G. E. (1996). *Creating the national pastime: Baseball transforms itself, 1903–1953.* NJ: Princeton University Press.

Wiggins, D. K. (1979). Isaac Murphy: Black hero in nineteenth century American sport, 1861–1896. *Canadian Journal of History of Sport and Physical Education, 10*, 15–32.

Wiggins, D. K. (1983). Wendell Smith, the *Pittsburgh Courier Journal* and the campaign to include Blacks in organized baseball, 1933–1945. *Journal of Sport History, 10*, 5–29.

Wiggins, D. K. (1985). Peter Jackson and the elusive heavyweight championship: A Black athlete's struggle against the late nineteenth century color-line. *Journal of Sport History, 12*, 143–168.

Wiggins, D. K. (1988). The future of college athletics is at stake: Black athletes and racial turmoil on three predominantly white university campuses, 1968–1972. *Journal of Sport History, 15*, 304–333.

Wiggins, D. K. (1989). Great speed but little stamina: The historical debate over Black athletic superiority. *Journal of Sport History, 16*, 158–185.

Wiggins, D. K. (1991). Prized performers, but frequently overlooked students: The involvement of Black athletes in intercollegiate sports on predominantly white university campuses, 1890–1972. *Research Quarterly for Exercise and Sport, 62*, 164–177.

Wiggins, D. K. (1992). The year of awakening: Black athletes, racial unrest, and the civil rights movement of 1968. *The International Journal of the History of Sport, 9*, 188–208.

Wiggins, D. K. (1997). Edwin Bancroft Henderson, African American athletes, and the writing of sport history. In D. K. Wiggins (Ed.), *Glory bound: Black athletes in a white America* (pp. 221–240). NY: Syracuse University Press.

Wiggins, W. H. (1971). Jack Johnson as bad nigger: The folklore of his life. *Black Scholar, 2*, 4–19.

Wolters, R. (1975). *The new Negro on campus: Black college rebellions of the 1920s.* Princeton: Princeton University Press.

Woodward, C. V. (1966). *The strange career of Jim Crow.* NY: Oxford University Press.

Yetman, N., & Eitzen, J. D. (1972). Black Americans in sport: Unequal opportunity for equal ability. *Civil Rights Digest, 5*, 20–34.

Young, A. S. (1963). *Negro firsts in sports.* Chicago: Johnson Publishing.

Zang, D. W. (1995). *Fleet Walker's divided heart: The life of baseball's first Black major leaguer.* Lincoln: University of Nebraska Press.

African American Predominance in Sport

Othello Harris

Abstract

This essay investigates the involvement of African Americans in collegiate sport and the attendance problems. The first part examines African American collegiate sport participation in the early years (the late 1800s until World War II); the post-World War II influx of Black athletes into athletic programs; and Black militancy and the predominance of African Americans in collegiate programs from the 1970s through the early 1990s.

Today, many revenue-generating collegiate athletic programs, particularly programs in the South, have a preponderance of African American athletes on their teams (although many of these athletically and academically prestigious colleges enroll few African American nonathletes). However, this change in the racial composition of teams has not been accompanied by the disappearance of athletic and academic problems faced by African American athletes in earlier decades. The second part of the essay addresses problems faced by present-day African American athletes at predominantly White colleges and universities. Among these problems are athletic concerns such as racist perceptions and stereotypes and a continuation of stacking patterns. The essay also addresses academic problems such as poor academic performance and low graduation rates. Finally, the NCAA's attempts to address the poor academic performance of African American student-athletes are analyzed.

Key Terms

- Black pride -
- Superspades -
- Stacking -
- Freshmen eligibility -
- NCAA reform -
- Marginal student—outstanding athlete -

Collegiate sport in America has become a showcase of African American talent. No longer denied athletic scholarships and opportunities at major colleges and universities, African Americans dominate the record books. Statistical leaders in categories such as rushing and receiving in football, scoring and rebounding in basketball, and sprints in track and field are, almost without exception in recent years, African Americans.

Television highlight films bring us replays of African Americans receiving passes, running into the end zone for touchdowns, scoring baskets, and anchoring suffocating defenses.

Their presence is required, it seems, for teams to compete, not to mention excel, in revenue-generating intercollegiate sports. For example, African Americans figured prominently in the New Year's Day bowl games that concluded the 1990–1991 football season, where an estimated $45 million was paid to participating teams for eight collegiate contests. Even at quarterback—a position that appears to have been, in the past, the domain of White players—the presence of African Americans was felt; the teams that received the AP and UPI polls' nominations as the top college team were both led by African American quarterbacks. (The AP and UPI differed on their choice for the "number one" team.)

In the 1990 balloting for the Heisman Trophy—the oldest and most prestigious of the individual player awards—three of the top four candidates were African Americans. That year, for only the third time in 17 years, the award was won by a White player—Ty Detmer of Brigham Young University. Like the two other White players who have won the award in more than a decade and a half, he played quarterback. (The last White player to win the award, other than a quarterback, was Penn State's John Cappelletti, a running back.) In the professional football draft that followed the 1990–1991 college football season, the top seven draft choices and 23 of the 27 first-round selections were African Americans.

In college basketball, many of the key players in the 1991 Final Four were African Americans. The University of Nevada, Las Vegas (UNLV), which was the top-ranked team from preseason until its Final Four loss, carried an all-Black starting five; four of them were taken in a two round draft by professional teams. The other was invited to camp by one of the professional franchises.

In short, there is no denying that intercollegiate sport has come to regard the presence of African American athletes as essential to its goal of presenting an exciting, professional-style game that will attract spectators and network dollars, but it has not always been that way. As recently as 40 years ago, intercollegiate sport was, on the whole, opposed to, or at best indifferent to, African American participation.

Athletes, Scholars, and Superspades

According to D. Wiggins (1991), during the latter half of the 19th century, sport was not of primary importance to African American student-athletes; they were more concerned about academic success. Many of these student-athletes were from upper-middle-class families and had attended private academies, prestigious public schools, or Black colleges in the South. Still, few schools, even in the North, accepted them on their athletic teams. The service academies—Army and Navy—Catholic schools like Notre Dame, and Ivy League schools like Princeton and Yale all shunned African American athletes, if not African Americans altogether. Athletic ability and a predisposition for academic success meant nothing to coaches and administrators if they were not cloaked in a White body.

During the next few decades, intercollegiate sport provided a few more opportunities for African Americans to participate, mostly in football and track and field. A larger number of northern schools had African Americans on their teams, but segregation still prevailed off the field. In many cases, there was only one African American on the team (and there were few on campus). As Behee (1974) notes, those who made varsity teams were "superspades." That is, they were expected to do more than simply participate in the team's success; they were expected to *carry* the team to victory. Willis Ward is a shining example of a superspade; he scored 13 of the University of Michigan's $18^3/4$ points to lead them to victory over Illinois in the 1932 Butler Relays. Three years later, Jesse Owens scored 40 of Ohio State's $40^1/5$ points in a win over UC-Berkeley. Paul Robeson, the lone African American on campus at Rutgers, was an All-American in 1917 and 1918. These and other African Americans were expected to provide super performances to justify their presence on athletic teams at predominantly White colleges and universities.

Super performances notwithstanding, African Americans were often treated shabbily by their schools. Campus housing was off-limits to most of them; they were refused service in restaurants and not allowed to stay at hotels with their White teammates (even in northern cities like Chicago and Buffalo, New York); and probably most humiliating, they were kept out of home and away games against southern teams. (When playing southern teams on the road, northern teams were expected to be *gracious guests* by keeping their African Americans—who were considered offensive to southern Whites—off the field. When northern teams played at home against southern teams, they were expected to be *gracious hosts*, again by keeping their offending players off the field.) The National Collegiate Athletic Association (NCAA) steered clear of these abominable practices, and the games went on as planned. Men like Paul Robeson—an All-American for 2 years and Phi Beta Kappa at Rutgers—and Willis Ward had to watch from the sidelines as their football teams sought to uphold the honor of the school without them.

Although a few African Americans (e.g., Robeson, Ward, Fritz Pollard, and "Duke" Slater) were found in football programs in the North, most were barred from athletic activities that required interracial contact. Until the 1930s, most of the participation occurred in track and field where, according to Behee (1974), there were 100–200 Black athletes competing for major colleges and universities at the time of the 1936 Olympics. Only later would football and basketball programs begin to accept African Americans in more than token roles.

The Aftermath of World War II

World War II brought about a number of changes in the status of African Americans.

They, like other Americans, had fought in Europe to eliminate Nazi racism, yet racism pervaded nearly every American institution. Upon their return, they (along with Black civilians) were prepared to fight for integration at home.

After the war, several factors combined to greatly increase the college attendance rates of African Americans. Congress passed legislation that created the G.I. Bill, which provided funds for the postsecondary education of returning servicemen. This allowed many Americans to attend college who otherwise would have lacked the finances to attend. More than one fourth of the students registered at colleges and universities in 1945 and 1946 were veterans of World War II (Andrews, 1984). Many African Americans were among the beneficiaries of the G.I. Bill (Green, 1982). In some cases, the veterans were former athletes who, in addition to furthering their education, were interested in participating in collegiate sports.

Also, President Truman appointed an interracial committee to study problems in higher education. This committee called for an end to discrimination in higher education, including inequalities in educational opportunities (Franklin & Moss, 1988). This recommendation, coming from a committee appointed by the nation's chief executive, made discrimination in colleges and universities a national issue (Wiggins, 1991) and, undoubtedly, made college desegregation a more acceptable, if not expected, practice.

Finally, after the war, professional sports—baseball, football, and basketball—began to accept more Black players on their teams. Collegiate sport was moving in the same direction.

The above factors resulted in the presence of more African Americans at predominantly White colleges and universities. Consequently, at a time when White Americans were more receptive to African Americans—at least at the level of secondary structural assimilation—there was also a larger pool of potential Black athletes available to collegiate athletic teams.

The change in racial attitudes in intercollegiate sport led to a new look in collegiate football. In 1944, two African Americans were selected to the *Look* magazine All-America team; no others were selected in the decade of the 1940s. However, during the 1950s, 15 African Americans made the magazine's All-America team (Behee, 1974).

Basketball experienced similar changes. By 1948, 10% of the basketball programs at predominantly White colleges and universities had African Americans on their rosters; one percent of all players at these schools were Black (Berghorn, Yetman-Hanna, 1988). Although this did not constitute a large number of African Americans, it was a sizable increase from the pre-World War II figures. No Black basketball player was named to *Look* magazine's All-America team until 1952. Thereafter, African Americans have been on every *Look* All-America team; twenty-one made the team during the 1950s (Behee, 1974). The Associated Press named five African Americans to the 1958 All-America team, the first of many times that this happened.

As more African Americans participated in intercollegiate sport, the superspade requirement was dropped. Still, a disproportionate number of these athletes were rookies of the year, conference most valuable players, and All-Americans. They, more than their White peers, were expected to turn in stellar performances in return for their athletic scholarships.[1]

The desegregation of collegiate sport did not mean, however, the integration of sport. African Americans in the 1940s and 1950s faced many of the same problems their predecessors faced. For example, while their teammates were quartered at prestigious hotels, they were often left to seek lodging at the "Black YMCA" or with Black families in town. When the University of Cincinnati team traveled to Texas in 1959, Oscar Robertson, the star of the team, had to stay at a Black college while the rest of the team were housed in Houston (Ashe, 1988). Even when the entire team stayed at the same hotel, segregation was carried out through racial pairing in the room assignments; Black and White players were seldom allowed to room together.

Housing was still a problem for African Americans, as they were often required to seek accommodations away from campus. The isolation from other athletes was magnified away from campus as Black athletes found many stores, restaurants, and movie theaters in college towns off-limits to them. To wander too far from campus could be risky, yet they were prohibited from most aspects of campus life.

What makes the opprobrious treatment of African American athletes described above even more untenable is that it occurred in northern, midwestern and western regions of the country. Southern schools' athletic programs, for the most part, remained segregated during this period. A 1956 legislative act that banned interracial sports in the state of Louisiana, and the riots that met Autherine Lucy's attempt to integrate the University of Alabama that same year (see Paul, McGhee, & Faut, 1984), were clear signs of a southern aversion to segregation. That this inclination to distance themselves from African Americans was not confined to intrateam competition can be illustrated by the Mississippi State University basketball team's decision to sit out NCAA tournaments in 1959 and 1961, and the University of Mississippi football team's willingness to forgo a 1961 bowl game rather than compete against integrated teams (Paul et al., 1984).

To the disappointment of African American athletes, the postwar period did not result in the collapse of discrimination in intercollegiate sport. Nevertheless, there were some changes

---

1. The NCAA did not allow colleges to award scholarships based solely on athletic ability until 1952. Before that, schools could award scholarships or jobs to athletes if they demonstrated financial need (Rader, 1990).

in the attitudes of Whites toward Black athletes. Many conferences dropped racial bans (Rader, 1990) and gentlemen's agreements (Behee, 1974) that prohibited African American participation in basketball and football (although schools continued to set quotas on the number of African Americans permitted on a team). Some schools canceled games with teams that refused to play against their Black players. More important, African American athletes were experiencing a change in attitude and demeanor; resistance to their maltreatment was growing. Discontent would soon turn into rebellious outbursts.

Black Pride and Protest

During the latter part of the 1950s, African Americans showed their impatience with America's unfulfilled promise of full equality by participating in mass demonstrations. Through peaceful forms of civil disobedience, they demanded an end to discriminatory practices, such as segregated seating on public transportation and the disenfranchisement of eligible Black voters. Participants in the protests were counseled not to retaliate against those who verbally and physically assaulted them as they opposed America's racist practices. Instead, they were advised to "turn the other cheek." Although their nonviolent tactics were often met with violence—by angry mobs, police clubs, attack dogs, and the spray of fire hoses—the demonstrators, for the most part, remained nonviolent.

As the decade of the 1960s began, a new weapon of peaceful protest was unleashed on southern businesses—sit-ins. In February 1960, four African American students who attended North Carolina A & T were refused coffee at a department store in Greensboro, North Carolina (Morris, 1984). Their response was to sit and wait for service, thereby depriving the store of the opportunity to profit from service to other customers, while bringing attention to their grievance. This movement spread all over the South.

At the same time, institutions of higher education in the South found themselves engaged in heated battles over the issue of desegregation. In 1962, it took a court order, deputy marshals, and the National Guard to enroll James Meredith at the University of Mississippi. The next year, in defiance of a court order, Governor Wallace stood in the door of the University of Alabama to prevent African Americans from enrolling and attending classes. He proclaimed segregation to be a way of life in the South; it was an unstated but widely acknowledged component of most organizations in the nation.

Although discrimination was a way of life in most American institutions, many thought sport, particularly college sport, was exempt from this pernicious treatment of participants; there seemed to be evidence to support this egalitarian notion of college athletics. By 1962, African Americans' presence in collegiate basketball was comparable to their distribution in the general population (Berghorn et al., 1988). Oscar Robertson was college basketball's player of the year in 1960 (for the third consecutive time); by 1966, when Cazzie Russell was player of the year, the All-America first team was predominantly Black. It would remain that way the rest of the decade. In 1963, Loyola University of Illinois started four Black players—a practice unheard-of at that time in college basketball—and won the national championship. The decade ended with Lew Alcindor (later, Kareem Abdul-Jabbar), also a three-time college basketball player of the year, leading UCLA to its third straight national championship.

Similar feats were accomplished by African Americans in other college sports. Many of the records in track and field, particularly in the sprints, hurdles, relays, and long jump, belonged to African Americans. Bob Hayes, Jim Hines, and Charlie Greene held the fastest times in the 100-yard dash in the 1960s; Tommie Smith topped the field in the 220-yard dash; Wyomia Tyus set records in the 100-yard and 100-meter dashes, whereas Wilma Rudolph did the same in the 200-meter dash; Lee Calhoun was the 120-yard hurdles champion; and

African American men owned the records in the 400-meter and 1600-meter relays (Edwards, 1969). Perhaps most impressively, Bob Beamon set a record in the long jump at the 1968 Olympics that lasted for more than 22 years. Moreover, African Americans were an integral part of many of the top collegiate track and field programs.

African American presence and stature on the football field were growing as well, as evidenced by the honors they were winning: Syracuse's Ernie Davis, in 1961, became the first African American to win the Heisman Trophy. Two others would follow in the decade of the 1960s—Mike Garrett and O.J. Simpson, both of USC. Other players, like Gale Sayers and Warren McVea, accumulated impressive rushing and passing statistics.

By the middle of the 1960s, even southern teams had begun to welcome Black athletes. The Southeastern Conference (SEC), one of the premier athletic conferences in the South, integrated in 1967; other southern conferences (e.g., the Atlantic Coast and Southwest conferences) had already desegregated. It seemed that programs all over the country sought Black athletes. African American athletes understood, however, the attention, adulation, and rewards they received from the athletic departments were ephemeral. They felt the sting of prejudice and exclusion that the Black athletes who preceded them had experienced. They began to perceive that "once their athletic abilities are impaired by their age or by injury, only the ghetto beckons and they are doomed once again to that faceless, hopeless, ignominious existence they had supposedly forever left behind them" (Edwards, 1969, p. xxvii). Once they left the confines of the athletic field, their treatment, like that of nonathletic African Americans, was at best insensitive and often abominable.

African American collegiate athletes began to rebel. They called for an end to stacking (in-traracial competition for team positions), racial stereotyping, policing of social activities (including interracial dating), and other forms of discrimination in athletic programs (Spivey, 1985). In some cases, they adopted the tactics of the Civil Rights movement—peaceful demonstrations. Black athletes, and sometimes White athletes, boycotted practices and banquets and refused to compete in events for organizations that discriminated against African Americans (e.g., the New York Athletic Club, which had discriminatory policies regarding accommodations). In other cases, African American athletes and activists announced their intention to cancel athletic contests staged by schools that mistreated them as students and/or athletes, "by any means necessary" (Edwards, 1969). By 1968, a movement by African American athletes to boycott the Olympic Games, to be held later that year in Mexico, appeared to be growing. Athletes were using athletics to bring about social change.

The proposed boycott of the 1968 Olympics never materialized; few prominent Black athletes declined to participate in the Games. However, the struggle for social equality by African American athletes and the willingness of some to sacrifice their athletic scholarships[2] for the movement brought about changes in college sport. For example, the Big Ten conference appointed a committee to look into the complaints of Black athletes. They found evidence to support the athletes' charges of academic neglect and athletic exploitation. Changes were then instituted to improve academic support and counseling for African American athletes, and efforts were made to recruit more African American coaches and other athletic personnel (Wiggins, 1991). Big Ten schools, like many other schools during the late 1960s and early 1970s, hired Black assistant coaches to serve as intermediaries for African American athletes and White head coaches. Problems of discrimination, social isolation, and ill treat-

---

2. Athletes at a number of universities had their athletic scholarships revoked for insubordination. Many others voluntarily gave up their scholarships because of the racism at their schools (see Edwards, 1969).

ment by coaches did not disappear during the 1960s and 1970s, but African American athletes were more inclined to confront coaches and administrators than they had been in earlier years. Their services were needed now more than ever. Some of their demands had to be met.

African American Predominance

The period since the mid-1970s has been one of increasing interracial participation in revenue-generating collegiate sports. Basketball and football command larger television contracts, and televised games result in more money for participating schools and their conferences. For example, in 1966, the NCAA received $180,000 from television for its basketball tournament. In 1988, the tournament was worth $58,000,000 to the NCAA; each Final Four team received in excess of one million dollars. By the early 1990s, the television contract called for payments of approximately $115 million per year. As the payoff for successful seasons has soared, the reliance on African American athletes has ascended (particularly in basketball, where one outstanding player can have a dramatic effect on the outcome of a game).

African Americans constituted more than one third of all male collegiate basketball players in 1975 (Berghorn et al., 1988). By 1988, over half (56%) of the male basketball players and one third of the female basketball players were Black (Center for the Study of Athletics, 1989). Southern teams have the highest percentage of African Americans; sixty-one percent of players on southern teams are Black. In many cases, they are the majority on the same teams that found them to be objectionable two or three decades ago. By 1985, 95% of NCAA basketball teams had Black players, and the average number of Black players on integrated squads was 5.7 (Berghorn et al.).

African Americans have dominated nearly every statistical category in college basket-

ball—scoring, rebounding, assists, etc.—especially in the more recent years. They have also garnered most of the player of the year awards (e.g., UPI, AP, U.S. Basketball Writers Association, Naismith, Rupp, and Wooden awards) and an inordinate number of the all-Conference and NCAA all-Tournament awards. Furthermore, since 1971, when the All-America first team comprised only African Americans, White first-team All-Americas have become more rare. In the 1980s, only 6 of the 53 All-America selections were White players[3], and no All-America team in the 1980s (or thus far in the 1990s) has had more than one White player on the roster.

Similarly, in football, African Americans have overshadowed all others in recent years in rushing, receiving, punt return and kickoff return statistics. In addition to the Heisman Trophy winners mentioned above, Blacks have won a disproportionate share of the other player of the year awards—Maxwell, Camp, and Rockne awards, and the recently inaugurated Thorpe award. Following the 1989 college football season, African Americans virtually swept the offensive and defensive player of the year awards winning the following: the Heisman Trophy and the Maxwell Award (top player), the Camp Award (top back), the O'Brien Award (top quarterback), the Rockne and Lombardi Awards (top lineman), the UPI lineman of the year award, the Butkus Award (top linebacker), and the Thorpe Award (top defensive back).

In track and field, African Americans continued to dominate the sprints, long jump, relays, and men's hurdles. However, their presence was felt most in the "money" sports of basketball and football. Although they were no longer plagued by problems of discrimination in public accommodations and housing, they faced some of the same difficulties confronted by African Americans of earlier generations (e.g., stereotypes and positional segregation)

---

3. In 1983, seven players were selected to the All-America team, whereas the 1985 team consisted of six players (Meserole, 1991).

as well as new crises (e.g., poor academic performance and new academic standards for acquiring and maintaining athletic eligibility).

Racist Stereotypes and Stacking

A stereotype is "a largely false belief or set of beliefs concerning the characteristics of the members of a racial or ethnic group" (McLemore, 1991, p. 137). It is a distorted picture of a category of people that the "out" group (and even "in" group members) accept as part of the cultural heritage. Furthermore, by ignoring or explaining away contradictory evidence, stereotypes become reified; overgeneralizations are treated as if they really exist (Davis, 1978). Stereotypes are resistant to change, although contemporary events may alter or weaken beliefs.

For much of their history in the United States, people of African descent were believed to be superstitious, lazy, happy-go-lucky and ignorant (McLemore, 1991). Secondary structural assimilation—the movement of African Americans into previously segregated schools, occupations, and other institutions—has been accompanied by a diminution in the salience of these stereotypes in many areas of life. However, major American sport, in spite of its inclusion of African Americans in player positions, has been resistant to the abandonment of racial stereotypes. Athletic excellence is believed to be determined by different sets of traits for African Americans and Whites. (See Edwards, 1973, for a discussion of myths about Black superiority in sport).

African Americans are thought to possess natural athletic ability in the way of speed and quickness and jumping ability—traits that many coaches believe cannot be taught; an athlete is either born with these qualities or does without them. That African Americans excel in sport, then, has little to do with their work ethic or their intellect, according to this perspective. This view allows for African Americans to be outstanding athletes without negating the belief that they are lazy and ignorant; in fact, this attitude reinforces the belief in their indolence and incognizance. This is what some sports fans (and fans of Black athletes) may have had in mind when they stated their admiration for the athletic gifts bestowed on African American athletes and followed that by asking, "without inborn talent, where would the Black athlete be? What do you think his fate would be if he had to work as hard as the White athlete?"

Whites, on the other hand, are believed to excel at sport because they possess traits that are valued both in and (especially) out of sport—intelligence, industriousness, and other unspecified intangibles. Athletic ability is a limiting but not a deciding factor in their sport participation. According to this view, they rely on other traits to overcome their mediocre endowment. An article entitled "The Best in College Hoops," which appeared in *Sport* magazine in January, 1991, p. 69, illustrates this point. In describing the top four point guards in college basketball, it pointed out the following:

1. Kenny Anderson (Georgia Tech)— ". . . Kenny has superb instincts, unbelievable quickness, and he's also amazingly mature for his age. . . . But . . . he often shoots when he should pass, a serious indictment for a point guard."

2. Bobby Hurley (Duke)—"So what's the deal here? Hurley's a team genius—the type of kid coaches love to love . . . From a team point of view—and what other point of view is there for a point guard?—this perceptive penetrator does every bit as much for the Blue Devils as Anderson does for Tech."

3. Chris Corchiani (North Carolina State)— ". . . If he gets the ball on the move, he's almost impossible to stabilize. Still, many experts question CC Rider's quickness and outside shot. Legitimate queries. But with a guy like Chris, his intangibles will always outweigh his ability."

4. Lee Mayberry (Arkansas)— ". . . Mayberry's a brilliant athlete and a great passer, but not

a true point guard. 'He just doesn't *think* like one,' says Hamilton. 'More often than not, I disagree with his decision making.' " (Emphasis theirs.)

Anderson and Mayberry are (of course) African Americans. The writer gives them credit for their physical ability but has reservations about their mental ability. The White players—Hurley and Corchiani—lack the physical skill of Anderson and Mayberry, but they make up for it with cognitive abilities and intangibles. Thus, although it appears the writer is honoring Anderson and Mayberry by their inclusion in this exclusive group, he is, in fact, reproducing one of the most pervasive stereotypes of African Americans—they have the tools, but their intellect is questionable. The real praise is reserved for the White players because they have managed to prevail despite what the writer perceives to be their modest athletic endowment.

The persistence of stacking in college football is a product of this stereotype. African Americans are still primarily relegated to positions that are said to require speed, quickness, and jumping ability. The rare player—Black or White—who occupies a position that deviates from the expectations for members of his group finds that his abilities are (re)defined in ways that are consistent with the race-linked stereotypes. To quote Tom Waddle, a White wide receiver for the Chicago Bears, "When you don't fit into the computer on things like size, speed and vertical jump, you are basically a reject. You are a possession receiver. A possession receiver is a polite term for slow" (quoted in Sprout, 1991, p. 3). *Possession receiver* is a term that is used almost exclusively for White receivers.

Even the presence of African Americans in positions that have been traditionally reserved for Whites (e.g., quarterback) tends to support rather than refute stereotypes about athletic ability. Many African American college quarterbacks are required to gain significant yards by

running the ball. They often accumulate as many yards as, if not more than, the halfbacks or tailbacks on their teams. In other cases, where they exhibit proficiency as passers, they still find it difficult for coaches and professional scouts to take their accomplishments seriously. For this reason, in the last 4 years, two African American quarterbacks who were runners-up for the Heisman Trophy, and one Heisman Trophy winner, had to watch lesser-rated White quarterbacks drafted ahead of them by National Football League teams, although each of the African Americans was the top-rated quarterback in the Heisman balloting. They probably would have fared better in the draft if they had entered it in "traditionally Black" positions.

Intercollegiate sport has made considerable progress in its treatment of African American athletes. They are found in programs all over the country and in every prominent conference. Few schools would deny athletic scholarships to very talented African American athletes. The overt racism that characterized earlier periods has dissipated. However, more subtle forms of racism continue to limit opportunities available to players (not to mention coaches and administrators). Racist stereotypes and stacking are examples of the racism collegiate athletes face. Their use by schools that value their athletic competency but not their academic potential is another.

Academic Concerns

Perhaps the most critical problems faced by African American collegiate athletes revolve around academic issues, particularly graduation rates. Consider the following:

• An annual NCAA survey ("Athletes in Division I," 1990) reported that Division I athletes graduated at a slightly higher rate than did nonathletes at those same institutions, but basketball and football players lagged behind participants in other sports, especially at public universities. Of student-athletes who entered college in 1983, only one third of all Division I basketball players graduated within 5 years; less than 25% of those at public universities graduated within 5 years. For football, slightly more than half the private university athletes and about one third of public university athletes graduated in 5 years.

- A *USA Today* study of student-athletes recruited between 1980 and 1985 found that most Division I basketball players failed to complete their degree 5 years after enrolling in school. Most consistently competitive programs had lower graduation rates than those of the less competitive schools. African American males had the lowest graduation rates—less than one third received their degrees. Eight schools recruited 10 or more minority male athletes and failed to graduate *even one* during the period studied. A dozen other schools recruited between 10 and 17 minority athletes and *only* graduated one (Brady, 1991).

- A survey by the Associated Press ("Athletic Notes," 1990) found that nearly two thirds of Division I athletes who were drafted by football and basketball teams in the spring of 1990 failed to graduate. Most of the nongraduates were more than one semester away from earning their degrees, and although some universities graduated most or all of their athletes (e.g., Notre Dame and Michigan State University), others graduated few.[4] For example, Florida State University and the University of Houston graduated none of their (total of 15) drafted athletes.

All of the nongraduating athletes are not African Americans, but a disproportionate number are. For example, football had 410 Proposition 48[5] casualties in the first 2 years of the rule's implementation, and 346 (84%) of them were African Americans. Of the 150 basketball players who were Proposition 48 casualties, 138 (92%) were African Americans (Bannon, 1988). African Americans are overrepresented among the Proposition 48 casualties—at-risk college student-athletes—in basketball and football.

Academic Performance

Some studies of the academic performance of student-athletes suggest sport and scholastic activities are compatible. For example, Shafer and Armer (1968) found athletes are not poorer students than nonathletes; athletes had a higher mean grade-point average. Another study (Picou & Curry, 1974) found a positive relationship between athletics and educational aspirations *for boys from lower-class backgrounds.* Although they did not perform well academically, boys from modest backgrounds who played sports expected to attend college more often than did their peers who did not participate in sports.

However, many scholars (e.g., Edwards, 1979; Meggyesy, 1971; Scott, 1971) contend that sport and academics are incompatible for most student-athletes. Student-athletes, they say, are shielded from demanding academic courses and programs, exempted from academic responsibilities, and often directed toward Mickey Mouse courses and programs (Edwards, 1969). This is especially true of African American collegiate athletes; as a result, they are less likely than their White peers to do well academically and to graduate from college. College and university officials have, for some time, recognized the poorer scholastic performance of student-athletes compared to that of student-nonathletes. The NCAA's Propositions

---

4. The low graduation rate of football players is even more problematic when you consider the fact that, as a result of red-shirting, many football players are enrolled in college for 5 years, although they may compete for only 4 years.

5. Proposition 48 required college freshmen to score a minimum of 700 on the SAT or 15 on the ACT and achieve a "C" average in 11 core high school courses to be eligible to participate in athletics at Division I colleges.

48, 42, and 16[6] were developed to address student-athletes' academic performance in colleges. These proposals were met by disapprobation from many African American educators, administrators, and leaders. Their concern was that the NCAA's reliance on test scores worked to the disadvantage of African Americans because the standardized tests reflect a cultural bias toward White students and White standards.

One thing that was painfully clear about the NCAA's position was that the onus was now on student-athletes to better prepare themselves for college (presumably by studying harder, longer, and better while training harder, longer, and better for a college scholarship); it was the fault of the student-athletes that they did not perform better in college. This NCAA position did not give proper attention to other factors that contribute to academic performance.

Marginal Students, Outstanding Athletes

One explanation for the poorer academic performance of African American compared to that of White American student-athletes is the singular emphasis on sport among African Americans: The student-athletes and their significant others (e.g., parents) attach more importance to doing well in sport than in school. However, research (Harris, 1990) indicates that African American high school student-athletes and their significant others are *more* concerned about academics than are their White peers.

A more plausible explanation would consider the conditions under which many African American student-athletes are expected to achieve academically. Although there are many success stories, a larger proportion of African Americans than other Americans are still poor or near-poor and attend schools in poor areas that are compromised by inadequate resources. Students from these schools in less privileged areas tend to exhibit poorer academic performances. A recent study (Banas, 1990) that documented the relationship between student achievement and property wealth of school districts found that students from school districts with the highest real estate property values scored substantially higher on standardized tests (e.g., state-mandated reading and mathematics exams and the ACT) than did those from poorer districts. This difference is largely attributable to per-pupil spending; rich districts spent 66% more per high school pupil than did poor districts. Many of these property-poor districts are the source of collegiate athletes; some schools in these districts annually send their top athletes to one or more colleges. Although their academic programs are inadequate to prepare a large number of students for Division I colleges, their athletic programs in basketball and football are exceptional in preparing athletes for athletic scholarships.

African Americans who attend private or predominantly White high schools often fare better academically than do their public school counterparts (Harris, 1990), but many of them have attended less affluent elementary schools and find themselves behind their high school classmates. When they are "recruited" by academically elite schools, it is often for the same reason they are recruited by colleges—for the rewards they bring to the athletic program.[7] In some cases, the students

---

6. Proposition 42 had the same minimum requirements for Division I athletic participation as Proposition 48. However, it would have denied financial aid to partial- or nonqualifiers. This was later amended to allow partial qualifiers to received aid based on need. In August 1996, Proposition 16 went into effect. It raised the standards for the combined GPA and exam score necessary to qualify through use of a sliding scale. For example, a student with a 700 SAT would need a GPA of 2.5 to qualify; a GPA of 2.0 would require a score of 900 on the SAT.

7. Some high schools use their national exposure, or the potential for national exposure—games on television and appearances in tournaments—to induce athletes to play for their school, even if it means the athlete has to change school districts. In this way, some high schools behave much like colleges, offering athletic shoes, clothing, and trips far away and abroad for student-athletes' services.

benefit little from the rigorous academic curriculum of the high school. They are there to render athletic services; academic concerns center on keeping them eligible, not preparing them to be scholars.

As a group, African American male student-athletes enter college with lower GPAs, and lower SATs and ACTs, than those of their White student-athlete peers and those of African American student-nonathletes (Center for the Study of Athletics, 1989). In short, they are at a disadvantage when they arrive on campus, and many schools do little to correct this academic deficiency.

When the marginal student-outstanding athlete arrives on campus, especially if he is a football player, he is likely to find that his first activity is not becoming acquainted with the library or the classroom, but getting to know the playing field. In fact, if he or she is like most football or basketball players, the student-athlete will spend more time on sports (about 28 hours per week) than attending class or labs (12 hours per week) *and* preparing for class or labs (12 hours per week).[8] He or she also will miss, on average during the season, 2 days per week of classes (Center for the Study of Athletics,1989); *the athlete will be absent from 40% of the class instruction.* It is small wonder that many of these student-athletes get "incompletes" and find themselves on academic probation.

Add to this the fact that, for males, the rewards for making a professional roster are enormous, especially given the marginality of their academic performance, and scholarly work becomes all the more problematic.[9] The fact that the athletes do poorly in the classroom may be less a reflection of what they value than what they see as within their grasp. This is not to say that student-athletes would forsake the "big bucks" of a professional sport career for a career as a modestly paid public servant. Rather, when one road appears to be a dead end they, like others, take an alternative path. For many of them, the road to academic success is not easily accessible. While others go speeding by, they sit idling.

Of course, many of them still hope that a professional sport career beckons, but only a small number of collegiate athletes will ever have an opportunity to play even one game of professional ball, and few of those who do will last beyond 4 or 5 years. Perhaps this is what led Joe Paterno, the football coach at Pennsylvania State University, to declare, "For at least the last two decades we've told Black kids who bounce balls, run around tracks and catch touchdown passes that these things are ends unto themselves. We've raped them. We can't afford to do it to another generation" (cited in Edwards, 1984, p. 14).

NCAA Reform

As the 1991 annual NCAA meeting neared, many expected reform, including academic reform, to be the theme of the assembly. Indeed, a number of proposals concerning academic issues were submitted, but they were rejected by the delegates, who chose to wait until 1992 to address academic reform. However, a measure was adopted that requires athletes to fulfill most of their major requirements by the start of their fourth year to retain their eligibility ("Sidelines," 1991a). Other measures were adopted that will limit the time athletes are allowed to spend on their sport to 20 hours per

---

8. This estimate for time spent on sport is low next to Edwards' (1984). He says, during season, major college Division I football players spend 45–49 hours per week on their sport, 60 hours per week if you count travel time.

9. Former collegiate student-athletes are not the only ones to benefit when they make it to the professional ranks. For the college coach, it reinforces his or her abilities and legitimates his or her coaching philosophy. It also leads to the acquisition of more blue-chippers, as a coach can point to professional athletes, formerly under the coach's tutelage, as examples of what the coach and the coach's system can do for prospective student-athletes.

week, shorten the length of the season, and reduce the number of games a team may play in a season ("Sidelines," 1991b).

Many of the issues taken up at the meeting concerned cost-cutting measures (e.g., a reduction in the number of scholarships allowed in all sports) and how to spend the $115 million—the first of seven annual payments from its television contract with CBS for basketball. The NCAA set aside $45 million to create a fund for needy athletes, to provide catastrophic injury insurance for athletes, to increase financing for championships, and to more than double the size of traveling parties (e.g., cheerleaders, bands, and university officials) for the Division I men's basketball tournament. Only $7.4 million was set aside for programs to enhance the academic performance of athletes. *This is less than seven percent of the funds, to combat the most serious problem facing collegiate athletics today.*

Although there has been much discussion about how teams that make it to the Final Four in the basketball tournament will fare financially,[10] very little attention has been paid to improving the academic performance of student-athletes. It appears that the 1991 NCAA meeting was business as usual—"Let's split up the money and figure out ways to make more." As an afterthought, the NCAA may remember the student-athletes who make the money are deserving of a quality education. In the meantime, the NCAA is helping to perpetuate the problem. It is time to seek solutions.

Suggestions

Two reasons for the poor academic performance of African American male collegiate athletes are that many come from less privileged school programs and all are expected or required by collegiate athletic programs to spend excessive hours on sports. A first suggestion (one that has been made by many people in and out of college athletics) is to curtail freshman eligibility. The student-athletes will benefit immensely from having their first year to concentrate on academics without the demands of athletics. Spending the first year on campus, instead of on the road, should afford student-athletes more time to spend preparing for classes, and they will not be required to miss an excessive number of classes. It is very difficult to be successful academically when one is required to miss in excess of one third of the class meetings; it is nearly impossible when one is a marginal student. Perhaps the reason a number of Proposition 48 casualties have been successful academically is that they were required to sit out intercollegiate athletics for a year, which gave them time to concentrate on academics.

The suggestion of freshman ineligibility causes tremors in some coaches and athletic directors. They want money and exposure, and they realize a talented athlete, albeit a freshman, can generate both, even if it is at the expense of education. Other coaches and sports administrators would like to see freshman ineligibility, but they fear they will be at a competitive disadvantage if their schools adopt changes and other schools do not. For example, the president of Iowa State University reported he was considering proposals from a faculty panel to bring about changes in the sports program (e.g., raising admissions standards for athletes and barring academically deficient athletes from competition). The men's football and basketball coaches promptly reported they would resign if these changes were implemented, because other schools would have a competitive advantage. It is hoped that if NCAA schools lack the sagacity to drop freshmen from competing in college athletics,

---

10. In 1991, the NCAA changed its distribution system for the basketball tournament so that performance in the last six tournaments determined a school's take. In 1991, Duke received over $790,000 of the ACC's nearly $4 million tournament pay ("NCAA Line," 1991). Schools in seven conferences received over half the $62.5 million paid out, with the rest going to the other 230 Division I schools ("NCAA Pays Out," 1991c). Five conferences received more than $2.4 million from the tournament payout.

some will have the courage of their conviction to act alone.

The NCAA's rule to limit the amount of time spent on sport to 20 hours per week is a good measure, but it needs to go even further. Therefore, a second suggestion is to restrict hours spent on sport to no more than the amount of time spent in class. If the mission of universities is to develop scholarship, then less, not more, time should be spent on athletic compared to academic endeavors. Put the emphasis back on academics.

Third, the NCAA should distribute a larger percentage of the money from television contracts to schools for academic enhancement. The NCAA should work with member schools to identify and develop programs that educate, not merely retain, student-athletes. Member schools have to go beyond providing study halls or "quiet times" and tutors to write papers and take notes for student-athletes. In addition, successful programs should be rewarded and duplicated.

The fourth suggestion is, perhaps, an unpopular one. NCAA schools and the companies that advertise during their games ought to contribute considerable money to the schools and communities these student-athletes come from. This would be an important step in aiding poor schools that produce collegiate athletes but have inadequate resources for academic programs. For example, a contribution of $50,000 could be made to the high school of each of the 12 basketball players on each basketball tournament Final Four team. The total amount (about $2.4 million) is less than a number of conferences received for their Final Four appearances in 1991. (A lesser amount could be paid to the high schools of football players whose teams participate in bowl games.) A large portion of the money, perhaps 80%, could be earmarked for the academic programs of the recipient schools. Most important, perhaps the sponsors of the NCAA telecasts will become as interested in some of the schools as they are in the athletes who come from these schools. (Of course, it does not have to stop here. Advertisers who use professional athletes to promote their products could, for philanthropic reasons, support the secondary and primary schools these athletes attended.) Advertisers give thousands of dollars to colleges in the name of "the players of the game" every week. Why not give some of that money to the schools and programs that need it most—the secondary and primary schools these student-athletes come from? Academic enhancement has to begin before student-athletes are in secondary schools and to continue, as necessary, throughout their college tenure.

Discussion

This paper has examined the predominance of African Americans in revenue-generating collegiate sports. It has traced their involvement on athletic teams from the era of superspades to today's "semiprofessional" players. In every era, race has played an important part in the acceptance or rejection and expectations of African American athletes. Although some forms of segregation have disappeared (e.g., segregation in public housing), other forms continue to exist (e.g., stacking). Furthermore, racist stereotypes are still prevalent in collegiate sport; virtually no television coverage (and little newspaper coverage) is without them.

African American collegiate athletes also encounter academic problems, particularly at predominantly White colleges and universities. If we include problems of isolation due to the scarcity of other African American students, faculty, and staff, and problems finding services such as churches, barbershops, etc., it becomes apparent that these student-athletes have special needs and concerns, many of which are addressed by neither their schools nor the NCAA.

Finally, a number of suggestions have been advanced to address academic problems faced by African American student-athletes. They are not expected to obliterate the problems that pervade revenue-generating, intercollegiate sports; nothing short of removing professional-style, interschool sport competition from institutions of higher education is likely to have that effect. However, they are an attempt to offer a corrective to a particular set of problems—those that create and maintain marginal academic performance among the most celebrated group of persons in institutions of higher learning: African American student-athletes. Hopefully, this paper makes a contribution to their well-being.

Study Questions

1. What options are available to the NCAA to deal with the apparent poor academic performance of African American collegiate athletes?

2. How does the public's image of the athletic prowess of young Black males continue to express racial stereotypes about African Americans today?

3. How did the activist movement try to bargain for better treatment of African American collegiate athletes by the sports establishment during the 1960s?

4. How does the media continue to perpetuate the belief that sports is the way to a better life for the African American community in the United States?

References

Andrews, D. S. (1984, September). The G.I. Bill and college football. *Journal of Physical Education, Recreation and Dance, 55*, 23–26.

Ashe, A. (1988). *A hard road to glory: A history of the African American athlete since 1946*. New York: Warner Books.

Athletes in Division I found graduating at higher rate than other students. (1990, July 1). *The Chronicle of Higher Education*, p. A29.

Athletic Notes. (1990, August 1). *The Chronicle of Higher Education,* p. A30.

Banas, C. (1990, June 21). Grades tied to school district property values. *Chicago Tribune,* Sec. 1, p. 3.

Bannon, J. (1988, Sept. 30). Proposal 48: Jury still out; foes vocal. *USA Today*, p. C1.

Behee, J. (1974). *Hail to the victors!: Black athletes at the University of Michigan*. Ann Arbor, MI: Ulrich's Books.

Berghorn, F. J., Yetman, N. R., & W. E. Hanna. (1988). Racial participation and integration in men's and women's intercollegiate basketball: Continuity and change, 1958–1945. *Sociology of Sport Journal, 5*, 107–124.

The best in college hoops. (1991, January). *Sport Magazine*, 69–79.

Brady, E. (1991, June 17). Players: 46% earn degrees in five years. *USA Today*, pp. 1A–2A.

Center for the Study of Athletics. (1989). *Studies of intercollegiate athletics. Report No. 3: The life experiences of black intercollegiate athletes at NCAA Division I institutions*. Washington, DC: American Institutes for Research.

Davis, F. J. (1978). *Minority dominant relations: A sociological analysis*. Arlington Heights, IL: AHM Publishing Corporation.

Edwards, H. (1969). *The revolt of the Black athlete*. New York: The Free Press.

Edwards, H. (1973, March). The myth of the racially superior athlete. *Intellectual Digest, 2*, 58–60.

Edwards, H. (1979, September). Sport within the veil: The triumphs, tragedies and challenges of Afro-American involvement. *The Annals of the American Academy of Political and Social Science, 445*, 116–27.

Edwards H. (1984, Winter/Spring). The collegiate athletic arms race: Origins and implications of the 'Rule 48' controversy. *Journal of Sport and Social Issues, 8*, 4–22.

Franklin, J. H., & Moss, A. A., Jr. (1988). *From slavery to freedom: A history of Negro Americans* (6th ed.). New York: Alfred A. Knopf.

Green, K. (1982). *Government support for minority participation in higher education*. Washington, DC: American Association for Higher Education.

Harris, O. (1990). Athletics and academics: Complementary or contrary activities? In G. Jarvie (Ed.), *Sport and ethnicity* (pp. 124–149). London: Falmer Press

McLemore, D. S. (1991). *Racial and ethnic relations in America* (3rd ed.). Boston: Allyn and Bacon.

Meggyesy, D. (1971). *Out of their league*. New York: Paperback Library.

Meserole, M. (Ed.). (1991). *The 1991 sports almanac*. Boston: Houghton Mifflin Co.

Morris, A. D. (1984). *The origins of the Civil Rights movement*. New York: Free Press.

NCAA line. (1991, April 2). *USA Today,* p. 4C.

NCAA pays out $31 million in television revenues. (1991c, September 25). *The Chronicle of Higher Education*, p.A43.

Paul, J., McGhee, R. V., & Fant, H. (1984, December). The arrival and ascendance of black athletes in the Southeastern Conference, 1966–80. *Phylon, 45,* 284–97.

Picou, J. S., & Curry, E. W. (1974, December). Residence and the athletic participation aspiration hypothesis. *Social Science Quarterly, 55,* 768–76.

Rader, B. (1990). *American Sports* (2nd ed.). Englewood Cliffs, NJ: Prentice Hall.

Schafer, W. E., & Armer, M. (1968, November). Athletes are not inferior students. *Transaction, 5,* 21–26, 61–62.

Scott, J. (1971). *The athletic revolution.* New York: Free Press.

Sidelines. (1991a, January 16). *The Chronicle of Higher Education,* p. A37.

Sidelines. (1991b, January 16). *The Chronicle of Higher Education,* pp. A1, A38.

Spivey, D. (1985). Black consciousness and Olympic protest movement, 1964–1980. In D. Spivey (Ed.), *Sport in America* (pp. 239–262). Westport, CT: Greenwood Press.

Sports briefs. (1985, December 27). *The Evening News* (Newburgh, NY), p. 8B.

Sprout, G. (1991, September 16). Openers. *The Sporting News,* p. 3.

Wiggins, D. (1991). Prized performers, but frequently overlooked students: The involvement of black athletes in intercollegiate sports on predominantly white university campuses, 1890–1972. *Research Quarterly for Exercise and Sport, 62*(2), 164–177.

The African American Athlete: Social Myths and Stereotypes

Gary A. Sailes

Abstract

The success and popularity of the African American athlete in the past three decades is unprecedented. African American athletes dominate the popular sports of professional football (60%), baseball (30%), and basketball (85%); in particular, in the United States they dominate the headlines of today's sports pages and are at the core of interest in American television sports programming. The accomplishments of the African American athlete have become an accepted facet of American culture. However, in an attempt to explain that athletic success, racial attitudes emerge that further polarize the two dominant ethnic groups in the United States today, African Americans and Whites.

The myths and stereotypes that attempt to explain the phenomenal success of the African American athlete are an indication of the deeply rooted divisions that exist in a racially segmented society. Consequently, they also perpetuate the development of structural barriers to entry into management and coaching positions in college and professional sport. This essay will examine the development and perpetuation of racial myths and stereotypes about the African American athlete and present the social conditions that rationalize his/her rise to prominence in contemporary American sport.

Key Terms
• African American •
• Athlete, Athletics/Sports •
• College/Intercollegiate •
• Discrimination •
• Myths •
• Prejudice •
• Racism •
• Stereotypes •

Introduction

American sport is a multi-billion dollar industry with unprecedented interest from fans and active participants in a global market (Coakley, 1998). No social institution in American culture receives the media attention generated by sport. American sport is currently televised globally into hundreds of international television markets. The most widely and internationally viewed American sport event is the Super Bowl (Coakley, 1998). Millions of viewers globally tune into college sports in March to watch the NCAA basketball tournament, affectionately called "March Madness!" The success of the 1996 women's Olympic teams, particularly the "Dream Team," has spurred the growth of interest in women's athletics. Title IX lawsuits and NCAA enforcement have increased, guaranteeing women's place in college athletics. Two women's professional basketball leagues have emerged (Women's National Basketball Association and the American Basketball League), and Nike has taken the lead in promoting interest in women's athletics through their commercial spots. Sport is big business and there is enormous interest. Virtually no one in the United States today is untouched by sport.

History

Concurrently, American college sport plays a significant role in popularizing sport in the United States. It has gained enormous popularity since the first collegiate event in 1852, a rowing race between Harvard and Yale universities. Most early college sports were nothing more than extramural contests organized and controlled by college students (Coakley, 1998). The "Golden Age of Sport," 1919–1930, set the stage for the commercialization and rise of college sport as we know it today. During that period in our history, American technology advanced, and consequently, so did American college sports.

A new invention, the assembly line, created jobs and enabled the mass production of goods that created wealth. As a result, there was a mass migration of Americans from rural areas of the country to major urban centers like New York, Chicago, and Detroit. Inventions like the radio, printing press, and wire service spurred the growth of the mass media. As an outgrowth, the mass media began to write about American sport and sports stars, thereby creating interest among the American public. Huge stadia were built, advances in travel (railroad) allowed schools, to travel and compete against other schools, creating rivalries. Consequently, conferences were established, and finally, the National Collegiate Athletic Association (NCAA) and other college sports organizations were established to control this tremendous growth (Coakley, 1998).

The media played a major role in the rise of American college sports. Coverage increased, leading to the emergence of sports heroes who later became professional athletes and sports legends. Collegiate rivalries were fueled in the press, adding to the popularity of this American pastime. The college All-American was established, and today, March Madness, the televised presentation of the NCAA Basketball Tournament, has become the symbol of college basketball's emergence as one of the most popular sports on television.

The Integration of American Sport

American college sport was a "Whites-only" institution, with only a few African American athletes participating on teams at predominantly White colleges and universities, until as late as the 1960s. For example, in the late 1920s, only Paul Robeson, who played football at Rutgers, and Fritz Pollard, who played football for Brown University, could be found (Ashe, 1993). African Americans played college sports at historically Black colleges and universities located primarily in the South. By the time Jackie Robinson broke the color barrier in Major League Baseball in 1947, African American athletes were being recruited to play on American college sports teams in relatively small numbers, particularly in football, basketball, and baseball. It was not uncommon for a predominantly White school to have only one African American player on its college basketball or football teams (Ashe, 1993). Today, however, African American athletes account for 67% and 44% of the athletes playing NCAA Division I basketball and football respectively. Moreover, 100% of NCAA Division I football programs and 98% of NCAA Division I basketball programs have integrated teams (Coakley, 1998).

The success of Jackie Robinson in Major League Baseball spurred the recruitment of African American talent from the Negro Baseball Leagues. Professional basketball and football emulated the trend and American colleges followed suit. By the late 1960s, nearly every major American collegiate and professional basketball, football, and baseball team was integrated (Ashe, 1993). As African Americans integrated American sport, they brought their special style of play that distinguished them from their White counterparts. For example, basketball was forever changed in its configuration when African American males began to dominate the sport with their numbers (George, 1992; Sailes, 1996). The "Whites-only" style of play was slowed down and consisted mostly of ball movement and outside shooting. Individual skills were sometimes sacrificed to augment team-oriented play. However, African American athletes played with a more athletic and aggressive game that highlighted individual skills like improvisational movement to the basket, slam-dunking, improvisational dribbling and passing skills, and aggressive rebounding (George, 1992; Sailes, 1996). For many inner-city athletes, these skills were developed in the parks and playgrounds of America's African American ghettos and have become the standard by which basketball is currently defined.

African Americans are also breaking ground in sports other than basketball, football, and baseball. African Americans have kept the doors of opportunity open in professional sports like tennis (i.e., Maliavia Washington, Lori McNeil, Zina Garrison, Chandra Rubin),

golf (i.e., Tiger Woods), swimming (i.e., Anthony Nesty), ice skating (i.e., Debbie Thomas), and gymnastics (i.e., Dominique Dawes). Consequently, however, the success of the African American athletes spurred the evolution of specific sports stereotypes and myths in an attempt to explain their success and the subsequent attack on the "White status quo" in American college sports. These stereotypes elevated the physical prowess of the African American athlete, but attacked the players intellectual capabilities. Simply put, the African American athlete was a spectacular physical phenomenon, but still a "dumb jock" (Sailes, 1993b).

Racial Stereotypes

The historical origins of the dumb jock stereotype can be traced to 500 BC, when Greek athletes were criticized for the inordinate amount of time they utilized in preparation for competition and for neglecting their intellectual development. Greek athletes were characterized by some philosophers of the period as useless and ignorant citizens with dull minds (Coakley, 1998). Media attention challenging the scholarship of college athletes, particularly in the revenue-producing sports of basketball and football, has tainted the academic credibility of college student-athletes (Sailes, 1993a). Reports of high school student-athletes not meeting NCAA minimum academic standards to establish college eligibility, accounts of college student-athletes failing their courses, and the particularly low graduation rates among major college basketball and football programs foster the belief that anti-intellectualism exists among college student-athletes (Sailes, 1993a, 1996). Unfortunately, Hollywood movies (Org character in the movies *Revenge of the Nerds, I & II*) and television situation comedies (Coach character in the television situation comedy *Cheers*) facilitate the perpetuation of the dumb jock stereotype through their characterizations of unintelligent sports figures.

Sailes (1993b) found that typical college students felt that college athletes could not compete with them in the classroom. Traditional students felt they could earn higher grades and had higher graduation rates when compared to student athletes. It was also felt that college athletes received unearned grades from their professors and took easy courses in order to maintain their athletic eligibility. Traditional students felt this fact accounted for any measure of success in the classroom among student athletes.

Although these perceptions were disclosed, most traditional college students were reluctant to reveal they felt that student athletes typified the dumb jock stereotype. Moreover, traditional college students felt that the African American athlete was least qualified to attend college and probably was admitted chiefly for athletic talent. In addition, they felt that the typical African American student-athlete was not sufficiently prepared to attend college and was least likely to be successful in the classroom. The negative stereotype of academic incompetence was perceived to be higher among African American athletes when compared to their White counterparts. In conclusion, Sailes asserted that traditonal college students felt that if the typical student-athlete was a dumb jock the African American student-athlete was the dumbest of all.

Beezley (1983) studied the development of the dumb jock stereotype traditionally associated with college football players. Although the dumb jock stereotype was prevalent in American sports culture, no substantiation could be generated to confirm its origin or its validity. Similarly, Nixon (1982) found no evidence to support the stereotype of the dumb jock. In a comparison of grade point average, graduation rate, and student perceptions, no significant statistical differences were found between typical college students and student-athletes. McMartin and Klay (1983) had similar findings and also reported that positive and favorable attitudes were held about students who were also athletes. Regardless of the low graduation rates of football and basketball players (53% and 46% respectively), which can be attributed to the time demands of these primary revenue-producing sports, the overall graduation rate for college student-athletes (58%) was slightly higher than for the ordinary college student (56%) (National Collegiate Athletic Association [NCAA], 1996). Despite the prevalence of the dumb jock stereotype, there appears to be no scientific basis for generalizing that the college student athlete is a dumb jock.

It is plausible to assume that the retention of unsubstantiated stereotypes about student-athletes emanates from a variety of circumstances. It is likely that most college students have very little, if any, contact with college student-athletes from which to draw factual information about student-athlete academic competence. Second, if generalizations about student athletes are continually perpetuated by the mass media in fictionalized depictions (television, movies, books), it is likely that those stereotypes will continue among the general public. In addition, it is doubtful that the general public reads scientific journals that clearly illustrate that student-athletes generally hold higher academic grade point averages and graduate in higher percentages than do traditional college students. Sailes (1993a) attributed this to tighter academic restrictions and requirements on student-athletes to maintain their eligibility to compete in college athletics.

Steele (1990) argued that one particularly sensitive race-oriented component of White superiority and African American inferiority is intelligence. Support for the physical superiority myth indirectly contributes to the belief that the African American athlete is mentally and intellectually inferior to the White athlete (Davis, 1990; Hoose, 1989; Sailes, 1991, 1993b). Conceptions about the dumb jock stereotype targeted at African American athletes are, therefore, related to racial stereotyping. This racist attitude contributes to the discriminatory practice of channeling African Americans away from the central (leadership and/or decision-making) positions in college and professional sport (Coakley, 1998; Eitzen & Sage, 1996; Leonard, 1998; Schneider & Eitzen, 1986).

Whites are reluctant to hire African Americans into management and head coaching positions in professional and major college sport because Whites do not have confidence in the intellectual capabilities of African Americans to manage or coach professional or major college ball clubs. Los Angeles Dodgers former executive Al Campanis illustrated this practice when he exposed racial stereotyping in sport on national television. He made the assertion that African Americans may not have the "necessities" to be managers in professional baseball (Hoose, 1989). Positional segregation (often referred to as stacking) is prevalent among college baseball, volleyball, and football teams (Coakley, 1998; Jones, Leonard, Schmitt, Smith & Tolone, 1987; Schneider & Eitzen, 1986). African Americans are systematically channeled away from the team leadership positions in favor of White players. Coaches are reluctant to entrust the leadership of the team to African Americans because they believe African Americans are not intelligent enough to be successful team leaders. This is characterized by the dearth of African American pitchers in professional and college baseball and quarterbacks in college and professional football.

Lombardo (1978) noted two distinct stereotypes that have emerged regarding African American males. Known as "the brute" and "the sambo" stereotypes, they were developed by Whites to maintain their superior position in society and to denigrate African American males, keeping them subordinate. The brute stereotype characterized the African American male as primitive, temperamental, overreactive, uncontrollable, violent, and sexually powerful. This stereotype intentionally separated the African American from intellectualism and mental control. White society placed importance on intellectualism and subsequently removed the African American from equal status by characterizing him with physical, primitive attributes. This stereotype has been popularly used to explain the dominance of the African American athlete in football, basket-

ball, baseball, and boxing (Sailes, 1996, 1993b, 1991). Consequently, the belief that intellectualism does not exist among African Americans has kept management and coaching positions in Division I college and professional sports mostly White (Coakley, 1998; Leonard, 1998)

The sambo stereotype depicted the African American as benign, childish, immature, exuberant, uninhibited, lazy, comical, impulsive, fun-loving, good-humored, inferior and lovable. These typecasts about African Americans have historical roots in American slavery. It was felt their characterizations relegated African American slaves to inferior status. Lombardo (1978) criticized the performance of the Harlem Globetrotters for their continued perpetuation of the sambo stereotype in sport and for compromising the integrity and positive image of African Americans in general and African American athletes in particular.

Other unsubstantiated, race-oriented sports myths have evolved in an attempt to explain the success and overrepresentation of African American athletes in certain American sports. Most myths attempting to rationalize the apparent dominance of African American athletes in specific sports generally have little scientific credibility. For example, there remains the popular belief that African American athletes are physically superior to White athletes, and that their superior body build is genetically determined, giving them an advantage over their White counterparts. Many believe this advantage accounts for the success among African American athletes in football, basketball, baseball, track and field, and boxing (Coakley, 1998; Leonard, 1998).

A 1988 investigative report by the *Philadelphia Inquirer* sought to answer the question: "Are African Americans better athletes than Whites?" (Sokolove, 1988). Similarly, a 1989 NBC special program hosted by Tom Brokaw, entitled *The Black Athlete: Fact or Fiction,* focused on the question: "What accounts for the success of African American athletes in American sports?" These two reports supported the theory of the physical or genetic superiority of the African American athlete. Although some physical differences are apparent between African Americans and Whites as a whole, it remains to be demonstrated that anatomical, genetic, and/or physiological differences between African American and White athletes contribute significantly to the dominance of either over the other in sports competition (Coakley, 1998; Eitzen & Sage, 1996; Leonard, 1998; McPherson, Curtis & Loy, 1989; Sailes, 1996, 1993b, 1991, 1987; Sokolove, 1988).

Davis (1991) argued that the need to analyze African American success in sport was a racist preoccupation emanating from fear generated within the White status quo. It was felt that White fear of loss of control of American economic, political, and educational institutions was the catalyst for investigating the so-called athletic superiority of the African American athlete. Historically, African Americans were barred from competing against Whites in sport for two reasons: 1. The country practiced segregation between Whites and African Americans. 2. It was believed that African Americans were mentally and intellectually inferior to Whites and posed no significant challenge on the athletic field. When African Americans integrated American sport and began to dominate in basketball, football, and baseball, Whites concluded that it was the natural physical and/or genetic superiority of the African Americans that enabled them to dominate those sports. Consequently, the stereotype that African Americans were naturally physically superior to Whites supported the racist notion that they were intellectually inferior and could not compete with Whites in America's corporate boardrooms. This stereotype facilitated the maintaining of White superiority and the White status quo.

Sports Myths

Many of the myths regarding African American athletes suffer from scientifically unacceptable assumptions and are not substantiated by research. Moreover, the variables impacting on the sport socialization and sport participation patterns of African American athletes in American sport emanate from the social constraints placed upon them by the dominant culture and the determination of African American athletes to overcome these constraints (Coakley, 1998; Eitzen & Sage, 1996; Leonard, 1998; McPherson, Curtis, & Loy, 1989; Sailes, 1987, 1991; Sokolove, 1988).

This author compiled a list of the prevalent myths held by college students about African American college student-athletes. Although this was informal qualitative research at best, the information gathered was collected every semester over a period of 10 years in a university elective course entitled "The African American Athlete in American Sport." Each semester, class enrollment was approximately 30 students, with one third African American and two thirds White. Students completed a course assignment that required them to list and explain every myth they heard or believed about the African American athlete. The assignments were maintained and organized for inclusion in a book. What follows is a summary of those assignments. It was interesting to note that most of the stereotypes attempted to answer two questions: 1. Is the African American physically superior to the White athlete? 2. Why does the African American athlete dominate American sport?

Matriarchal Theory

Many students in my course believed that most African American athletes came from a single-parent household with an absent father and with the mother as the head of the household. It was also believed that because of the absent father, the African American athlete was uncontrollable, hostile, and unfocused. He channeled his hostility into the sports area where he excelled. In addition, the absent father caused the African American athlete to seek and establish a bond with the coach. A paternalistic relationship developed, and the African American athlete became a better performer as a result of that special relationship. Evans (1978) and Anshel and Sailes (1990) found that most athletes, and African American athletes in particular, were suspicious and distrusting of the motives of their coaches. At best, the relationship between the head coach and the African American student-athlete was distant. The literature refutes the notion that a special relationship exists between the coach and the African American athlete because of an absent father and that it was that relationship that motivated the African American athlete to excel on the athletic field. Additionally, there is no evidence which substantiates the idea that the absence of a father, and the mother serving as head of the household, directly impact athletic performance.

Mandingo Theory

Jimmy "The Greek" Snyder popularized this theory with his candid remarks on national television. His remarks got him fired as an ABC sports analyst. It was believed that the physical superiority of the African American athlete emanated from the days of slavery. This theory holds that slave masters intentionally bred their slaves by requiring physically large, muscular male slaves to mate with physically large and muscular female slaves. The offspring were physically superior to the commonly reproduced slave child. This physically superior child, it was felt, would grow up to be a better laborer in the fields.

Snyder asserted this type of selective breeding caused the thighs and gluteal muscles in African Americans to become superior. This, he felt, accounted for their superior jumping and sprinting abilities over their White counterparts. Common sense dictates that even if this were true, there is no possible way this could account for the physical development of 34 million African Americans today. White slave masters had slave concubines, slave women were raped by White overseers, free Negroes could choose their own mates, most slaves were unrestricted in their choice of mates (Bennett, 1996; Franklin, 1994), and foreign immigration to the United States no doubt diluted the so-called "selectively-bred gene pool."

Interracial marriage and miscegenation were, and are, too prevalent in the United States for that gene pool to have survived and eventually accounted for any physical difference that would predispose itself in the contemporary athletic arena (Sailes, 1991).

History shows that large slaves were used as fighters, and heavy gambling by Whites took place on those fights. In fact, two slaves, Bill Richmond and Tommy Molineaux, were early fighters who won their masters enough money to earn their freedom (Ashe, 1993). Moreover, it is quite possible that slaves were used as breeders in isolated instances, but there were too many uncontrollable social variables in early and contemporary American society to give substance to this theory. It would be virtually impossible for slave masters to control all sexual relations between male and female slaves. Additionally, free Negroes chose their mates. History also shows that African Americans lived with Native Americans, intermarried, and had offspring as a result of those relationships. Common sense dictates that in all likelihood, the gene pool that might have originated from isolated cases of slave breeding was lost almost immediately and certainly was discontinued after the Emancipation Proclamation, which freed the slaves.

"Survival of the Fittest" Theory

It was felt that the physical superiority of the African American athlete was incidentally created by the survivors of the "middle passage" of African slaves to the Americas. The trip from Africa to America took several months. During that time, slaves were laid on their backs and chained together at hands and feet. They assumed this position for several days at a time, except for brief exercise periods on the deck of the slave ship. They were barely fed, became ill, and sometimes over 65% of the slave cargo was lost to dysentery, suicide, or murder (Bennett, 1996; Franklin, 1994). It was felt those who survived the middle passage were physically superior beings compared to those who perished.

Today's 34 million African Americans are supposedly the descendants of that superior gene pool and this accounts for their physical superiority on the athletic field. As indicated in the Mandingo Theory, immigration, miscegenation, and interracial marriage between African Americans, Whites, and individuals from other ethnic groups, especially after the end of slavery, would most assuredly have caused the dilution of any special gene pool supposedly created by the middle passage.

Genetic Theory

This theory assumed that African Americans had more white, fast-twitch muscle fibers and Whites had more red, slow-twitch muscle fibers, which predicted the potential in athletics. White muscle fibers were power-oriented and were better able to liberate greater force over a short period of time. White, fast-twitch muscle fibers would be most beneficial for sports activities which required agility, speed, quickness, jumping, lifting, and throwing. This explanation was used to justify African American dominance in sports activities like the jumping and speed events in track and field, basketball, baseball, football, and boxing. One of my White students believed that African Americans were able to run faster and jump higher than Whites because African Americans had an extra muscle in their legs. He asserted he was told this by a college professor/athletic trainer who held the Ph.D. at a predominantly White, medium-sized, midwestern college. There are no available data or research to confirm this belief.

The Genetic Theory also assumed that Whites had a preponderance of red muscle fibers, which were better-suited for endurance events. Red muscle fibers were better able to liberate oxygen from the bloodstream to replenish the muscles for long-distance activities. This was why Whites dominated the middle- and long-distance endurance sports. Examples are middle- and long-distance events in track and field, swimming, cross-country skiing, cross-country running, marathons, and skating. This theory was debunked when West African muscle fibers, cross-country skiing, cross-country running, marathons, and skating.

Americans began, and continued, to dominate the marathons and middle- and long-distance events in track and field. Olympian Kip Keno of Kenya and others who followed him have won international marathon competitions every year. In addition, no scholar or researcher was willing to step up and confirm through scientific research the claims made by this myth. There is overwhelming evidence that supports the conclusion that social variables, such as the sport opportunity structure, social and cultural norms about sport, personal aspirations, economic factors, coaching, and available facilities and programs, have a greater impact in explaining the recent success of the African American athlete in American sport. Perceived closed doors to opportunities in mainstream American society and peer pressure not to pursue mainstream opportunities channeled African Americans into the only avenues they felt were open to them, in entertainment, in sports (Sailes, 1987), or through the underground economy where they engaged in a life of crime (Oliver, 1994).

Psychological Theory

This theory presumed that African Americans were incapable of leadership in positions like quarterback in football, pitcher in baseball, or point guard in basketball. Moreover, Al Campanis, a former executive with the Los Angeles Dodgers, reiterated the belief of management in Major League Baseball on national television when he said that African Americans may not have the "necessities" to become managers and field coaches in Major League Baseball. This theory also claimed that African Americans did poorly under pressure and were not good thinkers, which was why they were under-represented in individual sports like tennis, golf, skiing, skating, gymnastics, and swimming. However, when given the opportunity, African Americans have excelled in individual sports, and in leadership positions in team sports, for decades. There are several African Americans who participate in professional tennis and golf and who serve as head coaches in Division I and professional basketball, football, and baseball. Several of these coaches and athletes have won national titles.

The National Brotherhood of Skiers, the American Tennis Association, and the National Golf Association are all African American national organizations. The American Tennis Association is the oldest African American sports organization in the United States today (Ashe, 1993). There are African American swimming and gymnastics programs and clubs across the United States to provide programs and instruction for adults in those sports (Hoose, 1989). These organizations also have junior development programs that have produced several national amateur champions.

African American athletes in leadership, management, and coaching positions have won national championships and titles in the United States. For example, John Thompson of Georgetown University and Nolan Richardson of the University of Arkansas have won NCAA basketball titles. Cito Gaston of the Toronto Blue Jays and of the New York Yankees have won World Series titles. Doug Williams was a winning quarterback in the NFL's Super Bowl. Tina Sloane Green of Temple University won two NCAA national lacrosse championships. However, the Psychological Theory is the primary reason many African Americans are not given management and/or coaching positions in professional and college sports today. White fear of African Americans invading the White status quo, and prejudicial attitudes about African American competence, are nothing new and continue to create barriers to African American success in the administration of American sports. Given the opportunity, African Americans can excel and have proven themselves worthy of inclusion in the sports marketplace as on-field leaders, managers, and coaches.

Dumb Jock Theory

A corollary of the Psychological Theory, this theory challenges the academic competence of student-athletes. It was generally felt that student-athletes could not compete with tradi-tional students in the classroom. In addition, it was felt student-athletes took easy, "jock" courses and majored in eligibility (general studies) rather than a legitimate academic major (Sailes, 1993b).

The stereotypes against African American student-athletes were even more denigrating. It was generally felt that African American athletes did not belong in college. Students felt it was the African American athlete's athletic talents, not intelligence, that provided admission to college. They felt that if athletic departments did not have special admission policies, most African American athletes could not get into college. Although this may have been the practice of athletic departments in isolated instances in the past, this is not possible today. The NCAA has minimum academic requirements for student-athletes to establish eligibility to participate in college athletics. For example, a graduating high school senior must score a minimum of 900 on the Scholastic Aptitude Test (SAT) and have a grade point average of 2.0 in order to receive an athletic scholarship and participate in Division I college athletics. Furthermore, the grade point averages and graduation rates of student-athletes are slightly higher than those of their nonathletic counterparts (Sailes, 1993b). The myth of the dumb jock is unfounded, and most of the literature indicates that student-athletes are doing better in school than are traditional college students.

Concluding Discussion

Racial myths and stereotypes are born out of ignorance. Lack of contact with different social and/or ethnic groups creates ideologies that are generated from social dissonance and are founded on subjective observations. Our interpretations of other cultures are filtered through our own life experiences. To define others and to derive meaning about others based on our own cultural values, without the benefit of personal contact with those other indigenous cultures, leads to conjecture, myths, stereotypes, and inaccurate depictions of what we see. In extreme cases, inaccurate depictions can generate fear, prejudice, and misunderstandings that can lead to confrontation. Myths and stereotypes are damaging in that respect. Until we are ready to step up and reintroduce ourselves to one another, social myths and stereotypes will continue to fuel the fires of racial hatred and bigotry that currently infest American society.

The fears and anxieties of White America cause it to subjugate other cultures and ethnic groups within this country to inferior status and to create the caste system of inequities that has kept us apart for decades. It is time to pursue the truth, to interact with one another, and to have meaningful dialogue about who we are. W.E.B. DuBois wrote that the greatest problem that would face America in the 20th century would be the race problem. Current researchers forecast that problem will continue into the 21st century. It is time to learn to respect one other, to dispel the myths and stereotypes that keep us hanging onto the dark past. We must shield ourselves from the blatant negative media depictions of African American athletes portrayed as mindless physical specimens whose success is predisposed by their genetic and physiological superiority to Whites. If we continue on the present journey of distrust, fear, and confrontation that is fueled by our unfounded mythological and stereotypical beliefs about one another, Americans will never reach the peace and harmony that are the rewards of enlightenment.

Suggested Readings

Coakley, J. (1995). *Sport in society: Issues and controversies*. St. Louis: Mosby Publishers.

George, N. (1992). *Elevating the game: Black men and basketball*. New York: HarperCollins.

Hoberman, J. (1997). *Darwin's athletes*. New York: Houghton Mifflin Publishers.

Hoose, P. (1989). *Necessities: Racial barriers in American sport*. New York: Random House.

Lapchick, R. (1996). *Sport in society: Equal opportunity or business as usual?* CA: Sage Publications.

Majors, R. (1992). *Cool pose: The dilemmas of Black manhood in America*. New York: Lexington Books.

Sailes, G. (1998). *African Americans in sport: Contemporary themes*. New Jersey: Transaction Press.

Shropshire, K. (1996). *In Black and White: Race and sports in America*. New York: New York University Press.

Study Questions

1. What are the origins of social myths and stereotypes?

2. What are some of the social stereotypes held in society about African American male athletes?

3. Define the term "stacking." How does stacking present itself in American football and baseball?

4. Why does social stereotyping exist in sport?

5. What do you feel is necessary to eradicate social stereotyping in American sport?

References

Anshel, M., & Sailes, G. (1990). Discrepant attitudes of intercollegiate athletes as a function of race. *Journal of Sport Behavior, 13*(2), 87–102.

Ashe, A. (1993). *A hard road to glory: A history of the African American athlete*. New York: Amistad Press.

Beezley, W. H. (1983). Images of the student athlete in college football. In S. Kereliuk (Ed.), *The university's role in the development of modern sport: Past, present, and future* (pp. 447–461). [Proceedings of the FISU Conference Universiade '83 in association with the Tenth HISPA Congress] Edmonton, Canada: University of Alberta.

Bennett, L., Jr. (1996). *Before the Mayflower: A history of black America*. Chicago: Johnson Publishing.

Coakley, J. (1998). *Sport in society: Issues and controversies*. Boston: Times Mirror/Mosby.

Davis, L. R. (1991). The articulation of difference: White preoccupation with the question of racially linked genetic differences among athletes. *Sociology of Sport Journal, 7*(2), 179–187.

Eitzen, D. S., & Sage, G. H. (1996). *Sociology of North American sport*. Dubuque, IA: Wm. C. Brown.

Evans, V. (1978). A study of perceptions held by high school athletes toward coaches. *International Review of Sport Sociology, 13*, 47–53.

Franklin, J. H. (1994). *From slavery to freedom*. New York: McGraw-Hill.

George, N. (1992). *Elevating the game: Black men and basketball*. New York: Harper-Collins.

Hoose, P. (1989). *Necessities: Racial barriers in American sports*. New York: Random House.

Jones, B., Leonard, W., Schmitt, R., Smith, D., & Tolone, W. (1987, March). A log-linear analysis of stacking in college football. *Social Science Quarterly, 70*–83.

Lederman. D. (1990, July 5). Athletes in Division I found graduating at higher rate than other students. *The Chronicle of Higher Education*.

Leonard, W. M., II. (1998). *A sociological perspective of sport*. New York: Macmillan Publishers.

Lombardo, B. (1978). The Harlem Globetrotters and the perception of the black stereotype. *The Physical Educator, 35*(2), 60–63.

McMartin, J., & Klay, J. (1983). Some perceptions of the student athlete. *Perceptual and Motor Skills, 57*(3), 687–690.

McPherson, B., Curtis, J., & Loy, J. (1989). *The social significance of sport*. Champaign: Human Kinetics.

National Collegiate Athletic Association. (1996). *1996 NCAA Division I graduation rates report*. Overland, KS: American Institute of Research.

National Collegiate Athletic Association. (1989). *The status of minority participation in intercollegiate sports*. Overland, KS: American Institute of Research.

Nixon, H. L. (1982). The athlete as scholar in college: An exploratory test of four models. In A. Dunleavy, A. Miracle, & C. Rees (Eds.), *Studies in the sociology of sport* (pp. 239–256). Fort Worth: Texas Christian University Press.

Oliver, W. (1994). *The violent social world of black men*. New York: Lexington Books.

Sailes, G. A. (1987). A socioeconomic explanation of black sports participation patterns. *The Western Journal of Black Studies, 11*(4), 164–167.

Sailes, G. A. (1991). The myth of black sports supremacy. *Journal of Black Studies, 21*(4), 480–487.

Sailes, G. A. (1993a, Spring). An investigation of academic accountability among college student athletes. *Academic Athletic Journal*, 27–39.

Sailes, G. A. (1993b). An investigation of campus typecasts: The myth of black athletic superiority and the dumb jock stereotype. *Sport Sociology Journal, 10*, 88–97.

Sailes, G. A. (1996). An examination of basketball performance orientations among African American males. *Journal of African American Men, 1*(4), 37–46.

Schneider, J., & Eitzen, S. (1986). Racial segregation by professional football positions, 1960–1985. *Sociology and Social Research, 70*, 259–262.

Sokolove, M. (1988, April 24). Are blacks better athletes than whites? *Inquirer: The Philadelphia Inquirer Magazine*, 16–40.

Steele, S. (1990). *The content of our character*. New York: St. Martin's Press.

Stacking in the Team Sport of Intercollegiate Baseball

Earl Smith and Debra A. Henderson

Abstract

This chapter is an analysis of the longest thread in sport sociology research: stacking. Most of the previous research has concentrated on the team sports of football, (professional) baseball, soccer, basketball, and to a lesser extent, volleyball. Missing from the literature is an examination of the intercollegiate sport of baseball. The analysis explains the stacking phenomena. Furthermore, previous research of stacking is most often severed from the structural changes in the larger society, economy, and polity, and herein we show that in fact these are the very determinants of stacking. Our research provides a different perspective by drawing attention to specific issues of discrimination and segregation that African Americans are in constant struggles to overcome and change. The central argument that we make is that the interrelated set of phenomena captured by the term stacking are primarily characteristics of social isolation, marginalization, and systematic discrimination against African Americans. What makes this analysis unique is the focus on the so-called level playing fields of America. That these practices take place on the playing fields of team sports, instead of in the more-established institutional settings (e.g., boardrooms of corporate America), adds to the uniqueness. This chapter concludes with an optimistic appraisal and strategies for eliminating stacking.

> Black people do not create their oppressive worlds moment to moment but rather are co-erced into living in worlds created and maintained by others; more-over, the . . . source of this coercion is . . . racism.
>
> Kimberly W. Crenshaw (1995)
> Race, Reform, and Entrenchment

> In our country, not just in athletics, there's a great deal of talent we let go unnoticed. Coming from an ethnic background, you see it. You see talent not being derived, not being noticed, not showing what it can really do. There are a lot of people who could be doing the job I am doing, given the opportunity.
>
> Tyrone Willingham
> Coach, Stanford University

Key Terms

- African American -
- Social structure -
- Stacking -
- Intercollegiate baseball -
- Social isolation -
- Student-athletes -

Introduction

The African American head football coach at Stanford University, Tyrone Willingham, echoing observations made herein, put it best in the above epigram when he talked about modern-day opportunities (Weiner, 1995). To be successful in modern times in the market-driven society, whether in the professions of business management, nursing, social work, medicine, advertising, aircraft repair, or university-level teaching, individuals need opportunities to enter into the ranks of these established professions (Tang & Smith, 1996). This is no less true for the sporting enterprise, including the "national pastime," baseball.

As is well known to sport scholars, several strong and well-placed empirical studies have demonstrated the continued existence of problems that some African American athletes have when trying to break into the games they want to play (Berghorn, Yetman, & Hanna, 1988; E. Smith, 1995). Some of the most important literature of this genre addresses the problems encountered when positional segregation (sometimes referred to as stacking) is allowed to persist in all of the major team sports (Eitzen & Furst, 1989; Loy & McElvogue, 1970) and, in particular, in Major League Baseball (MLB) (E. Smith & Seff, 1990). Most research scientists (Leonard, 1978, 1988; Sammons, 1994) who study this reccurring phenomenon do so by assuming that the underrepresentation of African Americans from key or central positions in MLB is enough to assert the existence of stacking (Eitzen & Furst, 1989; E. Smith & Seff, 1990). Is it? This remains, then, an area of research that can benefit from further extensive investigation, as we try to understand the changing social relationships extant in our society (Brooks & Althouse, 1993; Coakley, 1994).

Stacking: A Definition

This chapter is an analysis of stacking in intercollegiate baseball. In the hope of illuminating the topic, illustrative examples will be taken from the larger sports arena, as these are relevant to our overall understanding of this phenomenon. That said, it is important to note that the research literature on stacking at the collegiate level is almost nonexistent (Eitzen & Furst, 1989; Leonard, 1978). In conducting our analysis of the issues, we will review this literature on stacking and offer an explanation of the findings. What we attempt to do in this chapter is address a long-overdue subject: How well do team sports in our institutions of higher learning conform to, or depart from, patterns of stacking/positional segregation found in intercollegiate, Division IA baseball?

According to Adair, "the most important person on the team, in any one game is the pitcher" (1990, p. 21). Whether in college or in the professional leagues, this pitcher is most often White (Shropshire, 1996a,b; E. Smith & Leonard, 1997). Stacking and the political, economic, and social disparities that it spawns ensue from culturally ascribed beliefs about who should pitch, who should catch, and roles of superiority of Whites and inferiority of African Americans.

From the outset, we will define stacking so as to avoid ambiguities as we address our subject. Hence, although stacking is often studied in the context of centrality and dominance (Edwards, 1973), for this essay the authors have constructed an original definition, thus expanding the term, and define stacking as

> The placement of African American baseball players at specific playing positions, and not others. Stacking is to mean that African American baseball players are relegated to playing positions based on race/ethnicity and not on their playing abilities. African American baseball players are positioned on the field so that they, more so than White players, have less of a chance to play a leading, determining role in the outcome of the contest. Stacking is a discriminatory practice. It is used to keep the number of African Americans on the team low. The concomitant and therefore long-term ef-

fect of this practice is that African American players have less of a chance to assume leadership positions as coaches and managers when their playing careers are over.

The definition of stacking that we offer here did not exist historically. Why? We show below that African American and White baseball players did not play on the same teams, nor did they play in the same games: Stacking, then, is the result of social isolation (E. Smith & Leonard, 1997), which is one of the most common dimensions of discrimination and segregation. In defining stacking as the most institutionalized and systematic way of eliminating African American competition with Whites at power, or central positions in all team sports and, specifically, for this essay intercollegiate baseball, we are able to demonstrate stacking's pernicious effect on American ideals such as integration (Hochschild, 1995) and the development of interracial socialization via intercollegiate sport. In the final analysis, throughout this essay, the term stacking is used to refer to positional segregation by race/ethnicity.

The almost total exclusion of African Americans from all levels of organized baseball, including the minor leagues, resulted in the dual existence of White and African American baseball institutions (Wiggins, 1993). Therefore, in order to better understand stacking, we follow up on our definition above with a review of the stacking literature. Both sociologically and historically, stacking was and is a social reality that grows out of patterns of social isolation stemming from segregation and discrimination. In the next section of the essay, we offer a review of the more widely cited research literature readily available on stacking.

Review of the Stacking Literature: An Historical Overview

Although it remains important to discuss the successes in sports being made by African American athletes (Cose, 1993; Davis, 1995; Early, 1994), it is also important that we analyze specific patterns of discrimination that historically existed to block social progress for African American athletes, and determine especially if there are indicators that these patterns of discrimination remain a problem in sport today. Such is the case with stacking. Stacking research has been a staple in sport sociology, with a thread of existence that stems for at least 25 years (E. Smith & Leonard, 1997). While the reasons for this are many, the main one that drives our discussion is that stacking research is quantifiable. Being able to quantify data in baseball is an obsession. Furthermore, the issue of racial integration was in vogue in the 1960s and 1970s—that is, the racial climate was ripe, and therefore the timing correct, for raising critical questions about racial integration in sports and especially baseball (Birrell, 1989; Shropshire, 1996a).

This literature review for this essay, although selective, represents some of the most important research on stacking available. We do not come to this conclusion lightly, for it is evidenced by reoccurring citations in the overall stacking literature. The review begins with one of the early essays published by Aaron Rosenblatt, an essay important for its boldness at a time when segregation in sport and especially baseball was the rule of the day.

Rosenblatt, in "Negroes in Baseball: The Failure of Success" (1967), starts his essay, which covers the years from 1953 to 1965, by looking at the historical importance of the integration of Jackie Roosevelt Robinson into Major League Baseball. Rosenblatt felt that it was tokenism, not true integration, that propelled Robinson to the majors. He felt that simply the presence of African American players did not necessarily ensure that they would be treated equally and that, especially, they would have a hard time trying to play the central positions. He even went so far as to say that African American players had to be better than White players to win starting positions. Several key findings came from the study. One interesting finding was that for the entire 13-year period of the research, African American batters had batting averages superior to those of their White counterparts, thus supporting the belief about African Americans having to perform better than Whites if they expected to play the game. This last point has been carefully researched by Edwards (1973).

Rosenblatt showed that during the period of the research there were fewer than 30 African American pitchers and, for the same period, no African American managers, one coach, and one umpire. Rosenblatt concluded his work by saying,

> the distribution of both player and non-player positions in baseball hierarchy is different for the two races. Discrimination appears to operate for managerial jobs on the field and in the front office as well as for player positions below the star level. (p. 52)

Three years after Rosenblatt's essay appeared a paper by Loy and McElvogue (1970) was published. "Racial Segregation in American Sport" is considered one of the first full empirical research studies of stacking (E. Smith & Leonard, 1997). Using a sophisticated theory of "centrality," Loy and McElvogue set out to test Blalock's (1967) proposition that baseball, unlike other areas of occupational enterprise, is free of racial discrimination. What they found was that Blalock was "perhaps naive" (Loy & McElvogue, 1970, p. 6). They also found that only a small portion of African Americans occupied central or power positions; that is, positions such as pitcher, catcher, and third base, both on defense and offense. From there, the authors raised several interesting questions, one of which was, "does this finding [meaning the relationship between race and position] indicate the presence of racial segregation?" Although they do not fully answer the question, the authors speculate that there are many forms of discrimination other than full, outright segregation (Loy & McElvogue, 1970), which leaves the door open for further research, some of which was

carried out by Curtis and Loy in 1978.

Curtis and Loy (1978), in "Race/Ethnicity and Relative Centrality of Playing Positions in Team Sports," reviewed nine stacking studies in baseball. Asking if high-status, high-reward positions (such as those in corporate settings) apply to baseball, the authors' research questions were shaped around the center/periphery analogy. They found that stacking existed, which confirmed results of earlier research, but they were unable to offer an explanation for why stacking existed, thus leaving the causal factor unclear, and therefore, leaving room for further research, some of which was carried out by Medoff.

Medoff (1986), in "Positional Segregation and the Economic Hypothesis," took a different route to the question: His analysis focused squarely on the issue of training and development costs that accrue to players and their families. The researcher found that costs factor into decision making and impact what specific positions players ultimately end up playing.

Medoff (1986) felt that certain sports and certain positions in some team sports require expensive development costs, including expensive training, to master the game. The author offered three hypotheses to test this reasoning: (a) biological, (b) psychological, and (c) sociological. The author clearly felt that it was the sociological factor that explained best the choices players make when deciding on what positions to play. This has come to be known as the "economic" hypothesis (Medoff, 1986).

The researcher witnessed an increase in African American income and the concomitant decrease in discrimination against African American players as significant factors in the overall decline of stacking. The end of 1986–1987 saw questions being raised about the methodological factors inherent in stacking research. One scholar, N. Johnson (1988), addressed some of the particulars in this debate.

N. Johnson (1988), in "A Methodology for Studying Stacking in Football and Baseball," stated that stacking exists in baseball because coaches try to match athletes with positions they, the coaches, assume fit the athletes' specific personalities and physical characteristics. The author saw this as being highly problematic. To overcome this problem, Johnson suggested using research of a hypothetical nature to address the problem. He envisioned, for example, building player profiles or biographies as a way of assisting management when attempting to make player assignments. These biographies would be available to teams scouting prospective players. Although hypothetical, the reasoning behind the study is akin to that of the player profiles built for teams in college and professional basketball that are sold to teams scouting players.

Lavoie (1989), in "The Economic Hypothesis of Positional Segregation: Some Further Comments," unabashedly suggested that Medoff (1986) was wrong in his analysis of positional segregation. According to Lavoie (1989), African American athletes do not choose to play non-central positions, which was a central claim made by Medoff (1986). Lavoie (1989) believed that outright discrimination leads to the placement of barriers in front of African American players because their playing-position assessments are subjective. That is to suggest that playing-position assignments are not in the hands of the players, but, rather, are the sole providence of the coaches and managers (E. Smith & Seff, 1990). The research by Lavoie (1989) is supported in a paper published several years later by E. Smith and Seff (1990).

E. Smith and Seff (1990), in "Race, Position Segregation and Salary Equity in Professional Baseball," analyze data for all players, and, after computing the relationship between salary and productivity, argue that African American players have to be superior to White players if they expect to play on a regular basis. The data accompanying this essay clearly demonstrate that African American players are not mediocre: They have productivity statistics superior to those of their White counterparts (E. Smith & Seff, 1990). The authors also found that African American players were not considered for positions that have tra-ditionally been described as the "outcome/control" positions, that is, positions like pitching, where the player has a direct relationship to the final outcome of the game. E. Smith and Seff (1990) concluded their research saying that stacking or positional segregation in MLB still existed well into the 1980s.

Phillips's (1991) "The Integration of Central Positions in Baseball: The Case of the Black Shortstop" is an analysis of the four central positions of third base, first base, second base and shortstop. Phillips undertook the analysis to disentangle the more important central positions from the less central positions (e.g., first base from third base). Based on the collection of several years of data by position and race/ethnicity, Phillips concluded that by the mid-1980s African Americans began assuming the field at the position of shortstop. Thus, according to Phillips's research, this shows a decrease in racial discrimination in professional baseball.

As important as Phillips's (1991) work is, he fails to adequately demonstrate his conclusion: The demise of racial discrimination in professional baseball has to be proven via empirical data, and his essay does not do that. The paper by Lavoie and Leonard (1994) does a better job of demonstrating their thesis, which is presented next. Lavoie and Leonard, in a 1994 paper entitled "In Search of an Alternative Explanation of Stacking in Baseball: The Uncertainty Hypothesis," see the problem of stacking linked to the inability of good, solid assessment of a ballplayer's abilities at a given position. The authors put it thus:

> Stacking is due to a form of racial discrimination. The more difficult it is to accurately and objectively measure performance, the higher the probability that subjective and less relevant factors will be taken into account when hiring or promotion decisions are made. (Lavoie & Leonard, 1994, p. 141)

The authors follow closely the work of Blalock (1967), who insisted that the easier it is to evaluate individual performance, the less discrimination we will see in the workplace. This perspective assumes that a meritocracy is at work in baseball decision making, thus assigning positions to the most capable players, regardless of race. Although instructive, the reliance on Blalock (1967) takes away from the work, in that Blalock was wrong (E. Smith & Seff, 1990).

Most of the research presented here has stood the test of time. All of the authors have tried to address a very serious problem for sociology of sport scholars interested in social progress for minorities in general and African Americans in particular. Has sport transcended race? That is to ask, has sport delivered on its promise of equality of opportunities in sport? This question is difficult to answer, especially definitively. It requires a special insight in terms of how scholars from a variety of race/ethnic backgrounds address issues of integration and segregation in sport.

In a major survey of attitudes about athletic ability, the daily newspaper *USA Today* (Myers, 1991) repeated what many Americans discuss only in private (E. Smith, 1995), that is, the stereotypical beliefs that see African American athletes as "big Black dumb jocks" (Edwards, 1984; Hoberman, 1997). In the survey results published in *USA Today* (Myers, 1991), we learn that White athletes are intellectual, whereas African Americans are not intellectual but are physically gifted. These findings point in the direction of what we call "the logic of stacking." That is to say that intellectually gifted White athletes are assigned to positions of leadership, whereas African American athletes, who are seen as being only physically gifted, are assigned to non-core, non-central positions like the right field in baseball (Hoberman, 1997).

The Importance of Theory in Stacking Research

So much of what is assumed in the review of the literature above seems to be lodged within the structure of how the larger social, political, and economic segments of American society work (Wilson, 1991). Social structural factors, including race, are so very important to an understanding of stacking. Sociologist William J. Wilson (1996), in his explanation of social structure, points to the relevancy of its use in our discussion of stacking. He puts it thus:

> By social structure I mean the ordering of social positions (or statuses) and networks of social relationships that are based on the arrangement of mutually dependent institutions (economy, polity, family, education) of society. Race, which reflects both an individual's position (in the sense of social status defined by skin color) and network of relationships in society, is a social structural variable. (p. xiii-xiv)

Yet these societal structural functioning issues that impact how race/ethnicity are or are not accounted for in individual and group status are rarely ever visible in the previously noted stacking literature. We see this as a major weakness: the lack of and/or disregard for sociological theory. To be called or classified as "theory," the hypothesis found in the work should hold for all team sports, not just some of them. Second, sociological theories, whether addressing issues of urbanization, the family, or education, should at minimum meet a specific criterion. Thus, a theory of stacking should be a set of interrelated propositions that allow for the systematization of knowledge, explanation, and prediction of social life, and the generalization of new research hypotheses (E. Smith & Leonard, 1997; Ritzer, 1996).

Because of the historical neglect of theory in sport sociology (Nixon, 1991), it is important to draw on research from other areas of empirical sociological research that have a bearing on the topic under discussion. In our opinion, stacking is just one way of looking at a specific type of inequality in sport, and because it has so much that is similar to other sociological investigations, it is important to look elsewhere to further develop the line of reasoning presented here. We believe that in so doing we also extend further the 25-year thread of stacking investigations in sport sociology research (Smith & Leonard, 1997).

Housing Discrimination, Segregation, and Stacking

Is stacking any different than the processes that inform housing discrimination that urban sociologists have been researching and writing about since the end of World War II? Overall, we do not think so. Specifically, the problem at one end of the continuum can be viewed as "White flight." That is, White Americans flee their neighborhoods when the desire for limited interracial contact is threatened by an influx of African Americans. At the other end of the continuum, we find the problem of "piling up." Piling up is the phenomenon of placing a large number of African Americans in the same undesirable inner-city ghetto locations, thus limiting their access to better housing. Both White flight and piling up are very similar to our current understanding of stacking. Piling up, in fact, is extremely relevant and can be explored more in depth in the book entitled *The Negro Population in Chicago* by Otis and Beverly Duncan (1957).

The formation of urban ghettos took shape along specific, historically distinct dimensions. That is to say, their formation did not just happen by chance. When we look at the urbanization research of Degraff (1970), Du Bois (1896/1995), Frey (1979), Kushner (1979), Kusmer (1979), and Osofsky (1968), it becomes clear that all have demonstrated the existence of these sociohistorical patterns as well as the existence of severe racial antagonisms. These antagonisms were, stated plainly, the resistance by Whites to opening up their communities to upwardly mobile (Duncan & Duncan, 1957) African American families looking to escape the degradation of urban squalor (Kusmer, 1979).

Although these racial problems or antagonisms begin at the turn of the century and last through contemporary times, some of the authors listed above point to the post-World War II African American south-to-north migration trek as being a critical factor in the establishment of the northern urban ghetto (Duncan & Duncan, 1957; Lemann, 1991).

As more and more African Americans moved north, Whites fled to, among other places, suburban enclaves (Frey, 1979). As the northern ghettos solidified, bringing about the demise of the once racially mixed neighborhood, the expansion of the ghetto ceased: The lines had become completely drawn across both geographical and racial/ethnic boundaries.

Affordable and livable housing was difficult to secure for African Americans, especially the Levittown variety that has received attention in the now-famous, as well as important, nostalgic memoirs of the 1940s, 1950s, and the 1960s (Halberstam, 1993). Thus, African American individuals and families were forced to subdivide their living space, making ghettoization a living reality for the majority of northern urban African Americans (Bianchi, Farley, & Spain, 1982).

Urban ghetto population densities created the piling up phenomenon researched by Duncan and Duncan (1957). Instead of integrating into neighborhoods they could afford to live in, African Americans, regardless of their socioeconomic status, were piled up into human-made ghettos. It is the contention herein that piling up and stacking are similar phenomena. These have not been linked previously, for good reasons: Sport sociologists studying stacking have not been trained as urban sociologists.

There are other connections that can be made in terms of the special disciplinary language that we use to explain both our research focus and subsequent findings (e. g., not just in the areas of urbanization and sports). This connection is both relevant and troubling; that is to say that one arena of sports, baseball, can be linked theoretically and methodologically to some of the most virulent forms of racism seen in our society, that which unfolded and unfolds in the housing market. To be sure, it is also a research site that calls for more cross-comparative research.

One of the most recent reviews of stacking research (Smith & Leonard, 1997) reveals that from the front office, to the coach/manager ranks, to positions on the playing field, African Americans in baseball have been discriminated against (even to the point of total exclusion during the heyday of the Negro Leagues) and placed outside of Major League Baseball.

We are reminded that, unlike any other group in American society, African Americans did not choose to be socially isolated (segregated and discriminated against) from the time they arrived on these shores hundreds of years ago. The "Critical Race Theory" scholar, Crenshaw (1995), puts this best, as shown in the epigraph above, when she points out that "Black people do not create their oppressive worlds . . . but rather are coerced into living in worlds created and maintained by others" (p. 110).

Crenshaw's analysis on this all-important point is insightful. From the early research by Loy and McElvogue (1970) to the recent research by Lavoie and Leonard (1994), we find that what is being discussed by almost all of the stacking researchers is, in fact, discrimination and segregation. It will help to define both terms to make sure that the true meaning, as used herein, is being properly communicated.

Discrimination

The argument in this essay is that, when we refer to stacking, it may help to be forthright and say that we are also discussing discrimination. Robert K. Merton, professor emeritus (Columbia University), addressed the issue of discrimination many years ago (Merton, 1948), and it is still fruitful to make reference to his far-reaching analysis today.

According to Merton (1948), discrimination needs to be carefully addressed, for invoking that the great documents of our country stood and stand for equality for all—the Preamble of the Constitution, Declaration of Independence, as well as the Bill of Rights—we need to be clear what, exactly, in the final analysis the American creed stands for. For Merton (1948) these documents do not say that all humans are created equal in capacity and/or endowment.

That the great pugilist "Brown Bomber" Joe Louis is superior, not equal, to other bruisers is patently clear; that Einstein is superior to all other thinkers is also patently clear. What, in fact, the American creed does say is clarified by Merton (1948) when he informs us of the following: "Instead the creed asserts the indefeasible principles of the human right to full equity the right of equitable access to justice, freedom, and opportunity, irrespective of race or religion or ethnic origin" (p. 36).

From Merton (1948) we learn that what is necessary in a democracy like the United States is the extension of the opportunity to succeed. We believe that this feature of Merton's argument is the essence of the stacking analysis, articulated in a profound way by Harry Edwards in his book entitled *Sociology of Sport* (1973). There he notes this phenomenon "refers to the practice of stacking Black athletes in certain positions on athletic teams while denying them access to others" (p. 205). Edwards (1973) continues by noting, "thus, where leadership and outcome control role responsibilities are institutionally attached to a particular sports position, one should expect to find Blacks being excluded from that position." (p. 209–210). Edwards (1973) then concludes his stacking analysis, saying that since "control in sports [have] fixed zones of role responsibility" (p. 210), they invariably exclude African American players from leadership positions both on and off the playing field.

This is especially evident to the scientific observers when looking at the makeup of coaches and managers in college and professional sports today. The idea or the cement that holds stacking rationalizations together is that the aim is to keep African American athletes away from leadership positions. The paucity of African Americans in leadership positions today is the direct result of the truncated, segregated policies and practices fostered upon these athletes while they are playing (Shropshire, 1996a). This leads us directly to the next definition, that of segregation.

Segregation

It is hard to believe that a term so loaded as segregation gets buried in the polite language of sport sociology. In sport, both individual and team sports, the essence of an athlete's existence is whether or not the athlete can perform at her or his optimum.

The public consciousness about segregation is usually confined to the drab statistics meted out about the level of segregation in our public school system. We almost never discuss the social and political as well as the overwhelmingly economic consequences of public school segregation that gave rise to the equally pernicious practice of the rise of private schools. For example, when looking at public school segregation, we often see numbers like those appearing in Table 1, showing the growing segregation of students in public school systems around the country (Hacker, 1992). This portrait is, in our opinion, just the sort of empirical reference needed to be able to continue to compare sport and society, "sport as a microcosm of society" (Lapchick, 1995), most forcefully argued by two of the foremost sociologists of sport, Stanley Eitzen and George Sage (1997, p. 14).

Now, approximately 43 years after the 1954 *Brown v. Board of Education,* Topeka,

Table 1. African American Attendance at Urban Public Schools

City	% Black attendance at public schools
Washington, DC	95.5%
Chicago	84.7%
New York	75.0%
Philadelphia	73.2%
Baltimore	70.0%
Los Angeles	69.9%

Kansas decision (Smith, 1981; *Brown v. Board of Education, Topeka, Kansas, 1954*), it is clear that in sports the *Brown* decision had little to no genuine impact on who was allowed to play on collegiate and professional sport teams. The reality of this only becomes clear in 1997, as Major League Baseball celebrates the official integration of modern baseball by Jackie Roosevelt Robinson in April of 1947 (E. Smith, 1997).

Segregation was still almost complete at the time of the great African American revolution in sport. Jackie Robinson, Willie Mays, Jim Brown, Monte Irvin, Wilma Rudolph, Ernie Banks, Henry Aaron, Althea Gibson, Bill Russell, and others were largely individual superstars, segregated and socially isolated, on the teams and in the sports in which they competed (Spivey, 1983). Jim Brown (1989), the great running back for the Syracuse Orangemen and later the Cleveland Browns, put it thus:

> On the football field they wanted me to be brave. Wanted me to take the ball when we were all backed up, on our own one yard line, carry us out of there, where we could be safe. Away from the football, they wanted me to be another guy. They wanted me to be docile. (p. 47)

It is rather ironic, though, that out of this push to have African American athletes accept docility and accept second-class citizenship and player status that came hand-in-glove with segregated hotel rooms, eating alone, and accepting the code that one just did not speak one's mind and ask questions about one's status, there emerged some of the greatest African American athletes of the 19th and 20th centuries.

In a paper that finally provides a full and complete analysis of the problems African American athletes, collegiate and professional, face within a racially hostile sports environment, legal scholar Williams (1996) accepts the challenges that come with taking on this issue. In the beginning of her article entitled "Performing in a Racially Hostile Environment," she notes,

When informing some of my friends and relatives that I had decided to write about racial harassment of professional athletes, concerns were raised on more than one occasion that no one really sympathizes very much anymore with the "plight" of the Black . . . athlete. (p. 287)

This response, from African Americans and Whites, is not only typical, but predictable. Less clear, though, are the history of these hostilities and the ongoing extent of them as we move to the 21st century. What is amazing, nonetheless, is the depth of the hostilities. It is understandable, at one level, to hear what happened to home-run phenomenon Hank Aaron (Aaron, 1992) as he closed in on the all-time home-run career record of the great Babe Ruth (hate mail, threats against his life), yet it is another thing altogether to learn of the extreme hostilities heaped against a student-athlete, Patrick Ewing, when he played for the Georgetown University Hoyas basketball team.

During the 1982–83 season students at Providence College held up "Ewing Can't Read" signs. At the Meadowlands Seton Hall supporters unfurled a banner that read, "Think! Ewing! Think!" while in Philadelphia Villanova fans wrote "Ewing Is a Ape" on placards. T-shirts were sold at the Big East schools declaring, "Ewing Kan't Read Dis." Several Georgetown games were interrupted by bananas thrown on the floor.

Twice during the 1982–1983 campaign the Hoyas and chief rival St. Johns engaged in fist fights partially attributable to the Big East's ultra-physical style.

Thompson's team helped inspire as well the racial slurs from St. Johns student body. Far too many of the school's White working class Catholic student body used Ewing as a sounding board for their own latent racist attitudes. I am a St. John's alumnus, and I saw and heard things from them that brought dishonor on the school. "Ignorance has no color," Thompson told *Time*. "The point isn't that this season has been degrading to a Black man, it has been degrading to any man. On the airplane last week I asked Pat again how he was holding up. He told me, 'I've grown accustomed to it. I got so much of it in high school.' That made me saddest of all." (Williams, 1996, p. 288)

All of this occurred in a place, on a field, in a gym, in a game where discrimination and segregation are not supposed to be present, at least not as prevalent as they are in society at large (Shropshire, 1996a). Again, all this occurred in a place, a college, a university where opportunities are supposed to be available, especially for African Americans, many of whom play the games that make the sports so attractive to the hard-core fans and, more widely, the sporting public (Frey & Eitzen 1991; E. Smith, 1995).

Legal scholar Timothy Davis (1995), in his fictional voice, captured the essence of blocked opportunities and stereotypical thinking in his depiction of the student-athlete by the name of Mylan. Mylan is typical of many African American student-athletes who come from modest economic circumstances and a single-parent home (his father died when he was young). Similar to so many other student-athletes, Mylan sees basketball as his ticket away from the ghetto where his East Texas home is located.

What Davis makes clear in this story of Mylan is that the student-athletes often see the stereotype, work to overcome it, and remain clear about who they are and their place in the university setting. This portrait of Mylan is far different, say, from those painted about the Dexter Manleys of the intercollegiate sporting world, who achieve athletically but fail, miserably, in their intellectual challenges and the challenges of life.

Having access to and achieving a university education are the major goals for all college-attending students. Nothing in the educational experience in America ranks higher. This is what we are told by the coaches as well as by university administrators, but, when time permits, athletically gifted students can pursue the opportunities afforded to them through a variety of levels of sport activities. These include, but are not limited to, intramural play (most often found organized around the Greek system on campuses that have fraternities and sororities and housing assignments), club teams (as is the case with many women's rugby teams), and the institutionally supported, competitive, varsity athletic teams.

All students, even women, have a chance to play for these teams, including the varsity teams (Yarbrough, 1996). In the case of *Blair v. Washington State University* (Yarbrough, 1996), the belief in equal educational opportunities was redefined to include the opening up of all aspects of athletic opportunities to female athletes. This case has rather important sociological consequences for issues of exclusion, underrepresentation, and racism in college sports. The meaning we take from *Blair* is that underrepresentation and exclusion are not supposed to be taking place in college sports today. If underrepresentation is still happening, then we must explain the reason for its persistence. To try to understand what is really going on, we examine the African American presence in college baseball.

Focus of This Essay

This essay extends the long stacking research thread into the realm of Division IA collegiate baseball. We decided to return to what Merton defined (1987) as the strategic research site (SRS). According to Merton, scholars select their SRS because this is where one finds the empirical materials that exhibit the phenomena to be explained and/or interpreted (Merton, 1987). The concerns of this paper address one of the most important empirical research topics in sport sociology. Lest we forget, stacking research, stretching now for approximately 30 years (E. Smith & Leonard, 1997), has the longest run among all research interests in the field of the sociology of sport.

The Problem

The prevailing sentiment of the late 1960s up through the mid-1970s as far as race relations were concerned (meaning in this context African American and White relations) was that African Americans wanted to integrate with their White neighbors, coworkers, and fellow citizens (Hacker, 1992; Terkel, 1994). Although this may be true (or the issue of integration may be more complex than how it has been portrayed heretofore), it is important to point out that African American baseball players at all levels of play simply wanted an opportunity to play the game. Moreover, although this question applies to all of team sports with which African Americans are involved, the limitations of a book essay force us to focus our time on one sport, and we choose college baseball.

Empirical Reference

To examine our hypothesis that stacking remains a problem in major team sports—the problem of who plays, what positions they play, when, and (just as importantly) performance and how this impacts access to other forms of relationships (for instance, coaching, after the playing days are over), we analyzed a very limited amount of data from two NCAA Division IA baseball teams. The teams were not chosen at random but represent universities where we had access to the data. By all indices, both teams have been successful in their conference competitions.

Sample

Team "A" is located in the Pacific Northwest, and Team "B" is located in the Midwest. We have team roster data and team performance data, by race, for Team "A" for the years 1987 to 1996. We have team roster data and team performance data, by race, for Team "B" for the years 1991 to 1996. These data were obtained (a) from contacts we had at both institutions and (b) access to media guides at both institutions.

For the period from 1991 to 1996, Team "B" had two African American players, one playing the junior/senior years and the other playing the freshman/junior years. One player who was on the team for his freshman/junior years was an outfielder, and the second player was an infielder, but not a catcher or pitcher. Each of the two players from Team "B" was moderately productive.

Discussion

For the period 1987 to 1996 team "A" had three African American players. One player was on the team for his freshman/sophomore years, the same for the second player, and the third player looks to have played only one season (1992). One African American player from the 1995 and 1996 team was a catcher. This player (Player #1), the catcher, looks to have been just as successful as the other two, with a batting average of .301.

Table 2 illustrates, then, in summary format, the productivity of the African American players from the two teams surveyed. As can be seen from the data in the table, the five players had good playing experiences in terms of their overall individual performances. Although the numbers have not been overwhelming—none of the players was on his respective teams for more than two years—they are respectable.

In total, both Team "A" and Team "B" had a combined number of five African American players across a total of 10 baseball seasons. These low numbers for Division I baseball

players capture the sentiment of a long time fan of Team "B" who was concerned that at the college level there should be more of a diversity of players in the 1990s than there was in the 1950s. It also captures the meaning of the *New York Times* Op Ed column by Rhoden (1990) in which he (and players and coaches interviewed) raised several concerns that Division I was not progressing in terms of recruiting native-born minority baseball players.

Do Division IA college baseball teams even want African American players? The team located in the Pacific Northwest has been accused (by students, faculty, and administrators) of not wanting African American players, and one coach from the Midwest team shared with us his observations that they, too, have been guilty of "overlooking" African American ballplayers. Some of the reasoning (read: stereotypes, myths) that we have come up with is:

- African American athletes want to play basketball only.

- African American athletes have abandoned the sport of baseball.

- Those African American players who can play the sport of baseball with a high level of skill forgo college altogether and take the farm-team route to the professional teams.

Whatever the purported reasons for the minimal numbers of African Americans in colle-

Table 2. Summary of Performance Statistics

| | Team "A" | | | Team "B" | |
	P1	P2	P3	P1	P2
At Bats	208	104	178	155	193
Hits	69	50	56	43	60
Homers	09	10	03	O5	O2
St Bases	03	O9	12	O5	11
Errors	O5	12	09	02	02
RBI	44	16	30	22	37
B Avg	.332	.221	.219	.234	.289

giate baseball, and there seem to be many, it remains a mystery even to those African American players themselves as to why so few play the college game. For instance, one player, (Jones, University of Southern California), responding to questions from reporter Beaton in the *USA Today* story (1996) also cannot figure it out, yet Jones remains optimistic that if managers and coaches really wanted African American players, they could get them. We agree with his assessment.

Jones, for example, was a high school baseball superstar but was recruited by only one team out of high school, and he becomes very annoyed when coaches come up to him now, or became annoyed when he was practicing with the U. S. Olympic team, and ask about other African American players with comments such as "if only I had one of you" (see Beaton, 1996).

Can we conclude from the limited data available for these two college teams that stacking is a problem in intercollegiate Division IA baseball? Yes. By analyzing what we found and integrating our research with the relevant findings from the research of other scholars—to be sure, the analysis is also based on discussions with individuals who are a part of the college game, the players and coaches, thus employing a methodology so carefully explained and demonstrated as "social worlds" research—we are comfortable with the conclusions we have drawn. This perspective transcends some of the more narrow, methodological approaches to the study of sports (Unruh, 1983), allowing for an interdisciplinary, nonhomogenous investigation of race and college baseball.

This, we believe, is built around the fact that college baseball coaches, who are primarily White males, are not convinced that young African American males belong in "their" game and, therefore, fail to recruit African American baseball players to their institutions (Davis, 1995; Dodd, 1993; Dunning, in press; Rhoden, 1990). To refuse outright to recruit African American players from high school because one feels or thinks these athletes (a) do

not want to be there or (b) will not want to play the team sport of intercollegiate baseball because of an overriding interest in playing basketball feeds directly into the whole scenario of social stereotyping. It is also the deepest form of social isolation and racism (E. Smith, 1981).

Strategies for Eliminating Stacking

Although most of the stacking literature does not spend any time discussing ways to eliminate stacking (E. Smith & Leonard, 1997) and therefore leaves a void in terms of strategies to eliminate stacking, we feel that it is imperative to list several concrete examples that would begin this long process towards the elimination of stacking. The remedies and the ability to carry them out rest squarely with the baseball managers, baseball coaches, and presidents of institutions of higher education. These people are the decision makers within the sport who have the influence and power to correct wrongful and deceptive behavior that blocks African American student-athletes from realizing their goals in college sports. Several concrete strategies are available for the elimination of stacking:

- Hire competent managers and coaches.

- Reward managers and coaches for successful play (e.g., contract extensions).

- Hire African American managers and coaches.

- Scout high school athletes from the inner-city neighborhoods and recruit athletes from these communities.

- Stop the practice of switching incoming African American athletes from their high school positions (e.g., pitcher to outfield).

- Introduce a merit system, based on performance, for assigning players throughout the duration of the game, thus ensuring that all athletes get to play, if not the whole game, at least portions of the games.

- Put negative incentives into managers' and coaches' contracts for discriminating against certain race/ethnic players. These incentives could be as simple as year-end bonuses, more favorable resource allocation, etc.

- Openly advertise that the institution and teams welcome minority athletes. As it currently stands, many African American baseball players know which teams accept or reject their presence.

Although these strategies are not exhaustive, they do point to a beginning that has been missing from stacking literature: Responsibility for eliminating stacking is placed on the shoulders of the managers, coaches, and presidents.

Conclusion

Since the first intercollegiate competition that took place in 1852 in the rowing contest between Harvard and Yale, the American public has become intimately enthusiastic about and involved in college-level sports (R. Smith, 1988). In fact, the National Collegiate Athletic Association's (NCAA) Final Four basketball tournament has the distinction of being one of the richest and most watched sporting events in the United States. CBS television has a contract with the NCAA, through the year 2002, paying $215.6 million per year to televise the NCAA Final Four basketball tournament (Mangan, 1994). The crowds who watch this contest in person and on television grow each year.

Furthermore, intercollegiate athletics opens up many doors and is not just a conduit to the access road into professional sports for the young men and women who participate at the various levels of competition. Finally, sporting apparel, from baseball caps to team T-shirts to fancy jogging suits to the colorful player-named sneakers, has become a staple that Americans purchase on a daily basis, thus bringing them even closer to the college games and players they so adore.

All of this suggests that the institution of sports is very important in American life; that social scientists, including sociologists, should be paying more attention to the patterns of fan loyalty, issues related to women and sport, sponsored and contest mobility, career attainment, race relations, and other aspects of sport; that sport serves as a natural laboratory for relevant research questions that serve to tell us about the peculiarities of the society in which we live. It is high time we put to rest the silly notion that to study sport is to be involved in trivial research, falling outside the bounds of serious scholarship. This issue was taken up by philosopher Drew Hyland (1990) writing in *Philosophy of Sport*:

> There is a long tradition that calls on the academy, as one of its central tasks, to reflect on and analyze social phenomena that play an important role in a given culture. Thus, there are many varied considerations of the role of politics, religion, music, and the arts by the various disciplines in the academy, including philosophy. Arguably, however, that social phenomenon in American life which has the biggest impact on our culture, yet which receives the least serious attention from our intellectual standard bearers, is sport and athletics. There seems to be a long-standing prejudice that however popular a phenomenon sport may be, it is simply not "serious" enough to be a legitimate subject of intellectual inquiry. That has certainly been one of the long standing prejudices of professional philosophy. (p. xiii)

A further extension of this argument was taken up by Giamatti (1989). In his wonderful little book entitled *Take Time for Paradise: Americans and Their Games*, the late baseball commissioner and former president of Yale University had this to say:

> It has long been my conviction that we can learn far more about the conditions and values of a society by contemplating how it chooses to play, to use its free

time, to take its leisure, than by examining how it goes about its work. (p. 3)

Although Giamatti may have not meant it to sound that way, it would be wise to add here that work and leisure need not necessarily be separated from each other, as we continue to recognize the interconnections between the sports we participate in and the society we live in. Sport, it has been said over and over, is a microcosm of our society (E. Smith, 1995).

This essay has returned to one of the longest research traditions in the sociology of sport. Stacking, as we have defined it, has always been present in American team sports, from total exclusion of African American athletes to selective placement of African American athletes at specific positions and not at others, at all levels of sport. In this essay we have demonstrated the past existence and persistence of stacking well into the 20th century. This is especially true of intercollegiate baseball played at the Division I level of competition.

The governing body for college sports, the NCAA, which maintains a monopoly position of control over college sports and which holds the student-athlete to a large number of rules and regulations, somehow cannot and does not pay significant attention to the large-scale forms of discrimination and persuasiveness of racism taking place within college athletics. From our vantage point, we include stacking on the list of offenses that deny African American student-athletes all of the benefits that accrue to university students. The authors of this essay support the findings of Davis (1996), who arrives at similar conclusions in his work looking at the regulatory powers of the NCAA.

We are also mindful that a good portion of the discussion central to the stacking literature is the acknowledgment and acceptance of the athletic prowess of African American athletes. This is especially true of their speed. African American athletes in baseball can run fast and have very good jumping ability. Thus, they most often play the outfield positions. Yet a part of the rationale for the placement of African American players in non-central, non-decision making positions is that they cannot "think"; therefore we will find few African Americans in the leadership positions such as catcher and pitcher (Harris, 1993). The non-central or peripheral positions like right fielder are reserved for African American players. Davis (1995) notes the contradictions of these views in the following passage:

> The athletic success of African American athletes often has been attributed to physical characteristics of mythical proportions. . . . [Yet], the virtual exclusion of African Americans from organized collegiate sport during the Jim Crow era was rationalized by beliefs of inferiority and inhumanity. (p. 644–645)

Which is it? Innate inferiority or natural athletic powers? Because we cannot have it both ways, how is it that in a few decades the tides (or at least their perception) have been shifted from innate inferiority (E. Smith, 1995) to athletic predominance (Harris, 1993)? Also, why are so few sport scientists looking deeper into the juxtaposition of the inferiority/dominance perspectives that, from the looks of it, are competing against each other?

To recapitulate, thus returning to our opening question, the research problem addressed in this essay can be summarized this way: How well do team sports in our institutions of higher learning conform to or depart from patterns of stacking/positional segregation found in intercollegiate Division IA baseball? That is, if stacking does not exist in college baseball then why are so few African American players at the Division I level in intercollegiate baseball (Rhoden, 1990)? Furthermore, why, when the final choices were made for the 1996 U. S. Olympic Baseball Team (unlike basketball, where the players are from the professional National Basketball Association, Olympic baseball is still made up predominantly of college players), was only one African American player named to the team?

"The U. S. Olympic baseball roster is set. One player African American."

These words open the article by Rod Beaton, who writes for *USA Today* (1996). The article is indicative of the widespread problems of discrimination and segregation addressed in this essay, and still prevalent in collegiate sport. The longtime sport critic Harry Edwards (1994) puts this issue in a much better context than we have when he says,

> The ubiquitous and perplexing outcome of the socio-political dynamics of Black-White relations in post-integration America has been a shift not from Black segregation—or collective exclusion and subordination—to collective inclusion and equality, but rather, from Black segregation to selective inclusion and subordination. The resulting structure of Black-White role and authority relationships in consequence has come to approximate nothing so much as a plantation system of mainstream social and institutional organization. Consistent with this reality, in most mainstream sports, African Americans are woefully underrepresented or completely absent. In sports to which they do have access in numbers, African Americans tend to be significantly underrepresented in authority, policy, and decision-making positions, while being greatly over-represented in the least powerful, most exploitable, and most expendable production roles—primarily that of athlete. (p. 102)

Although the phenomenon of stacking is now well-documented, the social, economic, and even the psychological mechanisms that underlie it are only now being discussed. In this essay we note, without losing sight of our most important conclusions, one of the most important theoretical questions facing sport sociology is whether, and to what extent, race or ethnicity is directly related to participation in sports. Furthermore, how does race/ethnicity play out in terms of what positions in team sports African American athletes are allowed to compete for and actually get to play? To specify what we mean, it is important also to note that we are mindful that the overall makeup of the U. S. sports community reflects the values of the larger society in its social structure, beliefs, and attitudes. That is to say, we do not expect and cannot expect the sporting community to be socially constructed and different from the rest of U. S. society. Yet, as a society, we have expectations within sport, as these pertain to parity, that are greater than society at large. This point is crucial. The social historian Allen Guttman (1991) underscores this point when he says,

> If athletes rather than scholars are seen as representatives of educational institutions, the probable reason is that sports are a lowest common denominator, a signifier whose significance anyone can understand. Unlike the genetic code, Roman law, and Japanese grammar, the rules of the game any game, even cricket can be learned in a day. (p. 17)

This, we feel, is definitely the case, as we demonstrate in our research on Division IA intercollegiate baseball. Our research highlights the constraints of African Americans in intercollegiate baseball. The results provide a framework and guidance for future efforts to determine if African Americans are catching up to their White counterparts in playing positions and, just as important, in other aspects of career attainment.

It is the strength and persistence exhibited in the long history of stacking research that drives our own undertaking, and we hope that the contribution made here has some value for future research. For in the final analysis, to understand stacking, one has to account for social structure as addressed above and the ways in which stacking interacts with other forces in society to produce blocked resources and opportunities for African American student-athletes. African

American athletes are not stacked just because of their skin color or hue of skin color. This, we contend, has little to do with the matter, as evidenced by the placement of Black Latin American players at central positions (Phillips, 1991). African Americans are stacked for reasons of low expectations, negative social stereotyping, and their low socioeconomic status in American society.

Suggested Readings

While the reference section of our essay is a listing of all sources consulted for the essay, here we draw a selective list of easily accessed readings that are especially important for understanding the persistence of stacking in American team sports:

Brooks, D., & Althouse, R. (Eds.). (1993). *Racism in college athletics: The African American athlete's experience.* Morgantown, WV: Fitness Information Technology, Inc.

Davis, T. (1995). The myth of the superspade: The persistence of racism in college athletics. *Fordham Urban Law Journal, 22,* 615–698.

Edwards, H. (1973). *Sociology of sport.* Homewood, IL: Dorsey Press.

Lapchick, R. (1995). *1995 racial report card.* Boston: Northwestern University Center for the Study of Sport in Society.

Loy, J., & McElvogue, J. F. (1970). Racial segregation in American sport. *International Review of Sport Sociology, 5,* 524.

Phillips, J. (1991). The integration of central positions in baseball: The Black shortstop. *Sociology of Sport Journal, 8,* 163–167.

Sammons, J. T. (1994). Race and sport: A critical historical examination. *Journal of Sport History, 21,* 203–278.

Smith, E. (1995). The self-fulfilling prophecy: Genetically superior African American athletes. *Humboldt Journal of Social Relations, 21,* 139–163.

Smith, E., & Leonard, W. (1997). Twenty-five years of stacking research in Major League Baseball: A theoretical assessment. *Sociological Focus, 30,* 321–331.

Study Questions

1. Discuss the term stacking as presented by the co-authors of this essay.

2. Explain the theory of centrality and apply this concept to the sport of baseball.

3. Identify strategies to eliminate stacking in baseball.

References

Aaron, H. (1992). *I had a hammer.* New York: Harper Collins.

Adair, R. (1990). *The physics of baseball.* New York: Harper & Row.

Beaton, R. (1996, July 5). Jones one-of-a-kind on Olympic team. *USA Today,* p. A1.

Berghorn, F., Yetman, N., & Hannam, W. (1988). Racial participation and integration in men's and women's intercollegiate basketball: Continuity and change, 1958–1985. *Sociology of Sport Journal, 5,* 107–124.

Bianchi, S., Farley, R., & Spain, D. (1982). Racial inequalities in housing. *Demography, 19,* 37–51.

Birrell, S. (1989). Racial relations theories and sport: Suggestions for a more critical analysis. *Sociology of Sport Journal, 6,* 212–227.

Blalock, H. (1967). *Toward a theory of minority group relations.* New York: John Wiley.

Brooks, D., & Althouse, R. (Eds.). (1993). *Racism in college athletics: The African American athlete's experience.* Morgantown, WV: Fitness Information Technology, Inc.

Brown v. Board of Educ., 347 U.S. 483 (1954).

Brown, J. (1989). *Out of bounds.* New York: Zebra Books.

Coakley, J. (1994). *Sport in society: Issues and controversies.* Boston, MA: Mosby.

Cose, E. (1993). *The rage of the privileged class: Why are middle-class Blacks angry? why should America care?* New York: Harper Collins.

Crenshaw, K. (1995). Race, reform, and retrenchment. In K. Crenshaw, N. Gotanda, G. Peller, & K. Thomas (Eds.), *Critical race theory* (pp. 103–122). New York: The New Press.

Curtis, J., & Loy, J. (1978). Race/ethnicity and relative centrality of playing positions in team sports. *Exercise and Sport Sciences Review, 6,* 285–313.

Davis, T. (1995). The myth of the superspade: The persistence of racism in college athletics. *Fordham Urban Law Journal, 22*, 615–698.

Davis, T. (1996). African American student-athletes: Marginalizing the NCAA regulatory structure? *Marquette Sports Law Journal, 6*, 199–227.

Degraff, L. (1970). The city of Black Angeles: Emergence of the Los Angeles ghetto. *Pacific Historical Review, 39*, 323–352.

Dodd, M. (1993, January 11). Survey finds minorities rare in power positions. *USA Today*, p. A1.

Du Bois, W. E. B. (1896/1995). *The Philadelphia Negro*. Philadelphia: University of Pennsylvania Press.

Duncan, O., & Duncan, B. (1957). *The Negro population in Chicago*. Chicago, IL: University of Chicago Press.

Dunning, E. (in press). *Sport in the process of racial stratification: The case of the USA*. Center for Research on Sport & Society, University of Leicester.

Early, G. (1994). The Black intellectual and the sport of prizefighting. In (Ed.), *The culture of bruising*. Hopewell, NJ: The Ecco Press.

Edwards, H. (1973). *Sociology of sport*. Homewood, IL: Dorsey Press.

Edwards, H. (1984). The Black "dumb" jock: An American sports tragedy. *The College Board Review, 13*, 8–13.

Edwards, H. (1994). Playoffs and payoffs: The African American athlete as an institutional resource. In B. Tidwell (Ed.), *The state of Black America* (pp. 85–111). Washington, DC: National Urban League.

Eitzen, S., & Furst, D. (1989). Racial bias in women's collegiate volleyball. *Journal of Sport and Social Issues, 13*, 46–51.

Eitzen, S., & Sage, G. (1997). *Sociology of North American sport* (6th ed.). Madison, WI: Brown & Benchmark.

Frey, J., & Eitzen, D. S. (1991). Sport and society. *Annual Review of Sociology, 17*, 503–522.

Frey, W. (1979). Central city white flight. *American Sociological Review, 44*, 425–448.

Guttman, A. (1991). The anomaly of intercollegiate athletics. In J. Andre & D. James (Eds.), *Rethinking college athletics* (pp. 17–30). Philadelphia: Temple University Press.

Hacker, A. (1992). *Two nations: Black and white, separate, hostile, unequal*. New York: Ballantine Books.

Halberstam, D. (1993). *The fifties*. New York: Villard Books.

Harris, O. (1993). African American predominance in collegiate sport. In D. Brooks & R. Althouse (Eds.), *Racism in college athletics: The African American athlete's experience* (pp. 51–74). Morgantown, WV: Fitness Information Technology, Inc.

Hoberman, J. (1997). *Darwin's athletes: How sport has damaged Black America and preserved the myth of race*. New York: Houghton Mifflin.

Hochschild, J. (1995). *Facing up to the American dream: Race, class, and the soul of the nation*. Princeton, NJ: Princeton University Press.

Hyland, D. (1990). *Philosophy of sport*. New York: Paragon House Publishers.

Johnson, N. (1988). A methodology for studying stacking in football and baseball: A preliminary note. *Sociology of Sport Journal, 5*, 270–277.

Kushner, J. (1979). Apartheid in America: An historical and legal analysis of contemporary racial residential segregation in the United States. *Harvard Law Journal, 22*, 547–560.

Kusmer, K. (1979). *A ghetto takes shape*. Urbana, IL: University of Illinois Press.

Lapchick, R. (1995). *1995 racial report card*. Boston: Northwestern University Center for the Study of Sport in Society.

Lavoie, M. (1989). The economic hypothesis of positional segregation: Some further comments. *Sociology of Sport Journal, 6*, 163–166.

Lavoie, M., & Leonard, W. (1994). The search for an alternative explanation of stacking in baseball. *Sociology of Sport Journal, 11*, 140–154.

Lemann, N. (1991). *The promised land: The great Black migration and how it changed America*. New York: Alfred A. Knopf.

Leonard, W. (1978). Stacking in collegiate basketball: A neglected analysis. *Sociology of Sport Journal, 7*, 294–301.

Leonard, W. (1988). Performance characteristics of white, Black and Hispanic Major League Baseball players: 1955–1984. *Journal of Sport and Social Issues, 12*, 31–43.

Loy, J., & McElvogue, J. (1970). Racial segregation in American sport. *International Review of Sport Sociology, 5*, 5–24.

Mangan, K. (1994, September 21). Paying for athletics. *The Chronicle of Higher Education*, pp. A43–44.

Medoff, M. (1986). Positional segregation and the economic hypothesis. *Sociology of Sport Journal, 3*, 297–304.

Merton, R. K. (1948). Discrimination and the American creed. In J. Stone (Ed.), *Race, ethnicity, and social change* (pp. 26–44). Belmont, CA: Wadsworth Publishing.

Merton, R. K. (1972). Insiders and outsiders: A chapter in the sociology of knowledge. *American Journal of Sociology, 78*, 7–47.

Merton, R. K. (1987). Three fragments from a sociologist's notebooks: Establishing the phenomenon, specified ignorance, and strategic research materials. *Annual Review of Sociology, 13*, 1–28.

Myers, J. (1991, December 16). Race still a player: Stereotypes pit ability vs. intellect. *USA Today*, p. 1A.

Nixon, H. (1991). Sport sociology that matters. *Sociology of Sport Journal, 8*, 281–294.

Osofsky, G. (1968). *Harlem: The making of a ghetto*. New York: Harper and Row.

Phillips, J. (1991). The integration of central positions in baseball: The Black shortstop. *Sociology of Sport Journal, 8*, 163–167.

Rhoden, W. (1990, June 11). A scarcity of Black Division I college players raises concern. *New York Times*, p. B11.

Ritzer, G. (1996). *Sociological theory*. New York: McGraw Hill.

Rosenblatt, A. (1967). Negroes in baseball: The failure of success. *Transaction, 4*, 51–53.

Sammons, J. (1994). Race and sport: A critical historical examination. *Journal of Sport History, 21*, 203–278.

Shropshire, K. (1996a). *In Black and white: Race and sports in America*. New York: New York University Press.

Shropshire, K. (1996b). Merit, ol' boy networks, and the blackbottomed pyramid. *Hastings Law Journal, 47*, 455–472.

Smith, E. (1981). An analysis of the social stereotype with special reference to Afro Americans. *Humboldt Journal of Social Relations, 8*, 61–82.

Smith, E. (1995). The self-fulfilling prophecy: Genetically superior African American athletes. *Humboldt Journal of Social Relations, 21*, 139–163.

Smith, E. (1997, April 12). 50 years ago: Jackie Roosevelt Robinson and the integration of Major League Baseball. *Winston-Salem Journal*, p. B1.

Smith, E., & Leonard, W. (1997). Twenty-five years of stacking research in Major League Baseball: A theoretical assessment. *Sociological Focus 30*, 321–331.

Smith, E., & Seff, M. (1990). Race, position segregation and salary equity in professional baseball. *Journal of Sport and Social Issues, 13*, 92–110.

Smith, R. (1988). *Sports and freedom: Rise of big time college athletics*. New York: Oxford University Press.

Spivey, D. (1983). The Black athlete in intercollegiate sports. *Phylon, 44*, 116–125.

Tang, J., & Smith, E. (Eds.). (1996). *Women and minorities in American professions*. New York: State University of New York Press.

Terkel, S. (1994). *Race: How Blacks and whites think & feel about the American obsession*. New York: Anchor Books.

Unruh, D. (1983). *Invisible lives*. Beverly Hills, CA: Sage Publishers.

Weiner, R. (1995, October 14). Stanford coach was ready for call. *New York Times*.

Wiggins, D. (1993). Critical events affecting racism in athletics. In D. Brooks & R. Althouse (Eds.), *Racism in college athletics: The African American athlete's experience* (pp. 23–49). Morgantown, WV: Fitness Information Technology, Inc.

Williams, P. (1996). Racial harassment of Black athletes: Another paradigm for understanding African American experiences. *Marquette Sports Law Journal, 6*, 287–314.

Wilson, W. J. (1996). *When work disappears: The world of the new urban poor*. New York: Alfred A. Knopf.

Wilson, W. J. (1991). Studying inner-city social dislocations: The challenge of public agenda research [Presidential address, American Sociological Association]. *American Sociological Review, 56*, 1–14.

Yarbrough, M. (1996). If you let me play sports. *Marquette Sports Law Journal, 6*, 229–238.

Yetman, N. (1987). Positional segregation and the economic hypothesis: A critique. *Sociology of Sport Journal, 4*, 274–277.

African American Head Coaches and Administrators: Progress But. . . ?

Dana Brooks and Ronald Althouse

Abstract

Since 1968, the involvement of African American head and assistant college coaches has increased slowly. Yet African American male and female coaches and administrators have not attained parity and remain underrepresented in college athletics. As recently as 1997, eight African Americans were hired in Division IA as head football coaches: Ron Cooper, Louisville; John Black, Oklahoma; Bob Simmons, Oklahoma State; Tony Samuel, New Mexico State; Tyrone Willingham, Stanford; and Jim Caldwell, Wake Forest ("Ceiling Breakers: Black Coaches," 1997). Only one African American female (Vivian Fuller) held the title of athletic director at an NCAA Division I institution. Tony Samuel, New Mexico State, added to the list of African American head football coaches (Wojciechowski, 1997). Throughout this essay, the authors update their 1993 essay, and identify and describe conditions leading to racial imbalance in coaching and administrative positions among National Collegiate Athletic Association (NCAA) member institutions. Previously identified racial issues of opportunity and discrimination focused on stacking, structural barriers, coaching mobility patterns, and media publicity; "old-boy networks" have been revisited, and discussions link African American coaching career mobility to the historical development of the NCAA on college campuses. College coaching success has been tied primarily to the organizational structure of football and basketball. The authors maintain that strategies to increase the number of African Americans in coaching and leadership positions must begin with an understanding of the organization of college athletics and multiculturalism and pluralism.

Edward Stanley Temple

Coach Ed Temple served as head coach of the USA Junior Team at the 1982 and 1986 Pan American Junior Games, and head coach of the USA National Junior Women's Track Team at the dual meet with Romania in Bucharest, and the first-ever World Junior Championships held in Athens, Greece in 1986. He is a past member of the USA Olympic Committee and for forty-four years served as head women's track coach at Tennessee State University. During his coaching career (1940–1994), forty members of his Tigerbelle teams (including Wilma Rudolph, Wyomia Tyres, and Lucinda Williams) represented Tennessee State University in the Olympic Games. Coach Temple's honors and awards are numerous: elected to the National Track and Field Hall of Fame, the Tennessee Hall of Fame, and the Pennsylvania Sports Hall of Fame.

Photo courtesy of Ed Temple.

John B. McLendon, Jr.

Coach John B. McLendon, Jr. attended the University of Kansas and was an advisee of Dr. Naismith, basketball's inventor. Records suggest that Coach McLendon premiered the full court basketball game, featuring the fast break and the full court press defense. His distinguished coaching career is as follows: North Carolina College, 1937–1952; Hampton Institute, 1952–1954; Tennessee State, 1954–1959; Kentucky State, 1964–1965; and Cleveland State 1966–1969. He was the first coach in college basketball to win three consecutive national championships (NAIA 1957, 1958, and 1959) while at Tennessee A & I State University. Coach McLendon, Jr. was elected NAIA Coach of the Year in 1958; inducted into the National Basketball Hall of Fame in 1978; and selected to The Cleveland Sports Stars Hall of Fame in 1998. He also spent a year coaching the Denver Rockets in the American Basketball Association.

Photo courtesy of John B. McClendon, Jr..

Key Terms

• Stacking •	• Coaching subculture •
• Black Coaches Association •	• Network structure •
• Social mobility •	• Coaching •
• Racism •	

Introduction

Over the past 25 years, *Sports Illustrated* published a series of articles painting a picture of the experiences of African American male and female athletes at the college and professional levels. Headlines included "The Black Athlete: A Shameful Story, 5 Part Series, Part 1: The Cruel Deception" (Olson, 1968); "An Assessment of Black is Best" (Kane, 1971); "Equality Begins at Home: It's Time to Give Black Football Coaches a Chance" (Reed, 1990); "The Eye of the Storm: The Lives of the U.S. Olympians Who Protested Racism in 1968 Were Changed Forever" (Moore, 1991); "Minority Opinion: Major League Job Openings Aren't Open to Everyone" (Scher, 1991); "We've Got to be Strong: The Obstacles Facing Black Women in Sports Have Scarcely Diminished with Time (DeFranz, 1991); and "No Room at the Top" (K. Anderson, 1992).

A set of landmark articles appeared in *Sports Illustrated* (August, 1991) when the magazine printed a series on the "Black athlete" comparing the African American athlete's present experience with conditions 23 years ago (Johnson, 1991). In canvassing African American and White male athletes from the NFL, NBA, and big-league baseball teams about their professional experiences, the writers asked the athletes how their sport treated them: how "Blacks" were treated by coaches and management, what their chances were of moving into management, and how communities accepted "Blacks." Results suggested that Black athletes believed they were treated worse than White athletes; they received lower pay and had to be better athletes to succeed professionally.

About four months later, *USA Today* published a four-part series dealing with race and sport (*"USA Today* Poll," 1991; "Black Access," 1991; "Money and Fame," 1991; "Stacking," 1991; "Black Access," 1991) that asked: "What makes a great athlete?" The series then described the extent of stacking practices, the culture of playground "hoops," NBA minority hiring, and Black access/White flight. These articles were sensational, once again provoking awareness about racial discrimination in American sport.

A prominent theme in both series was the continuing conspicuous absence of more minorities in coaching or management positions. In virtually all these reports, minority attention is concentrated almost exclusively on men. In 1991, a *USA Today* survey of 63 Division I college programs found only 12.5% of 3,083 athletic department positions were held by Blacks, Hispanics, Native Americans, and Asians. Only 2 minority members were athletic directors; 10 were sport information directors; and some 43 held the head coaching position (Boeck & Shuster, 1991).

In less than one year after the survey, the number of African American head football coaches among the 105 big-time Division IA teams had declined to zero. Ron Dickerson, assistant football coach at Clemson University and president of the Black Coaches Association, said, "It is truly frightening that this is 1992 and we don't seem to have progressed at all" ("And Then There Were None," 1992, p. A36). Shropshire (1996) reported that, in 1994, of 107 schools with football programs in NCAA Division I, only three of the head coaches were African American. C. S. Farrell (1994) found that from 1991 to 1993, there were 10% new head coaches (excluding historically Black colleges), yet Blacks made up only 143 (12.9% of the new head coaches.) The opportunities for African American men and women to enter coaching ranks or to achieve parity within the administrative ranks has shown little evidence of overcoming the subtleties of unconscious racism over the past 40 years. A very alarming 1994 report, the NCAA's Minority Opportunity and Interest Committee 4-year study, found that there had been no significant increase in the number of members selected as athletic administrators over the past 4 years (C. S. Farrell, 1994). Rudy Washington, executive director for the Black Coaches Association, said, "If you look at the whole scope of things, we've only come a little way. There is not a level playing field by any stretch of the imagination" (Farrell, 1995, p. 32). These findings and others led Cedric W. Dempsey, president of the NCAA, to say, "Institution's general failure to hire Black athletic directors is 'hard to defend'" (quoted in Naughton, 1998, p. A29).

In the summer of 1998, there were 28 African American athletic directors in NCAA Division I institutions. It is important to note that 20 of the athletic directors work at historically Black colleges and universities, and the remaining 8 African American athletic directors are as follows:

1. Irvin A. Cross, Idaho State University
2. Michael Garrett, University of Southern California
3. Tom A. Goss, University of Michigan
4. Lee A. McElroy, American University
5. Orby Moss, Jr., Georgia State University
6. Merritt J. Nowell, Jr., Michigan State University
7. Eugene D. Smith, Iowa State University
8. Nelson E. Swanson, State University of New York at Buffalo (Naughton, 1998).

What conditions feed this racial imbalance in coaching and administrative positions among NCAA member institutions? This essay will focus on the relationships among six primary factors: race, college athletic participation, ability to mobilize resources, organizational structure, impact of structural barriers, and subsequent career mobility to the ranks of coaching. The lack of African American men and women in head coaching positions and other leadership positions in college athletics may be a result of one or more of the following conditions:

1. Overt discrimination on the part of the NCAA athletic directors;
2. African Americans not playing "central positions" during their collegiate careers;
3. African Americans not having the same professional pathways available to them as those available to White coaches;
4. African American coaches not having access to existing head coach recruiting networks (Brooks, Althouse, King, & Brown, 1989).

Throughout this essay, we will examine how these factors can affect career mobility patterns of college coaches, particularly African American head and assistant college coaches. At the end, we will discuss strategies and recommendations that might increase the opportunities of African American men and women to attain new avenues of access to coaching and managerial positions and reduce barriers organized along gender lines.

Sport Participation and Subsequent Mobility

It is a long-held belief in American society that athletic participation provides African Americans the opportunity to gain social mobility. Braddock (1980), for example, stated that athletic achievement has a positive impact on orienting African American males toward college. The focus of this section is to summarize the effects of athletic participation on educational attainment of high school and college athletes. What is the relationship between race, athletic participation, and social mobility?

The literature written on this issue can be divided into two categories: (a) sport participation enhancing mobility (Braddock, 1980; W. Leonard & Reyman, 1988) and (b) sport participation limiting mobility (Edwards, 1973). J. W. Loy (1969) identified four consequences of sport participation that enhanced upward mobility:

1. Developing selected physical skills and abilities that could then lead to direct entry into professional sports;
2. Facilitating educational attainment through a college scholarship;
3. Leading to occupational sponsorship;
4. Fostering attitudes and behavior patterns valued in the wider occupational world.

A major research question addressed by scholars was the relationship between athletic participation (high school and college) and future educational and occupational goals, aspirations, and attainment; the findings have promoted conflicting results (Buhrmann, 1971; Coleman, 1961; Hanks & Eckland, 1976; Otto and Alwin, 1977; Picori, 1978; Rehberg and Schafer, 1968; Shafer & Armer, 1968; Snyder & Spreitzer, 1989; Spady, 1970; Stevenson, 1975). Nevertheless, there still was a consensus with regard to high school and college athletic participation's increasing the student-athletes' educational and occupational aspirations and attainment leading to social mobility.

According to Braddock (1980), it is important to differentiate between direct and indirect mobility. *Direct mobility* occurs when a lower-class youth acquires wealth and status and becomes a coach or sports personnel director. *Indirect mobility* takes place when formerly successful athletes are given the opportunity to occupy prestigious positions in the nonsport sector (Braddock, 1980).

Since the 1960s, studies investigating mobility of athletes through educational opportunities have been widely discussed. However, relatively few researchers have studied the career mobility patterns of college coaches and administrators. What literature does exist supports the position that sport participation does increase both direct and indirect social mobility. It would also hold true, then, that sport participation would provide former athletes with the opportunity to become head coaches and athletic administrators.

Miller and Form (1964) organized career mobility into four stages: (a) preparatory stage, in which the individual is influenced by significant others to choose an occupation, (b) initial stage, in which the individual takes a first job, (c) trial stage, in which the individual begins full-time employment and may change jobs three or four times, and (d) retirement, or disengagement from work.

Rosenberg (1980) argued that Miller and Form's (1964) stages of career mobility may be acceptable for the study of professional athletes. The application of their model to the study of career mobility patterns of college coaches and other administrators may also be appropriate. American college sport has become a big business, generating millions of dollars annually for the various colleges or universities. Yet the roles and responsibilities of coaches within these institutions have not been clearly defined. Ball and Loy (1975) remind us that college coaches function within an organization that is relatively formalized, highly structured, and bureaucratic. College coaching, similar to any social system, requires that individuals must be recruited to occupy the various positions within the system. According to Ball and Loy (1975), the recruitment of college coaches can be viewed from two standpoints: (1) The coach chooses an occupation, and (2) the athletic department makes a deliberate effort to draw recruits to their institution.

It appears that occupational coaching careers may be a factor of personal attributes, luck, and/or access to networks of professional ties/relationships.

Career Path or Dead End for African American Athletes?

Coakley (1986) believed that attaining sport-related career alternatives (i.e., coaching and administrative positions) requires skill in interpersonal relations, advanced education, knowledge of training, strategies, experience in sport organizations, and connection with individuals who provide job recommendations. These requisite skills are important because sport, as a social institution, reflects the basic values within society. Possessing such skills is not a

guarantee of being hired as a head coach. Edwards (1979b) contends that racism exists in American sport and has an impact on hiring decisions and subsequent mobility. Racism throughout the larger society accounts for the disproportionately high percentage of African American athletes in some sports.

Oliver's (1980) review of existing literature concluded that both race and social class standing have a very important impact on determining social mobility via sport. The following hypotheses were developed to test the relationship between these two variables:

1. The lower the social class background, the more likely people are to believe in the notion of upward social mobility through sports participation.
2. Members of minority groups, particularly Blacks, are more likely than Whites to believe in the notion of upward social mobility through participation (Oliver, 1980, p. 66).

The data gathered on 9- to 11-year-old African American children and their parents revealed that African American families were more likely than White families to associate with a potential career in professional sport. Earlier research conducted by Rosenblatt (1967) suggested that African American youth assign high self-esteem to participation in professional sport.

McPherson (1975) suggested that for African American males, professional athletes provide a visible, high-prestige role model. Young African American children are socialized by their parents, friends, and relatives to emulate successful professional athletes. On the other hand, there is a general belief among the American population that sports participation provides the African American with the opportunity to gain upward mobility. For example, the *Miller Lite Report* (1983) found approximately 50% of the respondents (White and African American) reported that athletics is one of the best ways for African Americans to advance their social status. However, according to Snyder and Spreitzer (1989), few

African American athletes have an opportunity to become professional athletes. A coaching career is a channel for social mobility and may provide an alternative career path.

Position Discrimination

During the decades of the 1970s, 1980s, and 1990s, social scientists investigated the relationships between athletic playing position and social discrimination in sport (D. Anderson, 1993; Best, 1987; D.B. Chu & Segrave, 1981; Curtis & Loy, 1978a,b; Eitzen & Sanford, 1975; Eitzen & Tessendorf, 1978; Massengale & Farrington, 1977; Medoff, 1977). Initial research focused on participation and racial discrimination in professional, college, and high school sports.

Blalock's (1962) research remains a significant piece of work providing insights into occupational discrimination, particularly into positional racial segregation in sports. Arguing that the importance of individual performance affected the degree of minority discrimination, Blalock (1962) proposed a set of organizational principles. Athletes know that the performance appropriate at various playing positions is much the same from one team to another, but player performances cannot be completely measured or summarized. This uncertainty allows for a quality of control by employers, for the factor of race to influence the playing life of the athlete. If uncertainties about assessing performance can affect a player, then uncertainty will affect hiring and careers of coaches and managers. Measurements of performance are less reliable, allowing a greater influence of the racial factor.

Blalock (1962) recognized that African American players had not attained parity and faced discrimination; eventually, African Americans would encounter more severe difficulties in obtaining coaching and managerial positions.

Grusky (1963) added to Blalock's (1962) work by investigating the relationship between an individual's position in the social structure and subsequent career mobility patterns, and arguing that

All else being equal, the more control of one's spatial location,

1. the greater the likelihood dependent or co-ordinative tasks will be performed;
2. the greater the rate of interaction with the occupants of other positions; and
3. performance of dependent tasks is positively related to frequency of interaction. (p. 346)

This spatial model was applied to the study of professional baseball teams. Findings suggested that major league managers were primarily selected from high-interaction positions. Numerous researchers immediately began to investigate these conclusions.

Segregation by Playing Position: The Outcome of Stacking

Hypothesizing that African Americans would more likely occupy noncentral positions than central positions. J. W. Loy and McElvogue (1970) applied Blalock's (1962) and Grusky's (1963) ideas of formal structure to the analysis of professional baseball and football. Results showed that African American athletes were underrepresented in central positions (positions that require a high degree of interaction) and overrepresented in noncentral, peripheral positions. J. W. Loy and McElvogue (1970) concluded that social segregation in professional sport was positively associated with centrality of playing position. The term *stacking* is the disproportional allocation of persons to central and noncentral athletic positions on the basis of race or ethnicity (Jones, Leonard, Schmitt, Smith, & Tolane, 1987).

Stacking and Leadership Recruitment

Over the past 25 years, the study of stacking and racial discrimination in high school, college, and professional sports has received considerable attention. These stacking and leadership recruitment studies (W.M. Leonard, 1977; W. Leonard, 1986, 1987) ask the same basic question: How are positions and reward structures allocated? More recently, researchers have begun to integrate the two areas to better understand the relationship between position occupation and future career mobility in sports.

The stereotype explanation of stacking concludes that African Americans are excluded from occupying central positions (quarterback, linebacker) because coaches act according to stereotypes that African Americans lack the leadership abilities necessary to occupy these positions (Edwards, 1973; Eitzen & David, 1975; Eitzen & Yetman, 1977; Williams & Youssef, 1975). The stereotypical beliefs that Whites hold about African American athletes still exist today.

A survey of 159 Blacks and 395 Whites conducted by USA Today ("USA Today Poll," 1991) polled attitudes about athletic abilities, which indicated a belief that African Americans are more physically gifted, but Whites possess intellect and leadership. Images found in popular media assist in institutionalizing stereotypes by reinforcing the gap between "Black" and "White," crediting African American athletes with physical prowess but reserving judgment on mental abilities. Adeno Addis chides, "Hell Man, They Did Invent Us." Davis (1995) maintains that the unconscious racism that occurs in college sport is tied to stereotypes about Black athletes' physical superiority.

Eitzen and Sanford (1975) initially reviewed the career patterns of African American athletes and found that as they move from high school to college to professional sports, they move from central to noncentral positions. Steve Weiberg (1991), a reporter for USA Today, claims that stacking is seen when a high school football player goes on to play college football. African American quarterbacks become wide receivers and running backs. The researchers concluded that discrimination is the source of racial segregation by position, and African American positions (noncentral) are not considered to be leadership or thinking positions. Consequently, playing noncentral positions is inadequate training for a career in coaching (Eitzen & Sanford, 1975).

This finding was further supported by Fabianic (1984), who studied the absence of minority managers in professional baseball. Between 1921 and 1980 a larger percentage of professional baseball managers were recruited from the infield positions. It was concluded that minority managers would have been expected to appear more frequently in the managerial ranks in 1980 than they actually did.

Similarly, Massengale and Farrington (1977) were interested in determining the relationship between centrality and the recruitment of college coaches. During the 1975 season, press guides from NCAA Division I head and assistant football coaches were used to determine previous playing positions. Massengale and Farrington (1977) concluded that playing central positions positively related to upward career mobility in college football.

Finally, D. B. Chu and Segrave's (1981) analysis of college and professional basketball players found that African American athletes were overrepresented (stacked) at the forward position and less prevalent at the guard position (leadership position). This is interesting to note because Whites who played at the guard position in college basketball dominate the college and professional coaching ranks. This study further supported the segregation-by-playing-position hypothesis and tied coaching mobility to previous playing position.

Similarly, Eitzen and Tessendorf (1978) applied the stereotype hypothesis to basketball. They found that African Americans were overrepresented at the forward position. This position requires speed, quickness, strength, and rebounding ability. African Americans were underrepresented at the guard and center positions (leadership positions). These findings further supported the segregation-by-playing-position hypothesis.

Berghorn, Yetman, and Hanna's (1988) results conflicted with Eitzen and Tessendorf's (1978) findings. They concluded that stacking at the guard and forward positions was in existence in 1970 but was eliminated by 1975. Berghorn et al. (1988) also observed that stacking in basketball no longer exists. Berghorn et al. (1988) argued that the elimination of stacking in college basketball was associated with the increase in minority participation in basketball. With more minority players, it was more difficult to exclude them from central positions through sheer force of numbers.

Best (1987), however, contended that positional segregation is still prevalent in professional football and that African American career earnings, postcareer earnings, and postcareer opportunities are negatively affected. This ties into the existence of a racial wage discrimination in professional sports, documented by Christiano (1986, 1988), W. M. Leonard (1987), and Mogull (1975). Basically, African American athletes were paid less when compared to their White counterparts.

More recently, the economic factors tied to positional segregation have received considerable attention (Yetman, 1987). Medoff (1977) suggested that positional segregation was a result of differential training and development costs associated with playing specific sports. Medoff (1986) extended his argument by concluding that stacking results from free choice by the African American athlete. These athletes choose to play noncentral positions on their own and are not coerced by coaching staffs to play these positions.

As an alternative to the stereotyping and economic hypotheses of stacking, McPherson (1975) supported role modeling as the foundation to position segregation. The author hypothesized that African Americans segregate themselves in specific positions because they wish to emulate successful African American athletes who previously played the same positions. Edwards (1973) advocated the outcome-control hypothesis and argued that Blacks were excluded from those sports and positions that have the greatest opportunity for influencing the outcome of the contest (quarterback, tennis, golf). More recently, D. Anderson (1993) traced college head-coaching career paths and subsequent mobility and concluded that becoming an assistant coach often is a pre-

requisite to becoming a coordinator, and becoming a coordinator is a prerequisite to becoming a head football coach. D. Anderson's results are significant because the author concluded that race still matters, and racism functions to keep Blacks from entering the pool from which head coaches are selected: White assistant coaches were twice as likely to have played the quarterback position (central) in college (D. Anderson, 1993).

Edwards (1987) reached the conclusion that cultural and social explanations provided the explanation of African American success and overrepresentation in the athletic role. The following explanations were offered:

1. The African American community tends to reward athletic achievement.
2. The overwhelming majority of aspiring African American athletes emulate established African American role models and seek careers in basketball, football, baseball, boxing, and track.
3. The American media have increased the visibility of the African American athlete.

Numerous theories (stereotyping, economic, and role modeling) have been suggested to address the relationship between race, playing positions, and subsequent sport-mobility career patterns. The majority of these studies focused on African American and White male athlete comparisons. Emphasis is placed upon a failure to evaluate social mobility patterns of Chicanos, Asian Americans, Jews, and Native Americans (Birrell, 1989), as well as those of African American female athletes.

The focus on stacking has been treated within the context of racism and, specifically, racism directed toward the African American males. One of the initial studies to investigate the relationship between stacking and racism among women was conducted by Eitzen and Furst (1989). They studied the extent to which stacking was evident in women's collegiate volleyball. White female athletes were found to dominate the setter position (leadership and high degree of interaction required) whereas

African American females were occupying the hitter and blocker positions. These positions require quickness, agility, and jumping ability. This finding suggests there may be less opportunity for African American females to gain access to coaching and other managerial positions in volleyball and, by extension, in other sports.

According to Schneider and Eitzen (1979), stacking research can be summarized into the following topical areas: interaction and organizational centrality (Grusky, 1963; J.W. Loy & McElvogue, 1970); responsibility for outcome control (Edwards, 1973); role model socialization (McPherson, 1975); and stereotypes of social class (Edwards, 1973; Eitzen & David, 1975; Eitzen & Tessendorf, 1978; Eitzen & Yetman, 1977).

One of the major points to be drawn from all of this literature is that African Americans were not considered for coaching or managerial positions in college or professional sport because during their playing careers, they did not occupy positions requiring leadership and decision making. None of the theories presented in this section can explain how African Americans who played noncentral positions became coaches or managers. Clearly, the positional segregation and career-mobility model literature cannot fully explain career mobility patterns of coaches. Additional models and explanations must be explored.

Coaching Mobility Models

In contrast to investigating the relationship between position segregation in sport and future mobility opportunities, researchers have begun to develop alternative models to explain career mobility in sport. Scholars are now interested in identifying how geographical patterns, career patterns, managerial changes, organizational effectiveness, and personal attributes for coaches explain, describe, and predict the developmental pathways.

In dealing with coaching mobility, Eitzen and Yetman (1977) applied Grusky's (1963) earlier hypothesis of the relationship between the roles of administrative succession and the degree of organizational effectiveness. They systematically studied male college basketball team records between 1930 and 1970 to determine the relationship between coaching tenure (number of years covered in the period, divided by the number of coaching changes) and team effectiveness (winning percentages). The results of this study provided support for Grusky's (1963) model. Turnover rates and organizational effectiveness were negatively related. Coaching changes had no effect on team performance during the following year. However, the longer a basketball coach remained at an institution, the more successful he tended to be. Beyond a tenure of 13 years, coaching effectiveness began to decline. Coaches who left the profession after 8 or 9 years tended to have higher win-loss percentages at the end of their careers than in their earlier years of coaching.

Eitzen and Yetman's (1977) study was significant because the researchers challenged the belief that a turnover in coaching would result in immediate changes in team performance. It has also been an accepted belief that managerial change is dysfunctional to the organization. Too often the coach is given responsibility for the success or failure of the team. Historically, head-coaching mobility patterns have been tied to the success or failure of the team. It is important to note that formal organizations (athletic programs) seek to maintain relatively stable populations and must fill vacancies either internally or externally (J. Loy, McPherson, & Kenyon, 1978). Eitzen and Yetman's (1972) study examined coaching turnover rate and team performance among college basketball teams. The researchers found that unsuccessful teams had the highest rate of coaching turnovers. This finding further supported the relationship between organizational effectiveness and personnel replacement rates in college sports.

Career Mobility Patterns

G. H. Sage and Loy (1978) were two of the first researchers to investigate systematically the career patterns of college athletic coaches.

Initially, they applied Rooney's (1974) concepts of spatial organization and migration patterns to analyze the geographical movement of college head basketball and football coaches. G. H. Sage and Loy (1968) found that the majority of basketball (43%) and football (36%) coaches attended small private or public colleges. California, Illinois, New York, Ohio, and Pennsylvania were identified as the five leading states in producing college football and basketball coaches.

One of the most significant findings obtained by G. H. Sage and Loy (1978) was that most coaches attended colleges in their home states or bordering states (81%). In addition, a majority of coaches obtained their first coaching positions at senior high schools near their undergraduate institutions.

The G. H. Sage and Loy (1978) data clearly identify the regional nature of college coaching career-mobility patterns. That is, coaches often remained in the same NCAA districts. Coaches often changed coaching assignments as much as four or five times prior to obtaining their current head coaching positions. G. H. Sage and Loy (1978) concluded that the athletic prestige of the colleges from which the coaches graduated was a factor influencing their current coaching positions. Further strengthening their ties to their alma mater, basketball and football coaches were first employed by their alma mater as graduate assistants or assistant coaches. The "internship" program provides the new coaches with experience and visibility.

G. H. Sage and Loy (1978) adapted Turner's (1960) concepts of elite status and mobility. Links were found between serving as a head coach and assistant coach at a high-prestige university and moving between institutions. High-prestige organizations provided more than their fair share of assistant coaches.

Data obtained from the head basketball and football coaches in 1979 provided support for the sponsored mobility model. For example, the athletic prestige of undergraduate colleges had more influence on the career-mobility patterns of football coaches, and the athletic prestige associated with coaching apprenticeship had greater influence on those patterns for basketball coaches. Surprisingly, variables such as educational status, athletic achievement, coaching experience, and coaching success had very little effect on the athletic prestige of the coaches' first or present jobs.

The authors concluded by pointing out that the relationship between coaching career patterns and institutional prestige does not fully explain the mobility patterns of college coaches. Additional factors such as old-boy networks, athletic farm systems, publicity offered by the mass media, and the extent to which social exchange exists in the coaching profession must be analyzed. One must also realize that racism and discrimination may negatively affect coaching career patterns of minorities.

Social, Educational, Athletic, and Career Backgrounds: Organizational Structures

Early research focused primarily on the coaching mobility patterns of White coaches. Comparatively, we have not seen significant career paths for African American males. By and large, most studies have centered on coaches at the endpoint positions (head coaching roles). To better understand the coaching career process, we need to look at social mobility and organizational structure within these organizations.

Latimer and Mathes's study (1985) represents one of the first attempts to investigate the relationship between social, educational, athletic, and career backgrounds of African American football coaches (1 head, 79 assistant). Data from this study permit researchers to begin to understand similarities and differences in the coaching career-mobility patterns of White and African American coaches.

Latimer and Mathes's data revealed that 66% of the African American coaches attended colleges and obtained their first coaching positions in their home NCAA districts. This is about the same level that G. H. Sage and Loy (1978) found in their study of White coaches (fifty-nine percent of the White football coaches initially began their coaching career at the high school level). Apparently, half of the coaches began their careers as high school coaches. Similarly, about 50% of the African American coaches began their first coaching assignments at the college level.

Over the past two decades, there has been a gradual increase in the number of African American head coaches, especially in basketball. Berghorn et al. (1988) found the number and percentage among Black males participating in college basketball from 1970 to 1985 increased dramatically.

According to these researchers, in 1985, 61% of male and 30% of female players in Division I were African American. The greatest increase in the number of African Americans participating in college athletics was found in the South. Although there has been a significant increase in the number of African Americans participating in college athletics, there has not been a correspondent increase in the number of African American head coaches.

The apparent lack of African Americans in integrated coaching positions was also noted at the high school level. According to Eitzen and Yetman (1977), African Americans historically obtained coaching positions at predominantly African American high schools, especially in the South.

One consequence of integrating schools in the South during the 1960s resulted in eliminating African Americans from head coaching positions. Unfortunately, many of the former African American head coaches were not hired at the predominantly White schools. This finding led the researchers to conclude that two forms of discrimination existed that prevented African Americans from becoming head coaches at the professional sport level: (a) overt discrimination when owners ignored qualified African Americans for available head coaching positions because of prejudice and (b) a fear that White fans would react negatively if an African American were the coach or manager.

More recently, research has focused upon coaching success and career mobility paths by identifying relationships between personal attributes and job responsibilities of successful coaches. Banks (1979) surveyed African American football coaches to identify the significant attributes a head coach at a major college looks for in selecting an African American assistant coach. The coaches identified knowledge of the game, implementation of methods on the field, recruiting skills, personality, ability to get along with others, ability to communicate with both White and African American student-athletes, and personal appearance as important selection criteria.

The results of this study showed that approximately one half of the African American assistant coaches served as graduate assistants before assuming assistant coach duties. In addition to the selection attributes, the data revealed that at least three fourths of the African American coaches agreed that the college or university at which they played had an influence on securing a major college coaching position. This finding further supports the relationships between college prestige and career mobility indicated by Loy and Sage (1978) and Latimer and Mathes (1985).

Occupational Demands

Grenfell and Freischlag (1989) recognized that the career mobility paths for men may differ from those for women. In consideration of these differences, the researchers hypothesized that a complex set of personal and professional attributes was related to successful coaching. Grenfell and Freischlag (1989) developed a model representing role responsibilities of coaches (Freischlag and Jacob, 1988) through use of questionnaires solicited from 84 men's and 81 women's NCAA Division I basketball coaches. The results included the identification of five factors contributing to coaching success: communication skills, administrative support, public image, dress, and NABC membership in the professional coaches' associations.

Based upon data found in their study, the researchers outlined the attributes of a typical head coach, because they found both successful male and female college basketball coaches exhibit some career-path similarities. The ability to identify the typical coach with certain attributes tends to support the idea that there is a set of minimal competencies that successful coaches are expected to have. Among these competencies are experience, membership in professional associations, clinic attendance, participation in summer camps, and holding of at least a master's degree.

In 1980, G. Sage identified the need to analyze the occupational demands of the coaching position. His work provides the reader with an excellent review of the literature covering such issues as personality of the coach, leadership styles, social and political attitudes, and value orientation. The literature in 1980 could not clearly differentiate between successful and unsuccessful coaches. During the decades of the 1960s and 1970s, articles appearing in local newspapers, magazines, and books were very critical of the role of the coach. G. Sage (1980) concluded that a majority of these attacks focused upon the personal attributes of coaches. Clearly, the role of the coach and the ultimate success or failure of the athletic program are influenced by more factors than merely the personality of the coach. Indications are that by the time people apply for head or assistant coaching positions, few attributes will distinguish African American coaches from White coaches. Selection will be based on some other criteria!

Coaching Subculture

West (1994) writes in *Race Matters* to engage in a serious discussion of race in America. We must begin not with the problems of Black people but with the flaws of American society, flaws rooted in historic inequalities and long-standing cultural stereotypes. How we set up terms for discussing racial issues shapes our perception and response to these issues. As long as Black people are viewed as a "them,"

the burden falls on Blacks to do all the "cultural" and "moral" work necessary for healthy race relations. The implication is that only certain Americans can define what it means to be American and the rest must simply "fit in" (West, 1994, p. 67). The following analysis of coaching as a subculture represents an attempt by African Americans to "fit in" to what is perceived by some members of the lay public to be a closed coaching fraternity.

Massengale (1974) agreed that an understanding of coaching as an occupational subculture might provide additional insights into the coaching role. Coaches display distinctive ways of thinking, feeling, and acting in a given environment. Coaches are promoted upward through the system, and Massengale (1974) pointed out that young coaches learn what is expected behavior within the profession. Subcultures are relatively closed systems, and coaches learn that obtaining a coaching position may be tied to the amount of support that other members of the coaching profession are willing to offer. He also stated that "the subculture can become a referral system to vested interest groups such as alumni organizations or athletic booster clubs, or it can become an acceptable sponsor and offer unsolicited firsthand personal recommendation" (Massengale, 1974, p. 141).

The extent to which African American coaches are recruited and become members of the dominant White subculture of college coaching and "fit in" is not clearly understood. The application of Massengale's (1974) "favored models" argues that members of the subculture value the credentials of coaches who have values, beliefs, and behaviors similar to those of recognized successful coaches. African American coaches who serve as assistant coaches under very successful head coaches learn these values and begin to imitate their mentors. As a result, the African American coaches become part of an informal recruiting and referral coaching system operating in college athletics. Sperber's (1990) critique of NCAA college sport concluded that most Division I head coaches are White males, early-to-late middle age, and part of an old boy network. As a result, coaches and athletic directors perpetuate their subculture by hiring their duplicates. Similarly, Shropshire (1996) concluded that the old boy networking cycle is hard to break. The researcher based this belief on the fact that informal social and managerial networks have long been institutionalized in sports. To date, there are no formal, structured recruiting systems in the NCAA that have been established to identify potential college coaches.

"Basically, there is no feeder system for athletic departments. An athletic program is so small there aren't enough positions to really work your way up and cultivate young and new managers. The system is 'self-fulfilling'" (Krasnow, 1988, p. 11). John Chaney (men's basketball, Temple University) voiced similar concern and advocated that the NCAA become more proactive and begin to give access to African American members for coaching positions (C. Farrell, 1987a).

Network Structure, Mobilization of Resources, Coaching Mobility, and Organizational Structure

Brooks et al. (1989) wanted to begin to lay a foundation investigating the political economy of college sport related to the African American coaching experience. The primary goal of their study was to explore various models in an attempt to explain why few African Americans occupy head coaching positions. Their research represented new alternatives to analyzing coaching career-mobility patterns.

In the initial stage of the interviews, researchers conducted telephone discussions with members of the Board of Directors of the Black Coaches' Association (BCA) (1988–89), regional directors of the BCA, and two members of the BCA recommended by the executive director. The researchers asked the following questions: What were the standout qualifications that must be shown on the re-

sume in order to achieve a "real shot" at head coaching positions; what did they perceive to be their strongest attributes as coaches—did they have a desire to become head coaches; what benefits versus cost are associated with assistant coaching versus head coaching; and who does one have to talk to in order to be recruited as a head coach?

The interviews permitted the researchers to confirm the existence of four coaching avenues. The avenues are (a) Blalock Talent Avenue, (b) Personal Attribute Avenue, (c) Internal Mobility Career Avenue, and (d) Coaching Mobility Network Avenue.

Blalock Talent Avenue

Bell (1992) put forth the proposition that Black people will never gain full equality in this country. Even those herculean efforts we have as success will produce no more than temporary "peaks of progress," short lived victories that slide into irrelevance as racial patterns adapt in ways that maintain White dominance. This is a hard-to-accept fact that all history verifies. We must acknowledge it, not as a sign of submission, but as an act of ultimate defiance. (p. 12)

Disputing this proposition, Blalock (1967) argued that sport creates an opportunity for African Americans to gain mobility by making individual skill the most important determinant to success. Blalock's (1967) argument was based on the following arguments: (a) The lower the degree of purely social interaction on the job, the lower the degree of racial discrimination; (b) to the extent that performance level is relatively independent of skill in interpersonal relations, the degree of racial discrimination is lower; and (c) the greater the importance of high individual performance to the productivity of the work group, the lower the degree of minority discrimination by employers.

Blalock (1967) also believed that African Americans did not attain parity in athletics and that they would encounter difficulties in obtaining coaching and managerial positions. It was argued that African Americans would require special training and that vague standards for evaluating leadership effectiveness would serve to discriminate against these individuals getting coaching positions.

In addition, Blalock (1967) contended that African American coaches who demonstrate excellence in coaching can be expected to be recruited for additional coaching responsibilities. Some scholars, most notably Edwards, take exception to this assumption. Edwards (1973) argued that Blacks do not gain upward mobility via sport and that, in fact, very few Blacks gain access to participate in professional sports.

Blalock's Talent Avenue deserves further investigation. College athletic programs, like many other highly structured organizations, have been established to recognize and reward talent. Coaching talent may be rewarded in the form of extended coaching contracts, higher salaries, or upward mobility into directorships.

Personal Attribute Avenue

The personal attribute avenue suggests that coaches gained upward mobility as they acquired the attributes necessary to perform the functions of head coach. Brooks et al. (1989) showed that coaches perceived they had the following attributes:

(a) communication skills, (b) motivation, (c) listening (supportive) skills, (d) job experience, (e) honesty, and (f) ability to relate to students. These coaches believed that certain personal attributes were associated with coaching success. The researchers were unable to explain the fact that the majority of these coaches perceived they had the necessary personal attributes yet remained assistant coaches. Additional factors, such as the ability to fit into the institution and compatibility with other coaches, alumni, and the athletic directors must be considered.

Internal Mobility Careers Avenue

This idea suggests that coaching mobility depends heavily on recruiting network ties and communication links with individuals in decision-making positions. Interpretation relies on Collins's (1975) examination of the relationship between individual success and social mobility. Basically, the ability of an assistant coach to achieve upward mobility is tied directly to the success of the head coach. If the head coach is labeled as unsuccessful, his or her assistant coach is also labeled unsuccessful. Negative labeling by those in power (athletic directors, college presidents) makes upward mobility for assistant coaches nearly impossible. The assistant coaches lack power and influence in the decision-making process (Brooks et al. 1989). It is important for upwardly mobile assistant coaches to build acquaintance networks with athletic directors and other head coaches to assist them in acquiring head coaching positions.

Coaching Mobility Network Avenue

Coaching mobility networks or ties are related to Internal Mobility Careers Avenue. Some evidence indicates successful coaches function as key links in networks that generate other successful coaches. Such "recruiting trees" are affected by an organization's level of success with its athletic program as well as its conference affiliation. Comments made by members of the BCA, such as, "people who have been associated with successful programs become head coaches" and "being associated with 'big-time' institution increases your chances of being hired" pointed to the existence of perceived structural opportunities to career-coaching mobility (Brooks et al., 1989).

Brooks et al. (1989) were unable to account adequately for the relatively low upward mobility and the fairly slow development of African American assistant coaches promoted to head coaching positions. Most of the assistant coaches who were identified remained assistant coaches or left the coaching ranks. Those who became head coaches appeared to take years to get there. This suggests that different factors may be influencing features of recruitment and that both levels (micro and macro) will be important if we are going to understand the recruitment and career-mobility coaching patterns.

Friendship networks, professional contacts, and acquaintances are important influences on the upward mobility of African American coaches. According to Young (1990), networking benefits are similar to those provided by mentoring: encouragement, support, advice, increased knowledge base, the establishment of new networks, and assistance with job placement. It is apparent in college athletics that network relationships tie together coaching mobility and head coaching positions. Coaching careers are considered to be unique for each individual, but networks represent the way in which organizations allocate and mobilize the opportunities for mobility.

Brooks, Althouse, and Brown (1990) also looked at structures of the mobility exhibited in the career paths of 28 African American head coaches in Division I basketball who held positions in 1989. Notable coaches such as Lefty Driesell, Denny Crum, and Digger Phelps were recruiting "gatekeepers" (mentors, who hired African American assistant coaches). Career-path sponsorship also appears to have depended on the success of athletic programs, conference affiliation, and type of institution (public or private). Evidence suggests that the process can work for African American assistant coaches as African American head coaches begin to hire more African Americans as assistant coaches. In some measure, as African American head coaches establish their own recruiting system, they can increase the potential pool of available coaches. The expanded network may result in increased access to coaching openings. Some evidence (e.g., formation of the BCA) suggests that African American assistants have begun to expand their occupational network, both in their own professional associations and through employment in sports and related commercial jobs. These assistant

coaches may be keenly aware of power brokers (i.e., alumni, presidents) within the recruiting and hiring structures, and indications are that failure to identify their influence in decision making will result in token interview sessions. Women coaches and administrators are also encouraged to develop network ties to overcome barriers in the male-dominated athletic field (Young, 1990). In fact, the author found that network ties tend to hasten career development, and recommendation by network contacts often takes precedence over the candidate's experience in the field.

A better understanding of career mobility is likely to await a more thorough investigation of the network relationships among the career resources acquired by coaches and the rate of organizational turnover and change in mobility among coaches. Turnover among head coaching positions at NCAA levels I, II, and III will vary, but probably amounts to no more than 10%. This results in only a few head positions available before the next season. This rate of coaching turnover among NCAA division institutions has not been documented, and the NCAA has only recently started to monitor this situation.

Brooks et al. (1990) were able to identify four mobility career paths characterizing experiences among African American basketball coaches:

1. Professional road (previous college playing experience, professional playing experience, assistant coach under successful head coach);
2. Internship (previous college playing experience, assistant coach under two or more head coaches, head coaching position);
3. Stepping-stone (previous college playing experience, head coach for small college with low student enrollment, head coach Division I level); and
4. Developmental (mentorship—previous college playing experience, assistant coach under successful head coach at College X, head coach at College Y).

Further investigation suggested that an individual may experience more than one coaching career path. We simply need to recognize that a good deal of coaching ends at the assistant-coach level and that coaching jobs are a source of alternative careers. Sometimes an early job involves a secondary school or prep school position; the individual may later move into a mobility path at a new entry point. The young, upwardly mobile African American coach may travel more than one of these paths. However, differences in league structure, league ranking of the college, prestige of the college, athletic program cost, and type of sport (individual/team) may affect the path followed by African American coaches. Thus, each career path represents potential opportunity and vulnerability to achieve success.

Study of these career patterns can and must focus on internal factors affecting the allocation and distribution of organizational resources. Specifically, we suggest study of the relationships between coaching networks and cycles of athletic participation, coaching schedules and loads; and of the schemes and mobilization of alumni support, as well as administration support and future coaching-career mobility.

Different career paths in basketball appear to extract different costs of success; many African Americans may drop out as well as be "forced out" of coaching. Understanding the standardized, but differentiated, career paths of coaches may depend on seeing how assistant coaches are tied together by their occupational level and the chances for coaching mobility from different segments of that labor force. Research is needed to determine whether similar careers exist for men or women, and among revenue or nonrevenue sports.

Persistent Discrimination or Progress?

During the past 20 years, more African Americans have won jobs as head coaches, and the number of assistant coaches in the NCAA also appears to increase, especially in the sport of basketball. Popular magazines such as *Ebony* and *Jet* applaud these achievements, but also reflect on continuing aspects of discrimination. *Jet*'s 1979 article "NCAA's First Black Head Football Coach is Ready to Tackle the Pressure" traced the career of Willie Jeffries, the first African American coach of a major White institution (Wichita State). Prior to accepting the position at Wichita State, Jeffries declined interview offers from predominantly White institutions because he felt these institutions were "interviewing Black coaches (only) to fill one kind of criteria" ("NCAA's First," 1979, p. 48).

In 1981, before moving to the 49ers, then Stanford, and recently to the Minnesota Vikings head office, Dennis Green was the only head African American football coach in the Big 10 Conference. He coached at Northwestern University, where his teams had limited success. Two years later, Tony Yates and George Raveling accepted head basketball coaching positions at the Universities of Cincinnati and Iowa, respectively. Nolan Richardson, previously the head basketball coach at Tulsa University, accepted a head coaching position at Arkansas. Richardson became the first African American head coach of any men's sport in the Southwest Conference ("Black Head Coaches," 1982). Perhaps a more notable hiring was that of Kenneth Gibson as head track coach at the University of Mississippi in 1985, the first African American coach of any sport in the school's history. The Southeastern Conference had been the last major college conference to integrate its sports teams, not having done so until the late 1960s. Finally, when the University of Tennessee hired Wade Houston as the head basketball coach in 1989, Tennessee became the first college in the Southeastern Athletic Conference to hire an African American head basketball coach (Oberlander, 1989).

Ebony saw some new balance as African Americans won these positions ("Black Head Coaches," 1982). Although the number of head coaches at the college level was few, the number was slowly increasing. Of the 276 Division I colleges, 13 had hired head African American basketball coaches. The majority of the coaches being hired for college positions were in basketball, track and field, and football. The magazine's interviews with these African American coaches revealed that tokenism and decreased support by the alumni still seemed to weigh heavily in accounting for the persistently low percentage of African American head coaches.

Reports suggest that since 1986, there has been a notable increase of head African American college basketball coaches. Several prominent African American men's and women's head basketball coaches were noted by *Ebony* during that year. (See table 1.)

By 1991, 34 African Americans had head basketball coaching assignments. This amounts to a 500% increase from the 1978–79 season, when only 7 African Americans were head coaches (Keegan & Towle, 1991). It is important to note between 1991 and 1997 African Americans continued to gain some measure of access to head basketball coaching positions at the NCAA Division I level. In fact, in 1997,

African Americans occupied 55 among 289 Division I head basketball coaching positions ("Ceiling Breakers,"1997). It is also important to point out in Division basketball, Whites make up 68% of assistant coaches. Comparatively, African Americans make up 31.2% of assistant coaching positions (R.E. Lapchick & Matthews, 1997).

Dealing only with basketball (football is a totally different power game), the listing shows the following: (a) Only 13 of the 35 African American head basketball coaches occupy positions in major conferences; (b) the majority of coaches have little head-coaching experience; and (c) half of the 34 coaches were hired within the past 3 years.

As a major longtime advocate for social justice and the rights of the African American athlete, Edwards (1969, 1979b, 1982a,b)contends that the revolt of the Black athletes in the 1960s was a major factor influencing the increase in Black coaches. The Black assistant coaches' core activities have changed since the 1960s. Determined specifically by the existing exigencies of each college/university, assistant coaches serve as recruiters, scouts, academic advisors, and public relations officers. Yet today, it is generally acknowledged that one of the major tasks of the African American coach is to recruit African American players (Lederman, 1988). Edwards believed many African American coaches fill dead-end jobs with no chance for promotion (Dent, 1987).

Table 1. Head African American College Basketball Coaches (1986)

Coach	College/University
Walt Hazzard	UCLA
Tony Yates	Cincinnati
George Raveling	Iowa (Men's)
Vivian Stringer	Iowa (Women's)
Larry Farmer	Weber State
Nolan Richardson	Arkansas
David Gaines	San Diego State
John Chaney	Temple
Clem Haskins	Western Kentucky
Bob LeGrand	University of Texas Arlington
Charles Coles	Central Michigan
Vernon Payne	Western Michigan
Wilkes Rittle	University of Illinois Chicago
John Thompson	Georgetown

("A Boom in Black Coaches," 1986)

Power Structure of NCAA Division I Football

Some progress has been made to hire African American head and assistant Division I NCAA basketball coaches. Unfortunately, head college football coaching remains primarily a White male domain. Football conferences have been slow to hire Black coaches. In 1993, Jim Caldwell became the first Black head football coach in the ACC, and in 1995, Bob Simmons became the first Black head coach (Oklahoma State University) in the Big Eight Conference. By 1995, there were six African American Division IA football coaches: North Texas, Matt Simien; Oklahoma State, Bob Simmons; Stanford, Tyronne Willingham; Louisville, Ron Cooper; Temple, Ron Dickerson; Wake Forest, Jim Caldwell (Campbell, 1995). Hill (1997) identified 16 current or previous African American head football coaches at Division IA institutions (see Table 2). Rudy Washington, executive director of the BCA, reviewed the progress made in the hiring of African American head football coaches: "If you looked at the whole score of things, we've only come a little way. There is not a level playing field by any stretch of the imagination" (quoted in C. S. Farrell, 1995, p. 32). Reed (1990) also sounded a pessimistic note and said, "There is the persistent notion that football is less a Black coach's sport than basketball is" (p. 138). The author further stated, "The

situation in football is so bad that only a handful of Blacks have risen to offensive or defensive coordinator, jobs that are springboards to head coaching positions." According to Hill (1997), during the 1995 football season, 213 of 972 assistant coaching positions were occupied by Blacks. The author noted since 1982, there have been 263 head coaching vacancies, but only 14 Black coaches were hired to fill these vacancies.

In a manuscript titled "African American Male Head Coaches: In the 'Red Zone,' but Can They Score?" Brooks, Althouse, and Tucker (1997) concluded that Temple University has been very successful in its efforts to identify and have African American men and women head coaches. In 1993, Temple University had the following head coaches on staff: Ron Dickerson, football; John Chaney, basketball; Nikki Franks, fencing; and Tina Sloan Green, lacrosse. It became apparent to the authors that Temple University's hiring success was directly attributable to the University's cen-

Table 2. Black Head Football Coaches at Division IA Institutions

Name	Employing Institution	Years of Employment
Willie Jefferson	Wichita State	1979–83
Dennis Green	Northwestern	1981–85
Cleve Bryant	Ohio	1985–89
Wayne Nunnley	Nevada-Las Vegas	1986–89
Francis Peay	Northwestern	1986–91
Dennis Green	Stanford	1989–91
Willie Brown	Long Beach State	1989–91
James Caldwell*	Wake Forest	1992–97
Ron Cooper	Eastern Michigan	1993–94
Ron Dickerson	Temple	1993–97
Matt Simon*	North Texas	1995–97
Ron Cooper*	Louisville	1995–97
Bob Simmons*	Oklahoma State	1995–97
Tyrone Willingham*	Stanford	1995–97
John Blake*	Oklahoma	1996–97
Tony Samuel*	New Mexico State	1997

* Currently employed at this institution (as of 1997).

NCAA News (1997)

tral administration and athletic department commitment to diversifying its coaching ranks.

African American Female Coaches

NCAA athletic observers attribute the greater representation of African American head coaches to an increase in the number of African Americans participating in college sport. According to Yetman, Berghorn, and Thomas (1982), racial participation rates in men's and women's college basketball changed dramatically. In 1948, only 1% of all players at predominantly White institutions were African American. Participation increased to 45% in 1975 and 49% in 1985, and the greatest increases were found in colleges located in the southeastern United States. Although participation improved for African American women athletes, as late as 1985, fewer than one fourth of all women players were African American (Berghorn et al., 1988). According to Siegel (1994), African American females made up 5.3% of all college students during 1992–93. It was important to note the African American female athletes represented 2.1% of all African American females. The African American female athletes tended to be found primarily in basketball (42%) and track and field/cross-country (41%) (Siegel, 1994).

It would be logical to conclude that the increased female participation would impact coaching opportunities for African American females. In fact, between 1948 and 1985, the number of African American assistant coaches increased more and more rapidly than did the number of head coaches. It is disturbing to note that only 3% of all NCAA women's teams had African American head coaches. Acosta and Carpenter's (1990b) longitudinal study of women in intercollegiate sport showed a dramatic increase in participation rates by African Americans but also reported a significant decline in female coaches and administrators. Acosta and Carpenter (1990a & 1994) argued convincingly that the decline of female leadership in athletics is a result of (a) the success of the old-boy network, (b) the weakness of the

old-girl network, and (c) lack of support systems for females. Acosta and Carpenter (1998) updated their original research on women in intercollegiate sport (1977–1998) by concluding that 47.4% of the coaches of women's teams are females, down from 47.7% in 1986 and 58.2% in 1978. In addition, the researchers found that women hold 59.8% of the 6,767 paid assistant coaching positions for women's teams. On a very discouraging note, 19.4% of all women's programs were headed by a female administrator.

The decline in the number of female head coaches led George (1989) to say, "as men replace women as coaches of women, the coaching profession is viewed increasingly as a nontraditional vocational field for women" (p. 6). More recent data continue to suggest that opportunities for women to gain upward mobility to coaching, officiating, and administrating remain limited, especially for the African American women. Racism, sexism, and structural barriers make it very difficult to gain access to high-quality programs (Eitzen & Sage, 1989). Knoppers (1989, 1992) reminds us that we must not overlook the structural causes of inequity and the institutionalization of sexism in sport. Reinforcing the point, Acosta and Carpenter (1998) found the percentage of women coaching men's teams stands at 2%.

However, conditions for African American women in NCAA leadership positions continue to deteriorate. In 1993, a national forum was organized to examine discrimination complaints by Black women in college sport (Blum, 1993). African American women at this conference echoed that they face discrimination based on their gender and race. As of January 1, 1999, there is only one African American female athletic director at an NCAA Division I institution (Vivian L. Fuller, initially at Tennessee State University, now at Northeastern Illinois University). James L. Whalen, president of Ithaca College, stated, "Black women bear the consequences of having the opportunities and the least amount of support" (Blum, 1993, p. A39).

Equal access for African American females to the coaches, ranks has moved slowly. In the spring of 1994, the top ten African American females in NCAA Division I included C. Vivian Stringer, University of Iowa; Marian Washington, University of Kansas (first Black female at a predominantly White college; Cheryl Miller, University of Southern California; Jessica Kenlow, University of Houston; Charlene Curtis, Temple University; and Marianna Freeman, Syracuse University ("Women Basketball Coaches," 1994). In 1997, Vivian Fuller was hired as athletic director at Tennessee State University, thus becoming the first African American female to head a NCAA Division I program that supports football. Nonetheless, the BCA remains concerned about the lack of African American women holding coaching and athletic administrative positions ("Black Coaches Association," 1994).

R. E. Lapchick and Matthews's (1997) extensive analysis of Division I, II, and III athletics revealed some rather alarming data. The authors found African American women coached 1.5% (106) of the 6,881 college women's teams. At the Division III level, 3.3% of the women's teams were coached by African Americans. These and other data permitted the authors to conclude that college sports has the worst record of all for hiring practices for women and people of color.

Discrimination: Underrepresentation

The representation of African American males coaching in college basketball has been hotly debated in college ranks, and the NCAA has been credited with taking positive steps to reduce disparities in recruitment and to correct inequalities found in association with the head coaching position, but reviews of the NCAA initiatives yield mixed results. In interviews of college coaches and administrators, Charles Farrell (1987a) found disparity with the NCAA's efforts to hire more African American coaches. For example, hiring data showed the following:

1. Only two athletic directors in the 105 member Division IA are Black.
2. No major college athletic conference, except those composed of Black colleges, has a Black commissioner.
3. Three head football coaches in Division IA are Black.
4. About 25 of the head basketball coaches at the 273 predominantly White institutions in Division I are Black (Farrell, 1987a).

Surveying the employment efforts of the NCAA, Wulf (1987) concluded that the NCAA had a poor record in minority hiring. Dent (1987) maintained that the NCAA's poor record is tied to racism. Dent reported on an interview with Peay (a former offensive lineman for the Kansas City Chiefs), "You've got influential people in booster clubs and alumni organizations, and it's very hard for an athletic director to go to them and recommend that an assistant coach be promoted to head coach to fill a vacancy" (Dent, 1987, p. 34). These institutional barriers prevent African American assistant coaches from becoming head coaches. Conditions led Shropshire (1996) to say, "In the harshest of terms, the sport industry resembles a Black-bottomed pyramid: large number of African American participants, but few African Americans in non-playing positions at the highest levels" (p. 456).

The view from the top is a little different. Charles Harris, athletic director at Arizona State, does not believe the lack of African American head coaches is due to racism. In his estimate, employment opportunities are tied to previous coaching success and the ability to establish network ties among other professionals that would be used to establish career paths that currently do not exist for African Americans (C. S. Farrell, 1987b). Charlie Harris and Rudy Washington reiterated the belief that the problem is "getting to the mainstream" and "there are no feeder systems for athletic departments" (Krasnow, 1988, p. 11). In effect, slow turnover in the college coaching ranks makes it very difficult for African Americans to work their way up the coaching-mobility ladder. Thus, the lasting effects of racism and oppression still produce discrimination and barriers to success, whether the discrimination is regarded as intentional or not.

The NCAA claims to be taking positive steps to identify and establish policy and guidelines to deal with the underrepresentation of African Americans in NCAA coaching and managerial positions. One action has been to establish an NCAA subcommittee in 1988 to review and promote minority opportunities in college athletics. For the first time this subcommittee surveyed the current status of minorities in the NCAA across Divisions I, II, and III. The data (NCAA, 1988) collected from 74 Division IA institutions, 51 institutions from Division IAA, and 54 IAAA schools revealed that African Americans hold six percent of full-time administrative positions (athletic directors, sport information directors, ticket managers, equipment managers, business managers), that two percent of full-time administrators at the conference level are African American, and that African Americans hold approximately five percent of the full-time men's head coaching positions and about five percent of full-time head coaching positions of women's teams.

The minorities' report showed a different pattern for African Americans in the assistant coaching ranks, especially in men's basketball. Across NCAA Divisions I, II, and III, African American men hold 29% of all assistant coaching positions in basketball and 47% of the full-time assistant coaching positions in cross-country in Division IA.

The survey concluded on a discouraging note, suggesting that mechanisms to promote minority participation in college athletics will be getting worse. The survey showed that very few African American graduate and undergraduate students are involved in any of the athletic administrative positions that would be essential to building the basis for leadership in colleges and universities: "The only identifi-able pool of talent from which to draw minority applicants within collegiate athletics administration is composed of the student-athletes themselves" (NCAA, 1988, p. 1).

In summary, the arguments found in the literature attempting to justify the lack of African Americans in NCAA Division I coaching and leadership positions were as follows: (a) complacency on the part of NCAA athletic directors to recruit and hire African Americans, (b) super "O" expectations by hiring administrators that African Americans have to have significantly more talent and greater experience when compared to their White counterparts, (c) lack of alumni support to hire African Americans to sport leadership positions, and (d) lack of qualified African American applicants available to fill the number of limited vacant positions (Brooks & Althouse, 1999).

After a comprehensive review of the literature, Brooks and Althouse (1999) were able to conclude that head coaching and administrative career-mobility paths of African American men and women differ significantly from those of their White counterparts. The authors were able to identify structural and behavioral barriers to success: differentiated salary structures, old-boy and old-girl networks, chilly campus climate, tokenism, stereotyping, and sexism and racism on campus. College administrators must develop strategies to redress the inequalities identified above.

In conclusion, although there have been some marginal gains, NCAA football continues to lag behind in the hiring of African American head coaches. Reed (1990) said, "There is the persistent notion that football is less a Black coach's sport than basketball is" (p. 138). Reporting in the *Chicago Tribune,* Al Gonzales (athletic director at New Mexico State University and one of only two Hispanic athletic directors) said,

There are a lot of talented Black coaches out there, . . . being totally honest, you're looking at these coaches and you know that some of them aren't sorry to get an opportunity, aren't going to be looked at because they're Black. (quoted in Wojciechowski, 1997, p. 11)

Strategies for Change

The BCA recognized the paucity of African Americans in head coaching and other managerial positions in the NCAA. Rudy Washington, first executive director said,

"What initially motivated me to form an association was 15 years of frustration. I've been in the game in various capacities on different levels: as a head coach, as an assistant, and as an administrator. I've watched my (White) colleagues obtain jobs that I know and know I'm qualified for, and I don't even get a phone call for an interview . . . and still haven't after a year of success with the association. Sharing these thoughts with other frustrated Black coaches became the basis for the BCA creation." (Quoted in Ivey, 1988, p. 1)

The BCA, a voluntary, nonprofit organization, was primarily created to deal directly with minority issues in sports. Issues included the stereotyping of minority coaches and administrators, the lack of minorities in key decision-making roles and the lack of media coverage. In 1987, members of the BCA met with the NCAA executive director to request a review of minority opportunities in college athletics. The association leadership took the position that if the NCAA is committed to increasing the number of Black coaches, institutions have to get away from the buddy system and use affirmative action plans. Membership in the BCA has grown from over 2,000 in 1988 to over 3,000 in 1991, and the association has been able to establish lines of communication with the NCAA to establish a job-line assisting with the identification of potential head coaches. The BCA has broadened its base of support away from NCAA Division I concerns and now includes NCAA Division II and III coaches. Association structure continues to ex-

pand, and BCA chapters (based on five geographical regions in America) are organized to address mainly issues on the local level. Chapter officers include president, vice-president, secretary, and treasurer. Each chapter is governed by the BCA constitution, which states, "the Black Coaches Association shall be dedicated to the logical, reasonable, and natural investigation and application of methods to reconcile the disparity of head coaching positions, administrative and decision making rules of Black coaches in comparison to their majority culture counterparts." (The Constitution of the Black Coaches Association, 1987, p. 1)

Membership in the BCA continues to escalate to a point when nearly 600 delegates attended the 1996 BCA annual meeting May 23–25, 1996, in Orlando, Florida. This was the largest attendance at this conference in its history since 1987.

More recently, the BCA has expanded its advocacy role to redress issues of gender equality, athletic eligibility, Propositions 16 and 48, and the hiring of African American graduate assistants. Stating their propositions are not in the best interest of African American youth who desire to attend college, the association has publicly gone on record to repeal Proposition 16 and 48.

The BCA gained national prominence in 1993 when it voted to boycott an "issues forum" conference organized by the National Association of Basketball Coaches. The purpose of the boycott was to draw national attention to the lack of African Americans in NCAA administrative positions.

The congressional Black Caucus initially failed to moderate this impasse, and the BCA threatened to boycott basketball games (Davis, 1995). Wolff (1994) reported that the boycott became realized when the NCAA voted in 1994 to decrease the number of men's basketball scholarships. It is important to understand that the BCA agenda also called for the addition of minorities to NCAA coaching staffs and made a request for the NCAA to reconsider the mandates of Propositions 42 and 48

(Wolff, 1994). Reporting in the March 1994 edition of the *BCA Journal*, the BCA met with the NCAA to mediate the following concerns:

1. Academic standards for eligibility
2. Gender Equity concern that gender equity would have a negative impact on African American females
3. Limited access to student-athletes at issue, current rules that preclude coaches from being role models and mentors to African American youth
4. Minority opportunities in athletics, an on-going concern given the following data (3 Divison I head football coaches, 6 athletic directors [1 female], 22 female Division I head women's basketball coaches) ("Black Coaches Association Takes Stand," 1994).

The congressional Black Caucus continued to meet to resolve the differences between the NCAA and the BCA. After much debate, on March 23, 1994, the NCAA and the BCA signed an agreement that was mediated by the U.S. Department of Justice. The agreement contained some of the following statements:

1. The NCAA was to review its commitment to ensuring as a primary goal the significant participation by Blacks and other ethnic minorities in every aspect of NCAA governance.
2. Legislation to allow student-athletes who were partial qualifiers and nonqualifiers to earn a fourth year of eligibility would be presented to the NCAA Council and President's Commission for their consideration.
3. Progress to increase the participation of Black, ethnic minorities and females in sports would be enhanced.
4. The goals set forth in this agreement were to be maintained.

Davis (1995) concluded that this agreement was important because it set governing principles providing a framework for future discussion between the BCA and NCAA.

The BCA remains committed to eradicating social injustice for African Americans in col-

lege athletics. In 1996, the association began to discuss how the proposed restructuring of the NCAA would impact minorities, and the growing trend of high school seniors and underclassmen leaving college prior to graduation and declaring their desire to play professional basketball, and the increasing problems associated with sport agents on the college campus ("Black Coaches Association," 1996).

The Rainbow Coalition for Fairness in Athletics, founded in 1993 by the Reverend Jesse Jackson, began to work with the BCA to monitor college hiring practices. In 1994, the Rainbow Coalition developed the "seven point diversity and affirmative action plan" to specifically assess progress Division I NCAA institutions were making in the areas of graduation roles, number of head coaches, and number of minority vendors doing business with athletic departments ("Rainbow Coalition Develops Diversity Plan for Institutions, 1994). The Coalition continues to support annual conferences highlighting issues facing African American student-athletes, coaches, and administrators.

Brooks et al. (1989) concluded that the BCA was meeting stated goals clearly:

• To strengthen commitment to diversity within the membership of the NCAA;
• To create professional development seminars and workshops for BCA members;
• To encourage and solicit support for the enhancement of opportunities for minorities in athletics from other sports and non-sports organizations;
• To assist members in their foundation of career development strategies; and
• To keep the membership and the general public informed of relevant BCA activities.

("The History of the Black Coaches Association," 1997, p. 1)

The association continues to (a) use (gather) statistical data to show the need to hire more Black head coaches and (b) make institutions aware that Blacks are more than just performers on the field, that they have head coaching ability.

Change is on the horizon, though, as the political base of the association has expanded to include Division II, III, junior college and high school coaches (African American and White). The BCA is gaining recognition as a major advocate for social justice issues in intercollegiate athletics, and it has the potential to affect policy decision making and implementation affecting the future status of African Americans in college sport.

The role of advocate for social justice in college athletics goes beyond that of the BCA. The Center for the Study of Sport in Society has assumed a major leadership role in this area. R. E. Lapchick (1989), director, has also recognized the lack of African Americans in head coaching and other administrative positions as an issue facing African American athletes in the 1990s. He offered the following suggestions and recommendations to increase the number of African American head coaches:

1. More Blacks must become college presidents and athletic directors.
2. Black head coaches should be represented in all sports.
3. The number of Black assistant coaches must be increased.
4. Support for the BCA must continue.
5. The NCAA vita bank for minorities and women must be supported.
6. Sport information directors should be more aware of stereotypes of minorities (Lapchick, 1989).

Lapchick does not offer the reader a detailed plan on how to implement his six recommendations to increase the number of African American head coaches. We suggest there are two fundamental issues, internal organization of college sport and multiculturalism/pluralism, that must be understood and addressed if Lapchick's recommendations are going to be realized:

1. How is the organization of college sport tied to wealth (revenue vs. nonrevenue sport status), career, and professional achievement? Teachers, coaches, and administrators must gain insights into where African American

players and coaches came from. One could argue that classism, manifested in the form of the amount of resources spent on revenue sport as compared to nonrevenue sport, exists in college sport. This is of particular importance because a significant number of African American male athletes are recruited to play for revenue (football, basketball) teams.

2. A broader base for understanding racism in college athletics must include all ethnic minorities and not be limited to discussion of the African American athlete. Over the next several decades, more and more ethnic minorities will be seeking and gaining access to colleges and universities. These individuals will be competing with African Americans for playing and coaching positions.

The United States is becoming a nation of diverse cultures, and as a consequence, no real study of racism and dominance can be undertaken without including the various groups who participate on the various NCAA teams. Unfortunately, the experiences and achievements of individuals found within the various ethnic groups are missing from the sport sociology and history literature. A multicultural approach to critiquing racism in college sport would lead to a better understanding and appreciation of cultural diversity. In summary, the African American experience in college sport has been, and will continue to be, shaped by the structure of the NCAA. As people of color, African Americans share opportunities and potential liabilities for participating in college sport.

Expend Personal Acquaintances

Strategies to increase the number of African Americans in college leadership positions must first begin with an understanding of the political economy of college athletics. The ability of an assistant coach to achieve upward mobility is tied directly to the success of the head coach. If assistant coaches are going to achieve upward mobility, they must begin to develop acquaintance networks to help them gain head coaching positions. Athletic directors need to be in the network of personal acquaintances for assistant coaches. Athletic directors are a very important part of the recruiting process, and they ultimately make the decision to hire the head coach.

Future strategies and innovations must also take into consideration the plight of the African American female. Very few women occupy leadership positions at the high school or college level.

Green, Oglesby, Alexander, and Franke (1981) took a futuristic look at the role of the African American female athletes in the year 2000. They believed that African American females would find it necessary to create jobs in the African American community to gain the necessary skills to compete in the national market, and they advocated the establishment of coaching camps and clinics in the African American community. These camps would serve as internship programs and training camps to develop leadership skills.

Given the data and information presented in this essay, we do not believe we are going to see a significant increase in the number of African Americans (men and women) in leadership positions until we begin to address the social issues facing African Americans and other low socioeconomic families. Our school systems must develop and enhance programs to increase the high school graduation rate and college entrance and graduation rates of ethnic minorities. Once on campus, we must begin to address the chilly climate faced by African Americans and women. African American students in predominantly White institutions are apt to feel different from other students, feel isolated from other students, and feel racial isolation and discrimination (American Institute for Research, 1989).

A historical overview from 1972 to the present suggests that African Americans and other persons of color have experienced an unequal path through the education system, especially higher education. In 1972, African American students constituted 8.4% of the full-time un-dergraduate enrollment, but 4 years later, they received only 6.4% of the baccalaureate degrees (Watson, 1979). The data relative to high school graduation rates and going-to-college rates are very disturbing. From 1976 to 1988, the high school graduation rates for African Americans increased; however, the college participation rate dropped from 40% to 30% for low-income African American high school graduates and from 53% to 36% for middle-income African Americans (Carter & Wilson, 1989). The decrease in college participation may be due to the following factors: a reduction in available financial aid from the federal government, the high number of African Americans who fail to graduate, and weak educational foundations (Allen, 1988).

Increasing the high school and college graduation rates for African Americans should be a high priority. One of the many possible outcomes of this action would be a potentially larger recruiting pool from which to identify sport leaders.

Currently, there are several unique programs throughout the United States that could be modified to assist with the identification and development of coaching ability.

National Youth Sport Program

The National Youth Sport Program was organized in 1979 to provide economically disadvantaged youngsters between the ages of 10 and 16 with sport skills, drug awareness, and career advising.

Project directors and activities coordinators of these programs are encouraged to invite sport leaders (coaches, athletic directors) to their camps addressing career opportunities in college sport. As a follow-up, the NCAA and the state high school athletic federations host regional conferences/workshops, invite nationally known sport figures, and further explore career opportunities in college athletics. This particular recommendation builds on the existing National Youth Sport network structure.

After reviewing the data, the NCAA Subcommittee to Review Minority Opportunities concluded that the NCAA's member institutions need to address the lack of minorities in leadership positions. The NCAA Minority Enhancement Scholarship and Internship Programs were established by the NCAA to increase the pool of potential NCAA leaders.

The postgraduate scholarship program was designed to increase the potential pool of minorities pursuing and graduating with degrees in the field of sport administration. Ten scholarships are awarded annually to women and ethnic minorities. The internship program provides minorities the opportunity to gain on-the-job training at the NCAA national headquarters. Finally, the NCAA Ethnic Minority and Women's Vita Bank assists colleges and the private sector in identifying candidates to fill job vacancies.

Role of College Presidents

College presidents and athletic directors have a major role to perform in increasing the number of African Americans in leadership positions in college athletics. They can establish affirmative action goals and establish policies and procedures to enhance opportunities for African Americans. Shropshire (1996) identified four affirmative action strategies:

1. Make a focused effort to recruit members of the underrepresented group(s).
2. Utilize diversity and sensitivity training programs.
3. If necessary, modify employment practices that may tend to underutilize minority members.
4. Move towards preferential hiring and promotion of members of underrepresented groups.

The author does conclude that strategies must be developed (and supported by college presidents) that open up hiring networks. We support Shropshire's (1996) positions and suggest presidents play a major role in establishing affirmative action goals and strategies and in holding athletic departments responsible for meeting these goals.

In addition it is recommended that all Division I NCAA institutions appoint a senior-level minority athletic administrator and staff member. This would be a major administrative position with responsibility for overseeing student-athlete success, budget authority, staff evaluation, and public relations. The proposed model is based on the concept of the currently existing Senior Women's Administrator role.

Summary

College and high school sport are often viewed as two of the most responsive of many integrating mechanisms now active in American society. Yet from 1947 (when Jackie Robinson played for the Dodgers) until 1967, few African Americans participated or coached at the college level. After 1968, the increase in participation rates of African Americans can be attributed to a change in social climate, the Civil Rights movement, and recruitment policies (which view college athletics as big business). Sport provided an avenue for mobility for African Americans both socially and economically. The route followed by many African American athletes has been the early development of physical skills in order to get out of the ghetto and succeed professionally.

In this essay, the authors chose to identify and describe factors that explain the absence of African Americans in head coaching positions. Race, athletic participation, the ability to mobilize resources, the impact of structural barriers (i.e., conference affiliation, type of institution, and success of the program), and career mobility patterns were identified as variables influencing the coaching mobility process at the college level.

During the 1960s and 1970s, a large volume of research was conducted to determine the relationship between athletic playing position and racial discrimination. The early research papers utilized sociological theory as the conceptual basis for understanding segregation in American sport.

Literature revealed that coaching and managerial positions in college sports organizations are for the most part exclusively in the White domain. The absence of African Americans in head coaching positions, especially at NCAA Division I institutions, may be related to discrimination in recruiting at the college ranks, known as stacking. Stacking refers to situations in which African Americans are relegated to specific team positions (such as wide receiver and defensive back) and excluded from competing for others (quarterback). As a result, African Americans compete against other African Americans for a limited number of team positions. A number of theories (psychological and sociological) have been postulated in an attempt to explain this phenomenon.

The stereotype hypothesis has been one of the most widely accepted explanations for stacking in American college sport. The hypothesis states that White coaches believe that African Americans lack the leadership ability necessary to occupy control or leadership positions. One of the consequences of positional segregation, or stacking, is the relationship found between subsequent coaching mobility and previous position played. A high percentage of college coaches and administrators were recruited from central positions.

This finding suggests that White and African American coaches were thrust along different career paths to achieve coaching success. Coaching career mobility avenues were also developed in an attempt to describe these differential paths.

The personal attribute avenue holds that coaches gain upward mobility to the head coaching ranks as they acquire the attributes necessary to perform the duties of head coach. Communication skills, cultural values, administrative support, experience, and public image were identified as important characteristics of coaches. African American coaches also held the notion that selected personal attributes were directly associated with coaching success.

The personal attribute avenue could not explain that the majority of the African American coaches perceived they had the necessary personal attributes to become head coaches, yet remained assistant coaches. A possible explanation was that African Americans were hired primarily to recruit other African American athletes. The role of recruiter does not permit assistant coaches to gain the knowledge and experience necessary to become head coaches.

Career coaching-mobility patterns of college coaches demonstrated specific geographical movement patterns. The majority of White coaches attended colleges in their home states or bordering states. Likewise, African American coaches attended colleges in their home NCAA districts. The vast majority of the African American coaches came from the southeastern United States.

The demographic explanation viewed coaching mobility in terms of spatial production and consumption. Understanding geographical movement patterns of coaches was useful because it first specified sport regions and then identified such factors as the proportion of coaches recruited to various colleges and universities. Nonetheless, demographic analysis represented a somewhat simplistic causal relationship between coaching mobility and geographical regions.

None of the avenues presented in this essay could clearly explain the coaching-mobility patterns of coaches (White or African American). The career-coaching paths followed by individual head coaches were unique. It is impossible to conclude that the ability to negotiate various career stages successfully will lead to a head coaching career.

The essay does conclude that since 1954, the number of head African American coaches and assistant coaches in the NCAA did increase. This was especially true for NCAA basketball. The increase in the number of African American head coaches has been associated with the number of African Americans participating in college sport. Member institutions of the NCAA have taken steps to identify and establish policies to address the lack of African Americans in NCAA coaching positions.

Since 1986, African American head coaches have begun moving into positions of coaching and building their own recruiting and "stem-and-branch" structures. African American head coaches are strongly encouraged to hire other African American assistant coaches. This practice should result in increasing the pool of available African American coaches.

Throughout this essay we have documented that African American males and females have been underemployed and underrepresented in college athletic leadership positions. We do not believe America will witness a significant increase in the number of African Americans in leadership positions until we address the low high school graduation, college entrance and graduation rates of African Americans. Further, we must address the chilly climate faced by many African American students who attend predominantly White institutions.

Establishment of affirmative action policies and procedures has not been successful in changing the hiring practices of NCAA member institutions. College presidents, athletic directors, coaches, athletes, and faculty must engage in a program of social justice and equity if we are going to see changes in hiring and promotion practices as we look towards the next century.

We may be witnessing a redefinition in the display and control of collegiate sports and be on the edge of an NCAA athletic transformation: a rejection of old solutions and advocacy of those who have the most to gain (administrators, coaches, students). Normal practice is no longer going to be accepted by university administrators. This is the vision for change.

Suggested Readings

American Institute for Research. (1989). *The experiences of Black intercollegiate athletes at NCAA Division I institutions (Report No. 3).* Palo Alto, CA: Author.

Berghorn, F. J., Yetman, N., & Hanna, W. C. (1988). Racial participation and integration in men's and women's intercollegiate basketball: Continuity and change, 1958–1985. *Sociology of Sport Journal, 5* (20), 107–124.

Brooks, D., Althouse, R., & Tucker, D. (1997). African American male head coaches: In the "red zone," but can they score? *Journal of African American Men, 2*(213), 93–112.

Latimer, S., & Mathes, S. (1985). Black college football coaches social, educational, athletic and career pattern characteristics. *Journal of Sport Behavior, 8* (3), 149–162.

Study Questions

1. What factors explain the dearth of African American male and female NCAA head coaches and athletic administrators?
2. Discuss the relationship between athletic playing position (stacking), social discrimination, stereotyping, and career-mobility patterns of African American coaches.
3. Discuss how the following variables influence athletic coaching career patterns: migration patterns, athletic prestige of the colleges from which coaches graduated, old-boy networks, personal attributes of coaches, alumni support, and acquaintance networks.
4. What initiatives have the Black Coaches Association, the Rainbow Coalition, and the Study of Sport in Society recommended or established to increase the number of African American head coaches?

References

Acosta, R. V., & Carpenter, L. J. (1990a). *Perceived causes of the declining representation of women leaders in intercollegiate sport 1988 update.* (ERIC Document Reproduction Service No. ED 314 381)

Acosta, R. V., & Carpenter, L. J. (1990b, February). *Women in intercollegiate sport: A longitudinal study thirteen year update 1977–1990.* Paper presented at the Symposium for Girls and Women in Sports, Slippery Rock University, Slippery Rock, PA.

Acosta, R. V., & Carpenter, L. J. (1994). The status of women in intercollegiate athletics. In Birrell & Cole (Eds.), *Women, sport and culture* (pp.111–118). University of Illinois at Urbana-Champaign: Human Kinetics.

Acosta R. V., & Carpenter, L. J. (1998). *Women in intercollegiate sport: A longitudinal study—twenty-one year update (1977–1998)*. Unpublished paper, Department of Physical Education and Exercise Science, Brooklyn, NY.

Addis, A. (1993). "Hell man, they did invent us," the mass media, law, and African Americans. *Buffalo Law Review, 41*, 519–565.

Allen, W. R. (1988). Black students in U.S. higher education: Toward improved access, adjustment, and achievement. *The Urban Review, 20*, 165–188.

American Institute for Research. (1989). *Report No. 3: The experiences of Black intercollegiate athletes at NCAA Division I institutions*. Palo Alto, CA: Author.

And then there were none. (1992, January 29). *The Chronicle of Higher Education*.

Anderson, D. (1993). Cultural diversity on campus: A look at intercollegiate football coaches. *Journal of Sport and Social Issues, 17*(1), 61–66.

Anderson, K. (1992, September 28). No room at the top. *Sports Illustrated, 77*(10), 62.

Ball, D., & Loy, J. (1975). *Sport and social order: Contributions to the sociology of sport*. Reading, MA: Addison Wesley Publishing Company.

Banks, O. (1979). How Black coaches view entering the job market at major colleges. *Journal of Physical Education and Recreation, 50*, 62.

Bell, D. (1992). *Faces at the bottom of the well: The permanence of racism*. New York: Basic Books.

Berghorn, F. J., Yetman, N., & Hanna, W.C. (1988). Racial participation and integration in men's and women's intercollegiate basketball: Continuity and change, 1958–1985. *Sociology of Sport Journal, 5*(20), 107–124.

Best, C. (1987). Experience and career length in professional football: The effect of positional segregation. *Sociology of Sport Journal, 4*, 410–420.

Birrell, S. (1989). Racial relations theories and sport: Suggestions for a more critical analysis. *Sociology of Sport Journal, 6*, 212–227.

Black access, white flight: Where are they taking sports in the USA? (1991, December 19). *USA Today*, p. 9C.

Black coaches accept big college basketball jobs. (1983, April 25). *Jet*, 46.

Black Coaches Association concludes successful annual meeting. (1996, May 29). BCA news release.

Black Coaches Association takes stand against NCAA. (1994, March). *BCA Journal, 2*(1), 1.

Black head coaches: Taking charge in major campuses. (1982, May). *Ebony*, 57–62.

Blalock, H. M. (1962). Occupational discrimination: Some theoretical propositions. *Social Problems, 9*, 240–247.

Blalock, H. M. (1967). *Toward a theory of minority group relations*. New York: John Wiley and Sons.

Boeck, G., & Shuster, R. (1991, March 19). College "old boy network" hard to crack. *USA Today*, p. 11A.

A boom in Black coaches. (1986, April). *Ebony*, pp. 59–62.

Braddock, J. H. (1980). Race, sports and social mobility: A critical review. *Sociological Symposium, 30*, 17–38.

Brooks, D., & Althouse, R. (1999). The African American coaching experience: A case of social injustice? Trends and issues affecting ethnic minorities in health, physical education, recreation, and dance. AAHPERD: Reston, VA.

Brooks, D., Althouse, R., & Brown, R. (1990, March). *Black coaching mobility: An investigation of the stem and branch structural model*. Paper presented at the North Central Sociology meeting, Louisville, KY.

Brooks, D., Althouse, R., King, V., & Brown, R. (1989). Opportunities for coaching achievement and the Black experience: Have we put marginality into the system? *Proceedings of the 32nd Annual ICHPERD Conference*, 246–254.

Brooks, D., Althouse, R., & Tucker, D. (1997). African American male head coaches: In the "red zone," but can they score? *Journal of African American Men, 2*(213), 93–112.

Buhrman, H. G. (1971). Scholarship and athletics in junior high school. *International Review of Sport Sociology, 7*, 119–128.

Campbell, R. M. (1995, October 9). Five new division I football coaches unbeaten so far. *The NCAA News, 32*(35), 10.

Carter, D., & Wilson, R. (1989). *Eighth annual status report: Minorities in higher education*. Washington, DC: American Council on Education.

Ceiling breakers: Black coaches. (1997). *BCA Journal, 1*(4), 14.

Christiano, K. J. (1986). Salary discrimination in Major League Baseball: The effect of race. *Sociology of Sport Journal, 3*, 144–153.

Christiano, K. J. (1988). Salaries and race in professional baseball: Discrimination 10 years later. *Sociology of Sport Journal, 5*, 136–149.

Chu, D. B., & Segrave, J. O. (1981). Leadership and ethnic stratification in basketball. *Journal of Sport and Social Issues, 5*(1), 15–32.

Coakley, J. J. (1986). *Sport in society: Issues and controversies* (3rd ed.). St. Louis: Times Mirror/ Mosby.

Coleman, J. (1961). *The adolescent society.* New York: Free Press.

Collins, R. (1975). *Conflict sociology: Toward an explanatory science.* New York: Academic Press.

Curtis, J. E., & Loy, J. W. (1978a). Positional segregation in professional baseball: Replication, trend data and critical observation. *International Review of Sport Sociology, 4*, 5–21.

Curtis, J. E., & Loy, J. W. (1978b). Race/ethnicity and relative centrality of playing positions in team sports. *Exercise and Sport Science Review, 6*, 285–313.

Davis, J. (1994). Intercollegiate athletics: Competing models and conflicting realities. *Rutgers Law Journal, 25*(2), 270–327.

Davis, J. (1995). The myth of the superspade: the persistence of racism in college athletics. *Fordham Urban Law Journal, 22*(3), 615–698.

DeFranz, A. (1991, August 12). We've got to be strong: The obstacles facing Black women in sports have scarcely diminished with time. *Sports Illustrated, 75*(7), 77.

Dent, D. (1987). Black coaches remain scarce in college ranks. *Black Enterprise, 18*(5), 112.

Edwards, H. (1969). *The revolt of the Black athlete.* New York: Free Press.

Edwards, H. (1973). *Sociology of sport.* Homewood, IL: Daisy Press.

Edwards, H. (1979b, September). Sport within the veil: The triumphs, tragedies, and challenges of Afro-American involvement. *Annals, AAPSS, 445,* 116–127.

Edwards, H. (1982a). On the issue of race in contemporary American sports. *Western Journal of Black Studies, 6*(3), 138–144.

Edwards, H. (1982b). Race in contemporary American sports. *Phi Kappa Phi Journal, 62*(1), 19–22.

Edwards, H. (1987). Race in contemporary America. In A. Yiannakis, T. McIntyre, M. Melnick, & D. Hart (Eds.), *Sports in sport sociology: Contemporary themes* (3rd ed., pp. 194–202). Kendall/Hunt Publishing Company.

Eitzen, D. S., & Furst, D. (1989). Racial bias in women's collegiate volleyball. *Journal of Sport and Social Issues, 13*(1), 46–51.

Eitzen, D. S., & Sage, G. H. (1989). *Sociology of North American sport* (4th ed.). Dubuque, IA: Wm. C. Brown.

Eitzen, D. S., & Sanford, D. (1975). The segregation of Blacks by playing positions in football: Accident or design? *Social Science Quarterly, 55,* 948–959.

Eitzen, D. S., & Tessendorf, I. (1978). Racial segregation by position in sports: The special case of basketball. *Review of Sport & Leisure, 3*(1), 109–128.

Eitzen, D. S., & Yetman, N. R. (1977). Immune from racism. *Civil Rights Digest, 9*, 3–13.

Fabianic, D. (1984). Minority managers in professional baseball. *Sociology of Sport Journal, 1*(2), 163–171.

Farrell, C. S. (1987, September 23). NCAA effort to spur Black coach hirings gets mixed reviews. *The Chronicle of Higher Education*, pp. 39–40.

Farrell, C. S. (1987b, May 6). Scarcity of Blacks in top jobs in college sports prompts founding of group to monitor hiring. *The Chronicle of Higher Education*, pp. 40–42.

Farrell, C. S. (1994, September 22) NCAA: blacks make the plays but call few of the shots. *Black Issues in Higher Education, 11*(15), 34–36.

Farrell, C. S. (1995, September 7). Progress yet, but. . . . *Black Issues in Higher Education, 12,* 32–34.

Freischlag, J., & Jacob, R. (1988). Developmental factors among college men basketball coaches. *Journal of Applied Research in Coaching and Athletics, 3*(2), 87–93.

George, J. J. (1989). Finding solutions to the problem of fewer female coaches. *The Physical Educator, 46*(1), 2–5.

Green, T. S., Oglesby, C., Alexander, A., & Franke, N. (1981). *Black women in sport.* Reston, VA: AAHPERD.

Grenfell, C., & Freischlag, J. (1989, April). *Developmental pathways of men's and women's college basketball coaches.* Paper presented at the AAHPERD Convention, Boston, MA.

Grusky, O. (1963). The effects of formal structure on managerial recruitment: A study of baseball organization. *Sociometry, 26*, 345–353.

Hanks, M. P., & Eckland, B. K. (1976). Athletics and social participation in the educational attainment process. *Sociology of Education, 49*, 271–294.

Hill, O. F. (1997). Career opportunities or restricting employment barriers? The hiring patterns and experiences of Black football coaches at NCAA

Division IA colleges and universities. *BCA Journal*, *4*, 89, 14.

The history of the Black Coaches Association. (1997). *BCA Journal*, *1*(4), 1.

Ivey, L. (1988, Winter). An interview with Rudy Washington. *BCA Journal*, *1*, 45.

Johnson, W. O. (1991, August 5). A matter of black and white: An SI survey of professional athletes revealed some of the deep divisions between the races. *Sports Illustrated*, *75*(6), 44–58.

Jones, G. A., Leonard, W. M., Schmitt, R. L., Smith, D. R., & Tolone, W. L. (1987). Racial discrimination in college football. *Social Science Quarterly*, *68*, 1, 783.

Kane, M. (1971, January). An assessment of black is best. *Sports Illustrated*, *34*(2), 72–83.

Keegan, T., & Towle, M. (1991, January 17). Black coaches on the rise. *The National Sports Daily*.

Knoppers, A. (1989, March). Coaching: An equal opportunity occupation? *Journal of Physical Education, Recreation and Dance*, *60*(3), 38–43.

Knoppers, A. (1992, August). Exploiting male dominance and sex segregation in coaching: three approaches. *Quest*, *44*(22), 210–227.

Krasnow, S. (1988). Survey: Major colleges shun Black coaches. *Sport*, *79*(6), 11.

Lapchick, R. E. (1989, Spring). Future of the Black student athlete: Ethical issue of the 1990s. *Educational Record*, *70*, 32–35.

Lapchick, R. E., & Matthews, K. (1997, March 6). *1997 Racial Report Card*. Northwestern University Center for the Study of Sport in Society.

Latimer, S., & Mathes, S. (1985). Black college football coaches: Social, educational, athletic and career pattern characteristics. *Journal of Sport Behavior*, *8*(3), 149–162.

Lederman, D. (1988, April 13). Black coaches movement gains momentum: First annual meeting attracts 300. *The Chronicle of Higher Education*, pp. 43–44.

Leonard, W. (1986). The sports experience of black college athletes: Exploitation in the academy. *International Review for the Sociology of Sport*, *21*(1), 35–49.

Leonard, W. (1987). Stacking in college basketball: A neglected analysis. *Sociology of Sport Journal*, *4*, 403–409.

Leonard, W., & Reyman, T. (1988). The odds of attaining professional athlete status: Refining the computations. *Sociology of Sport Journal*, *5*, 162–169.

Leonard, W. M. (1977, June). Stacking and performance differentials of whites, blacks, and latins in professional baseball. *Review of Sport and Literature*, *2*, 77–106.

Leonard, W. M. (1989). Salaries and race/ethnicity in major league baseball: The pitching component. *Sociology of Sport Journal*, *6*(2), 152–162.

Loy, J. W. (1969). The study of sport and social mobility. In Gerald S. Kenyon (Ed.), *Aspect of contemporary sport sociology* (pp. 101–119). Chicago, IL: Athletic Institute.

Loy, J. W., & McElvogue, J. (1970). Racial segregation in American sport. *International Review of Sport Sociology*, *5*, 5–24.

Loy, J. W., McPherson, B., & Kenyon, G. (1978). *Sport and social systems: A guide to the analyses, problems, and literature*. Reading, MA: Addison Wesley Publishing Co.

Loy, J. W., & Sage, G. H. (1978). Athletic personnel in the academic marketplace: A study of the interorganizational mobility patterns of college coaches. *Sociology of Work and Occupation*, *5*(4), 446–449.

Massengale, J. D. (1974). Coaching as an occupational subculture. *Phi Delta Kappan*, *56*(2), 140–142.

Massengale, J. D., & Farrington, S. K. (1977). The influence of playing position centrality on the careers of college football coaches. *Review of Sport and Leisure*, *2*, 107–115.

McPherson, B. D. (1975). The segregation by playing position hypothesis in sport: An alternative explanation. *Social Science Quarterly*, *55*, 960–966.

Medoff, M. M. (1977). Position segregation and professional baseball. *International Review of Sport Sociology*, *12*(1), 49–54.

Medoff, M. M. (1986). Position segregation and the economic hypothesis. *Sociology of Sport Journal*, *3*, 297–304.

Miller, D., & Form, W. (1964). *Industrial sociology*. New York: Harper & Row.

Miller Brewing Company. (1983). *Miller Lite report on American attitudes towards sports*. Milwaukee: Author.

Mogull, R. G. (1975). Salary discrimination in Major League Baseball. *Review of Black Political Economy*, *5*, 269–279.

Money and fame: Who reaps the rewards and benefits? (1991, December 18). *USA Today*, p. 4C.

Moore, K. (1991, August 12). The eye of the storm: The lives of the U.S. Olympians who protested racism in 1968 were changed forever. *Sports Illustrated*, *75*(7), 60–66, 68, 70, 72–73.

NCAA's first black head football coach is ready to tackle the pressure. (1979, March 22). *Jet,* 48.

NCAA. (1988). Summary to the survey of NCAA member institutions and conferences on minority representation. *Report to the NCAA Council Subcommittee to Review Minority Opportunities in Intercollegiate Athletics.* Mission, KS: Author.

Naughton, J. (1998, July 3). Black athletic directors remain a rarity in NCAA's Division I. *The Chronicle of Higher Education,* pp. A29, A31.

Naughton, J. (1998). New report decries dearth of black coaches in football and basketball. *The Chronicle of Higher Education,* pp. A45–A46.

Oberlander, S. (1989, April 10). University-paid membership in all-white club ignite controversy after Tennessee hires Black head coach. *The Chronicle of Higher Education,* p. A33.

Oliver, M. L. (1980, Spring). Race, class and the family's orientation to mobility through sport. *Sociological Symposium 30,* 62–86.

Olson, J. (1968). The cruel deception. *Sports Illustrated, 29*(1), 15–17. [Part 1 of 5-part series, *The Black Athlete*].

Otto, L., & Alwin, D. (1977). Athletics, aspirations and attainments. *Sociology of Education, 42,* 102–114.

Picori, J. S. (1978). Race, athletics, achievement and educational aspirations. *The Sociological Quarterly, 19*(3), 429–438.

Rainbow Coalition develops diversity plan for institutions. (1994, November 7). *The NCAA News, 31*(40), pp. 1, 20.

Reed, W. F. (1990, November 26). Equality begins at home: It's time to give Black football coaches a chance. *Sports Illustrated, 73*(26), 138.

Rehberg, R. A., & Schafer, W. S. (1968). Participation in interscholastic athletics and college expectations. *American Journal of Sociology, 63,* 732–740.

Rooney, J. R. (1974). *A geography of American sport from Cabin Creek to Anaheim.* Reading, MA: Addison Wesley Publishing Company.

Rosenberg, E. (1980, Spring). Sports as work: Characteristics and career patterns. *Sociological Symposium, 30,* 39–61.

Rosenblatt, A. (1967). Negroes in baseball: The failing of success. *Transaction, 4,* 51–53.

Sage, G. (1980). Sociology of physical educator/coaches: Personal attributes controversy. *Research Quarterly for Exercise and Sport, 51*(1), 110–121.

Sage, G. H., & Loy, J. W. (1978). Geographical mobility patterns of college coaches. *Urban Life, 7*(2), 253–280.

Scher, J. (1991, November 4). Minority opinion: Major league job offerings aren't open to everyone. *Sports Illustrated, 75*(20), 11.

Schneider, J. J., & Eitzen, S. D. (1979). Racial discrimination in American sport: Continuity or change? *Journal of Sport Behavior, 2,* 136–142.

Shafer, W. E., & Armer, J. M. (1968, November). Athletics are not for inferior students. *Transaction, 5,* 21–26, 61–62.

Shropshire, K. L. (1996, January). Merit, ol' boy networks, and the black-bottomed pyramid. *Hasting Law Journal, 47*(2), 455–472.

Siegel, D. (1994, September). The black female scholarship athlete. *College Student Journal, 28*(3), 291–301.

Snyder, E. E., & Spreitzer, E. A. (1989). *Social aspects of sport* (3rd ed.). Englewood Cliffs, NJ: Prentice Hall.

Spady, W. G. (1970). Lament for the letterman: The effects of peer status and extracurricular activities in goals and achievements. *American Journal of Sociology, 75,* 680–702.

Sperber, M. (1990). *College sport inc.: The athletic department vs. the university.* New York: Henry Holt & Company.

Stacking: a widespread practice that determines who gets to play where. (1991, March 17) *USA Today,* p. 6C.

Stevenson, C. L. (1975). Socialization effects of participation in sports: A critical review of the research. *Research Quarterly, 46,* 287–301.

Turner, R. H. (1960). Sponsored and contest mobility in the school system. *American Sociology Review, 25,* 855–867.

USA Today poll shows blacks and whites often accept the same stereotypes about athletes. (1991, December 16). *USA Today,* p. 1.

Watson, B. C. (1979, October). Through the academic gateway. *Change, 11*(7), 24–28.

Weiberg, S. (1991, December 17). Stereotypical notions often come into play when finding athletes. *USA Today,* p. 6C.

West, C. (1994). *Race matters.* New York: Vantage Books: A Division of Random House, Inc.

Williams, R. L., & Youssef, Z. I. (1975). Division of labor in college football along racial lines. *International Journal of Sport Psychology, 6*(1), 313.

Wojciechowski, G. (1997, January 5). Going beyond the pool. *Chicago Tribune*, p. 11.

Wolff, A. (1994, January 24). In whose best interest? *Sports Illustrated*, *80*(3), 70.

Women basketball coaches: Grooming the overlooked stars of the collegiate sports world. (1994, April). *Ebony*, 122–126.

Yetman, N. R. (1987). Positional segregation and the economic hypothesis: A critique. *Sociology of Sport Journal*, *4*, 274–277.

Yetman, N. R., Berghorn, F. J., & Thomas, F. R. (1982). Racial participation and integration in intercollegiate basketball, 1958–1980. *Journal of Sport Behavior*, *5*, 44–56.

Young, D. (1990). Mentoring and networking: Perceptions by athletic administrators. *Journal of Sport Management*, *4*, 71–79.

The Glass-Ceiling Effect and African American Women Coaches and Athletic Administrators

Robertha Abney

Abstract

With the passage of affirmative action, the Civil Rights Act of 1991, and Title IX one would anticipate an increase in the status of African American women as administrators and coaches in intercollegiate athletics.

The 19-year update by Acosta and Carpenter (1996) revealed four interesting facts:

1. The number of women's teams per school is the highest it has ever been.
2. Women hold 35.9% of all administrative jobs in women's programs.
3. Of the coaches of women's teams 47.7% are females.
4. On an average, there is almost one female involved in athletic administration per school. It is unclear what percentage of these figures represent African American women and/or women of color. Research pertaining to the status of African American women as administrators is extremely limited and, perhaps, an unexplored area.

This essay will investigate the impact of the glass-ceiling effect on the status of African American women as athletic administrators and coaches in intercollegiate athletics. Suggestions for change will be discussed. Strategies and recommendations for recruiting and retaining African American women will be provided.

Key Terms

Affirmative action: A policy that seeks to ensure that individuals, regardless of their physical or personal characteristics, have fair and equal opportunities at education, employment, and promotion based on their abilities, performance or qualifications. Legislation regarding affirmative action prohibits quotas (Social Equity Office, 1997).

African American: Persons having any African ancestry, no matter how remote, are ascribed membership in the African American group (Nelson, 1982).

Athletic administrator: The various titles for the administrator who has direct oversight of and responsibility for the institution's program of intercollegiate athletics (Kinder, 1993, p. 16).

Civil Rights Act of 1991: Amendment to the Civil Rights Act of 1964 to restore and strengthen civil rights laws that banned discrimination in employment and to provide monetary remedies for victims of intentional employment discrimination (Social Equity Office,b, 1997).

Gender equity: An athletics program can be considered gender equitable when the participants in both the men's and women's sports programs would accept as fair and equitable the overall program of the other gender. No individual should be discriminated against on the basis of gender, institutionally or nationally, in intercollegiate athletics (NCAA, 1996–1997).

Glass-Ceiling effect: Organizational, attitudinal, and social barriers that effectively keep women and minorities from advancing up the career ladder (Morrison, White, Velsor, & The Center for Creative Leadership, 1987).

Title IX: No person in the United States shall, on the basis of sex, be excluded from participation in, be denied the benefits of, or be subjected to discrimination under any education program or activity receiving Federal financial assistance (NCAA, 1996–1997).

Introduction

Morrison et al. (1987) described the glass-ceiling effect as the organizational, attitudinal, and social barriers that effectively keep women and minorities from advancing up the career ladder. The glass ceiling is a more subtle form of workplace discrimination. With the increase of African American sport participants in intercollegiate athletics, the use of affirmative action guidelines, and the adoption of the Civil Rights Act of 1991, an increase in the number of African Americans as athletic administrators, head coaches, assistant coaches, and sports information directors could be anticipated. Unfortunately, that has not occurred. The affirmative action guidelines, the Civil Rights Act of 1991, and Title IX have served to overcome some of the glass-ceiling phenomenon.

Since the passage of Title IX, the opportunity for female athletes to participate in intercollegiate athletics has increased in the past 17 years (Acosta & Carpenter, 1994). In 1978, the academic year just before the Title IX mandatory compliance date, the number of sports offered women was 5.61 per school. In 1988, the number had grown to 7.31 (an all-time high), and in 1994 to 7.22 (a 4-year high) (Acosta &

Carpenter, 1994). However, the increase in the number of women, more specifically African American women, in athletic administrative and coaching positions is not reflective of the increased number of participants.

According to the 1993 NCAA Division I Graduation Rates Report, the number of African American administrators is well below the percentages of African American student-athletes in the Division I student-athlete population. African Americans made up 25.6% of the 58,398 total student-athletes in Division I. In revenue sports, African Americans provided 49.4% of the 22,376 student-athletes.

The purpose of this essay is to examine the existence of the glass-ceiling effect during the career progression of African American women within intercollegiate athletics. Women have made strides in intercollegiate athletics, and the number of women in coaching and administrative positions within intercollegiate athletic departments has increased; however, there are very few African American women in the top- and middle-level administrative positions. Most African American women are concentrated in lower-level positions such as secretary, graduate assistant, assistant coach, administrative assistant, assistant athletic director, or athletic academic advisor/coordinator. A lack of representation of African American women has been apparent at all levels of intercollegiate athletics, for example, in officiating, coaching, administration, sports information, and athletic training (Houzer, 1974).

In Houzer's (1974) article, "Black Women in Athletics," the situation is stated well:

> . . . Black women have been irrespectably quiescent with respect to their status in athletics . . . participation in athletics by women has increased both in number of participants and variations of activity. This broad expansion of participation in sports and athletics by women has not been proportionately represented by Black women. (Houzer, 1974, p. 209)

Alexander (1978) examined the status of minority women in all active member institutions of the Association of Intercollegiate Athletics for Women (AIAW). Her study revealed the following facts:

1. There is a great underrepresentation of minority women athletes, minority women administrative personnel, and minority women coaches.

2. Sports where participation by minority athletes was greater than 10% were badminton, basketball, and track and field.

3. Administrative personnel positions where minority involvement was greater than 5% were assistant directors, sport information directors, and team managers. Only 5% of the athletic directors in women's athletic departments in the 213 member institutions of AIAW participating in the study were African American women. Also, only 2% of the assistant athletic director positions and 5% of the coaching positions were held by African American women. Instead of improving, the relative position of African American women remained virtually static during the 1970s.

Murphy (1980) examined the participation of minority women as athletes and coaches within the AIAW structure. According to Murphy (1980), in 1974 there were 556 head coaches in women's athletic departments, of whom 16 (3%) were African American women, 443 (80%) were White women, 4 (1%) were African American males, and 93 (17%) were White males. Among assistant coaches, 1 (2%) was an African American woman, 4 (6%) were White women, 13 (19%) were African American males, and 48 (73%) were White males. During the 1978–79 year, the number of head coaches increased to 1,009 (an increase of 79%). The number of African American women increased by only 23; that is, only 5% of the new head coaches were African American women. During the same period, 184 more White women head coaches were added, constituting 41% of the additional head coaches. The greatest change was recorded in the addition of assistant coaches. There were 296 (an increase of 48%) more individuals in that group in 1979 than in 1974. Of those new ones, 3 (1%) were African American women, 189 (64%) were White women, 3 (1%) were African American males, and 89 (30%) were White males. Murphy (1980) reported that the percentage of African American women occupying administrative positions in women's athletic departments, in all active-member institutions of the AIAW, was 15 (5%) in assistant coaching positions, 39 (5%) in head coaching positions, and 5 (2%) in athletic director positions. She further found that the percentage of African Americans, both male and female, occupying athletic administrative positions (5% head coaches, 8% assistant coaches, 5% other support staff) was close to the percentage (5%) of historically Black colleges and universities that participated in the study. She argued that it seems likely then that African American women hold a very limited number of athletic positions in traditionally White institutions.

In summary, in 1974 the White female held the highest percentage of head coaching and administrative positions in women's athletic departments, with African American females occupying a very small percentage. The support-staff category was dominated by White women, followed by White males. African American men and women occupied a small percentage of positions in this category.

African Americans are restricted to certain roles in college sport. African Americans at White institutions tend to be underrepresented in roles associated with leadership and decision making. They are "assistants to"; that is, they serve as coordinators or assistants to a major decision maker. As long as racist and sexist practices influence hiring practices, the numbers of African American women in high-authority sport positions will not increase.

Efforts to assess the effects of the glass ceiling on coaches and athletic administrators can be difficult because hiring and promotion decisions can be subjective, and universities use different criteria in making decisions to hire and promote. However, the experiences of individuals during their career development and statistics indicating the number of African American women employed in coaching and athletic administrative positions can be used to determine the glass-ceiling effect phenomenon. The hiring problem has been blamed on the position held by African American women during their career development.

Abney (1988) investigated the career development of African American women coaches and athletic administrators in intercollegiate athletics at historically Black colleges and universities and predominantly White institutions. The women were asked to complete a survey questionnaire, and interviews were conducted with 10 women from the historically Black institutions and 10 women at predominantly White institutions. From a list of obstacles or problems that were listed in the survey questionnaire, the women were asked to identify whether or not the problems or obstacles were major, minor, no problem, or not applicable in their careers. Abney (1988) reported the 10 highest ranking obstacles for African American

women coaches and athletic administrators at African American institutions were inadequate salary, lack of support groups, gender, employer discrimination (sexism), low expectations by administrators and others, male coworker resentment (sexism), youth, sense of tokenism, lack of cultural and social outlets in the community, and burden of being the official minority spokesperson. The African American women at White institutions indicated inadequate salary, lack of support groups, being African American, gender, lack of cultural and social outlets in community, sense of tokenism, employer discrimination (sexism), employer discrimination (racism), burden of being the official minority spokesperson, and male coworker resentment (sexism). The African American women at White institutions differed from the African American women at historically Black institutions in that the former selected being African American, and employer discrimination (racism), as significant factors. The women were very similar in that both groups selected inadequate salary, lack of support groups, gender, employer discrimination (sexism), male coworker resentment (sexism), sense of tokenism, lack of cultural and social outlets in the community, and burden of being the official minority spokesperson as obstacles or problems during their career development.

The interviews with the women revealed additional details about the obstacles encountered in developing their careers. Problems encountered as a result of being a woman consisted of constant questioning of their abilities; people who resented women being in key positions; dead-end positions or lack of upward mobility; lack of respect from the administration; and lack of support from bosses, coworkers, and the administration. Several women stated that women in athletics have a problem in that people do not perceive them as being competent. These women also dealt with the problem of people who felt the women should not have had the position or did not promote women. One woman stated her experience as such:

He [coworker] was the one that probably created the most problems. He [coworker] felt that some of the other schools that he had dealt with did not have a women's Athletic Director, and he didn't see the need for [this institution] to have a women's Athletic Director. (quoted in Abney, 1988, p. 91)

Some women recalled discriminatory practices during career interviews:

I interviewed for a major job last year which I did get, but I subsequently decided not to take it. Their questions to me were different than their questions to the White candidates, and I happen to know that because I happen to know other people who were interviewing. Their concerns were about what I could do, were more based on my color rather than my record. (quoted in Abney, 1988, p. 93)

The majority of the women believed their biggest obstacles or problems related to sex and/or race. Several African American women vividly recalled being excluded from participating in events, from leadership positions, and from membership on key committees. Both sexual and racial discrimination are burdens that African American women bear in the university setting and in American society. This "double jeopardy" adds to the difficulty of African American women who are seeking career advancement. Alexander (1978) described the double jeopardy as "preventing Black women from formal networks such as higher educational training, and informal networks in which social relationships could possibly generate career benefits" (Alexander, 1978, p. 106).

The women provided reasons why very few African American women were in coaching and athletic administration. Their responses were attitude of society toward minorities and women, sexism, racism, lack of qualifications, lack of interest, lack of role models, lack of mentors, family responsibilities, time constraints, dead-end positions, politics, stereotypes, lack of opportunity, and lack of networks.

Many African American women have a common value of high achievement and the desire to pursue a coaching and/or administrative position in institutions of higher education. However, there are societal and institutional barriers that are hindrances, and thus, many Black women are denied the opportunity of achieving such positions. "The perpetuation of fatalistic stereotypes coupled with contradictions in the literature concerning the images of African American women have had a profound effect on personal relationships and professional opportunities for African American women in a society" (Stratta, 1995, p. 50).

Several explanations have been advanced to explain the small number of African American women as coaches and administrators in sport. Houzer (1974) stated that fewer African American women prepared for professional occupations in sport. Perhaps the lack of role models and mentors has been a deterrent. According to Smith (1991), planned interventions with adult role models and mentors do appear to have a positive effect on the career behavior and aspirations of African American youth. The majority of the African American women occupying positions as administrators or coaches in sport are former athletes. In most traditionally White institutions, the African American woman athlete lacks African American women administrators and coaches with whom she can identify. In most traditionally Black institutions, African American males occupy a large percentage of the positions in sport. As a result, professional occupations in sport are not perceived as a "visible" goal for the African American woman; therefore, she may not desire to pursue the area.

Career mentors are of special value to African American women during their career development process. Unfortunately, a small number of women are in positions in athletic departments to provide the type of mentoring desired. African American women are rarely hired in high-level coaching and/or athletic administrative positions in colleges and universities. African American women continue to be underrepresented as administrators and coaches. Consequently, there are fewer African American women role models and mentors available to African American student-athletes.

Evidence of the glass ceiling can be traced back to the experience of and team position held by African American women as student-athletes. Many educators will attest that the sports experience prepares the student-athlete for career and life experiences. According to Malveaux (1993), "the teamwork needed to participate in sports teaches students life lessons about cooperation, human relations, dignity and poise" (p. 54). The role that the student-athlete plays on a team can serve as the basis for career preparation. Sport sociologists have presented the theory that African American athletes are stacked in positions that do not require them to become leaders of their teams and are scarce in positions that are more central to the team's operations. Fuller stated, "Even in sports in which African American women are represented in significant numbers, basketball and track, they are often not in decision making, or what she called 'control' positions" (quoted in Blum, 1993, p. 40). She further stated, "Look at the point guards on many of the teams. The African American women are out there in the scoring positions and making big contributions, but they are not directing traffic" (quoted in Blum, 1993, p. 40).

If African American student-athletes have a quality intercollegiate athletic experience, an experience where they believe that they are being provided a legitimate opportunity to succeed and prosper, they will be more inclined to invest in a career in intercollegiate athletics. If more African American student-athletes graduate, the pool of those individuals able to consider a career in college athletics will expand (Vance, 1984). A better sporting experience means more interested and qualified candidates for positions as coaches and athletic administrators.

African American student-athletes must be provided leadership and graduate school opportunities after their playing days are over. Although progress has been made in creating new internships and postgraduate scholarship opportunities at the institutional, conference, and national levels, these opportunities must be expanded (Gerdy, 1994). Our current African American student-athletes should be our future coaches, athletic administrators, and conference commissioners. Unfortunately, very few African American women student-athletes are being hired into intercollegiate athletic departments.

There has not been significant hiring of African Americans within intercollegiate athletic departments over the last 10 years. A 1986–87 study reported the total number of African Americans holding athletic administrative positions was .156 per school, for a total of about 123 in National Collegiate Athletic Association (NCAA) schools. Thus, it was concluded that there is a minority group member in only one out of five of the athletic administrative structures found in NCAA member colleges and universities. The total number of head coaches was .494 per school, for a total of about 387 in NCAA schools. There is no minority group member serving as head coach in either the men's or women's programs in one out of three colleges and universities. Assistant coaches were 1.350 per school, for a total of about 1,065 in NCAA schools (Acosta & Carpenter, 1987).

It was concluded that the number of representatives of minority groups who hold a position as administrator, coach, or assistant coach in all of NCAA sports is about 1979; in other words, about 2.5 per school (from a pool of all levels of administrators, coaches for all teams in women's programs and men's programs, as well as assistant coaches in these programs (Acosta and Carpenter, 1986–87).

In 1990, it was reported that minority women comprised fewer than 5% of all women coaches (Grant & Curtis, 1993). In 1996, Acosta and Carpenter reported that 6,580 head coaching jobs existed in 1996 for coaches of women's NCAA teams, an increase of 209 jobs from 1994. Women held 3,138, 9 less than in 1994 in spite of the growth in number of teams by 209. Women hold 61.1% of the 5,902 paid assistant coaching positions for women's teams. Women hold 35.9% of all administrative jobs in women's programs. Today, there are fewer programs totally lacking women than in any of the last years. It was concluded that on an average, there is almost 1 female involved in athletic administration per school; this is up from 0.96 in 1994 and up from 0.83 in 1992 (Acosta & Carpenter, 1986–87).

The NCAA Minority Opportunities and Interests Committee conducted a 4-year study by race demographics of NCAA member institutions. Data were collected from annual certification reports that provided a breakdown of the number of administrators by race from 1990–1991, 1993–1994, and 1995–1996. Administrators were defined as those in the following positions: administrative assistant, associate athletic director, assistant coach, academic advisor, athletics director, assistant athletics director, auxiliary services, business manager, compliance coordinator, equipment manager, eligibility officer, faculty athletics representative, graduate assistant, head coach, promotions/marketing director, strength coach, sports information director, ticket manager, and trainer (The NCAA Minority Opportunities and Interests Committee's Four-Year Study of Race Demographics of Member Institutions, 1994).

The report presented several significant findings:

1. From 1990–91 to 1993–94, there were 5,889 additional athletics administrator positions. Of those positions, African Americans represented 597, or 10.1%, of the new administrators. With historically Black colleges and universities excluded, these were 5,843 additional athletics administrators. The increase in the overall percentage of African American administrators was 0.8%, from 5.4% to 6.2% however, this increase was still well below the percentage of African American student-athletes in the Division I student-athlete population.

2. There were 124 additional athletics directors. African Americans represented 19, or 15.3%, of the new athletics directors; however, when historically Black institutions were excluded, there were 15, or 12.3%, in the additional positions and 3.6% of the 897 total athletics directors in 1993–94. There were 29 more African American associate athletics directors, an increase from 4.2% to 5.6%, from 1990–91 to 1993–94. When historically Black schools were excluded, African Americans represented 11 of 127 new associate athletics directors, or 8.7%.

3. Assistant athletic directors' percentages are bleaker. There was an increase of 333 assistant athletics directors from 1990–91 to 1993–94. African Americans represented only 20, or 6.0%, of the additional assistant athletics directors, since the percentage of these individuals has not grown since 1990. The data suggest that future African American athletics directors will not come from the current ranks of associate and assistant athletics directors because the percentage of these individuals has not grown since 1990. The data suggest that there has been an increase in representation, though not dramatically, among the numbers of head coaches.

4. There were 1,109 additional head coaches, excluding historically Black schools. African Americans represented 143, or 12.9%, of the additional coaches, but only 3.9% of the total number of head coaches (10,176). For revenue-producing sports, excluding historically Black schools, African Americans represented 86 of 417, or 20.6%, of additional head coaches. In nonrevenue sports, African Americans represented 57 of 692, or 8.2%, of the additional head coaches.

5. The number of assistant coaches increased by 2,394, but African Americans represent only 213, or 8.9%, of these additional assistant coaches. Over the last 4 years, there has

been no percentage increase in the total number of assistant coaches. (The NCAA Minority Opportunities and Interests Committee's Four-Year Study of Race Demographics of Member Institutions, 1994). The two previously mentioned reports provide data regarding the status of women and African Americans in intercollegiate athletics; however, specific data pertaining to the status of African American women as athletic administrators and coaches in intercollegiate athletics remain unclear.

In 1998, the NCAA Minority Opportunities and Interest Committee released the findings of a two-year study on race demographics of NCAA member institutions' athletics personnel. In general, the data revealed that there has been no improvement in Black representation in the athletics departments at NCAA member institutions, with the exception of the following areas:

• Academic advisors show the greatest percentage increase of all administrative positions both overall and in Division I groups.

• The Division I assistant coaches show marked increases in both men's and women's teams, as well as in men's and women's revenue sports.

• Division I shows an increase in overall administrative positions held by African Americans.

• Division II shows the greatest percentage decrease in African American administra-

tors and head coaches of both men's and women's sports teams.

• There has been relatively no change in Division III in any of the categories.

Although the number of women and minorities within intercollegiate athletics departments has increased, the number of African American women as athletic directors, associate athletic directors, and head coaches has not increased significantly and continues to be disappointing.

Abney (1997) investigated the positions held by African American women in intercollegiate athletic departments of member institutions within the NCAA, the National Association for Intercollegiate Athletics (NAIA), and the National Junior College Athletic Association (NJCAA). A total of 1,300 survey questionnaires were mailed. Six hundred ninety-three, or 52%, were returned. The results were that a total of 1,912 African American men and women were identified as holding athletic administrative and coaching positions, with 475 or 25% identified as African American women athletic administrators and coaches.

See Table 1.

Of the 475, **304,** or 64% were coaches. Of the **304** coaches, 12 were identified as graduate assistants, interns, or volunteers, and 26 of the women held another position; that is, coached another sport or were administrators. One hundred seventy-one, or 36%, were athletic administrators. Of the 171, 6 were identi-

Table 1. **DATABASE**

	NCAA	NAIA	NJCAA	TOTAL
Total number of African American names submitted	0.90% (1736)	0.01% (12)	0.09% (164)	100% (1912)
Total number of African American women	0.94% (449)	0.01% (4)	0.05% (22)	100% (475)
Total number of African American men	0.89% (1287)	0.01% (8)	10% (142)	100% (1437)

fied as interns or graduate assistants, and 7 held another position. These percentages are much smaller when compared to the overall number of positions, male and female, within intercollegiate athletic departments. The top five administrative positions held by African American women in intercollegiate athletic departments were secretary/receptionist, academic counselor/student services, athletic trainer, administrative assistant, and business manager/account executive (see Table 2).

According to Fuller, "There are seven African American males who are athletic directors at White schools and there is one African American woman: me" (quoted in Blum, 1995, p. A39). Abney (1997) identified 0.44%, or three, African American women as athletic directors. All three women were employed at NCAA member institutions. One was employed at a Division I White institution, whereas the other two were employed at Division II, historically Black institutions.

The top five head coaching positions held by African American women in intercollegiate athletics departments were basketball, volleyball, track and field, cheerleading, and softball. The top five assistant coaching positions were basketball, track and field, volleyball, cheerleading, and softball.

The void of African Americans as coaches and athletic administrators has been attributed to a number of factors: "not enough jobs available in collegiate coaching or athletic departments" and "difficulty in identifying qualified African American coaches" and the "reluctance to hire African American coaches for fear of booster backlash" (Farrell, 1992, p. 36). The data do not support these justifications. It was

Table 2. TOP FIVE ADMINISTRATIVE POSITIONS

POSITION	NCAA	NAIA	NJCAA	TOTAL
Secretary/Receptionist	7.8%	0.0%	0.0%	6.2%
	(42)	(0)	(0)	(42)
Academic Counselor/				
Student Services				
Director	2.4%	0.0%	0.0%	1.9%
	(13)	(0)	(0)	(13)
Assistant	0.93	0.0%	0.0%	0.73%
	(5)	(0)	(0)	(5)
Athletic Trainer				
Head	0.75%	0.0%	0.0%	0.59%
	(4)	(0)	(0)	(4)
*Assistant	2.2%	0.0%	0.0%	1.7%
	(12)	(0)	(0)	(12)
Administrative Assistant	2.8%	0.0%	0.0%	2.2%
	(15)	(0)	(0)	(15)
Business Manager/Account				
Executive				
Director	1.5%	0.0%	0.78%	1.3%
	(8)	(0)	(1)	(9)
Assistant	0.56%	0.0%	0.0%	0.44%
	(3)	(0)	(0)	(3)

*Note: Six (6) of the assistant trainers were employed at one institution.

1995–1996 photo of Marianna Freeman, head coach of women's basketball at Syracuse University. Photo courtesy of athletic communications at Syracuse University.

reported that there are 800 NCAA members in all divisions, with an average of 15.5 teams per school, or 12,400 teams. NCAA teams have an average of two assistants per team. The National Association for Intercollegiate Athletic (NAIA) has 503 members, with an average of 7.66 teams per school and 1.5 assistants per team. There are approximately 68,888 college sport-related jobs (Lapchick, 1989).

Richard E. Lapchick released *The 1997 Racial Report Card*, a report on the hiring practices by professional sports teams and college athletics. The report revealed the following findings pertaining to Black women as collegiate athletic directors and head coaches:

- One percent of the athletic directors at Division I institutions, 0.8% of the athletic directors at Division II, and 0.3% of the athletic directors at Division III were Black women.
- Of the head coaches at Division I institutions, 2.1% were Black. 1.6 percent of the head coaches at Division II and 1.0 percent of the head coaches at Division III were Black women (Naughton, 1998).

In 1993, the Black Coaches Association (BCA) threatened a boycott unless its concerns about equity in intercollegiate athletics were addressed. The congressional Black Caucus intervened, getting the United States Department of Justice to mediate an agreement between the two parties to make significant steps toward the ex-

pansion of educational, employment, and governance participation opportunities for African Americans and other ethnic minorities. Cedric Dempsey, NCAA executive director, conceded at the BCA annual convention that there was "a moral obligation for women and minorities to have better opportunities to become coaches and administrators" (quoted in Farrell, 1994, p. 22). An agreement was developed. Dempsey agreed that the state of minority hiring in the NCAA was "simply indefensible," but vowed that an upper-management position in the association would soon go to an African American.

Change has to occur at the top of an organization in order to impact the entire organization. Until diversification occurs within the offices of national organizations, and the administration and athletic departments on college campuses, the glass ceiling will remain for African American women.

African American women who aspire to obtain and advance in positions within intercollegiate athletic departments are faced with a shatterproof ceiling. The positions are available, but significant numbers of African American women are not being hired in decision-making positions within intercollegiate athletics departments, and those who have been hired are in dead-end positions. If hired in the middle- or low-level positions, they are not rapidly advancing up the career ladder.

African American women must develop strategies to *reach* and shatter the glass ceiling. Changes in the following areas would increase the number of African American women in athletics: society's attitude towards African American women; affirmative hiring procedures; more African American women interested in the area; elimination of sexism and racism; and more mentors, role models, networks, and opportunity for African American women. African American women should make themselves more visible and qualified, and design or develop programs to help prepare student-athletes for careers in athletics.

The following are recommendations and strategies for shattering the glass ceiling:

1. Efforts to achieve diversity within athletic departments should be an integral part of strategic plans, and the administration must be held accountable for progress toward breaking the glass ceiling.
2. Organizations must expand their traditional recruitment networks and seek candidates with noncustomary backgrounds and experiences.
3. Formal mentoring and career development programs can help stop minorities from being channeled into staff positions that provide little access to the decision-making positions.
4. The top leadership of colleges and universities must demonstrate its commitment to the recruitment and advancement of African Americans by removing obstacles embedded in personnel practices.
5. African American women must receive challenging job assignments and the necessary training to advance.
6. Organizations must establish ongoing training and educational programs on race relations for all organizational members. Such training can help to eliminate many of the barriers of the African American experience of racism and prejudice.

Abney and Richey (1991) provided the following strategies to African American women who aspire to pursue a career in intercollegiate athletics:

1. Start support groups, organizations, and/or programs to exchange ideas and share experiences.
2. Investigate initiating formal and informal mentoring programs within the athletic arena and the governing bodies of sport.
3. Become qualified and compete for leadership roles at all levels in sport; become actively involved in sport associations, organizations, committees, and/or governing bodies.
4. Be confident, competent, determined, and willing to persevere when unpleasant experiences arise.
5. Develop and maintain a positive sense of self while remaining in sport; be inspired to meet sport challenges.
6. After having secured career positions in athletic-related professions, help other African American women with career development.

Although laws have opened the doors of opportunity for African Americans in intercollegiate athletics, stereotypes, ignorance, societal attitudes towards differences, and discriminatory institutional practices have limited employment in athletic leadership positions such as athletic administrators, coaches, officials, commentators, athletic trainers, and sports information directors. Political constraints in sport organizations also hinder the opportunities and/or advancement of African American women in intercollegiate athletics. Building the ranks of African American women in athletics department decision-making positions will require a change in the organizational mind-set. Those individuals in positions to hire must be committed and sensitive to diversifying the ranks of college coaches and athletic administrators. The college athletics community, both collectively and individually, and institutions, must make a firm commitment to improve African American representation at all levels and positions.

Study Questions

1. Define the glass-ceiling effect.
2. Discuss the glass-ceiling effect as it relates to African American women coaches and intercollegiate athletics administrators.
3. List several strategies to assist African American women in overcoming the glass-ceiling effect.
4. List several strategies that can be implemented by the NCAA, conferences, universities, and intercollegiate athletics departments to shatter the glass ceiling.

References

Abney, R. (1988). *The effects of role models and mentors on career patterns of Black women coaches and athletic administrators in historically Black and historically white institutions of higher education.*

Unpublished doctoral dissertation, The University of Iowa, Iowa City.

Abney, R. (1997, April). *The impact of gender equity on the status of African American women as athletic administrators and coaches in sport.* Paper presented at the meeting of the American Alliance for Health, Physical Education, Recreation and Dance, St. Louis, MO.

Abney, R., & Richey, D. (1991). Barriers encountered by Black female athletic administrators and coaches. *Journal of Physical Education, Recreation, and Dance, 62*(6), 19–21.

Acosta, R. V., & Carpenter, L. J. (1987). *Minority group members in athletic leadership.* Unpublished manuscript. [Available from Carpenter/Acosta, Department of Physical Education, Brooklyn College, Brooklyn, NY 11210]

Acosta, R. V., & Carpenter, L. J. (Eds.). (1994). *Women in intercollegiate sport: a longitudinal study seventeen year update 1977–1994.* Unpublished manuscript. [Available from Carpenter/Acosta, Department of Physical Education, Brooklyn College, Brooklyn, NY 11210]

Acosta, R. V., & Carpenter, L. J. (Eds.). (1996). *Women in intercollegiate sport: a longitudinal study nineteen year update 1977–1996.* Unpublished manuscript. [Available from Carpenter/Acosta, Department of Physical Education, Brooklyn College, Brooklyn, NY 11210]

Alexander, A. (1978). *Status of minority women in the AIAW.* Unpublished master's thesis, Temple University, Philadelphia.

Blum, D. E. (1993, April 21). Forum examines discrimination against Black women in college sports. *The Chronicle of Higher Education,* pp. A39–A40.

Farrell, C. S. (1992, December 3). NCAA minorities committee addresses absence of Black football head coaches. *Black Issues in Higher Education, 9,* 36–37.

Farrell, C. S. (1994a, June 16). Jump ball: Black coaches, NCAA have benign standoff. *Black Issues in Higher Education, 11,* 22–24.

Farrell, C. S. (1994b, September 22). NCAA: Blacks make the plays but call few of the shots. *Black Issues in Higher Education, 11,* 34–36.

Gerdy, J. R. (1994, August 11). You reap what you sow. *Black Issues in Higher Education, 11,* 30–31.

Grant, C., & Curtis, M. (1993, December 2). Women in sports. *Black Issues in Higher Education, 11,* 25.

Houzer, S. (1974). Black women in athletics. *Physical Educator, 31,* 208–209.

Kinder, T. (1993). *Organizational management administration for athletic programs.* Dubuque, IA: eddie bowers publishing, inc.

Lapchick, R. E. (1989, Spring). Future of the Black student-athlete: Ethical issue of the 1990s. *Educational Record, 70,* 32–37.

Malveaux, J. (1993, December 2). Sports scholars aren't the only outstanding students. *Black Issues in Higher Education, 10,* 54.

Morrison, S., White, R. P., Velsor, E. V., & The Center for Creative Leadership. (1987). *Breaking the glass ceiling.* Reading, MA: Addison Wesley Publishing Company.

Murphy, D. M. (1980). *The involvement of Blacks in women's athletics in member institutions of the AIAW.* Unpublished doctoral dissertation, Florida State University, Tallahassee.

National Collegiate Athletic Association. (1994, August). *The NCAA Minority Opportunities and Interests Committee's four-year study on race demographics of member institutions.* Overland, KS: Author.

National Collegiate Athletic Association. (1996–1997). *Achieving gender equity, a basic guide to Title IX and gender equity in athletics for colleges and universities* (2nd ed.). Overland, KS: Author.

National Collegiate Athletic Association. (1998, April). *The NCAA Minority Opportunities and Interests Committee's two-year study on race demographics of NCAA member institutions' athletic personnel.* Overland, KS: Author.

Naughton, J. (1998, March 6). New report decries dearth of Black coaches in football and basketball. *The Chronicle of Higher Education,* pp. A45–A46.

Nelson, W. J. (1982). Society defining its members. In *Racial definition hand-book* [On-line]. Available: http://www.webcom.com/intvoice/handbook.htm/

Smith, Y. R. (1991). Issues and strategies for working with multicultural athletes. *Journal of Physical Education, Recreation, and Dance, 62,* 39–44.

Social Equity Office. (1997a). Social equity at Slippery Rock University [Poster]. Slippery Rock, PA: Author.

Social Equity Office. (1997b). Social equity office policies [Brochure]. Slippery Rock, PA: Author.

Stratta, T. M. (1995). *An ethnography of the sport experience of African American female athletes.* Unpublished doctoral dissertation, Southern Illinois University, Carbondale.

Vance, N. S. (1984, April 25). Football study links race, player positions; Reasons aren't clear, 3 researchers caution. *The Chronicle of Higher Education,* pp. 21, 24.

SECTION 2

RECRUITMENT, RETENTION, AND LIFE AFTER PARTICIPATION

African American Student-Athletes: Opportunity or Exploitation?

Robert M. Sellers

Abstract

The present essay examines quality of life that African American student-athletes experience after their retirement from athletics. Student-athletes' life experiences on the college campus play an important role in influencing their subsequent life experiences. Specifically, it is argued that African American former student-athletes will show more positive psychological adjustment to the extent that their university experiences offered them true educational opportunities rather than exploitation of their athletic ability and to the extent that student-athletes themselves took advantage of educational opportunities. Data are presented that suggests that African American student-athletes have a very unique college experience in that they both share similarities with and show important differences from other African American college students and White student-athletes. African American student-athletes come to college with poorer academic preparation and from poorer socioeconomic backgrounds and, once enrolled, perform more poorly academically.

Unfortunately, conceptual and methodological flaws in the research literature make it impossible to reach any definitive conclusions about the typical African American student-athlete's postathletic experiences. However, the literature does suggest that, at least for high school athletes, athletic participation may be associated with indicators of upward social mobility. In lieu of empirical documentation of the quality of the postathletic lives of African American student-athletes, the essay presents a framework by which to evaluate the quality of the educational experiences of African American student-athletes. It is argued that universities are obligated to provide African American student-athletes with access to a college education consisting of opportunities to develop personal competence, enhance social mobility, and earn a degree in exchange for the athletes' full participation in athletics. A critique of the current reform movement within intercollegiate athletics is presented as a backdrop for a set of proposed reforms to the current system. These reforms focus on proactive steps that the NCAA, individual institutions, and African American student-athletes and their families can take to enhance the educational experiences of African American student-athletes.

Key Terms

- Opportunity •
- Exploitation •
- Motivation •
- Structure •
- Proposition 48 •
- Proposition 16 •

One of the most hotly debated arguments surrounding the African American athlete focuses on the role of sports in the African American community. Specifically, has sports helped or hindered the African American community? Those who argue that sports has been a benefit to the African American community point to the relatively color-blind nature of athletic competition. Sports is viewed as one of the few meritocracies in this country. On a football field, skin color is not as important as speed, strength, and skill level. Those who argue for the benefit of sports point to the fact that despite constituting only 13% of the population, and around 4% of the student body at the predominantly White division I universities, African American athletes constitute 37% of the football players, 33% of the women's basketball players, and 56% of the men's basketball players (Center for the Study of Athletics, 1989).

The proponents of the "sports provide opportunities to the African American community" perspective also focus their arguments on the social mobility that sports has provided those who are athletically gifted and financially smart enough to exploit the sport system. Because of the *relatively* few racist barriers in sports, barriers that are prevalent in most of the other legal avenues of social mobility in this country, proponents argue sports provides African Americans with one of the few legal opportunities to change their station in life.

Sports provides educational and career opportunities to African American athletes from underprivileged backgrounds that are often beyond the reach of some of their more academically gifted, but less athletically endowed African American classmates. The opposing side contends that sports has exploited African American athletes. This argument focuses not on the successful African American athletes, but instead focuses on those athletes who do not reap the benefits of sports participation. Those who focus on the exploitive nature of sports emphasize the extremely long odds that face any high school athlete with career aspirations of playing professional sports. For example, an African American high school football player has a 1-in-43 chance of playing for a Division I college football team (Lapchick, 1991). His chances of playing in the National Football League (NFL) are 6,318 to 1 (Lapchick, 1991). An African American male high school basketball player has about a 1-in-130 chance of playing for a Division I basketball team, and the odds are 10,345 to 1 against his playing in the National Basketball Association (NBA) (Lapchick, 1991). The supporters of the exploitation argument also point out that only one out of four African American Division I athletes has graduated from his/her university five years after arrival (National Collegiate Athletic Association, 1991).

Also, those who support the "sports exploits the African American community" perspective argue that participation in sports does not enhance most African American athletes' opportunities for upward social mobility. On the contrary, they argue that the lure of sports blinds too many African American athletes to other, more stable avenues up the social stratum, such as academic excellence. The sports establishment benefits from the African American athletes' skills and labor by providing the illusion of an opportunity at fame, fortune, and education. However, in the end, the majority of the African American athletes are exploited without any measurable compensation for their service. Noted sport sociologist Harry Edwards (1979) eloquently sums up this argument:

> This channeling process tragically leads millions of blacks to pursue a goal that is foredoomed to elude all but an insignificant few. . . . The impact of what would otherwise be personal career tragedies reverberates throughout black society both because of the tremendous proportion of black youth channeled into sport and the fact that serious sport involvement often dictates neglect of other important spheres of development. Further the skills cultivated through sport are utterly worthless beyond the sport realm. (p. 119)

Whereas those who view sports as a positive force for the African American community point to the potential benefits that can be reaped from participating in sports, such as obtaining a college education and/or playing professional sports, their opposition argue that far too few African American athletes receive a college education and even fewer get the opportunity to play professional sports.

This debate over the value of sports to the overall welfare of the African American community hinges on the question of what happens to African American athletes after their athletic careers are over. Unfortunately, there is very little empirical work to document what actually happens to African American athletes after their college careers are finished. Much of the evidence regarding the influence athletics has on the quality of life of former African American college athletes is limited to anecdotes. For

example, there are the stories like Kevin Ross's. Kevin Ross was a basketball player at Creighton University. Ross spent 4 years at Creighton as a member of the basketball team and, ostensibly, a member of their student body. However, after his athletic eligibility was exhausted and he was unable to make it with an NBA team, Ross found himself a functional illiterate with over 70 credit hours of college course work. He made national headlines by enrolling in Marva Collins's Westside Preparatory school in Chicago and beginning as a fifth grader. At present, Kevin Ross is suing Creighton University.

However, there are also other stories similar to the one experienced by Thomas LaVeist. LaVeist grew up in a rough section of Brooklyn. Although very intelligent, LaVeist never truly applied himself academically during his high school days. He was a student with A ability, but performed at C level. He was fortunate enough to receive a football scholarship from the University of Maryland Eastern Shore (UMES). While at UMES, LaVeist became a more diligent student. He went on to receive a Ph.D. in medical sociology. Today, Dr. Thomas LaVeist is a very successful professor at the Johns Hopkins University School of Public Health. LaVeist credits a lot of his success to the educational opportunity he received. Because of his poor high school academic record and his family's financial situation, he would never have been able to go to college without an athletic scholarship.

Unfortunately, we do not know which ending is most typical of the athletic experience of the African American athlete. Does participation in college athletics provide African American student-athletes with the opportunity for an education, or does it exploit their physical skills without providing fair compensation? This is the central question of the present essay. In general, the quality of life for African American student-athletes will be better if they have received a college education than if they participated in college athletics without receiving a fair opportunity for an education. In order to properly address this question, the present essay will also examine a number of other relevant questions. Are the life experiences of African American student-athletes unique? What does the research literature say about the influence of athletic participation on the quality of life of former African American student-athletes? What should African American student-athletes reasonably expect to receive as compensation for their athletic exploits? How will the current reform movement within intercollegiate athletics affect the quality of postathletic life for African American student-athletes? What can be done to improve the quality of African American student-athletes' postathletic lives?

First, I will provide a brief description of the African American student-athlete at NCAA Division I schools. Next, I will briefly review the relevant research that has focused on athletic retirement, as well as race differences in career aspiration. Then, I will present a framework by which to evaluate whether a college student-athlete is provided equitable compensation for participation in intercollegiate athletics, followed by a discussion of the current reform movement within the NCAA and its impact on the postathletic career of the African American student-athlete. Finally, I will present some recommendations that I feel will provide the African American athlete with a better opportunity to maximize his collegiate experience.

Before I begin to address these issues, it is important that I provide an overview of my perspective on the African American athlete. Any analysis of the life experience of the African American athlete must view the African American student-athlete as both a unique entity as well as a composite of other, related groups of students. At first glance, this perspective may seem paradoxical. However, any meaningful investigation of the African American student-athlete must be aware of both the similarities and the differences in the life experiences of African American student-athletes as compared to those of all student-athletes and all African American college students. The life experiences of these analogous groups should be used as a point of reference, not an evaluative yardstick. African American student-athletes' experiences can only be evaluated from their own worldview. However, African American student-athletes also do not exist in a vacuum. They are a function of their environment. Thus, we should also be aware of the societal context and its influence on African American student-athletes' life experiences before, during, and after their college athletic careers.

The major premise of the present essay is that the quality of African American student-athletes' postathletic lives is significantly influenced by the extent to which their college experience was one of opportunity or exploitation. Because of the lack of systematic evidence on the processes involved in the postathletic adjustment of African American student-athletes, the present essay will avoid the temptation to develop a model based on idiosyncratic anecdotes. Instead, the focus will be on ways to enhance the educational experiences of African American student-athletes during their stay in college with the assumption that these experiences will have a positive influence on the quality of postathletic life.

African American Student-Athletes: Experiences and Worldview

African American student-athletes represent unique entities on our college campuses. They often come from very different backgrounds than the rest of the student body. Moreover, African American student-athletes are different from the two student constituencies with whom they share the most in common—White student-athletes and African American nonathletic students (Sellers, Kuperminc, & Waddell, 1991). Whereas the median enrollment of African American students at Division I universities is approximately 4%, Blacks constitute approximately 12% of the student-athlete population. Interestingly, the proportion of

African American student-athletes roughly corresponds with the proportion of Blacks in the overall population (13%). The problem is not that Blacks are *overrepresented* in college athletics, the problem is that African American students are *underrepresented* in college.

In one of the few studies to focus specifically on the unique college experiences of African American student-athletes, Sellers and his colleagues (1991) compared African American student-athletes to White student-athletes and other African American college students on four important areas: demographic and academic background, college life experiences, mental health, and social support. The data came from a national, representative survey of African American and White student-athletes in revenue-producing sports (football and men's and women's basketball) at 42 NCAA Division I schools. The study also surveyed a random sample of nonathletic African American students from these same institutions. The study found interesting differences between African American student-athletes and both comparison groups across all four domains.

One important finding was that African American student-athletes enter college with very different educational and sociocultural backgrounds than both White student-athletes and other African American students. African American student-athletes come from families with significantly lower incomes that are headed by less educated parents. Once enrolled, African American student-athletes perform worse than their counterparts (Ervin, Saunders, Gillis, & Hogrebe, 1985; Kiger & Lorentzen, 1986; Purdy, Eitzen, & Hufnagel, 1982; Sellers, 1992; Shapiro, 1984). With regard to academic performance, the average African American student-athlete hovers perilously close to the NCAA minimum requirements for initial eligibility (average SAT score of 753; score of 700 necessary for eligibility). This trend continues after entering college (average GPA of 2.14; GPA of 2.00 necessary for eligibility).

Broadly stated, African American student-athletes' experience of college life appears more similar to that of White student-athletes than to that of other African American students (Sellers et al., 1991). African American and White student-athletes do not differ in the importance they ascribe to earning a degree, their satisfaction with their relationship with coaches, and their overall satisfaction with life. For the most part, African American and White student-athletes also perceive similar levels of difficulty in achieving personal growth as a result of athletics. However, African American student-athletes feel that it is easier to become more assertive as a result of being an athlete. African American student-athletes seem to be aware of the increased status that is accorded them as a result of being an athlete. This elevated status often results in them having greater and more familiar access to influential alumni and university officials. At the same time, their relationships with other African American students (who may have the least access to important individuals within the university) make African American student-athletes more conscious of their opportunities to be assertive than White student-athletes.

African American student-athletes are more likely to report experiencing racial isolation than White student-athletes. This finding is consistent with the reported increase in overt racism on campuses and the racial makeup of most universities. However, African American student-athletes reported feeling less different as a result of being athletes than did their White counterparts. While these last two findings seem contradictory, they are actually complimentary. Because they are more likely to experience racial isolation, African American student-athletes may be attributing their feelings of being different more to the fact that they are African American and less to the fact that they are athletes. For African American student-athletes, being African American makes them different from the mainstream. But, being student-athletes provides them with some privileges that are not experienced by the average African American student.

For instance, African American student-athletes seem to feel that their college experience is more worthwhile and more satisfying than do other African American students. This may be as much an indicator of the social difficulties that many African American students experience at predominantly White colleges as it is a measure of the quality of the African American student-athlete's college experiences (Allen, 1988). Although both groups are highly motivated to obtain a degree, African American student-athletes perceive greater personal growth from being an athlete than African American students perceive from being students (Sellers et al., 1991). African American student-athletes also reported feeling less racial isolation than other African American students. Sellers and his colleagues attributed this finding to the possibility that African American student-athletes' enhanced status as athletes provides them with opportunities to socialize with people who are inaccessible to other African American students. Thus, it may be easier for African American student-athletes to interact with White students from very different backgrounds because of their status as athletes. White students are more likely to make an effort to get to know the African American student-athlete than they would be for a nonathletic African American student.

With regards to social support, the study found that African American student-athletes are less likely than White student-athletes to report that they have someone to talk to about their problems. African American and White student-athletes also differ in the groups of people with whom they are most likely to discuss their problems. African American student-athletes are less likely to discuss their problems with peers (teammates, other students, and other friends) and more likely to talk with an academic advisor. The study concluded that the relative social distance that African American student-athletes report from their teammates and other students on campus may be a function of sociocultural background

differences. The greater utilization of and contact with the academic advisor for emotional support may be a function of African American student-athletes' poorer academic performances, which may in turn lead to greater contact with academic advisors. While African American student-athletes and other African American students are more similar in their perception of overall emotional support, the structure of that support does differ. African American student-athletes are less likely than other African American students to talk to peers (other students and friends) and are more likely than other African American students to receive support from loved ones who are not on campus (parents and siblings).

African American student-athletes' reliance on support located off-campus may interact with their socioeconomic background to place them at greater risk. African American student-athletes come from poorer families and their support systems are more likely to be located away from campus. Thus, it is more difficult for them to personally access their support systems. This problem is exacerbated by the fact that NCAA rules forbid athletes from working during the school year. And yet, the NCAA does not permit universities to provide athletes with any money beyond tuition, room, and board. Another potential problem for African American student-athletes is that although their support networks may be very effective in providing emotional support, they may have more difficulty garnishing instrumental support. Instrumental support refers to the type of support, such as information, which helps the individual to solve the problem. In the case of problems associated with being a college student, oftentimes instrumental support can only be provided by a person who has had some college experience. It would be difficult for someone without any college experience to advise a student interested in medical school on whether to major in pre-med versus biology. Because the average African American student-athlete has parents who have never attended college, and is more likely to seek support from parents, s/he is often limited in the type of support that her/his networks are able to provide (Sellers et al., 1991). The NCAA must look at developing legislation that will provide a means by which African American student-athletes may access their support systems more frequently. For example, the NCAA could subsidize an annual visit home. On the other hand, universities must also be aware of the potential of inadequate educational experiences from some African American student-athletes' support networks. The universities should make every effort to provide African American student-athletes with access to persons who have the experiences necessary to provide instrumental support.

Tracking the Problem

As stated earlier, there is a dearth of empirical studies that have specifically documented what happens to African American student-athletes once their athletic careers are completed. However, there are two areas of study that may aid in providing a glimpse of what former African American student-athletes may be experiencing. First, there is a growing literature that has investigated the retirement process of student-athletes in general. This literature examines the psychological consequences associated with the end of an athlete's sport career. The second area of study has focused on the relationship between athletic participation and career attainment. This area of research typically examines differences between athletes and nonathletes on such direct measures of career attainment as postathletic career occupation, as well as such indirect measures as career aspirations and academic performance. The main emphasis in this area of research is on what impact being a student-athlete has on the person's social status later in life.

Athletic Retirement and Psychological Adjustment

The research literature has approached retirement from sport from the perspective that sport retirement leads to a significant adjustment

within the life of the student-athlete (Danish, 1987; Harris & Eitzen, 1978; Lerch, 1982). The quality of the athlete's adjustment is influenced by whether the athlete was forced or voluntarily retired from his/her sport. In general, athletes whose athletic careers ended abruptly because of such things as career-ending injuries report less satisfaction than those who were able to complete their athletic careers without an unexpected disruption (Kleiber, Greendorfer, Blinde, & Samdahl, 1987). Harris and Eitzen (1978) suggest that those individuals who feel that their athletic careers end as a result of their own failure are at a greater risk of having problems adjusting to life after athletics. They argue that such an experience can damage the individual's athletic self-esteem. This damage may be especially extensive and pervasive if the individual's athletic self-esteem is central to his/her overall self-concept. Thus, " . . . the consequences of failure for an athlete who intends to be an athletic success and has no alternative can be quite serious" (Harris & Eitzen, 1978, p. 185).

Other research suggests that for many former student-athletes the adjustment to life after an athletic career is not particularly difficult. Greendorfer and Blinde (1985) surveyed 1,123 former male and female athletes from the Big Ten conference on their experiences during their athletic career, their postathletic career sport participation, and their adjustment to sport retirement. The majority of the sample did not report experiencing any long-lasting emotional hardship as a result of the completion of their sports career. The study paints a picture in which most student-athletes adjust to life after their athletic careers by slowly de-emphasizing the importance of athletics in their lives while at the same time continuing to participate in athletic activities. This pattern does not seem to differ for either men or women. Coakley (1983) has even suggested that retirement from sport may actually be a rebirth. It may allow an athlete the opportunity to pursue other activities and roles which had to be sacrificed or de-emphasized as a consequence of the demands associated with being a college athlete. Retirement from an athletic career may also signal the end of an unpleasant association with a coach or teammates. It is not uncommon for college athletes to talk about how much their college athletic experience differs from their high school experience. Often they perceive this change as being for the worse, lamenting the fact that they no longer play the sport out of love but out of obligation instead.

Unfortunately, the research literature on the psychological consequences of athletic retirement have several conceptual shortcomings which severely limit our understanding of postathletic life for African American athletes. First, the research literature has conceptualized postathletic retirement as a monolithic event, with all athletes having similar reasons for their participation in athletics. It is assumed that all athletes participate in intercollegiate athletics because of their love for the sport. Such an assumption overlooks those student-athletes who view participation in college athletics as an experience that is to be tolerated in exchange for an opportunity for an education. Another limitation of the research literature in this area is that it has ignored the possible influences that race and socioeconomic status may have on postathletic career adjustment. A number of authors have argued that there are race and socioeconomic status differences in the orientation to sport such that athletics is more central for Blacks from poorer backgrounds than for middle-class Whites (Cashmore, 1982; Eitzen & Tessendorf, 1978; Snyder & Spreitzer, 1978). Such cultural and structural differences in sport orientation suggest that there should be similar cultural and structural differences in postathletic career adjustment. However, to date there is little evidence to either support or refute this hypothesis.

Along with the conceptual shortcomings, the research literature on the psychological consequences also suffers from methodological limitations. Most of the research has utilized retrospective techniques to assess changes in individuals' perceptions of their athletic experience and adjustment. In other words, the former athletes are asked questions in the present about what their perceptions of their experiences were at a previous point in time, when they were athletes. Such techniques are vulnerable to distortions and deficits in the subjects' memories, as well as the possibility of the athletes providing responses that make them appear more favorable. Another limitation of many of the studies in this area is their failure to use representative samples of student-athletes. This shortcoming severely limits the generalizability of the findings beyond those student-athletes who participated in the study. Finally, the lack of clarity and uniformity in the definition of such concepts as athletic retirement, psychological adjustment, and life satisfaction has resulted in the use of imprecise measures of these concepts.

Athletic Participation and Career Attainment

Another area of relevant research is the literature on the influence of athletic participation on career attainment. Over the past twenty years, a number of studies have attempted to determine whether participating in athletics enhances or detracts from the athlete's subsequent career status. Does athletics build skills and provide opportunities that translate into success outside of the playing field? Or, do the role demands of being an athlete exact a toll on preparation and performance in other domains outside of athletics? The research in this area has taken two approaches in investigating this link. These approaches consist of studies which have tried to (1) examine a direct association between athletic participation and career attainment, and (2) examine an indirect association between athletic participation and career attainment through intermediate processes such as educational and career aspirations and academic performance.

The literature that has analyzed the direct relationship between athletic participation and subsequent career status has been somewhat inconclusive. In his extensive review of the literature regarding race, sport, and social mobility, Braddock (1980) delineates two opposing hypotheses within the literature. The *sport enhances mobility* hypothesis argues that traditionally sport has served as a vehicle to social mobility for minority groups. The *sport impedes mobility* hypothesis argues that the deceitful allure of an athletic career, with its truncated career options, has blinded minority groups from other, more viable career paths. Braddock noted that both hypotheses assume that lower-class, minority youths would place greater importance on sport than White, middle-class youths. Interestingly, Braddock (1980) presented little empirical evidence to support the notion that Blacks place more importance on athletics than Whites. In fact, he cited evidence that suggests that younger White males may actually place a greater value on sport (Hurtsfield, 1978). However, with regards to the present essay, the most relevant finding of his review was that out of the 16 studies which investigated the direct relationship between sport participation and occupational attainment, only 1 study found that nonathletes obtained higher status occupations, and 3 studies found that athletes obtained higher status occupations. The other 12 studies found no statistically significant difference between the two groups. It should be noted, however, that 7 of the 12 studies found a statistically nonsignificant relationship for athletes obtaining higher career status.

Braddock's (1980) review of the research focusing on the influence of athletic participation on intermediate process of social mobility suggests that there may be moderate support for the notion that athletics has a positive influence on educational and occupational aspirations. Of the 25 studies that examined educational and occupational attainment, 19 studies (6 statistically significant) yielded differences that favored athletic participation. This is in contrast to only 2 studies which yielded statistically nonsignificant differences in support of non-athletes. For example, Picou (1978) examined the achievement behaviors and social mobility attitudes of 691 male athletes and 838 male nonathletes from a representative sample of Louisiana high school seniors. Picou found that participation in athletics was associated with higher educational aspirations. He also found significant race differences in his results. For African American students, there was a direct association between athletic participation and educational aspirations. On the other hand, for White student-athletes, Picou found the association was mediated by a college-oriented peer group such that White student-athletes were more likely to interact with a college-oriented peer group, which in turn was associated with higher educational aspirations.

There is growing evidence that suggests that participation in intercollegiate athletics, in at least some sports, is associated with poorer academic performance. Purdy, Eitzen, and Hufnagel (1982) examined the academic potential and performance of more than 2,000 student-athletes from the Western Athletic Conference across a ten-year period. They found that student-athletes came to college with significantly lower academic credentials and performed poorer academically while there. In contrast, Shapiro (1984) studied the graduation rates at Michigan State University (MSU) from 1950 to 1980 and found that MSU athletes graduated at a rate similar or superior to MSU nonathletes. However, recent evidence released by the NCAA strongly suggest that athletes are not performing as well academically as nonathletes.

In 1986, the Center for the Study of Athletics at the American Institutes for Research (AIR) was commissioned by the President's Commission of the NCAA to survey student-athletes at 42 Division I universities. In their initial report, the Center for the Study of Athletics (1988) found that student-athletes had lower college GPAs than a sample of students who participated in 20 or more hours of extracurricular activities. African American student-athletes had lower GPAs than both White student-athletes and other African American nonathletes (Center for the Study of Athletics, 1989; Sellers, Kuperminc, & Waddell, 1991).

Recently, the NCAA reported results from a five-year study of the graduation rates of Division I student-athletes (National Collegiate Athletic Association, 1991). The analysis of the graduation rates for the first cohort of student-athletes revealed that only 46% of the student-athletes in the sample had graduated five years after first enrolling in college. Within that group, White student-athletes graduate, at about twice the rate (52.3%) of African American student-athletes (26.6%).

As one can see, the findings in the research literature focusing on the links between athletic participation and career attainment are rather complex. It seems that athletic participation in high school may be positively associated with indicators of upward social mobility (e.g., Picou, 1978). On the other hand, participation in intercollegiate athletics is associated with poorer academic performance (e.g., Purdy et al., 1982). There also appear to be race differences between the relationship between athletic participation and career attainment. Unfortunately, limitations in the studies make any firm conclusions about this literature precarious. Prospective longitudinal designs are needed before any firm conclusions regarding the causal relationship between athletic participation and career attainment can be made. Subsequent research is also needed which utilizes large representative samples of both athletes and nonathletes from as similar backgrounds as possible, and which follows them throughout their high school, college, and postcollege years. Such research is quite expensive and time-consuming. However, it is the kind of research that is necessary to enhance our understanding of this phenomenon.

Framing Educational Opportunity: When Is the Check Cashed?

One of the objectives of this essay is to evaluate whether African American student-athletes receive fair compensation for their participation in sport. If African American student-athletes are receiving fair compensation, then athletics constitutes a valuable opportunity. On the other hand, if they are not receiving fair compensation then African American student-athletes are being exploited. The assumption here is that the exploitation of African American student-athletes results in their experiencing negative psychological, social, and financial adjustments to life after sports. In order to accurately evaluate the fairness of the exchange between African American student-athletes and their universities, a set of expectations to be met by both parties must be developed. With regard to their obligation to the university, African American student-athletes must participate fully in athletics, with a commitment to excel to the best of their abilities. In return for African American student-athletes' commitment to athletic excellence, the university is obligated to provide them with a viable opportunity to receive a college education.

One should note that I argue universities owe student-athletes the *opportunity* for a college education. That is because the most that a university can provide a student is an opportunity for an education. Ultimately, it is the individual's responsibility to take advantage of the opportunity. Nonetheless, it is the university's obligation to provide any support service that will enhance the African American student-athlete's chances of receiving a college education. These services include appropriate academic support programs and career counseling (I will discuss this point in greater detail later in the essay). The university must also insure that the student-athlete will have the time necessary to pursue an education. During the season, student-athletes in the revenue-producing sports spend more time participating in sport-related activities than they do preparing for and attending class (Center for the Study of Athletics, 1988). This is analogous to giving athletes a generous check for their athletic services but prohibiting them from going to the bank and cashing it. Although the athletes have something of great value in their possession, it is worthless to them because they are unable to convert it into usable currency.

It should also be noted that I argue for the opportunity for a college *education* and not a college degree. The two are not synonymous. A degree is a necessary, but not a sufficient, element of a college education. Not all individuals who receive degrees from accredited universities receive a college education. There are three elements to a college education that are important to African American student-athletes. These three elements consist of (1) the refinement of personal competency; (2) upward social mobility; and (3) earning a degree. All three elements of a college education are important to all student-athletes; however, the last two elements are especially significant for African American student-athletes.

College life consists of numerous experiences that help in the development of personal competence in students. Most of these experiences occur outside of the classroom. Student-athletes may have a head start over other college students with regards to personal competency. Danish (1983) argues that participating in athletics leads to experiences that may enhance personal competence. Personal competence consists of both interpersonal skills and intrapersonal skills (Danish, Galambos, & Laqquatra, 1983). Interpersonal skills can be simply defined as the individual's ability to relate well with others. Such skills are important in the garnishing of social support and the projecting of a positive image of oneself to others. Interpersonal skills allow one to "win friends and influence others." The novel experience of entering college forces freshman students to develop new social networks without the aid or hindrance of their previous social networks and reputations. On the other hand, intrapersonal skills refer to those skills that are associated with the development and successful completion of tasks that are important to the overall success and well-being of the individual. Intrapersonal skills associated with personal competence include goal setting, knowledge acquisition, risk taking, self-confidence, and self-discipline. Such collegiate activities as writing a research paper, being active in a student organization, and planning for one's career help to develop intrapersonal competency skills. Also, the lack of structure in college forces students to be responsible for their own actions, which in turn hones their intrapersonal skills.

A college education should also provide an opportunity for upward social mobility. African American student-athletes come to college from poorer socioeconomic backgrounds than White student-athletes and other African American college students at their schools (Sellers et al., 1991). The average African American student-athlete is also likely to be the first generation within the family to receive a college education. A college education can lead to upward social mobility for African American student-athlete in two ways. First, the skills and the credentials associated with having attended college provide African American student-athletes with greater access to higher status career opportunities. The second way in which it may enhance upward mobility for the African American student-athlete involves exposure. African American student-athletes on a college campus are often exposed to numerous career options that they never knew existed. For example, a student-athlete with an aptitude for drawing who has her mind set on becoming an architect may become exposed to a number of careers, such as drafting or graphic design, which she may find more appealing. College is also a setting in which African American student-athletes can form social relationships which may lead to career advancement in the future. The business world is replete with examples of successful partnerships that were forged from college friendships.

The final element of a college education that is important to African American student-athletes is earning a college degree. More than anything else, a college degree is, and has always been, a credential of achievement rather than a certification of competency. Traditionally, a college degree was a ticket to "the good life." Ironically, opportunities for obtaining college degrees were usually reserved for those persons whose family were already living "the good life." Those few individuals from less educated families who were somehow able to go to college and earn a degree greatly enhanced their social and financial status. In the past, a college degree was a great advantage in earning a good living, but it was not a requirement for earning one. Today, with the technological advances in the workforce, a college degree no longer means the same thing as it did 15 years ago. It is no longer an advantage in today's labor market. It is a necessity. There are fewer viable opportunities for non-college-educated persons to earn an income sufficient enough to support a family. Although the skills that African American student-athletes learn in college may or may not transfer to the performance of their jobs, the college degree is often required for them to get hired in the first place.

African American student-athletes who have fulfilled their athletic commitment to the university have the right to expect the university to provide them with the opportunity to develop personal competence, improve their social status, and earn a degree. In order for a university to live up to its end of the commitment, it must provide an environment that enhances African American student-athletes' chances for success. Paramount to that success is the balance between institutional support and personal freedom and responsibility. Later in this essay, I discuss some recommendations for building such an environment. However, we will examine next the direction taken by the current reform movement within intercollegiate athletics.

The Current Reform Movement Within Intercollegiate Athletics

Over the past 15 years, a reform movement has swept through intercollegiate athletics influenced in part by a number of embarrassing and tragic incidents. These incidents include point-shaving scandals at Tulane and Boston College; the NCAA's suspension of the football program at Southern Methodist University; the drug-related death of Lenny Bias and the ensu-

ing investigation of the University of Maryland Basketball Program; the academic indiscretions of such schools as the University of Iowa and Temple University during the trial of sports agents Nordby and Walsh; as well as the fiascoes associated with the University of Oklahoma football program. Incidents such as these have left big-time college athletics with a major image problem.

The negative publicity has forced university presidents to get involve with the management of their athletic programs. Up until recently, university presidents were content to delegate their responsibility of intercollegiate athletics to their athletic directors. At many institutions, it was as if the athletic department became an entity separate from the rest of the university. Indeed, some athletic departments became corporations in hopes of increasing their money-making potential. With athletic programs' increasingly negative publicity tarnishing the reputations of entire universities, the presidents were forced to get involved. Thus, the NCAA's Presidents' Commission was formed in the early 1980s. The organizations expressed goal has been to reform the current structure of intercollegiate athletics. The reform movement as led by the Presidents' Commission has focused on a number of areas within the governance of intercollegiate athletics, from institutional control to cost containment. However, the movement's most visible reforms have come from its efforts to restore academic integrity to intercollegiate athletics.

Recent NCAA conventions have been testaments to the President's Commission's commitment to reform. In 1989, the NCAA passed legislation (Proposition 42) that eliminated the partial qualifier from Proposition 48. Proposition 48 stated that potential student-athletes had to obtain a high school grade point average (GPA) of 2.0 in a set of 12 core-curriculum courses, as well as at least a 700 combined score on the SAT, to be eligible to participate in athletics during their first year. A potential student-athlete who met only one of the requirements was considered a partial qualifier and was ruled ineligible to compete during the first year. However, the partial qualifier was allowed to receive an athletic scholarship. As it was originally stated, Proposition 42 would not allow partial qualifiers to receive any financial assistance in their first year. (Proposition 42 was revised in 1990 to allow the partial qualifier to receive need-based financial aid.) In 1991, the NCAA also passed legislation that limits to 20 hours the amount of time an athlete can participate in activities related to his/her sport.

In 1992, the NCAA passed legislation, Proposition 16, that further raised initial eligibility requirements while at the same time adding a sliding scale for high school grade point average and SAT requirements. Proposition 16 went into effect in August of 1996. According to Proposition 16, a potential student-athlete with a 2.0 high school GPA in a set of 15 core-curriculum courses must now earn a score of 900 on the SAT in order to be eligible to receive an athletic scholarship; while a potential student-athlete with a 700 SAT score must have a 2.5 high school GPA in order to be eligible. A recent amendment to this criteria restores the partial-qualifier status to the increased initial eligibility requirements. (Partial qualifiers under Proposition 16 receive the same sanctions as those under Proposition 48.) Under this revision, a potential student-athlete who scores 600 on the SATs must have at least a 2.75 core grade point average to be considered a partial qualifier.

African American student-athletes have been affected more by the present reform movement than any other group. African American student-athletes score significantly lower than their White counterparts on the SAT and ACT (Center for the Study of Athletics, 1989). In a study conducted by the NCAA in 1984, two years before Proposition 48 went into effect, it was reported that 54% of African American male athletes and 48% of African American female athletes who attended and subsequently graduated from the surveyed institutions would have been disqualified from freshman eligibility by the standardized test re-

quirement (NCAA, 1984). Meanwhile, only 9% of the White male and female athletes would have suffered the same fate. Similarly, Walter, Smith, Hoey, and Wilhelm (1987) reported that 60% of the African American football players at the University of Michigan from 1974 to 1983 would not have been eligible under Propositions 48 and 42. Further, they found that 87% of those African American football players who would have been excluded under Propositions 48 and 42 actually graduated. This adverse impact on African American student-athletes should only get worse under the increased initial eligibility requirements under Proposition 16.

On the surface, the goal of restoring academic integrity in intercollegiate athletics is a noble one. Unfortunately, the reform movement has adopted a strategy that assumes that the problem regarding student-athletes' relatively poor academic performance resides in student-athletes' poor academic preparation prior to arriving to college. The movement's current strategy also assumes that the reasons for the poor academic preparation is that many student-athletes are not sufficiently motivated to achieve academically. The assumption is that student-athletes value athletics more than they do academics. Thus, by raising the initial eligibility requirements of student-athletes, the reform movement argues that they are sending a message to potential student-athletes that they must do a better job academically if they want to play college athletics. Supporters of the current reform movement have also argued that these increases in initial eligibility standards also will send a message to the secondary school systems throughout the country that they must also do a better job of educating high school athletes. Surprisingly, little research has investigated the role of motivation in the academic performance of student-athletes. What little evidence that does exist suggests that an overwhelming majority of student-athletes value a college education (Center for the Study of Athletics, 1988, 1989), and that at least for African American student-athletes, academic motivation is not a predictor of subsequent academic performance (Sellers, 1992).

The current direction of the movement is based on erroneous premises, and does nothing to address the real problems that are influencing the relatively poor academic performance of student-athletes. The student-athletes' lack of motivation is not the problem. As a result, the current movement takes an unnecessarily exclusionary approach which will lead to deleterious consequences for African American student-athletes. Much of the poor academic preparation of many African American student-athletes can be traced to the current state of the public education systems in our inner cities. For example, the Chicago public school system, which is 68% African American, has an overall dropout rate of 40%. Meanwhile, its neighbor to the north, Evanston, has a dropout rate of approximately 3 percent (Harrison, 1991). The national high school dropout rate is approximately 12 percent. Clearly, there is a great deal of variance between the educational experiences of students in our inner cities and those students who live just a few miles away in the suburbs. The current reform movement does not begin to address this societal problem which is adversely impacting the life chances of far too many potential African American college students and student-athletes. The present legislation on initial-eligibility requirements does nothing to alleviate these discrepancies in educational preparation. The present legislation does not provide the school system in Gary, Indiana with funds to help offset the fact that they spend 38% less per student than the public school system in Evanston (Harrison, 1991). Yet, the present NCAA legislation views the educational opportunities of students from Gary and the Chicago public school system as being equal to the educational opportunities of students coming from the Evanston public school system.

African American student-athletes are not only coming from poorer socioeconomic backgrounds, but they may also be coming to college from poorer school districts. They may represent a number of other African American students trapped in deplorable educational systems, for whom a college education is not a viable option. Given the frightening state of affairs associated with our inner-city schools, these African American students are not likely to meet the criteria for college admittance if that criteria is based on the academic performance of students who are coming from far superior educational environments. Universities, with a surplus of applicants for admission, seem to only show an interest in those individuals from poorer educational backgrounds who have skills that are unique and exploitable—such as the athlete. Nonathletic students from the same high school who have performed better academically than their athletic classmates may not have as many educational opportunities because they do not possess skills that the universities value. The poor reputation of their high schools undermines the African American nonathletic students' chances of being admitted to college. Thus, the problem of the relatively poor performance of African American student-athletes is not one of focusing too much on athletics. In fact, their athletic achievement may actually have provided them with an educational opportunity that would not have otherwise existed if they were not athletes. This is witnessed by the fact that roughly 1 out of 9 African American males on Division I campuses are scholarship athletes, as compared to a ratio of 1 out of 50 for White males (NCAA, 1995). In reality, the African American student-athlete is the only connection between the post-secondary school system and the problems of the inner-city educational system.

Recommendations and Solutions

Before recommending possible interventions that will enhance the quality of postathletic life for African American student-athletes, it is important to keep in mind the major premise of the present essay. The quality of African American student-athletes' lives after sports is directly influenced by the quality of their experiences in college, which in turn, is a function of the quality of the education that they received. If an athlete receives a quality education then s/he is more apt to have a productive and positive postathletic experience. On the other hand, if an athlete does not receive a college education then s/he is at greater risk for a poorer quality of life. One should remember that a college education consists of the opportunity to further develop personal competency, to move up the socioeconomic ladder, and to receive a degree. Clearly, there are exceptions from this premise. Perhaps the most obvious exceptions are those athletes who leave college without a degree to play professional athletics and are fortunate enough to use that experience to gain some of the same benefits associated with a college education. However, this is a rather rare occurrence. Very few athletes make it professionally. Too many of those who do make it do not learn the personal competence skills necessary to lead productive lives outside of sports. In general, African American student-athletes who receive an opportunity for a college education are going to be better-prepared for life after athletics than those African American student-athletes who did not receive that opportunity. Thus, the following recommendations focus on interventions directed at African American student-athletes' educational experiences during their tenure in college.

The problems facing African American student-athletes in their efforts to get a college education are quite complex and need solutions that are sensitive to these complexities. For some African American student-athletes, many of their academic problems stem from inferior academic preparation in the elementary and secondary school systems. This problem is not unique to the African American student-athlete. It is one that affects most of the students who are educated in these dilapidated systems. The African American student-athlete just happens to have skills that are coveted by universities. In fact, the graduation rate for African American male nonathletes is a disgraceful 34% for Division I schools (NCAA, 1995). Another problem facing many

African American student-athletes is the cruel irony that besides having poorer academic preparation, they also have to participate in an activity (athletics) which is comparable to working a full-time job. Add to this the fact that they are coming from very different backgrounds and experiences, and it is easy to understand why many African American student-athletes report feeling as if they are strangers in a strange land. There are a variety of influences that impact African American student-athletes' educational opportunities. These influences exist at a number of levels including the societal level, the institutional level, the departmental level, and the individual level. A presentation of recommendations to address societal influences is beyond the scope of the present essay. Suffice to say that the decay of our public school systems adversely affects the educational opportunities of many African American student-athletes. Instead, the following are recommendations that are designed to improve the quality of African American student-athletes' postathletic lives by enhancing their educational opportunity while they are in college. These recommendations are addressed to the following constituents: researchers in sport sociology and psychology, the NCAA, individual institutions, and the African American student-athlete and her/his family. Most of these recommendations would be beneficial to all student-athletes, but are especially proposed with African American student-athletes in mind.

Recommendations for Researchers in Sport Sociology and Sport Psychology

As stated earlier, there has been very little empirical documentation of what happens to most African American student-athletes after their playing days are over. Researchers in sport sociology and sport psychology must begin to build a systematic body of literature that addresses this issue. This literature must be sensitive to the unique life experiences of African American student-athletes when investigating possible factors that predict successful adjustment. Researchers who utilize control groups of nonathletes to examine the effects of athletic participation on the career achievement of African American student-athletes must be sure that their control group is an appropriate one. Because many African American student-athletes are coming from very different backgrounds from even other African American college students, it is more appropriate to use a control group of the student-athletes' high school peers. Future studies must also utilize longitudinal designs in order that we may have a better understanding of the different processes African American student-athletes undergo during their adjustment to life after athletics. How traumatic is the ending of an athletic career for African American student-athletes? Is the adjustment to life after athletics a gradual one? What variables mediate the success of this adjustment? These are all important questions that can best be studied within a longitudinal design.

Finally, researchers must also understand that African American student-athletes are a heterogeneous group. African American student-athletes vary with regard to gender and socioeconomic differences. Analyses of these differences should not simply be parcelled out, but fully investigated. They should be studied as contributors of important information. Thus, the postathletic career adjustment of African American student-athletes is a topic worthy of study, in itself, without other comparison groups to provide texture.

Recommendations for the NCAA

It is obvious to even the casual observer that intercollegiate athletics is in need of reform. However, it is imperative that reformists such as the President's Commission of the NCAA focus less on solutions that are designed to regain the public's confidence in intercollegiate athletics, and focus more on developing a system that will actually promote the educational mission of the colleges themselves. The NCAA should place greater emphasis on de-

veloping strategies that will provide student-athletes with the greatest opportunity to receive a college education while they are on campus. Less emphasis should be placed on legislation that focuses on student-athletes' academic preparation prior to college. The NCAA has no influence over the quality of the elementary and secondary school systems. The organization would be better served to focus its energies on enhancing the quality of the educational experience being provided by colleges—institutions over which the NCAA has some jurisdiction. The following recommendations are made in concert with this perspective.

First, the NCAA should adopt legislation that requires competent academic support systems for all student-athletes (Sellers et al., 1991). The NCAA should regulate these support programs. Although academic support programs for student-athletes are fairly widespread, many of them provide very little educational benefit to the student-athlete. Many of them are supervised by underqualified individuals such as assistant coaches and graduate students. The NCAA had implemented an accreditation process for athletic departments. At present the accreditation process uses rather general criteria to evaluate the academic support services that the university offers student-athletes. The vagueness of the criteria used to evaluate academic support undermines the effectiveness of such a process. There is also some question as to how much teeth is behind the accreditation process.

Second, the NCAA must enforce its legislation restricting the amount of time to 20 hours per week that student-athletes may spend involved with activities related to their sport. Anecdotal data call into question the extent to which this legislation is being enforced. Observations and discussion with current student-athletes at a number of universities suggest that a lot of the activities that are explicitly voluntary are implicitly mandatory. Student-athletes have complained that they are coerced to participate fully in such "voluntary" activities as conditioning, film sessions, and skill development, or extra practice. It is critical that student-athletes are given time to study, as well as interact socially with other students who are not athletes, if they are to obtain an education.

Third, the NCAA should make all student-athletes ineligible to participate as freshmen. Currently, at some schools, freshmen football players play in three games before ever attending their first class. Most freshmen would benefit from a year to adjust to college life without the added pressure of athletic competition. Freshman ineligibility would greatly enhance the academic potential of those African American student-athletes who are coming from academically impaired backgrounds by allowing them to take courses that teach basic study skills. Athletic programs should grant five-year scholarships that allow student-athletes to compete intercollegiately during the last four years. At many institutions, most nonathletic students take five years or more to graduate anyway. During their freshman year, student-athletes should only be allowed to participate in athletic-related activities for 15 hours per week. Fifteen hours per week is five hours less than the new NCAA time limit for all student-athletes. The five-hour difference per week in athletic participation roughly corresponds to the amount of time team sports spend watching film of an upcoming opponent. Recent legislation allowing partial qualifiers a fourth year of eligibility if they graduate in four years is a step in the right direction. However, this legislation does not address those student-athletes who were inadequately prepared academically for college and for whom a year of remedial training may be warranted.

The results of an NCAA report provide some evidence in support of freshman ineligibility (Blum, 1993). The report compared the graduation rates of student-athletes who were partial qualifiers under Proposition 48 with other athletes in their cohort who were eligible. By definition, the eligible athletes had higher grade point averages and test scores than the partial qualifiers. The report found that partial qualifiers graduated at a higher rate than the

student-athletes who qualified fully. These findings suggest that in spite the stigma attached to the label of "partial qualifier," having a year in which to get acclimated to the campus benefits student-athletes academically. Think how much benefit would be derived if the stigma of "partial qualifier" were to be removed.

Finally, the NCAA must take a more inclusive stance regarding admissions of student-athletes. I argue that such an approach would not undermine the academic integrity of our institutions of higher education. In fact, educating those student-athletes who come from disadvantaged backgrounds *enhances* rather than erodes academic integrity. It is the mission of most public universities to provide community service, and an important part of that mission is to provide access to educational opportunities for those who have been historically denied access. Public institutions are also responsible for educating citizens to help them become productive members of society. If America is to continue to compete effectively in the next century, it is clear that it is going to have to do a much better job of preparing its human resources. However, the most important argument for educating those student-athletes is that it is the mission of *all* institutions of higher education to pursue understanding and knowledge. Individuals from diverse backgrounds provide a valuable resource to that pursuit. Their unique life experiences provide important new perspectives on the theoretical and applied problems that face academia today. Thus, the emphasis in reform should not be to eliminate those individuals who "do not belong" in college, but instead to provide those same individuals with the best opportunity to succeed.

Anyone who has seen a playbook from any college football team would have to admit that it must take a great deal of intelligence and motivation to master it. Unlike in the classroom, where scoring 90% earns the student-athlete a spot on the Dean's List, on the football field it only earns him a seat on the bench. A coach will not allow a player to take the field if he knows that the player is going to miss an assignment one out of every ten plays. Yet, the same athletes whose SAT scores suggest that they are not qualified to be in college are able to master a playbook that is every bit as complex as any history textbook. For example, the date in which the Declaration of Independence was signed does not change from class period to class period, let alone during a single class period. However, players must think and adjust their assignments on the field almost instantly. On the playing field, the correct answer (reaction) to a set of test stimuli (plays) changes as a function of a number of game-situation variables such as down and distance, one's teammates' assignments, the time of the game, and the other team's tendencies. If the NCAA recognizes that these student-athletes from disadvantaged backgrounds *do* have the ability to be as successful academically as they are athletically and provides legislation that enhances the quality of student-athletes' educational opportunities, then the students cannot help but to have a better life chance after their athletic careers.

Recommendations to Individual Institutions

One structure which already exists in many institutions and which has enormous potential to nurture the overall development of African American student-athletes is the academic support programs. Most of the academic support programs for student-athletes are housed within athletic departments. In previous work, my colleagues and I have argued that these programs must focus on the long-term development of the student-athlete (Sellers et al., 1991). A program that focuses on the long-term development of student-athletes would emphasize future competence in areas both inside and outside of the classroom. Unfortunately, many support programs are forced to focus on the short-term goal of maintaining the student-athletes' athletic eligibility instead of their potential academic viability. This results in the student-athletes pursuing a curriculum that may be to their advantage in the short-

term, but undermines the pursuit of long-term goals. Another characteristic of such an approach is that the support staff (often tutors) are spending all of their efforts in getting student-athletes through their history courses instead of teaching them better writing skills.

On the other hand, an academic support program focusing on long-term development would emphasize academic skill-building activities. These academic skills consist of such activities as writing skills, note-taking skills, time management, and reading comprehension. Upon entrance to an institution, each student-athlete would be assessed for her/his strengths and weaknesses and a support program would be designed, tailored specifically for the student-athlete's needs. This means that many student-athletes, African American and White, would have programs that would have some remedial courses during their first year or two which may force them to adopt a five- or maybe even a six-year educational tract. A student-athlete who takes six years to graduate, but does so with a college education, is preferable to one who graduates in four or five years without a true education. This is especially important for African American student-athletes when only 1 out of 10 African American students has received a bachelor's degree within six years from their high school graduation (Chronicle of Higher Education, 1991). Institutions must be willing to redshirt student-athletes who have particularly deficient academic preparation and spend the time, money, and effort to strengthen them academically. This recommendation is for a commitment to the academic development of African American student-athletes that is no different than the current commitment athletic programs display toward the athletic development of African American student-athletes. Most athletic programs assess student-athletes' physical strengths and design individualized fitness regiments tailored specifically for the student-athletes' needs. The same practice should be done for student-athletes' academic needs.

A program with a long-term focus would

also emphasize a holistic approach to the student-athletes' development. Such a support program would facilitate African American student-athletes' efforts to further develop personal competencies as well as improve their chances for a successful career after athletics. With regards to the development of personal competence, the support program must allow student-athletes to feel a sense of power and responsibility over their education. Student-athletes should be encouraged to make decisions for themselves and allowed to experience the consequences of those decisions. Such an approach teaches self-discipline, responsibility, and decision-making skills. It also promotes an overall sense of self-efficacy. Unfortunately, too many institutions do not allow student-athletes the opportunity of developing the intra- and interpersonal skills that one must rely upon when one makes decisions. However, this does not mean that support programs should not assist student-athletes with many of these decisions. They should provide any resources that will help the student-athletes make the right decisions. The support programs must walk the often-fine line between being supportive and being controlling.

Academic support programs can do a lot to help African American student-athletes enhance their vocational potential by providing career-planning and placement programs throughout the student-athletes' tenure at the school. There is evidence that suggests that student-athletes may not be particularly sophisticated in their career aspirations (Blann, 1985). A study using a nationally representative sample of Division I student-athletes found that despite placing a greater importance on financial importance than nonathletes, the jobs the student-athletes hoped to have at age 40 were significantly lower in socioeconomic status than those of the nonathletes (Center for the Study of Athletics, 1988). Career counseling early in student-athletes' tenure at college has been shown to positively influence the student-athletes' career choices as well as their overall academic performances (Nelson, 1982).

The greater exposure to different career paths increases the chances of student-athletes finding careers that match both their aptitudes and their aspirations. Such a match can only increase the student's intrinsic motivation and performance.

Another area in which institutions can make an importance impact in enhancing the educational opportunities of African American student-athletes is in the hiring of more African American coaches and administrators within the athletic department (Sellers et al., 1991). African American coaches and athletic administrators (particularly former African American student-athletes) are more likely to understand the unique experiences of the African American student-athlete. Lapchick (1991) has noted that White coaches' treatment of African American student-athletes is sometimes influenced by their own stereotypical notions regarding African American athletes. Thus, African American coaches and administrators are more qualified to design programs that will enhance African American student-athletes' life chances. African American coaches and athletic administrators also provide important role models for both African American and White student-athletes. This is especially important to African American student-athletes because of their dependence on support systems located off campus.

In 1990, at predominantly White Division I schools, there were only 47 African American head coaches out of 1,165 head coaching positions in football, men's and women's basketball, track, and baseball (Lapchick, 1991). This equates to roughly 4 percent of the coaching positions. In 1990, African Americans made up approximately one percent of the athletic directors, assistant and associate athletic directors, business and ticket managers, and sports information directors at these schools. As of the 1995 football season, there were only 3 African American head football coaches at the predominantly White Division IA schools. African Americans were severely underrepresented as assistant coaches, as well. In many instances, the few African American assistant coaches at these institutions are relegated to recruiter status, where their primary function is to recruit African American student-athletes. Besides being a role that does not often lead to head coaching responsibilities, the role of recruiter also keeps African American coaches on the road for significant periods of time. The road-warrior existence of the recruiter makes it more difficult sustain a supportive relationship with the African American student-athletes who are on campus. Universities should not only hire more Blacks in their athletic departments, but they also need to place Blacks in a greater variety of positions.

Finally, universities should send admissions officers with their football and basketball coaches when they go to high schools to recruit students. It would be nice if universities would recruit the star students from economically impoverished high schools in the same manner that they recruit star athletes. One proposal would be to have each institution endow an academic scholarship to be given to a student at each high school from which a student-athlete is signed. This will help to provide more opportunities for academically achieving students from a more diverse sampling of high schools.

Recommendations for the African American Student-Athlete and Family

African American student-athletes and their families can also play a significant role in increasing the chances of the student-athlete receiving a quality college education. First, student-athletes and their families must understand that they are ultimately responsible for their education. They are the ones who will suffer the consequences of not receiving a college education. African American student-athletes and their families should adopt this understanding before choosing a college. They should make the quality of the educational opportunity offered a major criteria for evaluating which college the student-athlete will be attending. African American student-athletes and their families should be proactive in the recruiting process. They should evaluate every aspect of the school, from academics to athletics to social climate. An important part of any evaluation should be an examination and understanding of the graduation rates of previous student-athletes. (Recent NCAA legislation requires each school to provide information on their graduation rates of student-athletes over the past 10 years to student-athletes whom they are recruiting.) African American student-athletes and their families should also attain as much information about the educational experiences and career status of as many student-athletes from similar backgrounds as possible. The student-athletes and their families should also check out the academic support programs that are offered for student-athletes. Are the support programs adequate for the student-athlete's specific needs?

Once in college, student-athletes must be willing to take the extra steps necessary to receive a college education. These extra steps may mean that the student-athlete must go out of his/her way to interact with other students who are not student-athletes. This is especially important for African American student-athletes. Allen (1988) found that for African American students, interacting with other African American students was positively associated with academic achievement. Interaction with other African American students provides African American students with both the emotional and instrumental support necessary to navigate a sometimes-hostile environment. African American student-athletes should try to get involved with campus activities such as clubs, fraternities and sororities, and volunteer organizations. Besides providing a much-needed perspective of college life outside of the athletic realm, involvement with nonathletes also provides an opportunity to build a wider social network, which may lead to unforeseen benefits later in life. These unforeseen benefits include future business relationships, medical relationships, and legal relationships.

Conclusions

The quality of African American student-athletes' lives after their playing days are over is likely to be related to the quality of their college education. Those African American student-athletes who are able to get a college education are likely to enjoy greater economic, social, and psychological benefits than those who end their college athletic careers without receiving equitable compensation. Coming from very different backgrounds than their fellow student-athletes and fellow African American college students, African American student-athletes may have an unique postathletic career experience. Unfortunately, the research literature has virtually ignored this experience and the present reform movement in college athletics threatens to extinguishes it. More enlightened efforts by the NCAA and individual institutions can enhance the chances of African American student-athletes spending their postathletic days reaping the benefits of a college education instead of recovering from exploitation. Since African American student-athletes and their families are the ones who will have to endure the consequences of an exploitive athletic career, they are the ones who must ultimately shoulder the responsibility of obtaining a meaningful college education in a system that is not as responsive to their needs as it should be.

Study Questions

1. In what ways are African American student-athletes different from other students on campus ?

2. In what ways does your institution provide African American student-athletes with educational opportunities?

3. In what ways does your institution exploit African American student-athletes?

Suggested Readings

Braddock, J. H. (1980). Race, sports, and social mobility: A critical review. *Sociology Symposium, 2,* 18–37.

Chavous, T. M., & Sellers, R. M. (1997). National Collegiate Athletic Association policies and the educational opportunities of African American male athletes: A question of personal responsibility versus structural barriers. In C. C. Yeakey, B. A. Sizemore, & G. S. Johnston (Eds.), *Post Reaganism and the quest for social democracy in schooling.* New York and London: The Greenwood Group.

Lapchick, R. (1991). *Five minutes to midnight: Race and sport in the 1990's.* Lanham: Madison Books.

Sellers, R. M., & Kuperminc, G. P. (1997). Goal discrepancy in African American male student-athletes' unrealistic expectations for careers in professional sports. *Journal of Black Psychology, 23*(1), 6–23.

Sellers, R. M., & Damas, A. (1996). The African American student-athlete experience. In E. F. Etzel, A. P. Ferrante, & J. Pinckney (Eds.) *Counseling college student-athletes: Issues and interventions* (2nd ed.). Morgantown, WV: Fitness Information Technology, Inc.

References

Allen, W. R. (1988). Black students in U.S. higher education: Toward improved access, adjustment and achievement. *The Urban Review, 20*(3), 165–188.

Blann, F. W. (1985). Intercollegiate athletic competition and student's educational and career plans. *Journal of College Student Personnel, 26*(2), 115–118.

Blum, D. (1993, July 7). Graduation rate of scholarship athletes rose after Proposition 48 was adopted, NCAA reports. *The Chronicle of Higher Education,* p. A42.

Braddock, J. H. (1980). Race, sports, and social mobility: A critical review. *Sociology Symposium, 2,* 18–37.

Cashmore, E. (1982). *Black sportsmen.* Boston: Routledge & Regan Paul.

Center for the Study of Athletics. (1988). *Report No. 1: Summary results from the 1987–88 national study of intercollegiate athletes.* Palo Alto, CA: American Institutes for Research.

Center for the Study of Athletics. (1989). *Report No. 3: The life experiences of black intercollegiate athletes at NCAA Division I universities.* Palo Alto, CA: American Institutes for Research.

The Chronicle of Higher Education. (1991). *1991 Almanac, 38*(1).

Coakley, J. J. (1983). Leaving competitive sport: Retirement or rebirth? *Quest, 35,* 1–11.

Danish, S. J. (1983). Musings about personal competence: The contributions of sport, health, and fitness. *American Journal of Community Psychology, 11*(3), 221–240.

Danish, S. J., Galambos, N. L., & Laqquatra, I. (1983). Life development intervention: Skill training for personal competence. In R. D. Felner, L. A. Jason, J. Moritsugu, & S. S. Farber (Eds.), *Preventive psychology: Theory research and practice.* Elmsford, NY: Pergamon Press.

Edwards, H. (1979). Sport within the veil: The triumphs, tragedies, and challenges of Afro-American involvement. *Annals, AAPSS, 445,* 116–127.

Eitzen, S. D., & Tessendorf, I. (1978). Racial segregation by position in sports: The special case of basketball. *Review of Sport and Leisure, 3,* 109–128.

Ervin, L., Saunders, S. A., Gillis, H. L., & Hogrebe, M. C. (1985). Academic performance of student athletes in revenue-producing sports. *Journal of College Student Personnel, 26*(2), 119–124.

Greendorfer, S. L., & Blinde, E. M. (1985). "Retirement" from intercollegiate sport: Theoretical and empirical considerations. *Sociology of Sport Journal, 2,* 101–110.

Harris, D. S., & Eitzen, D. S. (1978). The consequences of failure in sport. *Urban Life, 7*(2), 177–188.

Harrison, C. H. (1991). *Peterson's public schools USA: A comparative guide to school districts* (2nd ed.). Peterson's Guide, Inc.

Hurtsfield, J. (1978). Internal colonialism: White, black, chicano self-conceptions. *Ethnic and Racial Studies, 1*(1), 60–79.

Kiger, G., & Lorentzen, D. (1986). The relative effect of gender, race, and sport on university academic performance. *Sociology of Sport Journal, 3,* 160–167.

Kleiber, D., Greendorfer, S., Blinde, E., & Samdahl, D. (1987). Quality of exit from university sports and life satisfaction in early adulthood. *Sociology of Sport Journal, 4,* 28–36.

Lapchick, R. (1991). *Five minutes to midnight: Race and sport in the 1990s.* Lanham: Madison Books.

Lerch, S. *Athletic retirement as social death: an overview.* Paper presented at the Third Annual Meeting of NASSS, Toronto.

National Collegiate Athletic Association. (1984). *Study of freshman eligibility standards: Executive summary.* Reston, VA: Social Sciences Division, Advanced Technology, Inc.

National Collegiate Athletic Association. (1991). *NCAA academic performance study report 91–01: A description of college graduation rates for 1984 and 1985 freshmen student-athletes.* Overland Park, KA: NCAA Publications.

National Collegiate Athletic Association. (1995). *1995 NCAA Division I graduation-rates report.* Overland Park, KA: Author.

Nelson, E. S. (1982). The effects of career counseling on freshman college athletes. *Journal of Sport Psychology, 4,* 32–40.

Picou, J. S. (1978). Race, athletic achievement, and educational aspirations. *The Sociological Quarterly, 19,* 429–438.

Purdy, D., Eitzen, D. S., & Hufnagel, R. (1982). Are athletes also students? The educational attainment of college athletes. *Social Problems, 29*(4), 439–448.

Sellers, R. M. (1992). Racial differences in the predictors of academic achievement of Division I student-athletes. *Sociology of Sport Journal, 9,* 48–59.

Sellers, R. M., Kuperminc, G. P., & Waddell, A. S. (1991, Fall). Life experiences of Black student-athletes in revenue producing sports: A descriptive empirical analysis. *Academic Athletic Journal,* 21–38.

Shapiro, B. J. (1984). Intercollegiate athletic participation and academic achievement: A case study of Michigan State University student-athletes, 1950–1980. *Sociology of Sport Journal, 1,* 46–51.

Snyder, E. E., & Spreitzer, E. A. (1978). *Social aspects of sports.* Englewood Cliffs, NJ: Prentice Hall.

Walter, T., Smith, D. E. P., Hoey, G., & Wilhelm, R. (1987). Predicting the academic success of college athletes. *Research Quarterly for Exercise and Sport, 58*(2), 273–279.

Racial Differences in Collegiate Recruitment, Retention, and Graduation Rates

Audwin Anderson and Donald South

Abstract

Among the rationales for intercollegiate sports is the belief that participation will provide individuals with educational and status-enhancement opportunities. For many athletes, and African American athletes in particular, this is not necessarily the case. Over the past 15 years, sociology and sport literature has documented racial differences in educational outcomes for college athletes. In fact, recent disclosures by the NCAA of graduation rates revealed that nearly twice the percentage of White athletes compared to African American athletes graduated from college over the past year. This work focuses on some of the circumstances which have not been favorable for the purpose of education for African American athletes. Our analysis starts by looking at the social meaning of African American maleness, followed by a section on recruitment and Proposition 48. Final discussion addresses the issues of economic and academic exploitation of African American athletes, and the issue of graduation rates.

Key Terms

- Intercollegiate sports -
- African american athletes -
- Graduation rates -
- Economic exploitation -
- Academic exploration -
- Retention of African American athletes -

Introduction

Sport in American society has a long history of development (Eitzen and Sage, 1993). Despite some early resistance from religious interests, sport rapidly became an integral part of American culture. Sport and higher education likewise had a sometimes uneasy relationship in earlier years, but that relationship was cemented and intensified over the years, as was the relationship between sport and the larger society (Chu, 1989). In fact, the collegiate-sports contexts have become so interrelated that aspiring professional athletes in football and basketball have little recourse except to prepare for a sports career by attending college whether or not they are "college material." In effect, this means that a number of athletes are in college with little enthusiasm for academic work. Thus, there are obvious implications for scholarship and subsequent graduation.

To appreciate the problem experiences of African Americans in big-time collegiate athletics more fully, issues of athletics and education must be addressed. A basic tension between big-time athletic values and goals and those of higher education has been widely recognized (Asher, 1986; Chu, 1989; Lawry, 1991). Traditional goals of higher education are to promote high levels of academic achievement and integrity. The overriding goal of big-time sports is to win—which translates into high-level entertainment and big revenues. It has been the task of the National Collegiate Athletic Association to promote and enhance the marketability of collegiate sports and simultaneously to maintain the sense of amateurism and academic integrity. The more successful the NCAA is in achieving one of these goals, the more difficult it becomes to achieve the other. The trend among NCAA institutions has been toward promoting entertainment. As a result, such a vast array of rules has been promulgated to regulate collegiate sports recruiting, and participation, that athletic programs and individual athletes are in constant peril of infractions. This context is applicable for athletes in general, but it is experienced variously by different categories.

Sociological analysis often focuses on differences among various social categories within a population. The act of using categories as a basis for analysis does not assume that such categories are necessarily different because of inherent biological or intellectual traits. Rather, the causal emphasis focuses on differential experiences by given categories. Among the more consistently important categorical differences are those of race, sex, class, and age.

Persons forming major social categories are likely to develop different worldviews and to experience different opportunities. In addition, individuals will be accorded different identities and statuses and exhibit different behaviors. In short, the authors acknowledge that race categories are not discrete biological entities. Yet, social notions of race categories do have meaning and consequences for those who are assigned to these categories by themselves or others. This essay will focus on differences in collegiate sports experiences by African American males. More specifically, it will investigate racial differences in collegiate recruitment, retention, and graduation rates.

If there is a position which we take in this work it is one of pro-education. Our wish is that this work will become part of the debate and dialogue of college athletes, coaches, counselors, and athletic directors. Our goal is to help facilitate changes which will make circumstances favorable for the purpose of educating the African American athlete.

The Problem

Sport participation in American society has long been viewed as a vehicle for the assimilation of newcomers. As a conduit into mainstream American life, sport has been viewed as teaching the values of hard work, teamwork, and discipline. Proponents of sports developed a number of rationales for sport in society, its inclusion in higher education, and in the character development of individual participants (Schendel, 1965; Webb, 1969). Detractors have pointed to excesses, dysfunctions, and conflicts of interest in sport (Edwards, 1969; Eitzen, 1989). Among the rationales for intercollegiate sports is the belief that participation in intercollegiate sports will provide the athlete with educational opportunities (Naison & Mangum, 1983). For many athletes, and African American athletes in particular, this is not necessarily the case. Over the past 15 years, sociology and sport literature has documented racial differences in educational outcomes for college athletes (Naison & Mangum, 1983; Raney, Knapp, & Small, 1986; Spivey & Jones, 1975; Warfield, 1986). In fact, recent disclosures by the NCAA of graduation rates revealed that nearly twice the percentage of White athletes compared to African American athletes graduated from college between 1990 and 1991. The numbers showed that African Americans graduated at a 26.6 percent rate compared to 52.2 percent for Whites.

African Americans were absent from big-time college sport for most of the twentieth century. In the first half of this century, African American college students attended historically Black colleges and universities (Willie & Cunnigen, 1981). This trend began to reverse itself in the years following World War II. At the beginning of World War II, of the approximately 45,000 African American students enrolled in higher education, only about 10% were enrolled in predominately White colleges or universities (Mingle, 1981). Presently, most African American college students attend predominately White institutions.

Several conditions were responsible for the above-mentioned trend, not the least of which was the 1954 *Brown* decision of the U.S. Supreme Court which outlawed separate educational facilities. Another important factor was the establishment of federal financial-aid programs for students and institutions. In the 1950s, the National Scholarship Service and Fund for Negro Students (NSSFNS) was established (Mingle, 1981). Legal and economic factors provided the foundation leading to the migration of African American students to predominantly White universities. This migration pattern also included African American student-athletes.[1]

Harry Edwards has been an important voice in bringing to the forefront the unique social and political situation of the African American athlete (Edwards, 1969). According to Edwards, the manpower vacuum created by World War II, the 1954 Supreme Court decision, and the urge by Whites to further exploit African Americans economically resulted in African Americans being allowed to venture into big-time college athletics (Edwards, 1969). African American athletes also found it to their advantage to play for predominantly White schools (Edwards, 1969; Eitzen, 1989).

College Athletics and Issues of Race

In *The Souls of Black Folk* (1969), renowned scholar W. E. B. DuBois proclaimed that the prevailing issue of twentieth-century Americans would be the problem of the "color line" (p. XI). Conservative thought in the latter half of the twentieth century presents us with an interesting version of "color blindness." The suggestion is made that our society does not have a race problem, because we judge people on the basis of character and merit, not skin color. Though disputed (Marger, 1985; Takaki, 1987), this view was held to be true especially in the area of sports. There is much evidence that in reality, skin color continues to have a dramatic impact on one's life chances and opportunities for improved mobility and success. To say that our society is color-blind at this moment in history amounts to aversion to, and neglect of, real problems and issues.

---

1. Our discussion will be concerned primarily with the African American male athlete. This is in no way meant to disparage the experience of the African American female athlete. There are two fine chapters on African American female athletes in this volume which do more justice to that experience than space permits here.

If our society is ever going to "solve" problems of race (assuming it is not an insurmountable problem), it must face, in an honest and humane manner, the issues and implications of race. Likewise, if big-time college athletics is going to solve its much-publicized problems and dilemmas, it also must face honestly the issues and implications of race and race relations.

In the spring of 1991, the Knight Foundation's Commission on Intercollegiate Athletics released a report on abuses in college athletics.[2] The Commission expressed concern that "abuses in athletics had reached proportions threatening the very integrity of higher education" (Knight Foundation, 1991, p. 1). The report highlighted some of the problems of college athletics and proposed some change and remedies. Yet the report (about 40 pages) makes only four indirect references to the issue of race in college athletics. In the first chapter of the report appears the statement, "Sports have helped break down bigotry and prejudice in American life" (Knight Foundation, 1991, p. 3). On page 8 in a section entitled "Focus on Students" appears, "Intercollegiate athletics exist first and foremost for the student athletes who participate whether male or female, majority or minority. . . . " (Knight Foundation, 1991, p. 8). Further on it is recommended that grants-in-aid for low-income athletes be expanded to the "full cost of attendance; including personal and miscellaneous expenses" (Knight Foundation, 1991, p. 19). And finally on page 31 in the Statement of Principles, "Every student-athlete—male and female, majority and minority, in all sports—will receive equitable and fair treatment" (Knight Foundation, 1991, p. 31).

The egalitarian principles put forth by the Commission are to be commended, and there is no intention here to question the sincerity of their effort. Yet, the issue of race and the educational condition of the African American athlete are not directly addressed.

We take the position that there is a considerable amount of exploitation or victimization of student-athletes in big-time collegiate sports. Further, we contend that African American youth are especially vulnerable. We are aware of inherent difficulties in making the case for exploitation. Exploitation involves both an objective condition and subjective evaluations. Some, in observing a situation, will emphasize the former, others the latter. We will argue that a number of structural conditions are favorable for outcomes which lend themselves to interpretations of exploitation.

Through socialization, by emulation of esteemed role models and as a consequence of subcultural values, African American youth are highly oriented to the goal of a sports career (Anderson et.al.; 1990, Rudman, 1986). Interacting with this condition is the fact of relatively few career options. The colleges need African American youth to help provide high-level entertainment to match large-scale revenue opportunities. There is virtually no avenue to professional sport careers, especially football and basketball, except through college participation. Colleges are faced with a paradox of maintaining academic integrity while providing entertainment with youth who are often academically ill-prepared. The athletes may not be particularly devoted to scholastic pursuit, but have few options for gaining social mobility in American society.

The differential in power for these two interests is immense. College can dictate that youth must be capable of generating big-time entertainment to generate big dollars in exchange for rather small amounts of compensation and the hope of securing a professional sports position. Intense competition results because the number of positions is small and the players, numerous. To gain one of the scarce positions the athlete, especially one with less talent, must single-mindedly pursue that goal to the exclusion of academic interests. There-

---

2. It should be noted that the Knight Commission is an independent organization and is not a part of the NCAA.

fore, the end result for many is little monetary reward, little education, and an accumulation of debilitating injuries.

It seems that the issue which most needs to be addressed is the educational experiences of African American athletes in revenue-producing sports (i.e., football and basketball) at our nation's universities. We currently are witnessing declining university-enrollment rates for African American students, especially African American males (Marden, Meyer, & Engel, 1992). This is occurring at a time when we are also witnessing conflicts over multiculturalism in university curricula, a backlash against affirmative action policy, cutbacks in student financial aid, "race" politics, political correctness, and questions about the appropriateness of quotas in hiring. In light of this, an argument can be made that the recruitment by universities of African American athletes provides these athletes with an increasingly unique opportunity for an education. We wish to bring particular attention to the word opportunity. *Webster's New World Dictionary* defines opportunity as "a combination of circumstances favorable for the purpose" (*Webster's*, 1988, p. 950).

For the remainder of this work we will focus on some of the circumstances which have not been favorable for the purpose of education for African American athletes. We will start by looking at the social meaning of African American maleness, followed by a section on recruitment and Proposition 48. We will then speak to issues of economic and academic exploitation of African American athletes, and the issue of graduation rates.

Social Meaning of African American Maleness

In a very important piece of work by Fordham and Ogbu (1986), it was found that many inner-city African American youth define academic success as "acting White." The implication of this position is that academic success is the domain of Whites. This perception leads Fordham and Ogbu to suggest that many African Americans discourage their peers, per-

haps unconsciously, from emulating White academic striving and achievement. As a result, African American students who are academically able do not put forth the necessary effort in schoolwork and, consequently, perform poorly in educational settings. To the extent that this is true, what does it mean to use the opposite term, to "act Black"?

In recent history, we have witnessed the label used to describe persons of African descent change from Negro to Black to Afro-American to African American. What do these changes connote? Does each label connote a different set of behaviors, attitudes, dispositions, or lifestyles which define and delineate? The view held here is that the changes connote an ongoing search for identity, a search for a home on America's cultural landscape, a quest for a self-generated definition of what it means to be of African descent and a native-born American.

Sports have been held up in our society as an arena in which African Americans, particularly males, could compete and achieve without the bane of discrimination, as an activity where merit was rewarded and achievement was unambiguous and evident to all. For the African American male, sport has provided an activity in which to forge an identity. But, one must ask, what of this identity? Where did it come from? Is it self-generated? Why does it involve such physicalness? Why was this identity not forged through medicine or law?

It seems plausible to argue that the aforementioned labels connote a different way of interpreting experiences during this ongoing quest for identity. Certainly the "angry Black man" of the 1960s interpreted his experiences differently than the "docile Negro" of previous times. In this vein the label African American has the potential for eliciting a new interpretation, a broader and fuller interpretation of maleness than is proffered by the American stereotype.

Since the *Moynihan Report* (Moynihan, 1965) there has been increased attention paid to the so-called "absent father" in the African American family. For Moynihan, one of the factors which directly led to the "deterioration" of the African American family was the high proportion of African American families headed by females.

Karenga (1980) took a different view, particularly as it applied to the African American male. He contended that the major problem in the African American community was the lack of a cultural base or cultural identity. He concluded with the contention that the media's influence on African Americans, in particular males, was maximized in the absence of a strong cultural base and identity. Karenga maintained that African Americans possessed a "popular culture" rather than a "national culture." Popular culture is defined as the "societal perception and stereotypes of your group" (Karenga, 1980, p. 18), whereas national culture is more of a self-generated (group-based) definition. The first is externally generated and imposed; the latter is a self-definition by the subject group.

Marable (1986) presents a similar position by suggesting that the essential tragedy of being African American and male is the inability of African American men to define themselves apart from the stereotypes which the larger society imposes on them. Marable contends that through various institutional means these stereotypes are perpetuated and that they permeate our entire culture. Marable's position is that not only have the stereotypes informed the larger cultural image of the African American male, but they have also had a longstanding influence on how the African American male develops a definition of self.

The historical stereotypes of the African American male have been very narrow and usually physical. The image has been of a "laborer," or "super athlete," or "sexual stud." The major point to be made here is that these are not self-generated definitions, even though they may be in part accepted by African American males.

Another argument given for the cultural identity of African American males is that within the African American community there is a lack of role models for youth outside the fields of entertainment and sport (Edwards, 1973). The argument is that our society fails to highlight the African American doctor, lawyer, and other professionals. As a result, many African American youth see their only opportunity for social success in terms of the narrow fields of entertainment and sport. As Edwards states, "Young Blacks are encouraged toward attempts at 'making it' through athletic participation, rather than pursuit of other occupations that hold greater potential for meeting the real political and material needs of both themselves and their people" (Edwards, 1973, p. 44). Others have pointed out that the large number of African Americans in certain sports does not so much indicate a freedom from discrimination as much as it reflects the lack of opportunities in other areas (Castine & Roberts, 1974). In a similar view, Lawson, commenting on African Americans in sport, points out, "The successes of a few have served to conceal the limited opportunities for the majority" (Lawson, 1979, p. 190).

If the label African American does have the potential for eliciting a new interpretation of identity, it must allow for a more multidimensional identity. Certainly it must include an educational dimension. The term African American suggests some cultural continuity between West Africa and America: the bringing forth of an emergent cultural legacy to the present; a cultural legacy which defines the male in broader and fuller terms than the American stereotype; a tradition which speaks to intellectual contributions, such as those made in the arts, sciences, and literature. A conscious awareness of these contributions by African Americans and others is critical if a transformation in meaning and identity is to take place.

Recruitment and Proposition 48

For Fifteen years we have had a race problem. We have raped a generation and a half of young Black athletes. We have taken kids and sold them on bouncing a ball and running with a football and that being able to do things athletically was going to be an end in itself. (Joe Paterno, cited in Coakley, 1986, p. 143)

The above remark by Pennsylvania State University head football coach Joe Paterno, spoken from the floor of the 1983 NCAA Convention, is said to have provided the emphasis which led to the passage of Proposition 48 [By-law 5-1 (J)]. This proposition was proposed by the American Council on Education and implemented for the 1986–87 academic year. The by-law establishes the academic requirements which high school seniors must meet in order to be eligible for participation as freshmen in NCAA-sanctioned Division I sports. The requirements were

1. High school seniors must maintain a 2.0 grade point average in a curriculum that contains at least three English credits, two math, two natural or physical science, and two social science courses. At least 11 academic courses in high school must have been taken by a prospective athlete.

2. High school seniors must achieve a combined score of 700 on the Scholastic Aptitude Test (out of 1600), or a score of 15 on the American College Test (out of 36).

More stringent revisions of these standards were passed by the NCAA in 1992, to go into effect for athletes entering college in August 1995 or thereafter. The number of "core" courses will increase to 13 from the previous 11. With a high school grade point average of 2.00 (C) the student now needs a minimum score of either 900 on the Scholastic Aptitude Test (SAT) or 21 on the American College Test (ACT) to gain full admission status. With higher grade point averages, a decreasing scale of SAT or ACT scores is required.

From its inception, Proposition 48 has been one of the most controversial proposals ever adopted by the NCAA (Picou, 1986). According to Sage (1989), Proposition 48 is a classic example of "blaming the victim." Sage contends that NCAA places the blame on the student-athlete for being academically ill-

prepared for college-level work. Yet, the cause of the problem is university officials have been willing to admit academically ill-prepared students for reasons of competitive sports success. Sage sees the NCAA's call for higher academic standards as a "charade" which has moved attention away from the "commercialized structure of major college athletic programs and focused it on the athlete" (Sage, 1989, p. 169).

Sage's points are well taken here. Clearly one of the major antecedents of the condition which led to Proposition 48 was the recruitment of academically marginal students and the employment of various methods to keep them eligible. Also, the admission of academically marginal students is primarily a problem of revenue sports (football and basketball).

One of the fallouts or latent functions of the by-law is that it created a situation whereby the nation's junior colleges, which are not governed by the by-law, act as a kind of "feeder" to Division I schools. Division I schools are in some cases only accountable for the education of the student-athlete for two years and, in some cases, a shorter period of time. It is likely that in some colleges and universities the junior-college transfer in football could exhaust athletic eligibility by maintaining academic eligibility for only two semesters. This situation does not facilitate education and creates a structural situation which lends itself to exploitation.

Indeed, over the past several years some African American youth have been following a course of attending community colleges with the expectation that they will be "taken care of" academically—that they will automatically qualify for admission to Division I programs, or that academic counselors in athletic programs can "arrange" matters to make them eligible. Such practices have led to allegations of questionable or fraudulent course credits (Chronicle of Higher Education, August 16, 1996, p. A37) and have resulted in athletic ineligibility for an unknown number of youth, and probation for some university athletic programs (Baylor University, for example).

The major fallout of the by-law has been its racial consequences. Reports show that 85% of those losing eligibility under Proposition 48 have been African American (Cross & Koball, 1991; Johnson, 1988). In addition, Proposition 48 disqualified a sizeable percentage of African American athletes who might have graduated. According to Grambling State University president Dr. Joseph Johnson (1988), 40 percent of the athletes that have graduated in the past would be ineligible under present rules. Chu (1989) gives figures which show that if Proposition 48 standards had been applied in the years 1977–1980 they would have disqualified 69% of the African American and 54% of the White athletes who went on to graduate.

Proposition 48 was also met by direct charges of racism by presidents of the nation's historically Black colleges. Joseph Johnson, who was chairman of the National Association of Equal Opportunity in Higher Education Athletic Committee at the time Proposition 48 was passed, speaking on behalf of 114 Black institutions, states,

> It was our collective view that Proposition 48 was a very poorly thoughtout proposal. We were concerned because we knew that the rule would impact most severely on Black athletes. It was thrust upon us; none of us were included in any of the debates about the proposition. That was the thing. We thought it was unfair because we are members of the NCAA, and the Proposition was brought to the floor by the American Council on Education without our input. (Johnson, 1988, p. 4)

Proposition 48 has a particularly negative effect on historically Black institutions, which have a long tradition of remediating the academic shortcomings of African American students. It has exacerbated the financial difficulties faced by athletic programs at these institutions (Edwards, 1989). As pointed out by Johnson, traditionally Black institutions do not have the economic resources to finance the education of students made ineligible by Proposition 48 until they are eligible. Some Black college presidents have even proposed that Black institutions be exempt from Proposition 48 standards or be allowed to establish their own standards (Edwards, 1989).

Harry Edwards is the most visible and well-known spokesperson on the plight of the African American athlete in American sports. His activist position on improving the academic condition and image of the African American athlete is well-documented. His work in the area is so important and persuasive that one cannot speak to the social condition of the African American athlete without recognizing the contributions of Edwards. He has taken a position (see Edwards 1984, 1985) which is at odds with many African American educators and coaches. Edwards sees the establishment of Proposition 48 as a method of stemming the exploitation of African American athletes in the collegiate setting. Edwards even goes as far as to argue that the cutoffs for ACT and SAT scores should be higher, which would result in less exploitation. Lowering the standard would send the message to African American athletes that they are not intellectually capable of achieving these standards. Edwards also contends (as do the authors here) that African American athletes themselves must take a hand against their own exploitation. They must have an interest in getting an education.

The idea of a universal academic standard seems to us to be a bit problematic. It seems to ignore the fact that some universities are more academically challenging and rigorous than others. A counterproposal which has some potential for remediating the problem of admissions and low graduation rates would hold universities responsible for not recruiting athletes who do not have a reasonable chance of performing up to that university's standards, whatever those standards may be.

We should mention two other issues currently being pursued which might present uncertain hope of circumventing eligibility guidelines. One of these is the possibility of invoking "learning disabilities" as a basis for academically qualifying with less than a standard score (Chronicle of Higher Education, January 5, 1996, p.A47).

The other item is that of homeschooling. Issues of determining athletic competition eligibility for both scholastic and collegiate participation for those experiencing homeschooling are currently being debated by school boards and by the courts (*The Chronicle of Higher Education,* January 5, 1996).

African American youth are ill-served by such schemes to circumvent academic eligibility guidelines. Their interest would appear to be better served by pursuing opportunities offered by the Princeton Review Foundation and promoted by the National Alliance of African American Athletes to enhance test scores (*USA Today*, October 30, 1996). The thrust of this new effort is not to "fight" standards of eligibility—though they may sometimes appear unfair—but to promote SAT workshops which provide practice and analysis designed to produce better test results.

Economic and Academic Exploitation

> The most reprehensible feature of College football today is that many universities engage in what amounts to professional football, but hold fast to the illusion that their athletes are amateurs. (Sack, 1987, p. 165)

Many authors have recently spoken to the influence of the profit-making ideology of corporate business on college sports (Eitzen,1989; Sack, 1988; Warfield, 1986). The NCAA can be viewed as a business enterprise whose primary function is the production of competitive sporting events (Sack, 1988). Without question the primary labor force for the NCAA is the student-athlete. Much debate has centered around the appropriateness of the label "amateur" applied to football and basketball players at universities which realize high profits from these sports (see Sack, 1988 & 1991).

Of the 45 universities placed on NCAA probation between January 1988 and November 1989, 34 cases dealt with improper benefits to athletes (Sack, 1991). Presently, of the 34 schools under NCAA sanctions, 27 involve improper benefits (*The Chronicle of Higher Education,* March 27, 1991).

Collegiate sport has a long history of abuses of the standard of amateurism (Sack, 1988; Sage, 1989). A case can be made that the athletic scholarship (grant-in-aid) is in fact a form of payment for athletic ability (Sack, 1988). Given the time demands as well as the physical and mental stress, college athletes rank as some of the most underpaid workers in the economy.

In a recent study of college basketball players, Sack (1988) reports that African American athletes are far more likely than their White counterparts to think they deserve workmen's compensation, the right to form unions, and the right to share TV revenue. Eighty percent of the lower-class African American males in the sample felt they deserved a share of the revenue. It was also reported that 55% of lower-class athletes, regardless of race, see nothing wrong with accepting illegal payments. A probable basis for this position is given by Davis (1996). He argues that the absence of a voice by athletes in the rules-making process and disregard of social and economic realities by the rules-makers leave many athletes with low regards of the rules.

A large number of the athletes who participate in big-time collegiate football and basketball are African American youth from working-class and lower-class backgrounds. It seems that if the NCAA is to remedy the problems of intercollegiate sports it must address not only the economic exploitation of collegiate athletes but also the racial nature of the exploitation.

Given the corporate structure of intercollegiate athletics and the huge profits realized from television contracts, the perpetuation of the notion of college athletes as amateurs appears questionable. The interests of universities and athletic departments are served by labeling as amateur the primary labor force of a multi-million dollar a year industry. A new voice has been added to the debate on whether to further compensate the college athlete. Walter Byers, former NCAA director and a longtime opponent of pay for college athletes, has changed his mind on this matter and now advocates, among other reforms, greater compensation for collegiate athletes (Byers, 1995).

It is not surprising that those who benefit most economically from collegiate sports resist the idea of paying college athletes. In rejecting the idea of paying athletes we often hear the argument that scholarship athletes are being paid in a most meaningful manner: with a free education. This notion begs not only the question of what is meant by "free," but more importantly what is the "nature" of the education.

Academics

Our previously stated goal in this work was to help facilitate changes which will make circumstances favorable for the purpose of education for the African American athlete. African American athletes at predominantly White institutions continue to be faced with a particular set of problems. One of these problems is overcoming the stereotype of being intellectually inferior while possessing innate athletic superiority. Often the message given to African American athletes is, "You are inferior intellectually. We do not expect you to achieve academically. You are here because of your athletic ability."

In a study by Kiger and Lorentzen (1987) it was found that type of sport and race were negatively related to university academic performance for males. Minority male athletes and revenue-producing-sport athletes tend to do less well. Adler and Adler (1989) found that student-athletes enter college with high expectations, then over the course of their college careers make a pragmatic adjustment and resign themselves to inferior academic performance. This adjustment on the part of the students is due to time demands of sport and the coaches steering them to manageable, athletic-related majors such as physical education and recreation. The athletes received greater reinforcement for athletics than for academics.

The above-mentioned studies point to some very serious problems for the educational experiences of athletes. In order to improve the situation we feel the following issues must become part of discourse on college athletes and education. These issues address problems faced by all student-athletes. However, in the context of this essay, it is important to note that African American athletes are more vulnerable to these conditions.

1. Except under unusual circumstances the athlete's academic schedule should not be made out by the athletic department with little or no student participation. The responsibility for academic careers must be the responsibility of the individual athletes. To treat them otherwise retards the opportunity for intellectual development. If the experience of attending college is to provide preparation for life, the athlete's dependency on the athletic department to "take care of things" retards maturation and provides no preparation.

2. The notion that sports is a fertile avenue of upward social mobility for African American males must be dispelled. Educational attainment provides far more upward social mobility for African American males than does sport. The emphasis should therefore be on education as the most fertile avenue of upward social mobility.

3. The one-year renewable grant-in-aid sends out an antieducational message. It says that you are an athlete first, and your opportunity to get an education is dependent on your athletic achievements. The grant-in-aid should be for five years and should be terminated only for academic reasons—not athletic incompetence.

4. Given the time demands of collegiate football and basketball it is difficult to stay on schedule for graduation. Some of the revenue generated by intercollegiate sport could be put into a fund which would provide financial resources for the completion of education once a player's eligibility is up.

Graduation Rates

The issue of graduation rates among college athletes has been given much scholarly as well as popular attention in recent times (*USA Today*, June 17–21, 1991; *The Chronicle of Higher Education*, March 27, 1991 and July 10, 1991). It has also resulted in federal legislation (HR1454) better known as the Student-Athlete Right-to-Know Act. This act requires federally funded colleges and universities to report annually the graduation rates of student-athletes by sport, race, and sex. These data are to be supplied to high school officials and made available to families so that more informed decisions might be made in choosing among college options. This proposal has spurred action by the NCAA to collect data from its member institutions beginning October 1991 to implement the intent of the congressional bill. Findings from preliminary survey data are given in Table 1.

In evaluating graduation rates for athletes, several considerations are in order:

1. How do athlete graduation rates compare with nonathlete rates?
2. How do categories of athletes compare with similar categories of nonathletes—viz., African American male athletes with African American male nonathletes?
3. Should graduation rates be accepted uncritically as a measure of institutional responsibility?
4. Do graduation rates reveal much, if anything, about academic counseling programs? Do the high graduation rates at Duke and Georgetown, for example, mean they have superior academic supports for their athletes in comparison with schools having lesser rates?
5. It is not purely a matter of whether a degree is obtained, but also a matter of what type degree.
6. Issues of uniformity in how graduation rates are compiled and defined must be addressed and solved.

Table 1. Academic Outcomes of Division I Athletes Entering College, 1984–85

Academic Standing			
	All	White	Black
Graduated within five years	45.7%	52.2%	26.6%
Left in good standing	29.0%	28.2%	30.9%
Left in bad standing	25.3%	19.6%	42.5%
Remained in college after five years	4.4%	4.0%	5.4%
Graduation Rate			
	Number	Number graduated	Percentage
All athletes	3,288	1,504	45.7%
White	2,453	1,282	52.3%
Men	1,646	819	49.8
Women	807	463	57.4
Black	835	222	26.6%
Men	686	170	24.8
Women	149	52	34.9

Source: Adapted from *The Chronicle of Higher Education* (July 10, 1991), reporting on NCAA survey.

Collectively, the research on student athlete graduation rates has reached the following conclusions among many.

1. The graduation rates of all college athletes (46%) are about the same as the graduation rates of all nonathletes (48%) five years after entering college. However, there are great variations by school, race, sex, and type of sport.
2. Minority athletes graduate at slightly higher rates (36%) than do their nonathlete counterparts (31%).
3. Generally, but with a few exceptions, the most competitive basketball program schools have graduation rates lower than those schools which do not make it to the NCAA tournaments.
4. Women basketball recruits have an appreciably higher graduation rate (60%) than does the general student population (48%). However, most of the big-time women's programs do not have such favorable rates.
5. African American male student-athletes in basketball have the lowest graduation rates of any category.

Critical Appraisal of Use of Graduation Rates

It is acknowledged that systematic attention to graduation rates may function to sensitize universities and some prospective students to the degree to which universities are adhering to academic goals, yet it would be a mistake to accept uncritically the position that such emphases are all positive.

A labeling theory perspective would project some unwanted or unintended consequences of the Student-Athlete Right-to-Know Act. Schools labeled as nonacademic through this procedure would likely be avoided by academically interested students and/or parents. Those students wishing a nonacademic athletic experience would have an officially recognized list of schools which would offer a nonacademic athletic experience. Thus, the effect would be to continue or even exacerbate the problem of low graduation rates for some schools.

Another, equally disturbing prospect is that the pressure for standard graduation rates could result in "special athletes curricula" or the awarding of meaningless degrees. The athlete's interest is not served by the granting of a degree which has little or no marketability or potential for other rewards.

Meaning of Graduation Rates

What does a low graduation rate mean? As some wags have indicated, it could mean that while we have lowered standards to let some athletes in, we have not yet gone the next step of according unearned degrees. It might mean that, but almost certainly it does not mean that schools with the highest graduation rates are expending the most effort on behalf of the athletes which they admit. Rather, it is much more likely that high graduation rates reflect selectivity in admissions. There is a finite number of blue-chip athletes who are also blue-chip scholars. Traditional programs are able to recruit these few. If other programs are to compete athletically they must accept good athletes with lesser degrees of scholastic potential. Finally, there are programs which will have to settle for athletes with still greater scholastic deficits. It seems unreasonable to expect similar admission standards and graduation rates in each of these situations.

Rather than promoting a national standard for admissions and graduation rates, perhaps it would be more reasonable to assess these measures against the mission of the school, its own admission standards and graduation rates. Perhaps it would be more meaningful to try to evaluate what a school does to advance the scope and skills of those athletes whom they do admit. A case study approach might yield some remarkable incidents of "scholastic progress" on the part of students who could never enter one of the more traditional programs.

Summary and Recommendations

The marriage between education and athletics is likely to endure for the foreseeable future.

There will be occasional spats, mediated by the NCAA and the Council of Presidents, but academic interests have become so interwoven with those of sport entertainment that dissolution is unlikely. Indeed, without well-planned policies it is likely that the economic potential of big-time sports will result in the sports partner dominating the union.

African Americans, particularly inner-city African Americans, have been socialized to expect sports careers all out of proportion to realities (Edwards, 1973). Given this condition, coupled with the relative lack of alternative occupational opportunities and virtually no other avenues to the pro game, African Americans are particularly vulnerable to exploitation. The colleges need manpower to produce an exciting spectacle in order to enhance revenue. African Americans want the experience and exposure necessary to get to the pros.

These basic facts are unlikely to change to any considerable degree, thus they must be taken as a given in proposing any solutions.

1. If more effective "minor league" or other preparatory arrangements were provided by the system, then there would be fewer athletes in academia who do not want to be there. In no other industrialized world power is the college expected to train for professional sports. Two new basketball leagues for teenagers now are being planned (Chronicle of Higher Education, May 10, 1996, p. A48) to provide developmental opportunities for youth who do not enroll in college. The Teenage Professional Basketball League is scheduled to begin play in the summer of 1997.

2. We should continue or develop policies which assure that the athlete can participate in a meaningful educational experience, once admitted.

3. Once in the collegiate setting the athlete should be paid in a manner somewhat more commensurate with his/her economic productivity.

4. The income from collegiate sports should be distributed among colleges more equitably than currently, thus removing some of the emphasis on winning at all costs.

5. The tenure of coaches should be determined in part by considerations other than winning, thus allowing them to be more responsive to academic and character-building concerns.

6. Universities should be prepared to spend some of the money generated by sports in assuring counselling, tutoring, and related services to those athletes in need because of time and energy expenditure on behalf of the school.

The issues which we raise and our proposals for solution certainly do not exhaust the possibilities. Some of our proposals would no doubt raise additional issues and problems of their own. Our views are shaped by the nature of our discipline and a combined experience of some 40 years of working with athletes in the academic setting. It is our sincere hope that the promise of higher education and status attainment will become a more universal reality for the African American student-athlete. We pledge our efforts to that end and trust that student-athletes will assume their individual responsibilities in this collective endeavor.

Study Questions

1. How can we account for the Knight Foundation Commission's failure to confront racial exploitation in collegiate athletics?

2. What are some of the issues relating to African American male self-definition and the impact of athletics in the African American community?

3. What are the underlying issues of racism in meeting Proposition 48 guidelines?

4. In what ways can graduation rates stand as proxies for academic exploitation of African American athletes?

References

Adler, P., and Adler, P.A. (1989). From idealism to pragmatic detachment: The academic performance of college athletes. In D. S. Eitzen (Ed.), *Sport in contemporary society: An anthology* (pp. 142–157). New York: St. Martin's Press.

Anderson, A., Warfield, J., Picou, J. S., & Gill, D. A. (1990). Race and the educational orientations of college athletes: Implications for career counseling. *Applied Research in Coaching and Athletics Annual, 27*–40.

Asher, M. (1986). Abuses in college athletics. In R. Lapchick (Ed.), *Fractured Focus* (pp.5–20). Lexington: D. C., Heath and Company.

Brady, E. (1991, June17). Players: 46% earn degree in five years. *USA Today,* Sec. A., pp. 1–2, 7–8.

Castine, S., & Roberts, G. (1974). Modeling in the socialization process of the black athlete. *International Review of Sport Sociology,* (9), 59–73.

Chu, D. (1989). *The character of American higher education and intercollegiate sport.* New York: State University of New York Press.

Coakley, J. J.(1986). *Sport in society: Issues and controversies* (3rd ed.). St. Louis: Times Mirror/Mosby.

Cross, L. H., & Koball, E. G. (1991). Public opinion and the NCAA Proposal 42. *Journal of Negro Education, 60,* 181–194.

Davis, T. (1996). African American student athletes: Marginalizing the NCAA regulatory structure? *Marquette Sports Law Journal, 6*(2), 199–228.

Dubois, W. E. B. (1969). *The souls of black folk.* New York: Signet.

Edwards, H. (1969). *The revolt of the black athlete.* New York: The Free Press.

Edwards, H. (1973). *Sociology of sport.* Illinois: Dorsey Press.

Edwards, H. (1984). The collegiate athletic arms race: Origins and implications of the "Rule 48" controversy. *Journal of Sport and Social Issues, 8,* 4–22.

Edwards, H. (1985). Beyond symptoms: Unethical behavior in American collegiate sport and the problem of the color line. *Journal of Sport and Social Issues, 9,* 3–13.

Edwards, H. (1989). The black "dumb jock": An American sports tragedy. In D. S. Eitzen (Ed.), *Sport in contemporary society: An anthology* (3rd ed., pp. 158–166). New York: St. Martin's Press.

Eitzen, D. S. (1989). Ethical dilemmas in sport. In D. S. Eitzen (Ed.), *Sport in contemporary society: An anthology* (3rd ed., pp.300–312). New York: St. Martin's Press.

Eitzen, D. S., & Sage, G. H. (1993). *Sociology of North American sport* (5th Ed.). Iowa: William C. Brown.

Fordham, C., & Ogbu, J. (1986). Black student's school success: Coping with the burden of "acting white." *The Urban Review. 18,* 176–206.

Johnson, J. (1988). Personal interview. *New Perspectives, 19,* 4, 10–12.

Karenga, M. (1980). *Kawaida theory: An introductory outline.* California: Kawaida.

Kiger, G., & Lorentzen, D. (1987). Gender, academic performance and university athletics. *Sociological Spectrum, 7,* 209–222.

Knight Foundation Commission on Intercollegiate Athletics. (1991). *Keeping faith with the student-athlete: A new model for intercollegiate athletics.*

Lawry, E. G. (1991, May 1). Conflicting interests make reform of college sports impossible. *The Chronicle of Higher Education,* p. A44.

Lawson, H. A. (1979). Physical education and sport in the black community: The hidden perspective. *The Journal of Negro Education,* (48), 187–194.

Lederman, D. (1991, March 27). College athletes graduate at higher rate than other students, but men's basketball players lag far behind, a survey finds. *The Chronicle of Higher Education, 37,* p. A1.

Lederman, D. (1991, July 10). Black athletes who entered colleges in mid-80's had much weaker records than whites, study finds. *The Chronicle of Higher Education, 37,* p. A31.

Marable, M. (1986). The black male: Searching beyond stereotypes. In R. Staples (Ed.), *The Black family: Essays and studies* (pp. 64–68). California: Wadsworth.

Marden, C. F. (1992). *Minorities in American society* (6th ed.). New York: Harper Collins.

Marger, M. N. (1985). *Race and ethnic relations: American and global perspectives.* California: Wadsworth.

Mingle, J. (1981). The opening of white colleges and universities to black students. In G. Thomas (Ed.), *Black students in higher education* (pp. 18–29). Connecticut: Greenwood Press.

Moynihan, D. P. (1965). *The negro family: Case for national action.* Washington, DC: Labor Department, Office of Policy Planning and Research.

Naison, M., & Mangum, C. (1983). Protecting the educational opportunities of black college athletics: A case study based on experiences of Fordam University. *Journal of Ethnic Studies,* 119–125.

Picou, J. S. (1986). Propositions 48, 49-B and 56: Implications for student-athletes, coaches and universities. *The Journal of Applied Research in Coaching and Athletics, 1,* 135–147.

Raney, J., Knapp, T., & Small, M. (1986). Pass one for the Gipper: Student athletes and university coursework. In R. Lapchick (Ed.), *Fractured Focus* (pp. 53–60). Lexington: D. C., Heath and Company.

Rudman, W. J. (1986) The sport mystique in Black culture. *Sociology of Sport Journal, 3*(4), 305–319.

Sack, A. L. (1987). Are "improper benefits" really improper? A study of college athletes' views concerning amateurism. *Journal of Sport and Social Issues, 12,* 1–16.

Sack, A. L. (1991). The underground economy of college football. *Sociology of Sport Journal,* (8), 1–15.

Sage, G. H. (1989). Blaming the victim: NCAA responses to calls for reform in major college sports. In D.S. Eitzen (Ed.), *Sport in contemporary society: An anthology* (3rd ed.). New York: St. Martin's Press.

Schendel, J. (1965). Psychological differences between athletes and non-participants in athletics at three educational levels. *Research Quarterly,* (36), 52–67.

Spivey, D., & Jones, T. A. (1975). Intercollegiate athletic servitude: A case study of the black ethnic student athlete, 1931–1967. *Social Science Quarterly, 55,* 939–947.

Takaki, R. (1987). *From different shores: Perspectives on race and ethnicity in America.* New York: Oxford University Press.

Underwood, J. (1980, May). The writing is on the wall. *Sports Illustrated,* 36–72.

Warfield, J. (1986). *Corporate collegiate sport and the rule of race issues for counseling. Debate and understanding* (pp. 30–36). Boston: Boston University Press.

Webb, H. (1969). Professionalization of attitudes toward play among adolescents. In G. S. Kenyon (Ed.), *Aspects of Contemporary Sport Sociology.* Chicago: The Athletic Institute.

Webster's new world dictionary of American English (3rd college ed.). (1988). New York: Simon and Schuster.

Willie, C., & Cunnigen, D. (1981). Black students in higher education. *Annual Review of Sociology,* 177–198.

SECTION 3

GENDER
AND
RACE
INTERSECTIONS
IN
COLLEGE
ATHLETICS

Sociohistorical Influences on African American Elite Sportswomen

Yevonne R. Smith

Abstract

The purpose of this essay is to explore intersections of race, gender, and class sociohistorical and cultural influences on the socialization and achievement experiences of African American elite sportswomen. Pertinent discourse relative to the female athlete in society, sport, and the African American community will be addressed. The essay will review the following themes/topics:

1. The History of African American Women in Society and Sport
2. Historical Movements in the U.S.A.: Impact of the Women's and the Civil Rights Movements
3. The Female Athlete in the African American Community (Gender Relations and Historically Black Colleges)
4. Sociohistorical Time Line of African American Women in Society and Sport.

Key Terms

African American: An ethnic group that has its social history and cultural heritage grounded in both Africa and America. Americans of African ancestry.

Blacks: A racial term often used to describe persons of African decent.

Classism: A discriminatory social system based on socioeconomic status and power.

Culture: Shared patterns of beliefs, meanings, values, behaviors, social interactions and commonly held understandings, ideology, concepts, symbolic meanings, rituals and creative expressions learned and shared by ethnic groups, social organizations or a particular society.

Elite athletes: Highly talented and skilled athletes participating and competing at the national and international level in sport organizations.

Ethnicity: Social-historical and cultural heritage of a particular group. "An ethnic group is a category of people regarded as socially distinct because they share a way of life associated with a common cultural background" (Coakley, 1994, p. 240).

Ethnocentric: Belief in the superiority of one's own ethnic group.

Eurocentric: European-centered. Establishing and prescribing dominant cultural values based on European values and traditions.

Gender: A social category of being female or male that has dynamic social consequences in power relationships, distribution of resources, and equity in sport and society.

Hegemony: Dominant power interests of government, economic systems, mass media, education, sport, etc. (Sage, 1990).

Physicality: The experience of vigorous bodily or physical activities through physical labor, exercise, and sport.

Race: All people are members of the human race.

Racism: A discriminatory social system based on pseudoscientific characteristics, stereotypes, and a racial supremacy ideology and race logic created and maintained by dominant groups (Coakley, 1994).

Sexism: A gender-based discriminatory social system based on stereotypes, patriarchy (male dominance), inequality, and oppression of women.

Socialization: A process of learning from one's social environment through interactions, role-modeling, observations, experiences, self-identity, values, meanings, and expectations for behavior from self and significant others.

Women of color: Ethnically diverse women such as African American, Latina, Asian American and Native American women who have been excluded from dominant feminist thinking. The term is meant to highlight the shared experiences of gender and ethnic domination, and differences in power and privilege of culturally diverse women. Although women of color may be a generic term for several groups of diverse ethnic women, any one of these cultural groups of women may also be described as women of color. For example, African American women are women of color.

Introduction

To understand African American sportswomen's social history, one must understand both dominant societal race, class, and gender traditions and cultural traditions within the African American community. This essay is written from a Black feminist standpoint (Collins, 1990) which suggests that African American women, because of their subordinated status within society, have a special angle of vision and core experiences that they bring to the knowledge-production process. The politics of difference in America suggests that African American women have a very different standpoint from European American women and African American males, because African American women are simultaneously affected by the intersections of their gender and ethnicity and have often been marginalized and exploited within both contexts. Due to relationships of power and domination in society and sport, their voices have often been silenced in discussions of both gender and race (Birrell, 1990; hooks, 1990; Smith, 1992). Therefore, there is a longing or yearning for critical voice

and empowerment (hooks, 1990), which is accomplished by telling the story of African American women's multiple experiences of gender, race/ethnicity, and class in American society and sport.

Most feminist theorists agree that the category of woman is a social and not merely a biological or a psychological construct (Collins, 1990; Davies, 1994; M. A. Hall, 1996, 1990; hooks, 1990, 1989, 1984, 1981). Women are not solely biologically constructed genetically different from men, nor individually psychologically different in personality traits, attributions, and attitudes. M. A. Hall (1996) has noted that in order to understand women in sport, we must go beyond the individualistic bias and understand "that sporting practices are historically produced, socially constructed, and culturally defined to serve the interests and needs of powerful groups in society" (p. 6).

Consistent with the concepts of the social construction of women, Davies (1994) notes the connection between economics and how African American women have been historically constructed: "Women's bodies become the locus for a certain social definition of gender with specific economic import to this social construction. The working class African peoples and Black women have historically been constructed and defined as inferior for economic gain" (Davies, 1994, p. 71). Accordingly, there is a theme of oppression and struggle to overcome structural social and economic obstacles. This theme of oppression suggests that all American women of African decent share a commonality of oppressive experiences despite economic status.

> All African American women share the common experience of being Black women in a society that denigrates women of African decent [sic] regardless of economic status, and suggests that certain characteristic themes will be prominent in a Black women's (experiences in America and, therefore, in her) standpoint. For example, one core theme is a legacy of struggle. (Collins, 1990, p. 22)

Therefore, a shared social and cultural experience, a common reality, is experienced by all African American women based on racial/ethnic and gender affiliation, regardless of economic status. As a cultural entity, African American women have been categorically discriminated against politically, educationally, and socially because of their racial and gender status. Consequently, to tell the history of African American sportswomen is to tell of interconnections between racism (White supremacy) and gender (male superiority) in American society and within the African American community. In telling the story, we must discuss the social reality and the "struggle to survive in two contradictory worlds simultaneously, one White, privileged and oppressive, the other Black, exploited, and oppressed" (Collins, 1990, p. 22).

Historical Traditions of Sports Participation

African American female athletes have a rich tradition of participation in tennis, basketball, and track and field in the African American community beginning in the early 1900s (Cahn, 1994; Costa & Adair, 1993; Gissendanner,1994; Williams, 1994). Participation patterns in sport and physical activity were directly influenced by racial traditions of exclusion from mainstream America and the dominant culture's sport structures. For example, in 1916, the American Tennis Association (ATA) began because African American people could not participate in the segregated United States Lawn Tennis Association (USLTA). Therefore, they founded their own tennis structure which culminated in an annual national championship tournament. Within one year of the founding of the ATA, African American women participated, and Lucy Stowe won the first women's singles championship (Costa & Adair, 1993). Documented coverage by the African American press attested to the popularity of basketball, tennis, and track and field in the segregated African American community among women. Basketball and tennis were more popular than track and field (Williams, 1994).

In the 1920s, after World War I, many African Americans migrated North to cities such as Philadelphia, New York, Cleveland, Chicago, and Washington, DC to get better jobs and escape racial and economic oppression in the South. This provided more opportunities for women and families to have a better quality of life, which included more leisure and athletic participation for some. Unlike most southern women, whose physical labor was co-opted in agriculture and domestic service to maintain the dominant culture's racial and economic privilege, African Americans and their families who had migrated to the North were able to take advantage of an industrial economy that provided more income, limited working hours, and more recreational opportunities (Williams, 1994). This eventually facilitated participation for some very skillful, economically and geographically privileged working-class women to participate in leisurely physical activity pursuits in the Black community at northern community YWCAs, athletic clubs, and in the integrated northern Amateur Athletic Union (AAU) track events, where African American women were included, unlike in many other sport structures in the North and South, where they were not allowed to compete against White women. The AAU structure in the North facilitated women's athletic participation in local neighborhood, district, city, and regional championships, and on national and international Olympic levels. In addition, Eurocentric Victorian gendered attitudes about White women's participation in sport also facilitated African American women's access to track and field at the national and international levels (Cahn,1994).

"African American interest in track and field and permissive attitudes toward women's athletics set the stage for the emergence of Black women's track at the precise moment when the majority of White women and the White public rejected the sport as undignified for women" (Cahn, 1994, p. 118). Thus, the movement for athletic empowerment of African American sportswomen grew out of both racist and gendered attitudes in the dominant culture. Race logic limited interactions between diverse groups of people and forced African Americans to live and participate in sports in a segregated community. Gender logic suggested that only certain activities were appropriate for dominant-race women. The intersection of these two power relations, plus the fact that track and field did not limit competition between the races, advantaged African American women in track and field. (Cahn, 1994; Williams, 1995).

Tuskegee Institute Women's Track and Field

Coaches at Tuskegee Institute in Tuskegee, Alabama seized an opportune moment in history during the late 1920s, at a time when other universities, because of dominant-gender ideology, were not focused on the sports achievements of women, and began an era of outstanding athletic achievements for African American women. At Tuskegee the coaches "established the prototype for the training of future women Olympians" in track and field (Costa & Adair, 1993, p. 1100). Track and field at Tuskegee was started in 1927 for men. One year after track was included in the Olympics, track for women was organized in 1929 at the college. In the Tuskegee Relays in 1929, two events were held for women, the 100-yard dash and the 400-meter relay. In a few years, the 50-yard dash and discus were added. During the period of the 1930s to the 1960s Tuskegee Institute women athletes were provided coaching by Amelia Roberts, physical educator; Cleveland Abbott; Christine Petty; and later, Nell Jackson, former Tuskegee Olympic athlete, which led to continued success in the AAU and Olympics (Cahn, 1994; Costa & Adair, 1993). Between 1937 and 1948, Tuskegee won 11 of 12 AAU outdoor championships (Cahn, 1994). The school also hosted Olympic semifinal tryouts because African American women and men could not participate with Whites in the segregated AAU meets in the South. Also, historically Black colleges and universities (HBCUs) were some of the only facilities in the South with athletic resources and professional coaches who had a vision for the athletic empowerment of African American women. Therefore, the Black college provided a semisheltered training and educational experience for women athletes, away from insensitive, southern, racially segregated and oppressive traditions. Tuskegee Institute provided the first highly competitive program for collegiate women in track and field in America, and the Tuskegee Relays were the first major track meets sponsored by a historically Black college. In order to fund the athletes, Tuskegee offered work-aid scholarships for the female athletes (Cahn, 1994; Costa & Adair, 1993).

In 1932, Louise Stokes and Tydie Pickett were the first African American women to qualify for the Olympics, but they were deprived of a place on the team due to racial and economic oppression. They qualified again and eventually participated in the 1936 Olympics in

Berlin, Germany (where Jesse Owens became famous for challenging the racial supremacy ideology of Adolf Hitler). As money was raised by donors, this allowed Stokes and Pickett to travel to the Berlin Games (Cahn, 1994). These athletes got their start on the northern playgrounds, at track clubs, and AAU meets, and they would not have been so advantaged if they lived in the South.

Due to World War II, no Olympics were held in 1940 and 1944. In 1948, Alice Coachman of Albany State College in Georgia, and Tuskegee Institute, became the first African American female athlete to win an Olympic gold medal in the high jump, clearing the bar at 5 feet 6$^1/4$ inches. She and another high jumper actually were both credited with a new Olympic record, but Coachman won the gold medal because she cleared the bar with fewer misses (Coachman, 1996; Welch, 1993). Beginning at age 16, Coachman had to leave Georgia to receive sports training, and she entered the Tuskegee Relay track meet. Prior to this, she had begun running on dirt roads because they were prevalent throughout the rural South and because limited sport structures were available to people of color. Also, there was a lack of economic resources and sports training programs other than those in African American, segregated schools. Alice Coachman, who attended Albany State College, broke high school and college records and was subsequently invited to participate and train with the Tuskegee team during the summer and to attend the Tuskegee Preparatory School (Welch, 1993).

Coachman and the other female athletes on the team were systematically oppressed, not only by race, but by economics and gender. Coachman and other ethnically diverse female athletes of the day could not attend predominantly White public or private schools and colleges in the South because of legalized racial segregation. This was why most historically and predominantly Black colleges had been founded in the first place, to educate African American youth and young adults because of

enforced discrimination and unequal educational opportunities. Many historically Black institutions at that time prioritized academic, vocational, and professional education and did not prioritize athletic programs for women. They prioritized educating the descendants of slavery (sons and daughters) and America's most disenfranchised peoples. Many African American families also did not prioritize sports and could not afford to finance sporting equipment and opportunities for their children. Many families were more preoccupied with economic, educational, and social struggles and concerned mostly with trying to work in order to afford the basic necessities of life, such as food and shelter. Throughout the South after the Civil War and the end of slavery, and during the 1900s to the mid-1950s, African Americans were heavily engaged in agricultural and domestic work where they physically worked very hard, for less pay than Whites, because of economic oppression due to racism and the legacy of slavery. This seriously impacted the availability of resources and opportunities for women of color. In addition, many female youth were not encouraged to play sports, even though they may have been encouraged to work hard and help their families. There was also gender bias and bias against leisurely pursuits, active play, and sports participation in some families. In *Stolen Childhood*, King (1995) argues that "enslaved children had virtually no childhood because they entered the work place early and were more readily subjected to arbitrary plantation authority, punishments and separations" (p. xx). There were times when youth were allowed to engage in representative play, dances, and games after their work was completed. This legacy for African American youth, which included doing hard physical work, being physically punished, and losing their childhood, endured even after slavery in the agrarian society. Thus, females who became athletes had to persevere to resist not only racial, but economic, gender, and physical oppression. These factors influenced elite athletes such as Alice Coachman from Tuskegee Institute; Wilma Rudolph, Lucinda Adams, and Willye White from Tennessee State College; as well as others, to feel privileged to have the opportunity to play sports (*ABC Sports*, 1995; Adams, 1988; Rudolph, 1977).

Alice Coachman's Experiences of Sport

Alice Coachman, the first African American woman to be the recipient of an Olympic gold medal, in 1948, recounted some of her youth experiences of gender, economics, race and physicality in sport:

> I played hard to out-jump the boys. I would say you can't out-jump me! And that is how I started. I got three whippings a day; I got one in the morning for math. At noon hour I would get tied up with someone on the playground fighting. The principal would whip me for fighting. When I came home I got another for going out to play. I played hard to out-jump the boys. Pop had a World War I belt, one to two inches thick. My father said his girls had to sit on the porch and we could not rip and run. I learned to jump high. When I went to Tuskegee, one coach didn't want me to go. Someone gave me some clothes—I had no shoes. Someone gave me some tennis shoes. (Coachman, 1996)

Therefore, one can see that issues of gender, poverty, and race intersected her physicality. Fortunately, Tuskegee Institute's coaches began to see the potential opportunities for women's sports achievements through track and field, and began to validate young women's physicality through athleticism. Collegiate sports, then, provided social sanctioning for women's interests and physical skill abilities. Coachman noted that she became important as a person and was noticed for her athleticism by her coach. This enhanced her self-image and both her educational and sporting opportunities. She stated,

> Coach found out I could run a little. I could also jump. I went to the Tuskegee May Relays. Everyone was there. I trained and ran behind the dormitory at Albany State. This was what I had to do. I won ten national high jump titles. . . . My goal was to complete the high jump record and win a Gold Medal. It took guts and determination, but that was what I had to do. (Coachman, 1996)

Alice Coachman, as the first African American female athlete to win an Olympic gold medal for America, in 1948, was both advantaged and silenced through sport. Because of her time and place in history and female status, she was socially constructed according to gender in her family and in society. Due to the historical context, she did not receive any radio or television endorsements or commercials when she won the gold medal in the high jump because this was not consistent with gender ideology, technology, or the race logic of the era. It was not the socially sanctioned norm to have African American women or men on mainstream radio, print media, or television commercials at that time in America. She said that she was, however, asked to endorse Coca Cola. "When I came back [from the Olympics], Coca Cola asked me to endorse Coke. Coke gave me a contribution but no tv endorsement or commercial. I started the kids being the ones to get endorsements" (Coachman, 1996).

Thus, race, economics, and gender ideology intersected in Coachman's sport socialization and experiences of physicality. She and other African American young women who looked for culturally similar role models with which to identify in the mainstream media could find none. No culturally similar heroines were evident in mainstream media, cinema, or on television at that time for African American girls, not even the first Olympic gold medalist, as this was not consistent with the race, nor gender, logic of the era. In addition, female track athletes were not glamorized in society. Therefore, most girls who wanted to relate to a female personality were co-opted into identifying with White female media stars such as Shirley Temple. Many young African American girls did not feel good about themselves, as their images were denigrated because of mainstream media and societal traditions that excluded or distorted African American women's images (Corbett & Johnson, 1993). Consequently, many young women, prior to the Civil Rights movement, did not take pride in their ethnic heritage, or they perceived White dolls more positively than Black dolls in research studies. Having few culturally similar role models beyond family and friends, young girls often attempted to model themselves after popular White images because they were exposed to them through the dominant print and electronic media, and through the dominant ideology of gender (Clark & Mamie, 1950; Davis & Dollard, 1940). Even though there were more diverse standards for gender in the African American community, some females received pressure from family members to be stereotypically gender appropriate according to dominant ideology and to emulate European Americans such as female child star Shirley Temple. Coachman acknowledged that this, too, was a part of her childhood experiences, given that African American female youth were infrequently exposed to a diversity of role models and culturally similar media images in the mainstream press. Coachman stated, "My sister told me I wasn't anything but a damn fool to be running up and down that hot road. My idol had been Shirley Temple, but my feet were too big to dance" (Coachman, 1996).

The dominant gender ideology of the era suggested that dance was a more appropriate activity for girls as opposed to the athleticism involved in running. Consequently, Coachman followed her own ambition, which was guided by her athletic skills, love of physical activity, and sporting opportunity, and became an outstanding Olympic female athlete, pioneer, and role model for younger female athletes.

Tennessee State Tigerbelles

Between 1956 and 1972 the Tennessee State Tigerbelles, initially coached by Jessie Abbott, daughter of Tuskegee's Cleveland Abbott, and later Ed Temple, began another dynasty in women's athletics. The president of Tennessee State drove down to Tuskegee to recruit Ms. Abbott for his program. The Tennessee State Agriculture and Industrial College of Nashville, TN sent athletes to the Tuskegee Relays and established their own program in 1945 (Cahn, 1994). The Tigerbelles, under the leadership of Ed Temple, won all six gold medals for the United States women's track team at the 1960 Olympics.

Thus, the Tigerbelles became the most successful women's track and field program in America. The most famous Tigerbelle was Wilma Rudolph, who was known as "La gazelle noire" or "Black Gazelle" by Europeans (Hine, 1993). Like Coachman at Tuskegee, Rudolph first came to Tennessee State at age 16 to train during the summer when she was still a high school student-athlete. In 1956, she won a bronze medal as the youngest member of the United States Olympic Team. In 1960, she was the first woman to win three gold medals in a single Olympics, winning the 100-meter and 200-meter sprints and anchoring the 400-meter relay team. Other famous Tennessee Tigerbelles were Mae Faggs, Barbara Jones, Willye White, Madaline Manning, Wyomia Tyus, and Lucinda Adams. National and international recognition of the women athletes brought pride, dignity, and status to the outstanding athletes, their schools, and to the African American community. National sport structures and racism, as well as sport and educational structures within historically Black colleges (such as dedicated coaches, teachers, athletic facilities, work-aid scholarships for women athletes, summer track programs, and the Tuskegee Relays), influenced track and field traditions for African American elite female athletes even though athletic budgets were small and unequally distributed between men and women.

Impact of Race and Gender Ideology

Coaches at Tuskegee Institute and Tennessee State University seized an opportunity in history to involve African American women in elite sport at a time when White women were being discouraged from participating in strenuous athletics due to dominant cultural, race, and gender ideology (Cahn, 1994; Costa & Adair, 1993). This suggests that the history of African American women in sport was created by joint forces within the dominant culture and within the African American community. First, there had to be the opportunity to participate in a larger mainstream sport structure within the dominant culture, such as the AAU and Olympics, in order to achieve national or international visibility and mainstream recognition. Also, there had to be an economic, socially supportive athletic training structure within the segregated African American community, which was provided by historically Black colleges in the South. Finally, a racial and a gender ideology outside and within the African American community facilitated the athletic participation of elite sportswomen of color. Track and field for women was perceived to be among the more "physical" or athletic sports as contrasted with the more aesthetic activities of dance and elitist sports, such as tennis and golf, which were also actively played in the African American community (Williams, 1995, 1994). These aesthetic and more elite sports, however, had segregated racial sport structures that did not allow non-White participation. Although physicality of women was not in conflict with African American ideals of womanhood (Captain, 1991), dominant race ideology outside of the African American community considered the sport of track and field less than feminine (Cahn, 1994). According to a Eurocentric feminine ideology, track and field was perceived to be too athletic for females. Cahn (1994) summa-

rizes the gendered ideology prevalent in the dominant culture that impacted women's track and field sports participation:

> By the mid-century the sport had a reputation as a "masculine" endeavor unsuited to feminine athletes. Few (White) American women participated, and those who did endured caricatures as amazons and muscle molls. In this climate, despite the temporary enthusiasm inspired by female champions of 1948, Olympic governing bodies of the 1950's once again considered eliminating several women's track and field events from the games because they were not too feminine. (Cahn, 1994, p. 111)

This dominant ideology of gender was not necessarily the dominant construction of femininity within the African American community (Hart, 1976), although there were some in the community who held dominant-gender ideologies in spite of the fact that African American women had been socialized to work hard through physical labor since slavery times. There were also those who desired to rise above social constructions of gender, but the history of African American women in sport was affected by both race and gender ideology and economic structures within the African American community as well as within the dominant culture. Acceptance of the physicality of African American women for economic gain by the dominant culture, but not for sport, self-development, educational opportunity, or recreation, put many women in a double bind. What reality were they to believe, or adhere to—the one they lived and accepted in their own experiences, families, and communities based on their social histories and experiences of physicality; or the one constructed for White women, particularly during a period of racial segregation by the dominant society? The only choice one has is to live her own social and cultural reality of physicality, and this is exactly what African American elite sportswomen have done. In doing so, they became pioneers in women's sports during a time when other women were being socially constructed and oppressed by a dominant cultural gender ideology of genteel womanhood.

Historical Movements: Impact of the Women's and Civil Rights Movements on African American Females

The Women's and Civil Rights movements have influenced the empowerment of African American women in society and sport. The historical significance of the Women's and Civil Rights movements will be discussed, followed by a discussion of sport-related consequences for African American women. Prior to the 1920s, women of color were denied the right to vote, as majority-race women were. They were also denied quality education, human dignity, and freedom, as African American men were during periods of slavery, segregation, and Jim Crow in the South through the period of the 1960s (Hine, 1993). Therefore, African American females, throughout the historical time periods in America since the introduction of Africans as indentured servants and slaves in 1619, have been impacted by the intersections of interlocking societal structures and cultural values of gender, class, and race (M. Anderson & Collins, 1992; Baca Zinn & Dill, 1994; Hine, 1993). Similarly, gender and race have historically impacted African American elite sportswomen in activity participation and in the amount of media coverage they have received in the mainstream sports media. A case in point shows that because of gender and race bias, stories of African American elite sportswomen have rarely been told in the mainstream media:

> The white press gave minimal coverage to black sports and seldom printed photographs of African American athletes. Black women found that sex discrimination, in the form of small athletic budget, half hearted backing from Black school administrators, and general absence of

support from White-dominated sports organizations, further impeded their development. (Cahn, 1994, p. 119)

In fact, African American sportswomen have only appeared five times on the cover of *Sports Illustrated* in a 35-year period between 1954 and 1987 (Lumpkin & Williams, 1991). Therefore, with the exception of a few outstanding athletes, Oglesby (1981) described the African American female athlete as "fleeting, if ever in the consciousness of the sporting public. Nobody knows her; not publicists, nor researchers, nor entrepreneurs, nor published historians . . . the Black sportswoman is unknown and of course unheralded" (Oglesby, 1981, p. 1).

Thus, because of invisibility in the dominant culture's mainstream print and visual media, and discrimination outside and within race, most African American sportswomen are unknown and silenced in society. The interconnections of gender and race have also affected their status and power relations in society during the early and contemporary Women's movements.

Women's Movements

Both early and contemporary Women's Movements have been influenced by the empowerment and physicality of African American women in the United States. During the first United States Women's Movement Convention for women's equality in May 1851, held in Akron, OH, Sojourner Truth, a Black female former slave, abolitionist, and women's rights activist delivered her famous speech, "Ain't I A Woman?" (Hine, 1993). Palmer (1983), in analyzing the economic strengths and events surrounding the speech of Sojourner Truth in 1851, recalled how feminists accepted the message that denounced the prevailing opinion of women as weak, fragile, and dependent creatures, but largely ignored women of color as a part of the feminist movement:

> They do not . . . use Sojourner Truth's battle cry to show that Black women are

not feeble . . . rather they have used Sojourner Truth's hardiness and that of other Black women as proof of White women's possibilities . . . women such as Sojourner Truth embody and display strength, directness, integrity, fire. (Palmer, 1983, pp. 152–153)

Collins (1990) noted that Sojourner Truth, when faced with the hegemony of stereotypical, controlling images of women, began deconstructing the dominant cultural ideology of womanhood, suggesting that she as an African American woman certainly did not internalize this dominant-race ideology. Sojourner Truth was discussing intersections of gender and race in relation to her own social construction of femininity in contrast to dominant-race ideology of femininity and male superiority. Interpreting her legacy of struggle against both racism and sexism, she suggested that between coalitions of Blacks in the South and White women in the North, " . . . *de white man would be in a fix pretty soon"* (quoted in Hine, 1993, p. 1173). Further, she noted disparities between racialized conceptions of femininity. Many African American women historically have not perceived themselves as weak and fragile, to be consistent with dominant cultural ideology, nor "as amazon or muscle molls," which were the negative stereotypes of athletic women (Cahn, 1994, p. 111). However, these stereotypes of femininity and elite female athleticism increase our awareness of the negative power of dominant cultural ideology of race and gender that impact women in society and in sport.

Impact of the Women's Movement in Sport

The contemporary Women's Movement beginning in the late 1960s and 1970s and Title IX legislation impacted sports participation for girls and women by increasing females' athletic participation in sports (Acosta & Carpenter, 1990; Birrell & Cole, 1994; Coakley, 1994). They did this by increasing the number of sports teams and offerings. In some schools

and colleges where there had been no sports or only one sport for females, other sports teams became available as schools attempted to comply with Title IX of the 1972 Education Amendments. Often the sports presented to African American females in segregated rural and urban schools were traditional sports, such as basketball, track and field, volleyball, and occasionally, tennis (Houzer, 1974, 1971; Smith, 1992b; Smith & Ewing, 1992, 1991). In a study by Houzer (1974, 1971), African American college women noted that they were interested in many sports and held negative attitudes toward track. They desired to participate in a variety of sports and dance activities. This suggests that many African American elite sportswomen have been channeled into sports activities that were made readily available to them by schools, community, and national sport structures. With an increased interest in competitive women's sports following the passage of Title IX, and better salaries for women's sports coaches, more men and fewer women physical educators began coaching women's teams (Acosta & Carpenter, 1992, 1990). Similarly, perceptions and realities exist based on the distribution of hierarchial-patriarchal leadership in women's sports. Sports programs in both historically Black colleges and universities and traditionally White colleges (and high schools) are headed and coached predominantly by men (Acosta & Carpenter, 1992, 1990; Coakley, 1994; Corbett & Johnson, 1993; Smith, 1992a). In 1972, when Title IX was passed, over 90% of women's teams were coached by female coaches. By 1992 only 48% of women's college sports programs were coached by women (Coakley, 1994). Presently, only 5% are coached by African American sportswomen (Alexander, 1978; Smith, 1992a, 1992b). Participation for women of color in the full range of sports offerings and sports leadership positions is limited in women's sports and has not been substantially impacted by the Women's Movement or Title IX, but exceptions do exist. Often the exceptions within college sports are former elite women athletes who have attained a high status in their sport, have followed through and obtained their college degrees, and therefore can command sport leadership positions if they choose to have careers in sport (Smith, 1995).

Over 90% of African American women participating in college sports participate in basketball and track and field mainly because of the availability of traditional programming and easier access to these programs within local schools and recreation centers in the African American community, not because these are the desired sports of most females (Coakley, 1994; Houzer, 1971, 1974; Smith, 1992b). Further, it has been perceived by some African American males, who control the Black church, civil rights organizations, and sport in the community, that the Women's Movement could cause African American females to switch their loyalties away from supporting race and ethnic survival priorities to a focus on gender equity. This would highlight patriarchal gender privileges, power, and resource advantages held by males within the community and in sport. In some cases, more equalitarian relations between males and females, as well as patriarchal power, have been used to support and structure female athletics at historically Black colleges and universities in the American Tennis Association (ATA) tennis structures, and in various track programs in the African American community. It has been recognized that female physical educators, male coaches, and family members have been responsible for the direct involvement of many elite female athletes (Costa & Adair, 1993; Smith, 1992b, 1990). In addition, the Women's Movement was perceived as a White middle-class women's movement that was not inclusive of diverse race or class perspectives. For these reasons, the Women's Movement has often received negative attention, alienating males and females in the African American community, for it has been perceived that the movement was designed to alienate the genders, and solidarity among men and women was a necessity within the community to fight racial oppression that impacts both African American men and women. Patriarchal community power structures, having prioritized racial equality as the predominant survival issue, were not interested in focusing on women's gendered power issues.

Yet Title IX of the 1972 Education Amendments, which legislated equality of opportunity for males and females in federally funded educational and sport programs, is associated with the contemporary Women's Movement in the 1970s and 1980s and with the increase in participation of female athletes in sports. Title IX which comes out of a liberal feminist theoretical perspective, stated,

> No person on the basis of sex (should) be excluded from participation in, be denied the benefit of or be subjected to discrimination under any educational program or activity receiving federal assistance. (Title IX of the 1972 Educational Amendments)

Title IX, however, has benefitted African American elite female athletes as well as female athletes from other races by increasing attention to, and addressing some past discrimination of, girls and women in sport and education programs based on unequal sporting opportunities, numbers of sports teams sponsored by schools, inequality in female and male coaches' salaries, and unequal scholarships and resources for female athletes. It has not been as effective in addressing the decline of women coaches in women's sports. Title IX, while increasing participation opportunities for women athletes, did not increase leadership opportunities for women coaches and athletic administrators, as women sport leaders declined significantly from over 90% to approximately 45% to 48% in college women's sports programs after the passage of Title IX (Acosta, 1985; Acosta & Carpenter, 1992, 1990; Coakley, 1994). Female coaches in some interscholastic programs declined to 35% (Smith & Ewing, 1992). Legislative acts such as Title IX were, therefore, seen as problematic by radical feminists because they do not actually confront and deconstruct the system of power relations involved in racism, sexism, and classism (Dewar, 1990; Douglas,1988). Title IX legislation was designed to work within the existing social and sporting structures, rather than challenging and radically transforming the existing structure. These situations were particularly evident in both historically Black colleges and traditionally White college sports programs that have discriminated against women.

In spite of this fact, a select group of historically Black colleges were early pioneers in women's sports. At Tuskegee Institute and Tennessee State College, African American sportswomen were encouraged to develop their skills and achieve elite athletic status in track and field, beginning in the late 1920s–1940s at Tuskegee and continuing from the 1950s through the 1970s at Tennessee State. However, in many other historically Black colleges, women's sports budgets and programs remained limited and were only expanded to include more sports for women, such as track and field, basketball, volleyball, golf, and tennis, after the passage of Title IX. Most of the women's sports programs in historically Black colleges have never received equal financial resources and attained the status of most male sports, although there have been increased efforts since Title IX (Corbett & Johnson, 1993). Tuskegee and Tennessee State College were exceptions because they provided work-aid and athletic scholarships very early for women. However, several other historically Black colleges, such as Prairie View College of Texas, South Carolina State College, Alabama State College, Alcorn of Mississippi, Florida A & M, Fort Valley State College, and Albany State College in Georgia also were involved early in women's athletics. Still, other more elite, historically Black schools adopted the professional physical education women's policies and dominant-gender ideology and did not sponsor or advocate competitive sports and athletics for women (Cahn, 1994; Gissendanner, 1994).

Although expanding opportunities for elite athletes to train and compete in sport at tradi-

tionally White colleges, Title IX did not significantly expand the diversity of sporting opportunities for African American female athletes to increase their skills and participate in a wide variety of school and college sports. In fact, Title IX statistics were never compiled based on racial distributions of women in designated sports, although the National Collegiate Athletic Association (NCAA) has recently started compiling this data. Therefore, at major universities there were actually no requirements for tracking of culturally diverse women's participation and involvement in the variety of sports activities (Mathewson, 1996), nor any conscious effort to expand opportunities for multiethnic women in different sports programs. What was sought with Title IX and liberal feminism was more equality or opportunity between men's and women's sports participation, not more equity for culturally diverse women to expand their sporting participation experiences in a greater array of sports choices. Over 90% of African American women today who participate in college sports play basketball or participate on track and field teams (Coakley, 1998, 1994). This again points out the exclusion and silencing of African American women's needs even with Title IX, which was designed to improve gender equity in sports. The legislation mostly increased opportunity for African American women to participate in more basketball, track and field, and some volleyball programs sponsored by public high schools and colleges. It did not significantly expand participation opportunity in a wide variety of sports for ethnically diverse women. It did afford more opportunity for outstanding, highly skilled high school female athletes in basketball and track and field to receive athletic scholarship funding at universities with segregated and integrated college sports programs. This means that Title IX mainly facilitated college opportunity for those women athletes who already had gained competitive sport skills prior to attending college. For example, Evelyn Ashford, track and field Olympian, attended the University of California at Los Angeles (UCLA) on one of the first athletic scholarships it provided for women. Having participated in high school physical education and track, she was a very fast runner who was able to beat the best boy in high school. Later, she was recruited by UCLA, and in 1983, she became the fastest woman in the world at the National Sports Festival; and in 1984 she won Olympic gold in the 100m run (Page, 1991). Similarly, Cheryl Miller, an outstanding Riverside Polytechnic High School basketball player who scored 105 points in one game and led her high school team to a state championship, was recruited by the University of Southern California (USC). Later, she became a member of the 1984 Olympic gold medal women's basketball team, was MVP in the Final Four basketball tournament in her freshman and sophomore years, and propelled USC both years to national championships. Graduating with a degree in broadcasting, she has become a sports commentator and head coach of a WNBA professional women's basketball team (after serving as the USC head women's basketball coach). Similarly, Olympic gold medalists Jackie Joyner Kersee, Valerie Brisco-Hooks, and Florence Griffith-Joyner were already outstanding high school athletes who were recruited by major universities to advance their programs (Page, 1991). Cheryl Miller has acknowledged that, had it not been for Title IX, she would not have had the sporting opportunities that were afforded her. However, had it not been for the Civil Rights Movement, prior to Title IX, Cheryl Miller and other contemporary elite women athletes may not have had the opportunity to attend a traditionally White college and participate in sports. The Civil Rights era radically expanded social, political, and educational opportunities for marginalized groups, students, and student-athletes.

Impact of the Civil Rights Movement on Sports

The impact of the Civil Rights movement was to integrate public education and to diminish the number of separate or segregated Black schools and sports programs in the South where African Americans were the predominant sports leaders as athletic directors and head coaches. As a result of the Civil Rights movement, more high school and college sports programs became racially integrated. Integration gave more opportunities for female and especially male athletes to enter nonsegregated, mainstreamed athletic programs and contests, and compete against individuals of other races, as well as attend majority-race schools. It caused the elimination of many African American public schools in the South because many Whites were unwilling to send their children to integrated schools or schools with another racial history, often built with inadequate facilities and fewer resources (*The South*, 1990). Integration facilitated more mixed competition and team rosters composed of African American and White female athletes. It, however, began the erosion of women's sports dynasties at historically Black colleges such as Tennessee State. As mainstreamed universities with more competitive scholarship offers, better athletic facilities, more specialized athletic training, national prestige, and higher visibility began recruiting top female athletes after the passage of Title IX, many majority institutions were able to siphon off athletic talent from historically Black colleges. Thus, a negative consequence of the Civil Rights era was that it began the decline of Black racial solidarity in the community, in education, and in the leadership of women's sports programs at HBCUs such as Tuskegee Institute and Tennessee State University. Therefore, the Civil Rights movement was a human rights movement that enhanced human dignity and united African American people and people of goodwill from different racial and ethnic backgrounds to challenge racial oppression in American society. The movement facilitated the integration of public education and school sports programs around the country. The Women's Movement focused on gender equality, but often alienated men and women in the African American community.

The Civil Rights movement acknowledged the importance of racial, economic, and student power, as well as equal educational opportunity, but it eventually was the catalyst for integration and siphoning off athletic talent from Black colleges to major White universities outside the African American community, particularly in track and field and basketball. Outstanding athletes increased their opportunities and options, but often they faced hostility, racism, and a bicultural reality (influenced by their African heritage and Eurocentric impositions) on major college campuses (Stratta, 1995). As a result, graduation rates often declined for athletes at colleges which were not as supportive and sensitive to ethnic diversity (Anderson & South, 1993).

Currently, a majority of the recognized African American elite female athletes competing in sports at the national and international levels are attending majority-race universities. Many of the women's sports programs at major colleges are better funded, more prestigious, and offer more visibility than do women's sports programs at historically Black colleges, which still face racial, gender, and economic discrimination (Brooks & Althouse, 1993; Corbett & Johnson, 1993). Examples of the wave of Olympic-level female athletes attending predominately major universities since the 1980s are Evelyn Ashford, Jackie Joyner-Kersee, Florence Griffith Joyner (Flo Jo), Gwen Torrence, and Gail Devers in track and field; Cheryl Miller, Lynette Woodard, Sheryl Swoopes, and Lisa Leslie in basketball; Dominique Dawes in gymnastics; and Debi Thomas in figure skating (M. Davis, 1992, 1981; Green, 1993).

Impact of the Civil Rights Movement on African American Sportswomen

Black Feminist/Womanist social science and literary scholars (hooks, 1989, 1984; Washington, 1990) have noted that the Black Power Movement did not advantage women leaders within the African American community. African American self-determination was often equated with men obtaining power. Sexism diminished the power of women and their accomplishments. Therefore, the Civil Rights Movement both benefitted and alienated many African American women leaders who felt the movement was dominated by male leadership just as most sports, educational, and religious programs are. The movement often reflected patriarchal values, "equating Black liberation with Black men gaining access to male privilege that would enable them to assert power over Black women" (hooks, 1989, p. 52). Thus, the force of racism and sexism within society and sexism within ethnic groups have collectively and effectively oppressed and informed the social and sport status of African American women as well as European American women, who hold fewer athletic director and head coaching positions than do men in high school and college women's sports programs (Abney, 1988; Acosta, 1993, 1986; Birrell, 1990, 1989; Douglas, 1988; Green, Oglesby, Alexander, & Franke, 1981; hooks, 1981; Palmer, 1983; Smith, 1992a & 1992b). The absence of status and privilege from mainstreamed and community political, religious, and educational power positions has served to maintain invisibility and underrepresentation in a variety of sports and sport leadership positions and has severely disadvantaged African American womens' sports leaders, as only 5% or less of the women's sports leaders serving as athletic directors, head coaches, sports educators, officials, and athletic trainers are African American sportswomen (Abney, 1988; Alexander, 1978; Janis, 1985; Murphy, 1980; Smith, 1995, 1992a, 1992b). Yet, African Americans constitute 12% of the American population. In spite of this disparity, some elite women athletes who chose to stay in sport after graduation from college have gone on to coach college-level sportswomen and become leaders of sport organizations after their own athletic careers were finished (Smith, 1995). Participating in sports at the elite level and obtaining one's college degree, therefore, provide some elite sportswomen with a measure of athletic status, economic opportunity, networking power, and achieved social status which facilitates their ability to command head coaching and sport leadership positions in college and professional sports programs. Notable elite African American sportswomen head college basketball coaches are Marian Washington of the University of Kansas, past president of the Women's Basketball Coaches Association; and Vivian Stringer, formerly of Cheney State, University of Iowa, and currently coaching at Rutgers University. Others with degrees in physical education, health, recreation, and related education fields, such as Alice Coachman, Nell Jackson, Willye White, and Lucinda Williams Adams (Olympians from Tuskegee Institute and Tennessee State College) have gone on to the public sector (schools or recreation departments) to teach, coach, supervise, and direct sports programs after their athletic careers were over.

Prior to the Civil Rights Movement, historically Black colleges and universities had a monopoly on the athletic talents of African American female athletes. Because of both racial and gender discrimination, traditionally White colleges did not systematically seek or recruit African American female student-athletes prior to the Civil Rights and contemporary Women's Movements and the passage of Title IX (Alston, 1980; Barclay, 1980). However, the Civil Rights Movement and the *Brown vs. Board of Education* Supreme Court decision of 1954 and the contemporary Women's Movement paved the way for highly skilled, culturally diverse female athletes to attend formerly all-White schools and universities. These social changes did not happen without much upheaval and unrest on many college campuses and throughout the South. Because of gender bias in college athletic programs and the commodification of African American male athletes, males were the first to be recruited by White colleges. Because women's sports programs were not yet equal to men's sports programs, women of color were not targeted for recruitment as early as male athletes. It took

the combination of both the Women's and Civil Rights movements to stimulate the trend toward recruitment of African American women at major college athletic programs.

The Civil Rights Movement called attention to the tremendous human indignities suffered by people of color all over America. Even elite female athletes and teams from Tuskegee and Tennessee State experienced racism as they traveled by car throughout segregated and racist towns in the South. Most of the earlier elite women athletes had to attend segregated high schools and colleges, drink out of "colored only" drinking fountains, and use "colored only" restrooms and sports facilities in the South. Consequently, African American sportswomen have experienced multiple and intersecting layers of racial, gender, and economic oppression. This impacted their personal, social, educational, and sporting experiences. At times, Ed Temple, Tennessee State University's renowned coach, observed that their traveling teams were refused service at restaurants in the South even after winning important national championships (*ABC Sports*, 1995). Consequently, the Civil Rights movement, with its many sit-ins, marches, demonstrations, and calls for raising the humanitarian consciousness of all Americans, subsequently challenged an oppressive social structure and enabled student-athletes to receive less discriminatory and more equal treatment within society and college sports programs. The movement expanded educational opportunities and pressured local, state, and national sport structures to integrate sports programs and expand participation opportunities to outstanding athletes regardless of race (Gibson, 1958; Smith, 1992b). The Civil Rights Movement which advocated peaceful, nonviolent protests, created more accessible educational and recreational-sports facilities for oppressed groups. Social institutions and social structures that had formerly been segregated or off-limits were made available to ethnically diverse youth and adults. However, integration of sport structures and social institutions was not achieved easily, and many city municipalities closed schools, swimming pools, and other indoor and outdoor facilities rather than integrate those programs and facilities. Many private clubs held fast to their racist policies of segregation and refused memberships even to outstanding, highly skilled African Americans with high professional, athletic, and economic status because all cultural and ethnic diversity was negatively stereotyped and perceived as undesirable (*ABC Sports*, 1995; Gibson, 1958; Hine, 1993). This certainly was the case for Althea Gibson, the first African American to win Wimbledon and the U.S. Open championships, in 1957 and 1958. She had won 10 consecutive American Tennis Association championships before being allowed to participate in the United States Lawn Tennis Association Championships (*ABC Sports*, 1995).

Thus, YWCAs, historically Black colleges and universities, public schools, the American Tennis Association, and other community-based educational and sport structures, including families, became the predominate social support networks for African American elite female athletes.

The Female Athlete in the African American Community

Going for Olympic gold medals, the female athlete has been challenged by her racial and ethnic social history (Acosta, 1993; Adams, 1988; Adkins, 1967; Barclay, 1980; Bentley, 1983; Biracree, 1988; Cahn, 1994; Giddings, 1984). The physicality and sporting experiences of the female athlete in the African American community are not based solely on dominant ideologies of femininity in the society, but rather they are associated more with historically oppressive race traditions in America during and since slavery. Physicality is intertwined with dynamic racial and gender relations, self-identity, agency, and economic class socialization experiences within families and selected historically Black colleges within the African American community. Therefore, in order to comprehend the social history of

women of color, one must focus on multiple dimensions.

> To chronicle the participation of Black women in sports in the United States is to tell the story of slavery, alternative communities, Black colleges of distinction, organizations that provided safe havens for participation, and modern heroines. Above all, it is to tell the story of courage, physical skill and centrality of purpose rarely chronicled in the sports pages and television shows of modern America. . . . (Costa & Adair, 1993, p. 1099)

Within the African American community, the tradition of athleticism for women comes out of a social reality and acceptance of physicality through the form of physical labor co-opted for economic gain, demanded from men and women of color. This shared tradition of oppression and physicality created a more equalitarian bond between the genders despite obvious patriarchy within the community, and fostered an awareness of the inner strength of women (without this reality contradicting ideals of Black femininity [Captain, 1991] and cooperative spirit between male and female coaches and female athletes). According to Hart (1976), it may be attributed to values of femininity within the African American Community, as she has suggested,

> In the Black Community, the woman can be strong and achieving in sport and still not deny her womanness. She may actually gain respect and status as evidenced by the reception of women like Wilma Rudolph, Wyomia Tyus Simburg and other great performers. The Black woman seems also to have more freedom to mix her involvement in sport and dance without the conflict expressed by many White women athletes. (Hart, 1976, p. 441)

Further, due to the legacy of racial struggle and segregation in America, there was a perceived need for many African American women and men to achieve excellence for their racial/ethnic group as well as pride and dignity themselves and for the team, and not to achieve sport status solely for the individual accomplishment that is so highly valued by the dominant culture. Historically, members of the community felt a common bond, a sense of racial pride when others of their racial and ethnic group achieved national and international distinction, because so few were accorded respect historically in American society. Examples of athletes who contributed to this historical sense of ethnic pride were Joe Louis, Jackie Robinson, Althea Gibson, Tuskegee Institute's women track Olympians, and Olympians Wilma Rudolph and the Tennessee State Tigerbelles track team. Contemporary women athletes, such as Jackie Joyner-Kersee, Florence Griffith Joyner, Debi Thomas, and Dominique Dawes, have instilled the same ethnic and gender pride. Thus, physicality through sport has become "a way out" for some elite female athletes to achieve dignity, respect, social status, and educational opportunity in society and sport.

Sociohistorical Time Line

African American women in sport have truly come a long way and have been pioneers in women's sports. Despite many negative situations in society, these women have persevered and overcome many obstacles, such as societal oppression, largely through the support of family members, historically Black colleges, and the community. Race, ethnicity, gender, and socioeconomic structures in society have intersected the experiences of elite women in sport. A historical time line has been developed by the author to document and highlight the sequence of important events in society and sport that have influenced achievements of African American sportswomen. The time line summarizes African American women's historical movement from exclusion in society during slavery, to living at the margins of society and sport due to legalized racial segregation, to more inclusion during the era of integration and gender equity in education and sports. Further, the time line also highlights women's movement toward empowerment through their achievements in sports and the attainment of sport leadership positions at the national and international levels.

TIME LINE

African American Women in Sports: From Exclusion to Margin From Margin to Inclusion

African American History Begins in Africa

- **1600s–1960s**: Slavery, dehumanization, and segregation in America.
- **1619**: Jamestown, VA, settlement of 1st African Americans in American colony. African American women's physical activity is conditioned by slavery, agriculture, servitude, and domesticity.
- **1600–Present**: Subordinated in race, gender, and class-power relations, in social institutions (sport, media, politics, education, economics, health, etc.).
- **1848**: Early Women's Liberation Movement.
- **1851:** Sojourner Truth's speech, "Ain't I A Woman?"
- **1863:** Emancipation Proclamation.
- **1865:** End of the Civil War—Thirteenth Amendment freed Americans of African descent.

- **1865–1900s:** Many historically Black colleges and universities founded (i.e. 1868, Hampton Institute founded by American Missionary Assoc.).
- **1896:** The U.S. Supreme Court rules that separate but equal public accommodations are legal. Legal segregation in America is enforced; *Plessy vs. Ferguson* Supreme Court decision: Separate but equal doctrine established.
- **1910:** The National Association for the Advancement of Colored People (NAACP) is incorporated.
- **1914:** All southern states now have Jim Crow laws relegating African Americans to a lower class and inferior status than White Americans.
- **1900–Present:** Sports participation—African American community influenced by racial traditions of exclusion from the mainstream American social institutions.
- **1900–1970s:** Segregated sports in African American community; the community supports women's sports at selected colleges.
- **1916:** American Tennis Association founded.
- **1917:** Women participate in American Tennis Association tournament: Lucy Diggs Slowe wins the first women's singles title.
- **1920:** American women win the right to vote with the passage of the 19th Amendment.
- **1920s:** Documented coverage of women's sports by African American press in basketball, track, and tennis. Northern migration of African Americans; participation in YWCA, NY Mercury Club, and Illinois Women's Athletic Club programs.
- **1924:** AAU track and field championships.
- **1927:** Beginning of the Tuskegee Institute Relays.
- **1928:** First year that track is added to the Olympics by the International Olympic Committee. Five events are included for women.
- **1929:** Track for women begins at Tuskegee Relays.
  - Anita Gant wins ATA; trains at Washington, D.C., YWCA facilities.
  - Inez Patterson, multisport champ at Temple University, Philadelphia; only African American on field hockey team, basketball captain, swimming, tennis, volleyball, and dance.
- **1931–40s:** *Philadelphia Tribune* sponsors women's basketball team founded by Ora Mae Washington, eight-time ATA champ, player-coach.
- **1930s–70s:** Track and field success in Olympics by Tuskegee Institute and Tennessee State College.
- **1932:** Tydie Pickett and Louise Stokes—First African American women to qualify for United States Olympic Team.
- **1936:** Tuskegee finishes second in AAU; sponsors eighth women's track and field championships; hosts Olympics semifinals tryouts.
- **1936:** L. Stokes and T. Pickett qualify for the second time and participate on the U.S.A. Olympic team in Berlin, Germany in the same Olympics where Jesse Owens wins four gold medals.
  - Prairie View College begins women's track.
- **1940s:** Renee Powell's family founds a golf club for African Americans.

- **1947:** Jackie Robinson reintegrates Major League Baseball.
- **1947–1960s:** Civil Rights movements for equality, empowerment, racial pride and unity.
- **1948:** Alice Coachman becomes the 1st African American woman to win Olympic gold medal in high jump, clearing the bar at 5 feet 6¹/₄ inches. (The only American woman to win an Olympic gold in 1948.)
    - Dr. Nell Jackson is on Tuskegee Olympic team at Tuskegee Institute. Former Olympian, educator and sport leader, later became an associate athletic director at Michigan State University and athletic director at State University of New York, Brockport.
    - Pressure to integrate sports begins.
    - American Tennis Association promotes Althea Gibson to integrate the United States Lawn Tennis Association; Alice Marble challenges USLTA's racism in an editorial.
- **1950:** Althea Gibson is invited to play at USLTA Open at Forrest Hills, NY.
- **1952:** Mae Faggs of Tennessee State Tigerbelles wins Olympic gold in 4 x 100m relay with Catherine Hardy and Barbara Jones.
- **1954:** *Brown v. Board of Education, Topeka, KN.*—reversed *Plessy v. Ferguson* in education institutions: Separate but equal doctrine is not equal. Topeka, Kansas public schools are ordered to integrate. Segregation in public schools is declared unconstitutional.
- **1955:** Rosa Parks refuses to give up her seat on a city bus to a White man. A bus boycott is organized by Rev. Dr. Martin Luther King, Jr..
- **1956:** African American women continue to play significant roles in American track and field. (Debut of Wilma Rudolph and Willye White in Olympics.)
- **1957, 1958:** Althea Gibson wins USLTA Open and Wimbledon in both years (first African American to win a grand-slam tennis tournament).
- **1958:** Althea Gibson becomes first African American woman on the cover of *Sports Illustrated* magazine. Her autobiography is published—*Somebody I Always Wanted to Be.* She receives Florida A & M athletic scholarship in tennis.
- **1950–1960s:** Racial segregation and Jim Crow laws are still evident. Public schools, many sport structures, and public recreation facilities in the South are still segregated.
- **1956–1972:** Tennessee State College Tigerbelles' track-and-field success in the Olympics.
- **1956:** Wilma Rudolph, most famous Tigerbelle, debuts and wins bronze medal in the Olympics 4 x 100m relay in Melbourne, Australia.
    - Willye White wins an Olympic silver medal in long jump. Willye White, member of five Olympic teams between 1956 and 1980; 1956 and 1972 Silver Medalist long jump, 4 x 100m relay, respectively, held American long jump record 16 years; currently, public health and recreation director, Chicago sport leader.
- **1960:** Wilma Rudolph wins three gold medals in 100m, 200m dashes and 4 x 100m relays; Lucinda Williams Adams, Barbara Jones and Martha Hudson are on a gold medal relay team with Wilma Rudolph in Rome, Italy Olympics.
- **1960s–1980s:** School desegregation; more sports programs are integrated.
- **1960s:** Althea Gibson becomes first African American woman professional golfer.
- **1963:** The March on Washington is held in Washington, D.C., for civil rights and social justice. Martin Luther King, Jr,. delivers "I Have a Dream" speech.

- **1964:** Civil Rights Act legislates more equal treatment for all.
- **1964:** Edith McGuire of Tennessee State wins 200m-run Olympic gold and two Olympic gold medals in 4 x 100m relay and 100m run.
  - Wyomia Tyus of the Tennessee State Tigerbelles wins an Olympic gold medal in the 100m run and a silver in 4 x 100m relay.
- **1965–1990s:** Contemporary Women's Movement.
- **1967:** Renee Powell, golfer, becomes member of LPGA.
- **1968:** Dr. Martin Luther King, Jr., is assassinated in Memphis, TN.
  - Wyomia Tyus of Tennessee State wins two Olympic gold medals, in 100m run and 4 x 100m relay.
  - Madeline Manning Mims, a member of four Olympic teams between 1968 and 1980, wins Olympic gold in the 800m run. African American women win gold in 4 x 100m relay.
- **1970s–1990s:** Opportunities begin for African American sportswomen to participate at majority race schools and colleges expand.
- **1970–2000s:** Outstanding, highly skilled African American women athletes in a few selected sports benefitted from Title IX at traditionally White institutions.
- **1972–1978:** Title IX Education Amendments is passed. Schools must increase educational and sport opportunities for girls and women; increased athletic scholarships for women at historically Black colleges and universities and predominantly White colleges.
- **1976:** Anita De Frantz, Connecticut College, wins bronze medal in rowing, later graduates from University of Pennsylvania with law degree and, in 1986, becomes first African American on the International Olympic Committee.
- **1977:** Wilma Rudolph's autobiography is published and made into a movie.
- **1979–1981:** Supreme Court expands the scope of Title IX, allowing individual discrimination suits.
- **1984:** Cheryl Miller, USC basketball, Olympic gold medal team; cover of 1985 *Sports Illustrated.*
  - Lynnette Woodard, University of Kansas basketball; Captain of U.S.A. gold medal Olympic team; scores 3,649 points in college, more than any other woman in Div. I; first woman to play with Harlem Globetrotters. (Later she becomes a WNBA professional basketball player.)
  - Valerie Brisco-Hooks, California State, Northridge, wins three gold medals (200m run, 400m run, and 4 x 400m relay).
  - Alice Brown of California State, Northridge, wins Olympic medal in 4 x 100m relay and again in 1988.
  - U.S.A. Women win Olympic gold medal in basketball. (Team members are Cheryl Miller, Lynnette Woodard, Teresa Edwards, and Pamela McGee.)
  - Flo Hyman, University of Houston, volleyball, silver medalist. Later, Flo died and the Women's Sport Foundation named an award after her.

- Evelyn Ashford, UCLA, wins Olympic gold medals in track; 100m sprint, anchored 400m relay, sets Olympic record in 100m run.
- African American women on Olympic gold 4 x 100m relay and 4 x 400m relay teams.

- **1984:** Supreme Court Decision—*Grove City College v. Bell* reverses effects of Title IX in sports programs not receiving federal funds.
- **1987:** Debi Thomas wins the U.S. Figure Skating championship.
- **1988:** Civil Rights Restoration Act to reverse *Grove City College v. Bell* decision. If the institution receives federal funds, sports programs must again abide by Title IX.
- **1988:** Jackie Joyner-Kersee, UCLA, wins two Olympic gold medals in long jump and heptathlon; 1984 wins silver medal in heptathlon, world's greatest woman athlete. In 1987 she wins Sullivan Award and U.S. Olympic Committee Sportswoman of the Year. In 1988, is named Amateur Sportswoman of the year by the Women's Sports Foundation.
  - Florence Griffith Joyner, UCLA, wins three Olympic gold medals in 100m race (10.54 sec. Olympic record), 200m race, 4 x 100 meter relay; total of four medals in a single Olympics—three golds and one silver. Also, she brings flair and fashion to track, reinforces feminine stereotypes and speed/athleticism.
  - Evelyn Ashford, UCLA, gold medal in women's 4 x 100m relay.
  - U.S.A. Women win Olympic gold medal in basketball. (Team members include Cindy Brown, Cynthia Cooper, Teresa Edwards, Teresa Weatherspoon.)
  - Zina Garrison wins Olympic gold medal in tennis.
  - Debi Thomas is the first African American skater to win an Olympic bronze medal.
- **1992:** Supreme Court decision. Women athletes, coaches, and administrators can sue schools and universities for financial damages. (Ruling supports HBCU and Howard University women's athletic director, who later sues the University for gender inequity in salary benefits and wins.)
- **1992:** Jackie Joyner-Kersee wins Olympic gold medal in heptathlon (beats nearest opponent by 199 points). World's outstanding female athlete.
- **1993:** Florence Griffith Joyner appointed co-chair of the President's Council on Physical Fitness and Sport.
- **1996:** Summer Olympics in Atlanta, GA. Jackie Joyner-Kersee wins Olympic bronze medal in long jump (joins women's ABA pro basketball team).
  - Gail Devers wins gold medals in 100m and 4 x 100m track and field relay.
  - U.S. Olympic gold 4 x 100m relay track team (Gail Devers, Gwen Torrence, Ingor Miller, Chryste Gaines).
  - Dominique Dawes, member U.S. gymnastics team, wins Olympic gold and individual bronze medals.
  - U.S. Women's Olympic gold basketball team dominated by African American sportswomen (Sheryl Swoopes, Dawn Staley, Teresa Edwards, Lisa Leslie, Carla McGhee, Venus Lacey, Katrina Mclain, and Nikki Mcray).
- **1996–98:** Women's professional basketball leagues (ABA and WNBA) begin and many African American women participate.

Summary

Historical patterns of oppression and resistance have been faced by all African American women and men. Historical traditions and power relations in American society are interconnected with the sporting experiences of African American sportswomen and clearly suggest that prior to the Civil Rights era sporting experiences of African American women were relegated to their segregated community, where historically Black colleges provided the major support link to women's elite-level sporting experiences. After the Civil Rights movement, integration slowly became the commonly accepted practice. With the advent of the contemporary Women's Movement, Title IX expanded sports participation opportunities for all women, but it did not expand opportunities for African American females in a variety of sports. After majority-race colleges began to offer athletic scholarships for women, this expanded their sports programs. Similarly, Black colleges increased equity opportunities for women, but no longer had a monopoly on outstanding female talent. This means that currently, most elite, well-known African American sportswomen are participating in sports at major universities with better funding and are more visible in women's athletics programs. Many of these institutions are now providing elite-level sportswomen with playing experiences and coaching opportunities, more visibility, and access to dominant cultural ideology and social networks in a few traditionally selected sports. Tuskegee Institute, Tennessee State College, and other historically Black colleges, however, were pioneers in women's sports. Thus, educational and sport structures within the African American community, as well as gendered and racial ideology in American society, have significantly influenced the social history of women of color in sports.

Suggested Readings

Cahn, S. (1994). *Coming on strong: Gender and sexuality in twentieth century women's sport*. New York, NY: The Free Press.

Collins, P. (1990). *Black feminist thought*. Boston, M A: Unwin Hyman.

Hall, M. A. (1996). *Feminism and sporting bodies*. Champaign, IL: Human Kinetics.

Hine, D. C. (Ed.). (1993). *Black women in America: An historic encyclopedia. Vol. I and II*. Brooklyn, NY: Carlson Publishing, Inc.

hooks, b. (1984). *Feminist theory: From margin to center*. Boston, MA: South End Press.

hooks, b. (1990). *Yearning: Race, gender and cultural politics*. Boston, MA: South End Press.

Gissendanner, C. (1994). African American women and competitive sport, 1920–1960. In S. Birrell & C. Cole (Eds.), *Women, sport and culture*. Champaign, IL: Human Kinetics.

Smith, Y. (1992). Women of color in society and sport. *Quest, 44*(2), 228–250.

Smith, Y. (1995). Women sport leaders and educators of color: Their socialization and achievement. In *JOPERD, 66*(7), 28–33.

Williams, L. (1994). Sportswomen in Black & white: Sports history from an African American perspective. In P. Creedon (Ed.), *Women, media and sport (*pp. 45–66). Thousand Oaks, CA: Sage Publications, Inc.

Study Questions

1. Discuss social-historical barriers in the lives of African American women. How have these barriers influenced females' sport participation?

2. How have the circumstances in the dominant culture, including racism, slavery, legal segregation, and integration, influenced the social construction of African

American women? How have these social structures disadvantaged and/or advantaged African American elite sportswomen?

3. Are there positive and negative consequences of the Women's and Civil Rights Movements on African American elite female athletes?

4. Discuss the female athlete in the African American community. What was the role of the following:
   a. Historically Black colleges
   b. Physical educators and coaches
   c. Family members
   d. Media
   e. Racial ideology
   f. Economics
   g. Feminine ideology

References

ABC Sports producer. (1995, May 2). *A passion to play: The African American experience* [TV sport special on women in sport]. New York: ABC Sports, PDR Productions, Inc.

Abney, R. (1988). *The effects of role models and mentors on career patterns of Black women coaches and athletic administrators in historically Black and historically White institutions of higher education.* Unpublished doctoral dissertation, University of Iowa.

Acosta, R. V. (1985). Women in athletics: A status report. *Journal of Physical Education, Recreation and Dance, 56*(6), 30–34.

Acosta, R. V. (1986). Minorities in sport. *Journal of Physical Education, Recreation and Dance, 57*(3), 52–55.

Acosta, R. V. (1993). The minority experience in sport: Monochromatic or technicolor. In G. Cohen (Ed.), *Women in sport: Issues and controversies.* New York: Sage Publishers.

Acosta, R. V., & Carpenter, L. (1990). *Women in intercollegiate sport: A longitudinal study thirteen year update.* Unpublished manuscript.

Acosta, R. V., & Carpenter, L. (1992). *Women in intercollegiate sport: A longitudinal study—fifteen year update, 1977–1992.* Unpublished manuscript, Brooklyn College, New York, NY.

Adams, L. (1988). My Olympic experience. *JOPERD, 59*(3), 35–36.

Adkins, V. (1967). *The development of Negro female Olympic talent.* Unpublished doctoral dissertation, Indiana University.

Alexander, A. (1978). *Status of minority women in the Association of Intercollegiate Athletics for Women.* Unpublished master's thesis, Temple University, Philadelphia, PA.

Allen, W. (1990). Family roles, occupational statuses and achievement orientations among Black women in the United States. In M. Malson, E. Mudimbe-Boyi, J. Barr, & M. Wyer (Eds.), *Black women in America: Social science perspectives* (pp. 79–96). Chicago: The University Press.

Alston, D. (1980, January 4). *Title IX and the minority women in sport at historically Black institutions.* Paper presented at the National Minority Women in Sport Conferences, Washington, DC.

Anderson, A., & South, D. (1993). Racial differences in collegiate recruiting, retention and graduation rates. In D. Brooks & R. Althouse (Eds.), *Racism in college athletics: The African American athlete's experience* (pp. 79–100). Morgantown, WV: Fitness Information Technology, Inc.

Anderson, M., & Collins, O. (Eds.). (1992). *Race, class and gender.* Belmont, CA: Wadsworth Publishing Co.

Baca Zinn, M., & Dill, B. (Eds.). (1994). *Women of color in U.S. society.* Philadelphia, PA: Temple University Press.

Barclay, V. (1980, January 4). *Status of Black women in sports at the Big Ten institutions.* Paper presented at the National Black Women in Sport Conference, Washington, DC.

Bentley, K. (1983). *Going for the gold: The Story of Black women in sports.* Los Angeles, CA: Carnation Company.

Biracree, T. (1988). *Wilma Rudolph: Champion athlete.* New York: Chelsea House Publishers.

Birrell, S. (1989). Racial relations theories and sport: Suggestions for a more critical analysis. *Sociology of Sport Journal, 6*(3), 212–227.

Birrell, S. (1990). Women of color: Critical autobiography and sport. In M. Messner & D. Sabo (Eds.), *Sport, men and the gender order: Critical feminist perspectives* (pp. 185–199). Champaign, IL: Human Kinetics.

Birrell, S., & Cole, C. (Eds.). (1994). *Women, sport, and culture.* Urbana—Champaign, IL: Human Kinetics.

Brooks, D., & Althouse, R. (Eds.). (1993). *Racism in college athletics.: The African American athlete's experience.* Morgantown, WV: Fitness Information Technology, Inc.

Britannica. (1988). Arthur Ashe. Chicago, IL: Encyclopedia Britannica, Inc.

Cahn, S. (1994). *Coming on strong: Gender and sexuality in twentieth century women's sport.* New York, NY: The Free Press.

Captain, G. (1991, Spring). Enter ladies and gentlemen of color: Gender, sport, and the ideal of African American manhood and womanhood during the late 19th and early 20th centuries. *Journal of Sport History, 18*(1), 81–102.

Clark, K., & Mamie, P. (1950). Emotional factors in racial identification and preference in Negro children. *Journal of Negro Education.*

Coachman, A. (1996, April). *Olympic athletes: Views from within* [An oral history of her Olympic experiences]. Presented by the NASPE Sport History and Sport Sociology Academies at the AAHPERD Convention in Atlanta, GA.

Coakley, J. J. (1994). *Sport in society: Issues and controversies.* St. Louis, MO: C.V. Mosby.

Collins, P. H. (1990). *Black feminist thought: Knowledge, consciousness and the politics of empowerment.* Boston, MA: Unwin Hyman, Inc.

Corbett, D., & Johnson, W. (1993). The African American female in collegiate sport: Sexism and racism. In D. Brooks & R. Althouse (Eds.), *Racism in college athletics: The African American athlete's experience.* Morgantown, WV: Fitness Information Technology, Inc.

Costa, M., & Adair, J. (1993). Sports. In D. C. Hines (Ed.), *Black women in America: An historical encyclopedia* (pp. 1099–1102). Brooklyn, NY: Carlson Publishing, Inc.

Davies, C. (1994). *Black women, writing and identity.* New York: Routledge.

Davis, A., & Dollard, J. (1940). *Children of bondage: The personality development of Negro youth in the urban South.* New York: Harper & Row Publishers, Inc.

Davis, M. (1992). *Black American women in track and field: A complete illustrated reference.* Jefferson, NC: McFarland.

Davis, M. W. (Ed.). (1981). *The contributions of Black women to America: Vol. 1.* Columbia, SC: Kenday Press.

DeFrantz, A. (1988). Women in leadership in sport. *JOPERD, 59*(3), 46–48.

Dewar, A. (1990, November). *Working against oppression in sport: Towards an inclusive critical sport sociology.* Paper presented at the North American Society for the Sociology of Sport Conference, Denver, CO.

Douglas, D. (1988a, May). *Race, class and sex: Toward a relational level of analysis of Black women's responses to oppression in sport.* Paper presented at the R. Tait McKenzie Symposium on Sport, Knoxville, TN.

Douglas, D. (1988b, November). *Discourses on Black women—A history of silence: A review of relational analyses in education and sport literatures.* Paper presented at the North American Society for the Sociology of Sport Conference, Cincinnati, OH.

Gibson, A. (1958). *I always wanted to be somebody.* Philadelphia, PA: Harper & Row Publishers, Inc.

Giddings, P. (1984). *Where and when I enter: The impact of black women on race and sex in America.* New York: Bantam Books.

Gissendanner, C. (1994). African American women and competitive sport, 1920–1960. In S. Birrell & C. Cole (Eds.), *Women, sport and culture.* Champaign, IL: Human Kinetics.

Green, T. S. (1993). The future of Black female athletes. In D. Brooks & R. Althouse (Eds.), *Racism in college athletics: The African American athlete's experience.* Morgantown, WV: Fitness Information Technology, Inc.

Green, T. S., Oglesby, C., Alexander, A., & Franke, N. (1981). *Black women in sport.* Reston, VA: AAHPERD—NAGWS Publication.

Hall, A. (1996). *Feminism and sporting bodies: Essays on theory and practice.* Champaign, IL: Human Kinetics.

Hall, M. A. (1990). How should we theorize gender in the context of sport? In M. A. Messner & D. F. Sabo (Eds.), *Sport, men and the gender order: Critical feminist perspectives* (pp. 223–240). Champaign, IL: Human Kinetics.

Hart, M. (Ed.). (1976). *Sport and the sociocultural process.* Dubuque, IA: Wm. C. Brown Co.

Hine, D. C. (1993). *Black women in America: An historical encyclopedia.* Brooklyn, NY: Carlson Publishing, Inc.

hooks, b. (1981). *Ain't I a woman: Black women and feminism.* Boston, MA: South End Press.

hooks, b. (1984). *Feminist theory from margin to center.* Boston, MA: South End Press.

hooks, b. (1989). *Talking back: Thinking feminist, thinking Black.* Boston, MA: South End Press.

hooks, b. (1990). The politics of radical black subjectivity. *Yearning: Race, gender and cultural politics.* Boston, MA: South End Press.

Houzer, S. (1971). *The importance of selected physical education activities to women students in predominantly Black South Carolina colleges.* Unpublished master's thesis, Springfield College, Springfield, MA.

Houzer, S. (1974). Black women in athletics. *The Physical Educator, 30,* 208–209.

Janis, L. (1985, September). Annotated bibliography on minority women in athletics, *Sociology of Sport Journal, 2*(3), 266–274.

King, W. (1995). *Stolen childhood: Slave youth in nineteenth century America.* Bloomington, IN: Indiana University Press.

Lumpkin, A., & Williams, L. (1991). An analysis of *Sports Illustrated* feature articles 1954–1987. *Sociology of Sport Journal, 81,* 16–32.

Mathewson, A. (1996, November). Nobody knows her name: The Black American sportswoman. *Journal of Sports Law, Black Women & Gender Equity, 6.*

Murphy, M. (1980). *The involvement of Blacks in women's athletics in member institutions of the A.I.A.W.* Unpublished doctoral dissertation, Florida State University.

Oglesby, C. (1981). Myths and realities of Black women in sport. In T. S. Green, C. A. Oglesby, A. Alexander, & N. Franke (Eds.), *Black Women in Sport.* Reston, VA: AAHPERD Publications.

Page, J. (1991). *Black Olympian Medalists.* Englewood, CO: Libraries Unlimited, Inc.

Palmer, P. (1983, Spring). White women/Black women: The dualism of female identity and experience in the United States. *Feminist Studies, 9*(1), 151–170.

Rudolph, Wilma. (1977). *Wilma.* New York: New American Library.

Sage, G. (1990). *Power and ideology in American sport: A critical perspective.* Champaign, IL: Human Kinetics.

Smith, Y. (1990, November). *Socialization and achievement of African American elite women athletes.* Paper presented at the North American Society for the Sociology of Sport, Denver, CO.

Smith, Y. (1991, March). Issues and strategies for working with multicultural athletes. *Journal of Physical Education, Recreation and Dance, 62*(3), 39–44.

Smith, Y. (1992, April). *Ethnicity in interscholastic coaching.* Paper presented at the AAHPERD Convention, Indianapolis, IN.

Smith, Y. (1992b, August). Women of color in society and sport. *Quest, 44*(2), 228–250.

Smith, Y. (1995, September). Women sport leaders and educators of color: Their socialization and achievement. *Journal of Physical Education, Recreation, and Dance, 66*(7), 28–33.

Smith, Y., & Ewing, M. (1991, November). *The underrepresentation of gender and ethnicity in coaching: Research results and sociological implications.* Paper presented at the North American Society for the Sociology of Sport.

Smith, Y., & Ewing, M. (1992). Diversity of coaches: The need for recruitment and retention of women and minority coaches. *NASPE News*, National Association for Sport and Physical Education, AAHPERD.

The South: Collection from Harper's Magazine. (1990). New York: Gallery Books of W. H. Smith Publishers, Inc.

Stratta, T. (1995). *An ethnography of the sport experiences of African American female athletes.* Unpublished doctoral dissertation, Southern Illinois University, Carbondale.

Title IX of the 1972 Educational Amendment Act.

Washington, M. H. (1990). The darkened eye restored: Notes toward a literary history of Black women. In H. L. Gates (Ed.), *Reading Black, reading feminist: A critical anthology.* New York: Meridian, Penguin Books.

Welch, P. (1993). Alice Coachman (1921). In D. C. Hines (Ed.), *Black women in sport: A historical encyclopedia.* Brooklyn, NY: Carlson Publishing, Inc.

Williams, L. (1994). Sportswomen in black and white: Sports history from an Afro-American perspective. In P. Creedon (Ed.), *Women, media and sport: Challenging gender values* (pp. 45–66). Thousand Oaks, CA: Sage Publications, Inc.

Williams, L. (1995). Before Althea and Wilma: African American women in sports, 1924–1948. In K. Vaz (Ed.), *Black women in America.* Thousand Oaks, CA: Sage Publications, Inc.

The African American Female in Collegiate Sport: Sexism and Racism

Doris Corbett and William Johnson

Abstract

The subject of racism and sexism in collegiate sport continues to be a complex issue that causes Americans to be particularly sensitive. The fact that there have been too few African American sportswomen celebrated as role models is a reflection of the problems in this area. Even as we swiftly approach the 21st century, the American society is vaguely aware of the sporting experience of the African American sportswoman. This essay addresses the cultural milieu of the African American sportswoman from a herstorical and sociological perspective; noted African American athletes are profiled; the cultural inclusiveness of the African American woman in sport is discussed; the impact of Title IX on women of color in the historically Black institutions of higher learning is evaluated; special attention is given to the unsung African American basketball-coaching heroines who have been historically overlooked in the sporting community; and an overview of Proposition 48 and Proposition 16 is presented, with a view on the effect they have had on African American sportswomen. In addition, a review of prominent African American women in sport who are in athletic administration or related fields is featured; racial and sexual barriers women of color face in sport are discussed; and last, the media's attitude toward the African American sportswoman is examined.

Key Terms	
• Racism •	• Elite athletes •
• Sexism •	• Achievement •
• African American women in sport •	• Administrators and leaders in sport •
• Black women in sport •	• Barriers •
• Women of color •	• Discrimination •
• Cultural inclusion •	• Media •
• Cultural consciousness •	• Herstorical •
• Title IX •	

A Herstorical and Sociological Perspective of the African American Female

The concern regarding women in sport has brought with it a focus on African American women in particular. A new scholarship about women of color has been strengthened by the growing acceptance of African American and women's studies as distinct areas of inquiry.

In order to better understand the psychological and sociological nature of the African American woman in sport, the cultural milieu of the African American woman in society must first be reviewed.

Society viewed and treated African American women differently from White women in the United States. African American women have suffered many hardships and have not been treated as status symbols of their spouses or placed in a protected position in society.

Although the women's liberation movement focused on a number of theories regarding female inequality, very few models have examined in depth the constraints of both racism and sexism. It is a herstorical fact that African American women were excluded and denied mainstream participation in the political-economic development of the larger society until the Civil Rights movement of the 1960s. Prior to that time, the law denied African American people normal adult prerogatives. Widely sanctioned acts such as rape, sexual exploitation of African American women, low wages, menial jobs, and substandard educational programs all functioned as stringent barriers to participation in the political and economic process.

Like the African American woman, the White woman has also been victimized. However, the stereotypic traits differ and are quite often the very opposite. For example, almost without exception, African American women have been portrayed as aggressive, whereas White women were pictured as passive or nonassertive. The stereotypic African American/White opposites include (a) independent-dependent, (b) loud-coy,

(c) dominant-submissive, and (d) castrating-seductive (Gump, 1975).

The herstory of the African American woman has shaped concepts of her identity as well as her ideals, attitudes, behavior, role, and responsibilities. The African American female is believed to be instilled with skills essential to her maintenance and conducive to her survival. Bonner (1974), Lewis (1975), and Staples (1973) have suggested that young African American women have not been socialized to conform to stereotypic behavior patterns. Instead, African American women have continually challenged the system to define and maintain their own personal being.

The African American Woman in Society and Sport

There are herstorical differences between the African American women and White women that tend to create a different social milieu that surrounds each race. Although the United States is ethnically diverse, the standard of feminine beauty has tended to be defined by European history and European literature. The standard for assessing feminine beauty has been, until recently, described as light complexion, golden hair, and fragile build; and she is soft, small, and delicate. White women have been portrayed as the ideal housewives and symbols of love and motherhood. The antithesis of this standard is dark complexion, kinky hair, and sturdy build. The Black woman was considered to be tough and a hard-working matriarch in the home (King, 1973).

Cultural and ethnic conceptions of masculinity and femininity, the degree of sex-typing according to class, and the dominant/submissive relationship between the sexes tend to vary within and among all the various ethnic groups. As individuals and families adopt the mores and folkways of the United States, each generation will tend to erase ethnic differences as their members are absorbed into the urbanized, industrialized culture. First-generation Americans and first-generation migrants from rural areas are usually more patriarchal and traditional in their conceptions of masculinity and femininity. This pattern varies according to the cultural heritage, the unique herstorical experiences of the group, and the current availability of educational and economic opportunities to various ethnic groups (Yorburg, 1974).

For the African American woman, there was the general presumption by society that because she represented an "inferior status" in society (not limited to, but featured as, a tough, hardworking domestic or working-class individual), the roughness and toughness of the sporting world would only be a natural and an acceptable place where she would be competent.

In an era when minorities have been vocal relative to a wide range of social issues, African American women have been relatively salient with respect to their status in athletics:

> The Black woman's role in sports in the so-called Golden Era of sports in the 1930's and 1940's was nearly non-existent. The shackle of segregation handicapped the Black female in sport, but a few did excel in several sports including basketball, tennis, track, and golf. (Pinkey, 1975, p. 58)

Women in general have protested the lack of attention, respectability, and professional opportunities available to them in sport that the male athlete has traditionally enjoyed. The African American male has aggressively sought leadership roles and careers in athletics beyond his active years of competition. The African American female has not been proportionately represented in athletics at all levels, such as interschool competition, coaching, officiating, administrating, policy making, and league work (Houzer, 1971).

Houzer (1971) reported that African American women appeared to be moving toward a position of lesser interest and involvement in sport and athletics. Her findings reflected a decline in interest and sport involvement by African American women due to socially based factors. Similarly, Alexander (1979), in a study of the status of minority women in the Association for Intercollegiate Athletics for Women (AIAW), suggested that various factors account for the underrepresentation of minority women in athletics: (a) lack of money for lessons and equipment, (b) availability and rental of facilities, (c) lack of racial role models, (d) time commitments for child care, study responsibilities, and wage-earning responsibilities, and (e) available opportunities in geographic areas of minority population concentration.

In spite of segregation and racism, many African American women had the opportunity to participate in sports through clubs organized especially for that purpose, such as the Alpha, Physical Culture Club, Smart Set, and St. Christopher (Young, 1970). African American women have been participating in sports and athletics for many years. During the years of Black-White segregation, however, they were forced to compete only against other Black women in tournaments that, to the country as a whole, "did not count." One of the most widely held myths about the African American woman in sport is the belief that African American women favor track and field, in light of their successes in these events.

According to Houzer (1971), there is no substantial evidence that African American women favor participation in track and field. A 1969 study sampled 265 women students enrolled in five predominantly Black colleges in the state of South Carolina. From data collected, it was found that the subjects were generally negative in their attitudes toward track and field. The sports and activities of softball, volleyball, basketball, modern dance, and bowling were identified as the top five preferences. The subjects also indicated significant interest in tennis, badminton, swimming, gymnastics, square dance, soccer, and archery. Metheny (1972) argues that participation in track and field was more related to limited opportunities than to individual preferences.

With an increase in interest and support in general for women in sport, particularly post-Title IX, more and more women are not only being physically active, but they are also more inclined to participate in sport competitively. Although the African American culture has traditionally embraced the Black sportsman, Hart (1974), after discussing the plight of the woman in sport, commented,

> In startling contrast is the Black woman athlete. In the Black community, it seems a woman can be strong and competent in sport and still not deny her womanliness. She can even win respect and status. Wilma Rudolph is an example. (p. 441)

Hart (1980) suggests that within the Black culture, sport involvement provides women of color status and prestige. Coakley (1982) has supported the notion that the African American community places few constraints on the Black sportswoman. If this is true, then it might be suggested that gender-role expectations for African American women are less constraining in the Black culture than they are for White girls and women in White culture. For example, Black women more often have traditionally been represented in the sports of basketball, softball, and track and field. For the White sportswoman, public acceptance toward participation in these sports has not been encouraged (Del Rey, 1977; Snyder & Kivlin, 1975; Snyder & Sprietzer, 1975). White women are most represented in the individual sports of tennis, swimming, and gymnastics. These sports still remain as the most acceptable sports for White women (Metheny, 1965). Metheny (1965) found that sports that require application of force to a heavy object, body contact, or hard running and throwing are generally discouraged for the White female.

Oglesby (1981), in her writings, "Myths and Realities of Black Women in Sport," differs with Coakley (1982) and Hart (1974). Oglesby (1981) submits that the socioeconomic, political, and psychological environment in the United States has not been supportive of the advancement of the Black woman in sport. Oglesby (1981) argues that Black women have been a casualty to the double affliction of racism and sexism. The fact that Black women have systematically been neglected in the research literature simply supports this point of view. Further, Oglesby (1981) reports that most of the investigations on minorities and women have examined the sporting experiences of the Black male and the White woman in sport, without exploring the sport experience with regard to the Black woman.

In our view, the limited number of studies that have been conducted are tainted in their findings because they do not examine the sporting experience of Black women in its context. Not only do the few studies that exist neglect the sporting activities of the African American woman, but they also fail to depict how African Americans perceive women of color participating in sport. Much of the literature documents the achievements of a select group of African American women in primarily one or two sports. For example, the struggles and accomplishments of Wilma Rudolph in track and Althea Gibson in tennis have been reflected as the norm for women of color in sport. Their stories are used to reaffirm the myth that sport is a mobility escalator, and therefore, the existence of racism and discrimination in sport and society becomes disguised. Their experiences reflect their fight to compete with Whites and to gain recognition from Whites. By focusing on the few available, highly acknowledged examples of African American athletes, such as Althea Gibson and Wilma Rudolph, the authors believe the stereotypes and myths regarding the African American sportswomen are reaffirmed. Although many African American women competed and contributed to sport before and after Althea Gibson and Wilma Rudolph, these two women are considered the most significant athletic forces among African American women in sport history. The reality that the participation of African American women has been restricted to just a few sports is an issue that has caused considerable discussion (Boutilier & SanGiovanni, 1983,).

African American women have shown courage and determination in sport and have been instrumental in playing an important role in breaking down color and gender barriers in society. There have always been great African American athletes, but awareness of the African American female athletes has changed dramatically in the last 50 years, primarily because of television. Cheryl Miller, in a 1995 *Ebony* magazine article, states that her father told her that

> . . . if a White coach had to choose between a Black athlete and a White athlete of similar skills, he would choose the White athlete. Every time. The moral therefore was that it was not enough for us to be good—we had to be flat out better. (quoted in "Slap," p. 25)

Miller (quoted in "Slap," 1995) goes on to point out that

> Being a Black woman athlete, I have personally seen a lot of racial and gender bias. I was 13 years old, for example, when I tried out for an all-male basketball team. The coach, who was White, told me that if I could beat his son in a one-on-one game to 11 points, I could play on the team. I trounced him, 11 to 1, and asked the coach when I should report to practice. He looked me straight in the eye and said, "Miller, the only court I'll see you in will be a court of law. No girls will ever play on my team." I ran home crying and told my dad that I was quitting and that I never wanted to play basketball again. He sat me up straight and said: "I didn't raise any quitters. Tomorrow you will try out for the girls team and become the best who ever played. . . . " This was a turning point in my life. From that moment on, I never accepted being second best. (p. 25)

The achievements of African American women in the areas of law, politics, science, medicine, education, religion, the military, business, the arts, and sports have been impressive. The following provides an inventory of just some of the many great African American athletes who excelled in sport despite racial and gender barriers.

Outstanding African American Women in Sport

Evelyn Ashford (Track)—Broke Wilma Rudolph's 20-year-old record in the 100 meters. In 1979 was considered the top sprinter in the world. In 1984 achieved an Olympic record and received a gold medal in the women's 100-meter run. In 1984 received the gold medal in the women's 4x100-meter relay. In the 1988 Olympics, won a gold in the 400-meter relay and a silver in the 100-meter dash. Selected as one of the 100 Golden Olympians.

Tai Babilonia (Ice Skating)—First African-American woman to make the U.S. ice-skating team and compete in world-class competition.

Camille Benjamin (Tennis)—Outstanding professional tennis player.

Renee Blunt (Tennis)—Outstanding professional tennis player.

Surya Bonaly—Five-time European skating champion.

Valerie Brisco-Hooks (Track and Field)—Set Olympic and American records in all her finals; in the 1984 Los Angeles Olympics she won three gold medals for the 200-meter, the 400-meter and the 1600-meter sprint relay; in 1988 she won a silver medal in Seoul as a member of the 2nd-place, 1600-meter relay team. Selected as one of the 100 Golden Olympians.

Lillian R. Greene-Chamberlain (Track)—Was the first U.S. national champion in 800m long before it became an Olympic event, and the first African American to represent the United

States in 400- and 800-meters in international competition. A three-time member of the United States women's All-American Track and Field Team, she set national and world records in women's middle-distance running events. Gold medalist in the 1959 Pan-American Games.

Alice Coachman (Track and Field)—Listed among the 100 Golden Olympians. Alice Coachman's high jump of 5-feet-6 and one-fourth inches earned her a gold medal at the age of twenty-six. Nearly fifty-one years ago, in 1948, Alice Coachman from Tuskegee Institute became the first Black female Olympic gold medalist when she placed first in the high-jump competition at the XIV Olympiad in London, England.

Cherly Daniel (Bowling)—Champion bowler.

Dominique Dawes (Gymnastics)—Competed in her second Olympics (1996) to help the U.S. women's gymnastic team to win its first gold medal in Olympic history. She won a bronze medal in individual competition. Dominique Dawes was the top U.S. overall scorer on the night the U.S. women's gymnastic team won its first gold medal in Olympic competition. Without her, there would have been no celebration, no gold medal.

Anita DeFrantz (Rowing)—A bronze medalist and captain of the U.S. rowing team at the 1976 Montreal Olympic Games, and a member of the 1980 Olympic Rowing Team. DeFrantz also won a silver medal at the 1978 world championship before taking up posts on the National Rowing Association and National Olympic Committee in the United States.

Gail Devers (Track)—Gold medal winner in the 1992 Olympics in the 100-meter sprint. Member of the women's 4x400 Olympic Relay Team; 1996 USOC Athlete. Three-time Olympic gold medalist sprinter. Listed in the Jan./Feb. 1997 edition of the *Olympian* as one of the top 10 sportswomen. She claimed the 100 meters in Barcelona in the 100-meter hurdles.

Carla Dunlap (Bodybuilding)—Accomplished and nationally acclaimed bodybuilder.

Diane Durham (Gymnastics)—Outstanding, nationally recognized gymnast.

Teresa Edwards (Basketball)—Member of the U.S. 1996 Olympic and National Basketball Team. Listed in the Jan./Feb. 1997 edition of the *Olympian* as one of the top 10 sportswomen. Is also listed among the 100 Golden Olympians.

Nikki Franke (Fencing)—1975 National Fencing Champion, 1975 Pan-American Team (second place), member of the 1976 Olympic Team.

Chryste Gaines (Track)—Member of the U.S. women's 4x100 relay team for the 1996 Centennial Olympic Games in Atlanta, receiving a gold medal.

Zina Garrison (Tennis)—Was the first Black player to win the junior singles championship at Wimbledon. At the XXIV Olympiad in Seoul, Korea, she won a gold medal for doubles tennis and a bronze medal in singles tennis. She was the first African-American woman to play at Wimbledon since Althea Gibson in 1958, and in 1988 was a member of the first U.S. Olympic tennis team since 1924. Zina became the first Black to rank in the top 10 since the women's pro tennis tour began in 1971. Selected as one of the 100 Golden Olympians.

Althea Gibson (Tennis and Golf)—Champion at Wimbledon and Forest Hill. First Black to win at Wimbledon and the U.S. Open. Outstanding golfer and a member of the LPGA.

Tina Sloan Green (Field Hockey and Lacrosse)—U.S. Women's Field Hockey Squad in 1969; U.S. Women's National Lacrosse team in 1968 and 1972.

Traci Green (Tennis)—Member of the U.S. National Tennis team, 1995 and 1996.

Florence Griffith Joyner (Track)—World record holder in the 100- and 200-meter events. She brought fashion, flair, and high finance to women's track; at Seoul Summer Olympics in 1988, she won three gold medals in the 100- and 200-meter races and the 400-meter relay, and a silver medal in the 1600-meter relay; she surpassed Wilma Rudolph's record. Selected as one of the 100 Golden Olympians.

Lucia Harris (Basketball)—Three-time All-American. Player averaged 31 points per game at Delta State; she dominated the 1976 Olympics and was later elected to the Hall of Fame. She is the 1977 Broderick Cup Winner.

Flo Hyman (Volleyball)—First-team All-American to the United States Volleyball Association (USVBA). Flo Hyman led the rise of United States women's volleyball. She became the most recognized, most influential, and most dominant player on the best U.S. women's team ever, the 1984 Olympic Team. The 6' 5" Hyman led the U.S. team to a fifth-place finish at the 1978 World Championships, the best performance for the United States in a major international competition.

Nell C. Jackson (Track)—American record 200-meter; member U.S. Olympic Track and Field Team, 1948; member U.S. Pan-American Track and Field team, 1951, in 400-meter relay.

Cheryl Jones (Tennis)—Outstanding professional tennis player.

Mamie "Peanut" Johnson (Professional Baseball). She was one of only three women to play in the Negro leagues, and the only one who pitched. At 63 years old, she is the only one of the three still alive. Johnson posted pitching records of 11-3, 10-1, and 12–4 in 1953, 1954, and 1955 with the Indianapolis Clowns of the Negro American League. She played with Henry "Hank" Aaron and against Leroy "Satchel" Paige.

Jackie Joyner-Kersee (Track)—At 34 won a bronze medal at the 1996 Olympic Games. She has won three golds, a silver, and two bronzes since 1984 in the long jump and heptathlon. Holds the world record in the seven-event heptathlon. She is a trustee, Women's Sports Foundation. Selected as one of the 100 Golden Olympians. She has signed a one-year contract, with a one-year option, to play for the Richmond Rage of the American Basketball League. She plans to compete in track after the ABL's season concludes in March.

Stacy Martin (Tennis)—Highly ranked doubles professional tennis player.

Mildred McDaniel (Track and Field)—In 1956 became the first American female to set an Olympic and a world's record in the high jump. At the XVI Olympiad in 1956 in Melbourne, Australia, she won a gold medal in the high jump.

Lori McNeil (Tennis)—One of the highest ranking professional players; often played as Zina Garrison's doubles partner.

Cheryl Miller (Basketball)—Former star, University of Southern California women's basketball team; won 1982 national championship. Gold medal winner as a member of the U.S. Women's Basketball Olympic team in 1984. Selected as one of the 100 Golden Olympians. A Wade Trophy Recipient.

Inger Miller (Track)—Member of the U.S. Women's gold medal 4x100 relay team for the 1996 Centennial Olympic Games in Atlanta.

Madeline Manning Mims (Track)—Member of four Olympic Teams—1968, 1972, 1976, and 1980; in 1968 became the first American woman to win a gold medal in the 800-meter run. Gold medalist in 800-meter run and set an Olympic record of 2:00.9.

Sharon Monplaiser (Fencing)—Olympic fencer at the 1996 Centennial Olympic Games in Atlanta.

Renee Powell (Golf)—The second African American female to tour the professional golf circuits since Althea Gibson; has been with the LPGA since 1967.

Wilma Rudolph (Track)—Was the first African American woman to win three gold medals in track at a single Olympics. At the XVII Olympiad in 1960 at Rome, Italy, she dominated the Olympics by winning three gold medals.

Chanda Rubin (Tennis)—Turned pro at age 15. Won a Grand-Slam event in 1995, the French Open; has reached the semifinals of the Australian Open; outstanding performance at the 1995 Wimbledon, playing the longest match of Wimbledon history. Has been ranked as high as number 10.

Kim Sands (Tennis)—Outstanding professional tennis player.

Leslie Allen Selmore (Tennis)—Turned pro in 1977 and won the women's singles at the ATA (American Tennis Association) National Championship, which earned her a wild-card into the U.S. Open. She was the 1981 Avon champion. Her last appearance at the U.S. Open was in 1986. She owns her own tennis academy in Jacksonville, FL.

Brianna Scurry (Soccer)—U.S. Women's soccer team member for the 1996 Centennial Olympic Games that won the gold medal game against China.

Debi Thomas (Ice Skating)—Became the first Black to win an Olympic medal (bronze) in figure skating on February 27, 1988. She was also the first Black skater to win both the U.S. and World Figure Skating championships, both in 1986. Thomas retired from skating in 1992 to enter medical school, and graduated from Northwestern University Medical School.

Verneda Thomas (Volleyball and Track and Field)—Member of the 1964 Olympic volleyball team; Member of the 1956 track and field team for the Pan-American Games.

Gwen Torrence (Track)—In 1992, won two gold medals and one silver medal at the XXV Olympiad in Barcelona, Spain. A world-champion sprinter and member of the U.S. Women's gold medal 4X100 relay team for the Centennial Olympic Games in Atlanta in 1996.

Wyomia Tyus (Track)—Gold medal in the 1964 Olympics for the 100-meter and a silver medal for the 400-meter relay; 1968 Olympics, won a gold medal for the 100-meter and another gold medal for the 400-meter relay. Selected as one of the 100 Golden Olympians.

Marian E. Washington (Basketball)—United States Women's National team—1969, 1970, 1971; and AAU All-American team—1972 and 1974.

Ruth White (Fencing)—In 1969 first African-American and youngest to ever win the national fencing title; won five major fencing titles.

Willye White (Track)—Considered the grand old lady of track; silver medal in the long jump; silver medal on the 400-meter relay team; and won four medals in the 1959, 1963, and 1967 Pan-American Games; 17 national indoor and outdoor track titles.

Lucinda Williams-Adams (Track)—Olympic gold medalist in track and field; the third runner on the 1960 Olympic relay team with Wilma Rudolph. They called her "Lady Dancer." At the Pan-American Games in 1959, with 33 countries competing, she won the 100- and 200-meter races.

Venus Williams (Tennis)—Seventeen-year-old Venus Williams has been playing tennis for 12 years. Williams has been the most heavily recruited and richly reimbursed American prodigy since Jennifer Capriati. She made her Grand Slam debut at the 1997 French Open. She has played on the WTA Tour since turning pro in 1994. She made it to the final round of the 1997 U.S. Open in Flushing Meadows, NY, inaugurating the newly renamed Arthur Ashe Stadium by being the first African American to play in the finals of the U.S. Open under the new stadium name. Venus became only the second unseeded female finalist in the history of the U.S. Open in 1997. In the spring of 1998, Venus made it into the WTA Top Ten, winning her first WTA Singles title at the IGA Tennis Classic in Oklahoma City. She is currently ranked number seven and is the first American-born woman to win the Lipton Championship in Key Biscayne, FL, since Chris Evert in 1986. She has been named to the U.S. Federation Cup team. In 1996 and 1997, Venus was ranked 204 and 25 respectively and with a prize-money earning from $12,750 in 1996 to $460,536 in 1997. In 1997, she earned *Tennis* magazine's Most Improved Female Pro award. Venus Williams and fellow American Justin Gimelstob defeated Serena Williams and Argentina's Luis Lobo to win the 1998 French Open Mixed Doubles title.

Serena Williams (Tennis)—Younger sister to Venus Williams and is expected to become a world-class tennis star herself. Serena is currently ranked number 27. Teaming with her sister Venus, she captured the doubles crown at the IGA Tennis Classic in Oklahoma City in the Spring of 1998.

Lynette Woodard (Basketball)—Had an enormous impact on women's basketball by becoming the first female to play with the Harlem Globetrotters. A Wade Trophy recipient.

These briefly profiled African American women have pushed and persevered to make a difference. As African American sportswomen, they represent a selected few of the noted and outstanding women of color who have excelled in basketball, fencing, golf, bowling, lacrosse, rowing, field hockey, ice-skating, tennis, figure skating, track and field, soccer, gymnastics, bodybuilding, baseball, and volleyball (Boutilier & SanGiovanni, 1983; Corbett, 1987; Green, Oglesby, Alexander, & Franke, 1981).

In the past two decades sport sociologists and other social scientists have challenged the fairness and objectivity of those who report the sport experience in American society. As we seek to know more about the sporting experience of African American women within the Black culture, icons such as Althea Gibson have made it clear that they did not perceive themselves as Negro champions, even though society perceived them as a model for Negroes. Gibson commented that she saw herself as a tennis player and that she "never set herself up as a champion of the Negro race" (Gibson, 1958, p. 35). Similarly, Venus Williams has stated that "we just want to get out there and play like the rest. We've shown that we can play just like any one else. We want to be a champion for people of all color of skin" (quoted in Leand, 1998, p. 10).

Oftentimes White America holds a different interpretation of the role and function of sport in the Black community, and as a consequence, ideological generalizations, stereotypes, discrepancies, and contradictions are promoted in society and in the research and popular literature. White America, for the most part, is unaware and perhaps even uninterested in the realities of the sport experience for the African American sportswoman.

Cultural Inclusiveness of the African American Woman in Sport

Researcher Terese M. Stratta (1995) conducted an ethnographic study on the relevance of intercollegiate sports to African American women athletes. Stratta (1995) attempted to understand and describe the cultural reality of African American female athletes. Her findings suggest that many of the White athletes viewed and interacted with people from other cultures on the basis of stereotypes and that many Whites were unaware of the cultural impact their actions and words had on people of color in general, and on African American female athletes in particular. For example, Stratta (1995) points out that when attempting to lead teammates, White athletes would frequently disregard the historical, cultural relations between White and Black people. White athletes failed to realize that traditionally, Black people have been "told" by White people what to do, how to do it, and in general, what constitutes reality. Given these types of historical tensions, African American athletes admitted that at times they were treated "like slaves" rather than as teammates. White athletes generally are unaware of the fact that White people have historically had the "power" to define contextual relations that resulted in cultural group tensions on the team when African American athletes attempted to offer alternative perspectives (Stratta, 1995).

Other important examples of racial tension are reported in Stratta's (1995) study, which speaks directly to some examples of subtle racism. She reports that White teammates ignored/disrespected the cultural existence of African American athletes and were unaware of their own White privileges. For example, when socializing before or after a sport event, African American athletes were expected to enter "all-White" contexts; however, White athletes would not consider entering a racially mixed or Black context because of the "inherent dangers" associated with these social set-

tings. In addition, whenever the parents and fans of White athletes formed cliques and socialized before, during, and after sport contest, many times they failed to invite the families of African American athletes to participate in these activities. As one athlete noted,

> When I come off the field, the parents of my teammates kind of shy away from me and don't speak to me. And they speak to everyone else's parents, even if they don't know them, but they don't speak to my parents. (quoted in Stratta, 1995, p. 54).

Unfortunately, this and similar behavior is too often found as the normative experience for African American athletes at majority-White institutions of higher learning. When White athletes, spectators, and sporting administrators do not support African American teammates and fans in settings outside of the playing field, African American athletes feel "used" for their athletic prowess with little or any regard for their cultural existence. In short, the cultural consciousness of those concerned with sport must be raised.

Twenty years after the passage of Title IX, the federal regulation prohibiting discrimination on the basis of sex in college education has gone a long way to enhance sporting opportunities for women in general, but particularly the African American woman in the historically Black institutions of higher education. Title IX has played an important role in the creation and development of program opportunities for the Black sportswoman.

The Impact of Title IX at Historically Black Institutions of Higher Education

Title IX assures everyone (regardless of sex) an equal chance to learn skills, choose an area of study, partake of an opportunity for advancement in status, participate in sport, receive a scholarship, or otherwise benefit from the contributions of any institution supported by federal aid (United States Commission on Civil Rights, 1980). The regulations apply in three main areas: admission of students, treatment of students, and employment in the institution. Treatment of students is related to access to and participation in course offerings and extracurricular activities including student organizations and athletics. It is the area of intercollegiate athletics that provoked bitter discussion and controversy. Compliance is determined by the elimination of discrimination in athletic programs. Title IX does not require equal aggregate expenditure for male and female athletics. Some of the provisions of Title IX regarding sports programs are summarized as follows (United States Commission on Civil Rights, 1980):

1. All physical education classes in elementary, secondary, and postsecondary schools must be offered to both sexes.
2. There shall be no discrimination in competitive athletics. The act allows, but does not require, separate teams for members of each sex; the "nature" of the particular sport should be taken into account. Contact sports need not be open to both sexes; however, institutions are required to open intramural and club teams to members of both sexes.
3. Males and females must receive equal opportunity in selection of sport, levels of competition, provision of equipment and supplies, scheduling of games and practices, coaching, academic tutoring, practice and competitive facilities, publicity, and athletic scholarships.

Despite the fact that some negative attitudes toward women in sport persist, major changes in the level and patterns of participation for women have occurred. Since the implementation of Title IX in 1975, the opportunity for female athletes to participate in intercollegiate sport has increased substantially. For example, in 1977, one year before the Title IX compli-

ance date, the number of sports offered women was 5.61 per school. In 1980, the number had grown to 6.48; in 1986, to 7.15; and in 1988, to 7.31. The number for 1990 dropped slightly, to 7.24 (Acosta & Carpenter, 1990).

Title IX has been beneficial to African American women in sport, for it has indeed stimulated some changes in the way African American women sport teams have been treated by largely male-dominated and controlled athletic administrators. Title IX has increased the participation opportunities at historically Black colleges and universities (HBCU). In 1993, for example, there were 1,012 Black women participating as athletes in intercollegiate athletics out of 17,298 women in some 213 colleges and universities surveyed by Blum. Another study found 2,760 Black women on athletic scholarships in National Collegiate Athletic Association (NCAA) Division I institutions in the 1990–1991 academic year (Abney & Richey, 1992). It would appear, however, that the power of Title IX to remedy the historical position or status of African American women in sports is limited.

Because most universities tend to provide more sporting opportunities for men than for women, Title IX requires colleges and universities to increase the opportunities available for, and the resources expended on, women in their intercollegiate athletic programs. As a result, many colleges and universities have sought to comply with Title IX by adding more sports to the women's program. The National Collegiate Athletic Association (NCAA), which originally opposed the enactment of Title IX, has now made gender equity a major concern, which has resulted in the formulation of the National Collegiate Athletic Association Gender-Equity Task Force, which has identified several sports for women that universities may consider for compliance purposes. These sports include ice hockey, rowing, synchronized swimming, team handball, water polo, archery, badminton, bowling, and squash. Unfortunately however, African American women from the inner city and from low-income backgrounds do not have ready access to the training and development necessary to compete for scholarships and collegiate opportunities in these sports.

The enforcement of Title IX has suffered setbacks in recent years. The 1984 U.S. Supreme Court *Grove City* decision effectively denied the application of Title IX to non-federally funded programs, such as college departments of physical education and athletics. In March 1988, however, Congress enacted, over a presidential veto, the Civil Rights Restoration Act, which effectively renewed jurisdiction of Title IX over college departments of physical education and athletics. The period of 4 years without Title IX were years in which athletic scholarships for women were reduced and other negative changes were made in some women's intercollegiate athletic programs (Acosta & Carpenter, 1990).

African American sportswomen and their athletic programs have also experienced the evils of sexism in the historically Black institutions of higher education. Male athletic directors at historically Black colleges and universities (HBCU) have been reluctant to share revenue with the female athletes. The enforcement of Title IX has posed some hardships for most institutions. Eliminating sexism, like eliminating racism, is not an easy goal.

According to Howard University's head women's basketball coach, Sanya Tyler, historically Black universities are very much a part of the core of collegiate athletics and do not escape the responsibility for compliance with Title IX. Howard University, a historically Black University, has long been a pioneer in matters of civil rights, but was thrust into the national spotlight when a six-person, D.C. Superior Court jury ruled in favor of the Howard University head women's basketball coach, Sanya Tyler, by awarding an unprecedented $2.4 million which was later reduced by the presiding judge to $1,454,000. The jury found that the university violated the D.C. Human Rights Act by discriminating and by retaliating against Tyler once she filed suit;

and that the university violated federal Title IX statutes by discriminating against Tyler (Blum, 1993; Hente, 1993). According to Tyler, Howard University found itself having to defend itself against sexism and discrimination in the 1991 SANYA J. TYLER (Plaintiff) v. HOWARD UNIVERSITY, et al. (Defendants) Civil Action (No. 91-11239) only because it chose to believe that the university was exempt from federal law. Black schools because they are historically Black are not excluded from having to comply with Title IX regulations (Tyler, 1998). This judgment now rests as the cornerstone of current litigation and has, it is hoped, moved fair-minded individuals to make fair-minded and equitable decisions within their institutions. Tyler points out, however, that "many institutions are still slow in putting in place functional plans to provide equal opportunity to women through athletics" (S.J. Tyler, personal communication, September 2, 1998).

Historically, Black male athletic programs have functioned as second-class citizens striving to emerge into a National Collegiate Athletic Association (NCAA) Division I program. The majority of the athletic programs in the Black institutions of higher learning have not been able to produce revenue at a level that would qualify them to be major players in the big league. Athletic administrators in these institutions have witnessed the success of the athletic programs in the major White institutions and have observed their White colleagues as they enjoy the financial rewards that come with bowl games and media coverage, as well as other lucrative benefits. Many of the males responsible for the implementation of athletic programs have taken the position that selected male sport programs, especially football and basketball, should not have to suffer in order to support the female programs (Alston, 1980). In reality, however, this concern is not a legitimate one. Very few football or basketball athletic programs generate sufficient revenue to support themselves (Begly, 1985). This is true also for not only the women's athletic programs, but even the minor male sport programs in the historically Black institutions. The majority of the money spent for intercollegiate athletics for both male and female programs is still derived from student fees.

Not until recently have many of the athletic programs in historically Black institutions sought to achieve Division I status. Because a commitment to achieve Division I status is a costly one, many of the Black institutions experienced difficulty in adhering to the Title IX mandate while at the same time building or rebuilding their programs with limited funds. Consequently, the decree to provide resources fairly has not received a warm reception in the Black institutions of higher learning (Simmons, 1979). The idealist, however, might argue that a minority institution's athletic program would be more receptive to providing equitable opportunities to women for moral and ethical reasons.

Unfortunately, Black institutions have attempted to take as long as they can to do as little as possible to comply, even today, with the inherent principles of Title IX. On the 25th anniversary of Title IX on June 23, 1997, only a few Black institutions could boast that they had moved ahead to comply with the letter and the spirit of the law of Title IX. In the area of scholarship, often no systematic approach to the financial-awards process has ever been used. For the most part, the commitment to equitable opportunity in the area of scholarships is no more than a paper commitment. Improvements have been found in travel and per diem as well as in dining and training facilities. The worst news, however, is in coaching. Fewer women are coaches, hold leadership positions, or have an opportunity to make important decisions regarding their athletic programs. Female coaches have to work longer hours with less pay and with a shorter contract term than do their male coach counterparts (Alston, 1980).

Although the African American sportswoman has tired of second-class status both in society and sport, she has long become accustomed to discrimination due to race and gender and, therefore, holds little expectation that equity in sport will exist for her. There is no doubt that the problems encountered at the historically Black institution are any different from the problems that exist at predominantly White institutions of similar size. Regardless, the historically Black institutions must seek to train, identify, and employ minority female coaches and administrators who are sensitive to the problems and are willing to stand tall to address the inequities, in order to enhance the welfare of the next generation of sportswomen of color.

Although Title IX has served to improve the status and program opportunities for women, racial and sexual barriers continue to exist and must be addressed.

Racial and Sexual Barriers in Women's Collegiate Sport

Racial and sexual barriers surrounding the involvement of the African American woman in athletics include

1. **Limited financial support**. The lack of funds diminishes the opportunity for the minority female to receive quality training and have access to the best equipment for use.

2. **Physical education teachers often are lacking in the background to coach competitive teams**. The success of African American women in the sports of basketball and track and field has real implications for the physical education teacher who is socialized to emphasize these activities as she prepares for her professional career. Myths and stereotypes continue to exclude and serve as barriers to the African American woman who wishes to develop coaching and teaching skills in the individual sports of golf, tennis, gymnastics, and swimming. The success of Black women in track and field and basketball has led many individuals to believe that these activities are the only ones in which Blacks are better prepared to teach, train/coach, and officiate.

3. **Lack of administrative support where competitive programs and interest exist**. The major problems surrounding involvement of African American women in sport include limited financial support for athletes and athletic programs; lack of encouragement and support to attend and participate in workshop and training programs; and, with the increase in the numbers of African American women entering collegiate sport programs with undeveloped skills, greater coaching attention.

4. **Lack of positive opinion leaders as role models who are African American sportswomen**. It is difficult for a minority to select to enter an organization that is 90% White male.

5. **Tendency of White coaches to associate the Black female athletes with only certain sports (i.e., basketball and track and field)**. The high participation in track and field by Black women is probably more related to limited opportunities than to individual preferences. The commonly accepted belief that women of color are naturally gifted athletes in some sports and totally inept in others creates a barrier for them to be accepted in other sports. The result is a limitation in the variety of sports offered to them. Opportunities must be provided to African American women who can derive benefits from athletic programs other than basketball and track and field.

6. **Discrimination in team selection, particularly in the sports of volleyball and basketball**. Racial stacking is also evident for the Black female in sport. In volleyball, Blacks are underrepresented at the setter position, and they are overrepresented as hitters, a position requiring jumping, agility, and reaction—all physical characteristics. Whites are found in positions high in interaction, coordinative tasks, leadership, and outcome control. Blacks, in contrast, are found in peripheral positions where these traits are low and physical skills are paramount. Stacking is found to be stronger in volleyball than basketball (Eitzen & Furst, 1989; Furst & Heaps, 1987; Kanter, 1977; Simmel, 1950; Yetman, Berghorn, & Thomas, 1982).

7. **Discrimination in hiring**. Women of color are less likely to be recruited as coach, athletic director, or official. Therefore, too few African American women are actively involved in preparing for careers in coaching, officiating, or athletic administration.

8. **Limited skill-development opportunities**. African American women athletes are underrepresented in such sports as tennis, gymnastics, and swimming. Minority women are nearly absent in these sports because they do not have access to both the human and financial resources to develop these skills. Special training, facilities, and equipment are essential in the development and maintenance of skills for these activities.

9. **Coaches' hours**. Female coaches have to work longer hours with a more difficult goal to attain, have fewer financial rewards, and have a shorter term of contracts than do male coaches. Coaches are required to take too many hours away from their family. All too often, the female coach, and particularly the African American female coach, is without coaching assistants, which would enable coaches to have more time to spend with their families. Long coaching hours and the lack of coaching assistants also deter many capable minority women from pursuing a coaching career.

10. **Officials**. Many women are not motivated to be officials because of the perception that officiating is considered something that men do, and not girls, ladies, or women. Officiating is also less appealing to some women because of the amount of

road time required to travel to officiating sites.

11. **Intimidation from male coaches and fans**. Support systems must be developed and maintained that will provide the African American woman with the confidence that she can do the job. There is an unspoken message conveyed by the "majority society" that she is not qualified, will never be qualified, and will never be as competent as a male coach.

12. **Unwillingness to travel**. The demands to travel are greater for the African American coach, who must often function without assistants and, therefore, must also serve as a coach, scout, recruiter, trainer, and counselor.

Understandably, the solutions to eliminating these barriers are not simple. Institutions must first develop a nurturing and supportive environment where concerns can be acknowledged, and admit that racism and sexism are legitimate issues and that there are problems to be solved. Professionals who express concern about both racism and sexism should be supported, not discouraged. Denying that the barriers exist only hampers progressive behavior by everyone. Administrators must closely examine their own programs and define avenues by which

1. A much greater number of African American women will hold positions of authority as athletic directors, coaches, athletic trainers, and officials. Role models in these positions are essential to the successful recruitment and retention of African American women in these roles.
2. Adequate financial resources are in place to develop, support, and maintain quality athletic programs.
3. Female coaching salaries must be comparable to the male coaches' salaries in the same sports.
4. African American women must be encouraged to participate in a variety of sports with-

out being singularly directed into the sports of basketball and track and field.

5. Institutions can expand and provide lockerrooms and other facilities, including training facilities, to accommodate increased female participation. In many instances in the historically Black institutions, the male athletes and coaches have not been willing to share these facilities.

Propositions 48 and 16: Is It Double Jeopardy— A Race and Class Bias?

Another barrier to participation in sport has been the institution of Propositions 48 and 16. At least this is the position of many African American college presidents, athletic directors, coaches, and some civil rights leaders (Johnson, J.B. & H.W. Lundy, 1988). These leaders strongly believe that Propositions 48 and 16 reduce participation opportunities for African American athletes.

Proposition 48, the predecessor of Proposition 16, requires student-athletes to have a minimum SAT score of 700 (ACT score of 17) and a minimum GPA of 2.0 in at least 11 courses in core subjects. The core course requirements include 3 years of English, 2 years of math, 2 years of natural or physical sciences, 2 years of social sciences, and 2 additional academic courses. Under Proposition 16, course work requirements increase from 11 to 13 courses with the additional stipulation that the number of English classes be increased to 4, the 2-course mathematics requirement include algebra, geometry, or a higher level mathematics course, and 1 additional academic elective. A student-athlete with an SAT score of 700 (ACT, 17) must have a minimum GPA of 2.5; alternatively, a student-athlete with an SAT score of 900 (ACT, 21) must have a minimum GPA of 2.0.

The storm surrounding Propositions 48 and 16 has been over those provisions specifying minimum test scores as a condition for sports participation. The critics have argued that these tests are culturally biased. The fundamental arguments against Proposition 48 and 16 are that (a) the minimum SAT score requirement is arbitrary and (b) the SAT and the ACT are racist diagnostic tests that only display a cultural bias that favors Whites. It is argued that the SAT and ACT score requirement is punitive for the African American student-athletes because statistics show that under Proposition 48, 55% of Black students generally score lower than 820 on the SAT, and 69% score lower than 15 on the ACT (Chu, Segrave, & Becker,1985).

Certainly, one could argue that Propositions 48 and 16 force the interscholastic athlete to take seriously the whole notion of being a student first and an athlete second. The controversy continues, and although there is some empirical evidence to show the impact Proposition 48 has had on the Black athlete, there are no data to date to show its effect specifically on the African American sportswoman. Generally speaking, the female athlete is more successful academically.

It has been argued that women of color and women from a low socioeconomic background are penalized due to their socioeconomic status and ethnicity on the standardized SAT and ACT tests. Because income level is a strong indicator of SAT and ACT test performance, average scores on standardized tests increase steadily with increases in family income. Research findings indicate that minority-group members score lower than Whites on both the SAT and ACT, but graduate at a higher rate than do White athletes who score low on standardized tests.

A study conducted by the Educational Testing Service found that the SAT underpredicts the academic performance for African American women more than for women of any other race (Final Report of the NCAA Gender-Equity Task Force, 1993). Because of these factors, African American female student-athletes who are poor or are from working-class families are less likely to meet the National Collegiate Athletic Association (NCAA) minimum eligibility requirements. In the end, African American student-athletes must meet the stan-dards. They may not like these standards, but they will have to rise to the challenge despite any real or imagined race and class or gender bias inherent in such standardized exams.

The Overlooked Stars: African American Women Basketball Coaches

Many of this country's best college and university basketball coaches are African American women. These women build winning teams, but must deal with sexism and racism in a male-dominated institution of higher learning. African American female collegiate coaches are not bringing in the highest salaries in coaching, and their talents have not earned them the public recognition and respect they deserve. Yet, despite the double whammy of sexual and racial prejudice and discrimination, African American women are among the leading basketball coaches at predominantly White and historically African American colleges and universities.

Some of the Top 10 leaders in the National Collegiate Athletic Association (NCAA) Division I include C. Vivian Stringer, who coached more than 11 years at the University of Iowa and earned her 500th career victory at that university. Stringer is now the head basketball coach at Rutgers University; and Marian Washington has been head coach at the University of Kansas for more than 21 years and is the first African American woman to ever coach women at a predominantly White institution.

Although historically Black institutions do not break into the Top 25, veterans like Shirley Walker, head basketball coach at Alcorn State University, is one of the game's most accomplished coaches, with 200-plus wins. Howard University's Sanya Tyler has on three occasions gained entrance to the National Collegiate Athletic Association (NCAA) Championship play-offs; Patricia Bibbs of Hampton State University has acquired over 160 career wins; and Bessie Stockard of the University of the District of Columbia is renowned for her historic winning teams.

With the inspiring performance of the U.S. Women's national basketball team in the 1996 Olympic Games, and their winning of the 1996 Olympic gold medal, women's professional basketball became a reality. The recent formulation of the two women's basketball leagues, the WNBA (Women's National Basketball Association) and the American Basketball League (ABL), which is two more than there were in 1996, will lead to greater leadership opportunities for many of the outstanding African American ABL and WNBA players (such as Sheryl Swoopes, Lisa Leslie, Teresa Edwards, Teresa Weatherspoon, Trena Trice, or Andrea Congreaves) who are destined to become primary candidates for coaching and senior-level athletic administration positions in the future.

Just as there have been many impressive achievements made by African American women athletes, and their story has been underreported in the media, it is equally important for the media to report the achievements of the African American leadership in the field of sport and physical activity. What follows is a bird's-eye view of the many accomplishments of role models who are carving their own place out at the top of their profession in the area of sport leadership in the academy, professional educational, and sport associations and organizations.

Selected African American Women Sport Leaders and Educators of Health, Physical Education, Leisure, and Dance

Lucinda Williams Adams

Former president of the National Association for Sport and Physical Education (NASPE); supervisor of health, physical education, and drivers' education, Dayton Public Schools, Dayton, OH.

Robertha Abney

Former president of National Association for Girls and Women in Sport (NAGWS); associate athletic director Slippery Rock University, Slippery Rock, PA.

Alpha Alexander

Director of health promotion and sports advocacy, YMCA, New York; vice chair, USOC Member Services Committee; member, USOC Board of Directors throughout the 1997–2000 quadrennium; recently awarded the 1996 Olympic Shield presented in recognition and appreciation for outstanding service to the organization. She is only the second woman in history to receive the honor.

Gwendolyn Calvert Baker

Member, USOC International Relations Committee; member of the USOC Board of Directors throughout the 1997–2000 quadrennium; president/CEO, U.S. Committee for UNICEF; past president of the YWCA.

Beth Bass

Women's Basketball Coaches Association.

Renee Brown

Director of player personnel for the Women's National Basketball Association; former Olympic coach; as one of five WNBA Directors, Brown is the highest ranking African American on the League's administrative staff.

Lillian Greene-Chamberlain

First and only woman and American to serve as director of the Physical Education and Sport Program for the 161 member nations of the United Nations Educational Scientific and Cultural Organization (UNESCO), headquartered in Paris, France (1978–1988); only woman to serve on the Board of Trustees of the American University in Paris, France (1979–1989); first and only woman to announce a major sporting event in Madison Square Garden in New York City, as the official announcer of the Colgate Women's Games, the largest (approximately 10,000 registrants annually) and longest running (21 years) all-female athletic competition in America (1989–present); International Committee chair and Vice President of Athletes on the Women's Sports Foundation (WSF) Board of Trustees; Board of Directors, National Fitness Leaders Association; Board of Maryland Special Olympics; Maryland Governor's Council for Physical Fitness; Board of Directors, the American Running and Fitness Association.

Carla Coffey

Head, track/field, Cross-country USA T and F Committees Smith College.

Rochelle Collins

National Collegiate Athletic Association (NCAA) assistant director of Youth Sports.

Doris R. Corbett

Professor of sport sociology, Howard University; member of the International Olympic Committee (IOC) Sports for All Commission; president, International Council for Health, Physical Education, Recreation Sport, and Dance (ICHPER.SD); former president, American Alliance for Health, Physical Education, Recreation, and Dance (AAHPERD); first African American president of the National Association for Girls and Women in Sport (NAGWS); former Association for the Intercollegiate Athletics for Women (AIAW) board member; initiator/facilitator of the Howard University Women's Varsity Sport Program (1973), having formulated and framed the Howard University Varsity Proposal for Women's Athletics, and acted as its first women's basketball coach.

ICHPER.SD President Corbett in an official meeting of the Asian Games Scientific Congress in Beijing, China, in 1991. Photo courtesy of Doris Corbett.

Charlene Curtis

Assistant basketball coach, University of Connecticut, Storrs, CT.

Anita DeFrantz

Attorney and director of the Amateur Athletic Foundation of Los Angeles. On September 4, 1997, at the International Olympic Committee's (IOC) 106th Session in Lausanne, Switzerland, Anita De Frantz again made history. She became the first woman in the 103-year history of the IOC to be elected to serve as one of the organization's vice presidents (the IOC is the supreme authority of the Olympic Movement); became a member of the IOC Board of Directors in 1992; member of the USOC International Relations Committee; member of the U.S. Rowing Board of Directors; current president of the Amateur Athletic Foundation of Los Angeles; member of the Executive Committee of the U.S. Olympic Committee; trustee of the Women's Sports Foundation; vice president of the 1984 Los Angeles Olympic Organizing Committee; awarded the bronze Olympic Order by IOC in 1980.

Evie Dennis

USOC special assistant to the president; member of the USOC Executive Committee, USOC International Relations Committee, and Minorities in Sports and Women in Sports Task Forces; assistant chef de mission for the XIIIth Pan-American Games in Winnipeg, Canada, in 1999; USA chef de mission for 1991 Pan-American Games; Technical Commission member for Association of National Olympic Committees; jury of appeal/running referee for USA Track and Field at 1996 U.S. Olympic Trials; recipient of the Olympic Order in 1992; 1976 and 1980 Olympic head women's track and field team manager; USOC vice president, 1985–1988; USOC chef de mission, 1988 Seoul Olympic Games delegation; retired superintendent of Denver Public Schools.

Kathy Ellis

First African American woman president of NDA (National Dance Association) 1980, 1990.

Vivian L. Fuller

Former director of intercollegiate athletics, Tennessee State University, Nashville; former director of intercollegiate athletics at Northeastern Illinois University, Chicago; former associate director of intercollegiate athletics at Indiana University of Pennsylvania.

Linda S. Green

Lawyer, administrator and professor; vice chair, USOC Audit Committee; member, Black Women's Sport Foundation, University of Wisconsin Law School.

Tina Sloan Green

Member of the board of directors for the National Collegiate Athletic Association (NCAA)—NYSP (National Youth Sport Program), Founder and Executive Director, Black Women's Sports Foundation.

Gwen Harris

Head track and field coach, James Madison University.

Wendy Hillard

Past president, Women's Sports Foundation; television sports commentator, coach, and former elite-level rhythmic gymnast.

Photo courtesy of Tina Sloan-Green

Tina Sloan Green.

Barbara Jacket
Head track and field coach, Prairie View A and M.

Sharon Jones
Former outreach director of the Oakland A's, which made her the highest ranking woman in baseball with the Oakland As World Series team in 1990; executive director of College Relations at Mills College, Oakland, CA.

Cheryl Littlejohn
Head women's basketball coach, University of Minnesota.

Sadie Magee
Senior woman administrator, Jackson State University.

Cheryl Miller
Sports announcer; former player and coach at the University of Southern California; named general manager and head coach of the Phoenix Mercury.

Benita Fitzgerald Mosley
1984 Olympic gold medalist hurdler; director of the ARCO Training Center; president, Women's Sports Foundation.

Camille O'Bryant
Sport sociologist, Ohio State University.

Bev Oden
USA Volleyball board of directors.

Lynette Overby
NDA (National Dance Association) past president; professor, Michigan State University, East Lansing, MI.

Marcia Oxley
Programme manager, Eastern Caribbean Community, Sport Development Programme.

Violent Palmer
First African American NBA basketball official.

Dorothy Richey
Former president, National Association for Girls and Women in Sport (NAGWS); first woman to be named athletic director of both men's and women's athletic programs at Chicago State University; chairperson, Department of Physical Education, Spelman College.

Robin Roberts
Television sportscaster and host of *In the SportsLight, ABC's Wide World of Sports,* and co-host of *Good Morning America/Sunday*. Roberts has also been a correspondent for ESPN's *NFL PrimeTime* (1990–1994); correspondent and then anchor for ESPN's *SportsCenter* (1990); host of ESPN's *Sunday SportsDay*, (1990–1995).

Yevonne Smith

Sport sociologist, Michigan State University, East Lansing, MI; 1995 NASPE Sport Sociology academy chair; Women's Sports Foundation Advisory and Research Council member; North American Society for Sociology of Sport Executive Board; co-chair of the Inclusion and Diversity Committee; member of the editorial board of the *Sociology of Sport* and *Quest* Journal.

Sonja Steptoe

Senior editor, *Sports Illustrated.*

Vivian Stringer

Head basketball coach, Rutgers University, NJ.

Denise Taylor

Head women's basketball coach, WNBA—Utah Starazz.

Delores "Dee" Todd

Assistant commissioner, Atlantic Coast Conference; co-chair, USOC Minorities in Sports Task Force, National Collegiate Athletic Association.

Sanya Tyler

Head women's basketball coach, Howard University, Washington, D.C.

Kathy Richey-Walton

Head basketball coach, Spelman College, Atlanta, GA.

Marian Washington

Head basketball coach, University of Kansas; an NACDA (National Association of Collegiate Directors of Athletics) and U.S. Olympic Committee Collegiate Olympic Coaches medal winner for the sport of basketball.

Willye White

USOC—USCSC committee; chair USOC Women in Sports Committee USA Track and Field.

Barriers can be overcome, and the media make a significant difference in determining the degree of public support in the promotion of African American women in sport at all levels of involvement.

Media Attitude Towards the African American Sportswoman

Too often the media serve to reinforce previously existing attitudes and behaviors rather than to introduce new ones. This view casts the media as preservers of the status quo rather than agents of social change (Rintala & Birrell, 1984). It has been well-documented that Blacks have made tremendous strides in American sport, but little research has examined the extent of media coverage highlighting the African American sportswoman.

The media coverage that women of color receive in the leading magazines reflects our public awareness and says a great deal about our level of acceptability for the sportswoman of color. What the leading magazines report serves as a medium to illustrate our cultural values and stretches our definition of excellence beyond just public recognition of one's success. The media's portrayal of the African American sportswoman serves as a mirror of society, and it is our truth teller.

If, for example, we reflect on our expectations before the 1984 Olympic Games began in Los Angeles, the majority of sport fans and athletes felt that the Games would serve as the impetus to lift the Black gold medalist into the world of commercial endorsements, unlimited exposure, and infinite respect. However, 48 gold medals and 14 years later, most of the Black Olympic heroes and heroines from the 1984 Games are still waiting to be celebrated. There has been a general lack of recognition and respect for even the latest group of African American Olympians from the 1996 Atlanta Games.

Since the 1996 Olympic Games have ended, it appears that an outpouring of affection and adoration, media exposure, and commercial endorsements has been directed at the United States swimming and gymnastic teams, whereas African American gold medalists who excelled in track and field and basketball have remained essentially on the sidelines. Williams, Lawrence, & Rowe (1985) explain this phenomenon by stating that women's increased participation is severely impeded by social inequities in society. One must remember that a considerable number of Whites perceive African Americans as natural athletes, and Whites therefore expect African Americans to excel in sports. Consequently, when women of color perform well, as they did in the 1984, 1988, and 1996 Olympic Games, there is often a feeling among the majority (primarily White America) that the sport achievement of Blacks, regardless of how exceptional, does not deserve special acclaim in the form of special recognition and awards. Edwards (1969) explains that

> Many Black athletes have felt at one time or another that they were discriminated against. Aside from the money, prestige

is the greatest incentive to professional sports participation. In amateur athletics, it is the main incentive, along with love of the game. Prestige is typically accrued and measured by the frequency and general tone of publicity that an athlete receives in the various reporting media. Black athletes as a whole feel many sports reporters have not always given credit where credit is due. (pp. 9–10)

Because the mass media are recognized as among the most powerful institutions in our society, the mass media serve as an important vehicle for communicating social values and identifying role models. Consider the fact that African Americans in general now outnumber Whites on the playing field and are beginning to rise in numbers in coaching and executive positions. Thus, it seems peculiar that White reporters still dominate sports journalism. It can be argued and reasoned that different sensibilities and insights are warranted in today's modern sports reporting given the racial and ethnic dynamic present on the playing fields. The extent to which women of color in sport are invisible in the media suggests a symbolic annihilation of them. The African American sportswoman's perspective in sport is lost to the public for examination.

Corbett (1987) investigated the portrayal of African American sportswomen in 14 leading magazines (*Cosmopolitan*, *Glamour*, *Good Housekeeping*, *Ladies Home Journal*, *Ms*, *Redbook*, *Women Sport and Fitness*, *Woman's Day*, *Working Woman*, *Black Family*, *Crisis*, *Ebony*, *Essence*, and *Jet*) for a 2-year period (1985 and 1986) immediately following the 1984 Olympic Games. Only 20 African American sportswomen were identified in the review of 286 magazines. Corbett's (1987) findings clearly indicated that sportswomen of color are underrepresented in the popular literature reviewed. The pattern of coverage revealed that the African American sportswoman is essentially invisible and more likely to participate in very specific individual sports; and the sports that she most often represents are the least costly sports. Athletes participating in basketball and track and field received more attention. The White female Olympian received considerable attention in the media and was represented in a variety of sports.

Although the media have the power to act as agents of social change and can impact on society's attitude toward the African American sportswoman, they have not done so in a positive and progressive way. It is revealing to note that Corbett (1987), in her 2-year study of the portrayal of sportswomen of color, reported that *Ms* magazine featured only one Black sportswoman (Lynette Woodard—basketball) in the 2-year period investigated. During this same time frame, three White women (Diana Nyad, swimmer; Greta Waitz, runner; and Beverly Francis, bodybuilder) were featured. Similarly, *Essence* magazine in May 1985 did a celebration of Black women without any mention of an African American sportswoman. *Ebony* magazine in its November 1985 edition depicted Black women in history who have made outstanding contributions to society. However, no mention or recognition was given to the African American sportswoman. Valerie Brisco-Hooks said it best in an interview in 1985 when she commented, "I'm still waiting for some good things to happen" (*Ebony*, 1985).

The pathetic reporting by the media on the achievements of women of color in sport and particularly on the African American woman in sport is reflective of the limited gains made by African American women not just as athletes, but also in the area of sport management.

African American (Black) women represent 15.5% (see Table 1) of the collegiate athlete population, yet they are significantly under-

Table 1. Percentage of College Student-Athletes

(Females: Division I)			
Black Women	Latino Women	White Women	American Indian/ Alaskan/American Women
15.5%	2.2%	82.1%	0.5%

Source: *1997 Racial Report Card* (Adapted and reprinted with permission)

Table 2. A Percentage Status Report on College Sport Leadership

DIVISION I

RACIAL GROUP	College Head Coaches (Women's teams)	College Assistant Coaches	College Athletic Directors	College Assoc./Assist. Ath. Direct.	College Senior Women	College Faculty Rep. Admin.
Black Women	2.1%	7.7%	1.0%	1.8%	8.4%	1.3%
White Women	40.3%	46.9%	6.3%	27.8%	89.8%	15.4%
Other Women	0.5%	1.8%	0.3%	0.1%	1.3%	0.3%
Black Men	3.2%	4.8%	9.1%	7.5%	0%	6.1%
White Men	52.1%	35.7%	82.2%	61.7%	0.4%	76.2%
Other Men	1.8%	3.0%	1.0%	1.1%	0%	0.6%

Source: *1997 Racial Report Card* (Adapted and reprinted with permission)

Table 3. A Percentage Status Report on College Sport Leadership
DIVISION II

RACIAL GROUP	College Head Coaches (Women's teams)	College Assistant Coaches	College Athletic Directors	College Assoc./Assist. Ath. Direct.	College Senior Women	College Faculty Rep. Admin.
Black Women	1.6%	3.9%	0.8%	3.5%	16.7%	2.2%
White Women	35.7%	48.6%	10.6%	31.4%	80.2%	12.6%
Other Women	0.9%	2.0%	0.4%	0.9%	0.6%	0.9%
Black Men	2.9%	3.8%	9.8%	4.4%	0%	7.4%
White Men	56.2%	38.7%	77.7%	58.8%	2.5%	75.2%
Other Men	2.8%	3.1%	0.8%	0.9%	0%	1.7%

Source: *1997 Racial Report Card* (Adapted and reprinted with permission)

represented at all other levels of sport leadership and administration.

Across all of the divisional levels (Division I, Division II, Division III) of sport, African American women hold few leadership positions (i.e., as a college head coach, associate or assistant athletic director, athletic director, or even as the college faculty representative to the National Collegiate Athletic Association [NCAA]). The percentage of African American women who have been included in the culture of sport as athletic sport leaders and administrators is limited as depicted in the following tables compiled by the Northwestern University's Center for the Study of Sport in Society in its *1997 Racial Report Card* (Lapchick & Matthews, 1997). Tables 2, 3, and 4 reflect the extent to which African American women are included in the sport culture in leadership positions.

The evidence as reported in the *1997 Racial Report Card* (Lapchick & Matthews, 1997) clearly shows that African American women are underrepresented in college sport leadership positions. Only in Division II do Black college senior women administrators, at 16.7%, even come close to the percentage of Black women athletes represented in college sport, at 15.5%. At all divisional levels (Division I, II, and III), in each of the leadership positions

Table 4. A Percentage Status Report on College Sport Leadership
DIVISION III

RACIAL GROUP	College Head Coaches (Women's teams)	College Assistant Coaches	College Athletic Directors	College Assoc./Assist. Ath. Direct.	College Senior Women	College Faculty Rep. Admin.
Black Women	1.0%	2.7%	0.3%	1.7%	2.8%	0.4%
White Women	46.2%	52.1%	24.4%	42.4%	90.3%	22.1%
Other Women	0.9%	1.0%	0.5%	0.3%	0%	0%
Black Men	2.3%	3.5%	3.4%	3.7%	0%	1.8%
White Men	47.6%	38.7%	70.9%	50.8%	6.9%	75.4%
Other Men	2.0%	2.0%	0.5%	1%	0%	0.4%

Source: *1997 Racial Report Card* (Adapted and reprinted with permission)

(college head coach, assistant coach, athletic director, assistant athletic director, college senior women administrator, and/or college faculty athletic representative), the African American woman is significantly underrepresented.

Summary

The experience of the African American female in society, and particularly in sports, has been different from that of the White female. For the Black woman, the Black community has played an instrumental role in protecting the self-esteem of the African American woman by functioning as a buffer to the negative influences of the larger society. The African American community provides a sense of personal security, identity, and belonging and a different criterion for self-assessment. The stage has been set for a workable solution to improve the status and overall conditions of athletic programs in the historically Black institutions. Title IX has made a difference. Although all is not well, significant changes have occurred post-Title IX. African American sportswomen have become more vocal about the issues of racism and sexism. There are supportive and caring networks of professionals who want to make a difference and are willing to provide a supportive sport environment. Society needs to know about the African American sportswoman's achievements and how her experiences compare with and/or relate to those of other women of color and cultures. The public must know that there are many African American sportswomen other than Althea Gibson and Wilma Rudolph who have made significant contributions. The attitude of the media towards the African American sportswoman continues to be an issue in that the nature and degree of coverage are primarily based upon economic considerations and the prevailing interest of "majority members" of society. The struggle continues as more media attention is expected and demanded. Similarly, more support and media coverage are expected and demanded from within the historically Black colleges and university sport programs for women. The recent successful litigation by Howard University's Sanya Tyler points the way for other Title IX complaints to be levied and successfully litigated. Administrators must now think harder and longer about whether they are willing to spend more dollars on women's athletic programs or take the risk of facing a lawsuit and a long judicial process.

Suggested Readings

Birrell, S., & Cole, C. L. (1994). *Women, sport, and culture*. Champaign, IL: Human Kinetics.

Corbett, D. R. (1997). *Outstanding athletes of Congress*. Washington, DC: United States Capitol Historical Society.

Dealy, F. X. (1990). *Win at any cost: The sell out of college athletics*. Secaucus, NJ: Birch Lane Press.

Funk, G. D. (1991). *Major violation: The unbalanced priorities in athletics and academics*. Champaign, IL: Leisure Press.

Gibson, A. (1958). *I always wanted to be somebody*. Philadelphia: Harper & Row Publishers, Inc.

Lapchick, R. E., & Matthews, K. J. (1997). *1997 racial report card*. Boston: Northeastern University Center for the Study of Sport in Society.

Nelson, M. B. (1991). *Are we winning yet?* New York: Random House.

Plowden, M. W. (1996). *Olympic Black women*. Gretna, LA: Pelican Publishing Company, Inc.

Ryan, J. (1995). *Little girls in pretty boxes*. New York: Doubleday.

Sperber, M. (1990). *College sports inc: The athletic department vs. the university*. New York: Henry Holt and Company.

Study Questions

1. Describe and contrast the cultural and herstorical milieu associated with the African American woman in society with that of the White woman.

2. Identify and discuss the achievements of five contemporary African American sportswomen who have excelled in sport.
3. Identify five contemporary and prominent African American women who hold or have held significant leadership or administrative positions in sport or related areas.
4. What has been the impact of Title IX for the African American sportswoman in the Historically Black Colleges and Universities?
5. Discuss what is meant by culture inclusiveness as it relates to the African American woman in sport.
6. Identify and discuss the racial and sexual barriers many African American sportswomen experience.
7. Show how Proposition 48 and Proposition 16 may discriminate against the African American female student-athlete from a low socioeconomic background.
8. Discuss the role of the media in acknowledging the contributions of the African American female athlete.

References

Abney, R., & Richey, D. L. (1992, March). Opportunities for minority women in sport—The impact of Title IX. *Journal of Physical Education, Recreation and Dance, 56.*

Acosta, R. V., & Carpenter, L. J. (1990). *Women in intercollegiate sport: A longitudinal study thirteen year update 1977–1990.* Unpublished manuscript, Brooklyn College, Brooklyn, NY.

Alexander, A. (1979). *Status of minority women in the Association on Intercollegiate Athletics for Women.* Unpublished master's thesis, Temple University, Philadelphia.

Alston, D. J. (1980, January). *Title IX and the minority women in sport at historically Black institutions.* Paper presented at the National Minority Woman in Sport Conference, Washington, DC.

Begly, G. (1985). The current economic status of intercollegiate sport. In D. Chu, J. O. Segrave, & B. J. Becker (Eds.), *Sport and higher education* (pp. 287–297). Champaign, IL: Human Kinetics Publishers, Inc.

Berghorn, F. J., Yetman, N. R., & Hanna, W. E. (1988). Racial participation and integration in men's and women's basketball: Continuity and change, 1958–85. *Sociology of Sport Journal, 5,* 107–124.

Blum, D. E. (1993, April 7). Forum examines discrimination against Black women in college sports. *The Chronicle of Higher Education,* p. A39.

Blum, D. E. (1993, July 7). Howard basketball coach wins $1.1 million in sex-bias lawsuit. *The Chronicle of Higher Education.* p. A45.

Bonner, F. B. (1974, Summer). Black women and white women: a comparative analysis of perceptions of sex roles for self, ideal-self and the ideal-male. *The Journal of Afro-American Issues, 2.*

Boutilier, M. A., & SanGiovanni, L. (1983). *The sporting woman.* Illinois: Human Kinetics Publishers.

Chu, D., Segrave, J. O., & Becker, B. J. (1985). *Sport and higher education.* Champaign, IL: Human Kinetics Publishers, Inc.

Coakley, J. J. (1982). *Sport in society: Issues and controversies.* St. Louis, MO: C.V. Mosby.

Corbett, D. (1987). The magazine media portrayal of sportswomen of color. *ICHPERD/CAHPER World Conference Towards the 21st Century conference proceedings.* Vancouver, Canada: University of British Columbia.

Del Rey, P. (1977). In support of apologetic for women in sport. *International Journal of Sport Psychology, 8,* 218–223.

Edwards, H. (1969). *The revolt of the Black athlete.* New York: Free Press.

Eitzen, D. S., & Furst, D. (1989). Racial bias in women's collegiate volleyball. *Journal of Sport and Social Issues, 13*(1), 46–51.

Furst, D. M., & Heaps, J. E. (1987). *Stacking in women's intercollegiate basketball.* Paper presented at the annual meetings of the North American Society for the Sociology of Sport, Edmonton, Alberta.

Gibson, A. (1958). *I always wanted to be somebody* (p.35). Philadelphia: Harper & Row Publishers, Inc.

Green, T. S., Oglesby, C. A., Alexander, A., & Franke, N. (1981). *Black women in sport.* Reston, VA: American Alliance for Health, Physical Education, Recreation and Dance.

Gump, J. P. (1975). Comparative analysis of Black women and white women sex role attitudes. *Journal of Consulting and Clinical Psychology, 43,* 858–863.

Hart, M. M. (1980). Sport: Women sit in the back of the bus. In D. F. Sabo, Jr., & R. Runfola (Eds.), *Jock: Sports and male identity* (pp. 205–211). Englewood Cliffs, NJ: Prentice Hall.

Hart, M. M. (1976). On being female in sport. In M. Hart (Ed.), *Sport in the sociocultural process* (p. 441). Iowa: Wm. C. Brown Co.

Hente, K. (1993, July 7). Tyler's shot at equity

rings clear—A Title IX victory for Howard coach. *The Washington Post,* p. B6.

Houzer, S. P. (1971). *The importance of selected physical education activities to women students in predominately Black South Carolina colleges.* Unpublished master's thesis, Springfield College, Springfield, MA.

Johnson, J. B., & Lundy, H. W. (1990, April 27–28). *The NCAA's Rule 48 and Proposition 42: An overview.* The Sport Leadership Conference, Grambling State University, Grambling, LA.

Kanter, R. M. (1977). Some effects of group life: Skewed sex ratios and responses to token women. *American Journal of Sociology, 82,* 965–1006.

King, M. C. (1973, March–April). The politics of sexual stereotypes. *The Black Scholar.*

Lapchick, R. E., & Matthews, K. (1997). *1997 racial report card.* Boston: Northeastern University Center for the Study of Sport in Society.

Leand, A. (1998, July–August). Smashing success. *Olympian, 10.*

Lewis, D. (1975, Fall). The Black family: Socialization and sex roles. *Phylon, 36,* 221–237.

Metheny, E. (1965). *Connotations of movement in sport and dance.* Dubuque, IA: William C. Brown.

Metheny, E. (1972). Symbolic forms of movement: The feminine image in sports. In Oglesby, C. A. (1981). *Myths and realities of Black women in sport.* Cited in T. S. Green, C. A. Oglesby, A. Alexander, & N. Franke (Eds.), *Black women in sport.* Reston, VA: AAHPERD Publications.

National Collegiate Athletic Association. (1993, July 26). *Final report of the National Collegiate Athletic Association (NCAA) Gender-Equity Task Force.*

Pinkey, R. (1975, June–July). Taking a sporting chance. *Encore,* 58–63.

Rintala, J., & Birrell, S. (1984). Fair treatment for the active female: A content analysis of young athlete magazine. *Sociology of Sport Journal, 1*(3), 231–250.

Simmel, G. (1950). *The sociology of Georg Simmel* (K. H. Wolff, trans.). Glencoe, IL: Free Press.

Simmons, G. L. (1979). *The impact of implementing Title IX in a predominantly Black public university.* U.S. Department of Health, Education and Welfare National Institute of Education.

Slap in the face. (1985, Summer). *Ebony, 6,* p. 25.

Snyder, E. E., & Kivlin, J.E. (1975). Women athletes and aspects of psychological well-being. *Research Quarterly, 46,* 191–199.

Snyder, E. E., & Spreitzer, J. E. (1975). The female athlete: Analysis of objective and subjective conflict. In D. M. Landers (Ed.), *Psychology of sports and motor behavior.* University Park: Pennsylvania State University.

Staples, R. (1973). The Black matriarchy. In *Race relations: Current perspectives.* New York: Winthrop.

Stratta, T. M. (1995). Cultural inclusiveness in sport: Recommendations from African American women college athletes. *Journal of Physical Education, Recreation and Dance, 66*(7), 25–56.

United States Commission on Civil Rights. (1980). *More hurdles to clear.* Washington, DC: Educational Clearinghouse, #63.

Williams, C., Lawrence, G., & Rowe, D. (1985). Women and sport: A lost ideal. *Women's Studies International Forum, 8*(6), 639–645.

Yetman, N. R., Berghorn, F. J., & Thomas, F. R. (1982). Racial participation and integration in intercollegiate basketball, 1958–1980. *Journal of Sport Behavior, 5,* 44–56.

Yorburg, B. (1974). *Sexual identity, sex roles and social change.* New York: John Wiley and Sons.

Young, V. H. (1970, April). Family and childhood in a southern negro community. *American Anthropologist, 72.*

The Future of African American Female Athletes

Tina Sloan Green

Abstract

The author provides a historical and social overview of African American women's participation in college athletics. Despite the lack of existing data, the author is optimistic about the future of African American female participation in sport. Organizations such as PGM Golf, YWCAs, Amateur Athletic Foundation of Los Angeles, Black Women in Sport Foundation, Sports Bridge, Girls Clubs, and the National Youth Sport Program will continue to enhance participation opportunities for females.

The essay targets the future of the elite African American female athlete. Particular attention is given to her capitalization on the American commercial market and greater prominence gained through media exposure. As we approach the next century, it is predicted that the number of African American females participating in college and professional sports in foreign countries and the United States will increase. However, barriers such as racism, sexism, and politics will continue in the 21st century.

Recommendations to eradicate sexism and racism include having African American females apply for sport-related jobs, creating jobs in the African American community, establishing sport camps and clinics, and having African American females serve as sport interns.

Key Terms
• Afrocentricism •
• ABL—American Basketball League •
• APG—Athletic Performance Grant •
• BEOG—Basic Equal Opportunity Grant •
• BWSF—Black Women in Sport Foundation •
• NCAA—National Collegiate Athletic Association •
• NYSP—National Youth Sports Program; Proposals 42, 48, 16 •
• Replacement phenomenon •
• Title IX; USOC—United States Olympic Committee •

Introduction

What is the future of African American women in sports and athletics? The predictions that follow are based on the author's discussions and interactions with contemporary African American female athletes, administrators, and coaches. All agree that economics will be one of the primary factors affecting the future of these African American women. Although limited research has been conducted on the contributions and participation levels of African American sportswomen, the literature available indicates that there has been limited but increased involvement during the 20th century.

In categorizing some current research on the representation of African American women in sport, Smith (1986) reported that 281 African American females made major contributions to sports between 1900 and 1979 in 35 different areas. Focusing on the mid-1970s, Alexander's (1978) data indicated there were 17,000 women athletes in the Association for Intercollegiate Athletics for Women (AIAW) during the 1976–1977 academic year, of whom 1,000 were African American (5.8%). Approximately one decade later, Acosta and Carpenter (1990) found that between 1986 and 1987 African American women accounted for 10.3% of intercollegiate athletic participants. A study reported by the American Institute for Research (1989) for the National Collegiate Athletic Association (NCAA) revealed that 33% of women's basketball players on NCAA Division I teams were African American, whereas African Americans accounted for 8% in all other sports combined. Findings from the NCAA Research Department state that of the African American female basketball players in 1995, 1,360 Division I and 735 Division II players received aid.

Evidence of an apparent lack of participation of African American female athletes in scholastic sport programs has also been documented. According to the Women's Sport Foundation report (1989) on minorities in sport, the National Federation of State High Schools Association found that about 5.25 million youths participated in varsity sports in 1987–1988, yet African American females represented only 4.4% of the total sample of varsity athletes in 1980–1982.

One factor that may allow more African Americans to participate in sport may be an increase in their economic status. Historically, African American women have not had time to participate in games or sports (Corbett, 1981). It was necessary to work for whatever salary was available, whereas nonworking hours were spent mothering and tending to household chores. Today, among the African American middle and upper classes, more time and money may be available to pursue sport activities, including enrollment of young children in sports programs. Regardless of some modest affluence, in the remaining years of this century, however, the majority of African Americans will continue to experience economic oppression, and a very large number will remain poor.

Among African American women who are struggling to provide the basic necessities of life while making financial ends meet for their families and themselves, sport will remain a frivolous commodity—one that they will have neither the time nor the energy to pursue. In my estimate, public schools must provide realistic and inexpensive lifetime sport and fitness training for African American females from childhood through high school. Perhaps if African American women develop positive attitudes and habits concerning physical activity when they are young, these practices will continue into their adult lives.

Recreational Sport and the African American Female

According to Warwick (1991), the scope of recreation programs in urban areas has improved and should continue improving in the future. If this is so, African American children growing up in low-income environments may have more access to recreational sports than has been the case in the past. A variety of reasons may help us to understand changes in participation levels.

First of all, Title IX legislation and feminist groups have pressured agencies and sports organizations to provide more recreational sports activities for females. We may see more and more African American girls involved in league basketball, track and field, and softball. Second, many facilities—tennis courts, pools, outdoor fields—in urban areas now are available for use by African Americans.

Finally, changes in residential patterns and neighborhood composition may also affect the availability of recreational resources: As Whites flee the city, they leave behind facilities that may be used by African Americans moving into these communities. The availability of facilities in African American neighborhoods, in turn, places pressure on local recreation leaders to provide instruction and supervision in swimming, tennis, field hockey, and other sport activities. This "replacement" phenomenon was best exemplified in some Philadelphia residential areas during the late 1970s, as African Americans moved into Germantown,

Former Coach Cathy Parsons, Washington Mystics.
Photo courtesy of Washington Sports Entertainment, NCI Center, Washington, D.C.

Mount Airy, and other residential areas of west and north Philadelphia. In areas like these, more African American children than ever before are swimming on a daily basis, participating in summer tennis camps, and playing basketball year-round.

Indications are that the local fiscal and budgetary crises confronting cities will force some regional and national sport-governing bodies, nonprofit associations as well as youth organizations and clubs, to assume more responsibility for providing resources for youth sports. Government funds and Olympic development funds may be more commonly available for sport programs that are offered as alternatives to drugs and that key on maintaining the fitness of our youth. Current projects undertaken by the United States Tennis Association, the Amateur Athletic Union, Track Athletic Congress, United States Field Hockey Association, United States Golf Association, and others may enhance sport opportunities for the inner-city African American population (Williams, 1990). Some observers suspect that tennis, golf, and other such sports may forge new economic markets by revealing that the African American population is a viable economic market for equipment, footgear, and athletic talent.

In the professional arena, the White-dominated sport organizations and associations raise millions of dollars using grassroots involvement as a giving incentive. Although domination has grown less blatant, economic influence continues to exclude African Americans from economic participation, certainly from economic power. One suspects that it is in the best interest of sports organizations to control the funding for minority programs and to continue striving to monopolize the administration of sports while also controlling how African Americans may be allowed to succeed. The following factor exists, however, to temper such oppressiveness: If these organizations do not build programs for minorities, they will be subject to lawsuits alleging discrimination. Likewise, providing minority programs also avoids the threat of African

Americans' developing their own programs, producing talented athletes, and bypassing the national organizing body.

For young inner-city women, the YWCA, Girls' Clubs, and the Girl Scouts have recognized that girls have an array of social and recreational interests and many have strong interests in sport (Alexander, 1991). These organizations will continue to encourage sports activities in their programs. Indeed, one suspects that because many clubs are located in the city and their former White clientele has moved to the suburbs, the clubs' leadership will be forced to gear their programs toward the African American, Hispanic, and other minority populations who now occupy the neighborhoods.

The YWCA initiated grassroots programs for girls in field hockey, basketball, tennis, volleyball, and gymnastics, as well as swimming and fitness. The YWCA has a long-standing commitment to providing leadership positions for women of color and to eliminating racism and sexism in sport programs. These efforts should also aid in promoting sports participation among minorities.

Another nationwide association of groups that is geared to fight minority oppression through the provision of opportunities for personal growth and social development by focusing on an array of recreational activities is the NCAA's National Youth Sports Program (NYSP). Largely the offspring of an activist public conscience spawned from the Civil Rights movement, the NYSP was created in the summer of 1968 and is presently administered by the Office of Community Services (OCS), United States Department of Health and Human Services (DHHS), the National Collegiate Athletic Association (NCAA), Administration for Children and Families, and selected colleges and universities. Since 1968, the NYSP has offered youngsters (age 10–16) drug education, job and educational counseling, free meals and free medical exams and instruction on such issues as AIDS and teen pregnancy. The sports program combines sports instruction with exciting educational activities.

Enrollment is free and open to all youngsters in the community whose parent(s) or guardian(s) meet Department of Health and Human Services income guidelines. The NYSP programs are now held during the summer at 170 universities across the country and continue to have an impact on increasing participation of young African American girls and women involved in sports and sport-related fields. In 1997 the NYSP serviced 66,191 economically disadvantaged youths between the ages of 10 and 16 in 149 different cities. Because the NYSP has strong affiliations with urban and historically Black colleges and universities, the majority of the participants are African Americans.

Elite Sport and the African American Female

It is likely that improved sport programs and facilities in urban areas will result in an increased recreational participation among young African American women and men. At the same time, what may be needed to raise the skill level of African American female athletes to that of the elite athlete is a significant improvement in the quality of programs (facilities, instruction, support services). Unless the programs in the African American neighborhoods can compete in quality with the established White programs, it is doubtful that significant numbers of African American female champions will emerge during the next decade.

The possibility to compete successfully for more athletic scholarships will encourage some exceptional African American female athletes in urban areas to pursue their sports seriously. Title IX has forced universities all over the country to offer scholarships for women. Just as African American men have used scholarships as a means to acquire an education and a profession, so too will African American women. Chances have increased for African American female athletes to attend "top-name" colleges that were previously out of their economic and social ranges. In the future, programs such as Project Challenge, which is based in Philadelphia, will provide long-term support for select African American girls so that they can qualify for athletic scholarships. Project Challenge is a program that was created in 1995 by the Black Women In Sport Foundation, a national nonprofit organization, with funding from the United States Tennis Association. Project Challenge provides the resources necessary to train and facilitate competitive experiences for 14 outstanding African American female student-athletes between the ages of 8 and 12 in an effort to produce nationally competitive players.

The exploitation of student-athletes is documented, and in their quest for a championship team, colleges must not exploit the African American female athlete as they have the African American male athlete (Wiley, 1990). For example, to maintain a competitive program, coaches are apt to place heavy, sometimes extraordinary, demands on their African American scholarship athletes. Even though African American women may come to college for academic achievement, sport forces them to devote long hours to practicing, traveling, and competing, with very little time left for their academic studies (see 1989 AIR Study for data). A demanding schedule, in turn, may encourage some African American female athletes to take easy courses held at convenient times. Faculty members may also contribute to the exploitative system by "giving grades" to female athletes who rarely attend class. Some also complain about being forced to compete when they are injured, about being prohibited from going home for scheduled holiday weekends, and about being restricted in their social development. In the end, the athlete is left too often with an inferior education and, in some cases, no degree.

The new NCAA legislation restricts practice and competition time. Practice is restricted to 20 hours per week, 4 hours per day, with one day off. A competition is equivalent to 3 hours per day. This legislation is intended to help eliminate exploitation of Africa American female student-athletes and reduce some of the injustices. Tutoring and academic support services—structures that should be included in every program, certainly in every Division I athletic program—may also help offset the effects of exploiting athletes. Focusing on equalizing the outcomes to ensure minority education, financial aid and academic advising must not only be available for the student-athlete during her 4 years of eligibility but must also prove successful to support her after eligibility expires, to ensure her educational goals. When a university offers a minority student an athletic scholarship and accepts her into the institution, it is imperative that the institution also provide all the support the student needs for academic survival (Clark, 1988; Matthews, 1988).

The African American female athlete is no more prepared to define educational goals than is any other student and she may find it very difficult to refine and adapt her goals to be assured success. African American female athletes must make sure that they earn a degree as well as a varsity sport letter because, after four years of collegiate participation, the opportunity to enter the professional sport arena will be very slim. As a result of the national women's basketball team's gold medal performance and its commercial attraction in the 1996 Olympics, and the commercial success of women's college basketball, professional basketball for females will become a reality in the United States in the next decade. However, it is unlikely that professional track and field for females will flourish in the United States within 10 years, and the global market for sports will probably be even more confined for women than for elite male athletes.

Sexism has had and will continue to have serious penalties for women in professional sport. Sponsors and spectators spend millions of dollars in support of men's basketball and track teams, but sponsors and spectators do not support female athletes and teams in the same fashion. This is not simply a lack of parity; it is sheer exclusion, with the exception of a few White-dominated, media-driven games like golf and tennis, which receive scant attention and control from the NCAA. Although there have been several attempts to establish professional female basketball leagues in the United States, these efforts were unsuccessful. I believe the attempts failed because of a lack of public interest, low salaries, and lack of sponsorship. In the fall of 1996, eight cities were chosen as sites for the American Basketball League (ABL). Each ABL team played a 40-game regular season schedule, as well as playoffs. Players earned an average of $70,000 with top players earning as much as $125,000. Many of the U.S. national players, such as Dawn Staley, signed agreements and played with the ABL. The games were televised and the spectator support was fair.

The National Basketball Association (NBA) responded in late 1996 with the launching of its own league—the Women's National Basketball Association (WNBA)—which started play the summer of 1997. These were two very competitive, committed, and successful leagues in their own right, yet a comment circulating among fans of both leagues was whether the two leagues could survive.

The ABL, with its exclusive contracts, small city teams, small but loyal fan base, high salaries versus low promotions of its athletes, few sponsors, and minimal media coverage, struggled and finally went bankrupt on December 22, 1998.

Since the folding of the ABL, the WNBA no longer has to compete for the top talent. The WNBA is strong financially. Its games and playoffs are played in NBA venues during the off-season. With unionization, WNBA players' salaries and benefits should improve tremendously. The WNBA has a slew of sponsors, and their games are televised nationally three times a week on NBC, ESPN, and Lifetime, averaging 1.4 million households per game.

A few elite African American women athletes who are willing to travel will find greater financial opportunities in basketball or in track and field in the European and Japanese markets.

One suspects that African American female athletes who deal with economic hardships in new, largely corporate, and media-driven sports like golf and tennis will need to rely on new sources of backing. Currently, promising White tennis and golf pros begin to train very young, at ages six through eight. Parents usually are well-to-do business professionals, with access to sponsoring networks (money) and to expertise for training their daughters. In a 1988 report by the United States Tennis Association, Ron Woods, director of the Player Development Program, said, "We found that the average national junior player comes from a family that was making $80,000" (cited in Markowitz, 1991, p. 7). In addition, it is not uncommon for top juniors to move to warm climates in order to practice year-round.

Previously, in tennis, only Zina Garrison (a top-20 player), Lori McNeal, Stacy Martin, and Katrina Adams (doubles) were highly ranked professional players. People like Arthur Ashe, Althea Gibson, Bill Cosby, John H. Johnson, and organizations like the Johnson Publishing Company helped with the financial obligations of some of these African American female tennis players. Financial help from USTA Player Development and corporate sponsorship has enabled Chanda Rubin to break into the top 20 ranking. In addition, tennis prodigy Venus Williams has signed a lucrative contract with Reebok and has reached a top 10 ranking. Undoubtedly, improving the play, thus increasing the number of African American females playing tennis and golf, will rely on and awaits increased corporate sponsorship.

The absence and poor quality of existing facilities for training and tournament play of African Americans are barriers that can begin to be corrected with money. Not long ago, the chairman of the Black Tennis and Sports Foundation announced the formation of a minority support program to assist promising minority and disadvantaged junior tennis players. With such organizational and commercial assistance, promising upcoming players Traci Green (two-time National Junior Team member and member of the 1998 University of Florida NCAA championship team) and Alexandra Stevenson (National Junior Team) could possibly break into the top professional tennis ranks. Venus Williams in 1998 broke into the WTA Top 10, and her sister, Serena Williams, broke into the Top 20.

Especially since the success of Tiger Woods, there are strong indications that initiatives are also being implemented to attract and support young African American females in golf. For example, since 1971, the PGM Golf Clinic, Inc., a golf program for African American youth in Philadelphia, has been responsible for introducing golf skills to African American girls and boys on playgrounds and school yards, in church basements, and on public golf courses. The United States Golf Association has recently established a minority program to attract and retain minority junior golfers. Working with this program, Rose Elder has been very influential in raising funds for promising young African American golfers. Since 1993, the Black Women in Sport Foundation has sponsored golf clinics for African American girls in 10 major cities. Despite these and many other efforts, the chances are still slim that the African American female tennis or golf pros will suddenly emerge from the collegiate scene in the next decade without extensive training, strong parental support, and broad media exposure beyond the collegiate experience. However, there are exceptions, as evidenced by the performance and ever-increasing popularity of Renee Scruggs and Nakia Davis, who are power collegiate golfers breaking into the pro ranks.

Role of the Media

Greater prominence through media exposure is an advantage that the new upcoming generation of collegiate African American women athletes can and will enjoy. For example, Nike's financial support for the travel and training and promotion of the national basketball team prior to the 1996 Olympics had a dramatic impact on the commercial and spectator value of these athletes after their gold-medal finish. Although media exposure will surely generate a more ubiquitous, and probably vicariously known,

African American female role model, chances are good that a collection of elite women will stand as candidates for this role model. African American youth hold to the old sayings "Seeing is believing" and "A picture is worth a thousand words." Minority role models (including African American males and females) in sport will make children and parents believers. If youngsters have the opportunity to watch highly skilled African American athletes on television, their motivation to pursue the sport as participants may increase.

In order for the elite African American female athlete to capitalize on the United States commercial market, the sport as well as the athlete must appeal to the White upper-middle classes. We can compare this to fashion, where many trends originate in lower-class subcultures but usually do not become popular until they are sanctioned by the socially elite. Sport practitioners must work together to get the White economically elite to value and identify with the Dawn Staleys and the Chanda Rubins.

Top-level women's team sports like field hockey, lacrosse, and soccer have been and will continue to be predominantly participation sports rather than spectator sports and have little chance to capture very much media exposure without some support from corporate sponsors. In the past, Florence Griffith Joyner (Flo-Jo) has been one of a few African American talents able to take advantage of commercial markets. Her unique running attire appealed not only to female track stars but also to female joggers, walkers, and fitness buffs. She also became a sex symbol for men. In general, not many women have lucrative endorsement contracts, but most women who do possess Eurocentric features and manners: Jennifer Capriati, Monica Seles, and Chris Evert (all tennis players) represent types of female images appreciated by the upper-middle-class White establishment. However, Lisa Leslie, gold medalist in basketball in the 1996 Olympics, has received lucrative media exposure as a fashion model.

It has been the author's experience that racism and sexism are critical forces that will prevent the African American female "star" athlete from achieving commercial success. Either she will have to be talented and also portray an appealing middle-class image, or she will need to possess exceptional talent. Like successful entertainers who create a flamboyant and creative image package, she may have to develop something (hair, clothing, or personality) that makes her stand out from the crowd. Venus and Serena Willams have done a marvelous job of marketing their Afrocentric hairstyle, beaded braids.

The media should be more accessible to women and more vulnerable to concerted efforts among African Americans. African American political factions, especially women's groups, must put pressure on the media and sponsors for greater coverage. Sponsors must be convinced that there is an untapped economic market in African American communities for sport gear. The African American media must also play a greater role in promoting African American female athletes. African American female athletes may find more financial success in foreign markets like Europe or Japan where their Afrocentric differences have gained recognition.

According to June Rogers, professor of African American studies at California State University at Fresno, "Afrocentricism is an important new educational emphasis on the African and African American experience and contributions to human culture" (cited in Wiley, 1991, p. 1). Afrocentricism gives credibility, respect, and value to the African American heritage, which oftentimes in the past has been ignored or misrepresented by the dominant, American, Eurocentric ideology (Wiley, 1991). Dark skin, curly hair, large facial features, and body shape prevent many African American females from fitting the profile of the All-American White girl, a fair-skinned, blue-eyed blonde with petite hips and waist. Cultural differences in speech, body language, and customs prevent many African American females from being accepted by the dominant White culture. For purposes of social and eco-

nomic mobility, African Americans sometimes find it necessary to modify their behavior and appearance so that they can resemble the dominant model.

From a personal perspective, I toured with the United States Women's Lacrosse team to Australia and Japan in 1969, and for the first time in my playing career, I felt like a star. Much to the surprise of my White teammates, in these countries I was given very special treatment and media publicity. The Australians and the Japanese had many questions about the African American experience in White America. Eurocentricism does not encourage the African American athlete to feel good about her differences, but Afrocentricism encourages the African American athlete to value her diversity.

Merv Jones, academic counselor for student-athletes at Temple University and former video and film producer, states, "The media perception of African American female athletes is probably the most difficult element to change. While there have been small strides in the participation of African American females, like Cheryl Miller and Robin Roberts in the broadcast booth, the number of African American females involved in the overall decision-making process of what actually is shown on the air is minuscule, especially in sports television. Training programs, internship opportunities, mentoring, and creating minority awareness of career possibilities behind the camera are just a few of the ways to increase representation in these decision-making occupations.

Despite the limited number of African American females making decisions behind the scenes, the future of positive television exposure is bright. Several conversations I've had with high-school-aged African American females have revealed that, especially in women's basketball, these young girls are familiar with the names and faces of the stars of the game. A mere 5 years ago, this would not have been the case. This is partially due to efforts such as ESPN's investment of millions of dollars for the exclusive rights to televise the NCAA Women's Basketball Tournament, mainly because there are many who feel that as more women participate in sports, they will become both spectators and viewers of women in sports. This potential market of viewers has the kind of purchasing power that makes television executives take notice.

Even though the African American female athlete will have greater career opportunities in foreign countries in the year 2000, she will face other obstacles that will affect the longevity of her playing career. Isolation from family and friends will be a very significant problem. It will be very difficult to establish and retain a romantic relationship. Likewise, it will be very costly to call home to say "Hi" or "Happy birthday," or to attend family funerals, weddings, or parties. Other obstacles to overcome include demanding travel schedules; limited availability of African American hair care or cosmetics; and the absence of favorite foods, music, and cultural events. In order to make positive adjustments, it is imperative that the gifted African American athlete experience travel to foreign countries early in her career. It is also important that she have enough corporate sponsorship so that she can travel not only with a coach but also with family members or a significant other or both.

School Sport and the African American Female

The role of school sport and athletics has changed dramatically over the decades. The extent to which the gifted African American female athlete will be able to advance in her sport in a school setting will depend on her educational background; the positive advice and support that she receives from family and coaches/teachers; and her own self-discipline, work ethic, and motivation. Sport should be used by educators as a vehicle for fostering academic achievement. Some literature tends to support this concept. For example, a study by the Women's Sport Foundation (1989) concluded that athletic participation enhanced involvement in school and community activities. It was interesting to note that minority athletes actually performed better academically than

did nonathletes. In addition, sport involvement lowered the dropout rate among some minorities in suburban and rural schools.

These findings justify the inclusion of a variety of sports in schools to capture the interest and talents of a variety of students. In order for the student to participate in high school sports, however, there should be minimum academic requirements, such as (a) regular class attendance, (b) an acceptable GPA, and (c) good citizenship. It is my belief that if the student does not meet these requirements, she should not be allowed to participate in sports.

Students should know that coaches care about and monitor their progress. Once students know that they need to fulfill certain requirements for participation and that the rules will be enforced, they are more likely to assume responsibility for their actions and adjust their behavior in order to play. Coaches should inform parents if they think the student-athlete has potential for college athletics, but is not achieving academically. Maybe the home and school together can find an answer for the student's lack of success.

Student-athletes who think they want to go on to college should see their counselors and/or coaches in the 8th or 9th grade to plan their course selections. The academic school policy for athletic participation should be well publicized and enforced. In addition, each student-athlete and coach should be made aware of NCAA Proposals 48, 42, and 16, which define GPA standards, core curriculum minimums, and minimum standardized test scores. High schools must invest in tutoring programs, and student-athletes must be encouraged to take advantage of them. Each school district should offer a college board preparatory course or make available to students information on extension courses that deal with how to take the SAT and ACT. Students should be encouraged to take the exam in 10th grade, just for practice. The outstanding academic achievement of student-athletes should be publicized in the school and local papers, and coaches and staff should send letters of commendation to such students.

Student-athletes should sit down with their coaches and parents and establish career goals at the start of the 9th and 10th grades. Too often, students reach the 12th grade only to discover that they have not taken the right courses for entrance to college. Students should be encouraged to dream, to strive for excellence, to take risks, and to love themselves.

In my conversations with Merv Jones, he had the following to say:

In my experience, these eligibility requirements do not affect the African American female student-athlete in the same way that it affects the African American male student-athlete. Just as the statistics point to African American females, in general, out-performing African American males at both historically Black institutions and predominately White universities, the same can be said for African American female athletes. I suspect this may occur because, traditionally, college sports for all women athletes represented the highest level of competition. In other words, there were few, if any, opportunities for women to earn money as professionals after college so they had to be more serious about their studies to gain employment in "the real world." African American male student-athletes, on the other hand, traditionally look at college as a bridge to the pros. Most enter college believing that they are the "one in a million" who has the skills necessary to make it at the next level. It is not until the dreams of the professional athlete die that the athlete comes to the "real world" realization. As professional women's leagues become more prevalent, this same attitude may creep into the psyche of some African American female athletes.

Despite the aforementioned differences, the plight of the African American male and female student-athlete who is identified as a "prop" is essentially the same. Both are expected to achieve academically at a higher level than ever, yet maintain their athletic excellence without the benefit of practice. If they survive their first year and continue to achieve academically, they are still not awarded an extra year of athletic eligibility to make up for the one they were denied entering school. As a result, their athletic growth is often stunted. Many never reach their full potential as athletes and some, because of the first-year penalty, never set foot on the field or the court. Although they are wooed to major colleges and universities with the dangled carrot of participating in a Division I program, many lack the basic skills needed to function properly in a college setting. They are afforded tutorial help and academic guidance, but many were pushed along in high school and expect the same treatment in college. Not much attention is paid to those who do not develop enough academically to earn the scholarship they are denied during their "prop" year. What happens to them? They are forced to fund that first year of school by any means necessary and even if they do make it, that money is owed back to the university. Many who don't make it are shipped back home after incurring thousands of dollars in financial debt. I am not aware of gifted musicians and/or artists who are treated in the same manner. Why should the world be denied a great talent because of a test score or a combination of test scores and high school GPA? (M. Jones, personal communication, May 2, 1997)

Coaches of schoolgirl athletes will influence the lives of many African American female athletes. They should not lower their expectations for the minority athlete, whether it be in academics or athletics. If their high school coaches had not encouraged academic achievement, many of today's professional people would never have earned a college degree. A good coach will assist her student-athletes and their parents with the selection of colleges (M. Jackson, personal communication, June 8, 1991). The coach should help the athlete realistically evaluate her ability and advise the athlete of the probability of her playing on a Division I, II, or III collegiate level. The coach should talk with these students and send them where they are most likely to survive academically and socially. Coaches should assist athletes with completing college forms and meeting deadlines, and encourage them to visit the school of their choice. Although the coach will be in a position to influence the college selection for some athletes, the African American student-athlete, along with her parents, should also take responsibility for evaluating all the given information and choosing the college that best fits her needs.

The high school student-athlete should also know the difference between BEOG (need-based grant) and an athletic performance grant. She should write the NCAA for a booklet about the recruitment rules. She should visit the colleges of her choice and interview the coaches. She should ask the coach about coaching philosophy, coaching style, practice and travel schedule, and the role that the student will have on the team. The coaches' answers should be honest and reflect a concern for the athlete as a student and a person. The student-athlete should find out how many minority athletes are presently enrolled in the university and how many have graduated from the college. She should talk with those minority female athletes on campus about the campus atmosphere and make sure the university offers her career choice. The urban high school African American student-athlete must realize that even though she has good grades and good study skills, and has completed all the college application procedures in a timely fashion, the possibility of a scholarship aid will be quite limited.

Unless academic performance drastically improves in the urban schools, the reduction of the number of NCAA athletic performance grants and the enforcement of NCAA rules that increase academic standards will negatively affect the numbers of African American female athletes completing degrees at Division I universities. Those exceptional athletes with strong academic credentials will be highly recruited and financed by Division I colleges. Basketball and track and field will continue to have a high African American participation rate on many campuses (Acosta & Carpenter, 1990). However, those African American student-athletes who are educationally disadvantaged will be denied entrance to, and financial support from, Division I institutions. Some will choose not to attend college, thus ending their athletic career. Others, hoping to transfer to a major institution at a later date, will attend junior college.

Attending a junior college is an excellent alternative for those who do not qualify academically or financially for a 4-year institution. Many community colleges are less expensive than 4-year institutions and are more sensitive to serving the needs of educationally disadvantaged students. According to Triplett (1991), "One fourth of the students enrolled in Junior Colleges are minorities" (p. 88).

For a variety of reasons, however, community-college students have a low transfer rate, and African Americans and Hispanics have a lower transfer rate than that of both Whites and Asians. Because the community colleges are possible sources for increasing the pool of minority professionals, there is presently a concerted effort to encourage community-college students to transfer to 4-year institutions. Four-year institutions are developing transfer agreements with community colleges and establishing better community-college recruitment programs. Programs that target minority community-college students will address two critical issues facing the nation: increasing the total number of African American students earning baccalaureate degrees, and providing a large pool of prospective teachers (Triplett, 1991).

Many community colleges are trying to establish a campus-like environment that will encourage students to stay on campus after classes. Intercollegiate athletic programs are being created and improved to enhance campus life. This will have positive implications for the student-athlete who does not initially qualify academically for a 4-year institution. The community college will provide the student the opportunity to maintain her athletic skills, improve her academic skills, and transfer in good standing. Because of the expected increase in academic standards in the next decade, I see community colleges playing a greater role in providing opportunities for African American female athletes to attend a 4-year institution.

Historically Black colleges will also continue to play a major role in providing educational opportunities for educationally disadvantaged female student-athletes. With the proper nurturing, some of these student-athletes will thrive academically and receive their degree. However, because of the inequality of competition, lack of media exposure, and lack of political connections, many of these athletes will not receive top recognition in their sports. After they receive their degree, will there be opportunities for these African American female athletes in sport-related fields?

Sport Careers and the African American Female

With the projected increase of sports participants and evident affirmative action guidelines, it would seem natural that one would predict an increase in the numbers of African American females in sport-related fields such as administration, coaching, commentating, officiating, athletic training, and sports information. However, in the past 18 years, the number of female coaches and athletic administrators has drastically decreased. Furthermore, African American women as athletic directors and coaches in sports are rapidly becoming invisible (Acosta & Carpenter, 1990). I believe that there will continue to be great barriers to increasing the numbers of African American females in high-authority sport occupations.

Abney and Richey (1991) surveyed and interviewed African American female administrators and coaches at both Black and White institutions and recorded the social and institutional barriers that affect their mobility. The African American women at both White and Black institutions listed low salaries as a great obstacle in their career development. It is well established in this country that African American women are paid less than White men, African American men, and White women. Abney and Richey's (1991) study also revealed that African American women lacked support groups. There was an expressed need for role models and mentors. Being a woman was listed as another barrier that was cited by these women. In addition, they constantly had to deal with challenges to their competence and with peer disrespect. Many, especially those employed at White institutions, expressed a feeling of isolation and loneliness because of the lack of cultural and social activities. Being Black presented another barrier for African American women at White institutions where they were expected to be the Black expert on all African American issues. Employer discrimination in the promotion practices was another cited barrier. Last, low expectations by administrators and others was mentioned. In other words, African American women were given titles without significant or challenging responsibility.

It was believed that these barriers could be reduced if African American women could continue to compete for jobs and maintain a strong self-concept in spite of the obstacles. They were encouraged to create or find mentoring programs. It was suggested that African American women constantly improve their administrative skills and actively seek administrative leadership roles in sports organizations. They should also try to replace themselves by mentoring promising African American females who have an interest in sports (Abney & Richey, 1991).

My experiences as a former All-American collegiate athlete in field hockey and lacrosse, and former head coach and current professor of physical education in an urban university, and as a result of conversations with other players and colleagues, indicate that racism, sexism, and politics continue to influence hiring practices. The African American male has dominated the sports of basketball and football, but how many African American head coaches, athletic directors, sports promoters, and commentators have been seen in the past 20 years? As coaching female athletes becomes more financially and socially lucrative, the White male, the White female, the African American male, and other minorities will compete with the African American female for the same job. Lack of sufficient experience will be the cited reason for not hiring African American females (Edwards, 1983). Those few African American females who are hired will be either superqualified or young graduates who can enter the work force at minimal salaries.

The current trend, which will continue over the next decade unless there are significant affirmative action efforts, is a decrease in the numbers of female athletic directors and coaches. Mergers of departments will force reorganization and, in many cases, create male leadership. I believe that those few African American females who are currently athletic directors or associate athletic directors will be replaced by men or by White women. The trends indicate that the "old White girls" have been replaced by the "old White boys" and, in a few cases, by the "old Black boys" in administration and coaching (Acosta & Carpenter, 1990). In 1972, 90% of women's programs were headed by a female. In 1990, only 16% of women's programs were headed by a female. The NCAA has made an attempt to reverse the trend by proposing that each school that receives NCAA basketball revenue have at least one senior female administrator for women's sports.

Sport in the New Millennium and the African American Female: Future Strategies

My experiences have led me to believe that racism, sexism, and politics will still exist in the next century. Even though we erase or change discriminatory laws and practices, racist and sexist attitudes and feelings will be hard to change. Minorities must continue to insist on representation in the administrative committee structure and professional staff of each sport organization. We need sensitive minorities on each committee to scrutinize the process, to protect the welfare of our African American athletes, and to support inclusive rather than exclusive legislation. We also need to encourage the hiring of minority role models on every level of sport.

Young African American athletes must be prepared for the racist, sexist, and political roadblocks that they will face. They have to realize that to be successful they cannot be just average but must be high achievers, superstars. There must be strong support systems for the African American female athlete at every level. Even after she works hard and achieves, there will be times when she will be frustrated and disgusted. In times like these, she will need reassurance from her support group or mentor. The few African American pioneers who succeed as coaches, commentators, or athletic administrators will become important role models for others.

It is important that African American women continue to apply for sport-related jobs. After applying for several jobs and being rejected time and time again, it is only natural to lose some self-confidence and to adopt a negative attitude. However, it is important not to become lost in self-blame but to look at the employment system and the process. A large-scale study of high-achieving students in historically Black colleges showed that these students were able to perceive appropriate levels of system blame (Epps & Gurin, 1975).

It will also be necessary for African American women to create jobs in the African American communities so that they can obtain the experience necessary to compete in the national market. It appears that young African American women are prevented from getting jobs, but how does one obtain experience if one is not hired?

Sports camps and clinics have traditionally been excellent training grounds for aspiring young coaches, officials, and clinicians. It is very difficult for the young African American woman to find work at well-established camps and clinics. African American females are encouraged to establish camps and clinics in and for the African American community. They can then gain coaching, officiating, and administrative experience.

According to Merv Jones, "It is important for the prominent African American female student-athlete to participate in camps, clinics, sports clubs and recreation centers as volunteer coaches, referees, and administrators. In my experience as an academic counselor for female student-athletes, there is an underlying perception, even among African American females themselves, that male coaches are more knowledgeable and competent than female coaches. In other words, given the choice between a male coach and a female coach with the same credentials, the athletes would choose the male. This definitely hinders the progress of African American females who choose to enter the coaching profession. The best way to counter this underlying perception is to create positive experiences for African American girls interested in sports with respected African American female athletes. I believe this perception exists today because many of athletes' first coaches were male." (M. Jones, personal communication, May 2, 1997)

Volunteering to be an intern in established programs in community Ys, recreation centers, or schools is another way of gaining valuable work experience. The United States Olympic Committee (USOC) and the National Collegiate Athletic Association (NCAA, 1988) have excellent internship opportunities for athletes pursuing experience in sports administration. The NCAA also provides graduate scholarships to promising minority and female applicants who wish to complete master's or doctoral degrees in sports administration. Some African American females have taken advantage of these programs, and I suspect others may take advantage of these opportunities in the future.

Finally, because sport reflects society, it is highly unlikely that the African American female athlete in this country will receive the recognition and status of the male athlete. It will continue to be a struggle to eliminate sexist attitudes about the role of sport in the lives of girls and women. Based on my experience as a college coach and former athlete, once girls participate regularly in a sport, it is likely that their spectator interest will also increase. Young African American girls must see and identify with their mothers, sisters, and friends who enjoy competing in sport, in order to reinforce their own participation as being normal, acceptable behavior. The possibility of obtaining an athletic scholarship and media exposure has helped to positively influence mothers' and fathers' opinions about women in sport. As a result, many more parents are encouraging their daughters to participate in sports in hopes of their earning a college degree, as well as fame and fortune.

In spite of racism, sexism, and inadequate financial support, we will still find those African American women who will succeed and break barriers in sport. Why? Because of their internal fortitude, desire, and courage to overcome the obstacles placed before them. The real future of the African American woman in sport rests in the strength of the African American girl. Will she be able to endure the struggle? Will the struggle be worthwhile? There will be some women willing to fight and to sacrifice for a goal or a dream. In the next 20 years, those who attempt to achieve excellence in sport will have the exhortation and the knowledge of those who have endured and succeeded

The challenge in the future will be for Whites, African Americans, and other people of color to work together to support and encourage African American female participation in sport and athletics. By valuing diversity and making every effort to eliminate sexism and racism in sport, together we can improve the quality of life for all Americans.

Additional Resources

Video—*Amazing Grace:* Black Women in Sport.

After The Whistle Blows: Black Women in Sport.

For more information contact Black Women in Sport Foundation, P.O. Box 2610, Philadelphia, PA 19130. *Website:* www.blackwomen insport.org

Merv Jones, academic counselor for student-athletes at Temple University; former producer and director of the *Greatest Sports Legends* television series; writer and director of the made-for-television production, *Can't Wait;* and coauthor of *Recipes for Success: Ingredients for Raising Elite Black Female Athletes*

Study Questions

1. What are socioeconomic factors that have affected sport participation of African American females?

2. How has corporate America influenced sport participation of African American females?

3. What image does the African American female superstar athlete need to portray in order to secure media coverage and endorsements? Give examples.

4. Identify and explain some of the strategies one might use to assure the success of the African American female collegiate athlete.

5. Describe and give examples of nonprofit groups that have positively influenced sport participation of African American females.

6. What are some of the problems African American females face when seeking sport careers? What are some solutions to these problems?

References

Abney, R., & Richey, D. (1991). Barriers encountered by Black female administrators and coaches. *Journal of Physical Education, Recreation and Dance*.

Acosta, R. V., & Carpenter, L. J. (1990). *Women in intercollegiate sport: A longitudinal study thirteen year update 1977–1990*. New York: Brooklyn College, Brooklyn.

Alexander, A. (1978). *Status of minority women in the Association Intercollegiate Athletics for Women*. Unpublished master's thesis, Temple University, Philadelphia.

Alexander, A. (1991). New programs in girl-serving agencies. *Women's Sports Foundation annual conference proceedings* (pp. 101–107). New York: Women's Sport Foundation.

American Institute for Research. (1989). *Report No. 3: The experiences of Black intercollegiate athletes at NCAA Division I institutions*. Palo Alto, CA: American Institutes for Research.

Clark, G. (1988, February 15). Campus environment critical to minority retention. *Black Issues in Higher Education, 4*(26), 12.

Corbett, D. (1981). *Learned social identity of the black female athlete and non-athlete*. Paper presented at the North American Society for Sociology of Sport, Fort Worth, TX.

Edwards, H. (1983, August). Educating Black athletes. *Atlantic Monthly*, 31–38.

Epps, E. E., & Gurin, P. (1975). *Black consciousness identity and achievement: A study of students in historically Black colleges*. New York: Wiley Publishers.

Markowitz, D. (1991, February 12). Charges of racism now a tennis problem. *New York Times*, p. 7.

Matthews, J. (1988, June 1). Mentor program brings students, faculty together. *Black Issues in Higher Education, 5*(7), 11–16.

National Collegiate Athletic Association (1988). *Summary to the survey of NCAA member institutions and conferences on minority representation*. KS: Author.

Sloan, T., Oglesby, C., Alexander, A., & Franke, N. (1981). *Black women in sport*. Reston, Virginia: AAHPERD.

Smith, B. A. (1986). *Contributions of Black women to sport in America: A reference catalog.* Unpublished master's thesis, Temple University, Philadelphia.

Triplett, J. R. (1991, August 29). The nation's community colleges are an untapped resource for new minority teachers. *Black Issues in Higher Education, 8*(14), 88.

Warwick, R. (1991, October). African American recreation participation trends 1980–88. *1991 Leisure Research Symposium.* Baltimore, MD.

Wiley, E. (1990, May 10). Forum addresses solution to education plight of Black athletes. *Black Issues in Higher Education, 7*(5), 18–20.

Wiley, E., III. (1991, October 24). Afrocentricism: Many things to many people. *Black Issues in Higher Education, 8*(18), 1–20.

Williams, R. (1990, November). Is tennis doing the right thing for Blacks? *Tennis,* 46.

Women's Sport Foundation. (1989). *Minorities in sport.* New York: Author.

Women's Sport Foundation. (1996). *ABL announces sites for inaugural season.* New York: Zuk, Rachel, 4–5.

SECTION 4

ANALYSIS
OF
RACISM
AND
PROSPECTS
FOR
CHANGE

Race, Law, and College Athletics

Timothy Davis

Abstract

This essay examines the intersection of race and law in intercollegiate athletics. It argues that racism continues to adversely impact the interests of African American administrators, coaches and student-athletes engaged in college sports. Notwithstanding the persistence of racism in college sports, traditional civil rights laws are largely ineffective vehicles for protecting the interests of African Americans. The limited utility of these laws is a product of evidentiary standards that plaintiffs must meet to prevail in traditional civil rights suits. These standards and the covert nature of the racism that imbues college sports create obstacles that are difficult for plaintiffs to traverse. Given the constraints placed on traditional civil rights laws and increasing judicial hostility to affirmative action, this essay examines alternative approaches—legal and nonlegal—to remedying the harm racism inflicts upon African Americans in college sports.

Key Terms

Antidiscrimination norms: Statutory and common-law remedies available under the law for discriminatory conduct.

Circumstantial evidence: Indirect evidence from which a judge or jury may infer the existence of a fact issue, but which does not prove the existence of the fact directly.

Direct evidence: Evidence that affirmatively proves the existence of a fact. If the direct evidence is a witness's statement, the statement must be based on a fact perceived with one of the witness's five senses.

Invidious discrimination: Discrimination based on ill-will or resentment.

Judicial review: The process by which an appellate court reviews the decisions of lower courts, tribunals, and administrative authorities.

Prima facie evidence: The first step in a plaintiff's case that consists of presenting evidence that will establish a fact or raise a presumption of a fact that is essential to a plaintiff's legal claim(s).

Proposition 48: Effective in 1986, the NCAA rules (commonly referred to as initial eligibility standards) that provided that a student-athlete enrolled in a Division I or Division II institution as an entering freshman was eligible for financial aid, practice, and competition during his or her first year only if he or she scored 700 or 17 on the SAT or ACT, respectively. The student was also required to have attained at least a 2.0 GPA in a core curriculum that consisted of 11 courses in high school. This standard has been superseded by Proposition 16.

Proposition 16: Effective in 1996, these NCAA initial eligibility rules superseded Proposition 48 standards. Proposition 16 standards provide that a student-athlete who enrolls in a Division I or Division II institution as an entering freshman must comply with academic requirements measured by an indexed scale in order to be eligible for financial aid, practice, and competition during his or her first academic year. For example, high school graduates with a 700 or 17 (820 and 68 on recentered scales) on the SAT or ACT, respectively, must have at least a 2.5 GPA in a core curriculum that consists of 13 courses in order to be deemed eligible. A prospective student-athlete with a 2.0 GPA would be required to score at least 900 or 21 (1010 or 86 on recentered scales) on the SAT or ACT, respectively.

Racial animus: Motive or intent to discriminate.

Rational basis standard of review: Under this standard of judicial review, a court will uphold a challenged action or regulation if it has a rational relationship to a governmental objective that is not prohibited by the United States Constitution.

Strict scrutiny standard of review: Under this standard of judicial review, a court will uphold a challenged action or regulation if the charged party can demonstrate that its practices or policies are narrowly tailored toward furthering a compelling interest.

INTRODUCTION

The study of sport provides an excellent forum within which to examine complex social issues that confront American society. Given that sport can be viewed as a microcosm of American society, the issues that arise therein often involve the intersection of law, economics, and sociology. An issue that clearly displays this convergence of disciplines is the impact of racism on the interests of African Americans engaged in intercollegiate sport. As the following essay reveals, a collaborative effort by those from varied professional disciplines will be required to address effectively the harmful consequences of racism in college athletics. Consider the following scenarios.

In *Jackson v. Drake University* (1991), an African American student-athlete recruited by Drake University to play basketball brought suit alleging that the institution engaged in conduct that amounted to a breach of contract and educational malpractice. Jackson also alleged that a pattern of abusive conduct by Drake's basketball coach constituted a civil rights violation pursuant to 42 U.S.C. Section 1981. The federal district court rejected Jackson's claims.

A few years earlier in *Hysaw v. Washburn University of Topeka* (1987), several African American student-athletes recruited to play football alleged that the college's coaching staff and administration treated them in a racially discriminatory manner. In addition to allegations that the college infringed upon their contractual right to play football, the plaintiffs asserted that the institution afforded White football players more favorable treatment than their African American counterparts. The preferential treatment allegedly included the provision of better opportunities to White players to enter into favorable scholarship arrangements and to participate in Washburn's football program. The federal district court rejected these claims.

In 1990, Marvin Cobb, assistant athletic director for the University of Southern California, filed racial discrimination and breach-of-contract claims against the University (*Cobb v. University of Southern California,* 1996). He charged that he was denied promotions and harassed because of his complaints regarding the academic abilities and preparation of African American student-athletes (Hudson

& Sandoval, 1996). Specifically, Cobb alleged that the University failed to afford many of its African American student-athletes with an educational opportunity. He also alleged that USC's recruitment of academically underprepared student-athletes, with only a minimal likelihood of succeeding academically, constituted exploitation. Cobb's discrimination claim was dismissed. A jury award of $2.1 million dollars on the breach-of-contract claim was overturned by the trial court judge (*Cobb v. University of Southern California,* 1996). Cobb is currently appealing these rulings.

In 1995 Donnie Edwards, a former UCLA football player, was suspended for one game and ordered to make full restitution for accepting $150 in groceries from a sports agent. Under NCAA rules, an athlete can lose his or her eligibility to compete by accepting cash or other benefits from professional sports agents. Edwards denied that he knew that the groceries were from an agent, but acknowledged that there were times when he did not have the money to buy food. The NCAA concluded that suspension was warranted (Wilner, 1995).

Reacting to the NCAA's decision, Edwards urged a one-day boycott of college football players to protest their alleged exploitation (Springer, 1995). According to Edwards, "A lot of minority student-athletes who play football or basketball have parents who don't have any money. We're lucky to get a scholarship. But once we get here, what do we do? The money we get is not enough to even live on, especially in Westwood." (Springer, 1995). Edwards added, "Look at how much money they make from college football alone, all those TV deals, the shoe deals, the jersey deals. There's a lot of money around here. Who's getting it? All the schools. Who's being exploited? Us" (Springer, 1995, p. 1).

Finally, in 1998, Northeastern University's Center for the Study of Sport in Society released a report of its first comprehensive analysis of hiring practices of women and people of color in intercollegiate athletics. Although the report noted that progress has been made in opening access to African Americans, it provided the following illustration of the barriers that persist in the hiring of African Americans to coaching and administrative positions.

> At the end of the 1996 season, there were 25 openings for head coaching positions in Division IA [football]. New Mexico State, the last of the 25 to choose, was reportedly the only school even to interview a Black candidate. It chose Tony Samuel, who joined Ron Dickerson (Temple), Jim Caldwell (Wake Forest), Ron Cooper (Louisville), Tyronne Willingham (Stanford), Robert Simmons (Oklahoma State), Matt Simon (North Texas) and John Blake (Oklahoma) as the only Black head football coaches in NCAA Division IA.
>
> At the end of the season Cooper was fired and Dickerson resigned. [Simon was also fired in early 1998]. There were 12 openings at the end of the 1997 season. No Blacks were interviewed. Floyd Keith (Rhode Island) and Alex Woods (James Madison) were the only Blacks coaching in Division IAA. In the entire history of college football, there were only six other Black head coaches in Division IA. In the history of Division IA football, there have been thousands of college football teams that took the field, 51 have been led by a Black head coach!
> (Lapchick, 1997, pp. 4–5).

Notwithstanding factual differences, the foregoing scenarios illustrate the enigmatic role of African Americans in intercollegiate athletics. They also suggest that despite distributive justice in some sports—principally football, basketball, and track—a lingering question is whether African Americans are full participants at all levels of the collegiate sport enterprise. Indeed a case can be made that African Americans remain outsiders and consequently are not fully integrated into the academic, social, and administrative mainstream of college sport.

No single variable is responsible for producing the marginalizing of African Americans in college sport. Yet the failure of African Americans to achieve full equality is, in large measure, a product of the unconscious racism that results from the "internalization of stereotypes concerning Black athletes. . . . " (Davis, 1995, p. 644). Prior to World War II, stereotypes of African Americans as not being serious, but rather "docile, subservient, good-natured, childlike and slightly exotic" were used to exclude African American athletes (Lombardo, 1978, p. 61). Their athletic accomplishments were often defined in terms of "natural ability" and other stereotypes which belittled individual effort and achievement (Coakley, 1994).

Today, derogatory images persist, but in more subtle forms (Davis, 1995, pp. 647–48). These images and myths ultimately rest on beliefs that the success of African American athletes results more from innate physical skills than from hard work and determination (Wiggins, 1993, p. 42).

As discussed below, these stereotypes manifest to harm African Americans in three principal ways: (1) the lack of administrative and coaching opportunities for African Americans in college sports; (2) the disparate impact on African American student-athletes of NCAA rules and regulations; and (3) the academic and social devaluation of African American student-athletes.

Examining access to athletic administration, a NCAA study reported in 1994 that African Americans are underrepresented in the upper echelons of collegiate sports and NCAA management. The study revealed, among other things, that African Americans accounted for approximately 9.6 percent of all athletic administrators, including coaches. (NCAA Minority Opportunities and Interests Committee, 1994). Moreover, the study reported that although African American male student-athletes accounted (during 1993–94) for 65% of Division I basketball players, only 41 or 14% of the then 302 Division I basketball coaches were African American.

The *1997 Racial Report Card,* prepared by the Center for the Study of Sport in Society, reached similar findings. As Table 1 depicts, in 1996 African American males accounted for 61 and 52 percent of Division I basketball and football players, respectively. On the other hand, Table 1 also shows that 17.3 percent of Division I head basketball and 7.2 percent of head football coaching positions were held by African Americans in 1996.

Table 2 depicts similar disparities in Division I women's sports. With respect to both men's and women's sports, it is not necessary that the numbers of African Americans in coaching and administrative positions mirror the percentage of African American student-athletes participating in particular sports. Gaps, however, of the magnitude of those reported are disturbing.

The underrepresentation of African Americans in college sports administration is derived in large measure from negative stereotypes that

Table 1. African Americans as a Percentage of Male Student-Athletes and Head Coaches in Division I Basketball, Football 1996

	Male Student-Athletes Division I		
	Basketball	**Football**	**Baseball**
White	37.4%	47.2%	89.4%
Black	61%	52%	6.5%
Latino	1.6%	1.8%	4.1%
Male College Head Coaches Division I (Division IA Football)			
White	81.5%	92.8%	97.6%
Black	17.3%	7.2%	0%
Other	1.0%	0%	2.4%

Adopted from Lapchick, Richard E. (1997). *1997 Racial Report Card: College Special Edition.* Boston: Northwestern University's Center for the Study of Sport in Society.

nurture unconscious racism. "The inequality of access for Blacks to the administration of college athletics demonstrates the persistent influence of a particular racial stereotype: the Black

Table 2. African Americans as a Percentage of Female Student-Athletes and College Head Coaches for Division I Women's Teams 1996

Division I Female Student-Athletes		Division I College Head Coaches Women's Teams	
White	82.1%	White Men	52.1%
Black	15.5%	White Women	40.3%
Latino	2.2%	Black Men	3.2%
Other	0.5%	Black Women	2.1%
Other Men	1.8%		
Other Women	0.5%		

Adopted from Lapchick, Richard E. (1997). *1997 Racial Report Card: College Special Edition*. Boston: Northeastern University's Center for the Study of Sport in Society.

athlete as inferior to the White athlete regarding intellectual and leadership abilities" (Davis, 1996, p. 657).

In the case of African American student-athletes, a mindset nurtured by these stereotypes results in the exclusion of "African American student-athletes from the academic and social mainstream in many predominately White colleges and universities" (Davis, 1995, p. 699). Graduation rates provide some support for arguments concerning the devaluation of the African American athlete's educational interests (Harris, 1993). Male African American football and basketball players are graduating at rates that exceed those they achieved prior to the enactment of Proposition 48. Despite these gains, the most recent NCAA report of graduation rates reveals that at many institutions graduation rates for African American male student-athletes in revenue-producing sports lag far behind those of other male student-athletes. For instance, 39 percent of African American basketball players who entered college in 1990–91 graduated within six years of their matriculation. This figure is appreciably lower than the 58% graduation rate for White basketball players and the 58% rate for all male student-athletes who matriculated in 1990–91 (*NCAA News Digest*, 1997, p. 2). African American male football players who en-

tered college at Division IA institutions in 1990–91 posted a 45 percent graduation rate in contrast to a 61 percent rate for their White counterparts. (*NCAA News Digest*, 1997, p. 2).

These statistics highlight the concern that too little is expected academically of the African American student-athlete. Indeed, as some assert, African American student-athletes have become commodities serving the financial interests of the institutions for which they compete (Davis, 1995, p. 669). As evidence, critics point to the dominance of African Americans in the revenue-producing sports (Smith, 1996, p. 348).

Moreover, critics assert that NCAA rules and regulations impact African American student-athletes disproportionately. For example, the *Report of the McIntosh Commission for Fair Play in Student-Athlete Admissions*, released in December 1994, asserted that "[r]ather than increasing standards, Proposition 48 has increased discrimination by excluding large numbers of otherwise-qualified African American athletes, . . . who would have gone on to graduate." The report further alleged that Proposition 16 will worsen this situation (*Report of the McIntosh Commission for Fair Play in Student-Athlete Admission*, 1994).

Recent data lends credence to the concerns raised in the McIntosh Commission report.

NCAA research data reveal substantial increases in the percentage of Division I and II prospective student-athletes who were ineligible to compete in 1995 and 1996 as a result of the more stringent requirements of Proposal 16. The report notes significant differences "among ethnic and income groups in eligibility rates for freshman at NCAA Division I institutions." For example, in 1996, 26.9 percent of African American prospective students were ineligible. In contrast, 6.5% of White prospective student-athletes were ineligible. Moreover, 34.7 percent of African American prospective student-athletes from families with incomes under $30,000 were deemed ineligible. (*NCAA News*, 1998).

Proceeding on the assumption that racism impacts African Americans adversely in college sport, at least in the ways defined above, an obvious inquiry is what legal mechanisms are available to redress the harm. More specifically, is there a role for the law to play in addressing the harm caused by adherence to stereotypes and unconscious racism? As the remainder of this essay demonstrates, the role of the law will vary depending on whether the alleged harm is (1) underinclusion of African Americans and other ethnic minorities at administrative levels of college athletics; (2) the neglect of the academic interests of African American student-athletes; or (3) the alleged racial insensitivity that contributes to the disparate impact of NCAA rules and regulations on the interests of African American student-athletes.

Notwithstanding the issue addressed or the norm implicated, however, at least two generalizations seem appropriate. First, established antidiscrimination norms are of limited effectiveness in remediating the harm which racism inflicts upon African Americans in college sport. This limited role arises largely out of the nature of the racism that predominates in college sport—unconscious racism—which antidiscrimination norms are ill-equipped to address.

Second, alternatives must be considered, given the difficulties that African Americans will encounter. These alternatives include examining common-law doctrines as a basis for establishing antidiscrimination norms. More significantly, however, nonlegal alternatives may hold greater promise for redressing the adverse consequences of the unconscious racism that permeates college athletics.

Traditional Antidiscrimination Norms Access to Athletic Administration

The limited role of traditional antidiscrimination norms can be illustrated by examining the concerns previously identified. As previously noted, opportunities for African Americans have been limited in the coaching and administrative levels of college athletics. For example, the 1990s witnessed progress in the hiring of minority athletic directors. Nevertheless, the 11.4 percent of minorities who are athletic directors at Division I colleges lags behind the percentages of minorities who hold general manager positions in professional sports. (Lapchick, 1997, p. 9). In 1995–96, 1,523 associate and assistant athletic director positions existed at NCAA colleges. The minority representation was as follows: Black men (6.0%), "other minority" men (2%), Black women (2%), and "other minority" women (0.2%) (Lapchick, 1997, p. 9).

In seeking redress for barriers to entry and promotion, coaches and administrators would more than likely turn to Title VII and Section 1981 of the Civil Rights Act. Title VII prohibits discrimination in employment. Section 1981 is broader in scope in that it applies to the making, performance, and enforcement of all contracts, not just employment contracts. As the following discussion reveals, the nature of the proof required to establish a cognizable Title VII or Section 1981 action limits the potential effectiveness of these antidiscrimination norms.

Title VII Analysis

Title VII of the amended Civil Rights Act of 1964 renders it unlawful "for an employer . . .

to fail or refuse to hire or to discharge any individual, or otherwise to discriminate against any individual with respect to his compensation, terms, conditions, or privileges of employment, because of such individual's race, color, religion, sex or national origin." The thrust of Title VII is to prohibit employers from discriminating against any individual with respect to that individual's compensation, or privileges of employment.

With respect to allegations that racism impedes access to employment opportunities in college sports, two types of Title VII cases appear particularly relevant: (1) disparate treatment actions, in which plaintiffs allege intentional discrimination on account of race; and (2) disparate impact actions, in which plaintiffs allege the use of facially neutral employment practices unjustifiably discriminate, against members of a protected group.

Disparate Treatment: In a Title VII claim based on disparate treatment, a plaintiff alleges that he or she has been treated less favorably than his or her peers on account of race. To prevail on such a claim, the plaintiff must prove discriminatory purpose on the part of the employer (Modjeska, 1993, p. 24). Thus the key to proving disparate treatment is intent to discriminate (*St. Mary's Honor Center v. Hicks*, 1993; *Anderson v. Douglas & Lomason Co., Inc.*, 1994).

A plaintiff can prove discrimination by producing direct evidence of racial animus. As noted by Professor Kenneth Shropshire, "[t]his would be the rare smoking gun event where the employer says 'we don't want to hire you because you are Black.' " (Shropshire, 1996, p. 64). Professor Shropshire further notes that where direct evidence of discriminatory intent is unavailable, a plaintiff can establish discriminatory intent pursuant to a formula approved by the United State Supreme Court in *McDonnell Douglas Corp. v. Green*. There the court held that a prima facie case of racial discrimination can be established by showing that a) the plaintiff belongs to a racial minority; b) the plaintiff applied and was qualified for a vacant

employment position; c) the employer rejected the plaintiff despite his or her qualifications; and d) after the plaintiff's rejection, the employer continued to accept applications of persons similarly qualified (*McDonnell Douglas v. Green* 1973, at 801-04; *Washington v. Garrett*, 1993, at 551). Defendants can rebut evidence of discriminatory intent (whether direct or indirect) by proving the allegations are false or by establishing a nondiscriminatory reason for rejecting the African American applicant.

The requirement that the plaintiff prove discrimination is a formidable obstacle to prevailing in a Title VII disparate treatment case. As noted by one legal scholar, only in cases of extreme discrimination can a plaintiff demonstrate the requisite intent to discriminate, short of an admission of culpability by the defendant (Suggs, 1991, p. 1275). As discussed below, the manner in which hiring decisions are made in college sport makes it unlikely that prospective African American coaches or administrators will be able to prove that discriminatory motivation lies behind a college's negative promotion or hiring decision.

Disparate Impact: In *Griggs v. Duke Power Co.* (1971), the Supreme Court held that Title VII, in addition to banning intentional discrimination, also bans neutral employment practices that have a disparate impact on Blacks, unless those practices are shown to be justified by business necessity (*Griggs v. Duke Power Co.* 1971, at 431). In this regard, the Court stated that facially neutral practices which "operate as 'built-in headwinds' for minority groups and are unrelated to measuring job capability" violate Title VII regardless of the employer's good intent or lack of discriminatory intent. (*Griggs v. Duke Power Co.* 1971, at 432). The Court further stated as follows:

> The objective of Congress in the enactment of Title VII is plain from the language of the statute. It was to achieve equality of employment opportunities and remove barriers that have operated

in the past to favor an identifiable group of White employees over other employees. Under the Act, practices, procedures, or tests neutral on their face, and even neutral in terms of intent, cannot be maintained if they operate to "freeze" the status quo of prior discriminatory employment practices. (*Griggs v. Duke Power Co.* 1971, at 432)

In prevailing on these types of cases, plaintiffs must establish by statistics that the practice at issue results in a substantially disproportionate underrepresentation of statutorily protected persons. However, they cannot sustain an action simply by proving the existence of a racial or other imbalance in the employer's work force. A disparate impact claimant must also demonstrate that this imbalance was caused by a specific discriminatory practice and "that each challenged employment practice causes a disparate impact" (*Wards Cove Packing Co., Inc. v. Atonio*, 1989, p. 657).

The most viable suits in this area are those brought by a party denied a job opportunity based on a discriminatory selection device or hiring practice. Examples of employment practices that might be deemed discriminatory because of their consequences include standardized tests and educational requirements (Shropshire, 1996).

To summarize, the burden of proof in disparate impact cases has been described in part as follows: "An unlawful employment practice based on disparate impact is established under this title only if (i) a complaining party demonstrates that a respondent uses a particular employment practice that causes a disparate impact . . . and the respondent fails to demonstrate that the challenged practice is job related for the position in question and consistent with business necessity . . . " (*Civil Rights Act of 1991, 42 USC § 2000e-2(k)(I)(A)(i)*, 1994, p. 114).

Features of sports-hiring create potentially insurmountable evidentiary barriers to sustaining a Title VII disparate treatment or disparate impact claim. In making hiring decisions in sports, employers typically will not use a selection device or specific hiring practice. Indeed, a recent NAACP study revealed an absence of hiring or promotion practices in sports that amount to disparate impact or treatment (Shropshire, 1996). In this regard, Professor Shropshire has concluded: "Employers in sports tend to use a series of subjective criteria, varying among employment decisions, with no elements necessarily being weighed more heavily than others. With no unique practice to target as discriminatory, it is difficult to bring an action under Title VII no matter what the statistics show regarding the underrepresentation of any group at any job level" (Shropshire, 1996, p. 65).

It is important to note, however, the use of subjective hiring criteria will not provide an absolute shield against a Title VII disparate impact claim. In *Watson v. Fort Worth Bank & Trust* (1988) the United States Supreme Court held that subjective criteria under which employers or their agents have substantial discretion in identifying desired traits or characteristics are subject to disparate impact theory. In deciding that subjective criteria are subject to impact analysis, the Supreme Court noted the difficulty in showing what is sufficient to make out a prima facie case. This difficulty was expressed by another court as follows: "The difficulties are obvious: how does one show that the application of variable concepts such as 'experience' create racial disparity between those hired and those qualified for jobs?" (*Atonio v. Wards Cove Packing Co., Inc.*, 1992, at 1498).

Once again, however, plaintiffs are confronted with a formidable obstacle: establishing the requisite relationship between particular subjective employment practices and disparities in the work force (*Johnson v. Uncle Ben's, Inc,.* 1992). Subjective criteria are subject to the requirement that the plaintiff identify the specific criteria and demonstrate that it is responsible for the statistical disparity (*Atonio v. Wards Cove Packing Co., Inc.*, 1993). Given these evidentiary requirements, African Americans are likely to find that disparate impact theory offers little recourse as a basis for challenging employment practices in sports.

The controversial hiring of Rick Neuheisel, who is White, rather than Bob Simmons, who is African American, as head football coach for the University of Colorado illustrates this point. In justifying its hiring of the less-experienced Neuheisel, Colorado officials made reference to various subjective criteria. As one commentator wrote, "Neuheisel was the right hire at Colorado because he was an extraordinary coaching prospect, and because, not incidentally, he was a good fit for Colorado, a maverick campus, and for Boulder, a cosmopolitan college town along the picturesque Flatirons. Bob Simmons wasn't rejected; he just wasn't the No. 1 choice" (Frei, 1995, p. 26).

The hard-to-quantify factors on which hiring decisions are based in sport were identified by former University of Colorado President Judith Albino as including "proven coaching ability, recruiting ability, management skills, communication skills, public relations skills and ethical standards" (Willis, 1995, sec. 8, p. 1). She concluded that "[o]ver all, we found that our appraisal of [Neuheisel] was the highest of those we interviewed. . . . Any one of the four candidates could have done the job. But we weren't in the business of picking an acceptable coach. We were in the business of picking the best possible coach" (Frei, 1995, sec. 8, p. 1).

Thus the absence of objectively quantifiable factors on which employment decisions are made will pose difficulties for African Americans challenging hiring and promotion decisions. Such a challenge is all the more difficult to establish inasmuch as courts—which presume to lack the requisite expertise—are reluctant to second-guess hiring decisions in sports (Shropshire, 1996, pp. 114–15).

Voluntary Affirmative-Action Plans

The ineffectiveness of the law as a means of diversifying the positions of authority in college athletics underscores the critical role of college presidents and athletic directors in achieving this goal. As noted by Professor Shropshire,

the limited utility of the law and the impact of the old-boy network lead inevitably to the conclusion that "[a]ffirmative action must be taken for more African Americans to become a part of these hiring networks" (Shropshire, 1996, pp. 114–15). Yet the uncertain state of the law regarding affirmative action efforts creates potential impediments for voluntary affirmative action initiatives.

Briefly reviewing this case law, in *University of California Regents v. Bakke* (1978), the Supreme Court addressed the significance of diversity in the context of university admissions programs. Justice Powell, writing alone, concluded the University of California at Davis's race conscious dual-admissions policy was unconstitutional under the strict scrutiny standard of review (*University of California v. Bakke* 1978, at 320). In reaching this conclusion, however, Powell conceded that diversity was a compelling governmental interest in the context of university admissions programs (*University of California v. Bakke* 1978, at 313). In support of his position, Justice Powell attributed special significance to diversity in the higher education context because of the intimate experiences, varying outlooks, and the "robust exchange of ideas" that are essential to the quality of higher education (*University of California v. Bakke* 1978, at 313). He added that the "atmosphere of 'speculation, experiment and creation'—so essential to the quality of higher education—is widely believed to be promoted by a diverse student body." (*University of California v. Bakke* 1978, at 312).

The Supreme Court examined the importance of diversity within the broadcasting industry in *Metro Broadcasting v. FCC* (1990). The Court held that the FCC's program, seeking to enhance minority ownership within the broadcasting industry, did not violate the constitution under the intermediate scrutiny standard of review (*Metro Broadcasting v. FCC* 1990, at 564–66). In so holding, the Court stated, "[the] broadcasting industry with representative minority participation will produce more variation and diversity than will one whose ownership is drawn from a single racially and ethnically homogenous group" (*Metro Broadcasting v. FCC* 1990, at 579). It concluded that "the interest in enhancing broadcasting diversity is, at the very least, an 'important' governmental objective. . . ." (*Metro Broadcasting v. FCC* 1990, at 564–66). The Court also analogized the importance of diversity of views and information over the airwaves to that of the robust exchange of information and ideas in the university setting (*Metro Broadcasting v. FCC* 1990, at 568).

Recently, in *Hopwood v. State of Texas* (1996), the United States Court of Appeals for the Fifth Circuit revisited the issue of diversity in the context of higher education. A three-judge panel decided that consideration of race or ethnicity by the University of Texas Law School for the purpose of achieving a diverse student body is *not* a compelling interest under the Fourteenth Amendment (*Hopwood v. State of Texas* 1996, at 943). The court argued that Justice Powell's view in *Bakke* was not binding precedent, because he failed to represent a majority of the Court on the issue of diversity as a compelling governmental interest (*Hopwood v. State of Texas* 1996, at 943).

Obviously, the Supreme Court will have the final say on the question of racial diversity in the educational setting. Nonetheless, *Hopwood* seriously clouds the question of the constitutionality of employing race-conscious affirmative action initiatives premised on promoting diversity. Such uncertainty is heightened given the Supreme Court's holding in *Adarand Constructors, Inc. v. Pena* (1995), to the effect that all race-conscious affirmative action policies are unconstitutional unless the policy is "narrowly tailored" to further a "compelling governmental interest" (*Adarand Constructors, Inc. v. Pena* 1995, at 2113).

Thus after years of debate concerning the appropriate standard of review of race-conscious affirmative action policies, the Supreme Court, held that " . . . all racial classifications, imposed by whatever federal, state, or local governmental actor, [whether benign or invidious],

must be analyzed by a reviewing court under strict scrutiny" (*Adarand Constructors, Inc. v. Pena* 1995, at 2113). It should be noted that in dissent, Justice Stevens argued that the Court's opinion in *Adarand* did not diminish the important interest of fostering diversity which was recognized in *Metro Broadcasting* (*Adarand Constructors, Inc. v. Pena* 1995, at 2127). The Supreme Court's holding in *Adarand* has unequivocally answered the question concerning the proper standard of review to be applied in race-conscious affirmative-action programs; however, the question remains open as to whether "diversity" is a compelling governmental interest.

In summary, given the current status of the law regarding affirmative action, programs aimed at diversifying the administrative ranks of collegiate sports will, at a minimum, be subjected to a high level of scrutiny.

Disparate Impact of NCAA Rules: Equal Protection and Title VI Analysis

Overview of NCAA Rules

A principal function of the National Collegiate Athletic Association (NCAA) is the promulgation of the rules and principles with which its member institutions must comply. It is through the NCAA's rule-making and enforcement processes that the association articulates adherence to values long perceived as fundamental to intercollegiate athletics: educational primacy and amateurism. These values are articulated in the NCAA's statement of its primary purpose: "to maintain intercollegiate athletics as an integral part of the educational program and the athlete as an integral part of the student body and by so doing, retain a clear line of demarcation between intercollegiate athletics and professional sports." (NATIONAL COLLEGIATE ATHLETIC ASSOCIATION, 1996–97 NCAA MANUAL art. 1.1.3. [hereinafter NCAA MANUAL]).

With respect to the amateurism value, NCAA Bylaws enumerate the requirements with which a student-athlete must comply in order to retain amateur status. For example, student-athletes are prohibited from accepting pay for the use of their athletic abilities (*NCAA Manual 1996–97*, arts. 12.1.1.(a) & 12.1.1). With respect to the educational value, the NCAA considers intercollegiate athletics programs as vital components of an institution's education program (*NCAA Manual 1996–97*, art. 2.4). Rules reflecting the educational value include those regulating initial eligibility (*NCAA Manual 1996–97*, art. 14.3.1).

Critics question the legitimacy of amateurism and educational values as providing the cornerstone for NCAA rules in the context of big-time intercollegiate sports and given present-day commercial realities. In addition, although the NCAA's uniform rules and regulations are premised on the notion of color blindness, they have been "assailed as racially and culturally insensitive to ethnic minorities." (*NCAA Manual 1996–97*, art. 14.3.1). Among the rules that allegedly reflect racial or cultural bias are a) NCAA initial eligibility standards; b) rules restricting the money student-athletes are permitted to earn; and c) legislation that limits the access of coaches to student-athletes and prospective recruits. Thus, while facially neutral, these and other NCAA rules and regulations are believed to disparately impact African American student-athletes.

At the 1996 NCAA Convention, delegates rejected a proposal to modify Proposition 16. The proposed modification would have redefined partial qualifiers so as to include student-athletes who would be qualifiers under the standards known as Proposition 48 (Mott, 1996, p. 7). The delegates' rejection of the effort to soften academic standards for first-year athletes represents the latest chapter in the ongoing debate concerning the fairness of initial eligibility rules.

The perceived unfairness of NCAA initial eligibility rules illustrates the racial tensions surrounding the academic experiences of African American student-athletes. Tensions rose to the surface after the National Collegiate

Athletics Association (NCAA) adopted stricter standards—commonly known as Proposition 48—for determining the eligibility of prospective first-year student-athletes to receive athletic scholarships. Critics challenged Proposition 48 as racist "not only for the projected negative impact on African American enrollment but also for the lack of inclusion of African Americans in the original creation of the rule. . . . " (Mott). In addition, criticism of initial eligibility standards focuses on the significant extent to which they are based on standardized tests. A common complaint regarding such tests is that they are culturally and racially biased against minorities.

Not just initial eligibility, but other NCAA rules, such as those involving financial limitations imposed on student-athletes, disparately impact African American student-athletes (Davis, 1996). At their 1996 convention, NCAA members also defeated a proposal that would have exempted from scholarship athletes' grant-in-aid limits money that they earned from employment during the academic year when their sports were not in season (Mott, 1996, p. 7). Like initial eligibility rules, restrictions on the amounts student-athletes are permitted to earn represent an ongoing controversy. Critics of financial limits argue that the limited access that student-athletes from economically disadvantaged backgrounds—a high percentage of whom are African Americans—have to resources justifies easing such restrictions. Responding to criticism, the NCAA recently relaxed limitations on earnings by student-athletes. At their 1997 convention, the delegates adopted Proposal 62, which provides that "a student-athlete on a full grant-in-aid can work part time in the academic year, provided he or she is academically eligible and signs an affidavit confirming that he or she can earn only the difference between a full grant-in-aid and the cost of attendance." (Farrell, Fernandez, & Niland, 1997, p. 5).

In sum, critics assert that as a whole NCAA facially neutral rules operate to produce disproportionate injury to African American student-athletes. This concern invokes the question of the propriety of these athletes asserting denial of equal protection claims.

Equal Protection Analysis

The Equal Protection Clause of the Fourteenth Amendment (U.S. CONST., AMEND. XIV) and Section 1983 might be resorted to by plaintiffs challenging the legality of NCAA initial eligibility and other rules that allegedly disproportionately impact African American student-athletes. The equal protection clause of the Fourteenth Amendment "guarantees that similar individuals will be dealt with in a similar manner by the government." (Nowak & Rotunda, 1995, p. 597). Section 1 of the Fourteenth Amendment states in pertinent part:

> No state shall make or enforce any law which shall abridge the privileges or immunities of citizens of the United States; nor shall any State deprive any person of life, liberty, or property, without due process of law; nor deny to any person within its jurisdiction the equal protection of the law.

Thus, while the equal protection clause does not deny the right of the government to classify individuals in creating and applying laws, it requires that any such classification not be done arbitrarily to burden a group or pursuant to impermissible criteria (Nowak & Rotunda, 1995, p. 597). It guarantees that similar persons will be treated in a similar manner. Therefore the central purpose of the equal protection clause is preventing government conduct that discriminates on the basis of race (*Washington v. Davis* 1976, at 239).

42 U.S.C. § 1983 creates a cause of action whenever one acting under color of state law denies an individual a constitutionally protected right. This section states in pertinent part as follows:

> Every person who, under color of any statute, ordinance, regulation, custom, or usage, of any State or Territory of the District of Columbia, subjects or causes

to be subjected, any citizen of the United States or other person within the jurisdiction thereof to the deprivation of any rights, privileges, or immunities secured by the Constitution and laws, shall be liable to the party injured in an action at law, suit in equity, or other proper proceeding for redress. (Civil Rights Act of 1871)

As is true of their administrative counterparts, African American student-athletes will encounter significant impediments to mounting a successful constitutional challenge to NCAA rules and regulations. The reasons that underlie the limited utility of these established causes of action are next examined.

State Action Requirement: To successfully challenge NCAA rules and regulations on equal protection grounds under Section 1983, the NCAA would need to be classified as a state actor. Without such a classification, an equal protection claim fails. In short, the state action concept distinguishes between private conduct, which is beyond the prohibiting reach of constitutional requirements; and state action, which is subject to constitutional requirements; (Baruch & Cassidy, 1991, p. 76). In other words, the Fourteenth Amendment's guarantee of equal protection applies only to governmental action (Nowak & Rotunda, 1995, p. 597).

Early United States Supreme Court decisions narrowly defined state act to include formal acts of government. Over time, this definition was expanded to extend to private conduct that "may become so entwined with governmental policies or so impregnated with governmental character as to become subject to the constitutional limitations placed upon state action" (Evans, 196, at 299). Factors critical in determining whether a private organization's conduct amounts to state action include whether the organization assumes a public function, whether a symbiotic relationship exists between the organization and the government, and whether the private organization impacts private rights to such an extent as to warrant use of constitutional requirements to preserve such rights (Baruch, 1991, p. 77).

Prior to 1984, federal courts with the opportunity to consider the issue held, with one exception, that NCAA decisions constituted state action. This holding was premised primarily on the notion that the NCAA performs a public function in regulating college sport (*Parish*, 1975). The precedential value of these decisions proved, however, to be short-lived. Subsequent decisions, such as *Arlosoroff v. National Collegiate Athletic Association* (1984), relied on changes in the Supreme Court's definition of state action in concluding that NCAA decisions did not amount to state action.

Any lingering doubt as to whether NCAA decisions constitute state action was removed in 1988 when the United States Supreme Court rejected a "state action" classification of NCAA conduct. In *NCAA v. Tarkanian* (1988), the NCAA imposed penalties and pressured UNLV to suspend Jerry Tarkanian. Tarkanian obtained an injunction that enjoined UNLV from implementing his suspension. After several appeals, the case ultimately reached the United States Supreme Court. The Court emphasized the challenged actions were committed by UNLV, the state actor, and not the NCAA, the private actor. UNLV's adoption of NCAA rules was not sufficient to transform the NCAA's conduct into state action, despite Tarkanian's claim the organization's actions were the result of power delegated by UNLV. In *Tarkanian*, the Supreme Court acknowledged that while the NCAA is not a state actor, state-run colleges and universities are state actors. This aspect of the case has led some to argue that even though *Tarkanian* imposes a tough burden in challenging NCAA requirements, plaintiffs should sue individual institutions.

If a challenge to Proposition 48 and 42 can be brought successfully against a public college or university, the suit would diminish, if not eliminate, the NCAA's ability to enforce its current academic standards. This is because if one NCAA member public institution were legally prevented from implementing Proposition 48 or 42, challenges to the implementation of the rules at other public institutions could be expected to follow. Soon no public institutions could implement the Bylaws which contain Propositions 48 and 42. (Lufrano, 1994, p. 109)

Assuming the state action obstacle can be traversed as suggested above, African American student-athletes challenging initial eligibility standards must still prevail on the merits. Their ability to prevail will be determined to a large extent on the standard of review—which determines the degree of independent judicial review—adopted in assessing whether the challenged rule violates equal protection rights (Nowak & Rotunda, 1995, p. 600).

Equal Protection

Standard of Review: The constitutionality of a facially neutral law is determined pursuant to either a rational basis or strict scrutiny standard. Under a rational basis review, a regulation will be upheld as long as it conceivably bears some rational relationship to a governmental objective not proscribed by the Constitution (Nowak & Rotunda, 1995, p. 601). The rational basis test creates a strong presumption that the questioned governmental action is constitutional (Nowak & Rotunda, 1995, p. 605). Consequently, this standard of review affords legislatures considerable deference in rule-making.

In contrast, a strict scrutiny standard authorizes the judiciary to engage in a significant degree of independent assessment in determining whether the law in question conforms to the Constitution (Nowak & Rotunda, 1995, p. 601). This test requires a defendant to demonstrate the actions or policies that underlie a law are closely related to furthering a compelling interest.

To invoke the more favorable strict scrutiny standard, a plaintiff must establish membership in a protected class. The courts have limited the list of protected classes to race, ethnic identity, national origin, legitimacy, and gender (see *Coral Construction Co. v. King County* 1991, at 931). African American student-athletes challenging NCAA regulations, by virtue of their race, are members of a protected class and thus qualify to invoke the strict scrutiny.

In order, however, for African American students-athletes to invoke the strict scrutiny standard they must also establish that invidious discrimination was a motivating factor behind enactment of the regulation. The intentional discrimination requirement was articulated by the United States Supreme Court in *Washington v. Davis* (1976). In that case, Black police candidates challenged a civil service examination as a racially discriminatory and violative of the Equal Protection Clause (*Washington v. Davis* 1976, at 236–39). Notwithstanding the test's disparate impact on African Americans, the court held that plaintiffs failed to establish a discriminatory purpose behind its implementation (*Washington v. Davis* 1976, at 246). Thus a law or official governmental act is not unconstitutional merely because it has a racially disproportionate impact (*Washington v. Davis* 1976, at 239). According to the Court, the law or conduct must be "traced to an intentionally discriminatory purpose" (*Washington v. Davis* 1976, at 240). As summarized by one commentator:

> The case law is clear that where the discriminatory action is unintentional, but results in a discriminatory impact, rational basis review is the proper standard. A plaintiff would prefer the higher standard of strict scrutiny review. To get there, however, the plaintiff must show discriminatory intent. (Lufrano, 1994, p. 111)

Establishing Discriminatory Intent: It is unlikely that African American student-athletes would provide direct evidence of discriminatory intent. Where such evidence is lacking, a plaintiff can resort to circumstantial evidence. The Supreme Court, in *Village of Arlington Heights v. Metropolitan Housing Development*

Corp. (1977), stated that determining invidious discrimination "demands a sensitive inquiry into such circumstantial and direct evidence of intent as may be available" (*Village of Arlington Heights v. Metropolitan Housing Development Corp.* 1977, at 266–68). Evidentiary sources for proving discriminatory intent include evidence that the impact of the official action bears more heavily or one race than another, the specific sequence of events leading up to the challenged decision, the historical background of the decision, and the legislative and administrative history of the decision. In short, it is possible to infer purposeful discrimination from a series of actions, none of which alone would support such a finding.

In addition, *Washington v. Davis* has been interpreted as leaving open the possibility that a test known to be discriminatory provides evidence of discrimination (Lufrano, 1994, p. 112). In *Dixon v. Margolis*, a federal district court allowed discriminatory intent to be inferred under circumstances where the defendants continued to use tests that they knew were discriminatory and failed to seek proof that the tests were rationally related to job performance. The *Dixon* case has been interpreted as holding that "the continuing use of a test that has discriminatory impact could factually rise to a level of discriminatory intent" (Lufrano, 1994, p. 112).

Commentators, relying on the standards established in *Village of Arlington Heights* and the precedent established in cases such as *Dixon*, have argued that several factors could be utilized to establish that the NCAA's academic requirements constitute purposeful discrimination. Producing evidence of the following could conceivably provide the necessary proof of discriminatory intent: knowledge that standardized test scores have a greater impact on African American athletes than on White athletes, failure to consider less exclusionary alternatives to the use of test scores, limited involvement of African Americans in the decision-making/legislative process, and the disparate impact of the rule on the eligibility of African American student-athletes (Baruch & Cassidy, 1991, p. 83; Lufrano, 1994, pp. 114–15).

These factors suggest that plaintiffs, given the right set of facts, might prevail in asserting challenge to invalidate NCAA academic requirements. Nevertheless, the current state of the law is such that plaintiffs may encounter considerable difficulty in proving intentional discrimination (Lufrano, 1994).

Under a rational basis standard, a plaintiff is required to show that the challenged action has a disproportionate impact on members of a protected class. The plaintiff must also demonstrate that the action has no rational relationship to its intended purpose. The NCAA has articulated academic integrity in intercollegiate competition as the goal of its initial eligibility standards. Accordingly, a plaintiff challenging such regulations would be required to prove that the NCAA's academic standards bear no rational relationship to its goal of achieving academic integrity.

Several considerations would be relevant in assessing the constitutionality of NCAA academic standards under a rational basis test. Such evidence would include the impact of such standards on the admissions rate of African American athletes; the impact of standards on the ability of African American student-athletes to obtain athletic scholarships; and the academic attainment of Black student-athletes—perhaps measured in part by graduation rates—before and after the enactment of stricter academic eligibility rules (Lufrano, 1994).

In summary, it is conceivable that with the appropriate convergence of factual circumstances, an African American student-athlete might successfully challenge NCAA regulations on equal protection grounds. Such a convergence appears to have occurred in a case challenging the legality of NCAA initial eligibility rules, but pursuant to Title VI.

Title VI Challenge

In January 1997, Trial Lawyers for Public Justice, a public-interest group, filed a lawsuit alleging that the NCAA's eligibility requirements discriminate against African American athletes. The lawsuit, *Cureton v. the National Collegiate Athletic Association* (1999 WL 118667 E.D. Pa.), is a purported class action filed by four African American student-athletes who allege that they were unlawfully denied educational opportunities as freshmen by virtue of NCAA initial eligibility rules. Plaintiffs failed to achieve the minimum standardized test score required in order for a student-athlete to receive an athletic scholarship and to compete in intercollegiate competition during his or her first year at a Division I institution. They sought a declaratory judgment invalidating the minimum standardized test component of Proposition 16 and an injunction permanently enjoining the NCAA from using it.

Plaintiffs turned to Title VI as their basis for recovery. Title VI provides that "[n]o person . . . shall, on the ground of race, color, or national origin, be excluded from participation in, be denied the benefits of, or be subjected to discrimination under any program or activity receiving Federal financial assistance" (Title VI of Civil Rights Act of 1964, 42 U.S.C. Section 20000d et seq [1995]). Specifically, they alleged that "these rules ('Proposition 16') utilize a minimum test score requirement that has an unjustified disparate impact on African American student-athletes" in violation of Title VI (*Cureton v. National Collegiate Athletic Ass'n.,* 1999). Plaintiffs further contended that the

> NCAA's use of scores on standardized college-admissions tests in deciding eligibility was "determined, implemented, and enforced by the N.C.A.A. without proper validation studies and with disregard for the unjustifiable disparate impact that the minimum test-score requirement would have on African American student-athletes." (*Cureton v. National Collegiate Athletic Ass'n.,* 1999, Complaint ¶ 28)

In an important decision, the federal district court held that the NCAA's initial eligibility rule unjustifiably discriminates against African American student-athletes in violation of Title VI. In reaching this decision, the court first had to determine if the NCAA is subject to suit under Title VI. The jurisdictional prerequisite to Title VI liability is a determination of whether the defendant receives federal financial assistance (*Cureton v. National Collegiate Athletic Ass'n.*, 1999). The court held that as a matter of law, the NCAA is subject to suit under Title VI. It reasoned that the record established that plaintiffs had demonstrated that they could establish that the NCAA is a recipient of federal funds on the following grounds: (1) the NCAA is an indirect recipient of federal funds and thus subject to Title VI through its control of federal financial assistance provided to the National Youth Foundation Sports Program Fund, by virtue of the NCAA's control over the Fund itself; and, (2) "the NCAA is subject to suit under Title VI irrespective of whether it receives federal funds, directly or indirectly, because member schools (who themselves indisputably receive federal funds) have ceded controlling authority over federally funded programs to the NCAA" (*Cureton v. National Collegiate Athletic Ass'n,* 1999).

Having decided the jurisdictional issue in plaintiffs' favor, the court addressed the merits of the legality of Proposition 16. According to the court, determining whether a plaintiff presents a prima facie case of disparate impact discrimination involves a two-step process: (1) determining if the record establishes that the application of a facially neutral rule causes an adverse disproportionate impact (i.e., "excluding the plaintiffs and similarly situated applicants from an educational opportunity"); and, (2) assuming such a showing is made, allowing the defendant an opportunity to demonstrate that the rule or practice that causes the disproportionate impact is justified by educational necessity. Relying on data, much of it from NCAA-sponsored studies, the court concluded that Proposition 16 disproportionately impacts African American student-athletes. As an example, the court pointed to NCAA data that re-

vealed that in 1996, 21.4 percent of African American student-athletes failed to meet Proposition 16 requirements, in contrast to 4.2 percent of White student-athletes. It also noted a decrease from 23.6 percent to 20.3 percent in African American student-athletes enrolled in Division I institutions for 1994–96. The court concluded that according to the data, this decrease is attributable to these student-athletes not having satisfied Proposition 16 requirements (*Cureton v. National Collegiate Athletic Ass'n.*, 1999).

Concluding that plaintiffs established a prima facie case, the court turned to the educational necessity defense, which asks whether the challenged practice serves a legitimate educational purpose. The court acknowledged that increasing student-athlete graduation rates—a principal justification offered by the NCAA—is a legitimate educational goal. Nevertheless the NCAA failed, according to the court, to produce evidence that established a nexus between using particular cutoff scores of 820 and 68 on the SAT and ACT, respectively, and its goal of achieving enhanced graduation rates. It concluded the "NCAA has not validated the use of the SAT, or any particular cutoff score of the SAT, as a predictor of student-athlete graduation rates" (*Cureton v. National Collegiate Athletic Ass'n.*, 1999). In rejecting the NCAA educational necessity justification, the court went on to state,

> . . . [T]he NCAA has failed to justify either (1) that its choice of a 820 cutoff score is reasonable and consistent with normal expectations of the acceptable proficiency of student-athletes towards attaining a college degree; (2) that its choice of a 820 cutoff score is the logical "break-point" in the distribution of SAT scores relevant to meeting its goal of raising student-athlete graduation rates (and increasing access to opportunities); or (3) that its choice of a 820 cutoff score is a valid measure of the minimal ability necessary to raise the graduation rates of

student-athletes above those achieved prior to Proposition 16 let alone Proposition 48. (*Cureton v. National Collegiate Athletic Ass'n.*, 1999)

In summary, the court found that the 820 cutoff was arbitrary given that the NCAA failed to produce evidence of a relationship between this minimum score and the goal of raising graduation rates.

In a ruling issued on March 16, 1999, the federal district rejected the NCAA's motion to stay the injunction prohibiting the use of the standardized test component of proposition 16 (*Cureton v. National Collegiate Athletic Ass'n.*, 1999). The NCAA has expressed its intention to appeal both the denial of its motion to stay the injunction and the court's ruling in favor of plaintiffs on the merits.

Academic Opportunity for Student-Athletes: A Section 1981 Analysis

Another particularly harmful consequence of racism in college sports is the devaluation of the African American student-athlete's academic interest. This devaluation raises again the question of exploitation of African American student-athletes who provide valuable services, yet leave their institutions of higher learning without having obtained the academic preparation necessary for them to cope successfully with life issues following their college careers. Notwithstanding this real harm that ensues from this devaluation, it is unlikely that traditional antidiscrimination norms will provides a means of redress.

42 U.S.C. §1981 prohibits racial discrimination in the contracting process. Notwithstanding the student-athlete's contractual relationship with his or her institution, the utility of Section 1981 is dubious. Section 1981, like most antidiscrimination statutes, proscribes only intentional acts of racial discrimination (*Edwards v. Jewish Hosp. of St. Louis*, 1987). Therefore, to sustain a Section 1981 claim, it would be incumbent upon the student-athlete

to show that the institution's conduct was motivated by race. However, except in rare instances, the academic neglect of African American student-athletes appears to result from unconscious rather than deliberately overt forms of racial discrimination.

Given the inherent nature of the racism implicated, the African American student-athlete is situated like many other plaintiffs alleging discrimination in the contracting process. Section 1981 claimants encounter an intent element which represents an almost insurmountable hurdle to establishing their claim. This likelihood mandates the search for other means of protecting the African American student-athlete's academic interests.

Indeed, African Americans' inability to rely on established antidiscrimination laws to achieve racial justice illustrates the limitations inherent in an antidiscrimination legal framework that fails to take into account unconscious racism (Lawrence, 1990, p. 319; see also Green, 1990, p. 1515). For example, in urging that the equal protection doctrine come to grips with unconscious racism, Professor Charles Lawrence commented that

> [t]raditional notions of intent do not reflect the fact that decisions about racial matters are influenced in large part by factors that can be characterized as neither intentional—in the sense that certain outcomes are self-consciously sought—nor unintentional—in the sense that the outcomes are random, fortuitous, and uninfluenced by the decision maker's beliefs, desires, and wishes.

In summary, we see once again the unavailability of antidiscrimination laws as a tool to combat unconscious racism in collegiate sport. As adroitly captured by Professor Rodney Smith,

> In the intercollegiate context, where persons of color predominate (at least in the numerical sense), inequitable treatment is often far more subtle and far less susceptible of proof than in a traditional

discrimination suit. The intent requirement, coupled with the Supreme Court's
present unwillingness to permit "affirmative action," makes it unlikely that
student-athletes of color will be able to
address racial inequities of the sorts that
exist in the intercollegiate athletics context, . . . through federal constitutional
or related means. Given these shortcomings in antidiscrimination law, Professor Smith and others recommend a
broad range of legal and non-legal approaches to combating racial inequities
in college sports. These approaches include resort to common law doctrine,
NCAA rule-making, state and federal
legislation and political action as means
of ameliorating racial inequities in
sports (Smith, 1996, pp. 378–79; Davis,
1995, pp. 695–97).

Alternative Approaches to Combating Discrimination in Collegiate Sport

Litigation Strategy— Common-Law Doctrine

African American student-athletes might resort to common-law doctrines in challenging
the devaluation of their academic opportunity.
For instance, student-athletes have challenged
the failure of their institutions to provide them
with an educational opportunity pursuant to
breach of contract and educational malpractice claims.

One such approach has been taken with respect to using the common law to protect the
academic interests of student-athletes. For instance, in *Ross v. Creighton University* (1992),
a student-athlete sought to impose a duty on
his college to provide him with an educational
opportunity. In asserting the existence and
breach of such a duty he asserted claims based
on common-law tort and contract theories such
as educational malpractice, negligent admission, intentional infliction of emotional dis-
tress, and breach of implied and express con-

tract. Similar allegations were made by Terrell
Jackson in his lawsuit against Drake University. In addition to the theories asserted in
Ross and *Jackson*, I have also argued that the
common-law contract principle of good faith
may hold promise as a basis for constraining
discriminatory conduct that harms the interests
of African American student-athletes.

Courts have, however, exhibited reluctance
to adopt these theories to protect the interests
of student-athletes. In addition to judicial refusal to acknowledge such theories, other limitations reside in a litigation-based strategy to
combat racial discrimination. Litigation is financially and emotionally costly. In addition, it
requires resources that may not be readily
available to student-athletes. Moreover, the
very nature of litigation is such that it provides
redress on a case-by-case basis. Consequently,
a litigation strategy effectuates change slowly.
"Given its expense and interstitial nature,
therefore, litigation is a weak strategy for
bringing racial . . . equity to intercollegiate athletics. Indeed, its major virtue may simply be
that it can encourage an important dialogue regarding equity issues, which may ultimately
help facilitate meaningful reform at the
broader legislative or rulemaking level."
(Smith, 1996, p. 367).

Alternatives to Litigation Strategy

Given these limitations to litigation as a strategy for achieving racial equity in college
sports, other alternatives must be pursued.
While most of these strategies are untested,
they may warrant consideration either singularly or in combination. Such strategies include
the following:

1. the initiation of congressional hearings
   regarding racial equity in college sport
   that would specifically focus on exploitation and access (Smith, 1996, p. 372);
2. state legislative hearings exploring issues
   of racial equity (Smith, 1996, pp. 378–79);
3. development at the institutional level of
   detailed and comprehensive plans to create racial equity;

4. requiring that NCAA legislation be subjected to racial impact studies which would consider the racial implications of proposed legislation;

5. requiring institutions to account for funds generated in the revenue-producing sports —basketball and football—as a means of avoiding the exploitation of African American student-athletes (Smith, 1996, pp. 379–80);

6. recognition by state legislatures that student-athletes possess certain contract and torts claims as a means of holding their institutions accountable for providing educational opportunity and avoiding exploitation.

7. establishment by institutions of affirmative goals and policies to enhance the opportunities for African American administrators and coaches;

8. expansion and extension of programs such as the NCAA's minority internship programs (Smith, 1996, p. 382);

9. collaboration between the NCAA and schools to identify and develop academic assistance programs geared toward the complete education and development of student-athletes; and

10. distribution of larger percentages of revenues for academic development of student-athletes.

None of the above suggestions will be without its own difficulties. However, they offer promise for addressing the range of problems stemming from racism in college athletics.

Conclusion

The foregoing discussion suggests that given the proper set of circumstances, traditional and nontraditional antidiscrimination norms may provide mechanisms for confronting the harm caused by racism in college athletics. Yet as a general proposition, it is fair to conclude that the role of the law—if the focus is on existing antidiscrimination statutes—will be limited. For example, instances will likely be few when an African American coach can proffer the evidence of racial animus necessary to prevail in a Title VII claim.

Consequently, litigation strategies for addressing the harm inflicted upon student-athletes and other African American participants in college sport will require honest and creative approaches that may transcend traditional doctrinal boundaries. Limitations inherent to a litigation strategy for effectuating social change moderate its effectiveness in achieving racial equity in intercollegiate athletics. As noted by Professor Smith, the principal role of litigation may be as supplemental to nonlitigation strategies. Ultimately achieving racial equity in sports will require a shift in attitude: Those in power positions in intercollegiate athletics must commit to achieving racial equity. This will require recognizing and moving beyond the stereotypes and assumptions that underlie the unconscious racism that permeates college athletics.

Suggested Readings

Anderson, P. M. (1996). Racism in sports: A question of ethics. *Marquette Sports Law Journal, 6,* 357–408.

Baruch, C., & Cassidy, E. O., Jr. (1991). Technical foul: The legality and wisdom of NCAA academic requirements. *Lincoln Law Review, 20,* 71–86.

Clark, L. D. (1993). New directions for the Civil Rights movement: College athletics as a civil rights issue. *Howard Law Journal, 36,* 259–289.

Davis, T. (1995). A model for institutional governance for intercollegiate athletics. *Wisconsin Law Review,* 599–645.

Davis, T. (1995). The myth of the superspade: The persistence of racism in college athletics. *Fordham Urban Law Journal, 22,* 615–698.

Davis, T. (1996). African American student-athletes: Marginalizing the NCAA regulatory structure? *Marquette Sports Law Journal, 6,* 199–227.

Green, L. S. (1984). The new NCAA rules of the game: Academic integrity or racism. *St. Louis Univiversity Law Journal,, 28,* 101–151.

Lufrano, M. R. (1994). The NCAA's involvement in setting academic standards: Legality and desirability. *Seton Hall Journal of Sports Law, 4,* 97–141.

Mathewson, A. D. (1996). Black women, gender equity and the function at the junction. *Marquette Sports Law Journal, 6,* 239–266.

Shropshire, K. L. (1996). *In black & white: Race and sports in America.* New York: New York University Press.

Smith, R. K. (1996). When ignorance is bliss: In search of racial and gender equity in intercollegiate athletics. *Missouri Law Review, 61,* 329–392.

Suggs, R. E. (1991). Racial discrimination in business transactions. *Hastings Law Journal, 42,* 1257–1323.

Williams, N. G. (1994). Offer, acceptance, and improper consideration: A common-law model for the prohibition of racial discrimination in the contracting process. *George Washington Law Review, 62,* 183–229.

Yarbrough, M. V. (1996). If you let me play sports. *Marquette Sports Law Journal, 6,* 229–238.

Study Questions:

1. Describe the ways in which racism negatively impacts the interests of African Americans in college athletics.

2. Describe the historical transformation of racism in college athletics.

3. What variables contribute to the racism that persists in present-day college athletics?

4. Given that racial discrimination negatively impacts the interests of African Americans in college sports, why are traditional civil rights laws of limited effectiveness as vehicles for combating it?

5. Inasmuch as traditional civil rights legislation is of limited utility in ameliorating racism in college athletics, identify alternative means of recourse.

References

Adarand Constructors, Inc. v. Pena, 115 S. Ct. 2097 (1995).

Anderson v. Douglas & Lomason Co., Inc., 26 F.3d 1277 (5th Cir. 1994), *cert. denied,* 513 U.S. 1149 (1995).

Arlosoroff v. National Collegiate Athletic Assn., 746 F.2d 1019 (4th Cir. 1984).

Atonio v. Wards Cove Packing Co., Inc., 10 F.3d 1485, 1498 (9th Cir. 1993), *cert. denied,* 513 U.S. 809 (1994).

Baruch, C., & Cassidy, E. O., Jr. (1991). Technical foul: The legality and wisdom of NCAA academic requirements. *Lincoln Law Review, 20,* 71–86.

Coakley, J. A. (1994). *The Sociology of sport.* Dallas, TX: Taylor Publishers.

Cobb v. University of Southern California, 45 Cal. App. 4th 1140 (1996).

Coral Construction Co. v. King County, 941 F.2d 910, 931 (9th Cir. 1991), *cert. denied,* 502 U.S. 1033 (1992).

Civil Rights Act of 1871, 42 U.S.C. Section 1983 (1988).

Civil Rights Act of 1870, 42 U.S.C. Section 1981 (1994).

Cureton v. National Collegiate Athletic Ass'n., 1999 WL 118667 (E.D. Pa.).

Cureton v. National Collegiate Athletic Ass'n., 1999 WL 118667 (E.D. Pa). Complaint, 28.

Davis, T. (1995). The myth of the superspade: The persistence of racism in college athletics. *Fordham Urban Law Journal, 22,* 615–698.

Davis, T. (1996). African American student athletes: Marginalizing the NCAA regulatory structure? *Marquette Sports Law Journal, 6,* 199–227.

Dixon v. Margolis, 765 F. Supp. 454 (N.D. Ill.1991).

Edwards v. Jewish Hospital of St. Louis, 855 F.2d 1345 (8th Cir.1988).

Evans v. Newton, 382 U.S. 296, 299 (1966).

Farrell, K., Fernandez, J., & Niland, B. (1997, January). Convention listened to concerns of athletes. *NCAA News, 5.*

Frei, T. (1995, October 30). Separate ways. *Sporting News.*

Griggs v. Duke Power Co., 401 U.S. 424 (1971).

Groves v. Alabama State Board of Education, 776 F. Supp. 1518 (M.D. Ala. 1991).

Harris, O. (1993). African American predominance in collegiate sport. In D. Brooks & R. Althouse (Eds.), *Racism in college athletics: The African American athlete's experience* (pp. 51–74). Morgantown, WV: Fitness Information Technology, Inc.

Haworth, K. (1997, January 17). Suit says NCAA's eligibility standards discriminate against Black students. *The Chronicle of Higher Education*, p. A46.

Hopwood v. State of Texas, 78 F.3d 932 (5th Cir. 1996), *cert. denied sub nom*, 116 S. Ct. 2580 (1996).

Hudson, M., & Sandoval, G. (1996, February 21). Garrett and the Trojans: Turmoil USC. *Los Angeles Times*, p. C1.

Hysaw v. Washburn University of Topeka, 690 F. Supp. 940 (D. Kan. 1987).

Jackson v. Drake University, 778 F. Supp. 1490 (S.D. Iowa 1991).

Johnson v. Uncle Ben's, Inc., 965 F.2d 1363 (5th Cir. 1992), *cert. denied*, 511 U.S. 1068 (1994).

Lapchick, R. E. (1997). *1997 racial report card: College special edition*. Boston: Northeastern University Center for the Study of Sport in Society.

Large eligibility differences noted by race, income. (1998, February 2) *NCAA News*, p. 1.

Lombardo, B. (1978). The Harlem Globetrotters and the perpetuation of the Black stereotype. *Physical Educator, 35*, 60–63.

Lufrano, M. R. (1994). The NCAA's involvement in setting academic standards: Legality and desirability. *Seton Hall Journal of Sports Law, 4*, 97–141.

McDonnell Douglas Corp. v. Green, 411 U.S. 792 (1973).

Metro Broadcasting, Inc. v. FCC, 497 U.S. 547 (1990), *overruled in part* by Adarand Constructors, Inc. v. Pena, 115 S. Ct. 2097 (1995).

Modjeska, A. C. (1993). *Employment Discrimination law* (3rd ed.). Deerfield, IL: Clark Boardman Callaghan.

Mott, R. D. (1996, January 15). Delegates reject modification to initial eligibility standards. *NCAA News*, p. 7.

National Collegiate Athletic Association. *1996–97 NCAA Manual*, Art. 1.1.3.

NCAA Minority Opportunities and Interests Committee, 1994.

NCCA News Digest. (1997, July 21). Graduation-rate comparison. *NCAA News*, p. 2.

NCAA v. Tarkanian, 488 U.S. 179 (1988).

Nowak, J., & Rotunda, R. (1995). *Constitutional Law* (5th Ed.). St. Paul, MN: West Publishing Co.

Parish v. National Collegiate Athletic Assn., 506 F.2d 1028 (5th Cir. 1975).

Regents of the University of California v. Bakke, 438 U.S. 265, 319–320 (1978).

Report of the McIntosh Commission for Fair Play in Student Athlete Admissions. (1994).

Ross v. Creighton University, 957 F.2d 410 (7th Cir. 1992).

St. Mary's Honor Center v. Hicks, 509 U.S. 502, 113 S. Ct. 2742 (1993).

Shropshire, K. L. (1996). *In Black and white: Race and sports in America*. New York: New York University Press.

Smith, R. K. (1996). When ignorance is not bliss: In search of racial and gender equity in intercollegiate athletics. *Missouri Law Review, 61*, 329–392.

Springer, S. (1991, October 19). UCLA's Edwards says athletes don't get enough money to live on, and he wants to see drastic measures taken. *L.A. Times*, p. 1.

Suggs, R. E. (1991). Racial discrimination in business transactions. *Hastings Law Journal, 42*, 1257–1323.

Title VII of the Civil Rights Act of 1964, as amended by the Civil Rights Act of 1991, 42 U.S.C. Section 2000e *et seq*. (1995).

U.S. Constitution, amend 14, 1.

Village of Arlington Heights v. Metropolitan Housing Development Corp., 429 U.S. 252 (1977).

Washington v. Davis, 426 U.S. 229 (1976).

Washington v. Garrett, 10 F.3d 1421 (9th Cir. 1994).

Watson v. Fort Worth Bank & Trust, 487 U.S. 977 (1988).

Wiggins, D. K. (1993). Critical events affecting racism in athletics. In D. Brooks & R. Althouse (Eds.), *Racism in college athletics: The African American athlete's experience* (pp. 23–49). Morgantown, WV: Fitness Information Technology, Inc.

Compensation and the African American Student-Athlete

Kenneth L. Shropshire

Abstract

How does the absence of compensation, beyond room, board, tuition, and educational fees, impact the African American student-athlete? This is a strikingly curious issue, because the African American student-athlete, relative to other races, makes up the largest percentage of participants in the collegiate revenue-generating sports of men's basketball and football. These sports are often viewed as the financial engine for nonrevenue sports such as lacrosse, swimming, wrestling, and tennis. Ironically, African Americans make up only a small percentage of the athletes participating in those nonrevenue sports. Those participants are primarily White. The National Collegiate Athletic Association (NCAA) rules against pay appear to have a harsher impact on African American student-athletes. This is particularly the case as the economic status of this student-athlete population is reflective of the economic demographics of broader America. This essay concludes that if an open market would dictate, all student-athletes should receive increased compensation. This could and should be moderated by the constraints of Title IX, requiring equity in treatment and opportunity for both male and female athletes, as well as the nonmonetary social value of nonrevenue-generating sports. The primary purpose of this essay is to focus on the need for increased compensation for student-athletes, particularly African Americans. The difficult mechanics of how to accomplish this goal of increased compensation should be discussed rigorously in other forums and not ignored or put aside as an impossible societal transition. It is these mechanics that, in the end, may make increased compensation difficult to deliver.

Key Terms

- Amateurism -
- Compensation -
- Antitrust -
- Olympics -
- Exploitation -
- Title IX -
- Commercialization -
- Competition -

Introduction

> The bottom line is this: intercollegiate athletics is primarily a mechanism whereby poor, primarily Black students are used to finance the educational and athletic activities of wealthy White students. (Noll, 1991)

I wrote a commentary for *USA Today* in 1996, and that newspaper elected to lead with the headline "College Athletes Deserve Pay." As this essay will detail, that headline represented an oversimplification of my view—but it was not far off. That commentary called for a reexamination of the compensation allotted to *all* student-athletes. I have written controversial pieces before, so I was ready for the mail that I knew would be forthcoming. Much did indeed follow. Among those letters, a prominent broadcaster and former college coach sent me these words: "I find it both sad and somewhat embarrassing that a man of your intelligence has taken such a position in regard to paying college stars."[1] People do not tend to have half-spirited views on this issue. There exist deep feelings—sometimes rational, other times not—regarding increasing compensation to college athletes.

The focus of this essay is on the additional circumstances impacting the compensation issue with regard to African American student-athletes. From the outset, I should make it clear that my concern is for greater compensation for all student-athletes, especially those involved in revenue-generating sports. Additionally, my desire would be to develop a system that completely meshes with the goals of gender equity in college sports, both from a legal and a fairness standpoint. Further, my concern is not for some extraordinary amount above whatever the market for college athletes actually dictates. In the end, the amount I would advocate probably falls below that level. Some of the revenues generated by these athletes should be invested for the broader good of collegiate athletics.

The African American athletes' case is but a small piece of the larger picture, but in many ways, as the epigraph quoting Noll illuminates, they well may be the most negatively impacted. The background of a large percentage of African American student-athletes, both socially and economically, is far different from that of those who make the rules regarding compensation.

NCAA Rules and Amateurism

One of the longest-running debates in college sports concerns the rules barring payments to student-athletes as compensation for the value their athletic performances bring to American colleges and universities. In this regard, National Collegiate Athletic Association (NCAA) rules are clear in forbidding any payments to student-athletes that are made as a result of their athletic talents. NCAA rules state specifically that "tuition and fees, room and board, and required course related books" are the only forms of financial aid a student may receive from a university. (NCAA Bylaw 15.2). These rules—varied but long-standing—are grounded in historic concepts of amateurism. The classic view of amateurism proclaims that college athletes should not be paid for their participation in athletics, no matter what value their skills as accomplished, entertaining athletes bring to an institution of higher learning. (There is certainly a degree of grimacing that occurs when the terminology *pay* is used. *Compensation* lessens this some. Shrouding the compensation as "room, board, tuition, and required course-related books" has had a further harshness-lessening impact.) This value, in some cases, is arguably phenomenal. It is also, as with compensation for most wage earners, impossible to quantify with precision.

---

1. Letter on file with author.

Probably the most cited estimation of the value generated by a top-level college player to a university focused on football (Brown, 1993). Brown (1993) concluded that a top-level college football player generates $538,760 per year, or over $2 million over a 4-year period. This is the net gain for an institution following the deduction of a scholarship valued by Brown at $20,000 per year. In another study, Noll (1991) estimated the revenue generated by a star quarterback at Stanford University in 1986–87 to be $200,000 for that year. Noll (1991) further found that the average incremental profit from what he termed "good" players was estimated to be about $150,000 per year.

The revenues generated by student-athletes are certainly varied. It is difficult for any study to peg a specific dollar amount of revenue to a specific student-athlete. There is obviously the direct dollar value from ticket sales, television rights fees, corporate sponsorship of teams and facilities, and other endorsement opportunities. These sources of revenue are fairly well established, but new sources arise periodically. Notably, in 1996, the NCAA was negotiating a deal with a network to hold a national football championship play-off, including a championship game. In exchange for the broadcast rights, the NCAA was to be paid $500 million. The entertainers on the field, the athletes, were, of course, scheduled to receive no direct cash payment from this windfall (Sandomir, 1996). The basic response from some is, yes, the athletes do receive payment: room, board, tuition, and educational fees; broadly too, they argue, athletes earn the right to receive an education.

One was formerly able to point to amateur athletes in the Olympic movement as comrades without pay for stellar performances. The Olympics, historically, were another venue where athletes participated in sports for the glory of sport alone. We had ingrained in us, for many reasons, that such participation was good and pure, but this Olympic phenomenon exists no longer. Many of those athletes now receive compensation. In the 1996 Atlanta Olympic Games, gold medalists from the United States received a minimum of $15,000 for their success. These payments were made by the United States Olympic Committee and the National Governing Bodies of their respective sports. The United States is not alone in this pay-for-performance mode. Taiwan announced that it would pay its gold medalists over $300,000. These direct payments are certainly strikingly different from what occurs in collegiate athletics (Heath, 1996).

Income from endorsements displays another contrast in philosophies between the NCAA and the International Olympic Committee. This was starkly evident again during the Olympics when we saw participants in this formerly amateur celebration of sports—such as Jackie Joyner-Kersee—featured in television commercials in between events. We also saw current National Basketball Association millionaire stars participate in the formerly all-amateur event. Athlete endorsements are, of course, strictly against the rules on the collegiate level. Colleges are able to sell items such as jerseys with numbers made famous by current student-athletes and souvenir books attracting purchases with that athlete's likeness. None of these dollars go to the athlete. Notre Dame earns about $6 million per year from licensing its logo. Michigan and Ohio State earn nearly comparable annual totals (Thurow, 1996).

A further irony, at the collegiate level, is the right of coaches to earn income from endorsements and other compensation where the athlete cannot. Athletic shoe contracts, for example, have been reported to bring coaches millions of dollars (Golden, 1995). The payments to coaches, and the simultaneous wearing of the contracted brand by the student-athletes, began in about 1978, with Nike leading the way (Golden, 1995). It was in 1993 that the stakes were raised tremendously with Adidas stepping in to lure Duke University's players from Nike, through coach Mike Krzyzewski, with payments to the coach of $375,000 per year and a $1 million bonus (Golden, 1995). One of the largest endorsement deals is held by Georgetown's John Thompson.

He is reported to receive $351,000 per year as a Nike consultant, $18,000 as a director, plus 1,000 shares of Nike stock with the option to buy 18,000 more shares. Although the coaches are paid (and sometimes their dapper apparel dictates that they not even wear the product on the sidelines), the athletes are not able to avail themselves of this income source. Further, top-level college coaches earn salaries in a range from $400,000 to $1 million or more annually (Golden, 1995), but a coach's or even a university's entanglement in money-earning commercial ventures generally escapes the NCAA's scrutiny (Golden, 1995). Though subject to criticism, there exist few regulatory constraints. Not that they should be regulated—the coaches are only being paid what the market dictates. So how did this disparate treatment of student-athletes by the NCAA come about?

Sources of Amateurism

The complex web of the creation of collegiate amateurism has been traced elsewhere but is important to recount in this essay. When we reflect on amateurism's origins, we most likely think of some ancient society—probably Greek—where the athletes participated in sports for the glory of sport alone. The athletes received no pay, no compensation in any form for their athletic prowess. Then, the progression is probably on to Victorian England, with a focus on rowing, cricket, and pre-*Chariots of Fire* track and field competition. The final image is a mix of *Chariots of Fire;* Jim Thorpe's medals taken away for lack of amateur purity; and finally, collegiate football, in the era of raccoon coats, rumble seats, and that "ol' school spirit." These images are all connected, but there is much reality blending with myth. How could a sector of society develop where individuals are not paid for the revenue their labor generates? Certainly, some requisite "management" fee should be taken from the gross revenues, but why not pay the labor? It is difficult to think of any other enterprise historically or in contemporary society where the same circumstances exist—well below market wages—other than slavery.

It was about 1990 when I and a number of scholars dusted off the work of a student of the classics, David C. Young, and in particular his work *The Ancient Myth of Greek Amateur Athletics*. The most relevant and telling information in that study was the following, where Young (1985) not only contends that the Greeks did not have a word for amateurism, but he also points out evidence of the concept of amateurism.

So how did this all evolve? Particularly relevant to the African American student-athlete, many point to exploitation as the goal in the creation of amateurism. The reality is that this form of no-compensation amateurism is much more a function of Victorian England than ancient Greece (see Shropshire, 1991).[2] Young (1985) chronicles a justification process for not compensating Olympic athletes. This then led to the same justification in college. One of the earlier misstatements cited by Young is from Paul Shorey:

> And here lies the chief, if somewhat obvious, lesson that our modern athletes have to learn from Olympia. . . . They must *strive . . . only* for the complete development of their manhood, and their sole prizes must be the conscious delight in the exercise . . . and some simple symbol of honor. They must not prostitute the vigor of their youth for gold, directly or indirectly. . . . [T]he commercial spirit . . . is fatal, as the Greeks learned. . . . Where money is the stake, men will inevitably tend to rate the end above the means, or rather to misconceive the true end . . . the professional will *usurp the place of the amateur.* . . . (Cited in Young, 1985, p. 9)

---

2. I elaborate on this conclusion in Kenneth L. Shropshire, "Legislation for the Glory of Sport: Amateurism and Compensation," *Seton Hall Journal of Sport Law* 1991, 7, 9.

Young asserts that this article, written prior to the first modern Olympiad held in Athens in 1896 and directed at the potential Olympians, was part of a large web of fallaciously cross-cited articles relying on each other.

I wrote, when I researched this area in 1991, that "in simplest terms, these scholars were part of a justification process for an elite British athletic system destined to find its way into American collegiate athletics" (Shropshire, 1991, p. 11). With Shorey and other scholars affirming this myth, nonscholars readily joined in. This includes leaders of the modern Olympic movement. The structure certainly enforced class separation in England. Although I wrote at the time that the British system was destined to find its way to the United States, it certainly did not have to and probably should not have.

In a broad sense, it is not difficult to understand how any business can be more profitable if the labor in the enterprise does not need to be fully compensated. Such was the case in the development of the Olympic myth. Similarly, the NCAA was formed in the early 1900s, just a few years after the first modern Olympiad held in 1896. Early on, the NCAA made clear distinctions between amateurs and professionals.

Prior to this model of amateurism, however, professionalism could readily be found in even the most elite American institutions of higher learning. For example, Harvard University students participated in rowing events winning as much as $500 in the 1850s. Schools in the United States in many ways openly competed for the services of superior athletes with various forms of "gifts" and "rewards" for success on the field. One of my favorites is the all-expenses-paid vacation to Havana, Cuba, awarded to a star athlete on an Ivy League football team (Shropshire, 1990).

Smith (1988) discussed the difficulty in bringing, without modifications, the British model of amateurism to the United States. In short, in England, the competition in athletics was predominantly between two institutions, Oxford and Cambridge, whereas in the United States, hundreds of institutions, eventually over one thousand, would compete for athletic superiority, essentially for the best athletes. According to Smith (1988),

> The English amateur system, based upon participation by the social and economic elite . . . would never gain a foothold in American college athletics. There was too much competition, too strong a belief in merit over heredity, too abundant an ideology of freedom of opportunity for the amateur ideal to succeed. . . . It may be that amateur athletics at a high level of expertise can only exist in a society dominated by upper-class elitists.

The NCAA has never placed this mythical, pure model of Greek amateurism at the forefront of its operations. In fact, although most today probably view the NCAA as an entity involved in preventing corruption and running championships, the NCAA was originally formed to promote safety, not to promote amateurism (Shropshire, 1990). At the turn of the century, then U.S. President Teddy Roosevelt brought together the leaders of college football following a number of deaths on the field from the use of the "flying wedge" and other violent tactics. Further, there is nothing done overtly by the NCAA to tie itself with Greek amateurism, but too, there is no effort to correct the misconception. It would be difficult, if not impossible, to make the case that the African American athlete was being specifically targeted by those who met to form the organization. In fact, very few African Americans participated in organized collegiate athletics in the beginning (Ashe, 1988).

Coupled with amateurism, the secondary argument for not paying collegiate stars is that such a constraint on pay actually promotes competition. The view is that if monetary compensation is limited to room, board, tuition, and educational fees, then all NCAA member institutions may equally compete for student-athletes. The larger, more successful institutions cannot use financial incentives in order to gain a competitive advantage (Goldman, 1990). This argument is flawed because little parity currently exists between the major and smaller collegiate sports programs. There is a further irony in that it is difficult to compete unless "bidding" can occur for athlete services with *varying* levels of compensation, not the same. The beauty of a respective campus, the varying educational opportunities, and other factors are forms of differentiation, but direct monetary compensation is not allowed.

One obvious way to give an advantage in this landscape is to find a way, maybe unscrupulously, to provide the compensation that other institutions of higher education will not. This is the opportunistic void that some colleges have filled directly and others have filled via overzealous alums. This landscape also provides the setting for the opportunistic behavior of sports agents, constantly in the news for making these types of payments to student-athletes for the opportunity to represent them in future lucrative contract negotiations (Shropshire, 1990). Overwhelmingly, it seems that African American athletes are victims of this opportunistic entanglement. Increased compensation should be viewed as a mechanism to, to a limited degree, address this problem as well.

Disproportionate Impact on African American Student-Athletes?

The "no-pay-for-play" scenario has been with us since long before African Americans began to play the dominant role that they now hold in college athletics. An issue one must raise in addressing this is whether the situation persists because those who are "in charge" of the NCAA are largely White and the stars of the game are primarily African American. I say those who are "in charge" with full knowledge that it is not NCAA administrators (that office has diversified immensely in the past few years), but the athletic departments and presidents of member institutions (Lapchick, 1998). These are the parties who actually make policies and vote at NCAA conventions. Would

their children be treated in the same way? That is, does there exist a lack of understanding and empathy toward the economic plight of African American student-athletes on the part of largely White collegiate sports administrators? Arguably, this is always the case whenever there is an absence of diversity in leadership positions.

The appropriate question is this: Does there exist a disproportionate impact on this group of student-athletes who arguably provide the greatest entertainment value? For this query, the answer is also yes. This is based on assuming that the scholarship athlete population simply constitutes a microcosm of broader America. A large number of African American student-athletes are from lower socioeconomic families (Davis, 1996; Sellers, Kuperminc, & Waddell, 1991). The median family income of African Americans has long been lower than that of Whites. In 1995, the family figures compared at a median of $35,766 for Whites and $22,393 for Blacks (Goldberg, 1997).

As further support for this disproportionate impact proposition, note that the majority of the athletes on scholarship in the major revenue-generating sports of the NCAA are African Americans. In 1994, of all Division IA athletes on scholarship in basketball, 50.7% were African American. In football 65% were African American. In nonrevenue sports in the same period, only 5.6% were African American. This excludes baseball and track. In baseball 7.3% were African American, and in track 28.4% were African American. African American athletes provide a large source of the funding for nonrevenue sports—sports African Americans do not in large numbers participate in nor in large numbers are African Americans recruited to play. Is this exploitation? It may not have been designed as such, but the financing structure of collegiate sports lends the argument a degree of credibility.

The largest trail of evidence that the African American athletes' concerns have not always been appropriately addressed is that of the initial eligibility rules. Those rules were developed without the appropriate input of historically Black colleges and universities, African American administrators, or student-athletes (Shropshire, 1996). If one walks into an NCAA convention, particularly with Division IA administrators, African American decision makers are largely absent. Representation is nowhere near that of their representation on the revenue-generating playing fields. (Lapchick, 1998; Shropshire, 1996)

Whenever there is a debate on the floor of the NCAA convention, a few voices speak frankly regarding the race issues. Others may try, but as Bell has phrased it in other contexts, there is an absence of "voices from the bottom of the well" (Bell, 1992). This was clearly the case when the initial eligibility rules were developed. This seems to be the case, as well, regarding increased compensation.

Is it exploitative to take the dollars generated by these primarily African American athletes to fund nonrevenue-generating, largely White sports such as lacrosse, gymnastics, wrestling, and volleyball? These other sports certainly provide a broad range of athletic opportunities for a large number of students—much more than those two revenue-generating sports, basketball and football. There is great value in funding these sports. At a minimum, however, one should be able to acknowledge a degree of unfairness in this current status.

The response to increased compensation to student-athletes is often "Let them turn pro." This attitude too bespeaks the throwaway attitude some have toward this group of primarily African American student-athletes providing this huge entertainment value to college sports. What amplifies this throwaway attitude further are the sad graduation rates of African American student-athletes. Again, there have been extensive litigation and documentation in this regard (Davis, 1992). The education that is often pointed to as the value these athletes receive for their services may never be received. The most glaring example of this exploitation was the illiteracy disclosed by former professional football star Dexter Manley. He was learning disabled and virtually illiterate, but he still graduated from Oklahoma State University (Cohen, 1996, cited in "A Star Turn," *Washington Post*, October 10, 1996, A21).

In 1997, a modest proposal allowing student-athletes to work part-time during the school year was passed by NCAA member institutions (Copeland, 1997). Not all student-athletes should utilize this option, but some must. Many might prefer to study longer hours, but financially they cannot afford to do so. Some have no other routes to obtaining the income they need other than through paths that violate NCAA rules, or worse, the law (Naughton, 1996). The issue of increased compensation needs more focussed attention than it has received. If dramatic changes are not made, it will remain difficult to argue with vigor against perceptions of African American student-athlete exploitation.

Antitrust Implications Regarding Student-Athlete Compensation

Much of what is wrong with regard to not paying college athletes and not *competing* for their services has been addressed in the legal literature as potential violation of antitrust laws.[13] The basic theory of such an action is fairly simple: The NCAA member schools are conspiring in the form of a "covenant not to compete" to keep the student-athletes' compensation fixed at room, board, tuition, and educational fees. In an open, competitive market environment, many athletes would receive greater compensation.

A number of scholars, including Goldman (1990), have addressed this complex antitrust

---

3. See e.g. Lee Goldman, "Sport and antitrust: Should College Students Be Paid to Play?" *Notre Dame L. Rev., 206* (1990); Note, "Sherman Act Invalidation of the NCAA Amateurism Rules," 105 *Harv. L. Rev.,* 1299 (1992).

issue. The analogy is a relatively simple one: If all employers of college graduates in a particular field, say electrical engineering, agreed that they would all offer only the below-market-value wage of $100 per week to these graduates, there is the potential for a finding of two broad violations of antitrust law. First, Section 1 of the Sherman Act maintains that conspiracies to fix wages (as well as other forms of conspiracy) are illegal. Section 2 of the Act similarly finds existence as a monopoly combined with exertion of that monopoly power to be a violation of the law as well.

The courts have addressed the validity of the NCAA's rule against compensation directly in the case of *McCormack v. NCAA*, which was heard by the Fifth Circuit United States Court of Appeals. The case grew out of the NCAA "death penalty" temporarily suspending the football program at Southern Methodist University due to continued violations of NCAA rules, including payments made to SMU athletes in violation of NCAA rules. The argument by the SMU affiliated plaintiffs was that the NCAA rules against compensation constituted price-fixing and therefore violated the Sherman Act. There were a number of procedural problems, but in the end the court ruled that the restraints were reasonable. Rationalizing the reasonableness of the restraints, the court stated,

> The NCAA markets college football as a product distinct from professional football. The eligibility rules [regarding compensation] create the product and allow its survival in the face of commercializing pressures. The goal of the NCAA is to integrate athletics with academics. Its requirements reasonably further this goal. (*McCormack v. NCAA,* 1988, p. 1344–1345, cited in *NCAA v. Board of Regents of the University of Oklahoma*)

The *McCormack* court concluded, essentially, that NCAA restraints on compensation are reasonable. The test for what is reasonable under antitrust scrutiny of NCAA rules evolved fully under *NCAA v. Board of Regents of the University of Oklahoma* (1984). The Supreme Court, in *Board of Regents,* asserted that the reasonableness of a rule under antitrust laws will be gauged as to whether it is a "justifiable means of fostering competition among amateur athletic teams, and therefore enhances public interest in intercollegiate athletics" (*McCormack,* 1988, p. 117) the NCAA made just that argument. The further argument is that the existing compensation structure promotes the NCAA's image and secures its competitive position among sports enterprises. Essentially, everyone expects that college athletes will not be paid, and the court supported this.

More recently, the broader issue of NCAA institutions acting in concert on a matter was reviewed by the Third Circuit United States Court of Appeals in *United States v. Brown* (1993). That case did not review pay to athletes, but the "uniform determination" by Ivy League institutions as to the amount of financial aid offered to individual needy students. Such agreements have been determined to be illegal. It is not difficult to make the leap in logic from that financial aid agreement constituting a conspiracy and a violation of the law to agreements to pay a set rate to scholar athletes. The *Brown* case certainly sets the stage for yet another potential "pay-for-play" lawsuit.

Finally, in 1998, a jury awarded a verdict of $67 million in holding that the NCAA's rules restricting the earnings of a class of coaches to an annual salary of $16,000 violated the antitrust laws ("NCAA Ordered," 1998). This serves as further amplification of the point that the NCAA can be found to violate the antitrust laws.

Antitrust laws provide us with an additional piece to the compensation puzzle. Any across-the-board fixed rate of compensation could be subject to antitrust scrutiny as well. Thus, an agreement by all NCAA members to pay all student-athletes a wage of, for example, $150 per month arguably violates antitrust laws. There must be competitive bidding for services.

Profit, Title IX, Nonrevenue Sports, and Other Legal Constraints

There are at least three broad issues, beyond those discussed thus far, that opponents to increased student-athlete compensation raise in asserting that it is impractical to pay college athletes: first, that most college athletic programs actually lose money; second, that Title IX of the Civil Rights Act of 1964, as amended by the Education Amendments of 1972, makes any form of compensation beyond the existing structure impossible; finally, that if only the revenue-generating athletes are paid, the nonrevenue sports and participants will be treated unfairly.

Regarding the first issue, the 1996 NCAA biannual study of the finances of colleges found that the typical Division IA program had an average profit of about $1.2 million, with revenues of $15.5 million and expenses of $14.3 million ("Study: Typical IA Program," 1996) Even with this profitable average, many athletic programs still operate in the red. Increased compensation to student-athletes would require a shift in institutional spending priorities. Any change in the compensation to student-athletes would have a dramatic impact on the budgets of these colleges and universities. Thus, restructuring of spending priorities would be a natural accompaniment. As in the rest of society, a great deal of reengineering would be necessary.

The positive role of Title IX and the nonrevenue-generating sports must be incorporated in any change as well. The restrictions of Title IX on this compensation issue are a classic example of regulations impacting market activity. The goal of Title IX is so important that any impact it would have on compensation to revenue-generating athletes is just part of the price that must be paid to bring about equity for women in athletics. With this in mind, one coach noted,

> I agree it [payment of stipends] would be wonderful if it could be done, but when you're looking at the number of athletic

departments that are running in the red already and the fact that if you are going to do it for revenue-producing sports—football and basketball—you also are going to have to do it for a similar number of female athletes. . . . I just don't think it's feasible. (Feigen, 1991, p. 1)

If increased compensation is allowed, some member institutions may determine that they would prefer not to pay athletes. Other decisions may be made on an NCAA sports-conference-by-conference basis. As the popularity of women's basketball continues to grow, so too will its revenue-generating potential. With this occurring, paying men's and women's basketball players and maintaining gender equity may be the initial step.

This essay does not seek to determine the manner or amount of payments. Others have presented suggestions, and these should be explored more fully (Goplerud, 1996). The point is that changes should occur. The rules against compensation are outdated and, according to recent antitrust decisions, may even be illegal, but any change must incorporate in its new structure the value of nonrevenue-generating sports and women's athletics as well.

Conclusion

Should student-athletes receive increased compensation, and is there any reason for a specific concern with African American student-athletes? *Fairness* strikes me as the clearest reason. If revenues are available, then they should be channeled directly to the revenue-generating athletes. Another reason increased compensation should be considered is the prevention of opportunistic behavior by sports agents and individuals.

The NCAA has, in recent years, made much progress in recognizing this problem, but unless the market for compensation is opened more broadly, the opportunistic problems will continue to exist. Sometimes there is a blur between opportunism, greed, need, and stupidity. In 1996, a top collegiate basketball player told a reporter that he accepted $1,000 from a sports agent to buy his family Christmas gifts. Increased compensation certainly will not alleviate all of these problems, but for many, a few additional dollars per month may prevent involvement in some very negative situations.

The limitations on the amount of compensation a student-athlete may receive allow for opportunism. If an athlete desires more than the amount allowed by the rules, where else might he or she turn? For some, the answer is not difficult: Call home to the family. The student-athlete's family may provide that difference in the amount received via scholarship and the amount above room, board, tuition, educational fees, and limited part-time work. The NCAA too allows for some emergency and additional grant support. Unfortunately, the gap between the maximum amount allowable and the amount a student-athlete might receive is genuine. Who is hit the hardest by this? The athlete from the family that cannot fill that gap. Those athletes, no matter the race, but certainly with regard to income level, are the most vulnerable. Student-athletes in the gap are predominantly African Americans. For this reason, African Americans are the most likely to be prey to opportunistic behavior.

Fairness is the major topic to be revisited, and in this, the valid query is whether this group of athletes, made up in large part by African Americans, should continue to be the disproportionate financier of collegiate athletics. The transition away from this mode is more difficult than just beginning to write weekly paychecks. All of this points to one certainty—NCAA regulations regarding compensation are due for a major overhaul.

Suggested Readings

Becker, G. S. (1985, September). College athletes should get paid what they are worth. *Business Week,* 18.

Byers, W. (1995). *Unsportsmanlike conduct: Exploiting college athletes.* Ann Arbor, MI: University of Michigan Press.

Davis, T. (1995). The myth of the super-spade: The persistence of racism in college athletics. *Fordham Urban Law Journal, 22,* 615.

Eitzen, S. D., & Sage, G. H. (1993). *Sociology of North American sport* (5th ed.). New York: WCB/McGraw-Hill.

Fleisher, A. A., Goff, B. L., & Tollison, R. D. (1992). *The National Collegiate Athletic Association: A study in cartel behavior.* Chicago: The University of Chicago Press.

Lawrence, P. R. (1987). *Unsportsmanlike conduct.* New York: Praeger Publishers.

McMillen, T. (1992). *Out of bounds: How the American sports establishment is being driven by greed and hypocrisy—and what needs to be done about it.* New York: Simon & Schuster.

Telander, R. (1989). *The hundred yard lie: The corruption of college football and what we can do to stop it.* New York: Simon & Schuster.

Trope, M. (1987). *Necessary roughness: The other game of football exposed by its most controversial superagent.* Chicago: Contemporary Books.

Wong, G. W. (1988). *Essentials of amateur sports law.* Newton, MA: Auburn House.

Study Questions:

1. Where were the collegiate concepts of amateurism developed? How valid is this foundation?

2. Are any restrictions on compensation to student-athletes specifically designed to target African Americans?

3. What rationale is there for allowing college coaches to receive additional compensation for endorsing products, such as sneakers, and not student-athletes? Is this differing treatment fair?

4. What are the distinctions between Olympic and collegiate amateur athletes? Should there be variations in the levels of compensation each is allowed to receive?

5. Are African Americans more negatively impacted by rules against compensation than White athletes? Why or why not?

6. Generally, what level of compensation may student-athletes receive?

7. What are the participation levels of African Americans in revenue vs. nonrevenue-generating sports?

8. What type of opportunistic behavior may occur due to the absence of adequate compensation to student-athletes?

9. Do the antitrust laws allow the NCAA to bar schools from paying student-athletes?

10. How difficult does it become to pay student-athletes in schools when Title IX is applicable?

References

Ashe, A. (1988). *A hard road to glory*. New York: Warner Books.

Bell, Derrick. (1992). *Faces at the bottom of the well: The permanence of racism*. New York: BasicBooks.

Brown, R. (1993, October). An estimate of the revenue generated by a premium college football player. *Economic Inquiry, 31*, 671.

Copeland, J. L. (1997, January 20). Delegates ok key athlete-welfare legislation. *NCAA News*, p. 1.

Davis, T. (1992). Examining educational malpractice jurisprudence: Should a cause of action be created for student-athletes? *Denver University Law Review, 64*, 57.

Davis, T. (1996). African American student-athletes: Marginalizing the NCAA regulatory structure. *Marquette Sports Law Journal, 6*(2), 199–227.

NCAA ordered to pay $67 million to Division I coaches. (1998, May 31). *Entertainment Litigation Reporter, 1*, 3.

Feigen, J. (1991, March 31). Green with envy: Athletes earn college and NCAA money, but what's in it for them? *Houston Chronicle*, p. 1.

Goldberg, C. (1997, January 30). Hispanic households struggle as poorest of the poor in U.S. *The New York Times*, p. A1.

Golden, D. (1995, March 26). Hoop schemes: coaches prosper from shoe deals. *Boston Globe*, p. 1.

Goldman, L. (1990). Sports and antitrust: Should athletes be paid to play. *Notre Dame Law Review, 66*, 206.

Goplerud, C. P. (1996, Spring). Stipends for collegiate athletes: A philosophical spin on a controversial proposal. *Kansas Journal of Law and Public Policy, 1*, 125–131.

Heath, T. (1996, July 6). For some Olympians, gold fetches top dollar. *The Washington Post*, p. A1.

Lapchick, R. E,. *1997 Racial report card, college special edition*. Boston: Northwestern University's Center for the Study of Sport in Society.

McCormack v. NCAA, 845 F.2d 1338 (5th Cir. 1988).

NCAA Bylaw 15.2, 1997–98 NCAA Division I Manual. Overland Park, KS: NCAA.

NCAA v. Board of Regents of the University of Oklahoma, 468 U.S. 85 (1984).

Naughton, J. (1996, August 2). NCAA panel seeks to allow athletes to borrow against future earnings. *The Chronicle of Higher Education*, p. A29.

Noll, R. G. (1991). The economics of intercollegiate sports. In J. Andre & D. N. James (Eds.), *Rethinking college athletics* (pp. 197–209). Philadelphia: Temple University Press.

Sandomir, R. (1996, July 24). ABC locks up bowl game for no. 1. *The New York Times*, p. B15.

Sellers, R. M., Kuperminc, G. P., & Waddell, A. S. (1991). Life experiences of Black student-athletes in revenue producing sports: A descriptive empirical analysis. *Academic Athletic Journal*, 21–38.

Shropshire, K. L. (1990). *Agents of opportunity: Sports agents and corruption in collegiate sports*. Philadelphia: University of Pennsylvania Press.

Shropshire, K. L. (1991). Legislation for the glory of sport: Amateurism and compensation. *Seton Hall Journal of Sport Law, 7*.

Shropshire, K. L. (1996a, September 18). College athletes deserve pay. *USA Today*, p. 15A.

Shropshire, K. L. (1996b) *In Black and white: Race and sports in America*. New York: New York University Press.

Smith, R. A. (1988). *Sports and freedom: The rise of big-time college athletics*. New York: Oxford University Press.

Study: Typical IA program is $1.2 in the Black. (1996, November 18). *NCAA News*, p. 1.

Thurow, R. (1996, November 12). Go, team, go. Win one for the logo! *Wall Street Journal*, p. B12.

United States v. Brown, 5 F.3d 658 (1993).

Young, D. C. (1985). *The Olympic myth of Greek amateur athletics*. Chicago: Ares Publishers.

Where Is the White in the Rainbow Coalition?

Carole Oglesby and Diana Schrader

Abstract

This essay focuses attention on racism: initially a creation of White people and a present and continuing dynamic from which each individual must actively disengage. Racial identity, as one aspect of personal identity among participants in the social institution of sport, is explored. Action plans are described whereby each of us may dedicate a "tithe of time" to color-affirming behavior. One person's journey, through experiential education, is detailed.

Key Terms

- Blame the victim -
- Cross-racial relationships -
- Comparison and contrasts between prejudice and racism -
- Institutionalized privilege -
- Personal, research, and programmatic action steps -
- Racial and ethnic identity -

Introduction

Over the past two decades, there has been occasional prominence of the term *Rainbow Coalition*, signifying a new majority composed of Blacks, browns, reds, yellows, and Whites working together towards a bright tomorrow for all. It was a shining promise exceedingly slow to materialize. One of the problems in the actualization of this coalition seems to be the weakness of White support, generally, for systematic efforts to mitigate the problem of racism in America. "We are not racists" and "No problem here" are comments that stand in the place of hard-eyed commitment to end the problem, and this is true in sports and athletics as well as in other aspects of American life (Lapchick, 1984).

This book is filled with "facts" cataloguing the existence of racism in sports and athletics. These facts range from exclusions of the past and present, stereotypes and myths that lead to stacking African American players in only some positions with life-long career effects, disproportionate ratios of African American players to coaches, to simple pay inequities (Case, Greer, & Brown, 1987; Lapchick, 1984; Leonard, Pine, & Rice, 1988). The list is endless and will not be the central focus of this essay. The spotlight here is on the White person, especially the career educator-professional, involved in sport and athletics. We will look at the following questions:

1. What is the "face" of the racism we practice daily—what does it look like?
2. What is our own White racial identity, and why do we so resist the idea that we have one?
3. What is the price we pay for any complicity in racism?
4. What are the steps we can take to change and enhance the future in our increasingly multiracial, multicultural society?

The Face of Racism on the Gym Floor, Court, or Field

As White persons in a White-dominant society, we have had the privilege to determine if, when, and under what conditions we would encounter African American people. In order to begin to comprehend the full meaning of racism in sport, we must remember that near-total segregation was the social rule until the early 1950s. Professional colleagues (coaches, administrators, officials) who are African American and over age 45 probably first attended regional or national tournaments or AAHPERD conventions while residing in "colored hotels" and eating in "colored restaurants." Their first professional memberships may well have been in Black coaching or teaching organizations. Black sport participation was limited to certain (far from ideal) facilities and leagues. The "breaking of the color line" by Jackie Robinson in professional baseball, Chuck Cooper in basketball, and Althea Gibson in tennis is an easily recalled personal, as well as collective, history for many of us. This segregation was rationalized and enforced by Whites, like slavery before it, on the basis of beliefs of racial inferiority, and we must acknowledge this reality.

Beliefs, practices, and policies that directly or indirectly have racial implications and impacts abound in our sporting past and have been eradicated slowly, unevenly, and only minimally. One of the principal obstacles to desirable change is the reluctance of the White athletic establishment to say straightforwardly, "We have a race challenge here, and we are prepared to work on it."

There is a deep misunderstanding of the power and institutionalized privilege vested in a White-dominant group. Precisely because one is a member of a dominant group, there is little awareness of group membership.

I have come to see White privilege as an invisible package of unearned assets that I can count on cashing in each day, but about which I was "meant" to remain oblivious. White privilege is like an invisible weightless knapsack of special provisions, assurances, tools, maps, guides, codebooks, passports, visas, clothes, compass, emergency gear, and blank checks. (McIntosh, 1998, pp. 94–95)

To be exercising the privilege of Whiteness is not necessarily to be hating Blacks but "simply" assuming that White is the norm. For example, nobody in the National Collegiate Athletic Association (NCAA) leadership thought it strange that the early work on the (then) "Prop. 48" regulations was conducted by a commission of college presidents who were all White, although the effects of the regulations almost wholly impacted on Blacks. The policies and practices of society, and its components, need not be malicious to be racist.

We really need to be clear about the distinction between two important words: prejudice and racism. Jones (1972) subsumed the work of Allport and others to develop helpful definitions of these concepts:

Prejudice is the prior negative judgement of the members of a race, or religion, or the occupants of any other significant social role, held in disregard of facts that contradict it. (p. 171)

Racism is the transformation of race prejudice through the exercise of *power* against a racial group defined as inferior, by individuals and institutions with the intentional or unintentional support of the entire culture. (p. 172)

Prejudices are attitudes or expectations that members of one group hold about another. On an athletic team where race-based conflict or alienation is prominent, the African American and White group members may each reflect highly prejudicial expectations. By definition, however, the African American group members are not *racist*. They cannot be. They do not have the institutionalized power to control or inflict damage on the White team members. For example, if some kind of grievance is brought by a Black athlete against a White, as the griev-

ance works its way through the "system"— NCAA, NAIA, or the college itself—the Black athlete will find her- or himself in an ever "Whiter" group as the proceedings go on. Whether in proceedings that are legal, political, scientific, medical, or economic, the African American is practically always playing a game made up by (and of) "White folks." Whites practically never face such a situation vis-à-vis African Americans. The *NCAA News* (October 10, 1988) banner-lined the underrepresentation of Blacks in all athletic jobs, with only 6% of full-time athletic administrative positions held by Blacks. (If numbers from the staffs at historically Black colleges were removed, the figures would be worse.) Smith (1991) stated that 92 to 95% of all physical education teaching, coaching, and sport leadership positions are filled by Whites. The sense of being the "different/other" in the surrounding social systems brings feelings of powerlessness and alienation that White-dominant group members have not, yet now must, come to understand.

Although we might wish to believe otherwise, our American collegiate sport system has functioned in accord with other elements of our racist society. By policy and practice, African American colleges, teams, and individuals have been excluded, controlled, labeled and stereotyped, and ignored. In sport, we know from Yogi Berra, "It ain't over 'til it's over," and in regard to racism and sport, it ain't over!

One exclusion of the past was the absence of coverage on the printed page. Another was absence from most important fields of play. Grambling's great football teams never got the chance to test the mettle of a Notre Dame or an Army. A "color line" is still there, however, and we have got to see it. Exclusion today principally takes the form of economic closed doors. The great majority of African American players are located in a few, public-school-accessible sports. Many other sports have few performers of color because of the high costs of equipment, apparel, coaching or lessons, facility rental, medical care, travel to competitions and housing, geographic limitations, and the pressure of home responsibilities for child care or earnings to supplement the family income. Certainly for the growing Black upper and middle classes, these are surmountable problems. For a larger segment of racial minority populations, however, without specific affirmative plans to change the status quo, the doors will not open. Another example of exclusion of the African American athlete, from the benefit of athletics, can be seen in the data from a recently published report of the Women's Sport Foundation (1989):

> Consistent with patterns of racial and ethnic inequality elsewhere in America, it was mainly Whites for whom athletic participation proved to be related to upward mobility after high school. With some exceptions, high school sport served as a reinforcer of White privilege, giving advantage to those already advantaged. (p. 4)

Our responses to data like this typically have been to define the academic or employment unreadiness of African American youth as an individual problem with each student's ability or effort. We have refused to see the complicity of our educational, social, and economic system in these results. This is cultural and institutional racism. It sits down to eat with us at every training table; it has a ringside seat on the bench and in the bleachers; it hangs on the lanyard of each coach and official. How have we acquired this unwelcome guest? One aspect of the answers to these questions involves personal racial identity.

White Racial Identity

In the late 1970s, there were at least two research efforts directed towards the examination of Black racial identity (Cross, 1978; Young, 1979). Young presented Hardiman and Jackson's five-stage model, which evolved through the application of Piagetian developmental psychology principles. Cross's theory of racial identity consisted of four stages, ranging from a denial of identity as an African

American to cultural acceptance of one's race and appreciation of other races.

The past 20 years have seen an exponential growth in research on racial identity including specific focus on Asians (Kim, 1981), Latinos (Acre, 1981; Garcia, 1982), African Americans (Helms, 1990; Parham & Williams, 1993), and Whites (Carter, 1995; Helms & Carter, 1990).

This essay does not attempt to summarize and describe the research on racial identity, its development and consequences. For such a review, the reader is referred to the line of work from Hall (Hall, 1996; Hall & Bowers, 1992; Hall & Green, 1995), the first to specifically examine racial and ethnic identity and athletic participation.

Of importance here is the recognition that "White" is a feature of identity among Caucasian Americans. Helms's work illustrates that racial identity is an integral aspect of self-perception and that both Black and White racial identities are influenced by the degree and type of contact with members of other racial groups.

After examining identity among African American and White athletes at both predominantly African American and White institutions, Hall (1996) concluded,

> Even though it is challenging for privileged groups to appreciate the relevance of their ethnic identity, a greater awareness of ethnic identity for White ethnic groups could enhance their own identity development, similar to the enhancement provided by athletic involvement and identity as an athlete. (p. 64)

In athletics and sports, today and in the future, the identities of color will be increasingly seen as influences in personal and social dynamics. To be successful and effective, White leaders and participants will need to find a way to perceive (and separate from) early stages of White racial identity. These early stages are simply a legacy of unconscious White privilege. Coming to terms with this past legacy is much more difficult than most are willing to believe.

The Price We Pay as Whites for Arrested Racial Identity Development

Being aligned with institutionalized power is highly rewarding in many respects. The automatic positive connotations associated with Whiteness are seductive to accept at face value, and attempts to be overtly antiracist can result in feeling outcast by Whites and Blacks. It is the contention of this essay that the "benefits" of accepting racism in one's social milieu must be balanced against the price paid, knowingly or not, by the complicit White. Part of the price is related to external considerations of "marketability" in a multicultural, global village. Another part of the price is clarified when we examine the profound psychological damage possible due to unexamined dominance beliefs.

The data are clear that today's "minorities" are tomorrow's numerical majority. The 1990 census documented a dramatically changing racial mix in American society. African Americans, Hispanics, and Asian Americans all form demographic cohorts that education, business, and political institutions are hurrying to court. White Americans who are unable to work, play, and be comfortable with diverse groups; who are resistant to yielding to a Black superior or establishing an equitable relationship with a Black coworker will simply be left behind in the 21st century. Duda and Allison (1990) recently have described how it will be extremely difficult to function appropriately in applied sport psychology research and intervention work without sensitivity to relevant racial/ethnic differences in life experiences, perceptions, and needs.

These authors make their point even more powerfully when they assert that "restricting the study of the psychological aspects of sport and exercise to predominantly one group (mainstream) is in conflict with the nature of scientific inquiry" (Duda & Allison, 1990, p. 129). In truth, to ignore the research and educational situation of the racially diverse is not simply to pass over a peripheral issue in sport

and athletics. It is a violation of core tenets of the scientific and educational process.

Increasingly, departmental curricula will not be judged acceptable by external reviewers without diversity issues being fully addressed. Even now, our various professional certifications are beginning to include competencies in working with diverse groups. Each of us, trained before such requirements were in place, must view this as an area where in-service training and upgrading experiences are necessary. An old spiritual has a refrain about "the freedom train leavin' better get on board." Surely it will be unaware Whites left at the station this time if we do not bestir ourselves from complacency.

Of even greater concern is the profound personal damage exacted when lengthy training and socialization in the fear and ignorance of racism create an insidious cruelty in the hearts of many White people. A recent Associated Press release (Welch, 1991) described the reasons we cannot simply discount the White "racial problem:"

> America's racial and ethnic make-up is diversifying, and so is hatred in this country. . . . A good deal of what is going on is genuine culture conflict, which then calls out the sort of underlying prejudice and racism that exists in society as a whole. . . . The majority of hate-inspired crimes, ranging from murders to vandalism, remain acts by Whites against Blacks, homosexuals, or Jews.

Hallie (1969) conducted an extensive study of cruelty as viewed in the medieval and modern world. In his section on slavery in the United States, he comments on the strange manner in which the practice of slavery led to a "savage, ignoble hatred of the Negro" (p. 106). He points out that not all slavery took the same form. In Spain, for example, slaves could marry in the church and remain together as a family, testify in court concerning cruelty by the master, and buy freedom upon earning a fixed sum. None of these options was allowed in America. We are heirs to a past with a particularly violent form of cruelty.

This scholarly analysis of cruelty reveals that it is not always practiced by a sadistic person, nor is it always in the form of dramatic torture. Hallie (1969) describes vividly how cruelty can be institutionalized in a faceless way and, in fact, be unintended: "A victimizer need not want to hurt a victim—he needs only to want something which requires him to hurt the victim" (p. 13). Particularly he defines cruelty as holding a person (as prisoner; controlling a person) without allowing the freedom of humane existence.

Thus, we are able to see cruelty in the treatment of African Americans in the sport system. To stack players is to control them, to restrict them from the opportunity to fill a position their talents might have earned. To utilize hiring criteria that keep racial minority people from being chosen also is a cruel act. The speed of enactment of the "Prop. 48 style" academic requirements, with so little examination of the ramifications for athletes, was a further recent example of institutional cruelty. This latter example appears to be a textbook case of "blame the victim." As Young (1979) states, "The logical outcome of analyzing social problems in terms of the deficiencies of the victim is the development of programs aimed at correcting those deficiencies. The formula for action becomes extraordinarily simple: change the victim" (p. 15).

From differing vantage points, and using differing analysis techniques, Young (1979) and Hallie (1969) come to similar conclusions. The devastating aspect of institutionalized cruelty, with regard to the *victimizers*, is that ultimately it "veils our precious disgust with the destruction of human life" (Hallie, 1969, p. 103) and decent, ordinary people (sometimes even the victims) go along with these systematic abuses. We can see this "loss of our precious disgust" today in the White flight from the cities and the lack of involvement most professionals exhibit with the terrible conditions physical educators and coaches face in many urban school systems.

Oh yes, we may think these various situations are "a shame," but what are we specifically *doing*, individually or in our associations, to make things different? Tolerating cruelty to others, like performing cruel acts, ultimately dehumanizes the victimizer, and our souls and hearts may be diminished beyond redeeming. This does not have to happen. There are examples before us of affirmative steps, small and large, that can be taken. As White professionals, we need to commit ourselves to continual involvement, for a portion of our working hours, in antiracist activity. We do this, not so much on behalf of African American people, but on behalf of ourselves. "The opposite of cruelty is not kindness; it is freedom" (Hallie, 1969, p. 159).

Steps to Enhance Our Multiracial Future

There are three differing types of steps to be described here. Some of the proposed steps are large in scope, and some are small. Many are related, not mutually exclusive of one another, and could be approached in clusters. In our own experience, however, it has proved valuable not to take on too much antiracist activity at one time. It has seemed most productive to make efforts a "tithe of time," which never stops yet never demands so much we burn out. Efforts will be described that are *personal*, *research oriented*, and *programmatic*. These are samples of types of steps that can be taken. Many other examples abound, and it is too bad that credit cannot be extended to all.

Personal Efforts

A first step for the antiracist White person is the pursuit of an "education" in African American studies, especially in regards to physical education and sport. Most institutions, even night schools or continuing education, at least have a class (perhaps much more) that would enable a deeper awareness of African American culture.

Some people reach out to racial minority acquaintances in hopes that "some of my best friends" can give a "quick read" on people of color. Certainly, I am indebted to many Temple University colleagues and students who have taken me as far as they could. It is not fair for us as Whites to place our whole burden of ignorance on our Black friends. It is up to us to attend lectures, read books, go to conferences, take classes, and do volunteer projects in order to increase racial awareness.

It has been pointed out that a person need not be born in the South, nor the urban Northeast, to develop racist attitudes. These can be learned in Wyoming, Minnesota, or any White suburb. Thus, racism is particularly a White creation and a White problem to be solved. The term "White on White" racial awareness training has been coined (University of Massachusetts School of Education) to designate the focus for White efforts at self-education, social consciousness-raising, and commitment to life change with regard to racism (Edler, 1974; Fromkin & Sherwood, 1976; Katz, 1978; Matthew, 1988; Smith, 1991).

Once educators learn something, they usually become invested in "teaching it." As these self-educational projects proceed, you may soon want to offer units or entire classes on these topics. "African American in Sport" units or classes can multiply information available, and school projects focusing on the local community can unearth remarkable local figures who have never been recognized for their sport accomplishments.

More difficult, more volatile, will be efforts to present experiential classes or units focusing on racial dynamics in school physical education classes and on sport teams. Such classes are very valuable, but specialized training in the conduct and handling of this type of psychological education is necessary for some (if not all) of the staff. It seems likely that only by proceeding through intellectual matters into the areas of emotions and past personal history will

emerge the identity we might designate as the *Color-Affirming White* (CAW)—the "CAWs with a cause!" This is a White individual who is committed to building an equitable, racially diverse network of relationships and an antiracist lifestyle. We need CAWs in physical education and athletics.

A case study of experiential education. One of the co-authors enrolled in a graduate course at Temple University devoted to expanding awareness of and commitment to improved race relations in sport. What follows are excerpts from her class journal.

Like many people who grew up in America during the 1960s, I have been interested in issues of racism and social justice since childhood. My parents were active in our community and when I was 10 years old, they participated in a local project designed to diversify the student population of our all-White high school. For 2 years, we had an African American high school student from an Alabama city living with us while he attended high school. He got an education and opportunities not available had he gone to high school in his hometown. I had an opportunity to know someone from a background much different from the small, Middle-Atlantic college town I knew.

After about 13 years working as a psychotherapist and activities therapist in hospitals and day-treatment programs with severely mentally ill patients, I was ready for a change and returned to school to study sport psychology. My commitment and interest in issues of racism, prejudice, and social justice were renewed with my first class, which was entitled "Minorities in American Sport." As would be expected, much of the class dealt with issues of institutional racism in various areas of sport participation, coaching, and administration, as well as our own experiences of race and prejudice. The class included a wide diversity of students, racially, ethnically, and attitudinally. Some were athletes, whereas others were studying marketing, education, psychology, or business. I renewed my interest and observations in areas of race and social justice and found that I could no longer deny the degree to which they affect my own life. I found the journey to be enlightening and confronting, rewarding, and challenging. I found myself engaged in new questions, experiences, and actions.

During the course of this inquiry, one of the things I began to confront was the whole concept of "White privilege." I have always believed that people should be treated fairly and with respect, regardless of skin color, age, sex, nationality, religion, or any other such attribute. As is often the case when one exists in some aspect of privilege, I believed that most other White people operated from the same beliefs. It had never seriously occurred to me that I was really treated differently simply by virtue of being White. The reality of White privilege struck me in a dramatic way following this incident involving a coworker, who happened to be an African American woman.

In my work as an activities therapist, I am engaged in leading a wide variety of therapeutic activities for psychiatric patients, both adults and adolescents. One day, a coworker called me and stated that she needed to use the grocery account provided by the hospital to facilitate shopping for cooking activities. She knew that I use the account frequently and asked if there would be a problem because she had forgotten her work ID. I responded that I did not remember ever having been asked for my ID. When she returned from the store, I was very surprised at the story she related concerning the difficulty she had encountered regarding being allowed to use the account.

Previously, I would probably have thought that this colleague was exaggerating or misinterpreting the situation, or that this was "mere coincidence." Due to new sensitivities sparked by our class, I began to listen more seriously to all such stories of discrimination that I heard from my minority coworkers, friends, and clients/patients. I began to take more notice of the way other people relate to and treat me, as distinct from their treatment of people of minority groups. I began to feel uncomfortable about the advantages I have had, of which I had

never before been aware, simply by virtue of being a White person and having been born into circumstances over which I had no control. Yet, along with the discomfort, I realized that I cannot always offer to my clients the same coping strategies that I employ myself. I began to explore new ways in which I can support them in building healthy, productive lives.

During the course of this inquiry, I also became aware that the number of minority patients we serve at work had been increasing, but it struck me most clearly when I sat down with the patients on the adolescent unit to start the scheduled activity and noticed that not one of them was White. The entire group was African American and Hispanic. Suddenly, I felt completely inadequate to the task, so essential for a psychotherapist, of establishing a basis for trust and relationship with them. I became aware at a much deeper level than before that my life experience has been very different from theirs, simply because I am White, without consideration of other important cultural, economic, and social factors. I began to wonder how these young people view yet another White woman who claims to want to help them. Of course, there continues to be a basis for relationship promoted in our shared humanness, rooted in the truth that I, too, was once a teenager with many of the same concerns and feelings that most teenagers experience. I am now aware that I can never fully understand what their lives are like, and I have become more aware of the cultural factors that so powerfully influence their lives. Rather than assume that I know what their life experiences have been like, I listen to them carefully and in a new way, in an attempt to gain a sense, however small, of their everyday experiences. I now work to support them in building new skills that will support them in living healthy lives in their own environments.

During the period of being in the course, I had an opportunity to attend a professional conference, "Race, Prejudice, and Psychoanalysis: Treatment Issues." All of the presenters were distinguished psychiatrists who are also trained as psychoanalysts, published and highly respected in their field. All were either African American or Hispanic, some men and some women. I noticed myself being surprised by some of the comments, not because of the comment, but because they were being made by people of color. They spoke about "Black on Black" prejudice, as some of the presenters spoke of experiences they have had in which their same-group patients had expressed a disdain for their minority-group psychiatrist or had expressed a preference for a White psychiatrist. I wondered if Black coaches deal with Black players who prefer a White coach.

When I returned from the conference, my supervisor asked me to give our staff an in-service about what I had learned. Though the in-service actually went very well, I was acutely aware of my own discomfort in discussing these issues of racism in psychotherapy with a staff that included two African American women, two White women besides myself, and our supervisor, who is a White man raised in Mississippi. Contrary to my expectation that my African American coworkers would be "experts" in the subject, I found everyone equally engaged in the discussion, each expressing personal frustrations and concerns with various aspects of the issue. We were able to discuss the issue as peers, cooperatively, without resentment or blame. I was pleased at our ability to deal productively with an issue that is so potentially divisive, and I experienced a new depth of relationship with my coworkers.

Even now, almost a year after the class, I am periodically alerted to the prejudice that breeds unbidden and unwanted inside, despite my conscious beliefs and efforts. Today, I had an initial appointment with a new doctor, well respected and affiliated with one of the Center City teaching hospitals. As I sat in the waiting room, I noticed that a large number of the patients were African American. It suddenly occurred to me that the doctor might also be African American, and I was dismayed to observe the immediate discomfort and anxiety that followed. I realized that I had never before

been bothered by the idea because I had assumed that the doctor would be White. I began to imagine myself being treated by an African American doctor, just as I have worked with very capable African American professionals in other areas.

Overall, I found this exploration of racial issues to be both uncomfortable and rewarding. Old awareness has been rekindled, and new awareness has emerged. I now believe my friends, coworkers, and clients who relate experiences of discrimination. I have become aware of the reality of White privilege and the effects it can have, both on myself and on others. I have discovered that I must develop and utilize new skills and coping strategies for my minority-group clients/patients that can be utilized in the environments in which they live. Particularly important for members of minority groups is learning when and how to speak up for themselves, and when to be quiet and cope in some other way.

I have also become more aware of the people around me and have become more sensitive to the ways in which I may be perceived by those of minority groups. I am learning that maybe I can impact the "instinctive" responses that minority individuals may have toward me by being more aware of ways in which I can present myself in order to be perceived according to my commitment to racial equity. I no longer subscribe to the idea that being racially color-blind is a solution to this very complex social problem. If I am to relate respectfully to those of minority groups, I must do so with the recognition that in this country, racial prejudice continues to be a subtle and pervasive reality. I must stop denying the unpleasant reality that institutional racism in this country persists and will not be eradicated for many years. I must acknowledge that I can be passive, which will continue to perpetuate the problem, or I can find ways to act as an ally, to use the advantages of White privilege to benefit my friends, coworkers, and clients/patients who happen to have been born into minority groups.

Research Efforts

For those of us whose careers entail scholarly work to advance the body of knowledge of sport and exercise science, a "tithe of time" devoted to race-related inquiry can be helpful. Several authors (Duda & Allison, 1990; Hall, 1996; Lapchick, 1984; Women's Sports Foundation, 1989) have commented on the paucity of such efforts in the past.

It probably needs to be pointed out that comparing subjects from differing race groups on an infinite variety of dependent variables is but the simplest form of any race-related study. That is the predominant form of race-related research in our field to date. Following are many other types of investigations which might valuably be undertaken.

Content analyses. A number of studies could investigate differential descriptors utilized in print-based assessments of athletes, coaches, and administrators of different races. Content analyses of visual materials could also be conducted. Scientific work on subjects from differing racial groups could also be content-analyzed regarding types of variables utilized, complexity of approach, or degree of funding available.

Demographic assessment. During the 1970s and early 1980s, a few demographic studies (Alexander, 1977; Barclay, 1978) first assessed the percentages of racial minority collegiate student-athletes, coaches, and athletic department personnel. Edwards (1983) and Lapchick (1984) have reported similar types of data for males. This effort needs to be maintained continually at national, regional, and local levels for all athletes and personnel. This is our clearest and most direct way to gauge the effectiveness of our efforts (a) to diversify the types of sports experiences of racial minority people; (b) to diversify the racial make-up of sports leadership.

Qualitative/Descriptive work. The efforts of racial minority people to achieve, to excel, and to overcome have created a cohort of "unforgettable people and stories" that essentially has gone untapped and untold. No questionnaire or inventory could capture the essence and the depth of these stories. Masses of undergraduate and graduate students could be sent out into the field to collect interviews and/or case studies of local, regional, and national racial minority figures in every sport. Every day that goes by without such major, systematic efforts means irreparable losses as death erases the story of people whose lives have never made the printed record book.

Experimental studies. A content area of exercise and sport studies might be formulated "race/sport relations." This content area would focus on a historically constructed pattern of power relations between the races. Researchers in this specialization would attempt to study the interactive effects of racial identity (including White racial identity) and all manner of sport-related variables. For example, we could research the possibility that a program to enhance racial identity would impact on the cohesion of a racially diverse sport team. Studies of the interactive effects of sport and racial identity seem important, though unpursued, in our multiracial society.

Outcome Research

Last, as we begin to design and implement programs aimed at enhancing racial understanding, equality, and identity, it will be important to monitor the effectiveness of such programs and constantly improve them. Ongoing outcome research is necessary to accomplish the goals of such efforts. Consistent funding for such research must come from the institutions of sport at the professional, elite amateur, collegiate, secondary, and youth sport levels.

The research efforts described here could be conducted by qualified scholars, whatever their racial background. It seems, however, highly desirable (perhaps necessary initially) for White scholars to team with racial minority students and/or colleagues in the conduct of such studies. It has been my experience that, without such collaboration, unrecognized racist assumptions are built into instruments, measurement procedures, and interpretations.

Programmatic Efforts

The type of antiracist effort that probably makes the greatest impact is one in which a *program* is created, supported within an ongoing organizational base, continuing into the future beyond the energies of those who initially instigated it. The institutionalized form of racism in our society will be fully eradicated only when we have installed enough *anti*racist institutionalized programs to neutralize the historical toxicity of ordinary social life.

One such program is a "low-income" focused swim program that has been running at Temple University for many years. The Tiger-Sharks were created by Malachi Cunningham and aided by Charles Lumpkin, a Temple University faculty member who had been a collegiate All-American in swimming. Both knew that few elite swimmers were African American and that the problem was opportunity and little else. Their program was specifically designed to attract and hold inner-city, low-income youth. The products of this program are now reaching Olympic levels, and there is a delicious irony for the leadership to savor. The success and accessibility of the program have led to an avalanche of requests from "suburban" parents to allow their children to join the Tiger-Sharks. The Sharks have an "affirmative action" program that allows a few suburban youth each year to join, without overwhelming in numbers those for whom the program was created (C. Lumpkin, personal communication, 1991).

A second effort has been the creation of a program at Ben Franklin High School, located within a mile of Temple. With the leadership and driving energy of Cassandra Jones, an Academy for Fitness, Health Promotion, and Sport Education (hereinafter the Academy) was instituted in 1989. This became the latest entry in a town-gown initiative in the city entitled Philadelphia High Schools Academies, Inc. The Academy is an enriched, secondary-school major that is provided to Ben Franklin and advised and supported by an advisory council of Philadelphia sport educators and outstanding business leaders in the local sport and fitness industry. A class of 25 students, from across the city and rigorously screened by Jones, is added each year. The seniors graduating from the Academy are prize candidates for admission to health, physical education, and/or sport management programs across the country.

The antiracist steps described in this last section must be undertaken with the recognition that progress may be slow and that one may well receive little or no recognition for one's efforts. We do these things for our own satisfaction and education and not for the applause or approval of Black or White colleagues and friends. We *can* make a difference, and the firming of the resolve to make a difference in racial matters is a very important step on the path to personal empowerment.

Summary

This essay begins with a description of racism as it has expressed itself in American athletics. The focus is on racism as a White creation, a White problem, and on the negative effects of racism on White racial identity.

It is recommended that each White person make a commitment to a regular "tithe of time and service" in order to become a more color-affirming person. The steps a person might take include personal educative efforts, conduct of research, presentation of workshops or classes, and support of programmatic experiences in schools and communities.

Suggested Readings

Asante, M. (1980). *Afrocentricity: The theory of social change*. Buffalo, NY: Amulefi.

Brittan, A., & Maynard, M. (1984). *Sexism, racism, and oppression*. Oxford, UK: Blackwell.

Cogdell, R., & Wilson, S. (1980). *Black communication in white society*. Saratoga, CA: Century Twenty One.

Comas-Diaz, L., & Green, B. (1994). *Women of color: Integrating ethnic and gender identities in psychotherapy*. New York: Guilford Press.

Dubois, W. E. B. (1903/1965). *Souls of Black folk*. In J. Franklin (Ed.), *Classics*. New York: Avon.

Freire, P. (1970). *Pedagogy of the oppressed*. New York: Seabury Press.

Gurin, P., & Epps, E. (1975). *Black consciousness, identity, and achievement: A study of students in historically black colleges*. New York: Wiley.

Myrdal, G. (1944). *An American dilemma: The Negro problem and modern democracy*. New York: Harper & Brothers.

Poussaint, A., & Comer, J. (1974). *Black child care: How to bring up a healthy black child in America: A guide to emotional and psychological development*. New York: Simon and Schuster.

Study Questions

1. Characterize the role of racial identity in the way power is exercised to ensure domination and control in the limited states.

2. What opportunities exist to use sports for programmatic action to achieve viable multiracial social change?

3. If racism in the United States is largely a "White creation," what kinds of strategies can be used to establish antiracist programs to transform prejudice for ordinary people?

References

Acre, C. (1981). A reconsideration of Chicano culture and identity. *Daedalus*, *110*, 177–192.

Carter, R. (1995). *The influence of race and racial identity in psychotherapy: Toward a racially inclusive model*. New York: Wiley Intersciences.

Case, B., Greer, H., & Brown, J. (1987). Academic clustering in athletics: Myth or reality? *Arena Review*, *11*(2), 48–56.

Cross, W. (1978). Models of psychological nigrescence: A literature review. *Journal of Black Psychology*, *5*, 13–31.

Duda, J., & Allison, M. (1990). Cross cultural analysis in exercise and sport psychology. *Journal of Exercise and Sport Psychology*, *12*, 114–131.

Edler, J. (1974). *White on white: An anti-racism manual for white educators in the process of becoming*. Unpublished doctoral dissertation, University of Massachusetts, Amherst.

Edwards, H. (1983, August). Educating black athletes. *The Atlantic Monthly*, 31–38.

Fromkin, H., & Sherwood, J. (1976). *Intergroup and minority relations: An experiential handbook*. LaJolla, CA: University Associates, Inc.

Garcia, H. (1982). Ethnicity and Chicanos: Measurement of ethnic identification, identity, and consciousness. *Hispanic Journal of Behavioral Science*, *4*, 295–314.

Hall, R. (1996). *Ethnic identity and cross racial experiences of college athletes*. Unpublished master's thesis, Temple University, Philadelphia.

Hall, R., & Bowers, C. (1992). Afrocentricity and womanhood. *Proceedings of the American Psychological Association Centennial Conference*. Washington, DC.

Hall, R., & Green, B. (1995). Cultural competence in feminist family therapy: An ethical mandate. *Journal of Feminist Family Therapy*, *6*(3), 5–28.

Hallie, P. (1969). *The paradox of cruelty*. Middletown, CT: Wesleyan University Press.

Helms, J. (1990). *Black and white racial identity: Theory, research, and practice*. New York: Greenwood.

Helms, J., & Carter, R. (1990). White racial identity attitude scale. In J. Helms (Ed.), *Black and white racial identity: Theory, research, and practice*. New York: Greenwood.

Jones, L. (1972). *Black psychology*. New York: Harper & Row.

Katz, J. (1978). *White awareness: Handbook of anti-racism training*. Norman: University of Oklahoma Press.

Kim, J. (1981). *The process of Asian American identity development: A study of Japanese American women's perception of their struggle to achieve positive identity*. Unpublished doctoral dissertation, University of Massachusetts, Amherst.

Lapchick, R. (1984). *Broken promises*. New York: St. Martin's Marek Press.

Leonard, W., Pine, J., & Rice, C. (1988). Performance characteristics of white, black, and Hispanic Major League Baseball players: 1955–1984. *Journal of Sport and Social Issues*, *12*, 31–43.

Matthew, J. (1988, June 1). Mentor program brings student, faculty, together. *Black Issues in Higher Education*.

McIntosh, P. (1998). White privilege and male privilege. In M. L. Anderson & P. Hill Collins

(Eds.), *Race, class and gender* (3rd ed., pp. 94–105). Belmont, CA: Wadsworth.

Parham, T., & Williams, T. (1993). The relationship of demographic and background factors to racial identity attitudes. *The Journal of Black Psychology, 19*, 7–24.

Smith, Y. (1991, March). Issues and strategies for working with multi-cultural athletes. *Journal of Physical Education, Recreation, and Dance*, 39–44.

Women's Sport Foundation. (1989). *The Women's Sport Foundation report: Minorities in sport*. New York: Author (342 Madison Ave., Suite 728, New York, NY 10173).

Young, V. (1979). *Towards an increased understanding of whiteness in relation to white racism.* Unpublished paper, University of Massachusetts, Department of Psychological Education, Amherst.

Racism in Big-Time College Sport: Prospects for the Year 2020 and Proposals for Change

D. Stanley Eitzen

Abstract

This essay summarizes where we are in race relations as a society and in big-time college athletics, where we are headed in the future, and what changes should be instituted to improve race relations in college sport. Examined first are the two contexts in which male African American athletes participate—the interracial climates of U. S. society and of big-time college sports. Second, this essay examines the trends occurring in society, universities, and in college sports, in order to assess the future for African American athletes. The final section asks and answers: What ought to be done to accomplish social justice for racial minorities in big-time college sports? The recommendations for reforming college sport to eliminate racism address several problems:

1. That African American athletes are sometimes ill-prepared for college academics;
2. That African American athletes often come from economically disadvantaged backgrounds;
3. That African American athletes who are admitted have relatively low graduation rates;
4. That African American athletes are usually isolated in athletic ghettos with racial segregation within them;
5. That African Americans are underrepresented in leadership positions within athletic departments;
6. That some coaches are racist; and
7. That racial stereotypes are sometimes promoted unwittingly by members of athletic departments.

The United States has never lived up to its promise of social justice for all. The essays in this volume show vividly that social justice for African Americans has fallen short, way short, in the college sports world. This is especially ironic because (a) sport is one arena where achievement, not ascribed status, should be the fundamental criterion for participation and reward; and (b) colleges and universities claim to hold progressive ideals, leading by example and by persuasive argument, one would hope, to accomplish a climate of positive race relations in higher education and in society.

Key Terms

- Racism -
- Hypersegregation -
- Role distance -
- Marginalization -
- Stacking -

The Contemporary Context for African Americans in Big-Time College Sports

The Societal Context

The evidence is clear and consistent that African Americans are disadvantaged in the United States. Information for this section is taken from Eitzen & Baca Zinn, 1997, pp. 236–243; Fletcher, 1998, and *The Kerner Report*, Milton S. Eisenhower Foundation, reported in Rubin, 1998. A few examples make this point:

- The median wealth for African American families is one tenth that of White families.
- The unemployment rate for African Americans is twice that for Whites.
- The median family income for African Americans and Latinos is roughly 55% that of their White counterparts. This is explained in part by the lower educational level of African Americans and Latinos, but when controlling for education, Whites still make more. For example, well-educated young African Americans earn only about 85% of what their White counterparts earn.
- African Americans experience discrimination in jobs (getting them, keeping them, and advancing within them).
- Thirty percent of African Americans live in racial isolation in segregated neighborhoods. Housing is where researchers find the most persistent open discrimination.
- Forty percent of minority children attend urban schools, where more than half of the students are poor and fail to reach even "basic" achievement levels. About one third of African Americans attend public schools that are "hypersegregated," that is, 90% or more African American.
- About 3 out of 10 African Americans live below the government's official poverty line. From two to three million poor African Americans are locked in an "underclass" of extreme and long-term deprivation.

Although some African Americans are eco-nomically successful, many are not. The accrued disadvantages stemming from discrimination lead to poorer life chances for most. For example,

- Whites live about ten years longer than African Americans; African American babies are nearly twice as likely as White babies to die within the first year; twenty-two percent of the African American population is without health insurance, compared to 14% of the White population.
- One out of three African American men between ages 20 and 29 is under the jurisdiction of the criminal justice system (in prison, on parole, or on probation), which is higher than the proportion of African American men this age in college (Miller, 1996).
- Fifty-seven percent of all African American children under the age of 18 in 1993 were living with a single parent. Thirty-one percent of all African American children were living with a never-married parent (Wilson, 1996).
- Urban, poor, African American neighborhoods are often saturated with crime, drugs, and dysfunctional schools.

The societal context is characterized by growing racial polarization. Race relations are growing hotter rather than cooler. Racially motivated attacks on individuals and organizations have increased in the past decade (Herman, 1996; Southern Poverty Law Center, 1996). The membership of White supremacist groups is on the rise. Racial tensions are often caused by deteriorating economic conditions—lack of jobs, housing, and other resources—that lead to minority scapegoating on the part of Whites. It is also fueled by the new patterns of immigration that are changing the racial composition of society (Pedraza & Rumbaut, 1996).

Bigotry is not confined to White working-class or poor settings. Racist acts are becoming widespread on college campuses. Instances at the Massachusetts Institute of Technology (MIT); Michigan; University of Massachusetts; University of California, Berkeley; and on other campuses reveal an extensive problem of intolerance in settings where tolerance is essential to the pursuit of knowledge.

Contemporary racial division has been exacerbated by reactionary government policies. Conservative economic strategies during the Reagan and Bush years accelerated the economic decline of racial minorities. These strategies continued during the Clinton presidency as the Republican-controlled Congress teamed with centrist Democrats and the president to reduce or eliminate many social programs and to appoint judges to the federal courts and the Supreme Court who favored the dismantling of civil rights legislation, especially affirmative action and other protections against discrimination for minorities.

Big-Time College Sport

Many economically, socially, and educationally disadvantaged African American males are recruited to play football and basketball in big-time university athletic programs out of this societal environment. These programs are big business operations (the following is taken from Eitzen, 1997; Eitzen & Sage, 1997, pp. 102–109). Some universities have athletic budgets that exceed $33 million. In 1998, each school participating in the Fiesta Bowl received more than $13 million, which it divided with the other schools in its conference. The annual incomes for some of the coaches (from salaries, bonuses, perks, endorsements, shoe contracts, and television and radio programs) approaches $2 million. In 1994, CBS agreed to pay the National Collegiate Athletic Association (NCAA) $1.725 billion ($215.6 million annually) for the television rights to the NCAA men's basketball tournament through 2002. The NCAA generated $234.2 million in revenue for the 1995–1996 fiscal year. Syracuse University has a basketball arena that seats 50,000 and the University of Michigan's football stadium seats 106,000 which it sells out. The University of Florida rents skyboxes at its football games for $30,000 a year, with a minimum 5-year lease. Each year, supporters of

university athletic programs donate about $400 million to them. An estimated $2.5 billion a year in college merchandise is sold under license, generating about $100 million to the schools in royalties. The University of Michigan receives the most income from this source—about $6 million annually. After Kentucky won the NCAA men's basketball tournament in 1996, it received about $3 million in royalties from the sale of basketball-related merchandise (Blumenstyk, 1996).

These examples show that big-time college sport is a large-scale commercial entertainment enterprise. The success of programs at individual schools (and of coaches) depends on winning, media interest, and attracting spectators. This requires getting the best athletes and extracting the most from them. In many cases, this search for talent has led to abuses such as illegal recruiting practices, alteration of transcripts, physical and psychological abuse of athletes, and exploitation of athletes (for summaries, see Byers, 1995; Eitzen, 1997; Sperber, 1990). These programs want winners, and if the past serves as a guide, the public have not cared how they won.

Young men are recruited into this setting. Some athletes are recruited even though their high school records and test scores show they have little hope of educational success in college.

Some athletes, perhaps, are not there for an education, viewing enrollment in the university, rather, only as a necessary avenue to the professional level (an unrealistic goal to all but a few). Those who want an education find that they have signed a contract that makes them an employee (not in the eyes of the NCAA, but an employee nonetheless), and the demands of sport come first. Achieving an education is incidental to the overriding objective of big-time sports. (There are exceptions such as Georgetown, Notre Dame, and Duke, but as exceptions they prove the rule.) Because a primary concern of some coaches is the eligibility of their athletes, rather than their education, the athletes are enrolled in phantom courses (correspondence or residence courses that give credit for no work or attendance) or in easy courses with professors sympathetic to the athletic department (for examples of these abuses, see McCallum, 1994; Wolff &Yeager, 1995, 1997).

The research by P. Adler and P. A. Adler (1985, 1991) shows how the athletic experience actually tends to extinguish educational goals of the athletes. The researchers found that most athletes entered the university feeling idealistic about their impending academic performance; that is, they were optimistic about graduating, and they considered ambitious majors. This idealism lasted until about the end of the first year and was replaced by disappointment and a growing cynicism as they realized how difficult keeping up with their schoolwork would be. The athletic role came to dominate all facets of their existence. Coaches made huge demands on the time and commitment of their athletes. The athletes received greater positive reinforcement from their athletic performance than from their academic performance. They were isolated increasingly from the student body. They were segregated in an athletic dormitory. They were isolated culturally by their racial and socioeconomic differences from the rest of the students. They were even isolated from other students by their physical size, which some found intimidating. They interacted primarily with other athletes, and these peers tended to demean academics. In their first year, they were given courses with "friendly" professors, but this changed as athletes moved through the university curriculum. The academic expectations escalated, and the athletes were unprepared. The resulting academic failure or, at best, mediocre academic performance led to embarrassment and despair. The typical response, according to P. Adler and P. A. Adler (1985), was role distancing: "To be safe, it was better not to try than to try and not succeed" (p. 247). This attitude, and the resulting behaviors, were reinforced by the peer subculture.

The noneducation and miseducation of college athletes is especially acute for African Americans. Every study that has compared African American athletes to their White counterparts has found them less prepared for college and more likely to fulfill this prophecy in college: African American athletes tend to enter college as marginal students and to leave the same way. Edwards (1984) has argued that the Black "dumb jock" is a social creation: "'Dumb jocks' are not born; they are systematically created" (p. 8).

This social construction results from several factors. First, African American student-athletes must contend with two negative labels: the dumb athlete caricature and the dumb Black stereotype. This double negative tends to result in a self-fulfilling prophecy as teachers, fellow students, and the athletes themselves assume low academic performance. Moreover, many African Americans are ill-prepared for college because of their socioeconomic background, inadequate schools, and the special treatment often given to athletic stars in junior high school and high school. This special treatment continues in college with professors who "give" grades, surrogate test takers, and coaches who intercede for the athletes with the police when necessary. Thus, there is "little wonder that so many African American scholarship student-athletes manage to go through four years of college enrollment virtually unscathed by education" (Edwards, 1984, p. 9).

Despite efforts to add African American, Hispanic, and Native American students and faculty, U. S. colleges remain overwhelmingly White (Schaefer, 1995). African Americans (athletes or not) on mostly White campuses typically constitute only 4 or 5% of the student body. Thus, they are frequently alienated by the actual or perceived racism they experience and by their social isolation.

A major unintended consequence of this situation in which African American athletes find themselves is that their individual adaptations—denigrating education, opting for easy courses and majors, not making progress toward a degree, emphasizing the athlete role, and eventually dropping out of education without a degree—reinforce the very racial stereotypes an integrated education is meant to negate. Thus, unwittingly, the universities with big-time programs that recruit marginal students and do not educate them offer "proof" for the argument that African Americans are genetically inferior to Whites in intellectual potential (Davis, 1995).

In sum, African Americans are disadvantaged in the United States. To use a sports metaphor, for them the playing field is not level—to succeed, they must advance *uphill*. For a few African American males, a way to advance is through athletic accomplishment, which will, at a minimum, provide a college education. The college scholarship, however, is no guarantee of a college education. Only about one fourth of African American males who play in big-time college programs graduate. Some of these young men are responsible for not graduating. They may have sought the easy way that did not lead to graduation. However, many of the three fourths of African American athletes who do not graduate have been victims. They have been exploited by universities who used their athletic skills for economic gain but did not help to develop the intellectual skills of these students in their employ.

Anticipating the Year 2020

Societal Trends Affect Future Race Relations

There are five major trends that will shape future race relations. The first is the dramatic change in the racial composition of the United States. Currently, one fourth of the people in the United States are nonWhite (up from 15% in 1960). Some communities already have non-White majorities. The 1990 census, for example, found that more than 2,000 counties, cities, and towns had nonWhite majorities. Hawaii and New Mexico have nonWhite majorities, with California joining them, probably in 1999. Soon after, Nevada, Texas, Maryland, and New Jersey are projected to become states with non-White majorities. Minorities make up the ma-

jority in six of the eight U. S. cities with more than one million people. Moreover, racial minorities are increasing faster than the majority population. As a result, by about 2050, racial minorities will be equal in size to the White population. Within the racial minorities, the mix is shifting as well. By about 2010, in a historic shift, Latinos will outnumber African Americans (U. S. Census Bureau, reported in "Hispanics a Decade Away," 1995). As a precursor to this shift, in 1996, Latino children outnumbered African American children 12 million to 11.4 million (Jones, 1996). The growing racial minority presence will add tensions in society. The growth will occur mostly in urban areas, straining already exhausted budgets. The urban, minority underclass will continue to grow. In cities and regions experiencing economic hard times, the presence of growing racial minorities will be a source of turmoil between Whites and the minorities and among the minorities themselves, as individuals compete for a shrinking number of jobs and decreasing civic resources and services.

The tensions among these groups increase when there is a perception that the economy is not expanding to include oneself and one's group. This leads to the second important trend: the unequal distribution of wealth and income in U. S. society, which has the greatest disparity in the industrialized world, is becoming even more disparate:

1. The top fifth of households in 1994 got 49.1% of the total income, whereas the bottom fifth received just 3.6% (Sklar, 1995).

2. Between 1977 and 1992, America's most prosperous fifth gained 28% in real (adjusted for inflation) income. The middle 60% held its own, whereas the poorest fifth became 17% poorer.

3. The gap between the affluent and poor is widening. "The top 1 percent of Americans have more wealth than the bottom 90 percent . . . placing the United States first among industrialized nations when it comes to wealth inequality" (Fletcher, 1998, p. 35).

These facts indicate that the gaps between both the rich and poor and the rich and the middle class are wider now than at any time since World War II. Ironically, the resentment fostered by this situation is not aimed at the benefactors—the rich—but toward the poor, who are viewed, typically, as wanting government entitlements for doing nothing. These feelings lead to combustible race relations because racial minorities are disproportionately in the poor category.

The third trend that does not augur well for race relations in the future is the transformation of the economy. There are four interrelated forces that are fundamentally changing the economy—new technologies based on microelectronics, globalization, capital flight, and the shift from manufacturing to services (Eitzen & Baca Zinn, 1997). As a result, the nature of work is shifting, and low-wage jobs are migrating to low-wage areas in the United States and to other countries. As a result, the employment status of minorities has fallen (employment rates, occupational standing, and wage rates), especially in areas of industrial decline. In effect, African Americans have fewer job opportunities, and what is available for minority skilled and semiskilled workers tends to have lower pay and fewer, if any, benefits compared to manufacturing jobs. Again, this increases racial acrimony as Whites and African Americans, affected by automation and competition from overseas, compete for fewer and fewer good jobs.

Fourth, although racial minorities have always been disproportionately poor, the outlook is for this to worsen. The data from 1996 indicate that although 11.2% of Whites were officially poor, some 28.4% of African Americans and 29.4% of Latinos were (U. S. Census Bureau, 1997). This disparity by race will be accentuated in the future by a number of factors. Some of these are competition for ever-fewer good jobs, the continuing deterioration of our urban centers, the unequal financing of education (i. e., schools are advantaged or disadvantaged by the extent of the tax base in their districts), and the increasing unwillingness of federal and state governments to provide assistance to the needy.

This last point is the final trend that is squeezing racial minorities. The current mood among the majority of politicians and the *voting* public is to lower taxes, reduce social spending, and shift the burden for social services to the states (this last is known as *devolution*). The emerging ideological consensus is that government subsidies exacerbate social problems rather than solve them and that individuals must rely on their own resources and motivations if they are to succeed. As a result, the welfare state, created over 60 years ago in the Great Depression, is being systematically dismantled (Eitzen, 1996). Programs to provide aid to the disadvantaged, such as preschool programs (e. g., Head Start), legal services to the poor, housing subsidies, and Aid to Families with Dependent Children, are reduced or eliminated. The welfare reform legislation passed in 1996, for example, will, according to the Urban Institute, increase the number of children in poverty by more than 10%, adding 1.1 million to the officially impoverished, and worsen the conditions for millions already below the poverty line (Shogren, 1996). Shifting the responsibility and funding to the states for welfare programs will only make matters worse for the unfortunate, because many states cannot afford the additional financial burden, and many will choose not to provide the services even if they can afford them. As a consequence of this ideological switch from the progressive politics of Franklin D. Roosevelt to the centrist politics of William Jefferson Clinton, life will become more harsh for the economically disadvantaged. This means, of course, that people of color will be disproportionately affected. In particular, the gap between Whites and African Americans will increase. This will be especially evident in education, as urban schools will be underfunded compared to affluent schools in the suburbs, fewer African American children receive an adequate preparation for college, and the cost of higher education becomes more and more costly.

Trends in Universities and Athletics Affecting Race Relations

One disturbing fact is that disproportionately fewer African Americans attend colleges and universities. This is the result of three factors: ever-higher tuition rates, combined with the lower federal contributions to scholarships (a legacy of the Reagan, Bush, and Clinton administrations) and the relatively low economic status of African American families. Rising tuition also squeezes middle-class families (White and African American) and makes a college education more difficult for their children to obtain. The result may be student bodies composed more and more of the children of the elite, with the shrinking number of African Americans on campus more isolated than ever.

There are two countervailing trends on college campuses regarding race relations. On the one hand, there appears to be a growing commitment on the part of many university administrators and boards of regents toward greater racial diversity in student bodies and faculties. Thus, there is extra effort to recruit minority students (not just athletes), faculty members, and administrators. At the same time, there is a backlash on the part of some within and outside the academic communities against what they consider racial favoritism (in scholarships and hiring), racial enclaves (e. g., "African American studies," "Asian studies"), and what they see as the erosion of Western values through the adding of multiculturalism to the curriculum. These efforts have and will continue to heighten racial tensions on college campuses.

A potentially favorable trend in universities is the changing of the professorate. During the 1990s, about one third of professors (overwhelmingly White and male) will retire, a trend that will accelerate after 2000. These powerful individuals (overwhelmingly White, male, full professors) will be replaced by much younger and more diverse (in terms of race, gender, and worldview) assistant professors and part-time faculty.

On the athletic side, there seems to be no letup in the quest by universities with big-time programs to succeed on the field and to profit from sport. When Richard Lapchick, director of the Center for the Study of Sport in Society, was asked the cause of the illness in college athletics, he replied,

> Beyond any question in my mind, the root of the problem is money. Only thirty or forty athletic departments in the country make a profit. But the rainbow that is out there is so extraordinary . . . what that thirty or forty *do* make . . . that the others want to chase it. (quoted in Marchese, 1990, p. 2)

A second trend is that the NCAA has begun, tentatively, to consider efforts to reform the wrongs in college sport. Throughout its history, the NCAA has been relatively powerless to control the scandals of big-time intercollegiate sport or to run sport congruent with the goals of higher education. The fundamental reason for this was that athletic directors at the member schools cast the votes for their schools, meaning that the rules were determined by the athletic establishment rather the academic establishment. This began to change in 1984 when a commission of university presidents was formed by the NCAA to help in the reform and redirection of intercollegiate athletics.

The Presidents' Commission had little impact on the rules of the NCAA until the 1991 convention. At that time, the major agenda items were the commission's, members of the commission lobbied actively for their proposals, and a number of presidents (about 100 more than usual) attended to cast votes for their institutions. Many observers felt that the passage of their reform package signaled a turning point. That's the good news. The bad news is that the proposals of the commission did *not* address many of the key issues. Rather, they concentrated on cost containment. Scholarships were reduced by 10% (reducing the number of athletes on scholarship by 1,500 nationwide) and coaching staffs reduced (limiting, by the way, the number of jobs for African American coaches). To their credit, rules were passed by the NCAA members to help student-athletes:

1. All Division I schools must make counseling and tutoring services available to all recruited athletes.
2. All athletic dormitories were to be eliminated by August 1996.
3. In-season practice time must be limited to a maximum of 4 hours a day and 20 hours a week.

Although these rule changes were in the right direction, that is, in the direction of bringing the "student" back into the student-athlete role, they were mild and timid moves at best. The NCAA did not address the issue of freshman eligibility. It did not confront the scheduling of games at odd times to convenience television but at the expense of athletes missing class time. A proposal was defeated that would have required Division I schools to graduate 50% of their scholarship athletes. The NCAA also defeated a proposal to require athletes to post minimum grade point averages each year. Thus, it appears that although the presidents seem to be taking more of a role in the NCAA, the resulting rule changes have been cosmetic, not really addressing the ills of big-time college sports. Clearly, the commercial nature of sport, and the problems related to this, have not been questioned by the presidents.

An important missing ingredient in big-time college sports is adequate compensation for participation. Compensation limited to room, board, tuition, and books is unfair given the many millions of dollars generated by the athletes. Moreover, athletes from economically disadvantaged backgrounds (as are many of the African American athletes) are left with little or no spending money (in sharp contrast to students from affluent backgrounds). The Black Coaches Association (BCA) has argued that student-athletes should receive stipends of $1,500 a year, but this has been rejected by the NCAA because it threatens the amateur status (and, therefore, tax-exempt status) of intercollegiate sport. The result, of course, is that whereas athletes work for minimum wages, the NCAA, the schools, coaches, local merchants, corporations, and the media profit handsomely from their labors. The NCAA recently threw out its long-standing rule that prohibited student-athletes from working in the off-season. Despite this change, athletes continue to be undercompensated. As a consequence, many athletes, especially minority athletes from economically deprived backgrounds, engage in the underground economy of college athletics. Sack (1991) found that 53% of the athletes surveyed (72% of African Americans and 47% of Whites) saw nothing wrong with accepting benefits in violation of NCAA amateurism rules. The improper benefits that athletes may receive (by NCAA edict) are clothing, money, use of cars, free entertainment, travel, scalping tickets, and the like. Exceptional athletes with professional careers awaiting them are especially tempted by the lucrative gifts from sports agents (Davis, 1996; Shropshire, 1996a). The amateurism rules, aside from being unfair, have the unintended consequence of marginalizing athletes in activities defined as deviant. As Leroy Clark suggests, "It has to be a dangerous thing for character-building to have these young athletes seduced or drafted into covert arrangements, which have the aura of criminality" (quoted in Davis, 1996, pp. 223–224).

Reforming College Sport to Eliminate Racism

Contemporary trends in society suggest that racism will intensify in the near term. Big-time college sport will occur in that environment, adding to the racism as it exploits African American athletes for profit, often discarding them without an education. When this occurs, the stereotype that African Americans have physical but not intellectual gifts is reinforced.

This section addresses what ought to be done by the NCAA, the schools, the coaches, and the athletes to correct this situation. I will not attempt to address how big-time sport itself should be reformed (for suggestions to reform the system see Eitzen, 1997; Eitzen & Sage, 1997, pp. 116–119; Lapchick & Slaughter, 1989, section 4). The discussion is limited specifically to racism and the general issues regarding exploitation of African American athletes in big-time programs and their miseducation. Although the following recommendations are made specifically for African American athletes, they often apply to all college athletes. (I am indebted to Lapchick & Slaughter, 1989, for many of these recommendations.)

A. Problem: African American athletes are sometimes ill-prepared for college academics.

1. Athletes should not be admitted into college unless there is evidence of their potential to graduate. In short, if the academic potential of recruits is doubtful, then they should not be recruited. If the recruits have potential, they must be provided with the academic assistance (tutors and remedial courses) to get them to their appropriate academic level quickly.

2. The strict guidelines of Proposition 16 (successor to Proposition 48 for the incoming 1996 freshman athletes) must be supported and even strengthened. The new rules provide for an indexed scale, which requires that high school graduates with a 700 SAT or 17 ACT must have at least a 2.5 GPA in a core curriculum that consists of 13 courses. Incoming athletes must be able to succeed in the college classroom. Low standards place them at high risk educationally. Motivated athletes will work harder to be eligible, which is a win-win strategy for them. However, we must guard against the tendency to blame student-athletes for their educational shortcomings, because schools at

all levels are often guilty of the educational exploitation of their athletes (Davis, 1996).

3. Middle schools and high schools must prepare their potentially college-bound athletes for college.

4. Athletes at all educational levels, as well as their parents and leaders from their communities, must be counseled to realize that (a) a college education is the most significant step they can take for success in American society and (b) the odds of a professional career in sport are very long, and even if such a career is attained, it will last but a few years.

B. Problem: African American athletes often come from economically disadvantaged backgrounds.

5. Athletes must be provided with a monthly stipend ($300 or so) for incidentals, clothing, and entertainment. This will provide some justice by paying the athletes a portion of the money they generate for their universities. Moreover, it will permit students from poor families a chance to fit it with their more privileged classmates. Walter Byers, former executive director of the NCAA, has suggested that student-athletes be allowed to endorse products, with the income going into a trust fund, then to the players when they graduate or complete their eligibility. Moreover, full-need student-athletes should be given additional financial assistance over the permitted grant-in-aid (Byers, 1995).

6. Athletes must be provided two trips home during each school year. Moreover, the parents of athletes should be provided with two trips to the university each year. These actions will accomplish three goals: (a) provide the athletes with a form of financial aid that they have earned, (b) promote better ties between the athletes and their communities, and (c) promote family bonding.

C. Problem: African American athletes who are admitted have relatively low graduation rates.

7. Freshmen must be ineligible for athletic competition so that they can concentrate on the adjustment to the social and intellectual demands of college.

8. The institution must provide adequate study time, counseling, and tutoring. The object of these aids is not eligibility for sports participation but satisfactory progress toward a degree.

9. The time demands of sport on the athletes in-season and off-season must be reasonable. Thus, (a) practice time must be limited, (b) the number of games in a season must be limited, and (c) the number of class days missed because of sport must be limited. The NCAA has begun to place some restrictions on excessive time demands in basketball, but there is a gradual tendency to increase the number of football games.

10. The athlete's academic progress must be closely monitored by the school's (not just the athletic department's) academic advisors.

11. Athletes must retain their scholarships, including housing, meals, and books, for up to 2 years, if needed, after their athletic eligibility is completed. This recognizes the necessity of at least 5 years for graduation in most cases. At present, many schools eliminate educational assistance to athletes who have used up their eligibility, making it especially difficult for the economically disadvantaged to continue.

12. Coaches should be evaluated in part by the graduation rate of their athletes. This form of institutional control of coaches will, of course, increase the efforts of coaches to recruit athletes with academic potential and to see that those whom they do recruit make progress towards a degree.

D. Problem: African American athletes are isolated in athletic ghettos, and there is often racial segregation within them.

13. Separate living situations and separate eating facilities for athletes must be eliminated.

14. Athletes should be encouraged to become involved in social, organizational, and academic activities within the school context. At a minimum, this means that coaches should not impose restrictions on the nonathletic campus activities of their athletes, which is often the case.

15. Housing arrangements, meals, and road trip accommodations must be integrated. This can easily be accomplished through random assignments.

16. Positional segregation by race (stacking) must be eliminated. Racial stacking promotes racial stereotypes (e. g., Whites are "naturally" more intelligent and better leaders, whereas African Americans are "naturally" more gifted physically). Moreover, it tends to make competition for starting positions intraracial. This is a difficult proposal to implement because the procedures are often subtle. However, at a minimum, coaches should declare their acceptance of open competition for each position, and the results of this competition should be monitored by the administration.

E. Problem: There are not enough African Americans in leadership positions in athletic departments.

17. African Americans must be considered seriously for positions of athletic director and head coach. In 1993, when African American athletes accounted for 53% of the football players at Division IA institutions (the highest level), African Americans accounted for only 4% of the athletic directors and 3.5% of the head coaches at those colleges (Shropshire, 1996b).

18. African Americans must be considered seriously for positions of assistant athletic director, trainer, and sports information director, positions where they are rarely found.

19. African American assistant coaches must be given more responsibilities beyond the typical ones of recruiting African American athletes and serving as liaisons between the African American athletes and the White coaches.

F. Problem: A number of coaches are racist.

20. Players must have a mechanism by which they can report the racist and dehumanizing acts of coaches and others in the athletic department to the administration without fear of reprisal.

21. The university and athletic department administration must take strong and immediate action to eliminate discriminatory and dehumanizing practices.

G. Problem: Racist stereotypes are sometimes promoted unwittingly by members of the athletic departments.

22. Athletic department personnel must be educated about the subtleties of racism, including the negative use of language. In particular, the sports information director must be sensitized to the negative and sometimes subtle ways that minorities are often portrayed in press guides, press releases, and in the media.

There are three fundamental requirements if these recommendations are to be implemented. First, the NCAA must expand its recent reforms, focusing on the explicit goal of promoting educational and humane values in college athletics. All other goals, including making money, are secondary to meeting the educational needs of student-athletes. Put another way, the operating principle must be that the health and education of student-athletes are infinitely more important than television ratings, corporate sponsorships, and making money. If the NCAA does not prove capable of this, and there is reason to suspect that it is not (see Sperber, 1991), then the member universities, through their presidents, must form an organization that will.

Second, university presidents must make a commitment to their athletes as students. They must take responsibility for the educational and moral integrity of their institutions. They must set up mechanisms to monitor their athletic programs, set up rules to insure compliance with educational goals, and budget the necessary monies to implement those rules.

Finally, money must be raised by the NCAA and distributed to the schools equitably to fund the expensive items in these recommendations. This is not as difficult as it seems. Richard Lapchick has proposed an "Academic Superfund" that would tap the various profit centers in sport:

> One of my suggestions was that for every player who makes it to the pros, the NBA and the NFL would donate the equivalent of a full four-year scholarship to the Superfund. The money would then be used for those players who don't make it to the pros, to continue their educations in a fifth or sixth year.
>
> Given that 50 players a year enter the NBA and 150 the NFL, and given an average of $10,000 a year for tuition costs, the total comes out to about $8 million a year. That sounds like a lot of money, but consider that the telesports are worth $1.675 billion a year.
>
> I also proposed a 1 percent federal tax on ticket sales for all sporting events. Even on a $30 ticket, the tax would cost you only 30 cents; yet, that 1 percent would raise $33 million a year, because we sell $3.3 billion in tickets.
>
> I've also written to NCAA Executive Director Dick Schultz, suggesting that 10

percent of the increase in the NCAA's television revenues . . . just of the $83 million *increase* . . . go into the Super-fund. That's another $8.3 million.

The total amount in this new Super-fund would be something like $50 million a year (Lapchick, quoted in March-ese, 1990, p. 4).

To conclude, despite the impediments to achieving social justice in college sport, the situation can be improved mightily. We know what's wrong. That's the easy part. We must acknowledge the problems and demand that sport be cleaned up. The NCAA has allowed social injustice to occur and is now only beginning to reform, but these efforts, so far, are weak. That organization or one like it must oversee university sport to insure that educational values prevail. The administrators at each university, along with faculties, staffs, students, and the public, must insist on the same. At present, these groups demand excellence on the fields and in the arenas. This type of tunnel vision is at the heart of the problem because it has led to abuses, compromises, and hypocritical behaviors that are contrary to educational goals. Most important, it has allowed athletes, most often African American athletes, to be used by these schools for their athletic skills and then discarded without diplomas. That is not only embarrassing, but it also is immoral. Because educational institutions exist to serve their students, it is obvious that big-time college sport must be restructured to focus on the educational outcomes of athletes. To do otherwise makes a mockery of the educational mission of universities.

Summary

African American athletes in big-time college athletic programs are part of two contexts, both of which disadvantage them. The first context is the interracial climate of U. S. society. On every dimension related to health, housing, work, income/wealth, and education, African Americans, when compared to Whites, are disadvantaged. Conservative economic strategies have cut back social programs that might help reduce the problems of the disadvantaged. Moreover, racial tensions are increasing. Bigotry, even on college campuses, is real. The situation will not ease in the near term as politicians focus on the needs of the middle class, the competition for jobs intensifies, and racial/ethnic minorities increase their proportion of the population.

African American athletes recruited to big-time college programs are also part of a corporate/entertainment world. They are hired (for room, board, books, and tuition) to perform on the athletic fields and in the arenas to generate monies, media interest, and public relations for universities. They are recruited for their athletic talents but not necessarily for their intellectual abilities. Because African American athletes come disproportionately from economically, socially, and educationally disadvantaged backgrounds, the situation is loaded against them. From the perspective of many coaches and athletic administrations, these individuals are athletes first and only incidentally students. As a result, many of these athletes who are marginal students retain their athletic eligibility by being "taken care of" through phantom courses, "friendly" professors, surrogate test takers, and the like. This means, of course, that many African Americans will not graduate, even though they have played for 4 years. In effect, they have been used by the universities.

The NCAA has begun to take tentative steps to reform the wrongs in college sport, but these weak steps are not enough. The universities, through the NCAA (or another organization), need to be bold in their initiatives. As they consider reforms to eliminate racism, the following broad changes are essential:

1. Athletes admitted to universities must be prepared for college-level academics.
2. Athletes should receive fair compensation for their work, which will especially help athletes from economically disadvantaged backgrounds.

3. Athletes must be provided with whatever it takes for them to achieve educational goals.

4. Racial/ethnic minorities must be integrated into all athletic and university activities.

5. The staff of athletic departments must be integrated at all levels.

6. Athletic departments must be monitored carefully to determine that procedures are fair and nonracist, and to ensure that educational goals have the first priority.

Suggested Readings

Adler, P. A., & Adler, P. (1991). *Backboards and blackboards: College athletes and role engulfment.* New York: Columbia University Press.

Byers, W. (1995). *Unsportsmanlike conduct: Exploiting college athletes.* Ann Arbor: University of Michigan Press.

Davis, T. (1995). The myth of the superspade: The persistence of racism in college athletics. *Fordham Urban Law Journal, 22*(3), 615–698.

Eitzen, D. S. & G. H. (1997). *Sociology of North American sport.* Madison, WI: Brown & Benchmark.

Hamilton, D. C., & C. V. (1997). *The dual agenda: The African American struggle for civil and economic equality.* New York: Columbia University Press.

Hoberman, J. (1997). *Darwin's athletes: How sport has damaged black America and preserved the myth of race.* Boston: Houghton Mifflin.

Shropshire, K. L. (1996). *In black and white: Race and sports in America.*

Sperber, M. (1990). *College sports, inc.* New York: Henry Holt.

Symposium on race and sports. (1996). *Marquette Sports Law Journal, 6.* [entire issue].

Study Questions

1. Big-time college sport is a large-scale commercial entertainment enterprise. What are the negative consequences of this for athletes?

2. What does Harry Edwards mean by "The Black 'dumb jock' is a social creation"?

3. How does the social organization of society, universities, and sport work to keep African Americans in subordinate positions?

References

Adler, P., & Adler, P. A. (1985). From idealism to pragmatic detachment: The academic performance of college athletes. *Sociology of Education, 58,* 241–250.

Adler, P. A., & Adler, P. (1991). *Backboards and blackboards: College athletes and role engulfment.* New York: Columbia University Press.

Blumenstyk, G. (1996, April 19). Money-making champs. *The Chronicle of Higher Education,* p. A49.

Byers, W. (1995). *Unsportsmanlike conduct: Exploiting college athletes.* Ann Arbor: University of Michigan Press.

Davis, T. (1995). The myth of the superspade: the persistence of racism in college athletics. *Fordham Urban Law Review 22*(3), 615–698.

Edwards, H. (1984, Spring). The black "dumb jock": An American sports tragedy. *The College Review Board, 131,* 8–11.

Eitzen, D. S. (1996, June 15). Dismantling the welfare state: Is it the answer to America's social problems? *Vital Speeches of the Day,* 532–536.

Eitzen, D. S. (1997, December 1). Big-time college sports: Contradictions, crises, and consequences. *Vital Speeches of the Day,* 122–126.

Eitzen, D. S., & Baca Zinn, M. (1997). *Social problems* (7th ed.). Boston: Allyn and Bacon.

Eitzen, D. S., & Sage, G. H. (1997). *Sociology of North American sport* (5th ed.). Dubuque, IA: Wm. C. Brown.

Fletcher, M. A. (1998, March 9). The Kerner Report at 30. *Washington Post National Weekly Edition,* p. 35.

Herman, E. S. (1996, July–August). America the meritocracy. *Z Magazine, 9,* 34–39.

Hispanics a decade away from becoming no. 1 minority. (1995, April 16). *Denver Post,* p. 21A.

Jones, R. L. (1996, July 2). Hispanic children biggest majority. *Denver Post,* pp. A1, A11.

Lapchick, R. E., & Slaughter, J. B. (1989). *The rules of the game: Ethics in college sport.* New York: Macmillan.

Marchese, T. (1990). After the cheers: Is higher education serving its student-athletes? An interview with Richard E. Lapchick. *AAHE Bulletin, 42,* 1–l0.

McCallum, J. (1994, November 28). Paper trail. *Sports Illustrated,* 45–48.

Miller, J. G. (1996). *Search and destroy: African American males in the criminal justice system.* New York: Cambridge University Press.

Pedraza S., & Rumbaut, R. G. (1996). *Origins and destinies: Immigration, race, and ethnicity in America.* Belmont, CA: Wadsworth.

Rubin, A. J. (1998, March 1). Report updates racial division. *Denver Post,* p. 2A.

Sack, A. (1991, March). The underground economy of college football. *Sociology of Sport Journal,8,* 1–15.

Schaefer, R. T. (1995, Winter). Education and prejudice: Unraveling the relationship. *The Sociological Quarterly, 37,* 1–16.

Shogren, E. (1996, July 26). Welfare reform could impoverish 1 million kids. *Fort Collins Coloradoan,* p. A5.

Shropshire, K. L. (1996a, Spring). Sports agents, role models and race consciousness. *Marquette Sports Law Journal, 6,* 267–285.

Shropshire, K. L. (1996b). *In Black and white: Race and sports in America.* New York: New York University Press.

Sklar, H. (l995). Back to the raw deal. *Zeta Magazine, 8,* 19–24.

Southern Poverty Law Center. (1996, March). Klanwatch: Monitoring hate and fighting for justice. *Southern Poverty Law Center Report,* 12–13.

Sperber, M. (l990). *College sports, inc.* New York: Henry Holt.

Sperber, M. (l991). Why the NCAA can't reform college athletics. *Academe, 77,* 13–20.

United States Census Bureau. (1997). *Poverty 1996: Graphs.* Census Bureau website: www.census.gov/hhes/poverty/poverty96/povrac96.html.

Wilson, W. J. (1996). *When work disappears: The world of the new urban poor.* New York: Alfred A. Knopf.

Wolff, A., & Yaeger, D. (1995, August 7). Credit risk. *Sports Illustrated,* 46–55.

Wolff, A., & Yaeger, D. (1997, July 7). Troubling questions. *Sports Illustrated,* 70–79.

Epilogue:

Dana Brooks and Ronald Althouse

"Never let an injustice become yesterday's news."
—Johnnetta Cole (1997)

Fifty Years After Jackie Robinson: Equal Access but Unequal Outcome

On May 5, 1997, *Sports Illustrated* published an article, "The Breakthrough," a tribute to Jackie Robinson's career with an overview of his contribution to Major League Baseball and to race relations in America. We were particularly struck by the headline, "Fifty years ago, over fourteen games in May, Jackie Robinson erased any doubt that he belonged in the majors, clearing the path for other Black players" (Nack, 1997, p. 57). Today, it is a widely held belief that Robinson's signing with the Dodgers did more to alter the nation's race consciousness than any other single act during this time period.

When we reflect on the occasion, it is important to ask the following question:

> How would we measure the progress made by African Americans in college and professional sports since Jackie's signing with the Dodgers in 1947?

What variables or social conditions should be used to serve as the barometer? It is within this context that we would like to highlight the essays presented in this text and to address some of the unanswered questions about the current and future status of racism in college sports.

The first essay, by David Wiggins, provides the reader with an excellent social-historical analysis of racism in professional and college athletics. The author accounts vividly that African American athletes have been the target of discrimination throughout American history. Discrimination manifested itself in the form of segregated football, basketball, and baseball teams. Ostensibly, the White owners and managers followed the doctrine of "separate but equal" (legally sanctioned by *Plessy v. Ferguson*, 1896) during the first half of the 20th century, thus denying African Americans access to professional sport.

Signing Jackie Robinson in 1947 to play for the Dodgers was one of the most significant events in the history of professional and college sports. In spite of its significance, colleges and professional teams moved slowly to integrate their athletic teams. In the decades of the 1960s and 1970s the public outcry by African Americans for justice and equality resulted in the Civil Rights movement and the revolt of the Black athlete. The theme has shifted from "lack of access to sport" to "conditions of exploitation, discrimination, and inferiority-superiority, social barriers and sport participation, academic standards (Propositions 48-42-16) and concern over the graduate rate of African American athletes."

It appears that overt forms of discrimination against African American athletes have decreased since the early 1900s. However, Wiggins reminds us that individuals still hold racial and stereotypical beliefs about the African American athlete.

In "African American Predominance in College Sport" (Essay 2), Othello Harris initially traces the historical roots of African American participation in intercollegiate athletics. Too often, the early African American college sport participants were identified as "superspades," simply because higher levels of athletic prowess and performance were expected from these individuals as compared to their White counterparts.

Immediately following World War II, colleges began to witness a discernible increase in the number of African Americans attending colleges and participating in sports. Most notable, college football and basketball began to select more African American athletes in their respective teams. Yet, Harris is wise to note that desegregation of college sport was not equated with the integration of sport and society. Many of the colleges and public schools remained segregated in the decades of the 1940s and 1950s.

African Americans made progress against social barriers in the decades of the 1960s and 1970s as a result of the Civil Rights movement. Similarly, the African American athlete began to gain a significant prominence in college sports. It should be noted that the sheer number of African American athletes participating on the various athletic teams continued to increase during the decades of the 1970s and 1980s. The African American athletes were dominating statistical categories in baseball, basketball, football and track and field. Nonetheless, with these advances and increased levels of participation, there were some lingering setbacks. Concerns about racist stereotyping, stacking (segregating by playing position), the need for National Collegiate Athletic Association (NCAA) reform, and the need to address graduate rates of African American athletes persisted. Harris believed that this latter issue is one of the most critical issues facing the African American college athlete today. The authors insists to remedy this situation:

1. Freshmen athletes should be declared ineligible to participate, thus, provide more opportunity to prepare for the academic demands of college.
2. The amount of time in sport should be limited to 20 hours per week.
3. The NCAA should distribute a larger%age of the money generated from television contracts back to the colleges.
4. The NCAA should reallocate money back to the high schools and communities from which the student athletes were recruited.

These recommendations represent significant NCAA reform; however, unless these recommendations are implemented, we may continue to see patterns of oppressions and exploitation in college sports.

Gary Sailes's essay (3), "The African American Athlete: Social Myths and Stereotypes," focuses discussion on the role of the media in perpetuating racial stereotypes in college sport. The author challenges traditional stereotypes such as the "dumb jock", White superiority and African American inferiority in intelligence, the Brute and Sambo. Sailes's analysis of racial stereotypes and sport participation goes far beyond the traditional rhetoric and begins to describe the foundation on which race-based participation theories are based. A complete discussion of the following theories are presented in the text: matriarchal, mandingo, survival of the fittest, genetic, and psychological differences. The author dares to ask new questions and begins to raise our awareness of how racial stereotypes are perpetuated especially in the sport arena.

The essay concludes by stating, "Racial myths and stereotypes are born out of ignorance." Clearly, the role of the parent, coach, media, and athletic administrators is to dispel these negative and degrading images about a race of people. The media can and should play a significant and positive role in educating the lay public about the negative aspects of stereotyping.

Popular media continue to institutionalize stereotypes about African American athletes. Brooks and Althouse (1996) said, "If education can destroy ignorance and open doors, mis-education can academically marginalize and close doors. The presumed value of the African American student-athlete as a prized sports commodity is apt to be tendered in an institutional environment that fuels harmful racism because of notions of neutrality and color blindness of the rules sanctioning eligibility and participation in collegiate sport." (p. 1)

"Stacking in the Team Sport of Intercollegiate Baseball," written by Earl Smith and Debra A. Henderson (Essay 4) presents a refreshing look at an "old problem": the persistence of stacking in college athletics, especially baseball. The two sociologists analyze the social, economic, and psychological mechanisms that underlie stacking. Stacking was viewed as characteristic of social isolation, marginalization, and discrimination.

The essay begins with a definition of the term *stacking*: "African American baseball players . . . relegated to playing positions based on race/ethnicity and not on their playing abilities." This definition permits the authors to conclude that stacking is the result of social isolation.

Smith and Henderson's historical critique of the 30 years of stacking literature provides an excellent overview of this important line of research in the sport sociology literature. Suggested strategies for eliminating stacking include hiring competent managers, stopping the practice of switching African American athletes from central to noncentral positions, and providing a warm and caring athletic environment for African American athletes. Smith and Henderson are applauded for their groundbreaking analysis and the readers are encouraged to address many of the questions presented in this essay.

"African American Head Coaches and Administrators: Progress But . . . ?" (Essay 5), written by Dana Brooks and Ronald Althouse, identifies certain factors (i.e., racism, differential salary, tokenism, stereotyping) as contributing to the dearth of African American male and female head college coaches. The authors begin this discussion with a review of stacking and positional segregation research. It is not surprising to find a relationship between position segregation and social discrimination at the college coaching level. Further critique of African American head coaching career-mobility patterns permits the authors to conclude that coaching represents a distinctive subculture (consisting mainly of White males), and that a relationship exists between coaching careers and institutional prestige. Network and professional linkages can hasten career development. The authors conclude that no one coaching career model exists. The career coaching paths followed by individual head coaches were unique.

Over the past 20 years there has been some progress in the hiring of African American males into head coaching positions, especially in basketball. Unfortunately, college football, tennis, gymnastics, and baseball have not been receptive to hiring African American head coaches. A more recent study found very little change in the percentage of Black head coaches of men's teams at member institutions from 1995 to 1997 (7.6% to 7.8%, respectively) (Brown, 1998).

Employment data for African American females continue to suggest that these women are not gaining access or upward mobility in the coaching and administrative college ranks. It became apparent that African American females faced discrimination based on their gender and race. It was alarming to note that in 1997 only one African American female occupied the position of athletic director at an NCAA Division I institution.

There is some hope: The Black Coaches Association and the Rainbow Coalition developed specific goals, objectives, and affirmative action plans to assist NCAA institutions to diversify their coaching and administrative positions. Breaking down coaching career barriers means that NCAA member institutions must begin to value diversity, to initiate plans to target recruitment and retention of African American male and female coaches, and to develop strong mentoring and support systems within the organization.

Essay 6, written by Robertha Abney, "The Glass-Ceiling Effect and African American Women Coaches and Athletic Administrators," investigates the glass-ceiling effect on upward coaching mobility patterns of African American female coaches and administrators. Title IX legislation has increased the number of female (White and African American) athletes participating in college sport. Yet, African American females have not been afforded the opportunity to become officials, head coaches, administrators or athletic trainers. Abney is able to identify obstacles to African American female coaching and administrative mobility: inadequate salary, lack of support groups, race, gender, tokenism, and sexism.

On a positive note, the author recommends strategies to shatter the glass ceiling in college athletics: Recruit and diversify the athletic department, develop mentoring programs, establish training and educational programs, establish support groups, develop a sense of self-confidence, receive strong administrative support from the President and athletic director. Brooks and Althouse (1996) review of research dealing with the intersection of race, gender, and intercollegiate athletics led to their conclusion that "redressing the inequalities that now exist for African American women may not happen easily or quickly; administrative dedication to revenue generating practices, and discrimination in recruitment and racial stacking, as well as conflicts over scholarship entitlement, such as Title IX, may foster renewed racist challenges as well as oppressive sexist gender barriers."

Essay 7, "African American Student-Athletes: Opportunity or Exploitation?", by Robert M. Sellers, challenges the reader to answer the following questions: To what extent does college athletics provide African American student-athletes with the opportunity for social mobility, or does college athletics represent an institutionalized form of oppression and exploitation? Sellers presents a strong argument that student-athletes' life experiences on the college campus play a critical role influencing their subsequent life experiences. The author presents some compelling data showing that African American student-athletes enter college with poorer academics and have lower graduation rates than their White counterparts.

Sellers's essay breaks new ground in this topic and proceeds to answer his research question by analyzing the college life experiences of the African American student-athlete as compared to those of all student-athletes and all African American college students. In general, Sellers found that African American student-athletes experienced a college life similar to that of White student-athletes. Notable differences were that African American student-athletes were more likely to report experiencing racial isolation than White student-athletes were.

Sellers concludes by insisting that colleges owe student-athletes the opportunity for a college education. Nearly a half century has passed and it's time to transcend any racial barriers. All student-athletes should be offered the opportunity to develop personal competence and to earn a college degree.

Suggested strategies to realize these important institutional goals:

1. The NCAA should adopt legislation that requires competent academic support systems for student-athletes.
2. The NCAA should enforce legislation restricting the amount of time that student-athletes spend involved with sport-related activities.
3. The NCAA should make all student-athletes ineligible to participate during their freshman year in college.
4. The NCAA should develop a more inclusive position regarding admission requirements of student-athletes.

According to Audwin Anderson and Donald South's essay (8), "Racial Differences in Collegiate Recruitment, Retention, and Graduation Rates," there is a considerable amount of exploitation or victimization of student-athletes (especially African Americans) in college sports. Unlike Sellers (a psychologist) in Essay 7 these authors (sociologists) argue that structural conditions contribute to exploitation. Exploitation is presented in the context of self-identity, market and business concepts, and access to resources and power.

Anderson and South provide an excellent discussion relative to the social meaning of African American maleness and the sport experience. Citing the work of noted Afrocentric scholar Karenga, the concepts of popular culture (stereotypes of groups) and national culture (group-based) were well-articulated.

After reading this section of the essay, one can better understand the historical development of the African American male as laborer, superathlete, or sexual stud. The authors conclude that it becomes a tragedy when African American males are unable to define themselves apart from the stereotypes put forth by the larger society. Clearly, the heart of their thesis is the African American males' search for identify and self worth. Unrealistic academic entrance requirements (Propositions 48 and 16) and economic and academic exploitation (recruiting academically marginal students) will hinder the African American male's quest for identity and will continue to marginalize his presence on campus.

The stated purpose of this essay is to facilitate change and enhance the educational experiences of all student-athletes. Recommended changes include holding the student-athlete academic unit responsible for advising student-athletes, placing more of an emphasis on completing the college degree, making all grants-in-aid a 5-year commitment, and providing funding to those student-athletes who need it once their eligibility is complete.

There are individuals who argue the term *student-athlete* is a contradiction. Anderson and South provide strong arguments that the emphasis must be placed back on the student first if we are truly committed to eliminating the perceived exploitation of our student-athletes.

Yevonne Smith's essay (9), "Sociohistorical Influences on African American Elite Sportswomen," makes a significant contribution to the African American female sport literature. Writing from a Black feminist perspective, the author begins her discussion with the social history of African American women in American society. Throughout this presentation the theme of African American female oppression becomes apparent.

Historically, African American female oppression has taken the form of inadequate wages, slavery, sexism, segregation, racism, and lack of power and visibility. These factors also contributed to the lack of participation of African American females in early sports.

Initially denied access to formal, structured sports, African American females gained access to YWCAs, amateur athletic unions, and historically Black colleges and universities. African American female athletes gained early recognition in track and field and the Olympics.

Notable performances and track and field participants include Alice Coachman, first African American female to receive a gold medal in the Olympics (1948); Tennessee Tigerbelles Willye White, Wyomia Tyres, and Lucinda Adams; Wilma Rudolph (1960 Olympian); and Jackie Joyner-Kersee. African American tennis greats include Althea Gibson, Tina Garrison, and Lori McNeil.

Smith's ability to weave an analysis between biographies, career mobility, the Civil Rights movement, and the women's movement makes an important addition to the African American female sport literature. The elite African American female athlete, similar to her White female partner, faced oppression in the form of sexism in college sport. However, the African American female came to realize that "sport is just as 'gendered' as it is 'racially feared' and organized as a class system" (Brooks and Althouse, 1996, p. 51). Unfortunately, the opportunity for women to gain parity in college sports barely exists today.

Smith concludes her essay on the elite African American female athlete by stating that race relations, ethnicity, family relations, social class relations, socialization, and community sport structures, are significant structures *that ought* to be analyzed as well to gain an understanding about women's sporting achievement experiences.

Essay 10, "The African American Female in College Sport: Sexism and Racism," written by Doris Corbett and William Johnson, builds on the concepts presented in Essay 9 and presents a historical critique of the intersection of racism and sexism in college sport. After reading this essay one can reach the conclusion that, similar to their African American male counterparts, African American females have experienced a hard road to glory in sport. Historically, there have been sociocultural and structural barriers such as racism, sexism, lack of access to facilities and equipment, lack of role models, the negative impact of Proposition 48, and poor media images of the African American female athlete. Yet, there have been some success stories for the African American sportswomen: Cheryl Miller, gold medal Olympian basketball player; Nikki Franks, national fencing champion; Tina Sloan Green, U.S. Women's Lacrosse Team; Debi Thomas, ice-skating Olympian; Althea Gibson, Wimbledon tennis champion; Jackie Joyner-Kersee, track Olympian; and Wilma Rudolph, first African American female to win three gold medals in one Olympiad.

Notable African American female coaches and administrators include Robertha Abney, assistant athletic director; Renee Brown, Director of Player Personnel for the WNBA; Anita DeFrantz, International Olympic Committee board member; Vivian Fuller, director of athletics; and Marian Washington, head basketball coach, University of Kansas. It is important to note that the authors remind us that African American females have limited professional pathways available to them compared to White females. Unfortunately, very few empirical research studies have been conducted to analyze the African American female experience in sport.

Adding to the debate, the authors begin to question the impact of Title IX legislation on the African American female athlete. It is a general belief that the passage of Title IX had a major impact on increasing opportunities for females in sport. However, the authors do not believe that Title IX has been beneficial to African American females in sport. Women's sports such as synchronized swimming, water polo, archery, rowing, and badminton have been added to college sport programs since 1975, yet, "African American women from the inner city and from low-income backgrounds do not have access to the training and development necessary to compete for scholarships and collegiate opportunities in these sports." Clearly, this condition must be rectified if African American females are going to gain access to women's sports in the next century.

To achieve full equality in sports, African American females must overcome the following racial and sexual barriers: (a) limited financial support, (b) physical education teachers who lack the background to coach competitive teams, (c) lack of administrative support where competitive programs and interest exist, (d) lack of positive opinion leaders as role models who use African American sportswomen, (e) White coaches' tendency to associate the Black female athlete with only certain sports (i.e, basketball), (f) discrimination in team selection, particularly in the sports of volleyball and basketball, (g) discrimination in hiring, (h) limited skill development opportunities, (i) coaches, (j) lack of officials, (k) intimidation from male coaches and fans, and (l) unwillingness to travel.

Breaking down these institutional barriers is difficult. Yet, external and internal pressure must be consistently exerted on NCAA member institutions to expand opportunities for African American female athletes, coaches, and administrators. Eradicating the double-edged sword of racism and sexism means eliminating structural and institutional barriers to career success.

Tina Sloan Green, president of the Black Women in Sport Foundation and author of "The Future of African American Female Athletes" (Essay 11), demonstrates why she is recognized as one of the country's outstanding African American female coaches and scholars. Similar to Smith's essay, Green's contribution targets the future status of the elite African American female athlete. Historically, African American females were denied access to participate on high school and college athletic teams. Over the past two decades, there have been some political and economic changes leading to increased participation opportunities for African American females: increased economic status, Title IX and the feminist movement, and changes in residential patterns and neighborhood demographics. Yet, Green clearly acknowledges that social, structural, and economic factors such as stereotyping, poor facilities, sexism, lack of media exposure, and lack of support systems serve as barriers impeding the development of the elite African American female athlete. Many of these same barriers join forces to deny African American females access to coaching and administrative positions within NCAA institutions. It should be pointed out that there is a sense of optimism in Green's writing: "In spite of racism, sexism, and inadequate financial support, we will still find those African American women who will succeed and break barriers in sport." The author predicts additional participation opportunities for African American females in foreign countries to outperform African American males. In the academe, coaches remain significant individuals in the lives of student-athletes, and historically Black colleges will continue to play an important role in providing sport and educational opportunities for African American females.

Green challenges the majority establishment and African American female athletes to fight against all forms of social injustice; and en-

courages African American females to apply for sport-related jobs, to participate in sport camps and clinics, and to believe in themselves.

Timothy Davis and Kenneth L. Shropshire (two attorneys) are rapidly gaining national recognition for their scholarly works intersecting law, sociology, and the African American athlete experience. Timothy Davis writes in "Race, Law, and College Athletics" (Essay 12) that racism persists in college athletics and traditional civil rights laws are largely ineffective for protecting the interest of African Americans. At first, one does not want to accept this statement! However, like a good attorney, Davis builds his case by introducing court cases—*Jackson v. Drake University* (1991), *Hysaw v. Washburn University of Topeka* (1987), *Cobb v. University of Southern California* (1996),—documenting alleged racism, oppression, and exploitation in college athletics. Additional evidence is presented to the jury: NCAA rules and regulations (Propositions 48 and 16) that disproportionately impact African American athletes, and the lack of African Americans in head coaching positions. Reviewing Title VII of the amended Civil Rights Act of 1964 and, specifically, disparate treatment and disparate impact court cases, Davis reaches the following conclusion: "The absence of objectively quantifiable factors on which employment decisions are made will pose difficulties for African Americans challenging hiring and promotion decisions." He further believes that nonlegal alternatives may hold promise to readdress the various forms of oppression currently existing in college sports.

Effective strategies to increase diversity and to provide an environment conducive to learning begin with establishing a proactive affirmative action policy and plan by the athletic department, congressional and state legislative hearings regarding racial equality in college sport, analysis of NCAA legislation prior to implementation to determine racial implications, demand that colleges be accountable for funds generated in revenue-producing sports, and expansion of the NCAA minority internship programs. The judge has given the charge to the jury. The plaintiff and the defendant have presented their arguments. You, the jury, must now determine the future direction of NCAA member institutions.

Shropshire's essay (13), "Compensation and the African American Student-Athlete," opens by asking the question, "How does the absence of compensation, beyond room, board, tuition, and educational fees, impact the African American student-athlete?" The author presents the thesis that student-athletes, especially African Americans, should be provided additional compensation. The foundation of his argument is grounded in the debate over amateur athletes and professional sport. After we review this section of the essay, it becomes apparent that the British and NCAA concept of amateurism (throughout history this concept was revised to include those individuals who do not receive material benefits directly from participation) is obsolete. Amateurism in its original form (invented by the Victorian middle class) created an elite class system of participants.

Educators and the lay public who argue against paying students turn to the amateur foundation of the NCAA and say that paying student-athletes fosters competition. Of course, Shropshire does not support this "flawed" argument. He states, "Little parity currently exists between the major and smaller collegiate sports programs." The author notes that paying student-athletes consistently raises the following points: Most athletic programs lose money, Title IX makes any form of compensation beyond the existing structure impossible, and one would have to compensate revenue and nonrevenue sports participants. To bring resolution to these issues, NCAA institutions would have to set priorities in their spending and budgeting. Shropshire brings a refreshing look at this very important issue facing the African American student-athlete. Going "outside the box," the author motivates the reader to explore the legal and racial consequences of compensating

student-athletes for services rendered to the institution. After we read this essay, it is understandable that in 1995, Walter Beyers, the long-time advocate for amateur athletes and former executive director of the NCAA, reversed his position, finally acknowledging that big-time college sports is, in fact, a profit-making industry and that student-athletes are laborers.

Essay 14, by Carole Oglesby and Diana Schrader, "Where is the White in the Rainbow Coalition?", makes an excellent addition to the race relations literature. The authors begin their essay by presenting four very important questions:

1. What is the "face" of racism we practice daily—what does it look like?
2. What is our own White racial identity and why do we so resist the idea that we have one?
3. What is the price we pay for any complicity in racism?
4. What are the steps we can take to change and enhance the future in our increasingly multiracial, multicultural society?

In a beautifully developed script, the authors offer a discourse to the questions listed above. They controvert the concept of power and privilege currently vested in the White dominant groups, and they challenge the White community to reassess its own belief systems.

Oglesby and Schrader are strong advocates supporting antiracist activities. As White educators, the authors recommend educating the White population about African American culture so they will hopefully become color-affirming Whites—committed to developing equity and diversity.

A case study involving an activities therapist is presented to illustrate how a class in minorities in American sport can provide the spiritual journey and level of inquiry to confront the concept of "White privilege." They became more aware of and sensitive to other cultures and concluded that "I found this exploration of racial issues to be both uncomfortable and rewarding." In the final analysis, the therapist was able to develop new skills and strategies when working with minority patients.

The authors conclude their essay by encouraging scholars to employ a wide array of research methods (qualitative, experimental, demographic, content analysis) to expand the body of knowledge and understanding of the relationship between race, racism, power, oppression, and social justice in sport.

The final essay (15) in the text, "Racism in Big-Time College Sport: Prospects for the Year 2020 and Proposals for Change," was written by D. Stanley Eitzen. The author provides an excellent review of race relations in American and college sport in general. It is alarming to read that "race relations are growing hotter rather than cooler." The rise in the number of hate crimes, bigotry, and the unequal distribution of resources are factors leading to the author's conclusion that sport is not immune to these social forces. The commercial enterprise of college athletics has resulted in the miseducation of student-athletes, perpetuation of the dumb jock stereotype of African American athletes, and lower college graduation rates for African American athletes.

In general, it is believed that racism and exploitation of the African American athlete in big-time college athletics does exist. Eitzen ends his essay by suggesting the following action strategies to readdress these problems: Support the academic standards of Proposition 16; provide financial support to student-athletes—especially those from low socioeconomic backgrounds; support the concept of freshman ineligibility; have faculty monitor the academic progress of student-athletes; encourage student-athletes to attend social and cultural activities on campus; eliminate stacking; hire African Americans to the position of head coach and athletic director; and conduct multicultural awareness programs for the athletic department staff. Implementing the recommendations means the NCAA must undertake immediate reform; college presidents should be held more accountable for the academic integrity of the athletic programs, and funds generated from NCAA revenue should be redistributed to create a superfund.

Fifty Years After Jackie Robinson: A Dream Deferred?

The year 1997 marked a milestone in race relations and sports participation as American local media, magazines, radio, and television paid tribute to Jackie Robinson and the "American Dream." Yet, writing in his autobiography, Robinson said,

> I have had a great deal of support and I have tried to return that support with my best effort. However, there is one irrefutable fact of my life which has determined much of what happened to me: I was a Black man in a White world. I never had it made. (Duchett, 1995, p. 275)

Jackie Robinson, the athlete, civil rights activist, and humanitarian, had two dreams for sport in America: (a) increased player opportunities and (b) increased coaching and administrative opportunities for African Americans (Lapchick & Matthews, 1997). In the pages that follow, we will attempt to see if Jackie's dreams have been realized or deferred.

Noted sport sociologist and activist Harry Edwards (1979) reminded us that since 1947, Black Americans have dominated all sports to which they have had access. However, Edwards (1979) also pointed to the fact that as late as 1957 (10 years after Robinson's major league appearance) there were only 18 Blacks in professional baseball.

The 1960s witnessed tremendous racial unrest, leading to a moral crisis in America. The March on Washington, DC, on August 28, 1963, became synonymous with the Civil Rights movement of the era. Jackie Robinson and Dr. Martin Luther King, Jr., shared a similar dream—to live in a nation where individuals would not be judged by the color of their skin but by the content of their character. Federal legislation, in the form of Title VII of the 1964 Civil Rights Act and the Voly Rights Act of 1965, was passed in an effort to ensure African American and female civil rights. In 1968 the Kerner Commission (a presidential advisory body) concluded that America was becoming two nations: one Black and one White. The commission report condemned racism in America and called for financial assistance to African American communities to stem the tide of racial segregation. It was within this context that the popular sport magazine, *Sports Illustrated,* provided a criticism of the African American sport experience at the end of the 1960s.

In 1968, *Sports Illustrated* published a five-part series of articles surveying the experiences of the African American athletes in America: "Part 1: The Cruel Deception"; "Part 2: Pride and Prejudice"; "Part 3: In An Alien World"; "Part 4: In the Back of the Bus"; and "Part 5: The Anguish of a Team Divided", (Olson, 1968a). Throughout the five-part series the author reminds us how African American athletes became exploited and victimized—it was a truly shameful story!

Twenty-three years later (1991), *Sports Illustrated* ran another five-part series examining the African American experiences in sports. Topics included "How Far Have We Come?" (Johnson, 1991); "A Matter of Black and White (Johnson, 1991b); "Things Seem Better, But. . . . " (*Sports Illustrated*, 1991); "Reach Out and Touch Someone" (Swift, 1991); and "A Courageous Stand" (Moore, 1991).

One of the more significant findings of the 1991 five-part series can be found in the opening paragraph in the article "A Matter of Black and White" (Johnson, 1991b). Johnson drew out attention to the fact that more than 44 years after Jackie Robinson signed with the Dodgers, African Americans remain marginalized and experience racism and discrimination. A survey of NFL, NBA, and Major League Baseball teams revealed deep disagreement between African Americans and Whites on the extent of racial discrimination in professional sports. For example, 61% of the Black athletes believed that their salary and/or contract terms were less favorable than those of Whites. Sixty% of the African American athletes thought they were not treated as well by team managers as Whites were, 73% believed that their opportunities to endorse products were worse than Whites, and 77% believed that management in their sport was not doing enough to put Blacks into coaching or field-managing positions. African Americans and Whites continue to differ in opinions regarding the existence and magnitude of racism in America today.

As early as 1979, Edwards (1979) began to look towards the future of Black-White relations in America. Edwards's critically acclaimed works, "Sport Within the Veil: Triumphs, Tragedies, and Challenges of Afro-American Involvement" (1979), "The Source of the Black Athlete's Superiority" (1973), and "Black Athletes: 20th Century Gladiators for White America" (1974), viewed Black athletes as valuable performers. African American Black Coaches Association Executive Director Rudy Washington reached a similar conclusion and believed that the African American community must shoulder some of the responsibility for the emphasis placed on sport as a measure to gain social mobility and visibility. It is a widely held belief that sport is the "great equalizer," providing equality of opportunity and sportsmanship.

Since1947, data depict that the number of African American athletes participating in high school, college, and professional sport has increased. Equal access to "outcome" experiences did not accompany equal access.

More recently, G. H. Sage (1993) was deeply concerned about social practices that have "heaped injustice on African Americans in a sector of human activity—intercollegiate sport—that is typically admired for its commitment to opportunity and justice" (p. 1). Similarly, after an extensive review of the literature, Brooks and Althouse (1996) concluded,

Sports have been an arena of creativity and personal success for some African

Americans, and among the stand-outs, sports have been a source of money and respect. Michael Jordan's is likely the most recognized face in the world, just as Muhammed Ali's was earlier. Among those who are especially talented and lucky, sports are a mechanism for mobility. For many devoted fans, sports are viewed as one of the most responsive integrating mechanisms functioning in American society. Nonetheless, racism persists in sports, although exclusionary conduct and blatant discrimination are no longer legally countenanced. (p.vii)

In 1995 Davis documented the impact of unconscious racism in sports and argued that college sport served as a metaphor for the racism encountered by African Americans in our society.

An extensive review of the popular media, newspaper articles, and the sport sociology journals appearing in the *African American Resource Directory* permitted Brooks and Althouse (1996) to write that

> Racism and discrimination appear in the forms of salary inequities, racism, economic discrimination (i.e., unequal access to commercial endorsement opportunities), under-utilization of African Americans in coaching and other front office leadership positions, limited opportunities for speaking engagements, media perpetuation of racial stereotyping and athlete play discrimination." (p. 59)

Approximately 20 years ago, in 1979, Harry Edwards addressed what he perceived was the current status of race relations:

> Patterns of opportunity for Blacks in American sports, like those in the society at large are shaped by racial discrimination. This phenomena [sic] explains the disproportionately high number of talented athlete in certain sports and the utter exclusion of Blacks from most other American sports. (p. 374)

In essence, the author concluded that Black-White race relations in America remained unchanged. Lapchick and Matthews's (1997) *Racial Report Card* provides an excellent comprehensive analysis of the hiring practices of women and people of color in the NBA, NFL, Major League Baseball, and NCAA institutions. In some measure, the data represents a barometer of the progress or lack of progress made in race relations in American sports some 50 years after Jackie Robinson's signing. Reading the results contained in the report card, we were alarmed to read the conclusions reached by Lapchick and Matthews (1997), "the results showed no significant overall breakthrough in any of the categories covered in professional sport" (p. 1). The authors further concluded, "College sport, often assumed to be a more equitable arena in terms of race and gender, was actually behind pro sport in most categories in which comparisons could be made" (p. 1.).

In part, the authors reached their conclusions based on the following summary data:

1. Only 17% of Major League Baseball players are African American.
2. No African Americans or Latinos are majority owners in Major League Baseball, The National Basketball Association, or the The National Football League.
3. In college baseball, there are no African American head coaches of the 249 Division I schools.
4. Fifteen of the 547 college football coaches are African Americans.
5. Of the 301 Black men as head coaches, 205 coach basketball, track, or cross- country.
6. Only 8.3% of the men's assistant coaching jobs were held by Blacks.
7. Stacking is a problem in the NFL and Major League Baseball.
   a. Ninety-one percent of the quarterbacks and 72% of the centers are White.
   b. Six percent of the Major League Baseball pitchers are Black.

Conditions for the African American female athletes and coaches are equally deplorable.

The opportunity for women, and especially African American women, to gain parity in college and professional sports barely exists. Relatively few sport scientists have focused their research efforts on the study of the African American female athlete. The limited number of studies conclude that African American females are the target of stereotypes, myths, and gender bias that adversely affect their mobility.

Black College Sport, written by O. Cania Chalk (1976), represented a significant social-historical analysis of the African American male student-athlete's experiences on predominantly White campuses and at historically Black colleges and universities. Chalk's analysis was extensive and focused primarily on baseball, basketball, football, track and field, and the Olympics. Writing in the foreword to his book, Chalk said, "The writer awaits a definitive treatment on the accomplishments of Black women in sports" (p. v). More recently, African American female scholars Robertha Abney, Doris Corbett, Yevonne Smith, and Tina Sloan Green have taken leadership roles investigating the African American female athletes' experiences in sport.

Writing in the very controversial text, *Darwin's Athletes,* Haberman (1997) said, "Yet the Black male intelligentsia that has denounced almost every other form of cultural entrapment has never mounted a campaign against the sports fixation" (p. 76).

Contrary to this statement, the female African American scholars identified in the above paragraph and their African American male counterparts Othello Harris, Gary Sailes, Earl Smith, Robert Sellers, Audwin Anderson, Billy Hawkins, Keith Harrison, Delano Tucker, and William Johnson continue to write against the sports fixation. Their scholarship is stimulating, original, and thought provoking, and challenges the very nature of institutionalized racism in college sport.

The African American scholars and their allies (i.e., George Sage, Stanley Eitzen, Carol Oglesby, and David Wiggins) are committed to exposing and eradicating all forms of oppression and discrimination in American sport.

Over the past 50 years, progress has been made, and in the same measure, Jackie Robinson's dreams are being realized. Yet, the literature clearly indicates that the African American student-athlete's experiences differ significantly from those of his/her White counterparts. Today, the issue is no longer gaining equal access to the sport arena. Rather, the question is how does the African American student-athlete gain equal outcome?

On a very somber note, athletic administration and coaching at the college and professional levels still remain primarily White and male professions. Effecting some measure of change in this area of employment has been slow.

On an optimistic note, Robinson's dream is still alive, and organizations such as the Rainbow Coalition and the Black Coaches Association are committed to increasing the number of African Americans in sport leadership positions.

Arbitrariness and Discrimination: Notes About NCAA Initial Eligibility Rules

It's May 1999; we are approaching the middle of the last year of the millennium, almost half a century after "separate but equal" was declared "dead" in America's public schools and the new age of equality was to have been heralded, in part at least, by Jackie Robinson's contract to play baseball with the Brooklyn Dodgers.

The end of exclusionary racism in the face of civil rights actions promoted opportunities for today's athletes that were unavailable a generation ago, but these opportunities also grew when discrimination became incompatible with successful financing of professional and big-time collegiate sports. Yet, racial discrimination in sports continues to erode remarkable accomplishments that are being realized among African American athletes in the United States as well as globally.

A good deal of the work assembled in this book shows that the presumed value of the African American student-athlete as a prized sports commodity is tendered in an institutional environment that fuels harmful racism because of notions of neutrality and color blindness of rules sanctioning eligibility and participation in collegiate sports. Some considerable controversies have been pinned on the legality of NCAA eligibility rules because of alleged discrimination against African American student-athletes. Since 1983, when Proposition 48 was enacted during the NCAA convention at the bidding of university presidents who wanted tougher academic standards, the legitimate use of "cutoff" scores as predictors of successful graduation has been questioned. There is an persistent arbitrariness that clings to the use of "cut off" scores on tests as the principal link between minimal ability and graduation rates.

At the beginning of 1999, an important decision by the federal district court in Philadelphia struck down the NCAA's eligibility standard, known as Proposition 16, because application of the standard had an unjustified disparate impact against African American student-athletes. (Please refer to Essay 12 by Timothy Davis for more discussion on this subject.) The standard was challenged by four African American student-athletes who alleged they were denied athletic scholarships or sports eligibility because they did not score the minimum on the standardized tests. As a matter of finding, data showed an decrease in percent of African American student-athletes in Division I schools and a marked disparity in the percent of African American compared to White student-athletes failing to meet Proposition 16 requirements.

NCAA spokespersons insist that some minimal standards are needed to avoid revisiting more blatantly exploitative past abuses of student-athletes, yet increased access does not ensure a climate of racial acceptance, and African American student-athletes seem to come up on the short end of egalitarianism. Bringing student-athletes to campus is likely to prove inadequate to tasks of building opportunities to attain higher education. The court's conclusion about Proposition 16 serves to remind that sports are cultural arenas in which power, hegemony, and resistance are played out, and that sports are also about racism. It reminds us that the history of civil rights is a chronicle of lethargy, defiance, and unwillingness to abide by the mandates of entitlement; that the unresolved problems must still be resolved; but that looking at still-unresolved problems about African Americans in sport also can be about promise and hope in the future.

References

Brooks, D., & Althouse, R. (1996). *The African American resource directory*. Morgantown, WV: Fitness Information Technology, Inc.

Brown, G. (1998, May 25). Rate of minority hiring level over last two years. *The NCAA News*, 35(21) 1, 8.

Chalk, O. (1976). *Black college sport*. New York: Dodd, Mead & Company.

Cole, J. (1997). *Dream the boldest dreams: And other lessons of life*. Atlanta: Longstreet Press.

Davis, T. (1995). The myth of the superspade: The persistence of racism in college athletics. *Fordham Urban Law Journal, 22*(3), 616–698.

Duchett, A. (1995). *I never had it made: An autobiography of Jackie Robinson*. Hopewell, NJ: The Ecco Press.

Edwards, H. (1970). *Revolt of the black athlete*. New York: Free Press.

Edwards, H. (1973). The source of the black athlete's superiority. *The Black Scholar, 3*, 32–41.

Edwards, H. (1974). Black athletes: 20th century gladiators for white America. In A. Yiannakis, et al. (Eds.), *Sport sociology: Contemporary themes* (pp. 103–170). Dubuque, IA: Kendall/Hunt.

Edwards, H. (1979). Sport within the veil: Triumphs, tragedies, and challenges of African American nvolvement. *Annuals of the American Academy of Political and Social Sciences, 44*(5), 116–127.

Edwards, H. (1985). Educating black athletes. In D. Chu, J. O. Segrave, & B. J. Becker (Eds.), *Sport and higher education* (pp. 373–384). Champaign, IL: Human Kinetics.

Hoberman, J. (1997). *Darwin's athletes: How sport has damaged Black America and preserved the myth of race.* Boston, MA: Houghton Mifflin Company.

Johnson, W. O. (1991a). How far have we come? In 1968 SI surveyed the plight of the black athlete in America. *Sports Illustrated, 75*(6), 38–41.

Johnson, W. O. (1991b). Matter of black and white: An SI survey of professional athletes revealed some of the deep division between the races. *Sports Illustrated, 75*(6), 44–47.

Lapchick, R. E. , & Matthews, K. (1997). *Racial Report Card.* Boston: Northwestern University Center for the Study of Sport in Society.

Nack, W. (1997, May 5). The breakthrough. *Sports Illustrated, 86*(18), 56–67.

Olson, J. (1968a). [Part 5 of a 5-part series, *The black athlete*: A shameful story]. The anguish of a team divided. *Sports Illustrated, 29*(5), 21–24, 29–35.

Olson, J. (1968b). [Part 1 of 5-part series, *The black athlete*: A shameful story]. The cruel deception. *Sports Illustrated, 29*(1), 15–17.

Olson, J. (1968c). [Part 3 of a 5-part series, *The black athlete*: A shameful story]. In an alien world. *Sports Illustrated, 29*(3), 41–45.

Olson, J. (1969d). [Part 4 of a 5-part series, *The black athlete*: A shameful story]. In the back of the bus. *Sports Illustrated, 29*(4), 39–41.

Olson, J. (1969e). [Part 2 of a 5-part series, *The black athlete*: A shameful story]. Pride and prejudice. *Sports Illustrated, 29*(2), 15–17.

Sage, G. H. (1993). Introduction. In D. Brooks & R. Althouse (Eds.), *Racism in college athletics: The African American athlete's experience* (pp. 1–17). Morgantown, WV: Fitness Information Technology, Inc.

Subject Index